"William Burke" and Francisco de Miranda

The Word and the Deed in Spanish America's Emancipation

Dr. Mario Rodríguez

Professor of History (Retired)
University of Southern California
Department of History
University Park
Los Angeles, California 90089-0034

UNIVERSITY
PRESS OF
AMERICA

Lanham • New York • London

Copyright © 1994 by
University Press of America®, Inc.
4720 Boston Way
Lanham, Maryland 20706

3 Henrietta Street
London WC2E 8LU England

Library of Congress Cataloging-in-Publication Data
Rodríguez, Mario.
William Burke and Francisco de Miranda : the word and the deed in
Spanish America's emancipation / Mario Rodríguez.
p.   cm.
Includes bibliographical references and index.
1. Miranda, Francisco de, 1750–1816. 2. Venezuela—History—
1810–1830. 3. Burke, William, fl. 1805–1810—Influence.
4. Latin America—History—Wars of Independence, 1806–1830—
Foreign public opinion. 5. Public opinion—Europe. 6. Public
opinion—United States. I. Title.
F2323.M6R68   1994   987'.04—dc20   94–4182 CIP

ISBN 0–8191–9485–9 (cloth : alk. paper)

Contents

PREFACE

The quincentenary of America's Discovery, so recently upon us, has much in common with this work's major theme: the anticolonialist propaganda of Spanish America's Wars of Independence, especially from 1763 to 1815. Those years of the "Revolutionary Age" marked the beginnings of the "American Revolution" and the Emancipation of Spanish America, ending with the fall of Napoleon Bonaparte. Spanish colonials found it advantageous to question Spain's motives in the "Conquest," her "Theory of Empire," and the tyrannous record of three centuries which brought about the despoilation of great Indian civilizations, enslaving the natives of the New World, and violating with impunity the "natural rights" of all Americans. Such comportment was not reasonable to human beings in those times of the Enlightenment. Professor Herbert Eugene Bolton at the University of California (Berkeley) rightfully called the period from 1763 to 1826: the "Greater American Revolution," when most of the Americas gained their freedom from European mother countries and faced their independence with optimism and courage.

A celebrated war hero of that revolutionary era, Francisco de Miranda (1750–1816) figures largely in the following pages. This work, however, is not just another biography of the famous Venezuelan. It is more than that. Miranda is the "*Deed*" in our title, the man of action and the entrepreneur who prepared the grounds, as well as the ideology, for the Emancipation of Spanish America. Moreover, he was also a significant part of the "*Word*,"—the intellectuals whose writings inspired the "Liberation" of Spanish America during those initial years.

v

Chapter One: "A Scipio Africanus from Caracas" highlights Miranda as the man of action as well as an intellectual in his own right, well versed in the culture of the Classical Era and the Enlightenment. This image of Miranda, which he cultivated throughout his career, was a key ingredient of his personality as a "Universal" man. It attracted intellectual thinkers to his program of *Colombeia*—that is, all aspects of his beloved *Colombia*, the term he favored for a liberated Spanish America. At the end of the "American Revolution," U.S. leaders welcomed their Venezuelan ally into their life for a year and a half, inspiring him, with their example, to revolutionize the "other" Americas to the south. In Europe, he won the support of men like Thomas Pownall, the ex-Governor of Massachusetts, who was highly regarded by North Americans for his defense of their cause in the English Parliament. Jeremy Bentham and James Mill, well known political thinkers of that day, in England, likewise aided Miranda's crusade in every way possible.

Yet, as it turned out, his greatest collaborator in London was an obscure journalist who called himself "William Burke." In two publications of 1807 and 1808, this young writer focused and elaborated upon the argument against Spain's title to her New World possessions, defending the cause of the Indians and the Americans for independence. Furthermore, he argued that it was to Great Britain's best interests to assist in the Emancipation of Spanish America. Later, Burke's ideas flowed once again onto the pages of the *Gaceta de Caracas* from 1810 to 1812, urging Venezuelans and all other Spanish Americans to study and follow the model of the United States from 1787 to 1810—a miraculous period of peace and prosperity that was attracting the attention of the entire world. Without a doubt, at this point, "William Burke" was the Mr. "*Word*" of this study—its second hero, so to speak.

Our main concern throughout this book had been to identify this brilliant writer and philosopher by studying his analyses of the Napoleonic era, the imperative need for Britain's commitment to Miranda's cause in Spanish America, and his expert presentation of the grand model of the "American Revolution" and its institutions in those miraculous years from 1787 to 1810, guided by a new Constitution and Alexander Hamilton's financial reforms. "William Burke," in the process, helped to invent the key concept of the "Western Hemisphere Idea"; and he encouraged Inter-Americanism and the establishment of a super-government called the "United States of South America and Mexico," offering us new perspectives on the Independence of Spanish America.

During the Bicentennial of the American Revolution, I was in Madrid completing the research and writing of a volume on the origins of Spanish liberalism, leading to the famous Constitution of 1812, and the contributions of Spanish Americans to this formidable achievement. It resulted in a book published by the University of California Press: *The Cádiz Experiment in Central America, 1808 to 1826* (Berkeley, Los Angeles, London, 1978). Thanks to a Fulbright grant to Spain, I was able to complete the book cited, as well as to explore extensively Bolton's thesis of a "Greater American Revolution," improving upon my command of the Bourbon Reforms of the late eighteenth century, of all Spain's attempts and measures to dissuade her colonials from following the example of England's Americans from 1763 forward, and of Spain's role in the American Revolution and what impact it had upon the thinking of Spanish Americans. In addition, I recalled the various references to the "American Revolution" in the parliamentary debates at Cádiz, in southern Spain, etc. Prior to my arrival in Madrid, moreover, I had delivered a lecture in Washington, D.C. at the Library of Congress, entitled: "The Impact of the American Revolution on the Spanish- and Portuguese-Speaking World." In short, the Cádiz and Bolton thesis projects—both in the "Revolutionary Age"—merged to allow me to focus on the propaganda movement in Spanish America, underscoring her indebtedness to the model of the United States of America. In Chapter Four: "William Burke: Front and Center," you will find additional details on how the present book took shape over the years.

In a topic of this scope, travels to foreign countries were indispensable and time-consuming. It involved repeated visits to Spain, England, and Venezuela, not to mention depositories of documents in these United States.

In Spain, my good friend Ramón Bela, Director of the Fulbright Commission, provided me with credentials that opened doors everywhere: in Madrid, to the Archivo Histórico Nacional, the Biblioteca Nacional, Real Academia de la Historia, and the Biblioteca del Instituto de Cultura. *La revolución americana de 1776 y el mundo hispánico: Ensayos y documentos* (Editorial Tecnos, Madrid, 1976) mentions the names of the various directors of Spanish archives in

Sevilla, Cádiz, Valladolid, Bilbao, and San Sebastián—all of them were generous with their time and help. And Don Ramón's demise has saddened his old friends.

In England, my experiences there since 1958 have facilitated my labors at the Public Record Office, the British Museum (now British Library), and the Colindale Newspaper Collection. Professors John Lynch and Harold Blakemore of the University College of London and the Institute of Latin American Studies made many suggestions; and I proceeded to the Science Division of the University College Library, which housed the manuscript collections of Henry Broughman and Jeremy Bentham. On my last two visits to London, I also became a frequent reader at the Manuscript Division and the North Library of the British Library. Although I never got to Liverpool to study the Blanco-White documents, I much appreciate the help extended to me by Professor John Fisher. And I am still looking forward to visiting that city and perusing the materials mentioned. Our next visit will also take my wife and me to Edinburgh to learn more about the university and its distinguished authors.

In Venezuela during the past decade, Professors Pedro Grases and Manuel Pérez Vila have advised me on the available documentation there and elsewhere, discussing historiographical tendencies and problems with me in person and by letter. The personnel at the Academia Nacional de Historia in Caracas has always been exemplary in their dealings with me, especially helpful in allowing me to work with the microfilm of Miranda's original manuscripts—a rewarding experience in every sense.

Much of my material in the United States has been located in the Library of Congress, especially in the Manuscripts Division where I found Richard Rush's evaluation of General Miranda in 1805. On other collections in the East, my good friend Harry Bernstein, formerly of Brooklyn College and Columbia University, briefed me with discernment and to my advantage. His death in January, 1993, was a shock to me. Our mutual colleague Bailey Diffie, who has since left this vale of tears, read my earlier chapters critically and with enthusiasm. Indeed, I treasured his comments, as well as his presence with me at USC, where he taught his final classes. For the past two decades—my final university stand—the members of the History Department have been a constant source of encouragement and help in reading my publications. Among them, let me mention John Schutz, an expert on Thomas Pownall, who provided me with valuable insights into that famous personage. On an earlier version of Chapter Two "A British Star in Spanish America's Emancipation," I received valuable input from Franklin Mitchell, Lloyd Moote, Brendan Nagle, and John Wills. Joseph A. Styles' comments and materials were especially useful on the "Scottish Enlightenment." Our administrative personnel has always been exceptional; and I wish to remember that priceless Australian chief, Isabel J. Mahoney, and her talented successor Lori A. Rogers. There was also that stern tyrant on the computer, the indispensable Brenda R. Johnson who recorded my entire manuscript with patience and understanding.

During the past year (1992), I counted heavily upon the encouragement of two colleagues in the historical profession: Professor Wilcomb E. Washburn, a U.S. colonialist and Director of the Office of American Studies at the Smithsonian Institution, who helped me meet key figures at the recent AHA meeting in Washington, D.C.; and Professor David Bushnell, former Editor of the *Hispanic American Historical Review*, whose comments and suggestions helped to improve our final product. In geographical matters, I am deeply indebted to Professor James Curtis (Oklahoma State University), his interns, and staff, for the maps in this study. And Jeff Reid from Stillwater's Vocational Technical School provided valuable computer expertise. Thank you, colleagues.

Sergeant Mario Rodríguez of the U.S. Army married Mildred P. Shepherd, a recent graduate of Oklahoma A. & M., in Champaign-Urbana, Illinois, on September 3, 1943. After half a century with her historian, it is appropriate to dedicate this work to her and her closest kin: Rosetta Pearl Shepherd, her nonogenerian mother; Jacqueline Mattice (Wayne), our daughter and teacher of sciences in Akron, Ohio; and Valerie Tesmer (John), our granddaughter, who is a Ph.D. candidate in Biochemistry at Purdue University, along with her husband; and my lovely little Christina, Valerie's sister who never made it beyond her sixth year—all of them, the author's pride and joy.

Finally, the contents of this volume are fully my responsibility.

Mario Rodríguez

Chapter One

A Scipio Africanus from Caracas

There was no one who spent his hours of leisure with elegance . . . ever engaged in the improvement of the arts of either war or peace. Addicted wholly to arms or books, he never relaxed the exercise of his body, in danger, or his mind, in application to study.

Velleius Paterculus[1]

Dr. William Thomson, a well-known British historian, felt a great indebtedness to Francisco de Miranda for his impressions of French military campaigns in the 1790s. The English savant acknowledged emotionally the Venezuelan's contributions to his book: *Military Memoirs, Relating to Campaigns, Battles, and Strategems of War, Ancient and Modern* (London, 1804), in which he likened Miranda to Scipio Africanus, as described by the Roman historian Paterculus. Miranda pretended to deny this flattering comparison in a moment of embarrassment.[2] And yet, this would-be liberator of South America greatly appreciated a positive international image, especially as he boarded the *Polly* at Gravesend, England, on September 2, 1805. A veteran of the "American" and "French" revolutions, Francisco de Miranda was sanguine that his good friends in the United States would support him in the impending months, as he prepared to liberate his beloved "Colombia."

Born in Caracas, Venezuela, in 1750, Francisco de Miranda was the son of a merchant from the Canary Islands, who traced his lineage to northern Spain. As the son of a *Canario*, young Francisco sensed the discrimination of the well-established American families (*Mantuanos*) in the Captaincy General of Venezuela. Elements of this local oligarchy of Creoles (*Criollos*) lobbied aggressively against his father's use of an honorary title granted to him by the Spanish Government.[3] This slight offended the Mirandas to the core. Given this hostile context, young Francisco chose to seek his career elsewhere. Not yet twenty-one, he left for Spain to pursue a military career. After presenting the required legal papers, Francisco de Miranda purchased a captain's commission on January 7, 1773, in the reputable Princess' Regiment.[4]

At the University of Caracas, Miranda began a lifelong concern for the study of classical Greece and Rome. He learned Latin early in life and continued to perfect it by much reading. At forty, he took up the passionate task of learning Greek. By then, because of his varied travels, he also spoke French, Italian, and English. His German, however, was just passable.[5] Such a conscientious preparation in languages opened up horizons for the pursuit of knowledge and for a special expertise on the Greeks and the Romans—their history, philosophy, literature, art, architecture, etc. This deliberate classical emphasis developed into a hallmark for the Scipio Africanus from Caracas—an image that he nurtured assiduously throughout his life.

Following the pattern of Scipio Africanus, both the Elder and the Younger, Miranda served as a military official in Spain and Africa. The Elder (Publius Cornelius Scipio, 236 to 183 B.C.) won recognition for ousting the Carthaginians from Spain and chasing them back into Africa, while the Younger (Publius Cornelius Scipio Aemilianis, 184 to 129 B.C.) destroyed Carthage in Africa (146 B.C.) and Numantia in Spain (133 B.C.). The historian Paterculus' reference was to the Younger in the opening quotation. A believer in the Stoic philosophy of the Greeks, Scipio Africanus gathered around him such scholars as Polybius, Panaetius, and others who consciously tried to blend the better elements of Greek and Roman life. The Younger was a worthy model, indeed. Many years later, Captain Miranda went into his first combat at Melilla (1774), in Africa, a minor skirmish with Moroccan forces. Most of Miranda's service, however, took place in southern Spain at the famous port of Cádiz.[6]

Always striving to improve his mind, young Miranda labored conscientiously on French and English. He hoped one day to make himself eligible for more imaginative assignments in the Spanish service. His constant reading of classical historians, moreover, helped him to acquire an expertise in military strategy and theory which he used to advantage throughout his career. Miranda's practical experience in the American and French revolutions improved upon the final product, impressing North Americans and Europeans alike. President John Adams once commented that Miranda knew more about the military history of the American Revolution than the officers involved.[7]

As Miranda focused on the politics of the Classical Age, he improved his command over the period. Moreover, his concern for the arts and sciences complemented the Venezuelan's broad grasp of man's experiences on earth. While in Caracas, Miranda also cultivated an abiding interest in music and architecture. Throughout his personal archives, there were programs of operas and recitals, as well as architectural plans and designs of buildings. His comments on music, art, architecture, and literature were sophisticated by any standards. Judging from his attainments, the calibre of education at the University of Caracas must have been notable. *El indio*, as one of his European friends called him affectionately, was an educated world citizen in every respect.[8]

In keeping with his intellectual curiosity, Miranda appreciated the importance of diaries while recalling events accurately. He kept good notes of his various stops in Spain, providing us with priceless details about her people, their customs, conditions, and institutions. His description of "sloth" in Extremadura was priceless. His impressions of buildings and the type of architecture throughout Spain were sensitive. In addition, he left us keen evaluations of various libraries and art collections that he found here and there; and he rewarded the diary reader with perceptive remarks that highlighted an acute power of observation. He always posed the right questions, thus gaining valuable insights into his fellow man. A penchant for the collection of books, documents, works of art, and other forms of historical evidence was a major characteristic of his long career.[9] His extensive travels and his mastery of writing a diary prepared Francisco de Miranda to become one of the great memorialists of the "Revolutionary Age" in the Western World.

Before leaving for an assignment in Cuba, Captain Miranda listed all the books and items that he had purchased in Europe before April, 1780. This remarkable document exposes a genuine autodidact whose goal was to advance in the military at a good pace, while at the same time becoming a veritable *philosophe* of the eighteenth century.[10] The compilation underscores the fact that intelligent people in the Hispanic

World had no real obstacle in keeping up with worldwide intellectual developments—a conclusion that is no longer in doubt, thanks to the research of this century.[11]

For his military career, Miranda included books on mathematics, geography, topography, and other relevant sciences and applications. Psychology, political science, history, and economics were considered useful fields of inquiry for this ambitious *Caraqueño*. A student of languages, of course, needed dictionaries, grammars, as well as the works of literary greats: Cervantes, Corneille, Molière, etc. Classical books were also plentiful: studies of Roman revolutions, Cicero's thought, Caesar's commentaries, histories, etc. Hispanic history was a favorite field; yet Miranda also included the "Age of Louis XIV" in France and his contemporaries in seventeenth-century England. Among French writers, we note the surnames of Diderot, D'Alembert, D'Argens, Rousseau, Voltaire, Raynal, Montesquieu, and La Bruyère; English authors: Locke (two different works of his), Hume, Burke, Swift, Wollaston, Chesterfield, Ferguson, Pope, etc.; and, the works of Grotius and Pufendorf, among others. This thirty-year-old Venezuelan, in short, possessed a fairly sophisticated library. And the process had only begun. By 1807, Francisco de Miranda had one of the best known libraries in London, containing some six thousand volumes that were valued at over nine thousand pounds sterling.[12] Dr. Thomson's simile of Miranda and Scipio Africanus was no exaggeration at all.

* * * * * * * * * * * *

Spain declared war on Great Britain in 1779, just as France had done in the previous year. It thus bolstered the cause of the English colonials; and the Caribbean area assumed greater importance. The clandestine activities of the Bourbons were now out in the open. From New Orleans, Louisiana, General Bernardo de Gálvez wasted no time in clearing out all pockets of Englishmen from the Mississippi Valley area. Spanish forces from Cuba, headed by Field Marshall Juan Manuel de Cagigal, cooperated with Gálvez in the capture of Pensacola in 1781. Captain Miranda was a participant in that famous battle as the assistant of Cagigal, his ex-Colonel in the Princess' Regiment at Cádiz, which explains Miranda's assignment to Cuba. His mentor also held the appointment of Habana's governor. Subsequent combat in the Bahamas raised Miranda's rank to that of Lieutenant Colonel and won him the appointment as Cagigal's aide-de-camp. Thoroughly impressed with the intellectual and linguistic talents of his young friend, Cagigal sent him on a special espionage mission to Jamaica with the alleged objective of exchanging prisoners. This bold maneuver might have facilitated the capture of Jamaica by the forces of Bernardo de Gálvez. But other factors impinged at the time, lessening its overall importance. Cagigal, nevertheless, was much impressed with Miranda's performance in Jamaica.[13]

The wheels of fortune, however, were about to change for the young Spanish officer from Venezuela. The Minister of the Indies, José de Gálvez, had by this time become paranoid about the loyalty of Spanish Americans to the Crown of Spain. For personal reasons, or perhaps from annoyance at the Peruvian insurrections of the early 1780s, the Minister's warped mind was beginning to pit Spaniard against Spaniard on this issue, as well as alienating many good Spanish-American officers. Like his well-placed relative in Spain, General Bernardo de Gálvez also became suspicious of Miranda, whom earlier he had praised to the skies. On the basis of flimsy evidence, the Spanish government accused Colonel Miranda of permitting a captive British officer to examine key Spanish installations in Cuba—a ridiculous charge that General Cagigal rejected out of hand. The most serious accusation, however, was that Miranda, and his superior Cagigal, had willfully encouraged a contraband conspiracy with Jamaican interests. A lengthy investigation ensued; and the two men were not finally exonerated until 1799. General Cagigal went back to Spain to challenge the case; and his Venezuelan protegé opted to leave Cuba. The escape to the United States was remarkably easy, perhaps because Cagigal personally resented the trumped up charges against his young assistant. In fact, Miranda took with him a letter from Cagigal to General George Washington.[14]

During the next year and a half, Colonel Francisco de Miranda was in the United States of America. He landed in Newberne, North Carolina on June 9, 1783, and exited Boston on December 15, 1784.[15] It was an auspicious period in American history, not covered too well by foreign observers. Colonel Miranda had the opportunity to witness the last days of the "Revolution" and the crucial transition to a nation at peace. Thanks to his diary, we have an excellent record of this key period, written by a talented observer who covered ten states and most of the major cities. Because of his interest in military strategy, Colonel Miranda visited and investigated all the major battle zones of America with the spirit of an expert. North American officers were surprised by his insights. Miranda left us other valuable impressions on varied themes: the architectural features of urban and rural structures; the layouts of the major cities and their extensive facilities (the illumination of Philadelphia's streets fascinated him); the quaintness, as well as provincialism, of college life on the campuses of Princeton, Yale, and Harvard; the energy, resourcefulness, and optimism of the Americans in all walks of life; the faithfulness and subordination of American wives, as compared to their more rebellious spirit before marriage; the "leveling" nature of American society, which permitted Miranda's carriage driver to sit at the same table with him, or allowed the lower classes to mix promiscuously at a "barbecue" with their superiors, drinking from the same glasses and jugs, even though it was in celebration of the war's end; the apparent harmony of religious sects, despite some hypocrisy and a decided intolerance of the rights of Catholics (Samuel Adams had to grant the validity of Miranda's observations); and the New England "Blue Laws" which left the Venezuelan speechless on occasion, especially when he was caught with a deck of cards on the Sabbath! Francisco de Miranda's portrait of the young American Republic is a priceless reading experience. It was not available in English, however, until 1963.[16]

A consummate traveler, Colonel Miranda learned much about the art of writing a diary during his stay in the United States. A major requisite for travel in that era was a letter of recommendation. With letters from Juan Manuel Cagigal to Washington and to Francisco Rendón, the Spanish Representative in Philadelphia, and other recommendations by James Seagrove, a North American friend whom Miranda had met in Habana, the doors opened freely from the beginning of his visit to the United States. People everywhere took a liking to this charming young Spanish officer, so well educated and conversant on so many topics. Thus, more letters of recommendation were forthcoming for all parts of the new nation. The variety and range of Americans that he met was very impressive. Military leaders were everywhere: Nathaniel Greene, one of Washington's key collaborators, and William Moultrie enjoyed visiting with Miranda in Charleston, South Carolina. Governors, judges, mayors, religious leaders, and intellectuals looked forward to meeting the articulate foreigner in their midst. Wives and daughters were much smitten by his handsome features and cavalier ways. It was in the United States that Miranda perfected the technique of loaning and borrowing books and articles from the *right* people, thus building up his image as an intellectual. The historian David Ramsey, who had written about the revolutionary conflict in 1778, relished his talks with Miranda while he was in Charleston. Ramsey wrote a letter for him to Dr. William Smith in Philadelphia, one of the leading educators of the time and the provost of the Philadelphia Academy, later to be known as the University of Pennsylvania.[17] As a result, Miranda became a good friend of Dr. Benjamin Rush, a prominent medical educator at the same institution in Philadelphia and one of the key figures of the "Revolution."

Colonel Miranda met two Englishmen in Charleston who exerted a strong influence on his European career. He talked to Edward Penman, who along with his cousin James, were major figures in London's trade. Edward Penman introduced him to the Englishman Andrew Turnbull, a real estate developer who was known as "The Penn of Florida." Turnbull wrote key letters for Miranda to Lord Shelburne, Colonel Isaac Barré, and Dr. Joseph Priestly—two major political figures in England and a world-renowned scientist. Miranda never wanted for letters throughout the rest of his career; and his experiences in the United States, early in his life, helped him to perfect the technique to an art form.[18]

Although Cagigal's letter to Francisco Rendón in Philadelphia made no mention of Miranda's trouble with the Spanish government, the Venezuelan informed him unofficially when he was sure that he had won his confidence. Rendón took Miranda to meet General Washington on December 9, 1783. On the previous day, the General had entered Philadelphia to a victor's welcome. Washington thoroughly enjoyed Cagigal's flattering evaluation of his military ability; and he graciously invited Cagigal's aide-de-camp to share his table during his stay in Philadelphia—an excellent opportunity for Miranda to observe America's great hero. Washington's characteristics did not seem out of the ordinary, according to Miranda; but there was no question about his charisma among Americans. No matter what he did, he could do no wrong, as if there was an impermeable shield around him.[19]

Philadelphia was Colonel Miranda's favorite city, so beautiful and meaningful. It was clean, well-managed, and orderly with stately buildings, museums, libraries, and superior educational institutions. It had played a vital role in the "Revolution;" and Miranda marveled at its industry and commerce. It was a model worth emulation. Perhaps some day there would be Philadelphias all over the southern continent, the Hispanic section of the Western Hemisphere. Miranda hoped to

return to this model city in the future to imbibe further its implications
for his own people. In Philadelphia he met all of the leading figures
of the American Revolution: members of the Continental Congress,
preachers, educators, scientists, military greats, etc. They are all in
Miranda's diary, pouring out their dreams for their country's future.

Everywhere he traveled, Americans greeted him as an ally in the
recent war. All this changed when the news came out that he was in
exile, having abandoned the Spanish service. At this point, the
character of Miranda's visit took on another dimension—the
revolutionary cause of the Americas. He was a representative of the
"other Americas," who admired the courage of the English Americans
in fighting for their independence—an insight that flattered North
Americans immensely in this period of their political development.
Miranda sensed this pride and fed it with his remarks: Spanish
Americans likewise yearned desperately for "liberty" and "freedom" and
wanted to imitate what their northern brethren had accomplished.
Many years later, George Clinton, the Governor of New York in
Miranda's first visit, teased the Venezuelan affectionately about his
spirited advocacy of "republics."[20] Colonel Miranda discussed his plans
to liberate "Colombia," with Alexander Hamilton, who promised his
support. Stephen Sayre and William Duer, Miranda's constant
companions when he was in New York, likewise encouraged his
emancipation project. They wrote letters to England in his behalf, and
Duer loaned him a substantial amount of money for his trip to Europe.[21]
According to Susan Livingston, a young lady from a prominent New
York family with more than a passing interest in the dashing
Venezuelan colonel, Stephen and William were forever lifting their
glasses in toasts honoring the "Queen of the Incas." She wondered
innocently what meaning that toast might have![22] We do not know
what Miranda's answer was; but it probably had something to do with
the "Inca" insurrections of the early 1780s—proof of the revolutionary
ferment throughout South America. In Boston, Henry Knox, the
youngest of the revolutionary generals, adamantly supported the
emancipation of "Colombia" in the vaunted Bostonian "*simposios*" of
1784.[23] Later, General Knox forwarded a letter to Miranda estimating
what it would cost to support an expeditionary force of five thousand
men from the United States, presumably to be used in Miranda's
emancipation move.[24] Colonel Miranda's visit to the United States in
1783 and 1784 certainly aroused and inflamed the revolutionary spirit
of the Americas, the New World of the future as opposed to the Old

World. Miranda's American friends, moreover, maintained their constant loyalty to his cause during the next two decades, while the Venezuelan moved on to the European stage.

* * * * * * * * * * * *

After two months of sailing on the *Polly*, Miranda had sufficient time to think about his career. Although sanguine about the prospects of genuine support in the United States, he could not shake off the stark realities of his experiences in Europe during the previous twenty years. To be sure, he was known throughout the world, and especially in England, France, and Russia. The Spaniards, of course, did not think much of him. There was also the reality that time and time again he had been thwarted by the vacillations of English leaders like Prime Minister William Pitt. Had he played out his hand in life? After all, he was fifty-five years old; and the gray in his hair was not fiction. It mattered little that he fudged away a few years of his life in recent biographical articles.[25] Whether he chose to admit it or not, Miranda was sensing intuitively that perhaps he had passed to the other side of the ledger.

With letters to spare for dignitaries in England, Miranda resumed the life style of a world traveler. He arrived in London on February 1, 1785. His address book grew at a fast pace, as did the number of visiting cards. He seemed to be compiling a veritable "Who's Who." Among the notables were: Count Shelburne, Count Effingham, Lord Macdonald, General Melville, Edward Chamberlayn (Treasury), William Brummel (ex-Private Secretary of Lord North), Jeremy Bentham, and a host of British military figures and bureaucrats.[26] Thoroughly enjoying his sightseeing throughout the City, he was impressed with England's "opulence, culture, and magnificence." He loved to sit in on the debates in Parliament, "a sublime school of politics and legislation."[27] Moreover, Miranda soon contacted James Penman, whose cousin Edward had befriended him in Charleston. He also reestablished contact with the prominent merchant John Turnbull, whom he had met at Gibraltar in 1776, while in the Spanish service.[28]

Determined to keep all doors open, Colonel Miranda made his presence known to the Spanish Minister in London, Bernardo del Campo. The reception was friendly, so much so that Miranda was put at ease during his first visit to London. He also wrote to the Spanish Minister of State, the Conde de Floridablanca, and to King Charles III explaining his case and protesting his innocence. The Spanish government acknowledged his letters, and encouraged Miranda to think that perhaps the tactic was working.[29] He had little choice in the matter, of course. Miranda soon recognized that Great Britain was in financial straits because of the lengthy rebellion in English America, which, in turn, might pose a serious deterrent to British involvement in Hispanic America.

Miranda received joyous news several weeks after his arrival in London. His good friend Colonel William Stephens Smith, the aide-de-camp of George Washington, was in England serving as the Secretary of the American Legation under John Adams, the Minister Plenipotentiary. Thus a deep friendship between the two colonels was allowed to continue. A strong puritanical streak permeated Smith's character which made him an irrevocable champion of the New World's emancipation from the Old. He wrote to Francisco on July 4, 1785: "as a friend of the rights of man and of society's happiness."[30] Despite religious differences, William S. Smith was always Miranda's true friend. Moreover, they both liked to drink together—a trait which Miranda shared with many of his American companions. One night at Vaux Hall, Francisco made a suggestion that instantly appealed to William, if he could get a clearance from his superior in the Legation. At that time of the year, Frederick the Great of Prussia usually held a military review that involved from sixty to seventy thousand expert troops over a period of five days. Both colonels wanted to experience one of these famous annual reviews; and with remarkable speed, they made their arrangements. Smith got his clearance; and Miranda received a credit of 250 pounds sterling from John Turnbull. James Penman agreed to keep Miranda's papers and possessions until his return; and the Spanish Minister wrote to Spain's agent in Berlin, introducing Colonel Miranda.[31] On Saturday, August 13, 1785, the two travelers were in Amsterdam.[32] Although Miranda did not know it at the time, he had just commenced a four-year trek—it lacked only seven weeks—throughout the Continent; and, of course, there were more diaries for posterity to read.

Throughout Miranda's long and distinguished career, there were many anonymous publications associated with him that appeared in sundry places: newspapers, periodicals, pamphlets, broadsides, treatises, or books. Sometimes he or one of his allies wrote the pieces. Often his enemies were the authors. At any rate, the authorship remained in doubt or was nebulous. A good example of this was the editorial that appeared first in the summer of 1785 in the *Political Herald and Review* (London). It reached a wider audience when it came out in the *Morning Chronicle* (London) on August 20, 1785. Since Miranda was already on his trip, James Penman forwarded a copy to him, expressing his deep concern over its implications.[33]

Considering Miranda's relations with the Spanish Minister in London, it is doubtful that the Venezuelan "planted" that article before his departure. The contents suggest that it was written by one of Miranda's friends. The reader should savor this document in its entirety, especially since Miranda was going to utilize it in future propaganda campaigns:

> The flame which was kindled in North America, as was forseen, has made its way into the American dominions of Spain. That jealousy which confined the appointments of government in Spanish America to native Spaniards, and established other distinctions between these and their descendants on the other side of the Atlantic, has been a two-edged sword, and cuts two ways. If it has hitherto preserved the sovereignty of Spain in those parts, it has sown the seeds of a deep resentment among the people. Conferences are held, combinations are formed in secret among a race of men whom we shall distinguish by the appellation of Spanish Provincials. The example of North America is the great subject of discourse, and the grand object of imitation. In London, we are well assured, there is at this moment, a Spanish American of great consequence, and possessed of the confidence of his fellow citizens who aspires to the glory of being the deliverer of his country. He is a man of sublime views and penetrating understanding, skilled in the ancient and modern languages, conversant in books, and acquainted with the world. He has devoted many years to the study of general politics; the origin, the progress, and the termination of the different species of government: the circumstances that combine and retain multitudes of mankind in political societies; and the causes by which these societies are dissolved and swallowed up by others. This gentleman, having visited every province of North America, came to England, which he regards as the mother country of liberty, and the school for political knowledge. As friends to freedom, we forbear to be more particular concerning this distinguished character. He is a notable proof and an example of the fact that we wanted to illustrate. We admire his talents, esteem his values, and heartily wish prosperity to the noblest pursuit that can occupy the powers of any mortal, that of bestowing the blessings of freedom on millions of his fellow-men.[34]

The style, as well as the messianic flavor of the article, resembles that of Thomas Pownall, a former British governor of Massachusetts who became Miranda's trusted friend and advisor from 1790 forward. But Pownall and his second wife, whom he married in late 1784, were on an extended honeymoon in Europe for most of the following year.[35] Another possible candidate was Jeremy Bentham, although the learned political philosopher did not know Miranda that well at this time.

The logical author was William Stephens Smith, who was traveling in Europe with Miranda. The messianic note permeates his correspondence with the Venezuelan. Smith really believed with all his heart that some day Miranda would free his people. It is my contention—and we shall study the evidence that points to this conclusion—that Smith confessed to his Venezuelan friend that he was responsible for publishing that article in hopes that it would bring Miranda support for the "Colombia" project. It could be that Stephen Sayre and William Duer may have helped Smith compose the selection before he left the States. Miranda thanked his companion for the noble effort, but he pointed out that it left him in a delicate situation vis-a-vis the Spanish authority, who might resort to the use of foul means against him. We can imagine Smith's despair on hearing this. He had tried to help his friend; the result was negative, placing Miranda's life in jeopardy. The guilt he felt over this development lingered on for years. On the Prussian trip, however, Colonel W.S. Smith insisted that Miranda not return to England with him and that he should no longer continue the Spanish connection, lest a trap be set for him. Moreover, he loaned him two hundred and thirty pounds sterling to continue his stay on the Continent until it was safe to return. Here we have, in my opinion, the explanation for Miranda's change in travel plans, leading to almost four years of covering the Continent. The two American colonels separated in Vienna on October 26, 1785. Smith had been responsible for the "Diary" up to that point; now Miranda took over writing in Spanish rather than English.[36]

Here the plot thickened. Colonel Smith reached Paris in early November, 1785. Thanks to good detective work, he learned about a conspiracy in which the French Bourbons, cooperating with their Spanish allies, were planning to kidnap Colonel Miranda when he appeared in Paris. Smith immediately wrote to Miranda instructing him not to come to Paris at all—it was not safe for him. At this time, Smith did not supply the details of the conspiracy; he merely urged Miranda to take a circuitous route back to England via Amsterdam.[37]

This letter never reached Miranda. And for the next five months, Smith went through hell "from the most painful case of anxiety that I have experienced." When Miranda's letter from Naples (March 10, 1786) reached London, Colonel Smith felt some relief that Miranda had not been ensnared. In two letters of April 8th and 11th, Smith pleaded with Miranda to return to England as soon as possible.[38] Those two letters never reached Miranda.

On March 26, 1788, just before leaving London for the United States, Colonel Smith provided the details of the alleged conspiracy in Paris three years earlier. It was a fantastic story that even touched Thomas Jefferson, the representative of the United States in France. Smith went into detail on how he learned about the planned kidnapping of his Venezuelan cohort. One of his contacts was the man in charge of the Bastille. Jefferson playfully teased the serious colonel that he had better be careful, lest they lock him up in that famous Parisian jail! Colonel Smith continued his letter with another incident that had a bearing on the story. In the summer of 1787, Smith happened to be passing through Spain on his way to an assignment in Portugal. He heard the much publicized rumor that Spaniards had captured Miranda in England, taking him off a vessel that had entered the Thames River. The dangerous rebel Miranda was then spirited to Cádiz and later to Madrid, where he was a prisoner in the Court Jail. The whole story sounded false to Smith. It did not conform with the reports in England about Miranda's travels in Europe. Why would the Spanish government encourage such a false rumor to circulate? Smith's answer was that Spain wanted to impress her people with the fact that treason was impossible in their midst. The next obvious move for Colonel Smith was to visit the British Minister in Madrid. Great Britain would not have permitted such an infringement of her territorial waters. That, indeed, was the case; and Colonel Smith learned that the horrible tale about his Venezuelan friend was a brazen fabrication. It helped to relieve his sense of guilt for having published the prophetic editorial of 1785.[39]

Copies of Smith's final letter went to various points in Europe; but he decided to leave the original with James Penman in London. On June 18, 1789, Miranda returned to the English capital and learned for the first time about his dear friend's anxieties over the recent years. The news concerning Spain's intentions towards him did not come as any surprise. That hand had been exposed in Russia and in Sweden. Thanks to Catherine of Russia's protection, Miranda continued his travels with generous contributions by the Empress, who was determined to help Miranda liberate "Colombia" from the vicious rule of Spain. One final note on the 1785 editorial is that Miranda made no comments on it. Yet, he recognized its value as propaganda. One of his publicists cited it in 1808; and it was used again in January, 1809, in the *Edinburgh Review*—publications that will be analyzed later.[40]

Miranda perfected his world image during the protracted visit of the Continent—an intelligent and articulate Hispanic American who had fought in the American Revolution. Colonels Smith and Miranda told war stories that intrigued European officers, flattered by the genuine interest of these American colonels in the military systems of the Continent, as well as in their maneuvers and reviews. Moreover, the Americans insisted upon a first hand inspection of the famous battlegrounds of the Seven Years' War. After Smith's departure, Miranda carried on in the same effective manner. The European elites liked him, impressed with his politeness and delicacy of manner. He talked about the latest works, discreetly loaning books and articles to select individuals and borrowing others from them. It boggled the minds of Europeans to have in their midst such an urbane and cultured Hispanic American.[41] His command of the Classics especially singled Miranda out as a "Universal Man," a point underscored by a Swiss professor:

> He is the most extraordinary man whom I have ever met because of the extent of his travels in the four quarters of the world, because of the information that he has thus imbibed, because of the richness of his conversation, because of his knowledge of history, literature, fine arts,—in a word, because of a universality of which I had no idea and of which I had never beheld an example.[42]

The Austrian composer Franz Joseph Haydn, whom Miranda met at the Palace of the Esterhazy near Vienna, was likewise impressed with the Venezuelan's knowledge of music, as they discussed the merits of a little known Italian composer.[43]

With the winter of 1785 fast approaching, Miranda opted for a change in his itinerary. After visiting Trieste, he expected to proceed to Constantinople; and Emperor Joseph II issued him a passport to the Turkish city in glowing terms, as if he were a member of the nobility.[44] The dread of winter, and more importantly the proximity of his spiritual *patrias* (motherlands), dictated the decision to visit first the heartland of the Classical Age from November, 1785, to April, 1786 in Italy and the following three months in Greece. It was a highly emotional trip into the past, inspecting the reality of his studies and delights. The music and art of the Italians, and the visit to Greece and the Aegean region were the frosting on the cake.[45] The Scipio Africanus from Caracas had returned to his spiritual home. By July, 1786, Miranda was in Constantinople and the Black Sea area, still on his historical peregrination into Antiquity.[46]

In late September, 1786, Colonel Miranda made his way to the port of Kherson. Prince Gregory Potemkin had defeated the Turks in their last war (1769–1774) and then founded Kherson on the Black Sea, as a control center for Russian interests in the Crimea. The rumors that the Prince would soon visit Kherson undoubtedly motivated Miranda's visit to the land of the Tartars—a fortuitous decision, indeed. Prince Potemkin, former lover of the Empress, did appear on the scene and enjoyed Miranda's presence so much that he invited him to tour the Crimean Peninsula. Thanks to a clerical error in Constantinople, interpreting Joseph II's passport as worthy of a "Count," Miranda was able to leave his middle-class origins behind him.[47] The official connection with Potemkin, moreover, indicated that the Venezuelan traveler-noble was a guest of the Russian government. Not only did this mean an expense-free tour of the Crimean Peninsula, Poland, and Russia, but it also brought him loans, or grants of money to be more exact, that helped the new "Count" pay off his debts in England and elsewhere in Europe. It likewise financed the remainder of his trip to the northern part of the Continent, after he left Russia.[48] Miranda's diaries of Russian society before the French Revolution, the description of the trip through the Crimean Peninsula to Sebastapol, and the travels through Poland are all priceless historical documents left to posterity by one of the age's great memorialists.[49]

Catherine of Russia thought highly of her Venezuelan guest, whom she protected against the Spanish authorities.[50] He had authorization to dress in a Russian colonel's uniform, if he wished; and Miranda told Prince Potemkin that he ordered the dress of Catherine's Cavalry Regiment.[51] Moreover, she had issued a circular letter to her key diplomats in Europe to protect him in every way and to provide him with financial aid in her name.[52] With a Russian passport, Miranda was able to travel through other countries of Europe: Sweden, Norway, Denmark, the major Hanseatic Cities, and back to Amsterdam. In addition, his historical curiosity finally led him to Switzerland and then to France. Here his passport recorded the name, M. de Meroff, a Livonian gentleman. He first visited Marseilles and finally Paris, undetected by the French police. Monsieur de Meroff was the typical tourist who visited museums, bookstores, and military installations. Early one morning in June, 1789, Meroff slipped out of Paris on his way to London. It indeed was an eventful four years of Miranda's life.[53]

* * * * * * * * * * * *

Miranda's adjustment to the English milieu was rapid and smooth. He missed Colonel Smith, of course, especially after reading the letters about the Spanish conspiracy. It was no longer plausible for Miranda to continue the relationship with the Spanish Minister in London, although the latter seemed to be receptive.[54] To be sure, Smith was not there to accompany him in the nightlife of London, but another American filled the gap, none other than Stephen Sayre from New York! In the boastful manner of drinking companions, Miranda hinted at his close relations with Catherine of Russia. Stephen, of course, assumed that there had been sex as well; and he blustered to his Venezuelan colleague that he personally would not have left Russia under such favorable circumstances.[55] Along more serious lines, Sayre was the usual stalwart on the "Colombia" project; and it is conceivable that he introduced Miranda to Thomas Pownall, a favorite among Americans for having earnestly tried to settle differences between England and her colonies.[56] One of Pownall's biographers believes that it might have been James Bowdoin or John Adams who made the introduction.[57] Another possible candidate was Colonel Isaac Barré, who had cooperated with Pownall in the revolutionary crisis.[58] As a matter of fact, John Turnbull and Thomas Pownall were friends of longstanding; and it seems logical that this mutual friend might have been responsible for bringing the two men together.[59]

At any rate, the major consequence was the development of a very close relationship between the ex-Governor of Massachusetts and the vaunted liberator of South America. It lasted from January, 1790, until Pownall's death in 1805. Thomas Pownall and Francisco de Miranda had much in common. They were both inveterate champions and students of the Classical Age. They derived from the upper middle class and aspired for recognition by the higher classes of society. Pownall's second marriage in 1784 opened the doors to a more affluent existence for him; and "Count" Miranda thoroughly enjoyed his rank in the final phases of his trip on the Continent, leaving the impression that he was a progressive member of the nobility in Mexico.[60]   Both men were intelligent and perceptive; and they knew that Spanish America was on the threshold of emancipation from her European mother, following the precedent set by English America.   Pownall, in fact, published his views in London as early as 1780: *Memorial Most Humbly Addressed to the Sovereigns of Europe on the Present State of Affairs, Between the Old and the New World*.   Just as the British colonies had broken off from England, the same would happen in Spanish America.   "The falling off of South America," Pownall emphasized: "will be conducted in *its natural* progress, by the spirit of some injured enterprising Genius, taking the lead of a sense of alienation and of a disposition of revolt, to the establishment of a Great Monarchy."[61]   The anonymous editorial of 1785, it will be recalled, picked up Pownall's prophecy and applied it to Francisco de Miranda. Until his death, Governor Thomas Pownall was positive that Miranda would be Spanish America's "deliverer."   Be that as it may, from January 13 to 24, 1790, the two men worked feverishly to prepare their case for William Pitt.

A sincere British patriot and administrator, Thomas Pownall felt a deep concern for justice and natural law, the guidelines of his beloved Classical Age.   From 1755 to 1760, he served as the executive for English colonists in New Jersey and Massachusetts, who respected him for his fairness.   Later, from 1767 to 1780, he defended their cause with appeals for compromise and reconciliation in the halls of Parliament.   Yet, he fought in vain, thoroughly frustrated by his lack of influence among Englishmen.   The *Memorial*, reprinted in 1783 and followed by a second edition in 1803, delivered a concise message: the Anglo world should work together in a confederation advancing "free trade" in international affairs.   In linking up with Miranda, Pownall added to his confederation the Hispanic sections of the Western Hemisphere.   This great geographic zone would sponsor an economic customs union of "free trade" and the cause of international justice. Because of her advanced economic system of manufacturing, England was the major leader or guide in the Anglo-Hispanic union, collaborating in the promotion and improvement of the Americans in the Western Hemisphere.   Pownall's concern for England's leadership reflects his staunch nationalism.   Miranda, for his part, deliberately played upon the incentives for Englishmen in Spanish America that would secure England's predominance in world affairs, thanks also to her powerful naval and maritime facilities. England's prosperity, moreover, would guarantee Spanish America's independence from Spain. Presumably Brazil might also choose to join the alliance in support of free trade and constitutional monarchy. These two objectives would dominate the world and lead to its modernization, according to Thomas Pownall and his disciples.[62]

Those were the assumptions of the Pownall-Miranda team in their various projects from 1790 to 1805. Their program had a strong appeal to the merchants and industrialists in Great Britain and to Whig politicians as well. Prime Minister William Pitt, for example, yearned for such an economic boon that would help solve England's financial problems in the wake of the "American Revolution." The French disturbances from 1789 forward also weakened England's financial base; and here again the Pownall-Miranda projects seemed so tempting to William Pitt. Yet, the complex balance of power in the "Revolutionary Age" was itself a deterrent to the emancipation movement in South America.

Receptive to Pownall's overtures early in 1790, Pitt anxiously awaited the meeting with Miranda on Sunday, February 14, 1790, at Hollwood, his country house in the county of Kent. Nine years younger than Miranda, the Prime Minister showed special interest in the financial and commercial benefits suggested by Governor Pownall. Miranda assured him that South Americans would obligate themselves to pay the British government for the expenses of emancipation; they would also offer an annual stipend toward the reduction of the English debt. United by a "Solemn Compact" with the British, South America would establish a similar and free government; and she would join in a "Plan of Commerce" that would be reciprocally advantageous. The two nations together would form "the most respectable and preponderant Political union in the World." Pownall's influence was ubiquitous. Here was the alliance that he had written about in 1780. Another incentive for the British was the prospect of an interoceanic canal across the Isthmus of Panama. It would open up traffic between England and the Pacific, thus shortening lines to China and the South Seas. The governmental system envisioned by Miranda was consonant with the British pattern, both in theory and practice. A descendant of the Incas, the Emperor would constitute the hereditary executive power, who would share government with a bicameral congress. As devotees of Rome, the Pownall-Miranda team favored the use of censors, ediles, and questors: to watch over the morals of society; to supervise the infrastructure—ports, roads, monuments, etc.; and to oversee the nation's finances. The supportive documentation included statistics on population, trade, resources, etc. It was a thorough and persuasive presentation. Overwhelmed, Mr. Pitt decidedly favored the project.[63]

The strained relations with Spain also intensified Pitt's interest in the Miranda proposals. A dispute, threatening war, had arisen over an incident at Nootka Sound, off Vancouver Island in North America. It involved rival claims of sovereignty; and because of the Family Compact (Bourbons), it might also include France in the impending conflict. The instant that war began, the Miranda project would go into effect. But France and Spain were not in favor of a conflict at this juncture. In late July, 1790, the Conde de Floridablanca agreed to satisfy British claims on the seizure of property near Vancouver Island; the two countries signed an agreement to settle their differences several months later. Thus, Miranda's project was placed in limbo, until war with Spain once again threatened.

Commiserating with his advisor Pownall, Miranda despaired of Pitt's decision, angry at the way he was treated.[64] In his disillusionment, Francisco de Miranda even reconsidered the offer to serve in the military of the Empress Catherine. If Great Britain was not trustworthy, why not consult another European sponsor on his project? It might be appropriate to test the waters by returning to France and Russia. A revolutionary movement in France, for example, proclaimed a constitutional monarchy in 1789 with much fanfare about "liberty" and "freedom." These new French leaders might be interested in exporting those commodities to Spanish America. Miranda thus prepared his equipment and left London for Paris on March 20, 1792.[65]

The news of Miranda's presence in France immediately attracted the attention of the dominant Girondist party, whose leaders soon gathered with the Venezuelan. They anxiously hoped to spread their "Revolution" to Spain and her Empire. The Venezuelan remarked politely that it would be premature to push for the liberation of Spain; rather, France should capitalize on the rising sentiments for emancipation throughout the Americas. He reminded them that he had much to offer France in a project of this type; but he cautioned that it had to be properly organized to assure success. The French agreed, and it was understood that Miranda would be called when the time was ripe. At this point, early in August, 1792, Miranda made plans to visit

Russia for a few weeks before returning to London. He was sanguine that he had made some headway on his liberation project.[66]

The chaotic events of the French Revolution, however, were on the horizon. France declared war on Prussia and Austria in early August, 1792. Miranda had tickets to leave for St. Petersburg on the 12th; but orders went out prohibiting any exits from Paris. The Girondist leaders who had talked to Miranda, including General Charles F. Dumouriez, pleaded with him to join the French army in stopping the Prussian invasion. Their entry into Paris would jeopardize the lives of the royal family. If Miranda, an experienced officer of the American Revolution, would join France in stopping the northerners, it would expedite the realization of his great dream—the liberation and independence of "Colombia." Miranda thought about the proposition for several days and finally accepted it. He went into combat with General Dumouriez in the north holding the rank of Field Marshall. After a few months of brilliant fighting, he became Lieutenant General Miranda; and the Girondists hailed their American champion.[67]

There was talk, in late 1792, that General Miranda should head the government of Saint Domingue (Haiti) so that he could bring the querulous whites under control. As an American, argued the Girondist Jacques Pierre Brissot de Warville in a letter to General Dumouriez, Miranda would gain the support of the non whites—"the Idol of the people of colour." With the help of "10 or 15,000 brave Mulattos" and 12,000 regular troops, Miranda would be invincible against the Spanish Empire. Spaniards could not possibly counter his naval force. "The name of Miranda is worth an Army; and his Talents, his Courage, his Genius, all guarantee success." In this letter of November 28, 1792, Brissot emphasized that speed was imperative. "I know very well that his Appointment will strike Spain with Terror and confound Pitt with his poor dilatory Politics, but Spain is impotent, and England will not stir. Let us proceed, but ever be just and generous." If Dumouriez were willing to release Miranda, the plan would win approval in Paris, where everyone favored it.[68]

The Brissot suggestion, as worded, was too reminiscent of French colonial measures. When General Miranda learned of it, he cautioned prudence. He needed more information on St. Domingue and world developments. If France should take into account what had been proposed to William Pitt—and Miranda's papers were already available in Paris—the overseas project might achieve its objective.[69] Judging from his letters to Alexander Hamilton, Henry Knox, and William S.

Smith, Miranda was sanguine that "Colombia's" liberation was imminent. Colonel Smith, who was in London, again, urged his colleague to secure authorization for him to recruit foreign legionaries for the French cause in America and Europe.[70]

The ambitious Caribbean project had a dim future in the troubled political waters of France. Dumouriez sorely needed Miranda in the north where battle field reversals might occur if the French were not at full strength. Given the situation in Spain and England, it would be wise to postpone the Dominican venture. Others concurred with General Dumouriez; and that was as far as the "Grand Project" got—another reversal for the famous Venezuelan.

The rest of the French road was downhill for Miranda, during the new year 1793. The Monarchy turned into a Republic, and the King lost his head. General Dumouriez, defeated in some key battles, was accused of trying to restore the monarchy and to betray France. Miranda likewise ended up in a trial concerning negligence in battle. Absolved by the end of 1793, the Venezuelan emerged as a hero in France and elsewhere. Then the Girondists gave way to the "Mountain," controlled by the Jacobins and the spiteful Maximilien Robespierre, who hated Miranda with a vengeance. Indeed, it was a miracle that General Miranda survived eighteen months of incarceration under the Jacobins. In publications, Miranda spoke out against the radical change in the direction of the "Revolution." It heightened his notoriety and image among the enemies of radical revolution throughout Europe, those elites who feared the social direction that the French were taking. Somehow Miranda avoided the guillotine; and Robespierre died. But the Directorate was hardly better, Miranda again went to prison. There seemed no alternative but to return to Great Britain at the first opportunity.[71]

* * * * * * * * * * * *

On January 16, 1798, almost eight years since their first meeting at Hollwood, Miranda and William Pitt discussed the revival of the 1790 project. England was at war with Spain, who had signed a treaty of alliance with France in September, 1796. William Pitt feared the absorption of Spain by France and especially the prospects that the "abominable system" of the French Revolution might project itself into the Spanish Empire. Miranda deliberately capitalized on the French danger in America to stir the English into action. He reminded Pitt of strained relations between France and the United States, which might encourage North Americans to join the alliance with Great Britain and "the Sovereign States of the Spanish People of America." This Triple Alliance would have as its major objective: the invasion of Spanish America to avoid French dominance. Spanish colonials were now more receptive than ever for a liberating invasion that would bring them independence.[72]

The new European context, obvious to Miranda during his last year in France, led him to prepare the ground for another meeting with Pitt. He used John Turnbull as the intermediary who notified the Prime Minister of Miranda's latest thoughts on the 1790 project. Anticipating that Pitt might put up legalistic obstacles, Miranda called together in Paris a Junta of Spanish American Deputies, representing large sections of the Empire. These Spanish Americans signed a set of instructions on December 22, 1797, in which the Junta empowered Miranda to negotiate with Pitt. It is notable that the instructions followed the Hollwood guidelines with only few variations.[73]

According to General Miranda, the military force of the Triple Alliance would consist of twenty-seven British ships and an expeditionary force of fifteen thousand men: 8,000 English infantrymen, 5,000 North American troops, and 2,000 British cavalrymen. South Americans would join in large numbers as the invasion took place and advanced throughout their homeland. U.S. troops were to lead the assault on the Isthmus of Panama in the vicinity of Chagres; and there would be additional strikes into northern South America. Once the port of Cartagena fell to the liberators, a pincer from Venezuela in the east and one from Chile in the south would close together, thus securing the southern continent. Three British ships were to attack Buenos Aires and prevent the Spaniards from sending forces to the north; and additional English naval forces in the Pacific would patrol the coasts from Lima, Peru, to Acapulco, Mexico. The final attacks would be in Central America and Mexico.[74]

South Americans, of course, would throw off their chains and join the liberators. They would instantly form a new nation, which would show its gratitude to England by agreeing to pay a sum of about thirty million pounds sterling, a figure that emerged from the negotiations between Pitt and Miranda. English and North American merchants would pay lower tolls in the traffic across the Isthmus. It was also suggested that the Caribbean islands, with the exception of Cuba, might be placed under the control of the United States or Great Britain. The governmental system—the rule of an Inca and a bicameral parliament—was the same one discussed eight years earlier at Hollwood.[75]

The 1798 project seemed ideal for the conditions at the time. Rufus King, the new U.S. Minister in London, was a strong enthusiast of joint Anglo-American action on the "Colombia" dream. Alexander Hamilton wanted to lead the invading forces, but he had some reservations concerning the English role in the venture. British merchants like John Turnbull desired to open up new markets for their products and urged William Pitt to support Miranda in every way. Governor Pownall continued to advise his Venezuelan colleague. He reminded him that Providence had made him suffer in France in preparing him for a "Grand Role in the Drama of the World, I mean the New World. *Vive la liberté dans le Nouveau Monde.*"[76] Pownall's influence on governmental matters, so strongly Roman in inspiration, persisted in the 1798 project.

Although initially favorable to joint action with England, President John Adams decided against the expedition on grounds that the British might usurp the liberation of Spanish America. Besides, he had doubts about Miranda's quixotic schemes. Without the United States' support, unfortunately, the 1798 project was dead.[77] American reluctance merely permitted William Pitt to play his customary hand in the grand name of European diplomacy: the "Second Coalition" to prevent Spain's absorption. Miranda's dream was again stillborn. He demanded his passport to proceed to Trinidad; but the British government refused to grant it. Pitt wanted Miranda around, in the event England changed her mind. Miranda's presence in South America might also complicate matters for the British. Miranda was furious; and he persisted in his demands, to no avail.[78] In late 1800, he finally gained permission to go to France, where he hoped to recoup his unpaid salaries as a general. The Consul Napoleon, to Miranda's chagrin, was no improvement over the "Directorate." The Venezuelan again ended up in a French prison! Finally, on March 14, 1801, he was allowed to leave France.[79]

Europeans won a respite from war during the Truce of Amiens (1801–1803); and Miranda, who returned to England, settled down to his studies of the Classical Age. The Pitt ministry fell because of the King's opposition to the Catholic emancipation program in Ireland; and Henry Addington, one of Pitt's friends, formed the next cabinet. A member of Parliament chosen to serve in the Treasury, Nicholas Vansittart was a key figure in Addington's government. Thanks to John

Turnbull, Vansittart took a special interest in reviving Miranda's project. This was the beginning of another long-lasting friendship for Francisco de Miranda, who, in addition, gained a yearly allowance from the British government. In cooperation with Governor Pownall, Miranda worked on perfecting governmental institutions for "Colombia." The plans now called for two Incas serving for five year terms: one residing at the capital and the other traveling throughout the nation, as a trouble shooter. The Pownall-Miranda team also incorporated the Roman tradition of "Dictator" in cases of governmental crisis. The two Incas would agree on a candidate, giving him the full powers of a dictator for a year's time.[80] Miranda and Rufus King continued their collaboration, during which the U.S. Minister could not disguise his disappointment with President Adam's decision. When he left Great Britain in 1803, King asked Miranda to accompany him to the United States, assuring him that he could get all the aid he needed there for his "Colombia" project. Perhaps because of Vansittart, Miranda chose to believe that the British would not abandon him anymore.[81]

War broke out again in Europe on May 16, 1803; and it boosted the prospects for Miranda's expedition. The contractor Alexander Davison invested his money without hesitation; and the popular naval figure, Sir Home Popham, added to its credibility. Yet, the Addington cabinet likewise had a tendency to waver, so that Miranda was never sure of the future.[82] On May 12, 1804, a new cabinet took over, headed by William Pitt! Popham encouraged Miranda's project in an aggressive manner that convinced Pitt and the new Secretary of the Admiralty, Lord Melville. Napoleon was now Emperor of France; and in mid-December, 1804, a war crisis developed with Spain. Prime Minister Pitt felt it was time to renew his contact with the Venezuelan promoter in London.

The wary Miranda watched the feverish preparations of the Pitt ministry and the incessant negotiations concerning the expeditionary force to the New World. The Prime Minister's ways had not changed, as he launched the "Third Coalition" of Europe to stop the French Emperor. This would certainly restrain Napoleon from absorbing Spain; and it might protect England from a French invasion. Despite Miranda's entreaties, there were the usual delays. Somewhat paranoid in his third experience with William Pitt, Miranda suspected duplicity: Pitt wanted to keep Spain neutral so badly that he was holding out promises not to invade the Spanish Empire.[83] Whatever Pitt's motives were, General Miranda decided that he could wait no longer. In mid-1805, he was already demanding his passport to Trinidad or the United States. His sympathizers in the New World were insisting on immediate action.[84] "Colombia" was restless, and Miranda had to depend on his natural allies in the Western Hemisphere. Also, he was perhaps angry at himself for not having left with Rufus King two years earlier.

It was during the earlier negotiations with the Addington government that a sensitive and crucial issue came to the fore. The question, which had a highly emotional and nationalistic answer, was simply: Who was to be in charge of the "Colombia" enterprise? General Miranda? Or an Englishman? Considering all the major factors involved, the British, of course, would not tolerate a non-Englishman to head an expeditionary force that in almost every respect was British. Once the expedition landed on foreign soil and a new government was ready to assume power, then, and only then, could a non-Englishman take over.[85] This British position, of course, presented a disturbing predicament for Miranda since a liberation movement, by its very nature, presumed an invincible, national leader, not a "lackey" of invading foreign forces. This delicate situation, moreover, was made even more disruptive as long-standing charges resurfaced that Francisco de Miranda was a "soldier of fortune," "an adventurer," and "contraband trader." Officials of the Pitt government hastened to assure Miranda that they had no sympathy with such negative propaganda.[86] Unconvinced of these assurances, Miranda recalled that Pitt and other English officials, including Sir Home Popham, had a propensity for "Conquest" rather than the liberation objective that he championed. When he insisted upon his passport to Trinidad, Prime Minister Pitt apparently lost his patience with the Venezuelan: Miranda should be permitted to leave but under no conditions should he act in Trinidad without the approval of the Governor. Miranda was beside himself at this "personal insult," which was another expression of British superiority over his "Colombia" dream.[87] The final insult was the information that William Pitt really wanted Francisco de Miranda to wait around in England until European diplomacy reached the level of "convenient maturity."[88]

The decision to rely on his natural allies in the United States avoided the pesky nationalistic question. North Americans agreed with Miranda that only "Americans" should be responsible for forces operating in the New World proper. Europeans, on the other hand, would be tolerated on the waters off the coasts of America. Those born in the Old World found this attitude hard to understand. They apparently chose to ignore the historical process that had gotten underway in the New World during the 1760s, that wave of anticolonialism that poured over the Americas.

General Miranda did not break completely with the English in 1805. Pitt's final actions in his behalf were enough to convince Miranda that he could count on British support in the Caribbean, once his expedition had gotten underway and offered real promise of success. Nicholas Vansittart, in particular, would be the key middleman, or British spokesman, in what might be called an "unwritten alliance" with the Venezuelan promoter and his North American supporters. In this context, or perspective, there appeared to be a continuity with the rejected 1798 project.[89]

* * * * * * * * * * *

On November 9, 1805, the *Polly* made her way into the New York harbor; and her distinguished passenger disembarked under the assumed name of Mr.George Martin. Before long, the public learned that General Francisco de Miranda was in their midst. Henceforth, all over the world, people waited anxiously for news concerning the Venezuelan adventurer. The return to the United States brought on an emotional meeting with his friend William S. Smith, after so many years of absence. Now a Surveyor of the Port of New York, Colonel Smith had not changed one iota in his patriotic fervor. He still felt that Miranda was a man of destiny who would bring "freedom" to the Hispanic world and "the amelioration of the state of man." These poignant words record his messianic spirit:

> Our two Countries liberated from the galling yoke of oppression will furnish an expanded asylum for the injured and oppressed to fly to, and the northern and southern Continents will become the abode of freemen, sheltered from the assaults of Tyrants and the intrigues of vicious and Corrupt Courtiers. The oppressed European will find a tranquil and safe retreat; and the native American, embraced within the benevolent bosom of Civilization, will be under the protection of a well digested Constitution, a Government of Laws, (*not of men*), that written Constitution as a basis, firm and immovable as the pillar of Time.[90]

A skilled organizer and recruiter, Colonel William S. Smith hastened to complete the preparations for Miranda's expedition into the Caribbean. He introduced Miranda to Samuel G. Ogden, a patriotic merchant who was willing to risk much capital on the enterprise. Miranda also met the irascible "Commodore" Thomas Lewis who captained the main ship *Leander*, and whose brother Jacob controlled the service of another vessel. In short order, there were reportedly some fifty thousand dollars in the project. Materials came in for a total of five ships; and Colonel Smith personally supervised the recruitment of some two hundred men. He hoped to select the best qualified and motivated; but that was an impossible assignment considering the time element. The men were of varied backgrounds. Most of them were from the New York and the New England areas, adventuresome young men enticed by the rumors concerning the enterprise. Aware of the recruits' motives, Smith despaired that General Miranda might have trouble controlling them once the invasion began—the indomitable instinct of the "Conqueror." Perhaps his friend Miranda might request a leave of absence for him from the federal government that would permit Smith to join his old comrade. Yet, Colonel Smith doubted that President Thomas Jefferson would ever grant such permission. He was right. The government would not allow a federal employee to be involved in the expedition, unless he resigned his post and operated at his own risk. General Miranda advised his friend not to take such a gamble. Besides, he needed Smith's organizing genius in New York to expedite shipments of supplies and recruits after the expedition sailed to the south. Thus, the good colonel had no choice but to resign himself; and Miranda bolstered his spirit by accepting Lt. Colonel William Steuben Smith as his aide-de-camp. Thus, father and mother Smith still had a personal connection with the vaunted odyssey to the south. And General Miranda wrote to them periodically about their son's progress. Young Smith performed with distinction and fidelity in the 1806 expedition.[91]

It took only two and one-half months to complete the preparations for Miranda's expedition, an exceptional performance despite some anxious moments. To the surprise of Miranda, "politics" slowed matters down somewhat—the "Federalists" versus the "Republicans" of Thomas Jefferson. Perhaps the famous duel of July 1, 1804, had much to do with the tension of the moment—the death of the Federalist Alexander Hamilton at the hands of the Republican Aaron Burr, Jefferson's first Vice President. Rufus King was still preoccupied with the Hamilton estate when Miranda arrived in New York. The

Venezuelan's major collaborators in the United States were the Federalists Rufus King in New York and Christopher Gore of Boston, two men who for years had encouraged Miranda to undertake his expedition from the United States as a base. Yet, now, they seemed to be holding back their support.[92]

The Gore connection in Massachusetts was a dismal failure. Miranda's representative in the North was Major William Armstrong, another one of Colonel Smith's friends who was a key participant in the Caribbean effort. Armstrong proceeded to Boston with two key letters, one for Gore and the other for General Henry Knox, Miranda's old friend. Through Gore, Miranda hoped to interest Boston merchants in buying the necessary ammunition and guns, plus a financial support of from fifty to seventy thousand dollars. To begin with, Gore was so sick at the time of Armstrong's arrival that he could not attend his colleagues' meetings. These gentlemen, in turn, rejected the investment opportunity because it lacked a guarantee! Moreover, they feared that war with Spain would expose them to further complications and losses.[93]

As the "Mr. K." of the correspondence, Rufus King truly wanted to help his old friend Miranda because he knew that Nicholas Vansittart fully supported it. A few years later, in fact, Lord Castlereagh learned the unvarnished truth that Nicholas Vansittart, acting without any real authority, had encouraged Miranda's project in 1806.[94] To Rufus King, this meant that the United States and Great Britain were in fact both sponsors of the 1806 expedition—a reality that became even more patent during the year in question.

Hardly three weeks after his arrival, Miranda's plans were far enough along to permit him a visit to Washington, D.C. His objective was to obtain tacit approval for his expedition from the Jefferson government, a guarantee that Mr. K. and New York investors felt was necessary to assure their cooperation. With his ubiquitous diary, General Miranda left New York on November 29, 1805, recording, as he made his way southward, sundry data about the towns, places, and cities he passed. On the evening of November 30th, Miranda reached Philadelphia, his favorite city; and the love affair once again blossomed.[95] He spent three days there. Besides the sightseeing, Miranda revived his friendship with Dr. Benjamin Rush. The famous revolutionary figure gladly supplied his friend with a letter of introduction to Secretary of State James Madison, a good friend of the family. General Miranda also had the pleasure of meeting Richard

Rush, the doctor's son, who volunteered to escort Miranda around the city for a few days—a tour and commentary that will concern us later.

Miranda's diary of Washington, D.C. (December 6–17, 1805) is a fascinating account for anyone familiar with the area.[96] Despite the formidable plans for the city, founded in 1800, Miranda learned to his surprise that contemporaries were not sanguine about the implementation of said projects. The work was shoddy and the advances pitiful. Even the President's House had window frames without glass and the tiles on the roof were loose and missing. Mr. Richard Law claimed that he had invested forty thousand dollars in the project; and most people believed that Miranda's friend would be lucky to come out with eight thousand. The Naval Yard, on the other hand, seemed to be a progressive institution.

Housed at Stelle's Hotel on the Hill, General Miranda soon made friends with congressmen who invited their famous visitor to the Senate and the House of Representatives. Senators made no apologies for their hostility towards Napoleon; and after sitting through a session of the House, the Venezuelan observer noted in his diary that it appeared to be a cross between the phlegmatic Dutch Parliament and the tumultuous French Assembly.[97] One evening General Miranda attended a ball that he enjoyed immensely. He observed that American women had improved in their looks over the past twenty years! The inquisitive tourist found time to visit the home of General George Washington, offering his diary reader a lively description of Mount Vernon. He conversed with many members of the Washington Family and enjoyed a delicious meal with them. Judge Washington, the general's heir, asked Miranda to stay overnight, a kind offer which the general could not accept because of his schedule at the capital.

Miranda's interviews with President Thomas Jefferson and Secretary of State James Madison were informal, gracious, and straight-forward. On December 7, 1805, the morning after his arrival in Washington, D.C., Miranda presented his card and Rush's letter of recommendation. Jefferson was talking with some ministers and warmly greeted the Venezuelan while making some light remarks about the constant warfare in Europe. At the first opportunity, Miranda excused himself and headed for Madison's office. In few words he told the Secretary of State that he had serious business to discuss and recommended utmost secrecy. The business meetings took place at one o'clock on the afternoons of the 11th (Wednesday) and the 13th (Friday); and the social gatherings on the 13th at President Jefferson's house and on

Tuesday (17th) at Madison's home—sufficient time to present their positions and get to know each other.

At the first business discussion, Miranda presented his case by reminding Madison that for twenty years he worked for the "solid and absolute Emancipation of the Hispanic-American continent," in the mode that the United States had won its freedom from England. All that was needed now, to win the liberty of the Hispanic World, was the *"consentimiento tácito"* of the United States Government. The Executive Branch had only "to wink at" what Miranda was doing in New York City. And this would be the sign to friends in Boston and New York City to come forth with the needed financial support. Madison wanted to know which Hispanic provinces were involved in the liberation program. Miranda named them, inferring from Madison's question: "that they have their sights on Mexico—or that they are talking with Mexicans on the matter." Madison then briefly stated his government's position that citizens of the United States were free to assist such projects, according to international law. At any rate, he would confer with Jefferson and give Miranda a final answer at the Friday meeting.[98]

As the two met again, Secretary of State James Madison did not mince any words. The government of the United States could not officially support the Miranda project without violating its obligations to other nations with which it was at peace. Besides, the nature of Miranda's enterprise, risky and small in size, made it more appropriate for private parties to support, not a government that would be unduly compromised in case of a breakdown. Miranda replied spiritedly that all he wanted was the indirect aid, similar to that of the Bourbon powers before they entered the American Revolution. Besides, the United States would gain from the expedition. Mr. Rufus King had authorized him to say that the Federalists would supply the necessary money for the project "if the government would just give an approval and *Winked-at-it.*" He could not understand, Madison shot back irresistibly: "why the government had to *smile* or look angry at the project." Individuals were free to assist Miranda, providing there was no violation of the law. When Miranda noted that there was a legislative project in Congress to prohibit the exportation of arms and munitions of war, Madison assured him that the legislation in question would not go into effect for some time. Madison added that the success of the Miranda expedition would bring about the world's approval. At this point, Miranda recognized that he had heard the last word.[99] Besides, he was satisfied that the administration, in its own guarded way, had provided the "tacit approval" for his expedition. Rufus King understood it this way. He first assured Miranda of the needed financial backing in late December, 1805, and confirmed it absolutely by January 22, 1806.[100]

The social gatherings with members of the Jefferson government added another dimension of approval to Miranda's enterprise. Spanish agents had been watching Miranda carefully since his arrival in the United States; and the Marquis de Casa Urujo, the Spanish Minister in Washington, D.C., interpreted General Miranda's reception as sufficient proof of the intentions of the United States. He, therefore, alerted Spanish authorities in the Caribbean and in Venezuela to prepare themselves for the rumored invasion by General Miranda and his forces. France and Spain officially complained that the United States government had permitted the outfitting of Miranda's expedition in an American port. The clamor was such that President Jefferson had no alternative but to prosecute William S. Smith and Samuel G. Ogden for violating the laws of the nation. One of the famous legal cases of the times, the American public followed it closely for many weeks. The final verdict was the acquittal of General Miranda's two friends, although Smith eventually lost his federal post. The Jefferson administration won few friends by raising the case against Miranda's colleagues.[101]

Although Madison's remarks in their final meeting had left him somewhat dejected, Francisco de Miranda went over to the President's house for the 3:30 P.M. reception and subsequent banquet. He put on his best face for President Jefferson who talked to him incessantly about Hispanic America. The President paraphrased the great German scientist, Alexander Von Humboldt, on Spanish America; he talked of the possibility of building a canal from the Atlantic to the Pacific, a fascinating project; and he hoped that Americans, not Spaniards, would undertake the interoceanic passageway; he went on about the Apaches and Cherokees always urging him to permit an attack upon the possessions of Spain in the name of the United States government; and he thoroughly was amenable to Miranda's offer of a copy of a Jesuit Father's study on Chile. President Jefferson lamented, in conclusion, that he had been born too soon to witness "the glory and splendor of America, that was advancing by great strides towards her Universal Independence, the interoceanic canal, etc. etc."[102] General Miranda dutifully sent President Jefferson the Jesuit's work, recalling with feeling what Jefferson had said about "our dear Colombia" and her glorious destiny.[103]

Although General Miranda had some reservations about his achievements in the United States, he considered it a qualified success. Rufus King and his associates in New York followed through with their promises of financial assistance, although Gore's Boston crowd remained adamant in their negative stance. To make up for the Boston revenue, General Miranda drew some seven thousand pounds sterling from English associates: John Turnbull and Nicholas Vansittart in London and two merchants from Trinidad. None complained of Miranda's act of expediency.[104] These Englishmen were solidly behind his dream to liberate South America with the support of North American interests. Governor Thomas Pownall would have rejoiced at the "deliverer's" accomplishments in the United States, if his life had been extended one more year.

* * * * * * * * * * * *

Like his father Benjamin, Richard Rush was a Princeton graduate. As a legal student, he passed the bar in 1800. Although he later went into politics, his main career was in diplomacy. Acting Secretary of State under President James Monroe in 1817, he also received an appointment in that same year as Minister to Great Britain, a post which he held until 1825. He was the American representative who negotiated with George Canning at the time of Monroe's famous declaration of 1823. In the late 1840s he served in France. Recognized as a cultivated gentleman, Richard Rush was also a writer—the author, for example, of *Memoranda of a Residence at the Court of London*. Like Miranda, Rush went out of his way to interview scientists and intellectuals of his age. In 1836, he represented the United States in receiving the James Smithson bequest in London, his first connection with what was to become the Smithsonian Institution.

Such was the future of Richard Rush, who at twenty-five was to escort a famous personage around his beloved Philadelphia. On December 4, 1805, as General Miranda left for the nation's capital, this young man sat down at his desk to write his impressions of General Miranda.[105] Unaware of his future career and its accomplishments, Richard Rush was preparing himself for the role of interviewer which he did so well in later years.

General Miranda

I have passed a considerable part of the last two days in the company of this extraordinary man, at his own lodgings, at my father's house, or in walking about town. I have heard him say so many things, and so many of his sentiments and facts have been remarkable, that I must record a few of them while yet fresh in my memory.

He said the simplicity of manners he observed when before in this country, shortly after the revolution, seemed to have vanished; that a kind of *Plutocracy* has risen up; that he saw in our large cities ostentatious displays that tried to ape the luxury of Europe; that he was sorry for it; he had hoped this country would breed up an independent race of republicans, aiming to be great like the old Romans from integrity, talents, and illustrious deeds.

[Miranda's impressions of Napoleon Bonaparte were not complimentary, in the least. Note how the Venezuelan used his expertise on the Classical Age to portray Napoleon:]

When Caesar crossed the Rubicon all his soldiers chose to go with him. A great commander knows how to command *mind*, and makes his troops love, not hate him! He said there was a great difference between being at the head of an army, and being its *spring*. Julius Caesar was the spring of his army: Turenne of his, Frederick of his; Gustavus Adolphus of his. Bonaparte was the *head* of his army.

[Throughout the interview, General Miranda impressed his young companion with the great names he had known: Frederick the Great, Prince Potemkin, the Empress Catherine, the Archduke Charles, etc. etc. And he had kept a journal of his conversations with these eminent personages, he told young Richard. The writer continued:]

I was surprised at his various and apparently profound learning. He said that in London he had once, for three years in continuation, read 12, 14 and 15 hours a day. He went to a bookseller, and desired him to procure him every Greek author he could get. These he read in the course of those three years. He added that whatever a man's pursuits might be, letters were the most delightful resource for those hours which would certainly be left unemployed. He had ever found it so. He then quoted Cicero's fine eulogium upon them in his oration for the poet Archias. He said Aristotle had the greatest empire of mind of any mortal that had ever lived.

[As the General revisited some institutions and went to new ones that he had not seen in Philadelphia twenty years earlier, he provided his young companion with many insights:]

I took him to see the hospital. He said he had not seen so fine a one in Europe. When in the anatomical room he discovered, in conversation with the surgeon of the institution, a minute acquaintance with anatomy. Speaking of soul, he said we know no more of its immortality than Plato did. Looking on the large bronze statue of William Penn, I observed to him that Montesquieu had called him the Modern Lycingus. This led him to speak of Montesquieu whom I found he did not venerate highly. He said any man who lived a year in England, and was any thing above a mere vulgar observer, would find a great deal of what the 'spirit of laws' said about the British constitution, to be only theory.

I went with him to the Museum in Chestnut St. He displayed knowledge upon all the subjects that engaged his eye: coins, medals, animals, pictures, no matter what. The history of every American portrait appeared to be perfectly familiar to him. 'How much,' said he, 'it would add value to Plutarch if to every one of his lives were prefixed a good likeness. To see a good picture of Cato the Younger, one that I was sure was exactly like him, I would go a thousand miles.' He then referred to Sallust's account of Cato, and his parallel between him and Cicero.

I went with him to Mr. Hamilton's seat at the Woodlands. All that related to painting and statuary seemed to be known to him. He had cultivated a taste for both in Italy. He recommended some authors to me in each of these arts. In going through the greenhouse, his remarks showed that botany had also been among his studies.

When he entered the apartment of the Museum, where the skeleton of the mammoth stands, looking up at it he said, we have great *animals* upon this continent; we have great *mountains*; and we must have great *men.* He then spoke of South America. The inhabitants, he said, of North and South America should, in their government and interests, copy the union of the vast continent upon which they both live. He said South America was not yet, and he feared would not be, in our day, sufficiently understood; it was a country of infinite resources. The inhabitants, he added, were as enlightened as those of the United States when they began their revolution and could understand *Common Sense* as well. He here alluded to Paine's work.

[Elsewhere in the interview, Miranda said the following on the theme of man in history:]

He said that the great and striking events of the world, whether in political revolutions, science, morals, manners etc. had been brought about through the agency of single individuals, rather than combinations of men; that it was wonderful how much *one man* could do. He instanced Solon, Lycurgus, Numa, and others.

[Unable to get the French off of his mind, Miranda offered this final salvo:]

He said the French talked of imitating the Romans; but if they meant the Romans when they were sound, they did not imitate them, for if they had the spirit of the Romans, they would not so long have borne an usurper.

[Richard Rush finished the interview in this manner:]

The foregoing from some of the general topics he touched. I have given but a word, a single idea, where what he said might often have been spread over pages, and sometimes eloquent ones. He talked copiously, was always animated, and used great gesture of the countenance, arms, and even body. His ideas and knowledge were poured forth in floods at every question. He spoke much of our country, his inquiries respecting which were directed by a most intelligent curiosity. He expressed constant surprise and delight at its rapid advancement since he had last visited it.

There is little doubt that young Richard Rush had a rare talent for capturing the personality and essence of the person he was interviewing. He had been in the presence of a "Scipio Africanus from Caracas."

Chapter Two

A British Star in Spanish America's Emancipation

The injustice and stupidity of Spain now afford England an opportunity
of erecting in the rich savannas of South America another herculean and
indestructible monument to her genius, her virtue, her liberty, and her
power. May the illumining star of British glory light us to the right use
of the present inestimable opportunity!

William Burke, 1807[1]

Sir Home and Old England Forever

A cabal of naval officers and their political allies was conspiring
against Sir Home Riggs Popham—such a demeaning scheme against a
popular naval leader who only recently had captured the City of Buenos
Aires in Spanish South America. To be sure, he had no specific
authorization for that daring raid; but it must be admitted that it verily
electrified a war-weary nation of Englishmen. And British merchants,
fearful of Napoleon's designs on English trade with the Continent,
welcomed Popham's venture into Spain's Río de la Plata. To counter
the cabal's move, Sir Home prepared himself thoroughly for the court-
martial at Portsmouth on March 6, 1808.[2]

Public opinion differed widely on the momentous issue at stake in
the four-day trial at Portsmouth, while London's emotional press
coverage further impaled Englishmen on the horns of a dilemma. What
discretionary authority should British officers have in faraway posts?

Should they follow instructions to the letter, or might they take calculated risks that promised great gains for England? A recent report from the Plata, however, countered with the recapture of Buenos Aires by Spanish forces! Sir Home's victory was for naught? Many writers now began to wonder whatever possessed Popham to undertake such a mission with only seventeen hundred men.[3] The naval jurors, in the meantime, gathered at Portsmouth, studied the evidence carefully, and decided that Sir Home Riggs Popham should be "severely reprimanded."[4]

This embarrassing verdict threatened his future in the service; and, in all fairness, it would appear that Popham's arrogance at the trial had much to do with the jurors' vote. His attacks on the incumbent Admiralty were tenacious. Many of his superiors in the Navy resented Popham's meteoric rise to prominence. And Sir Home's fighting instincts led him to challenge the Portsmouth decision by marshalling his naval allies and by preparing a special edition of the trial proceedings. By taking his case to the public, he stubbornly hoped to sway public opinion against a narrow-minded party faction in His Majesty's Navy.[5]

Sir Home thus arranged a meeting with the leading merchants and underwriters of London for March 18, 1807. At three o'clock that afternoon, the Commodore strutted into Lloyd's Coffee-House and made his way up to the Subscription Room, which was unusually crowded. Three cheers greeted his presence, whereupon Sir Home spoke as follows:

> Gentlemen. It is impossible for me to express what I feel on this occasion, seeing myself surrounded by the most respectable merchants of the first City in the world, marking personally their opinion of my exertion to promote the public welfare; and although His Majesty's Government found it expedient to arraign my conduct on my return from abroad, I trust my defence will satisfy the respectable body to whom I have now the honour to address myself, that every action of mine was directed to promote the honour and glory of my country, and that I shall ever feel myself bound to employ my humble talents for the attainment of any object conducive to its prosperity, although I feel that wings of discretion have been materially clipt.[6]

A deafening applause welcomed the naval officer's speech; and the newspaper accounts portrayed Sir Home as the epitome of British courage and character. As he made his way down the stairs and out into the street, people everywhere shouted with enthusiasm: "Sir Home and Old England Forever."[7]

* * * * * * * * * * * *

Notoriety and controversy were indeed characteristic of Sir Home's career in the Navy. His personality seemed to invite attention to himself—a man who was aggressive, dynamic, arrogant, ambitious, and intelligent with a well-developed acquisitive instinct. Sir Home liked money and all that it could bring him—a trait described disparagingly by his critics who referred to him as a man of "speculative notions."[8] An entrepreneur at heart, Popham felt a close bond with the merchant class. He catered to its interests, as if aspiring to be a representative of the merchant community in Parliament. He admitted his political aspirations to his Venezuelan friend, Francisco de Miranda.[9] His clear commitment to the Whig Party of William Pitt pointed in the same direction. He was fiercely loyal to Pitt, and Lords Melville and Grenville. As a result, he inherited their enemies in and outside of His Majesty's Navy.[10]

Sir Home Riggs Popham was an unusually talented and versatile individual. He once wrote a book on telegraphic signals, for example.[11] When Lord Melville headed the Admiralty, Popham reported to him periodically on a secret research project involving carcasses. And there were frequent assignments of an undercover nature in which his political superiors allowed him considerable discretionary authority.[12] He seemed to anticipate the type of information wanted by Pitt, Melville, and Grenville; and he often offered invaluable suggestions on policy. They had full confidence in Popham, who thought like a politician. His superiors admired the wide range of his abilities: as a naval officer, researcher, diplomat, and strategist. That is why he received commands and assignments that, in truth, required men of higher rank. The fact that he bypassed the "common routine" made him suspect to many captains and admirals in the Navy. Sir Home, who was somewhat paranoid—even reporters commented upon his persecution complex—noted during his trial that there were more admirals than usual on the naval jury that was passing judgment upon him.[13]

Sir Home's advance in the British Navy after 1793 had been dramatic. Assigned to serve as "Agent of Transports" at Ostend—so his critics tell us—Popham became a "burgher" of that Belgian city, fattening his purse accordingly. Fortunate to be at the right place at the right time, Popham graduated to the assignment of "Superintendent of the Navigation on the Continent" as British forces landed in Belgium to cooperate with the Austrians. King George III assigned his second son to head the expedition; and the Duke of York, as it turned out, relied heavily upon Popham in carrying out his assignment. He placed him in command of transferring Russian troops to Belgium; and, apparently, Popham's performance was commendable. Promotions began to flow from the royal will in the next few years: first, as "master;" then as "Commander;" and, finally, as "Post Captain." The command with regards to the Russian troops was the first of many that Popham would receive, allowing him to advance over the heads of others. It made a mockery of the seniority system in the Navy. In 1800, Popham was successful in commanding British forces in the Red Sea area—again an assignment that resulted from a political decision—and his consumate diplomatic skill in Egypt two years later brought his name forth, once again, to the attention of the British public.[14] He was a naval officer with a future.

Sir Home joined the government's discussions on an expedition to South America in late 1803, a project that had intrigued William Pitt for years. Popham's involvement, of course, made him an inseparable friend of the Venezuelan Miranda. Sir Home's affinity to British merchants convinced him that Hispanic America was the land of the future, especially if it came under the guidance of Englishmen.

Popham's critics admitted that his defense at the Court-Martial was "ingenious" and even "poetical" although "by no means correct as to facts."[15] In light of the evidence, this was not an accurate charge. In fact, Sir Home presented exact information about the projected expedition to South America, even though it was slanted to convince his jurors. Certain omissions and points of emphasis were intended to show the jury that the Platine project was of long standing. Lord Melville testified that in the late 1790's he had considered an attack upon the Río de la Plata in the administrative post that he occupied at that time.[16] Sir Home followed with documentary evidence showing that the Platine project had been an option for years. He highlighted effectively the discussions with Pitt and Melville in the immediate period before the Platine invasion. All this was accurate. The distortion resulted, however, from Popham's emphasis upon the Río de la Plata as the primary objective of the British government. By using the general term "South America," he concealed the fact that the

English government's major concern had always been the northern part of South America. Recognizing Popham's strategy, Lord Melville supported the notion that the Plata had always been an option; yet, he admitted that the zone of primary interest was the northern coast of Venezuela.[17] The Miranda expedition had in mind this strategic area vis-a-vis the potential markets of South America and the Caribbean. And Popham was given a naval and political assignment in that Venezuelan project.

Action on the Miranda venture, it will be recalled, depended upon relations between Spain and Great Britain. War seemed imminent in November, 1804, as the British took over four Spanish frigates. Lord Melville asked Popham to supply him with the documentation concerning Miranda's strategy of attack in the New World. Meetings took place with William Pitt, and the Venezuelan again built up his hopes. Pitt and Melville, however, worked cautiously; and, at the last moment gave up the Venezuelan project for diplomatic objectives in Europe. When Sir Home returned to London in mid-1805, Miranda was disconsolate, even though Popham remained sanguine. The ubiquitous researcher, secret service agent, and what have you, Sir Home managed to learn from a very accurate source that Napoleon's Dutch allies at the Cape of Good Hope were in a weakened state. Popham thus suggested to Pitt that Great Britain waste no time in attacking the Cape. At the court-martial, Sir Home emphasized that Pitt chose to act on his suggestion.[18] As might be expected, Popham took command of the African expedition with a squadron of eight ships, including the *Diadem* which earlier had been specifically assigned to Popham for the Venezuelan project. General David Baird headed the accompanying military forces. Popham's jurors were led to believe that the Cape project was merely the first step before attacking Buenos Aires. Moreover, Sir Home's presentation stressed the fact that the Cape and the Río de la Plata were in the same navigational zone.[19]

Popham had a final conversation with Pitt on July 29, 1805, concerning the Cape assignment and the Platine project that might develop. Popham testified—and other witnesses did likewise—that Pitt had *not* given him instructions to proceed to the Plata. That was merely a contingency project in the event that the French should attempt to take Buenos Aires. The Admiralty, for example, had been notified of such a contingency program in mid-1805. Pitt explained to Sir Home that he had minimized the Platine objective out of deference to allies on the Continent who hoped to lure Spain away from the

French enemy. It was a weak strategy, Pitt admitted; but expediency dictated his acquiesence. Thus, Pitt opted to place the Venezuelan project in abeyance; and General Miranda left for the United States.

Popham's disclosure of the conversation with Pitt was vital information. Although it was "prescriptive" evidence, Pitt's major advisors confirmed it in their testimony. In view of Pitt's death on January 23, 1806, Sir Home argued that it was therefore as good as direct evidence.[20]

Swift and impressively successful, the Popham-Baird expedition took charge of the Cape of Good Hope in January, 1806. It was a model of teamwork, capped by the heroism of General William Carr Beresford. In short order, the English victors consolidated their control of the African area, improved the Cape's defenses, and conducted naval reconnaissance and intelligence concerning the French presence on the seas. By late March, 1806, Sir Home was ready to carry out his surprise move to the Río de la Plata.

The resourceful Popham had learned by then that the positions of Montevideo and Buenos Aires were in a poor defensive condition. Before he left London, British merchants, familiar with the Plata since 1802, volunteered this information. The major recent source was a North American merchant who knew the area well and was willing to join Popham's venture. The news from Europe further encouraged Sir Home's plans. Napoleon was the virtual master of the Continent: he had defeated the Russians at Austerlitz and the Austrians at Ulm and was in possession of Vienna. The Confederation, in short, had failed; and France and Spain were one for all practical purposes. Also influencing Popham's decision was Lord Horatio Nelson's victory over a French-Spanish force south of Cádiz (Cape of Trafalgar) on October 21, 1805, which, as it turned out, confirmed Great Britain's supremacy of the seas.[21] Aware of the geopolitics of his day, Sir Home sensed that it was time for a dramatic strike at the enemy in southern South America. The obstacles that Pitt had outlined to Popham, in their last conversation, no longer were valid. An attack in the Río de la Plata would capitalize upon the momentum of Nelson's victory in southern Spain.

It was this type of bold thinking that had won Sir Home various commands over men with much more tenure in the service. Leaving little to chance, Popham gained the cooperation of General Baird, who provided as many men as he could afford at that time. Sir Home did not seem to be aware of William Pitt's death before proceeding to the

Plata; but it is doubtful that it would have changed his mind. A major factor in the venture, we must stress, was Sir Home Popham's strong compulsion to get involved in South America—so evident in the deliberations from 1803 forward.[22]

To his naval critics, Sir Home's greatest sin was having been chosen for the Cape of Good Hope command, once again at the expense of many unemployed captains and admirals. That was the underlying theme of the court-martial proceedings. Sir Home knew it only too well, and the evidence exposing the Admiralty's inconsistency was devasting. While the news from the Río de la Plata was favorable, the Admiralty supported Popham. But when the recapture of Buenos Aires became known, the decision to punish him gained momentum. Although Sir Home refrained from directly accusing the Admiralty on this point, the insinuation was there nonetheless. There is little doubt that the final verdict against Popham was largely the result of his combativeness at the court-martial and the strong charges leveled at the Admiralty.[23]

Although technically "unauthorized," the Popham-Beresford expedition to the Río de la Plata kept the home authorities well-informed of its whereabouts. The squadron headed in a northwesternly direction to the Island of St. Helena which was over a thousand miles from the Cape, arriving there in late April, 1806. It is notable that the British Governor contributed a force of one hundred and fifty men—a strong indication of the government's real interest in Popham's decision to head for the Plata. On May 2nd, the ships set sail for the Plata Estuary; and five days later, Popham and a representative from General Beresford boarded the *Narcissus.* Her mission was to proceed ahead of the squadron on a reconnaissance of potential landing sites. Navigational obstacles, so typical of the route taken, held up the arrival of the entire squadron until June 13, 1806.[24]

In light of the available information, Popham and Beresford decided to attack Buenos Aires, rather than Montevideo. Assigning some ships to blockade the port of Montevideo and the installation at Maldonado at the entrance of the Estuary, they led the rest of the squadron slowly toward Buenos Aires. The obstacles were exasperating: fogs, adverse winds and currents, and the shallowness of the water. Inaccurate charts made it worse. On June 25, 1806, the English invaders reached Quilmes, twelve miles from Buenos Aires. While the English disembarked unopposed, the Spanish defender observed their movements closely from a ridge only two miles away. As it turned out, the green, gently-sloped plain between the adversaries was the next day's battlefield. The village of Reducción was on the left side of the ridge, and the Spanish defense line extended from that point to the right. There were two thousand men on the defense line, most of them cavalrymen, according to Beresford. Sir Home from his ship estimated the enemy at four thousand.[25]

At about noon on the 26th, Beresford lined up his men directly against the enemy, leaving the St. Helena force in a reserve position to maneuver against cavalry assaults from either flank. The British commenced a slow advance across the plain, not suspecting a boggy area in mid-field, which the Spaniards hoped would halt the Englishmen's forward movement. When the British reached the "tongue of swamp," as Beresford described it, they tried in vain to move their artillery pieces around the obstacle. The Spanish enemy hastened to open fire on the frustrated Englishmen; fortunately, their aim was poor. Beresford then ordered his troops to quicken their pace, which they did courageously. Sir Home noted proudly that the British ascended that hill with the "coolness and courage," so characteristic of the English soldier.[26] Apparently, the British charge also impressed the Spanish defenders who beat a hasty retreat to their next defense line at the Riachuelo, a small river—some thirty yards wide—three miles from Buenos Aires. Beresford congratulated his men and allowed them to rest awhile. The Spanish forces, in the meantime, burned the bridge over the river and consolidated their defense line.

On the next day, June 27th, a heavy artillery barrage from both sides started the hostilities. The British guns fired effectively enough to allow some of Beresford's men to cross the water on boats and rafts. Finding themeselves increasingly outflanked by Englishmen, Spanish defenders again retreated in numbers and bypassed the City of Buenos Aires. There was no desire to involve the City. The Viceroy of the Río de la Plata, the Marquis of Sobremontes, opted to withdraw his capital to the city of Córdoba in the interior. He ordered the public treasure loaded upon wagons for that destination.

With the enemy in flight, British troops walked into Buenos Aires and hoisted their flag at the Fortress on the afternoon of June 27, 1806. Although Buenos Aires' officials had wanted special concessions from Beresford in writing, the General merely gave his word that he would respect the life and property, as well as the religion, of the people in Buenos Aires. He did not want to interrupt the momentum of his forces. In the meantime, special English troops pursued the Spanish troops to Luján and other interior positions on the road to Córdoba, apparently welcomed by the people everywhere. The English pursuers, moreover, succeeded in capturing most of the wagons carrying the Plata's public treasure.[27]

Although the battles of June 26–27, 1806, did not involve much fighting, they have filled the pages of many history books. Every schoolboy in the Plata knows about the cowardice of the Viceroy Sobremontes and the retreating Spanish forces. Yet—to be honest—a strategy of withdrawal was good military tactics historically, given the circumstances. General Beresford, for example, admitted that it was an easy matter to figure out how many Englishmen marched out on the plain. Such a small and determined force might mean that there was a larger army of occupation at Montevideo. In that case, it would be foolhardy to expose the City of Buenos Aires to a needless bloodbath. It was wiser to regroup. Once they learned how many Englishmen were in the Plata, they could then engage them in a decisive battle. This is precisely what happened. The so-called "Reconquest" of Buenos Aires used Montevideo and Colonia del Sacramento, just opposite Buenos Aires, as the bases of operation, overpowering the small numbers of Englishmen in the Río de la Plata.[28]

However glorious his countrymen might consider his Platine victories, a seasoned fighter like General Beresford understood the implications of an easy military entry into a city out in the open. He requested reinforcements from the Cape of Good Hope; they arrived in October. By then, however, the Spanish enemy had retaken Buenos Aires. Given the limited number of Englishmen, Beresford had no choice but to make key concessions to the conquered. As Lieutenant Governor Beresford, he promised to respect the rights and privileges of the various corporations in the Río de la Plata—municipal, judicial, religious, commercial, and military. He was especially anxious to win the support of religious leaders, whom he reassured that Englishmen would not interfere with their spiritual life.[29] In a special proclamation, General Beresford promised that property rights in land, ships, and fishing equipment would not be taken over as war prizes. Moreover, as subjects of the English King, the people of the Plata were now free to trade throughout the British Empire on equal terms. He reminded them enthusiastically that the Island of Trinidad in northern South America, taken over by the English in 1797, had prospered significantly from its contact with Great Britain. The Plata could do the same.

As it turned out, Beresford's reference to Trinidad was an

unfortunate mistake since it touched a sensitive chord in the Platine psyche. The Plata's inhabitants recognized only too clearly—and this indeed was reflected in the various documents of the British occupation—that the English invader considered his presence in their area as a "conquest." In short, there had been a mere exchange of one set of European masters for another—a subtle point in the psychology of independence.[30]

Beresford's decision to return the boats and accompanying property was wise and expedient. It reflected British awareness of their short numbers while at the same time underscoring the main motive for the Popham-Beresford expedition of 1806. It aspired to establish commercial relations with the Río de la Plata in order to guarantee and sustain the prosperity of British industry and commerce. At the same time, it would protect Great Britain forever against such tactics as Napoleon's "Continental System," which excluded British manufacturers from European markets. Both economic and political, this was a basic concern in the thinking of British leaders like William Pitt.

Sir Home Riggs Popham certainly left no doubt about his commitment to British industry and commerce. It was explicit in the famous letter of July 1, 1806, that he sent to all of the major manufacturing centers of Great Britain. The content speaks for itself. Moreover, it should also help to explain Sir Home's popularity at Lloyd's Coffee-House in London and the enthusiastic reaction to the circular.[31] The following copy went to the Mayor and Corporation of Birmingham:

Buenos Aires   July 1, 1806

Gentlemen,

Although I may not have the honour of being personally known to some of your corporation, I nevertheless consider it a duty to the commercial interests of Great Britain, and a respect due to you as one of its great manufacturing towns, to state, in a few words, that the conquest of this place opens an extensive channel for the manufactures of Great Britain.

Hitherto the trade of this country has been cramped beyond belief, and the manufactures of Great Britain could only find their way to this rich province by neutral bottoms and contraband intrigues; but from this moment its trade will be thrown open. I need not point out to merchants of your extensive information, how beneficial the commerce of this hitherto neglected country will be; and you may form some judgment of its immense population by that of this city, which alone contains 70,000 inhabitants, wanting all sorts of goods of European manufacture.

The productions of this country are indigo, tobacco, Vicenta wool, cotton, tiger skins, seal skins, copperas, figs, dried tongues, beef and hams, saffron, cochineal, cocoa, hemp, hair, wheat, gums, drugs, gold, silver, and precious stones, exclusive of hides and tallow, which I consider the great staple, one million four hundred thousand of the former being annually exported. The short time we have been in possession, and the hurry of business, will not admit of my giving you any further information for the present; but if I can obtain a list of the articles most wanted, I will enclose it. I have the honour to be, Gentlemen, your most obedient humble servant,

Home Popham[32]

* * * * * * * * * * * *

The "Capture of Buenos Ayres" hit the London press like a bolt out of the blue on September 13, 1806. The *Narcissus* had just arrived at Portsmouth, and Captain Ross Donnelly was on his way to the City with dispatches from the Plata. In capital letters, *The Times*, in uncharacteristic ebullience, trumpeted the news: **"BUENOS AYRES AT THE PRESENT MOMENT FORMS A PART OF THE BRITISH EMPIRE."**[33] All newspapers in London agreed that the capture of Buenos Aires was unquestionably a key moment in history.[34] This was the type of news that the British public was thirsting to hear after so many years of sacrifices in the long struggle with Napoleon Bonaparte and his allies. The details appeared in most newspapers by September 15, 1806, as everyone read for himself the dispatches written by General William Carr Beresford and Commodore Sir Home Riggs Popham. *The Times'* editorial set the tone:

It is with great pleasure that we lay before our readers the Gazette Extraordinary of Saturday last, which announces the surrender of Buenos Aires to the British arms. This conquest is highly important from its intrinsic value, but still more so from the circumstances which attended it, and from the very critical time in which it is made known to the British public and to Europe. There can hardly be a doubt that the whole colony of *La Plata* will share the same fate as Buenos Ayres; and from the flattering hopes held out to the inhabitants in the proclamation of General Beresford, they will see that it is their true interests to become a colony of the British empire.[35]

The Times was especially sanguine about the impact of the Platine news upon the negotiations with France. "Bonaparte must be convinced that nothing but a speedy peace can prevent the whole of Spanish America from being wrested from his influence, and placed forever under the protection of the British Empire." The editor took pride in comparing the moderation and generosity of the English soldier to the plundering tactics of his French counterpart, all of which "will doubtless make the inhabitants of the Spanish colonies wish to be connected with Great Britain." "By such a union," concluded the editor, "we should have a never-failing market for our commodities, and our enemies would be forever deprived of the power of adding the resources of these rich countries to their other means of annoying us."[36] Many newspapers editorialized along a similar vein; and the British public reveled in the enthusiasm, pride, and patriotism of its writers. A new era in the history of the world had just begun, or so it seemed to many Englishmen. In a matter of days, advertisements for employment in South America began to appear; and books and pamphlets dealing with the Viceroyalty of the Río de la Plata were being prepared for publication, such was the demand for information about that part of the world.[37] The message throughout the numerous Platine articles was clear: here was a real British "conquest." To the victors went the spoils. When a handful of Englishmen, so to speak, could win such a gallant victory in faraway Buenos Aires, the future indeed seemed limitless and promising.

Nowheres did the euphoria of victory loom so large as in the processions that took place at Portsmouth and London in celebration of the "Landing of the Spanish Treasures," as *The Times* described it.[38] By two o'clock on the afternoon of September 17th, eight wagons were filled with mementoes, flags, and specie captured from the Spaniards at Buenos Aires. Valued at over one million dollars, the silver alone weighed well over twenty-seven tons.[39] "These proud and substantial testimonials of British valour were conveyed through the town, on their route to the Metropolis, in grand procession."

Colorful flags and standards waved over the wagons in careful and proper ranking. The first vehicle featured the Spanish colors; but, in front of them, sat a sailor holding the "English Jack." Some of the sailors were veterans of the Plata campaign, and they wore the clothing that had been used on that memorable occasion. Cannons followed, as did the excellent band of Royal Marines stationed in Portsmouth. "Vast numbers of seafaring persons in this port" went along with the procession enthusiastically "rending the air with their patriotic acclamation in honour of the bravery of their countrymen, and of the triumph and treasures they have gained from the foe."[40]

In London, the procession grew in size, the band played "God Save the King" and "Rule Britannia," and the crowds gathered with great rejoicing. The parade stopped momentarily at the Admiralty and then went up Pall Mall to St. James Square. There was a presentation in front of Colonel Davidson's house made by his wife. It was "a pair of colours, on which was written, with gold letters on blue silk, within branches of laurel, Buenos Ayres–Popham–Beresford–Victory." The "Treasure" passed through the City to the Bank, where a million dollars were deposited. Each wagon had the sign "Treasure Chest" in front. The crowds cheered the participants in the parade and shouted lustily for "Old England." Captain Ross Donnelly, who was the bearer of the good news from the Plata, rode in a special chair of honor.[41]

The response of the British government to the Platine news was likewise sanguine. It was in this context of national euphoria that the Admiralty responded to Sir Home's account of victory in the Río de la Plata. Although his naval superiors still felt that he should not have left the Cape unattended, they congratulated Popham and his men for the successful invasion of the Plata.[42] Also, the Board of Trade held a key conference on September 15th with Lord Auckland in charge. It was attended by several members of the Cabinet, as well as representatives of the Spanish houses in London, hoping thus to get the widest canvass of opinions on the trade with South America.

Although there was an initial proposal to throw open the trade of Buenos Aires to all neutrals, the protectionists at the meeting felt that such a program would benefit most the United States. Instead, they favored the control of licenses to neutrals, especially in products that competed with those of Great Britain. The message was again clear: the British victory at Buenos Aires was for the "national advantage."[43] This message understandably found its way into the Royal Order in Council of September 17, 1806. The British King invited all of his subjects to trade with his new possessions in the Río de la Plata. Platine subjects were warmly gathered into the economic and political union of the English empire, a source of prosperity and strength for all.

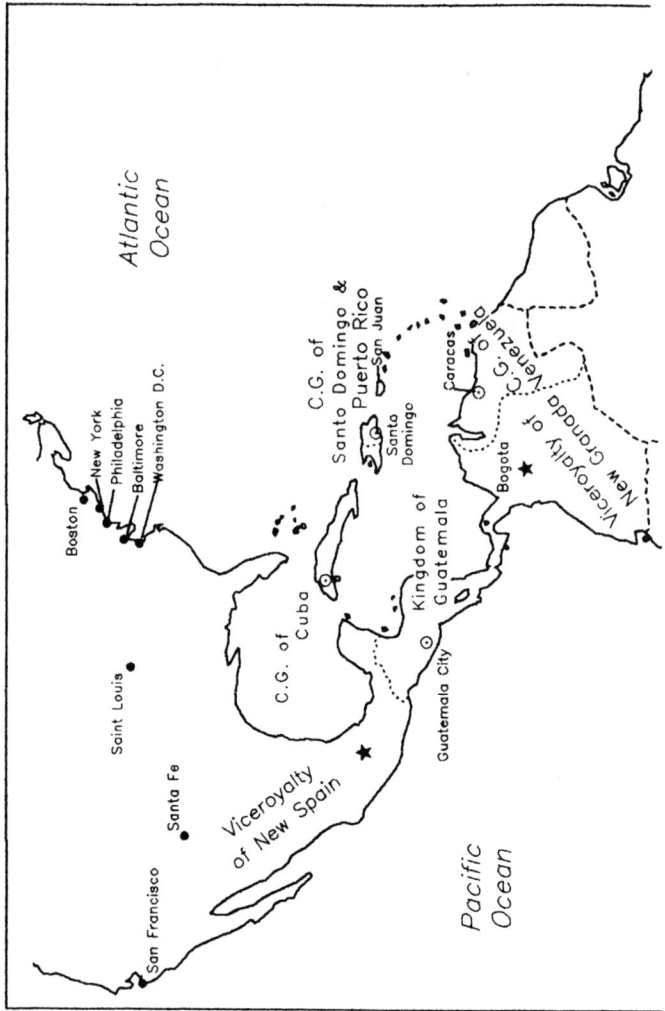

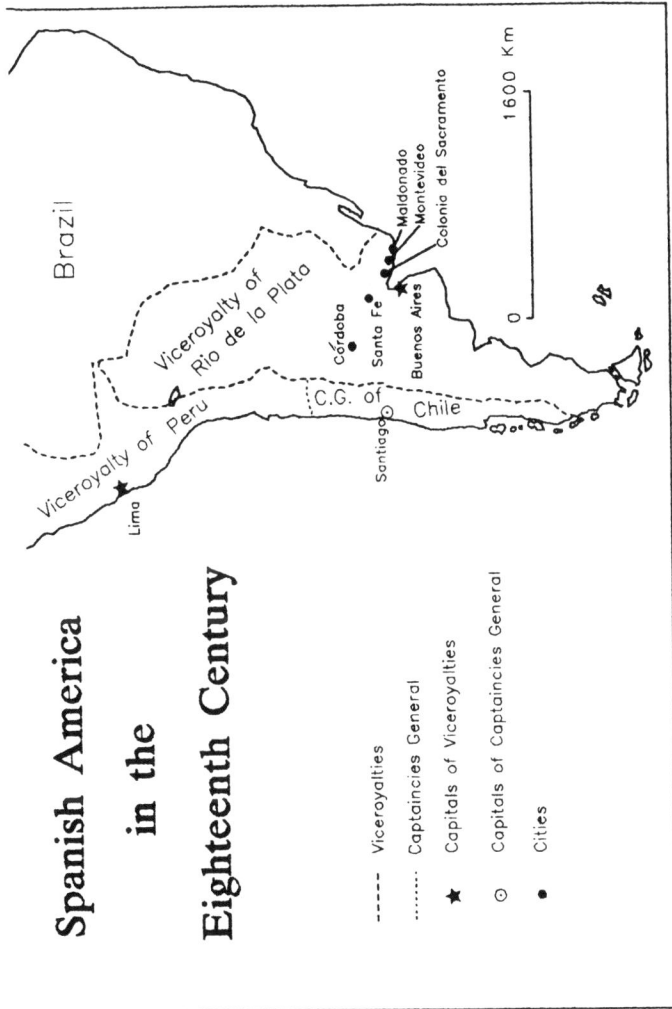

Spanish America
in the
Eighteenth Century

Viceroyalties
Captaincies General
★ Capitals of Viceroyalties
⊙ Capitals of Captaincies General
• Cities

Brazil

Viceroyalty of Río de la Plata

Viceroyalty of Peru

C.G. of Chile

Lima

Santiago

Córdoba

Santa Fe

Buenos Aires

Maldonado
Montevideo
Colonia del Sacramento

1600 Km

0

Instead of the preposterous duties of the Spanish government, estimated at thirty-seven and one-half percent ad valorem, the general British rate would be cut to just one third of that figure.[44]

The Popham-Beresford expedition to the Río de la Plata, to be sure, was technically unauthorized. Yet, some of the evidence suggests strongly that there was considerable authorization at various phases in the venture. There is no question at all, however, that the British government and the English public heartily approved of the Platine invasion. And the flow of reinforcements to South America left no doubt that the British government was keenly determined to secure a foothold in southern South America.

* * * * * * * * * * *

There was considerable speculation in the English newspapers concerning the leadership of the British forces in the Plata. At one time there was the conjecture that Arthur Wellesley, the future Duke of Wellington, might be placed in charge. It seemed fair at the time, however, to confirm General Beresford in the position of Governor.[45] The first large expedition from England as a base was under the direction of Sir Samuel Achmuty, whose forces left Great Britain on October 9, 1806.[46] Another large expedition under General Robert Craufurd went to the Cape of Good Hope and subsequently headed for an assignment in Chile. The Craufurd contingent also had instructions to stop in the Río de la Plata to assist the British forces there if needed. Finally, the major expedition under General John Whitelocke left England on March 11, 1807, arriving in the Plata two months later.[47] There seemed little doubt that Great Britain had welcomed the Popham-Beresford invasion and that Great Britain was seriously entertaining a colonizing presence in the Río de la Plata.

The presence of ten to twelve thousand Englishmen—soldiers, sailors, and marines—in the Río de la Plata seemed to be an awesome display of military power for the times. Yet, it was hardly sufficient to carry out British colonial aspirations in the area. The psychological mood of Spanish America at that time would not permit it. The Hispanic New World was in the throes of a revolutionary change in attitudes with regards to colonialism. This discontent had been stirred up by the Enlightenment and by the example of the English colonies from 1775 forward. Europeans had themselves experienced the same liberalizing climate of opinion that fostered the "Age of Democratic

Revolution," as Professor Robert R. Palmer has called it in his prize-winning work. These same Europeans, however, found it difficult to comprehend the New World's version of that liberalizing trend that gave birth to the first modern movement of anticolonialism. In the half century from 1775 to 1825, most of the Americas had realized their dream of independence from European mothers.

In this historical and philosophic context, the British faced a tremendous challenge in the Río de la Plata. Their offer of "freer trade" within the Empire was a welcome step in the right direction; but the problem was that Platine Americans, like their colleagues throughout Spanish America, were advocates of absolute "free trade." The Spanish Bourbons of the late eighteenth and early nineteenth centuries had officially encouraged the study of *laissez-faire* economics—the works of Adam Smith, Jean Baptiste Say, François Quesnay and his fellow physiocrats or *Economistes*—in the universities. The liberal orientation of the Bourbons was evident in Spain's official support of the research effort involving the Royal Economic Society of Madrid and leading to the publication of Gaspar de Jovellanos' *Informe de Ley Agraria* in 1795. That famous treatise recommended the new economic approach, as opposed to the mercantilism/paternalism of the past.[48] The Spanish Bourbons, moreover, had themselves provided Hispanic Americans with "freer trade" within the Spanish Empire in the 1770s. It stimulated production in the New World and, in turn, convinced Spanish Americans that the next step "free trade" was the proper solution. The Platine mentality, therefore, was much beyond that assumed by the British invader. The inhabitants of Buenos Aires and the Río de la Plata did not aspire to be subjects of the English monarch, or any other European king or emperor. Englishmen found this attitude difficult to understand, so did Napoleon after May 2, 1808, when he tried to revolutionize Spanish America under his brother's rule. This misreading of the American scene by Europeans is a major concern of subsequent chapters in this work.

"Recollector" wrote a letter to the *Morning Herald* in London in connection with General Beresford's mistake in mentioning the "Illusion of Trinidad" to the Platine people as the model of prosperity that they might expect from the British connection. The writer was well-informed, whoever he might have been. He comprehended and explained the Platine hostility toward the British under General Beresford, especially when the initial reaction to the invaders was one of friendship. "Recollector" noted that the Creole leaders had pleaded with Beresford to help them liberate the area for an independent government. Beresford apparently replied that he had no instructions from England on this issue. The disillusioned Creoles thus had no choice but to join their Spanish colleagues in ousting the hated English from the Río de la Plata. The "Illusion of Trinidad," as it turned out, was just that.[49]

The "Reconquest" of Buenos Aires on August 12, 1806, was a mismatch in light of the numbers and the fierce determination of the Spanish forces to rid the Plata of the British enemy. General Beresford had no choice but to capitulate. Sir Home Popham just managed to get back aboard his ship before the "Recapture" took place. Popham's squadron remained nearby in hopes that British prisoners would be liberated under the terms of the treaty. After waiting in vain, Popham protested to the authorities in Buenos Aires and Montevideo charging them of violating international law. The victorious Spaniards argued instead their version of the law of nations in an emotional exchange of letters and articles. Sir Home thus had no choice but to attempt a blockade of the Platine ports.[50]

In response to Beresford's first request for reinforcements from the Cape of Good Hope, Lieutenant Colonel John T. Backhouse reached the Río de la Plata in October, 1806. After conferring with Popham, the two decided upon an attack on Montevideo; but certain difficulties in getting English ships to a desired point forced the cancellation of the plan. Instead, the English attack focused on the port of Maldonado and its nearby island. The invasion here succeeded. The English still had a base in the Plata, an excellent position which, according to Sir Home, allowed the English to utilize their cavalry and mount their artillery.

General Samuel Achmuty arrived at Maldonado with his expeditionary force in early December, 1806. Admiral Charles Stirling was along as Popham's replacement. Although upset by his recall, Sir Home had an interesting interview with his successor. He suggested to him the policy that Achmuty should employ against the Spanish enemy in the Plata. He pointed out in detail why the British should first take Montevideo. Popham volunteered his services but apparently there were no takers. So he returned to England in a bad frame of mind.[51]

An imaginative and aggressive leader, General Samuel Achmuty readied his men for the attack upon Montevideo which fell to the British on February 3, 1807, another Platine victory for the English to savor, thanks to the "gallant Achmuty."[52] From Montevideo as a base, British cavalrymen were able to roam all of the territory on the eastern banks of the Río de la Plata, the *Banda Oriental*. A detachment of Englishmen occupied Colonia del Sacramento, across the water from Buenos Aires. In short, the British adopted the same tactics used in the previous year during the "Reconquest" of Buenos Aires by Spanish and Creole forces.[53] General Whitelocke's major expeditionary force arrived in Montevideo in May, 1807, before the start of the annual rains. It was the opportune time to strike. The British leader, however, chose to wait for Craufurd's troops to reach the Plata from the Cape of Good Hope before proceeding with the attack. By that time, the rains had started and would certainly present obstacles for the English invaders. The attack began in mid-June, 1807. The location of Spanish defenses, moreover, prevented Whitelocke from getting as close to Buenos Aires as General Beresford in 1806. He thus had to settle for a disembarkment point near the Ensenada de Barragón, some twenty-seven miles from Buenos Aires.[54] English columns marched overland toward the village of Reducción, the site of Beresford's first battle in the previous year. By this time English troops were exhausted and they had lost many guns and supplies going through swampy lands. The military adventure almost seemed ill-fated from the start; even liquor supplies had been lost—the impending battle would be a bitterly sober affair. Again, Spaniards consolidated their defense line at the Riachuelo. This time the position seemed impenetrable; and the Spanish-Creole force had been waiting for the fight, bolstering their morale with shouts of "*Santiago y vitoria.*"[55]

Rather than face the enemy head on, General Whitelocke surprised the Spanish-Creole resistance by skillfully bypassing its line of strength. He turned his forces to the left, into the interior, until he was able to ford the Riachuelo without any opposition. Thus, the British troops reached the suburbs of Buenos Aires in a place where they were not expected. One Spanish account admitted that if the English forces had invaded Buenos Aires on July 2nd, they would have taken the City.[56] But General Whitelocke decided to hold back. In the succeeding days, the Spanish defenders were able to prepare themselves even more for the onslaught on July 5th. Three British columns had instructions to take key fortified positions in the City and to rush through the streets hurriedly to their objectives employing "unarmed" tactics—that is, without firing at civilians on the way.

Combat situations are never as neat and as well-organized as they appear in the plans of military superiors before an attack. This was a bad day for the British; and only Sir Samuel Achmuty's column had any success. The other two got all mixed up turning in the wrong direction; and Whitelocke lost contact with his officers. The unnerving and unexpected factor in the combat of that day was the fierce resistance of the civilian population of all classes and races. They attacked the English invader with every conceivable weapon: grenades, guns, rocks, bricks, and so on, from every possible position: from the street, from corners, and from rooftops. They were out to destroy the hated British who in the days before the attack, according to their sources of information, had plundered the outskirts of Buenos Aires abusing women, children, and the defenseless. A spirit of revenge hovered over the horrible carnage of Englishmen on that day—two thousand five hundred dead and wounded, or one-fourth of the British expedition. To prevent any further casualties, as well as to pacify the angry citizenry of Buenos Aires, Whitelocke surrendered to his counterpart Santiago Liniers. The English general agreed to withdraw all British forces from Montevideo and Maldonado within two months; and the terms of the treaty were generous in providing for the care and evacuation of the British prisoners of war.[57]

The English defeat of mid-1807 was one of the most disastrous battles suffered by that country in the fighting against Napoleon and his allies. English grandiose aspirations in the Río de la Plata had been shattered to nothingness in just a year's time. It was that fatal year of the "Platine Fever," from September 13, 1806, when *The Times* trumpeted that the Plata was British to September 14, 1807, when the sorry news of Whitelocke's defeat hit the English nation. *The Times* captured the bitterness of that news:

> This had been a most unfortunate business from first to last. The interests of the country, as well as its military character, are deeply affected by it. The original plan was bad; the conduct of it has been equally so. There was nothing honourable or dignified in it; nothing worthy of the resources or character of this country. It was a dirty sordid enterprise, conceived and executed in a spirit of avarice and plunder, without a parallel, except in the disgraceful expeditions of the Buccaneers. How was it to be expected that either the hands or hearts of the people should be with us, when those who first seized upon the settlement were seen to be less anxious to conciliate the inhabitants, than to place the spoils which they obtained out of the reach of danger? There was a radical vice in the original plan, which no subsequent exertions could remedy. Had the unauthorized projectors of the first disembarkation landed with a force equal to that which has been since

driven out of Buenos Ayres, the country might now be in our possession.[58]

The Times, to be sure, had lectured on occasion against a British policy of violence throughout the world, advocating a more enlightened international order that respected the rights of nations and peoples.[59] Yet, this great newspaper avidly shared the conquest of the Río de la Plata and the attempts to consolidate British rule in South America. In the above quotation, moreover, the editorialist seem to be saying: *if* Popham had taken 10,000 troops to Buenos Aires, *we* would have succeeded. This is hardly a quotation of repentance!

As moods changed from one September to the other during the year of the "Platine Fever," the British public suffered an enormous letdown. Fiercely deceived, Englishmen demanded and needed a scapegoat. Sir Home Popham was the target in the initial phase of the "Platine Fever." He was "severely reprimanded" at his court-martial. But the public still admired their hero for having brought them that glorious news of victory in the Río de la Plata. The British Government, moreover, responded with an energetic follow through program of reinforcements. And, surprise of all surprises, it promoted Sir Home Riggs Popham to the rank of Captain of the Navy, only a month or so after his reprimand. His naval critics were beside themselves, and they now came out into the open to question Sir Home's command of the British attack upon Denmark. Eventually the complainants—captains and admirals—got some satisfaction but nowheres near enough to placate them. Even *The Times* exposed Sir Home's various lapses.[60]

The fate of Lieutenant General John Whitelocke was another matter, a hopeless case in view of the bitterness and hostility that prevailed among Englishmen at the end of the "Platine Fever." Perhaps they were angry at themselves for having been so gullible and innocent about matters in the Río de la Plata. The British press literally tried Whitelocke in public and found him guilty without question.[61] The military jurors followed suit and cashiered General Whitelocke from the service. It was a vicious judgment.[62] Whitelocke had pleaded in his defense that the unexpected "hostility" of the Platine inhabitants, as Sir Samuel Achmuty averred in his testimony, was the decisive factor in that tragic defeat, not his military leadership. Critics found this defense inadmissible. Napoleon and other military figures had not been deterred by the animosity of enemy forces.[63]

Platine Fever: Conquest or Liberation?

The "Platine Fever" of 1806–1807 aroused the attention of a bright young journalist in London, compelling him to ponder the implications of that disastrous and humiliating defeat in the Río de la Plata. Since Great Britain was facing a life or death struggle against Napoleon, he felt the urgent need to express his ideas and conclusions on recent Platine matters in order to avoid measures of revenge by the English government that would only compound the mistake. Violence was no solution, for the long run. It would merely weaken England's situation and keep her from realizing her full glory and destiny as the world's leading economic and political power. The liberation of Spanish America, on the other hand, would open doors to Great Britain's future!

Yet, in the bitterness that survived the "Platine Fever," this message of good intentions might not be well-received by his emotional countrymen. Life in London, for the past five years, had not been as lucrative as he had imagined upon his arrival there. Although his marriage had not set him back financially and his position as editor of the *Literary Journal* was respectable, yet, it was not as remunerative a lifestyle as one might want, or expect, living in an expensive city, especially after the birth of his son. Under the circumstances, therefore, it would be wise to take precautions. He decided to use a penname: "William Burke." This practice was common in those days for supplementing one's income. We shall identify this personage, in due time, an author whose writings appeared in the Western World from 1807 to 1812. He seemed capable of becoming one of the great intellectuals of the early nineteenth century. Until we are ready to identify him—"William Burke, Front and Center" is the chapter heading—we shall drop some hints about his training and education to explain his various stands. To begin with, "William Burke" published two treatises dealing with the implications of the "Platine Fever:" first, *South American Independence: or, the Emancipation of South America, the Glory and Interest of England* (London, 1807) and second, *Additional Reasons for Our Immediately Emancipating Spanish America* (London, 1808), both issued by the J. Ridgway Company.[64]

As editor of the *Literary Journal* the young journalist displayed exceptional depth and grasp of many disciplines: history, economics, political science, psychology, and international relations. He felt he knew exactly what was going on in the world and what it all meant for Great Britain, thus encouraging him to suggest imaginative policy decisions to the English government. With Popham's initial capture of Buenos Aires, "William Burke"—if we may use quotations one last time, at least for the present—foresaw that Napoleon would challenge immediately the British attempt to break his "Continental System." The war would extend into the New World: to control its resources. Now, young Burke concluded: Napoleon's hegemony in the Old World would be countered effectively by the British navy, as well as the English presence in South America. If this hypothesis were valid, it followed that the time was ripe for a *modus vivendi* between the two contending powers. In the preface of his first treatise, Burke explained that a compromise-project occurred to him before the Truce of Amiens (1801–1803), hoping that it would bring the war to an end. Rather than violence (war), the two powers would stress a cooperative program of "free trade" throughout the world. Burke's goal was to open up "new, wide, and free channels to the commerce and industry of both nations." Given world geography and the location of key resources, Burke concluded that "the most just, eligible, and efficient part of the earth, for the accomplishment of the above desirable purpose was Spanish America." When the Truce of Amiens ended, Burke again turned to his project, still convinced that South America was the logical place for the two contenders to take up a peaceful collaboration in free trade.[65]

At first glance, the idealism of the projected trade program with France appears somewhat naive and its underlying pacifism is about what would be expected of a young man trained for the ministry. Yet, Burke completely understood world realities and reasoned that further resort to exhausting warfare, year after year, was counterproductive for both sides. It was conceivable, therefore, that the French might be ready at this point to listen to such a proposal. After all, what was there to lose in trying it? The young author revealed his hopes in these words:

> It should be hoped the governments of these two great nations, are actuated by feelings of a more dignified policy, than to allow themselves to be surprised, from any ignoble opposition, to the best rights and interest of humanity.It will be a pleasing though somewhat curious spectacle, to behold the two great rival nations engaged, in forwarding in different hemispheres, and in the moment of their own contention, the sacred cause of independence and melioration: how devoutly it were to be wished, their efforts could be combined in the same noble cause—then indeed must it proceed with sure and gigantic step; and the

herculean powers of both nations, no longer wasted in fruitless and distressing contentions against each other, would be applied to the more glorious and certainly useful purpose, of diffusing civilization and happiness over the globe.[66]

Just before sending the first treatise to the press—we suspect that it was in early January, 1807—Burke learned of the Buenos Aires' recapture. Although it weakened the British position, he hoped that the French might still be amenable to the trade program; the two powers would continue to focus on the emancipation of Spanish America for a "Free Trade" under their dual guarantee. The first section of his manuscript on "Free Trade" could be left as it was written originally; later sections would have to deal with the changes in the Platine situation. It was obvious that William Burke was a champion of "Free Trade," as well as an adamant defender of Adam Smith's *Wealth of Nations* (1776).

Part one raised the key question: "Ought South America to be emancipated by us?" In what was to become a typical Burkian presentation, the author reminded his readers that such a question required him to discuss three "distinct heads: namely, the justice, the legality, and the policy of the measure." Justice, he proceeded, looks

two ways: how peculiarly true is this, with respect to Spain and her American possessions! If Spain complains that the emancipation of those possessions would be committing an act of injustice against her; alas! how much more numerous and extensive—how much less merited, but more unjust and cruel, are the wrongs which those vast and favoured regions of the globe, have to charge against Spain?

In our age, young Burke argued, we cannot accept "the arbitrary claim of accidental discovery* [footnote on Columbus' discovery], of bloody and nefarious conquest, and consequent violent and tyrannical possession." Certainly, such claims cannot be placed "in opposition to the sacred and imprescriptible rights of nature and justice; or be converted into a warrant for acting the most foul, stupid, and inhuman oppressions against our fellow-men, that ever cursed and disgraced the earth."[67]

Apparently drawing from William Robertson's work on Spanish America, Burke resorted to the "Black Legend" stereotype that was so popular among English writers. Above all, William Burke, and the man who used that name, was a skilled publicist, or propagandist, who employed the best materials and approaches to prove a given point. His use of satire and ridicule was characteristic of his approach:

> I will not, therefore, insult the moral feelings of my readers, by tracing further the injustice of the Spanish claim to America, founded on the arbitrary and unqualified right of discovery: with as much justice might the Chinese or any other Asiatic people, who happened to be ignorant of the existence of such a country as Old Spain, on discovering her shores, land and claim it as their own, in defiance of its being possessed by the rightful owners. Such a proceeding now would undoubtedly and justly be pronounced a rank robbery by the Spaniards themselves: and yet where does it differ from the claim to America, set up by Spain three hundred years ago.[68]

Burke, however, did not want his reader to think that he was against imperialism:

> I do not mean to say, that a civilized people, having discovered an uninhabited country, or even one with a few rude and wandering tribes upon it, have not a right to occupy this newly-discovered country. This would be contrary to justice, because it would be in opposition to the happiness of mankind, which most undoubtedly is materially forwarded and expanded, by the settlement of new, distant, and widely-extended regions. Nay, I say more—that where the natives, by reason of their paucity of numbers and incivilization, are incapable of applying their country to the great purposes of civilized life; it is right and just that the superabundant population of other nations, should migrate to those neglected and abused regions, and by founding settlements, enlarge the means as well as the field of human happiness.

Burke insisted, however, that the right of settlement should be accompanied by the

> principles of strict justice and equal right towards the natives; who, it should not be forgotten, are the original owners; and that no nation, under the arbitrary and flimsy pretext of discovery and apostolic sanction, has the right to make an unqualified seizure of the country of another people, and appropriate it exclusively to themselves. The act is robbery.[69]

Since the Indians had advanced civilizations in Mexico and Peru, the Spanish claim, therefore, could not be the basis for a "preclusive right

to the people's property." Rather, it was the "right of the sword . . . the
right of robbery—of the strong over the defenseless and weak." Again,
Burke's sarcasm:

> But the pious Cortez and the humane Pizarro charged the Americans
> with being infidels; and this crime, no doubt, was sufficient in the eyes
> of those true believers, for despoiling such infidel dogs of their country,
> and exterminating them likewise! Alas! How dreadfully horrible are
> the crimes which avarice and fanaticism have perpetrated in the dark
> ages, under the cloak of religion and sanctity![70]

The relentless attack intensified: "The Americans, unfortunately, had a
country, in your eyes rich; and you, like highway assassins, robbed
them of this first . . . "and then butchered them. Spaniards used
"infernal means"—torture, slavery, extermination—to achieve "what
they called the conquest, but which was more truly the robbery of
America." Cortez and Pizarro

> both these ruffians ended their villainous career, by hanging the two
> unfortunate American Emperors, for an alleged conspiracy—in their own
> dominions, and against the plunderers of their native land and by
> burning alive or otherwise exterminating the wretched people, for loving
> their country, and for their dutiful and virtuous attachment to their
> lawful sovereigns!

Citing Bartolomé de Las Casas, the Spanish Dominican friar who
championed the cause of the Indians, Burke described the carnage of
the Spaniards in their hot pursuit of gold, treating the natives viciously
like "wild beasts." No matter how much Spaniards insisted upon their
claim to the Americas; it was a false one, based on robbery.[71]

The justice of America's right, on the other hand,

> remains uninjured and entire. There are certain constitutional properties
> belonging to vast and distinct regions of the earth, inhabited by large
> masses of men, which no human force can destroy: they grow out of
> physical circumstances, beyond the reach of man; and the right to
> independence of a continent is one of these.

Although Spain gained dominance over the New World because of such
inventions as gunpowder or the presence of the horse; yet "they could
not have transferred rights, without which dominion, however acquired,

is but injustice and oppression." Americans have their own rights like
other peoples of the world:

> They were given by the Great Creator to his children for the
> improvement of the countries which subsist them, and for their own
> happiness. With this view has he interwoven them in the frame of man,
> and in the disposition of the globe: and their enjoyment can neither be
> interrupted nor suppressed, even for a moment, without committing a
> high crime against the immutable laws of the Supreme Being, and a
> great and lamentable injury of his works.

Americans, therefore, "derive their rights to their country and
independence, from the best of all titles, nature and justice."[72] As a
good student of the classics, Burke made excellent use of the "natural
rights" thesis, a standard tool in his arsenal of propaganda. Spanish
claims were baseless against the "sacred and imprescriptible rights of
a people, determined and powerful enough to assert them." As their
spokesman, Burke stated the American view:

> We . . . are men like yourselves, and consequently have an equal right
> to happiness with you . . . America has been given to us, as Spain had
> been to you, for the subsistence and felicity of its inhabitants . . . If you
> assert, and justly, a preclusive right to your own country, because you
> inhabit and cultivate it; surely we, who inhabit and cultivate America,
> have the same right to ours.[73]

The American case continued on even stronger terms:

> You strangers . . . were not content to come and settle among us, and
> share with us the productions of our country; but you must seize all; not
> only our lands and houses you required, but also our labour and persons,
> as your property. For nearly three hundred years have you cruelly
> robbed and oppressed us—you have nearly exterminated the native
> inhabitants; and some of the finest and most extensive regions of the
> earth, are deserts and useless in your hands. Trampled to the dust in our
> own land, by an ignominious slavery, our country is but as a prison to
> us: without security for life, freedom, or property, our exertions are
> necessarily palsied; and the richest lands in the world consequently lie
> neglected and uncultivated. Your stupid oppressions have tied up the
> hands of industry: agriculture, arts, trade, science, and commerce—the
> inestimable sources of human felicity, are scarcely known among us;
> and countries, sufficient to contain double or treble the population of all

Europe, now barely equal that of two European islands* [footnote:
*The whole population of Spanish America does not exceed fifteen
millions!]. In vain therefore hath Nature created America, if her
benefits are thus to be suppressed by you: in vain hath she bestowed
upon her a fine sky, a wholesome air, and an exuberant soil; if man be
denied by a barbarous policy, from enjoying and using those first of
blessings.

Of what benefit are the extensiveness, the richness, and geographical
disposition of America, to us; enslaved as we are? We have numerous
and immense regions, unoccupied but by the inhabitants of the forest;
but, you prevent man from entering them. If we cultivate the ground,
you seize the principal part of the productions of our labour; and by
shutting up our ports, you render the finest harbours, and the most
extensive rivers in the world, nugatory or useless to us. You therefore
would leave us no country: the rapacity which first plundered and
oppressed us, would persecute us still; and hold us in the degraded state
of abject slaves. But God, who created America, made it for the benefit
of its people: and has given them a right and power to possess and
enjoy their country, free from the intrusion and interference of lawless
invaders. Withdraw then, strangers, your unjust claims and oppressions
from our land—America is our country, as Spain is yours—the right is
the same to both:—and now that we possess the means, we are
determined to assert the justice of our cause; and free forever from a
foreign, ignominious yoke, our children, our country, and ourselves.[74]

After this stirring and powerful defense of the American position,
William Burke exposed his own training as a minister when he
described the hand of Providence in a natural economic order of the
world:

The Americans, however, are not the only people whom the
Spaniards injure, by the barbarous oppressions, and stupid preclusions,
which they exercise against that devoted country: other nations and
people are necessarily affected in their interests; by the unjust and cruel
suppression of the industry, the productions, and consumption, of the
immense regions composing South America. They who suppose this
globe had not been made for general happiness; know little of the
economy of its productions; or of the beneficent views of Him who
created it. The whole earth may be compared to a large garden, divided
into numerous and distinct compartments or beds: each bed having a
different soil and climate, or different degrees of heat and cold, of
dryness and moisture, from the rest. It is evident from this difference
of soil and climate, that there must also be a difference in the

productions of this garden: but as these productions, however various in taste, smell, colour, and other qualities, are all good either for the nourishment, the comfort, or delight of mankind; and their variety is best suited to please the diversity of likings and desires, which characterises the inhabitants of this garden; it follows, that an interchange and reciprocal enjoyment of those various productions, will be most conducive to the general happiness; and the more so, as all the beds are calculated, when fully cultivated and attended, to yield a great superabundance of their productions, above the consumption of their respective owners; but which surplus is absolutely required, to satisfy the wants or desires of others of the inhabitants.

Undoubtedly this globe has not been given for partial purposes; nor has a right been vested with any man or set of men, to interdict the flowing of its benefits among the great mass of mankind: that power which attempts it, is an usurpation, and in direct hostility with the rights and happiness of the human race. Spain, therefore, by, as it were, hermetically sealing up her immense possessions in America from the rest of the world, excepting her own stupid despotism; commits an injustice against other nations, which it is both their duty and interest immediately to destroy.[75]

This metaphor of the "walled garden"—Spain's vicious monopoly of America's wealth—often appears in Burkian works.

The vision of South America's independence and its world impact, as articulated by William Burke, was prophetic, emotional, and sanguine:

What a cheering prospect of prosperous independence, would the boundless and luxuriant but now neglected savannas of South America, being thrown open to migration and settlement, present to the eager view of thousands of poor Europeans; who are now with large families, and notwithstanding their utmost exertions, struggling against want and wretchedness, at home. New towns and villages would soon rise up in the desert: the trackless wilderness would shortly become the habitation of civilized men; and its wild fertility be applied to the bearing of productions, which men wafted beyond the seas, would greatly alleviate the wants and distresses of other countries; while a population extending over an immense portion of the globe, and growing daily as well in numbers as in civilization, would by their increased consumption necessarily open new and numerous markets for the sale of European manufactures; and would also greatly enlarge the supply of materials upon which industry might expand her useful and profitable exertions.[76]

On the question of legality, Burke merely reviewed and concluded with the natural rights thesis: "That what is just, cannot be illegal, is a principle so self-evident, that it requires only to be expressed, to receive the universal assent of mankind." Spain's claim was "unjust and tyrannical," thus, so were her laws in America. Here, Burke used the "highwayman" analogy which he cited often in his writings:

> No law certainly can exist between oppressors and the oppressed, to sanction the injustice of the former: as well might he who robs another of his watch and other valuables, on the highway; and who after the robbery extorts by terror an admission, that the property is then become legally his, charge the rightful owner with transgressing the law; if he afterwards endeavours to regain the articles which had been plundered from him!

The highwayman Spain could not charge the Americans of having broken a law "which it is evident, could never have existed between them. Hence the emancipation of America, is as legal, on the part of the people; as it is just."[77]

At this point, the author moved to the legality as it applied to a third party: "Spain, though unable to refute the lawfulness of the Americans, to emancipate their country; would in all probability, view the interference of England for producing that effect, as a breach of the law of nations." Burke insisted that the injustice of the Spanish case applied, as well, to the interests of a third nation:

> Public law is public justice; and therefore, no nation is or can be bound, to support the aggressions, the usurpations, and oppressions of one people or spot of the earth, over another; on the contrary, humanity, generosity, honour, all the ennobling properties of our nature, not only forbid us from becoming accomplices, by giving our assent or sanction to the cruel and barbarous spoliation and destruction of whole masses of our fellow-creatures; but imperiously demand it of us as a duty (and a sacred duty, it is) to prevent, with our whole force, such crimes being perpetrated, against the peace and happiness of mankind; or, if unfortunately they have been already committed, to rescue and relieve the sufferers, as far as lies in our power.[78]

The "highwayman" analogy applied here: "Every honest man among us" would come to the aid of the suffering countryman, driving away "the villains." Nations should do the same: "South America, unfortunately, is in the situation of the countryman: and the injustice and illegality would be, not to rescue her."[79]

In times of war, however, the rules changed. As a pacifist, Burke needed to express his anti-war feelings:

> This dreadful condition of lawless force between nations; this awful state of violence, which subverts or suspends the fundamental principles and laws of society, which forcibly transfers property from the rightful owners to the strongest, and which not only sanctions robbery, but also legalizes murder!—under this terrible condition of things, undoubtedly the liberation of oppressed men cannot be charged as a serious illegality.

Burke's logic, straining and buckling to nationalistic emotion, led him to the following argument:

> But the insidious interference of Spain herself, in conjunction with France, in the memorable dispute between Great Britain and her North American colonies, and which precipitated the loss of the latter; though it had not been entered into with the same honourable motives of extending freedom and of doing good, yet furnishes a practical and unanswerable argument in favour of the legality of England, to effect in her turn, the emancipation of Spanish America.

To justify his stand, Burke further argued:

> In doing so, Britain undoubtedly will have but followed the steps of Spain and France: and as in war, reprisals are held to be lawful, the injustice and illegality of the act (if any injustice or illegality can be supposed to exist in doing good), can attach only to those, who set the first example.[80]

In the third part of his opening question, dealing with the policy of emancipating South America, Burke provided a more persuasive exposition as to why Great Britain should embark upon the liberation of the Hispanic New World, exposing in the process his excellent university training. Burke reminded his readers of new currents in the writing of history and international affairs, as well as revealing to us how modern the methodological practices of the so-called "social sciences" had become by this time. Burke explained:

> As the theatre of human affairs begins to be enlarged, so also, what is termed the policy of nations, expands with it. Formerly the shutting

up of a river, the exclusive trade to a port, or the appropriation of a single town or district, were sufficient to occupy the attention of statesmen, and to plunge whole nations into all the dreadful horrors of protracted war and misery. Now, on the contrary, those circumstances, rendered insignificant by the magnitude which the affairs of men begin to assume, have scarcely a place in the policy of great nations; and the national mind keeping pace with the extension of national interests, can comprehend the emancipation of a whole continent, as being worthy of its views, best suited to the grandeur of its exertions, and most likely to afford a return of the greatest permanent good. This progress in the policy of nations, is extremely gratifying to the well-wishers of their fellow-creatures: it both proves that the elements and constitution of human affairs are laid with the view of finally producing general civilization and happiness; and that man, so long embroiled in the labyrinths of ignorance and petty contention, has at length discovered the high road, and is preparing to march on, freely and with steady step, to the goal of his felicity.[81]

Sanguine about the emancipation of South America, Burke announced with exhuberance:

Heretofore, alas! policy and justice seldom went hand in hand; but, in the liberation of America, we shall serve the world, break the chains of millions of our fellow-men, enlarge the sphere of human subsistence and happiness, add to the production of the necessaries and delicacies of life, and both positively and negatively serve ourselves, by opening new, rich, and numerous markets for the sale of our manufactures, and by cutting off from our present powerful adversary the important resources which he derives from Spain possessing America.[82]

Burke no longer was thinking about his cooperative trade project with the French; it was British interests that preoccupied him. As he put it,

Hence justice and policy, duty and interest, all combine in recommending to Britain the glorious work of emancipating Southern America—perhaps no other undertaking had ever been entered upon by any one nation, for the benefit of another, supported by so many brilliant and just claims to success. England has already acquired the indelible glory of having laid in the deserts of North America the foundations of an empire, which promises, at no very remote period, to astonish the world with the stupendous magnitude of its results.

At this point, William Burke supplied us with the title of this chapter and the opening quotation . . . . "May the illumining star of British glory light us to the right use of the present inestimable opportunity!"

Burke's appreciation for the new trends in international relations formed this evaluation of the Napoleonic enemy:

> Besides the greater expanse of objects which the policy of nations begins to assume; besides that these objects are rising in importance, are more intimately and widely connected with human happiness; they are further imperiously pressed upon us by the irresistible surrounding circumstances of the world. The events precipitated by the French Revolution, have more or less changed the moral and political condition of all the nations of Europe; and consequently materially altered the relative connexion between those nations and Great Britain. Our commerce no longer enjoys, as formerly, a free transit to all the parts of the European continent. The continental preponderance of France has already succeeded in shutting us out from a great and flourishing portion of Europe; and not a single port friendly to the British flag presents itself along the immense line of coast, extending from the shores of Dalmatia to the banks of the Ems, with the exception of Portugal, whose friendship is necessarily precarious, from the imminence of her own situation: while there is danger, that fresh successes may serve to feed the gigantic schemes of the enemy, and increase still further the exclusion which injures us.
>
> Under such disabilities, which it is possible may accumulate, and with the dangerous foe against whom we have to contend, surely we should not hesitate for a moment what line of conduct to pursue. If the French Emperor attacks our commerce because he knows that its diminution must severely injure us and weaken our power; for the very same reasons are we imperiously bound to protect, to cherish, and extend that commerce: if he can forbid the consumption of our manufactures upon the continent of Europe, and exclude us from its ports, we undoubtedly are called upon by the best interests of the people and the safety of the state, to adopt immediately and energetically the only adequate counter-mode of proceeding left to us—that of opening new markets for the sale of the products of our labour and industry elsewhere: and certainly in no other part of the world can this be effected with so much ease and efficiency as throughout the immense and fertile regions of South America.*   [Footnote: *It is to be understood that under the general designation of South America, Mexico is also included in these views.][83]

South America, Burke emphasized again, was the ideal area for the English to cultivate because of its "inexhaustible resources."[84]   But,

Englishmen should recognize that their attitude toward South America should be imaginative:

> all selfish and narrow-minded calculations of present gain must be repelled far from us; and a system of political treatment should be adopted towards her, at once grand, extensive, and liberal, like the leading natural features of this luxuriant and majestic division of the earth.[85]

Determined to convince his readers that "Conquest" was no solution at all in South America, he wrote this telling statement:

> Undoubtedly, a liberal frame of policy, besides according most with justice and the welfare of nations, and being more truly suited to the grandeur and importance of the object, will also agree best with our own real interests, and will unquestionably afford us the most good. By entering South America, to emancipate her, the people will crowd to the standard of their deliverers, and with a comparatively trifling force and little expense, we shall succeed in a short time, and with only a few efforts, in separating forever from the aid of our rival and enemy, the resources of a great, rich, and important continent, which we shall at the same time liberate, and throw open to a general trade, and consequently to an interchange of benefits: while a contrary policy might hazard these results, and lead to less happy consequences.[86]

Although a policy of conquest might appear successful in the short run, the costs of such a program would be prohibitive. Burke noted persuasively:

> still must the charges for supporting the forces, which in that case it will be necessary to keep up, both for defending the conquered provinces from foreign invasion, and to keep down and overawe the colonists and natives, subtract considerably from the profits gained by the seizure and possession, and render them much less than might be obtained by an open trade with the South American states, free and independent; and which, as these states grew up and flourished, must necessarily expand and become more lucrative.

The best proof of this contention, the author noted was the

> well and happily illustrated case of the North American United States, whose rapid increase of trade, since the era of independence affords to

Britain several times the amount of the annual gain derived from them, while we held them as colonies. So true is it in political morality, that the just and lawful opulence of one nation adds to the prosperity of others.[87]

At this point, the astute propagandist marshalled a series of facts and notes that would make any patriotic British subject listen to the author with care and emotion. If force were the policy in South America, Great Britain would need to send out, and maintain constantly, a large army to South America at a time of danger, a "new relative situation" between Great Britain and France. He elaborated:

> We have seen the latter nation within a few years augment most alarmingly her population, already double our own: we behold at the present moment her extraordinary and powerful chief, meditating fresh conquest and fresh additions of people and strength on the continent, with the view, principally, of being enabled to overwhelm us by the magnitude of his force; and the crisis, perhaps, fast approaches, when in a dreadful collision with the immense power of France, England must, single-handed and of her own force, depend on the efforts of her population for salvation from humilitation and ruin. With this possible prospect before us, and circumscribed to our present numbers, as we necessarily are, by reason of our insular situation; added to the many inconveniences which commerce must suffer, from drawing too large a proportion of the people from agriculture and manufactures, it becomes of the highest import to husband the first element of our defence, and not waste even a single man, where, by a wise policy, he might have been dispensed with, and in the hour of danger be living, and on British ground, to repel the desperate invaders of his country.[88]

Burke argued, moreover, that the present situation in Europe was propitious for an English move to liberate South America. The French were distracted in the area north of Germany by the "Fourth Coalition," so that "no very great maritime expedition can be projected and dispatched by France for some time to come." A British program of emancipation, therefore, would face no great opposition from the French enemy. But, Burke warned,

> we must not forget that these moments are precious; that the fourth might be the last coalition to oppose France upon the continent; and that, having subdued his continental opponents, Bonaparte will be at full

liberty to apply much of his immense power to maritime and colonial enterprises.[89]

Young Burke's prognosis was indeed accurate—a master analyst of international relations.

* * * * * * * * * * * *

In his second treatise, *Additional Reasons for Our Immediately Emancipating Spanish America* (London, 1808), Burke had to deal with Whitelocke's tragic disaster in Buenos Aires and the bitterly intense reaction of his countrymen. He began as follows: "After the severe lesson, which we have lately received from experience, few, I should hope, will be so hardy, as to persist in the scheme of conquering, rather than of emancipating Spanish America." Yet, the British navy had escorted the Portuguese court to Brazil in late 1807; and the circumstances attending the transfer and establishment of a European government in South America might encourage military fanatics in England to seek revenge in the Río de la Plata. Convinced that this was a distinct possibility, Burke felt it necessary to sound the alarm:

> to warn the nation in time, from rushing to fresh and accumulated disasters and disgrace, by engaging in a second ruinous and inglorious attempt to subdue Spanish America by force, and which attempt, however it may succeed for a time, must, in the present circumstances inevitably lead, before long, to augmented losses and disappointment.[90]

What disturbed the young journalist most was that British "public censure" was directed exclusively upon General John Whitelocke, as if he alone had brought about the Platine disaster. Certainly, as a military leader, Whitelocke was accountable for any failure as a professional; but the British public should understand that the real causes for the defeat derived from an erroneous policy guiding the English government, long before the general set foot in the Río de la Plata. "The great and leading causes of our miscarriage in Spanish America," Burke argued, were independent of him:

> and that such was their strength and inveteracy, that had he even triumphed by force over Buenos Ayres, his success could have been but partial and temporary; and there is too much reason to apprehend, would

have been the means ultimately of enlarging and aggravating our defeat.[91]

As a keen student of public psychology, Burke developed his case in these words:

> For admitting, for the sake of argument, that General Whitelocke had succeeded in carrying Buenos Ayres: the means he must have employed so to do, by extending the destruction, and perhaps reducing that town to a heap of ruins, could have had the effect, in the then temper of the South Americans, of aggravating and augmenting still more, the general and determined enmity of the inhabitants against him; and surely the present day is not without awful proofs, how tremendous are the consequences of a whole people flying to arms, from a general sense of injustice and in their defence; and how futile it is for an invader to attempt, under those circumstances, to conquer them. But the advocates of conquest perhaps will say, that time, an additional force from England, and the benefits to be conferred upon them, would ultimately subdue and reconcile the South Americans to our reduction of their country. The reverse, however, I believe would have been the case: first, because in the highly exasperated state of the public mind, it is unnatural to suppose, that additional injury could have the effect, of lessening the force of the general hostility. Secondly, as the enraged people could draw their resources from the spot, they might have increased their means in a sufficiently rapid and formidable proportion to ours, to have overwhelmed General Whitelocke before a reinforcement could have reached him. And thirdly, with the hatred and distrust which our conduct had excited in the minds of the people; and the ideas of independence they entertained, the benefits promised by us, they would necessarily distrust or despise; compared with those which the full and complete independence of their country held out to their view.[92]

The "new circumstances" prevailing in the world made it imperative for England to pursue a policy of emancipation, as he recommended in his earlier treatise of 1807. Napoleon's control of the European Continent was now a fact, and not just conjecture. With new resources at his disposal, Napoleon looked forward to carrying

> his plans and influence into the other three quarters of the globe, and to endeavour to exclude us from them, as he has already done from Europe. Who could stop him? Anyone thinking that he could do so has

not deeply observed the causes of the present eventful times—he has not looked into the nature of the heart of man—his long sufferings, and the almost generally miserable condition which still benights and oppresses him, throughout the greater part of the globe.[93]

How do we explain this modern conqueror's success in Europe? It has been due to

> the comparative weakness of his enemies, arising from their greatly inferior political institutions; and which, while they directly, by oppressing the people, repressed the growth of their strength and energies, and the production and accumulation of the resources of their country, had also the effect, as was natural, either of neutralizing their affections, and rendering them indifferent to the fate of governments, for which they could have no love; or of disposing them to receive and embrace a change, which might make their situation better. —Hence the invasions of Bonaparte met no opposition from the people whose countries he overran: that conqueror marched successively to Vienna, to Berlin, and to Warsaw; and now spreads his armies over the principal part of Europe, without exciting a single combined national movement towards resistance, on the part of the people; who seem to view the fall of their old governments, with the same apathy they would do that of their old houses, when in the certain prospect of having them speedily replaced by new and more commodious ones.[94]

The French monopolist, moreover, employs an "insidious policy" that spreads French dominance with changes that improve the lot of the people. He replaces "old feudal oppressions" with a code of laws "calculated at once to regulate and restrain the noble, and to protect and secure the peasant." Thus, the majority of the people

> heretofore weighed down by the heavy pressure of feudality, must by the new modifications in their favour, feel their burdens considerably lightened. The new acts of constitution will give them a civil existence before unknown: They will at once rescue and secure them from the tyranny and exactions of the priests and nobles; security will beget industry—industry, wealth, and prosperity, which consecrated by a long internal peace, and aided by the diffusion of knowledge, and the spirit of improvement and of just and enlightened religious liberality, will hold out to the view of the Continent, a more flourishing and happy prospect than she had before enjoyed.

Such a policy cannot be easily thwarted. People who now feel that they have a stake in society will not want to return to "the bondage of their feudal lords. This indeed would be contrary to nature, as it is to reason; and what in the present state of the world, cannot be expected to happen."[95]

It would be foolish to assume, moreover, that Napoleon would refrain from using this "all-powerful principle of meliorating the condition of the people" in other parts of the world. And he would, indeed, be successful there: Asia, Africa, and South America would be responsive to such an approach considering the bare subsistence of their people. Some critics might disagree, Burke noted: "But I beg those persons to reflect, that both in Asia and Africa, man has nearly performed his long night of sleep; that the dawn of civilization, revolving from the West, already radiates the horizon of both." We must not forget that the "modern conqueror" has provided "sufficient proofs, of his ability to manage the prejudices of an uninstructed people, and to mould their rude efforts into a furtherance of his own designs."[96] The only way that Great Britain might meet this threat was by following a "liberating and conciliating policy" toward the natives of India. Yet,

> wielding the power of the European Continent, as the successful French chief now does; and susceptible as the present condition of Asia and Africa is, of the impressions both of his power and policy, no force of ours certainly can prevent him from penetrating to the banks of the Indus, and from compelling us once more, but under circumstances more awful, to contend on the plains of Hindostan: for our empire and interests in the East.

Burke's point had been made effectively: the alleged "mental darkness and superstitions" of Asia and Africa rendering their people "inaccessible to change," was no longer a tenable position.[97]

"Happily for England," Napoleon's "circumstance of continuity" that favored him in the Old World, and to a lesser extent in Africa and Asia, was not the case in the New World! The young essayist burst forth with some brilliant paragraphs explaining and defining the objectives of the British nation in the Americas:

> The intervention of the ocean which terminates the power of France, commences that of Great Britain: and while it removes the Western Hemisphere, to a distance too remote for the direct grasp of the

conqueror, offers to England grand and preclusive facilities, for a wide and happy exertion of her means; and by adopting the all powerful measures of conferring independence on the people, for founding in the new world, and upon the firmest of all human foundations—the interests and affections of emancipated millions, the fruitful elements of an intercourse and influence, which shall, in no great distance of time, and without any costly efforts on our part, more than counterbalance the loss of those now destroyed or withheld by our enemy, in the old.

Certain I am, circumstances rapidly combine, to force this policy upon England, as her best, and, as it may perhaps shortly be, her only ally. Threatened, as we are, with nearly a general exclusion from the old world: necessity naturally points our relations to the new. Where besides, can we expect to find, in sufficient abundance, the raw materials demanded by our wants: and the necessary markets for taking off the surplus of our industry? The new world, and particularly Spanish America, contains the elements for speedily, under proper management, furnishing both: and requires of us, but to employ the master-key of independence, to unlock her treasures to our use. And what other principle can Britain wield, so congenial with her constitution, and the genius and feelings of her people; so powerful in its effects, and therefore well-adapted to our present relative strength and situation; and which promises such speedy, great, and comprehensive success? By spreading emancipation, England will have conquered, almost immediately, and with scarcely any other force than that of the principle on which she proceeds, millions of rich friends, ready at the moment to enter into an important community of interests with us, and capable of affording many of those valuable commercial advantages, denied us in Europe; but which, it is so necessary to the continuance of our power and prosperity, to establish elsewhere. While, by creating new, independent, and powerful states, beyond the reach of our enemy, we shall have gained so many valuable and lasting friends; and through them, raised in the Western world, an influence, which will serve to hold in equilibrium, the great and excessive power acquired by our rival in the Eastern.[98]

The British government had to capitalize on its "vast naval superiority, and the dominion of the seas" in order to frustrate any efforts by Napoleon to intrude into the New World. "Shall Britons behold him seize, and successively turn against them the power and resources of a great portion of the old world," asked the writer,

and now see him making preparations for gaining possession of those also of a vast and important portion of the new; and not assume the measures evidently in their power, for preventing for ever the latter, and for counteracting the former? Forbid it common sense—forbid it the glory and the safety of the country—No—rather let us, elevating our views and efforts to the awful magnitude of the crisis, determine to surmount it. The principal nations of the world league against us—the power and resources of the vast and important regions of Spanish America, are now sought to be added. Let us then hasten, while yet the opportunity remains, to anticipate the lures of the enemy; and, with the cheap gift of independence, immediately secure forever on our side, by the sole means through which we can hope to succeed, the generous affections and multiplying strength and resources of a rich and rising people; who will feel gratefully indebted to us, to the latest time, for having conferred upon them the most invaluable of human benefits—the emancipation of their country.[99]

The urgency to move swiftly with the policy of emancipation was dictated by the general discontent throughout South America with their "present condition." There should be no "unnecessary delay." Burke focused expertly on the issue:

For can it be supposed Bonaparte will overlook this disposition of the Spanish Americans, so favourable to his views? Or that he, who has acquired so much in the Eastern world, by availing himself of a similar susceptibility of the public mind—and who, through the agency of prospective meliorations, had induced so large a portion of the people of Europe, to accept his changes, will not now try the same powerful expedient in the Western world, for the important purpose of creating in his favour that influence, which our interdiction of his passage thither, precludes him, for the present, from commanding? Surely not.[100]

Apprehensive about Napoleon's designs in Spanish America, Burke suspected that he would exploit Spain's subservience to him by getting her to introduce overseas

his new constitutions, containing a show of independence, and appearing to meet the wishes of the inhabitants, but really calculated and designed to entrap and organize the people and their resources, for the use and benefit of France.[101]

Here, young Burke actually anticipated a pattern used in Spain after May 2, 1808, when Napoleon's brother, as Joseph I of Spain, called a constituent assembly to enact the so-called "Bayonne Constitution." It offered the ex-colonials certain rights in the new government, etc. What could the British do to prevent such a takeover by the French? The Burkian assessment, as usual, was painfully realistic:

> Even our offers of independence, may then be rejected as unreasonable: and to the feelings of deep and severe disappointment, we shall have to add the mortifying and humiliating reflection; that our failure and the triumph of the enemy, were wholly owing to the great and unaccountable blindness of our own policy. With this dangerous prospect of anticipation then before us—with the great facility which we see France possesses, by her hold on Spain, for gaining a footing, if not for her actual power, at least for her influence in Spanish America; either of which may be fatal to our views—and threatened as we are with hostility and exclusion, by almost the rest of the world; surely the best interests of England require, that we lose not a moment in adopting that great and efficient measure which can alone defeat the views of the enemy, and ensure our own success.[102]

The youthful Burke, so obsessed with his commitment to the liberation of Spanish America under British auspices, lashed out with a cutting and sarcastic attack upon his critics:

> I am aware that some persons, no doubt differing from me in their view of the subject, still hold; that we ought to reassume the principle of conquest, with the view of retrieving the lustre of our arms; which, according to them, had been tarnished by our late failure before Buenos Ayres. This, supposing the ground of the proposition true, but which I can admit only in a certain light, may appear a good military reason; and in times more chivalrous and less enlightened than the present, would certainly have had its weight. To those, however, who would urge this barren and hopeless conduct in the present day, I beg to observe, that, to the credit of the age in which we live, other notions of honour and policy now prevail: and that as justice is almost universally recognized by the civilized world, to be the true foundation of honour between nations; so the deepest stain national honour can receive, is from a deliberate breach of the principle which supports it. I know that what are called the *laws of war*, will be urged against me, in defence of our late attacks upon Spanish America: but do those laws apply, to every enemy?—at all times?—and upon every occasion?—Nay, might not cases even occur, where the application of them, would be a gross and flagrant breach of the first principles of justice? If this then be admitted, as true in some instances; and, I believe, the most zealous advocates for conquest, will hardly deny it in the case of Spanish

America; and particularly after it is known, that we had held out hopes of a very different conduct to her people, as will be hereafter shewn; the consumation and not the failure of our late attack, would have been the disgrace.[103]

After exposing the basic points of contention with the adversaries of conquest, the young British publicist sharpened his tools of debate. First, he asked:

independently of our promises of a different treatment, what injury, let me ask the partizans of conquest; had the Spanish Americans inflicted upon us, that justified our going to seize and plunder their country: had they attacked, or threatened us with a similar conduct; or even breathed a single hostile design against us, that could warrant retaliation? No, Spanish America, lay the inoffensive victim of the despotism of Spain, which nation had been dragged against her will into the war, in her fetters upon the ground; and had neither the means nor disposition to injure us: but on the contrary, was ready and eager to join her friendship and her fortunes with ours; and only waited the expected signal from us, to break from her former masters forever, and arrange herself upon our side. What then in justice or honour, could sanction our injury of her? Our inglorious attempt to seize the country of a friend by force, to appropriate and carry off the properties of the inhabitants, and cruelly bury themselves and their families under the ruins of their homes? But it will be said, all this is allowable; Spain, to whom those provinces belong, being at war with us! Gracious Heavens, shall we permit such miserable pretexts, in the present day, to interpose and cloud our view of the great and immutable laws of right: and not think it dishonourable to commit in Spanish America, acts for the perpetration of which in our country, men are daily, and in the name of justice, consigned to infamy and the gallows?[104]

In his next point, Burke cut his enemies with ridicule and scorn as he wrote:

But let me inquire of those chivalrous gentlemen: where in Spanish America, has the lustre of our arms been so grievously tarnished by defeat, as they suppose? Was it at our capture and subsequent defence of Buenos Ayres, by a mere handful of men under General Beresford? Or was it at the reduction of Maldonado? Or the truly arduous storming of Monte-Video, by the gallant Achmuty and his brave followers? No. But, say these gentlemen, we have failed in a second attempt to take Buenos Ayres! We have, it is true, failed to retake that town: and as I

have observed, prevented, by the failure, the disgraceful consummation
of an undertaking founded in injustice; and perhaps generalship might
also have been wanting on the occasion: but has the honour of the
troops suffered by the failure? . . . . What troops, under all the
dispiriting and awful circumstances of that truly melancholy occasion,
ever displayed more intrepid constancy and steady valour; or returned
more frequently to the deadly and unequal contest, over heaps of their
slain companions? I believe none. What then is this insufferable stain
upon our arms, which would require us . . . to return to the charge
against Buenos Ayres: and, by burning their town to ashes, and
murdering its inhabitants, remove the stain, by proving to the world our
ability to have done so before? If any such stain, as they conceive,
exist; and I cannot see it in the same light; and if this be the mode
which they suggest for wiping it away, I must confess; that, in my mind,
the honour will consist in rather letting it remain . . . I most undoubtedly
agree . . . that the lustre of our arms has received a stain, a deep
stain—which ought immediately to be wiped away. But, as I also
believe this stain has been cast upon them, not so much by their failure
in Spanish America, as is erroneously supposed; as by the selfish and
ignoble policy and views, towards which, their operations had been
unfortunately directed: so I must now be permitted to offer a different
mode to the above, for retrieving their lustre; and which simply is, to
employ them again, and speedily upon the same Continent: but upon a
political principle, diametrically opposite to that which caused their
disgrace before: upon a principle, which, being founded on justice, and
having for its aim, not the continuance of her subjection, but the
liberation and independence of Spanish America; not the plunder and
abuse of her people; but the security of their persons and properties:
will, instead of exciting the whole of her population against us as
before, on the contrary raise them in our favour, and cause them to join
their exertions to ours, for consummating purposes, at once so happy,
and so glorious to themselves and their country.[105]

In this day and age, William Burke concluded: "the odious principle
of conquest" amounts to "rank folly."[106]   Force is costly, and less
profitable, than the imaginative principle of emancipation. France with
double the population of England looks upon "melioration" as the
cheapest and most efficient plan "for gaining reception and stability for
her influence over other nations." Should the English be different? In
a long and involved construction, Burke answered the question with a
question:

threatened with destruction and exclusion, as we have seen, from every side; and compelled to divide our means, to guard various points against our numerous enemies; madly waste our strength, and expose ourselves to defeat, in a hazardous enterprise to subdue the vast regions of Spanish America, by force; and at a time too, when the general, and rapidly rising views of national independence and elevation, already rouse, and, as we have said invigorate the public mind; when we might, by so much easier means and without the danger of loss, secure superior advantages?[107]

With respect to the tragic failure in Buenos Aires, Burke claimed that his information came from an unimpeachable source:

It is a fact, I believe, not generally known; but the truth of which I can assert, upon the best authority: that the great and principal cause of our late expulsion from Spanish America, was owing to our refusing to declare her independence: and the existence of this cause will appear the more unaccountably strange, when I also affirm upon equal authority: that the demand was made, in pursuance of hopes and promises repeatedly held out to the Spanish Americans generally, and particularly to the people of Buenos Ayres, through the medium of their agents in London; that England would send out a force, to aid them in establishing their independence. 'Assist us,' said the chief and people of Buenos Ayres, to our officers, 'in declaring the independence of our country, as your nation had promised to do: and in return, we pledge ourselves, to separate forever from Spain. We will receive and cooperate with you, as brothers; and throw open our ports to a general and free trade, with your country.' I wish, by stating these important facts, not to implicate individuals: but the awful condition of the country, and the incalculable importance of the subject before us require; that the great political faults, which have caused our misfortunes in Spanish America, be exposed; with the view of precluding a recurrence of those mischiefs in future.[108]

A Peruvian observer, who had witnessed the English experience in the Río de la Plata explained in detail to William Burke why there was such a deep rooted hostility towards his countrymen in Buenos Aires and its environs, spreading like wildfire throughout Spanish America. In Lima, Peru, he noted that about 25,000 men

instantly flew to arms, without distinction of rank or colour . . . resolutely determined, should we attempt their shores, to defend

themselves and their country, against, as they considered us, the unjust
and illiberal invaders of Buenos Ayres. It is melancholy thus to have
to observe the calamitous turn, given solely and entirely by our faulty
and injudicious policy, to the bright prospects which once opened in
favour of us, in Spanish America: and which, if they had been but
wisely and seasonably treated by us, would ere now have yielded results
far different to those, which at present we are compelled to deplore.[109]

It took a powerful and courageous individual to speak out, as William
Burke did in his second treatise, explaining why the "Platine Fever" had
failed so miserably in South America. Burke's message, however, was
overwhelmingly positive and imaginative in his suggestion of a new,
responsible position vis-a-vis the emancipation of Spanish America.
And his diagnosis of the Napoleonic Wars, especially his explanation
of Napoleon's tactics towards the people conquered, was highly
perceptive. Burke displayed a general and specific command of history
and the new currents in the "social sciences." In the last half of his
second treatise, he continued the positive message by offering the
British hope that Francisco de Miranda would assist them in the
implementation of the "No-Conquest" program for Spanish
America—the subject of our next chapter.

Chapter Three

The Expedition of 1806 to Venezuela in Perspective

> Whoever undertakes an enterprise of danger and novelty generally incurs the imputation of a Quixotte, or becomes the theme of universal admiration. No man appears to have hazarded more than the celebrated General Miranda in his scheme of conquering, or rather revolutionizing his native place, the Province of Caraccas.
>
> The slender means with which he has commenced this extraordinary adventure, the obstacle he has had to contend against, and the prejudices that have been excited against him, cause his situation to be as critical as it is unenviable; but before we hastily condemn the man, or his expedition, let us examine the one and the other dispassionately.
>
> "Rolla," September 6, 1806[1]

The "mysterious" adventures of General Francisco de Miranda continued to fascinate readers everywhere, especially in England and in the United States during the years 1806 and 1807. Reporters allowed their imaginations, following snippets of information, to go off in all directions. Accordingly, a fuzzy tale appeared before the world public. As months passed, however, the reports gradually took on a semblance of credibility. The best official account of the vaunted expedition to Venezuela was in William Burke's second treatise.[2] Newspapers in the United States accounted for the earlier releases; and the later reports—the most reliable, as it turned out—originated in the English Caribbean. Writing from Barbados, "Rolla" was indeed perceptive; and his views influenced the English principals involved. Two North Americans, who were officers in Miranda's force, wrote uncomplimentary accounts of the 1806 trip when they returned to the United States. Lieutenants James Biggs and John H. Sherman, moreover, revived the unfavorable sterotype of Miranda that emerged from the French Revolution—a matter of grave concern to Miranda and his publicists.[3] Thanks to Sarah Andrews (or Martin), the mother of Miranda's two sons in London, there is a lengthy scrapbook of newspaper clippings available on Miranda's career in the Caribbean. The British public unquestionably favored the Venezuelan's quixotic adventures of 1806. Influenced by the "Platine Fever" (September 13, 1806 forward), Englishmen fervently hoped that General Miranda's efforts might also serve to open up markets for their goods in northern South America.[4] The intimate connection, in the public's mind, of the two expansive thrusts of 1806: (1) into the Plata and (2) into Venezuela had a definite influence on London's policy decisions. It underscored the significance of Miranda's first attempts to invade Venezuela, as well as the preparation for the General's return to South America a few years later.

* * * * * * * * * * * *

Upon receiving the *Leander's* papers from the port authorities of New York, Captain Thomas Lewis guided his ship to Staten Island, where she took on the remainder of her cargo and passengers. On February 3, 1806, she left the harbor as inauspiciously as possible. Despite the exaggerated conjectures of the press, the *Leander* initially was the sole component of Miranda's heralded expedition. There were serious rumors that the *Emperor* and the *Hindostan,* two comparable ships, would join Miranda in southern Haiti, where Alexandre Pétion was anxious to support his fellow revolutionary.[5] It might be possible to recruit additional men in the newly emancipated nation of Haiti, the former French colony of Saint Domingue.

Despite the real weaknesses of the venture, General Miranda tried to inspire his followers with optimism as the *Leander* proceeded along the American coast and then cut across in a southeasterly direction toward Bermuda. All that he had at his disposal were some two hundred men. They included the members of the ship's crew, a prospective cadre of two to three dozen officers for the future "Colombian Army," and a hundred or more North American recruits from the Philadelphia-New York and New England areas.[6] Even if we were to add another hundred men, as Sherman alleged, this was still an insufficient force in the context of the Napoleonic Wars. Such a small body, of necessity, had to proceed with extreme caution; and its leaders were forever suffering highly stressful moments, painfully aware of their vulnerability. The frustrating delays, in turn, played into the hands of the French and Spanish enemies and gave them time to prepare their defenses.

The first challenge to the *Leander* came on the morning of February 12th. It occasioned, as Biggs tells us, "a thousand alternate hopes and fears." If the ship in the distance was French or Spanish, Miranda *et al* had no choice but "to overcome or perish."[7] Fortunately, the challenger was English: the H.M.S. *Cleopatra*, of forty guns, under the command of Captain John Wight. There were some apprehensive moments initially among Miranda's followers, as it became obvious that the principal British concern was the impressment of sailors. A British lieutenant came aboard the *Leander* to examine her "*role d'equipage*" and then arbitrarily called out "names and countenances," that he assumed were Englishmen or Irishmen. These poor fellows, Lt. Sherman observed: "very unwillingly went into the boat, and with them the Lieutenant returned to the frigate."[8] To register their complaint on the loss of crew, Miranda and others decided to pay the *Cleopatra* a visit.

"With his portfolio" in hand, the eloquent Venezuelan thoroughly charmed his quarry, the Englishman Captain Wight. Over the years Miranda had learned much about the English and their ways. It paid off handsomely on this occasion. Captain Wight was deeply impressed. Biggs and Sherman could hardly believe it. Sherman wrote:

> immediately afterwards a sociable circle was formed between them and the other officers, in the cabin; wine was introduced, and Miranda and Armstrong remained on board ship the whole night. In the morning, Miranda was conveyed on board the *Leander* with martial honors. With him came sixteen native Americans, who had been impressed by the *Cleopatra*, in exchange for the twenty-six impressed the day before.

To show his gratitude for the previous evening, General Miranda "made the British commander a present of a barrel of ale, and two or three cheeses."[9] Lt. Biggs added a philosophical note that underscored the historical significance of the *Cleopatra* encounter:

This event has confirmed our impressions, respecting the nature and objects of this expedition. General Miranda, I think, must have effected the release of the *Leander*, by explaining a part, or the whole of his plan, relative to South America; and, by producing credentials from the British government, authorizing, or at least protecting him in the undertaking. This idea is strengthened by Miranda saying that Captain Wight had promised to assist in the enterprise . . . I am extremely glad we were overtaken by this ship; for the result tends to put us at ease about the consistency of our design with the laws of nations, and proves to the world that we are not a 'band of desperate pirates,' a description given to us by some persons before we sailed from New York, and propagated afterwards, in whispers, through the ship. Besides, the expedition is now placed on a respectable footing, by having, as we presume, the acknowledgement and countenance of England. We are still in high spirits and high hopes.[10]

Buoyed by Captain Wight's assurances, General Miranda embarked upon a serious propaganda move to get out all the literature that he expected to circulate during the expedition of 1806: the manifestoes, proclamations, broadsides, and pamphlets, especially, the famous tract of Father Juan Pablo Viscardo Guzmán, the Peruvian Jesuit who called for the end of Spanish colonial rule in the Americas. In the 1790's, Miranda himself had been instrumental in the publication of the French and English translations. Now, his forces would officially introduce the original Spanish version among his fellow countrymen in Venezuela.[11] There were several printers among the North American recruits, who could operate the printing press that Miranda brought with him on his voyage. London editors acclaimed with enthusiasm Miranda's use of "that powerful engine, the press" as well as the political function of "Miranda's pegs."[12] These so-called "pegs," Miranda's printing press, remained in South America after the 1806 expedition.

Hopeful of the future, Miranda likewise commenced the process of issuing commissions in the "Colombian Army" to the cadre of officers who would lead his units into combat. On February 14, 1806, the process began and was continued into the Haitian phase. A General Order announced that the "Password" in battle was "America" and the "Countersign: Liberty."[13] Captain Thomas Lewis of the *Leander* received the rank of "Colonel" in the Colombian Army. The assumption was that Lewis and his sailors would submit to military training prior to their participation in the invasion of South America.

Thus, Miranda could use his human resources to the maximum; and the same would apply to other ships joining his expedition later.

Despite the psychological lift of the *Cleopatra* experience, Francisco de Miranda was still apprehensive and impatient as he neared the Haitian seacoast from the south, a mood that persisted even after the arrival at the port of Jacmel on February 17, 1806. Days passed without any evidence of Captain Wight's promises of help. Lt. Biggs was a faithful barometer who sensed his general's uneasiness:

> There are yet no signs of the *Cleopatra* . . . . Every vessel, that is described in the offing, excites his fears or curiosity; and he seldom fails to request somebody, first asking if they have good sight, to take the spy-glass, and see if that vessel is the *Cleopatra*; upon hearing an unfavourable report from the observer, he says, 'well, never mind, should she not join us here, she will come to us on the Spanish Main.' All this is calculated to make us imagine that the British interest themselves in our success. Yet, if this is the case, there seems to have been no plan for securing their aid.[14]

Another disturbing factor that hovered over the scene was the disagreeable quarrel that took place aboard the *Leander* prior to her arrival in Haiti between General Miranda and Captain Thomas Lewis. Both Sherman and Biggs instantly recognized the implications of this hostility. The former noted:

> A circumstance, about this time, took place on board the ship, between Miranda and Lewis, which, although trifling in its nature, gave rise to a difference between them, which was not completely healed up during the expedition, and to which perhaps, some serious consequences, relating to the fate of the expedition, may be attributed. The circumstance was this.—The steward of the ship was ordered to wait upon the table, during dinner, which he neglected to do. Armstrong chastised him—he then complained to Lewis.—Miranda interfered and ordered the steward to obey Armstrong.—Lewis then replied, that neither he [Miranda] nor Armstrong, had any control over the seamen while on board the vessel—that if any one did not do his duty, complaint ought to be made to him. Some further words ensued, and the affair was dropped.[15]

After the arrival at Jacmel, Lt. Biggs still felt uneasy about the incident:

The Captain is high spirited and unyielding; and the General, I am persuaded, is a man of unruly temper, obstinate and determined. The judicious interposition of a third person, in such a case, will sometimes be effectual; if this shall be necessary, I hope Major Roorbach, who is qualified for the office, will try his influence.[16]

North American editors, in the meantime, were competing fiercely for news about the Miranda expedition. The break came on March 1, 1806, when a celebrated letter exposed Miranda's plans to the world. It was written by one of Miranda's dear friends, none other than Stephen Sayre. By March 1st, Stephen explained, he assumed that his announcement would not embarrass the Miranda expedition. He felt certain that his old friend had already landed in South America and that the Spanish enemy could not have time to prepare any effective defense against him. Sayre's report spread throughout the United States like fire; the news reached London by April 12th in abbreviated form. But by May 24, 1806, *The Globe* had the entire story, in addition to some valuable commentaries on it. It had a vital impact on world opinion. Writing from Richmond, Virginia, Sayre revealed the following:

> Miranda has the permission from the British Government to make Trinidad the place of rendezvous; he has gone there; the delegates of Caracas, St. Fée and Mexico—are now there or expected to meet him. Some delay may take place; therefore it would be imprudent to name the place of attack, rather the place to be surrendered, to be made the seat of confederation. If Miranda is not gone to that island, you may laugh at my credulity. If you hear of his being there, you may put more confidence than heretofore in the communication I shall make as to the subject.[17]

A Richmond reporter commented that Stephen Sayre was visiting his son: "We hope he may be induced to reside here, as his only son has now a considerable property in the state." To impress his readers, he outlined proudly the senior Sayre's prominent role in the American Revolution:

> It is well known that Mr. Sayre was Sheriff of London at the commencement of our revolutionary war; that being too zealous in our cause, he was committed to the Tower under the pretense of treason against the government; that he quitted England, was employed by our commissioners in Paris, in 1777, to go to Berlin; that he first prevailed

on the King of Prussia to enter in the armed neutrality; he then
proceeded to Denmark and Sweden, united those two Powers in the
object, which was finally carried into effect in 1780, by the Empress of
Russia, who fitted out twenty ships of the line to support it.[18]

The Richmond writer, as most reporters of that time, harbored strong
views about the Miranda project: "the most extensive, and above all
things, most likely to change the face of affairs through the universe."
He did not agree, as northern papers had reported, that "Miranda's
object was to revolutionize Cuba." Moreover, there was no question in
his mind that the English government was "privy to his plan." How did
he know this? Miranda had received "60,000 pounds from a house in
New York, thanks to an English connection." Besides, he based his
conjecture "upon the unknown and mysterious destination of Sir Home
Popham's squadron.—true this squadron may not have arrived at
Buenos Ayres."[19] This was indeed an unusual and penetrating
speculation, months before the Popham-Beresford invasion of the Río
de la Plata was known to the world. There are also traces of the
Popham-Miranda alleged connection in the English coverage of the
Miranda expedition.[20]

In *The Globe* (London) of May 24, 1806, a New Yorker commented
on the Sayre letter, speculating on England's interest in the
"rendezvous" portion of the message. He guessed that the English
connection in the venture was exploratory, somewhat skeptical of the
Venezuelan's success. But what if Miranda managed to exceed British
expectations? His answer:

> if the delegates of Caracas and Mexico should meet him at Trinidad and
> prove to the satisfaction of the British Governor, that the People of
> South America are ripe for Revolution, and able to accomplish it, in
> such a case may he not expect more effectual succours from them than
> a place of rendezvous?

In such an eventuality, England "will expect some more substantial
compensation, some extraordinary privileges of trade, at least in the part
of the Provinces whose emancipation is to be attempted; perhaps the
surrender of some of their Ports into their own hands." Here Miranda
should be careful: "The lion and other beasts agreed to hunt in
partnership; and it would be wise in the Colonies of South America to
recollect the result of the fable."[21] The reporter raised other interesting
points: Trinidad had been taken over by the English in 1797, an act

which was later confirmed by an article in the Truce of Amiens (1802). Would the British stay on at Trinidad at the end of the War? "Will she [Spain] abandon to her [England] an island, which may in all future wars become an asylum for the discontented subjects, a place of rendezvous for a British expedition against her territories, and the very key of Caracas!" Moreover, General Miranda intended to liberate all of Spanish America, not just the three areas mentioned by Sayre. He dreamed of establishing a "new confederation of states" in the Americas, formerly of Spain:

> tumultuous, and chaotic at first, but through the aid of the Press, and the extending information of the people settling down by degrees, into some fixed and harmonious system—the people would become freer, as they became more enlightened. And the United States of South America, like the United States of the North, will present to, an admiring Europe, another Republic, independent, considerable, and happy.[22]

* * * * * * * * * * * *

The arrival at Jacmel on February 17, 1806, turned out to be an unfortunate step in Miranda's itinerary. It was a period of troubles for the young Haitian Empire of Jean Jacques Dessalines, who six months later was killed in an ambush by a mob of angry mulattoes from Port-au-Prince. The rebel leader Pétion, under the circumstances, could not spare many men for Miranda's enterprise. The chaos in Haiti, moreover, distracted the mission of Captain Thomas Lewis and Major Jonas S. Smith to Port-au-Prince, some twenty miles to the north of Jacmel by land. Projected as a five-day mission by Miranda, it took over ten days; and the results were negative. Captain Jacob Lewis, owner of the *Emperor* and brother of Miranda's representative, refused to make his thirty-gun vessel available to the Venezuelan, despite promises he had made earlier in the United States.[23] Nor was the third large ship, the *Hindostani*, at Miranda's disposal. Instead, two small schooners were made available to Miranda for a period of fifty days: the *Bee* and the *Baachus*. Only fifty additional men signed up as recruits for the Miranda expedition.[24] Given these overwhelming obstacles, Miranda suffered one delay after another. He did not leave for Venezuela until March 27, 1806—a five-week postponement that further undermined the expedition's prospects. Miranda's enemies, therefore, had more time to prepare themselves against an invasion.

Miranda suspected that the source of his problems was the spiteful and negative Captain Lewis, who had persuaded his brother to break his promise—an opinion shared by Sherman and Biggs. Indeed, it appears that even Captain Thomas Lewis had second thoughts about continuing beyond Haiti.[25] His decision to stay on, however, did not auger well for the future of Miranda's odyssey. Two schooners and fifty more men did not eliminate the inherent weakness of Miranda's expedition, especially since now the element of surprise was gone. The Spanish and French enemies were waiting for him. He knew this only too well; and yet, as if escaping his frustrations by fleeing into an imaginary refuge, he supplied William Burke with an explanation that appeared in the second treatise. On the coast of Venezuela, General Miranda "had reason to suppose that the Spanish government still continued ignorant of his movements." Yet, because of "secret and dishonourable means" employed by the Spanish Ambassador in the United States, Miranda was mortified "to learn, that the government of the Caraccas was in possession of his intentions; and had given the necessary orders for taking measures of defence, and for guarding the coasts."[26]

As Miranda's fleet approached the islands of Bonair, Aruba, and Curaçao, just off the Venezuelan coast, the festering feud between Lewis and the General broke out again. Miranda's staff, as a matter of course, presumed that the sailors would participate in the military training program—an assumption that could not stand the pressure and hostility of the two leaders who hated each other with a passion. In a fit of pique, the naval leader resigned his "Colonelcy" in the Colombian Army; and Lewis threatened to transfer his followers to the *Baachus*, thus leaving the Miranda expedition.[27] Less inflamed minds prevailed at the last moment, convincing Lewis to withdraw his threat as the ships appeared off the coast of Aruba. Seamen agreed to participate in the military exercises on board ship and on land.[28] Compromisers worked out a contract that was acceptable to Lewis and his men. Miranda signed it with some reluctance. Spirits picked up on April 15th as two English ships joined them: the *Echo*, of ten guns, and an armed brig, following the recommendation of Captain Wight. After two months of waiting, the English support finally materialized. The excellent weather further bolstered morale; Miranda's men could see the Venezuelan coast across the way. Suddenly the clouds gathered and a vicious storm scattered Miranda's fleet—another delay that postponed, for ten days, the projected invasion in the vicinity of Puerto Cabello, Venezuela. By then, the two English ships had left since they could not remain in the area more than eight days after their arrival at Aruba. That was the excuse that General Miranda dourly admitted to his men.[29]

Miranda's little force readied itself for the invasion of Venezuela on the evening of April 25, 1806. The *Bee* and the *Baachus* went ahead to explore the coast and to check for Spanish defenses. At dawn of the 26th, Miranda was aghast to see his two schooners fleeing in desperation from two Spanish coastguards, a brig of 22 guns and a schooner of 18. The inevitable battle lasted three-quarters of an hour. The schooners were forced leeward, while the *Leander* hesitated to pursue the enemy aggressively. Captain Lewis opted to withdraw momentarily; by so doing, he gave up any chance of victory. Sixty men were lost by Miranda—nine in battle and fifty one as prisoners, most of them North Americans. William Burke's account blamed the defeat at Puerto Cabello to "the indecision of Captain Thomas Lewis."[30] Although Sherman and Biggs recognized this point, they did not spare General Miranda, who, after all, had the ultimate responsibility. Readers of the Sherman and Biggs accounts were left with the insinuation that the negative judgments about Miranda's comportment in the battles of the French Revolution might have been justified.[31]

After the dismal failure at Puerto Cabello, according to the Burkian account, Miranda's forces "sailed directly for Trinidad, for the purpose of procuring a British auxiliary force; and without which, in the present circumstances, he could not hope to succeed."[32] That was all that Miranda wanted to admit about the period after the disaster at Puerto Cabello. Fortunately, for history, Lt. Biggs' letters tell us another story, a plausible explanation of a defeat in retreat—how an embattled expeditionary force limped on for weeks, suffering thirst, hunger, filth, disease, and the irrational outbursts of its leader. General Miranda, it would seem, came close to what is called "Battle Fatigue" in modern warfare. These selections from Biggs' account are self-evident and very much in keeping with the realities of the period. In the following, Biggs describes an unbecoming "instance of the General's violence, that made me blush for the honour of grey hair, learning, and experience." It happened "on the quarter-deck, in the presence of all the officers and the whole ship's crew, at Bonair, two or three days after our misfortune."[33] The incident concerned an engineer who complained too loudly about the lack of money and other annoyances of Miranda's rule, all within earshot of the Venezuelan. Miranda ordered him to be silent. When the engineer disobeyed, Miranda "seized him by the throat, and threw him off the ship's gunnel, where he had been sitting, on one of the guns, and after repeated twirls, shakes, and twists, dashed him slap on the deck." In the nasty exchange that followed, the engineer threatened to resign and demanded to be allowed to "go on shore at this island. 'Sirrah!' exclaimed Miranda in a rage, 'you shall be dismissed when I think proper, and not when you please; you are at *my* disposal, and I shall retain, or send you away, as it best suits *my* purpose.'"[34] The engineer heatedly refused to concede the point, whereupon the General lost his patience: "and this shameful and ridiculous affair concluded by a severe rub of his knuckles over the ridge of the engineer's nose, not a little to the annoyance of his under lip and chin." It was such a ridiculous and laughable incident, "as to provoke our risibles," as Biggs put it quaintly:

> But, neither I, nor any other, could suppress a feeling of disgust and abhorrence at the want of self-command and of dignity in the Commander-in-Chief. He had cause, undoubtedly, to resent the language of the engineer, who was a little excited with liquor; yet the proper course would have been to put him under arrest for trial. What security has any of us under the command of a man who can be carried away by brutal fury? God grant we may not find ourselves at the mercy of a tyrant. If this be a specimen of his administration among the free people of Columbia, I think we shall have rights on paper, and wrongs in fact.[35]

As unknown ships appeared upon the horizon, General Miranda experienced one anxiety attack after another. Biggs captured these moments dramatically:

> According to custom, we are crowding sail to get out of her reach. There can be no question but that the General is much afraid of the ships of his countrymen and their allies. We may indeed expect the worst, in the event of capture. Yet I would rather contend with double our own force, especially if the vessel were Spanish, than to be forever running away.[36]

On May 15, 1806, Biggs wrote:

> Our good ship is like a thief, who apprehends every person he sees may detect him. Had you been here, you would both have laughed and fretted with me, at the quandary our chief was in today. The ship we saw yesterday pursued us several hours, fired three or four shots, and hoisted several signals. All we did was to hoist the American ensign at

the mast-head, and run as fast as possible . . . Grant that we are not absolutely ruined by this running, it will make our passage a very long one; but we are now used to disappointment and hardships, and almost prepared for the worst. Added to hunger and thirst, we are distressed by day with extreme heat, and by continual calms, and the sight of land seen a week ago, from which we cannot move a mile; and by night, tormented with flies, cockroaches, and rats, of which the ship is full.[37]

Finally, near Grenada on May 24th an aggressive ship pursued the *Leander* and fired upon her, more as a threat than to hit her: Captain Lewis

being persuaded she was English, hove to, and she came up. Seeing a French distinguishing vane at her mast head, we began to flutter. But, on speaking to us, she proved to be H.B.M.'s sloop of war, *Lily*, who had been for some time searching for the *Leander*.[38]

Thus ended the perilous voyage of Miranda's group from Bonair to Grenada. The British ally was now within reach. The *Leander* took on supplies at Grenada where English authorities eagerly assisted General Miranda's project and objectives.[39]

General Miranda's first invasion of Venezuela, in short, was an unqualified failure, plagued by constant delays, internal difficulties and tensions, and doubtful military decisions. Moreover, it was an unmitigated hell for fifty-one men of the *Bee* and the *Baachus* who ended up in the cramped Spanish dungeons of the tropics. They had reason to curse the day that they had hired on at New York. Here again we find a conspicuous gap in the Miranda account of the 1806 expedition, not a very commendable omission under the circumstances. The U.S. prisoner story, however, found its way into the North American press and was, in turn, relayed to the rest of the world. It created a great deal of emotion and criticism. Lieutenants Sherman and Biggs now had a bonafide cause to provoke their hostility against General Miranda. Sherman was one of those prisoners!

An excellent source for the prisoner story was a Philadelphian, the owner of the *Bee*, whose name, we suspect, was William Cartwright. While in prison in Cartagena on August 11, 1807, he wrote to a friend of his in Philadelphia, the editor of the *Aurora*. This was over a year after the failure of Miranda's first invasion.[40] The Cartwright letter provides a graphic account of the short battle and its grim consequences for many young Americans: the *Leander* running away from them "leaving us to the Spaniards," the instant death of Captain Huddell of the *Bee*, the lengthy and unfair trials at Puerto Cabello that sentenced ten North American officers to death by hanging in the presence of their comrades and whose decapitated heads ended upon poles throughout the Captaincy General of Venezuela. The Spaniards' message was to remind Venezuelans everywhere of the fate of "pirates" and rebels who conspired against Spain. They were to think twice about joining the "traitor" Miranda, who had a price on his head. Most American prisoners received sentences of from eight to ten years in the famous "Castles," or dungeons, of the Caribbean—an actual death sentence for many of those prisoners who died of fevers and tropical diseases. Cartwright and others described their plight in emotional terms; and newspapers in the United States sold their product in greater numbers to a concerned public. Angry readers demanded action from the U.S. Congress; and politicians debated the issue heatedly but with little results, despite the memorials published in the Biggs and Sherman accounts. In late 1808, as constitutionalism gained sway throughout the Spanish-speaking world, American prisoners were hopeful that they would be released. Miranda himself wrote to people in Spain in hopes that they would be receptive to the cause of the American prisoners. The pressure for freedom in the Spanish colonies, however, tended to polarize European Spaniards, thus allowing the militarists, or "hawks," to influence a vindictive stand against revolutionaries and their abettors. The cause of the American prisoners appeared hopeless. Over the years, those who survived managed to escape or get off for one reason or another. Lieutenant Sherman, for example, escaped from the prison at Omoa, in Honduras.[41]

The American prisoner story, moreover, rekindled the smoldering hatred of North Americans for the English government. The Editor of the *Aurora* in Philadelphia was a key leader in this wave of anglophobia. Lord Melville (Henry Dundas), in his eyes, was the main conspirator of the revolutionary movement throughout Spanish America since the 1790s. The following blast against the English was typical:

> The British policy is to subjugate and not to set free. The British nation, since it has been a nation, never emancipated any people from thraldom. They have subjugated and tyrannised over Ireland, over the people of India, and over every portion of the globe where they have gained a footing. Can it then be credited that they were to free the people of Caracas? Their object was different. They wanted a foothold.

They would then have established a commercial monopoly—the
unfortunate subject, from groaning under the weight of Spanish
oppression, would have sighed in the trammels of British maritime
restrictions.[42]

With regard to the expedition of 1806, the Editor noted:

Miranda once disgraced or discomfitted, the British would not interfere.
The Lewises proved faithless to the adventurer, and he became
embarrassed; part of his equipment was taken, and he failed entirely.
The British, who had prompted him to the undertaking, abandoned him,
as they do all their allies in misfortune.[43]

A celebrated newspaper account of the American prisoner crisis
focused on William Steuben Smith, Miranda's aide-de-camp. It dealt
with an exchange of letters between the Spanish Minister in
Washington, D.C., the Marquis de Casa-Irujo, and Miranda's ex-
colleague William S. Smith, formerly the surveyor of the New York
Port. The Marquis noted that the surname Smith was common among
the prisoners taken in Venezuela and he surmised that one of them
might be the son of William S. Smith. If this were correct, young
Smith was also the grandson of the ex-President of the United States,
John Adams. At this point, Casa Irujo proposed a "deal"—a brazen
case of blackmail for the release of young Smith. According to the
proposal, Father Smith would divulge to him the names of all those
Spaniards, and others, who had joined in the Miranda conspiracy
against Spain. Father Smith would likewise reveal in detail Miranda's
plan for Venezuela and elsewhere in the Spanish domains. Incensed at
such a proposal, William S. Smith nonetheless replied as politely as
possible that his son was a man of principle; and, as such, he would
never forgive his father for saving his life at the expense of his
comrades in arms and the noble cause of General Francisco de Miranda.
It was a superb reply to the wily Spanish diplomat, for which Miranda
was grateful.[44] The Smith-Casa Irujo correspondence initially appeared
in New York; and was much publicized in Europe. It undoubtedly won
support for Miranda's cause.

* * * * * * * * * * * *

General Miranda's second invasion of Venezuela in August, 1806,
was a bonafide thrust into the area of Coro and Maracaibo by contrast

to the brief skirmish three months earlier at Puerto Cabello. Moreover, there was an expanded British presence and commitment that left little doubt among Spaniards and Frenchmen as to their enemy's intentions in northern South America. Miranda's consuming desire to free his countrymen was infectuous, it would seem, especially among English officials in the Caribbean who appreciated the fact that the liberation movement might be advantageous and profitable to Great Britain. These British officials, as well as individual Englishmen in the Caribbean, shared a pronounced sense of empire that in an appropriate moment might well help to shape policy and opinion in England. This imperial dream, with all its vagaries, inspired Miranda's second invasion of Venezuela as well as its denouement.

As the *Leander* pulled into Grenada on May 27, 1806, Miranda welcomed the governor's reception, grateful for the much-needed supplies offered to him. The English ally advised Miranda to send ahead Colonel William Armstrong with the bulk of his followers to the port of Trinidad, while he and others joined Captain Campbell aboard the *Lily* for a trip to Barbados. There he could meet the key officials of the British Command in the Eastern Caribbean: General Bowyer, the military chief, and Admiral Cochrane, the naval leader.[45] This was, indeed, a momentuous turn in Miranda's career—the meeting with Admiral Alexander Cochrane, who became one of his best friends and staunchest supporters in the next several years. Whereas General Bowyer had doubts initially about Miranda's project, this was not the case for his naval colleague who acted boldly and without hesitation.[46] Apparently—perhaps because he knew him well—Cochrane acted with full confidence that Governor Thomas Hislop at Trinidad would fully support the Admiral's determination to intervene in behalf of General Miranda. Cochrane volunteered to assist the Venezuelan with the *Lily*, two brigantines, and possibly a frigate if he could spare one. The question arises as to Cochrane's eagerness to risk such an unauthorized intervention in behalf of Miranda's cause. Was he cut from the same cloth as Sir Home Popham, who at that very moment was preparing to land in the Río de la Plata? Although not so reckless, Admiral Cochrane did share the hope of relieving England from Napoleon's economic pressures. The Admiral's keen interest in Miranda's expedition first came to light when he heard the report in early April, 1806—an erroneous one, as it turned out—that the General had taken the Island of Margarita, off Venezuela, and was on his way to attack Cumaná and Barcelona on the Spanish Main.[47] It impressed Admiral

Cochrane that so many Venezuelans on the Continent were anxious to join the liberator. As Cochrane explained to members of the Admiralty in London:

> Being confident the General has abundant partisans on the Continent;
> and conceiving that his late attempt only failed on account of his not
> having a Sufficient Naval Force to cooperate with him on Shore; and
> knowing no way in which I can so effectually distress the Common
> Enemy, as by promoting the Success of this Expedition,

Cochrane decided to help Miranda with supplies and ships that were not being used at the moment in protecting his naval jurisdiction.[48] On June 9, 1806, moreover, Cochrane and Miranda agreed to a trade contract that gave Englishmen equal protection and taxation with citizens of the new state to be created by the liberators:

> principally with a view to prevent any of the Powers that now are, or
> may be Hostile to Great Britain before Peace is concluded, from
> participating in this trade; and that after the War, Great Britain should
> be the most favored nation.[49]

Throughout Admiral Cochrane's explanatory report to the Admiralty, it became increasingly clear that England's economic welfare was his major concern. "If the General succeeds, of which I have very sanguine hopes, the vend for British Manufactures will be great!" At this point, the Admiral outlined an ambitious project which he hoped the British government would undertake and complete by sending to northern South America "an active general" supported by five thousand English troops. Such a move would help to "compensate" for the losses suffered by British manufacturers at the hands of Napoleon's followers. It should be noted that Cochrane did not state that Miranda knew of this project, or that it was a condition of his naval assistance in the Venezuelan's second invasion. Cochrane apparently had not thought that far ahead; he wanted, for starters, his superiors' approval for this "imperial" dream.

The bulk of Cochrane's report of June 12th dealt with the Orinoco river basin and the strategic port of Angostura. From Angostura, the River "takes a Western Direction, and I am told is navigable for small vessels and Boats until it joins to the Provinces bordering on the Pacific Ocean." This vast area "offers a field for great commercial speculation." "This great Continent being once made free the consumption will be immense"; and since Great Britain will have aided in its "liberation," this will entitle "Britain to expect better Terms than other nations." "I most anxiously hope that your Lordship will see the advantage of taking immediate possession of Angustura." This country, he averred:

> is one of the most healthy in the world, the climate although to the Southward is far more temperate than any of the Islands; and where abundance of Provisions are to be had at a rate too cheap to be believed, independent of which, Great Britain will thereby secure a Command of inexhaustible Woods, full of the finest Timber for Ship building in the world—incorruptible in quality, and where by the assistance of the Natives, Ships may be constructed of any size, at a far less Cost than in England, and there is enough water on the Bars of the different mouths of the River to float a first rate [ship?] out in Ballast.[50]

Trinidad's proximity to the Orinoco river system and Great Britain's fascination with the Guiana area were logical adjuncts and springs for the sanguine expectations of Admiral Cochrane and his ally Governor Thomas Hislop in Trinidad.

Colonel William Armstrong, who directed Miranda's followers to Trinidad, landed there on June 2, 1806, thoroughly impressed with the reception given to him and Miranda's men by Governor Hislop.[51] He wrote a series of notes to his brother in England that revealed graphically his motivation and expectations as a leader of the 1806 expedition. In an earlier letter to Donald Armstrong, a merchant, it seems that he exposed Miranda's plans for the invasion of South America. "We shall make two establishments at the same time;" he wrote to his brother on June 10th, "mine will of course be where I mentioned it was likely to be, in my last letter from New York." This suggests that Miranda's original strategy was to occupy Coro and Maracaibo and that he revived this plan for the second invasion. From these various notes written to his brother from June 7–15, 1806, we also learn that Colonel Armstrong was a "good friend" of Admiral Cochrane, who personally wrote to him "congratulating me on my new situation, and assuring me that he will give General Miranda every assistance in his power to insure the success of the expedition." Moreover, William had seen Cochrane's orders to Hislop; and the latter "assured me, that he will do every thing in his power to promote it." Colonel Armstrong told his brother that many persons in Trinidad had volunteered to serve in the Miranda expedition. The commercial expectations of Englishmen in the Caribbean seemed to dominate Armstrong's notes to his merchant-brother in England; and he urged him to rally together his "mercantile friends." "If I live" through the invasion of South America, William noted:

> my situation is and will be such as to insure you and them a decided preference. I give you this information at present, in order that you may have time to make the arrangements preparatory to the receipt of my next letter, which will I trust inform you of my hopes being realized.[52]

On June 15th, his final note, William relayed the news of the Cochrane-Miranda trade arrangement. "On this account," he concluded, "they agree to supply him with every thing necessary to almost insure the success of the expedition." In William's correspondence, he emphasized his growing friendship with Governor Hislop, who had the military rank of "General." Hislop assured William "that both in my public and private character, he will be happy to serve me and at the same time showed me a private letter which placed our business in so favourable a point of view, that he wished he might be allowed to take a share in it." Was this a reference to the commercial plans of the Armstrong interests? Although the meaning is somewhat ambiguous, it is nonetheless suggestive as to the economic expectations of British officials in the Caribbean. Since *The Times* of London published this correspondence on August 27, 1806, it certainly must have stirred a rising interest among British merchants in General Miranda's exploits, only about two weeks before the electrifying news of Popham's invasion of the Río de la Plata.

Governor Thomas Hislop, it should be noted, became an undying supporter of British intervention in Spanish South America in behalf of Miranda's liberation movement. This is not surprising considering the English takeover of Trinidad less than ten years earlier; and Hislop had thoroughly emersed himself in the study of the facts and personages involved in the British conquest of Trinidad. In the spirit of Lord Melville, he too wanted Great Britain to help liberate the nearby Spanish mainland so that his countrymen might reap the profits. His experiences in Trinidad, where many rival interests were in contention, made General Hislop recognize the importance of General Francisco de Miranda, "and he was determined to assist the Venezuelan's return to his homeland." As Admiral Cochrane, Hislop also became one of

Miranda's strongest supporters and friends in the Caribbean area. Colonel Armstrong, as we have seen, documented this point with his letter to brother Donald; and Hislop's encouragement of the recruiting program in Trinidad for Miranda's second invasion was a notable contribution. The estimated number of recruits ranged from four to eight hundred; but perhaps the most important result of the recruitment drive was that General Miranda inherited some of General Hislop's best officers: in particular, the Colonel Gabriel de Rouvray (Count de Rouvray), and John Downie, an able Scottish captain who had a weakness for the title of "Colonel." Colonel Rouvray and Captain John Downie were to play leading roles in Miranda's future activities.

Although there were some ten vessels, of varying sizes, that left Trinidad on July 23–24, 1806, for the vaunted second invasion of Venezuela, it was still a small force for any key takeover of Spanish South America. The presence of British ships, however, added a psychological factor to the invasion which enhanced its potential success. Moreover, the sanguine expectations, or the widespread conviction, that Venezuelans and especially great numbers of Indians would throng to Miranda's standard was a favorable omen. Despite some misadventures, the landing at Coro in early August, 1806, was a military success; and the subsequent occupation of Maracaibo as well. There were some publicists who believed that the Coro-Maracaibo operations might very well bring about the downfall of Spain's rule in the New World.

In early September, 1806, a remarkable English observer informed the people of Barbados that he had just learned of Miranda's victories at Coro and Maracaibo from colleagues of his at the Island of Saint Tomas. His commentary on this exceptional news appeared in *The Barbados Mercury* in two installments: one on September 2nd, a brief introduction for the final report on September 6th.[53] Using the pseudonym "Rolla," he was the author of the quotation that opens this chapter. His real name was William D. Robinson, a British merchant, well-known in the Caribbean, especially from Saint Thomas to the Spanish Main. In fact, in the seven years prior to his publications he had resided in Spanish Venezuela and therefore was an excellent reference for information about personages and conditions in that Spanish colony. He was a valued informant for the English government in the next eight years; and his speciality, it should be emphasized, was the emancipation of Spanish America. Moreover, William D. Robinson, or "Rolla," was a highly articulate observer, more than what one would expect from a man in business. We know very little about his personal life and upbringing at this point; yet, as the reader will note, there is a certain quality of expression in his writing that marks him above the average in education—a writer who in many respects reminds us of William Burke. Certainly, the two men shared a vision of "Empire" in which Great Britain would be the world's leader. "Rolla's" writings and presence reinforced the British officials in the Caribbean in their determination to support General Miranda's project.

As "Rolla" hailed Miranda's victories at Coro and Maracaibo in early August, 1806, he emphasized the Venezuelan's "genius" as a strategist:

> Coro is situated in the Gulf of that name, and the whole coast in its vicinity forms a Peninsula which is separated from Caraccas by marshes and mountains impracticable for the passage of an army. Maracaybo is likewise separated by similar obstacles from Caraccas, so that it is impossible for Miranda to be dislodged either from the one or the other position unless the Government at Caraccas had a maritime force (and which they really have not) to transport an army from La Guayra.
>
> Miranda, by thus having effected a footing, will at once endeavour to augment his army by succours from Jamaica, Barbados, and Trinidad, and by the natives of the Country. He will demonstrate to the world that though his enterprise has been called rash by some, Quixotic by others, and by all deemed dangerous, yet it is in his power to take and preserve a position on Terra Firma.[54]

Coro and Maracaibo were sites selected because they were "at the extremity of the Province."[55] Easily defendable against larger forces from Caraccas, the choice of the two sites should impress the British Government:

> that even with the petty force of 7 or 800 men, he is capable of maintaining a situation on the Spanish Main. Had he attempted to take any place in the vicinity of the city of Caraccas with such a trifling force as he has now under him, he ran a risk of being cut off, and his name descending to posterity on the same parallel with the hero of La Mancha: but as he had selected a spot where his standard will be joined by the natives, and where he can receive succours from Jamaica and the Windward Islands, there is every probability, nay almost a certainty of his accomplishing his views, unless the British Government should withdraw all aid from him.[56]

The merchant Robinson could not conceive of such a withdrawal: "on the contrary, honour, policy, and humanity dictate the hope that further succours will be sent him."

"Rolla's" essay on General Miranda concluded that England could not abandon the Venezuelan: the English flag was already committed to the second invasion of the Spanish Main: "that flag and those subjects are in a situation exposed to be sacrificed." Why Admiral Cochrane had approved of the action was now a matter of "secondary importance." There was no threat to Miranda by land, but "if two or three Spanish or French ships of the line, or frigates, should arrive at La Guayra, or Porto Cabello, the situation might become critical." Also, the situation might worsen "if it should be known in Spain, or France that the British Government have been, and are still, lukewarm on the expedition." Instead, the British stand should be clearcut: "All that was needed was three or four ships of the line and a few frigates," along with an infantry contingent of "1,500 or 2,000 troops."[57] This British force, accompanied by large bodies of Indians like the "*Bravos*" of the Maracaibo area who were sure to welcome the English allies and to join Miranda's liberating force, would bring about a swift victory.

To convince his readers, and especially the British Government, the merchant-writer reviewed and evaluated the defense machine of the Captaincy of Venezuela, an analysis based upon his seven years' experience in that area. His conclusions were intriguing, as well as invaluable. At most, Spain could not count upon more than 25,000 men to bear arms in Venezuela:

> These consist of Indians, Mulattoes, Samboes, *and a few Whites*. The Regular Troops from Spain are the remnant of the Queen's Regiment, and do not exceed 200 men. These are stationed in the city of Caraccas, and constitute the *Body Guard of the Captain-General*.

Considering the extent of the Venezuelan territory, Robinson asserted authoritatively "that in no one spot is it possible to collect more than 7 to 8,000 men." At present there were 6,500 men defending the city of Caracas, La Guaira, Puerto Cabello, and "all the adjacent seacoast." Out of the estimated 25,000 men, "Rolla" doubted that 500 "have ever seen an action, or know the use of an instrument of warfare." At this point, the writer portrayed an exceptional insight into a major weakness of the Spanish defense structure:

They are not like the militia of other countries, that by regular training are prepared to encounter an enemy, they are a body of people whose habits have been tranquil, and to whom the prospect of a battle will only be the signal of a general desertion. They are destitute of the great principle which frequently animates the multitude, and supplies the place of discipline—they have no patriotism. Nor indeed is it extraordinary that they are deficient in this virtue; for how is it possible for men to feel affection for a Government under which they are suffering the keenest oppression. Genuine patriotism springs not so much from an affection for our native soil, as from a conviction of the blessings we enjoy. Can any man suppose a native of Caraccas receives those blessings; or can be loyal to a Sovereign who takes from the produce of the soil near three-fifths; who prohibits all intercourses or commerce with the world; who forbids the use of the press; and in fine, whose cardinal maxim is to continue the reign of ignorance and superstition throughout all his dominions in America?

Such a defense force could not effectively resist Miranda's invasion, supported by the English forces that he had recommended. In fact, "Rolla" concluded, it "would dissolve itself by disaffection and fear." The Captain General of Venezuela shared the same view: "for which reason he has sent several expresses to Martinique and Guadeloupe begging some troops."[58]

The merchant Robinson's final paragraphs speak for themselves on the urgency of assisting Miranda's valuable project:

General Miranda knows well the temper of his countrymen, and which will account for his having commenced his operation with a force so contemptible that to the world the transaction has looked more like an effort of chivalry, than a rational enterprise. I trust that the British Government has already taken some measures to assist Miranda and that in a few days some order will reach here to enable this Commander of the Military and Naval force on this station to immediately cooperate with him.

As a friend to humanity, I feel the most poignant regret to behold one of the greatest projects that has been attempted for many ages, exposed to miscarriage merely for the want of a trifling and timely aid.

If the province of Caraccas had its independence guaranteed by Great Britain, or if it is taken by her as a conquest, I consider it as the most important event that Great Britain ever was engaged in. The position of Caraccas, the fertility of its soil, its extent, and a climate perhaps without exception, the first in the globe, renders the Colony of far greater importance to England than either Mexico or Peru. As a new channel for the vent of British manufactures, it is an object of the highest consideration; and on which subject, on a future occasion, I shall offer some ideas. As a political event it ranks among those of the first scale; for if the British flag is once raised on Terra Firma the sovereignty of the Spanish monarchy may nominally exist in South America, but its duration will be limited to a very *few years*.

If Great Britain desires to check the enormous power of France on the Continent of Europe, she can in no way so effectually gain that end as by enlarging her own resources of commerce and wealth. South America presents the desideratum; and the facility by which the conquest of one of the finest of its provinces may be accomplished may serve to demonstrate the ease by which this immense empire may be united to the crown of Great Britain.[59]

On September 10, 1806, William R. Robinson had a morning interview with Admiral Cochrane, making each other's acquaintance. The merchant informed him that he had come to Barbados expressly to join Miranda's expedition. The general's secretary had asked him to join at an early period while he was at St. Thomas; but his obligations in Venezuela had prevented it. Later, when he decided "to abandon some demands of a serious nature I had against the Caraccas government," the situation changed. He had come from his base in St. Thomas to Barbados expressly to join Miranda. After almost seven years residence in Caracas, he was convinced "that Miranda has the secret and warm support of every respectable creole in the province, the Instant he presents himself with some force to inspire some Confidence." Miranda's friends were disappointed that the General had been unable to make "his appearance with two to three thousand Troops, a force more than adequate to have placed him ere this *in possession of the Capital*." The merchant told the Admiral that he was "Rolla," the writer of the recent editorials; and he hoped to supply additional details and suggestions in this interview for the benefit of the British government. In discussing the role of the Indian *Bravos* of the Maracaibo area, Robinson emphasized that their value as auxiliaries depended upon their integration and training under regular English troops, some 1,500 of them. This would take time. Whatever the numbers of auxiliaries might be, the next was to have an adequate maritime force to transport Miranda's expedition to a location "about two Miles to leeward of La Guayra." This was vital, Robinson continued: "for the mountains and natural obstacles which prevents an army from Caraccas from dislodging him from his present situation likewise deprives him of marching by land to the Capital."[60] Robinson's insights on the Indians, the nature of the topography between Coro and Caracas, and the weakness of Spanish defenders were vital not only for understanding Miranda's second invasion but also for understanding the military situation in Venezuela for many years to come.

Robinson's suggestions for an invasion route to Caraccas were likewise insightful, starting from

> an excellent landing place out of reach of the fortifications of La Guayra. Fifteen hundred to two thousand Men supported by a few field pieces may proceed direct to Caraccas, as there is no Spot on the Road but by a few minutes of Gallantry might be taken. A march from 7 to 8 hours from the place alluded to would place Caraccas in the possession of Miranda. This assertion is founded on my being personally acquainted with all the principal Militia Officers and I know from their Character and temper; and the motley collection they command that fear and disaffection would probably save Miranda the necessity of a Battle. The City of Caraccas being taken all the rest of the Province must speedily follow. I am certain that Miranda has now no other danger to apprehend, but the possibility of being cut off by some squadron arriving from France or Spain; if that danger is obviated, the success of his enterprise will soon be established.

A "Ship of the Line and two or three Frigates" should cooperate with Miranda: "*even their appearance on the Main* would inspire his friends with hopes of success and his few enemies with consternation." English ships going from Barbados to Jamaica should take routes "along the Spanish Coast." It would produce "the most salutary effect" for Miranda's cause.

Another one of Robinson's recommendations concerned the Island of Curaçao: "the inhabitants are generally disgusted with the new Monarch that has ascended the throne of Holland, and I believe would capitulate to the first British force that may then appear." "The excellence of this Island as a naval depot," Robinson affirmed, "its vicinage to the Main and the importance it would be to Miranda's views, are too obvious to render it necessary for me to enlarge on."[61] Within a year's time, British forces did, indeed, occupy Curaçao and it became an important reality to Miranda when he returned to Venezuela in 1810.

Given the insights and quality of "Rolla's" reports to the English-speaking audience, as well as to the British government and officials, it is not surprising that the news and analysis from Barbados was highly regarded in connection with the Miranda story. Admiral Cochrane and Governor Hislop wholeheartedly agreed with "Rolla's" advice in early September, 1806, coinciding almost to the day with the Platine news about the conquest of Sir Home Popham and General Beresford. Thus, the Popham and Miranda ventures interacted almost immediately raising such issues as "Conquest" versus "Liberation" as a British motive for expansionism and the independence of naval officers like Popham and Cochrane to take the law into their own hands if the situation warranted it.

* * * * * * * * * * *

Notwithstanding Miranda's daring and imaginative strategy at Coro and Maracaibo, as the merchant Robinson noted, the prospects for a long-term victory were tenous at best. To sustain the beachheads, General Miranda desperately needed the ironclad assurance of a larger British naval force in addition to about two thousand experienced English infantrymen. A steady and adequate flow of arms and supplies was also imperative. Without such support, one of Miranda's basic assumptions about the invasion of Venezuela remained stillborn: the attraction and recruitment of Indians and dissident colonists to his standard. And that was the grim reality of Miranda's second invasion. However sympathetic the Indian leaders might be, they could not risk their future on prophetic words or dreams of a liberator who did not seem to have more than two or three hundred men in his expedition. Miranda understood their predicament, despite his disappointment; and so, he decided to send Captain Ledlie to Jamaica to seek immediate naval support and a sizable auxiliary force of infantrymen. Ledlie arrived at his destination on August 15th. In the meantime, Miranda withdrew his forces to the coast to a more defensible location, keeping in mind that within a month the Captain General of Venezuela would finally get his numerous troops to Coro. These pressing concerns led Miranda to transfer his troops to the Island of Aruba by August 14th.[62]

Over a month later, a key British observer arrived in the area to evaluate the Miranda episode for the benefit of the Admiralty in London. He was Captain George Dundas of H.M.S. *Elephant* who wrote a major analysis to the Admiralty on September 22, 1806, while off the Island of Aruba.[63]   In very blunt terms, Dundas described Miranda's second invasion of Venezuela as a disaster.   He explained forcefully why the Indians had failed to join Miranda while blaming him for what had happened: he "has been too sanguine in his ideas of the attempt to be made on the Spanish Continent of America."   The Captain continued:

> That many individuals are anxious to throw off the Spanish yoke appears evident—that the whole of the Province of Caraccas (from the best information) seems ripe for revolt is true,—but there is not a man in the country who will rally round the Standard of a leader who cannot support himself.

At this point, Captain Dundas offered an insight that requires further verification: he pointed out, and insisted that

> the name of Miranda was unknown to the populace, no Spaniards of the Middle Class, no Indian had ever heard the name of Miranda; yet these were the people he had depended upon . . . . It therefore appears to me that General Miranda has himself been deceived, and in consequence has deceived others.[64]

Such a report, of course, would not be helpful to Miranda's cause in Great Britain, nor would it help Admiral Cochrane for having authorized, on his own, British support to the Venezuelan's second invasion.

The question arises: Where did Captain Dundas get such a negative or "cynical" view of the liberator's cause?   Did he consult with the Spanish enemy who typically viewed Miranda as a traitor and an opportunist without any popular support in the region?   This is doubtful. It is much more likely that it came from within Miranda's ranks. It so happens that one of his officers was reaching the depths of disillusionment with his Don Quijote at this stage of the crusade. There is ground to believe that Lt. James Biggs may have been the guilty party, the author of *The History of Don Francisco de Miranda's Attempt to Effect a Revolution in South America, in a Series of Letters* (Boston, 1808, and London edition, 1809).

When he joined the Miranda expedition in New York, Biggs was a young idealist who had great hopes for the liberation of Spanish America from oppression. In his letters to relatives and friends back home, this young intellectual, perhaps recently graduated from one of the East's top colleges, wrote sophisticated descriptions of the events that he witnessed aboard the *Leander*—commentaries that revealed a deep concern for ethical and juridical principles. It is difficult to say how much he might have changed his original letters by the time of publication. The earlier ones perhaps were left untouched. Later experiences, after the failure of Miranda's first invasion, may have been retouched to reflect increasing disillusionment for his Venezuelan leader, a man in whom he wanted to believe so much despite the aberrations he had noted. Before the second invasion took place, on June 18, 1806, James was promoted from Second to First Lieutenant. General Miranda thought that he deserved the promotion. When Biggs became an author, Miranda thought less highly of him: "a wicked and despicable youth, possessing ingratitude and villany to an uncommon degree."[65] However bitter the young artillery officer might have felt about the unfortunate lot of his countrymen captured at Puerto Cabello, his acceptance of the promotion indicated that he had not yet lost hope in Miranda's crusade. His letter before the departure for Coro, however, reflected that his optimism was undergoing strain:

> The troops in general are in full hopes of success. Miranda says again, excepting the dangers of the sea, it is infallible. From the smallness of the force with which he proposes to enter the country, it is evident he must have great dependence on the readiness and the ability of the inhabitants to join his standard. The number of our force, including the officers and sailors who will land from the ships, does not exceed four hundred. The squadron consists of the *Leander*, 16 guns, *Lily*, twenty-four, *Express*, twelve, *Attentive*, fourteen, *Provost*, ten; *Bull-dog*, *Dispatch*, *Mastiff*, gun-boats of two and three guns; *Trimmer* and *Commodore Barry*, unarmed merchantmen.[66]

Aboard the *Leander* on August 14, 1806, the day that General Miranda transferred all of his troops from the mainland to the Island of Aruba, Lt. Biggs was unquestionably disillusioned with his Chief. He wrote a bitter letter that might very well have been the reference used by Captain Dundas:

> We are again disappointed and confounded. The dream called an expedition has vanished; all our anxiety, trouble, and enterprise have come to nothing; our big expectations and lofty hopes have fallen to the ground. We have visited the Spanish Main, had possession of La Vela de Coro, the city of Coro, and other places; all of which we have just

evacuated. The Spaniards [Spanish-Americans] would have nothing to say to us. They had no thoughts of accepting our proffer of liberty; and we could not oblige them to take it. Miranda, so long the idol of his foolish followers, is not known by them. They wondered who he was; and what brought him in such guise into their country. They viewed him as a marauder whom they were to fly from, or destroy, instead of a deliverer to be made welcome. There was no sign of any partisans of his in force, or likely to be so; and not a shadow of probability that any one of the leading officers of government, civil or military, had thought, or would think, of adopting his plans or joining his standard. Having left the country, we are going, I know not whither; but wherever the prince of visionary schemers chooses to say. You will imagine my disgust and mortification; perhaps repentance. For I assure you, it is not without compunction that I reflect how we have terrified and harassed the unoffending people of this region, as the event has proved, without sufficient pretence, and to no good purpose. I should pity our fanatical leader more than all, but he has an admirable constitution for bearing mortifications. His blunders do by no means put him out of countenance. I dare say that he will soon talk of beginning again without any confusion of face. Indeed he has reason to believe he may go any length in amusing our expectations, considering how fond of being deceived we have appeared.[67]

As indicated earlier, the Dundas mission to Coro and subsequently Aruba was not just one sent there by Admiral Cochrane to assist Miranda et al. if necessary; it also represented the Admiralty's authority to take decisive action. It is not clear just how this dual assignment affected the relations between Dundas and Cochrane; but there are indications, however slight, that the two naval officers were well aware of the division of opinion in England over the unauthorized actions of Sir Home Popham and its significance for all naval officers who acted in the same manner. Dundas apparently fell on the side opposing Popham's independence; and it would seem that it put Admiral Cochrane on the defensive. It is no coincidence that Lt. Biggs, off in Venezuela and at Aruba, where he certainly must have met Dundas in early September, 1806, should happen to know so much about Admiral Cochrane in one of his subsequent letters. The remarkable detail in Biggs' letter could only have been possible because of his personal contact with Captain Dundas. Be that as it may, the British officer took decisive action with regards to Miranda, as he explained:

The whole force of Miranda does not at present consist of more than 200 Irregulars badly appointed—and he complains he has not wherewith to support—much more to reward these few Men. Thus circumstanced, I have told him he must come to an immediate resolution either to retire to Trinidad, in which the *Seine, Lily,* etc. will protect him—or go to Jamaica in which place I will escort him.

Since General Miranda indicated the former, Captain Dundas wrote: "I shall therefore give Captain Atkens directions to see him safe to Trinidad, conforming to the orders of Sir Alexander Cochrane on that Subject."[68]

In William Burke's second treatise, we learn that Captain Ledlie went to Jamaica with dispatches for the naval and military commanders there.[69] Why was Ledlie sent to Jamaica and not to Barbados? Lt. Biggs, surprisingly, had the answer to this question: because Miranda's second invasion of early August, 1806, took place in the territorial zone of the Jamaica station, and therefore outside of Cochrane's jurisdiction. Fortunately, Biggs added, the two admirals knew each other very well and thus there was no conflict between the two naval stations. Lt. Biggs' insight on this matter again points to a connection with Captain George Dundas.[70] Burke wrote the following about the mission to Jamaica:

> Captain Ledlie sailed from Vela de Coro, on the night of the 9th of August, in one of our tenders, and arrived at Jamaica on the 15th, when he presented his dispatches to the officers to whom they were addressed. Sir Eyre Coote and Admiral Dacres, are understood to have expressed themselves in high terms of approbation, of the laudable purposes which General Miranda had in aim; and regretted much, that they were precluded from giving him the assistance which his views demanded; wanting, as they did, official instructions from home on this subject: Admiral Dacres, however, gave orders to his cruisers, to afford every possible protection. Captain Ledlie immediately returned to the Spanish main, with this answer to General Miranda; who, after dispatching that officer to Jamaica, to obtain succours he required, had proceeded himself with his little army to Aruba, a few leagues from Vela de Coro, with the intention of possessing himself of the strong post of Río de la Hache, and there waiting the arrival of the succors promised him.[71]

William Burke, in his second treatise, introduced another interesting facet to the Miranda story:

However, premature reports reaching the West Indies, that the preliminaries of peace, between Great Britain and France, had been signed by Lord Lauderdale at Paris: and these accounts being accompanied, by an intimation from a naval officer, that, in consequence, he would be obligated to withdraw the entire aid of the naval force from General Miranda; this General found himself under the necessity, of abandoning all further operations on the Spanish main; and retired with his brave but disappointed companions in arms, to Trinidad.[72]

The naval officer alluded to by Burke was Captain George Dundas. Thus, the impression was given that diplomatic matters in Europe had been responsible for Dundas' decision against the Miranda expedition. But this was not a fair assessment since it ignores the role of Admiral Alexander Cochrane at this time. In Cochrane's letter of June 12, 1806, to the Admiralty, he explained why he had decided to help General Miranda. A month and five days later, the Lords of the Admiralty replied that they

highly disapprove of your having taken upon yourself without instructions, to assist General Miranda, by cooperating with him with a part of the force under your orders, and even to conclude a treaty with him . . . and are pleased to direct that you take no further steps by which His Majesty can be further committed in this Enterprise.

Yet, his naval cohorts in London, perhaps appreciating his good intentions, allowed Cochrane to take discretionary action in order to protect the British honor in this delicate matter:

you will therefore continue to maintain the Naval force already applied to the Service, in such positions as may best enable you to prevent any succours from being sent to the Colonial Government of Spain, and to assist if it should be necessary in bringing off those whom you have engaged to support.

Furthermore, they urged him "to send home a fast sailing Vessel with accurate details of all the circumstances relating to this transaction."[73]

There is no question that the British Admiralty was anxious to learn more about the Miranda expedition and what had resulted from Cochrane's intervention, and especially in light of the report that a diplomatic settlement with France was in the offing. So, Captain

Dundas was the bearer of the Admiralty's rejection slip to Cochrane and was empowered to make the decision that he made to discourage Miranda under those circumstances of an impending peace with France. Dundas reached Barbados in late August or early September. By the end of the second week of September, he proceeded on his mission to the Spanish Main. Given the urgency of the matter, the Admiralty undoubtedly sent a copy of the Cochrane letter of rejection to Admiral Dacres at the Jamaica station, since the latter, it should be noted, put into action the discretionary moves authorized for Admiral Cochrane. After all, it was Dacres' jurisdiction. Captain Ledlie, of Miranda's army, reported to Miranda on this action, as well as the Anglo-French diplomatic rumor that Burke included in his account.

Thanks to James Biggs, we know that Admiral Alexander Cochrane was very much upset with his rejection slip and whatever else Captain Dundas might have said to him. Perhaps they even discussed Popham's abandonment of his South African post which subsequently led to his court martial; it came up as an issue in the Admiralty when it was first learned that Popham had left his post in Africa. Dundas, of course, sided with his superiors in the Admiralty for obvious reasons; and Cochrane was thus put on the defensive. He was contrite and perhaps even gave Dundas the impression that he was duped by Miranda. Where else could Lt. Biggs have gotten this insight:

> The Admiral is, beyond a doubt, heartily sick of being associated with his plans. He would be glad to forget the past, and never hear the name of the revolutionist again. Very far will he be from any further engagements in this business. He thinks himself fortunate in not being saddled with the expense of it, and made to fear for his command. He, perhaps, is sensible that he had occasion for his well-earned credit with his government, and his respectable name, to screen him from unpleasant animadversions, or proceedings of administration.[74]

Such was the innocence of a young American lieutenant during the aftershock of disillusionment with General Miranda.

As September, 1806, came to an end, the situation looked grim for the cause of Francisco de Miranda who by now had failed twice in trying to liberate Venezuela. Would this perennial optimist, as Biggs had characterized him, dare to come back again? Biggs was right. H.M.S. *Pickle* hastened to return to England bearing key letters by Miranda stressing the point that he had failed to succeed on this last occasion because of the failure of the British to help.[75] This would be the theme of the propaganda thrust that Miranda was ready to develop in the final days of September. William Burke hammered away at this message:

> Thus failed, merely for the want of two or three thousand troops, to give assurance to the inhabitants; an enterprise, which, from the views and principles on which it had been undertaken,—the spirit and ability with which it has been executed,—and the great and happy results, which, if successful, it would produce, deserved a better fate. Nor can it be for a moment doubted, that had General Miranda been seasonably supported by the cooperation of a British auxiliary force, as he had reason to expect, his success would have been complete.[76]

As General Miranda worked on the transfer of his troops back to Trinidad, he decided to return to Barbados with some of his officers to consult with his British allies. On November 3, 1806, he was aboard H.M.S. *Northumberland* in Carlyle Bay, sharing the company of his good English friends. There is no question that Lt. Biggs would have had a cerebral fit, of sorts, if he could have heard what General Miranda and his true friend Admiral Alexander Cochrane were planning for the future.

Providence, "Lady Luck," or what have you, appeared to be smiling upon the conspirators, if we may take the liberty of calling them that, and their ambitious plans to emancipate Spanish America. To appreciate the turn of events, let us go back to the scene of early August, 1806, when the Spanish authorities at Caracas learned that the "detestable" traitor Miranda had landed at La Vela de Coro, the port to the city. As "Rolla" had noted accurately: the Spaniards in Caracas feared for their lives. They were doubtful that ten thousand troops sent to Coro under the command of the Captain General would solve the threat even if they managed to get there. Needing financial aid in the worst way, the Caracas leaders wrote to authorities everywhere: to Cumaná, to Margarita, etc. These urgent letters went out from the port of La Guaira on mail ships that looked like oversized canoes. One of those canoes made its way out of port on or about September 11, 1806. No sooner was it out of sight that it was engulfed in a hawk-like maneuver by H.M.S. *Osprey*. There was no time to dump the mail bags overboard. The English captors hastened to Trinidad with their valuable cargo. Governor Hislop's exhilaration was overwhelming: the

English had struck it rich. The *Osprey* documents contained key intelligence about Spanish Venezuela at the time of Venezuela's second invasion by General Miranda. They revealed the Spaniards' weakness and vulnerabilitly to an invasion of liberation, especially one that might be fully supported by Great Britain. In short, this godsend collection of papers would help to convince English ministers, once and for all, that supporting another Miranda invasion of the Spanish Main would be to Great Britain's long-term interests. Hislop had the key papers translated into English in great haste, while he notified his colleagues in Barbados to join him at the first opportunity. Admiral Alexander Cochrane and General Boyer both reached Trinidad by September 20th; they too cheered Miranda's progress against the enemy.[77]   On September 22, 1806, just as Dundas was relaying his message-decision to the English Admiralty, Governor Hislop gleefully exposed the *Osprey* documents in a letter to General Miranda. Hislop's comments on the Spanish letters and events in Europe provide us with valuable insights into the mentality of British officers in the Caribbean who were anxious to advance Miranda's cause. Copies of all relevant letters were sent to Miranda, including the key letter of Dionisio Franco, the "Director of Finances" in Venezuela. Hislop noted, referring to Franco's comments:

> I have sent the one of greatest consequence to the Secretary of State and must hope it will draw the serious attention of our Ministers. Nothing can more strongly shew the real situation of the wretched people who you are endeavouring to relieve.—I think its publication by you and distribution throughout the Province must produce the most favourable Consequence.[78]

The Franco document, in other words, would receive the major emphasis in Miranda's propaganda campaign to influence British policy in Spanish America. A significant postscript on September 24, 1806, demonstrated conclusively to what extent British officials were willing to go in support of Miranda's campaign in behalf of British intervention in Venezuela:

> Since writing the foregoing, I have consulted with the Admiral on the propriety of sending you the Original Letters which were taken by the Osprey and in which we have both Concurred, in order that you may convince every one that there is no fabrication or forgery used on the Occasion.[79]

In his famous letter to the Governor of Cumaná (Juan Manuel de Cagigal), Dionisio Franco discussed the problems in the Captaincy of Venezuela—a letter that appeared, in part, in William Burke's second tract and which was quoted or paraphrased extensively in the British press of that period. It is well worth saboring the major passages:

Caracas, August 16, 1806

My very esteemed friend:

The truly detestable Miranda limited even to his own resources will give in my opinion a great deal more to do than we at first imagined and supported too as it appears he is by the English altho' the assistance which they have hitherto given him indicates no further than that they do not disapprove his enterprise.

He effected his landing at Coro without any resistance as the Garrison of this truly important point consisted only of 200 Militiamen so that altho' they might have armed more than 1,000 men there were no Arms to give them and in this very same case are all the inhabitants of these Provinces.

In Consequence of this News the Captain General has taken the field as you will be able to see by your Official dispatches with the Arm'd forces which he had here and which will be perhaps a Month before ever they can arrive at Coro where no doubt they will find him already entrenched and in a situation to ensure his own retreat which in my own opinion will be the least evil that can happen to us, because if the English give him any assistance let it be ever so trifling and offer to support him his situation is the most advantageous of any that he could possibly have chosen on all those Coasts on account of the Peninsula de Paraguaná where they may form a second Gibraltar as long as they are Masters of the Sea, so that this spark of fire which appeared nothing may ultimately devour the Continent.

In Consequence of these Circumstances and the continued draining of funds here within these five months, since we have in that time expended more than a million of Dollars in this part of this Country, it appears to me that this Government cannot depend upon further supplies except those which they will find within themselves.[80]

With surprising speed, the *Osprey* documents—"The Intercepted Correspondence to General Miranda"—filled the pages of *The Spanish Main* (Barbados) in late September, 1806, and by November 9, 1806, *The Statesman*, the *London Evening Post*, and the *Bells Weekly Messenger*, were happily commenting on the good news from the Caribbean: General Bowyer was now willing to cooperate with Admiral

Cochrane, the great English hero who had the imagination to help General Miranda in his time of need. There was no mistaking the British mood, solidly in favor of their Venezuelan champion. Since September 13th, when they learned the glorious news of the Popham-Beresford conquest of the Río de la Plata, the English were euphoric. The *Osprey* materials, therefore, raised their expectations to even a higher plane, now that Northern South America gave promise of becoming available to English interests. They were, therefore, rudely shocked by the subsequent news that General Miranda's second invasion had failed due to a lack of adequate British ships and infantrymen. It infuriated British editors that Admiral Dacres and Sir Eyre Coote in Jamaica would argue weakly that they had no instructions to assist General Miranda in a decisive way. The public reaction mounted and could not be ignored by the British Parliament.[81] On December 20, 1806, Lord Castlereagh himself assailed the Ministers' "indecision" in the Caribbean to provide "a little timely assistance on the part of the British Government to the operations of General Miranda." This help

> might have produced the most important advantages to this Country. We had sufficient force in the West Indies to have assisted General Miranda, but our naval and military officers in that part of the world could not venture to stir for want of instructions from the Government."[82]

On November 3, 1806, aboard H.M.S. *Northumberland*, Admiral Cochrane's flagship lying in Carlisle Bay, Barbados, there was a memorable reunion and meeting of minds that unanimously voted for the success of General Miranda's third attempt to invade his homeland. It is fairly easy to reconstruct that conference despite the fragmentary documentation.[83] Admiral Cochrane welcomed the General to his ship and assured him that he still believed vehemently in his cause and that he would do everything possible to convince his government that it was to England's best interests to advance the liberation of Spanish America. As the record will show in the next several years, these were indeed sincere words. Cochrane also assured Miranda that General Bowyer could be counted on to support the project, as well as other British officials in the Caribbean who knew him or Governor Hislop. Much to the surprise and excitement of Miranda and Colonel Gabriel de Rouvray, also known as the *Comte de* Rouvray, Cochrane proceeded to describe the *Osprey* documents, which had not yet reached the elated Venezuelan. Indeed, there was no trouble whatsoever in recognizing the significance of those documents for a final invasion of the Spanish Main. It was agreed that the Count de Rouvray should sail as soon as possible for England as the personal representative of General Miranda, armed with all the printed documents or manuscripts that might influence the British government to send aid immediately to Trinidad in preparation for a full-scale invasion of the Spanish Empire in Venezuela. After years of sheer frustration—promises and rejections—not to mention the recent fiascos of April and August 1806, "the prince of visionary schemers," as Biggs had called him, dared to believe once again. The Count of Rouvray was likewise a believer, so was Admiral Cochrane and General Bowyer who days later toasted Miranda's health and wished the Count goodluck on his mission to London.[84] The consensus was that propaganda would be the mighty tool in the impending crusade. Miranda went out of his way to instruct Rouvray carefully on how to place key articles, or documents, effectively in the French and English press. And when he was about to return from his European mission, Rouvray was urged to select a responsible person to direct the propaganda thrust in Europe. It was during the Count's stay in London that he discovered an ally, William Burke, as we shall see in the next chapter. After some delays, Rouvray finally sailed from Tortola Island on November 19, 1806; by December 17th, he was in London serving as the representative of General Francisco de Miranda. A few days later, Lord Castlereagh made his critical remarks in Parliament, so favorable to Miranda's cause.[85] The Expedition of 1806, in short, had not been in vain.

The Barbados meeting of November 3, 1806, was also crucial in that it brought to the fore a greater awareness of the Platine connection. Thus, it reinforced the theme that absorbed the two treatises written by William Burke: "Conquest" or "Liberation" as the motive for British policy in Spanish America. From 1807 forward, Miranda and his publicists hammered away incessantly at the importance of an enlightened British approach to the liberation of the Spanish Americas. The Venezuelan constantly reminded his allies—Cochrane, Rouvray, Nicholas Vansittart, among others—of what he had said aboard the *Northumberland* when they received the news of the Popham-Beresford victory at Buenos Aires. The "*Capitulación*" (Treaty of Surrender, that outlined the relationship between Great Britain and the people of the

Río de la Plata) had all the earmarks of a "Conquest," which could only lead to disaster for the British presence there. His prediction became meaningful when the news of the "Recapture" of Buenos Aires on August 12, 1806, reached Europe. This disconcerting news was not made public in England until the first week of 1807. To Admiral Cochrane, Miranda wrote:

> I hope that the fatal consequences attending the Possession of Buenos Ayres by conquest, will open the eyes of Great Britain and shew to Ministers that the only solid Basis for putting the Continent of South America in a perpetual separation from the Mother Country and France is *Independency*. It is a circumstance *sine qua non* and I remember when we received the *Capitulation* of Buenos Ayres on board the *Northumberland*, I had the honor to impart to you this *presentiment* and fears, which unfortunately were already realized at the very moment we were talking on the subject. You may depend, my dear Admiral, that whatever may be attempted upon the Continent of South America with any other views but absolute Independency, will never be *permanent* or satisfactory either to Great Britain or the Country itself.[86]

Miranda sent essentially the same message to his good friend Nicholas Vansittart: "The recent catastrophe at Buenos Aires should open the eyes of British ministers concerning the absurd ideas of conquest that some people have always had about South America."[87]

General Miranda saved his strongest message for his erstwhile friend, Sir Home Popham, who wrote to him on July 20, 1806, extolling the Platine area and its people and urging the Venezuelan to join him. Miranda fumed over this letter for days; finally, he answered it as politely as he could. Of course, the Platine people had received him as a friend; Miranda had told him this many years ago in the presence of Lord Melville. "But," Miranda added, beginning to lose his patience, "I never maintained that it was possible to establish anything solid in that country, nor even less survive among the inhabitants without declaring their absolute *Independence*." Then, he began to lecture Popham with some sarcasm:

> How could you, in effect, expect 18,000,000 inhabitants in such a vast and impregnable Continent, located at a distance of 4 or 6,000 miles from Europe, and possessing immense treasures and resources, to be conquered and subjugated in these times by a mere handful of people determined to command them as masters?

"Non, mon cher Ami," he continued in French: *"la chose n'est pas naturelle, ni practicable, ni possible."* And the best proof of this assertion today are "the very results of your enterprise."[88] As time passed, Miranda could never forgive Popham for his conquest mentality. In the meantime, he beseeched Colonel Rouvray to enlighten British ministers on the importance of liberation as the only solution to the emancipation of Spanish America. Lacking this, he wrote to Rouvray in Italian: *"Ogni fatiga e vana"* ("all efforts are in vain").[89]

After the November 3rd meeting with Cochrane, Miranda and his followers returned to Trinidad aboard the H.M.S. *Melville.* Governor Hislop welcomed his friend with enthusiasm. He and Miranda were constant companions who continued to work out the details of the projected third invasion of the Spanish Main, as if the British auxiliary force and the government's approval for a large scale naval detachment were imminent. There were signs of approval from many English officials in the area that were especially well received by General Miranda. On November 20, 1806, John Turnbull, who was the key spokesman for London's merchants, notified him that his letters of late September had reached their destination and were favorably received by British officials. Moreover, he gave him the good news that "your Business rather looked favorable—Indeed, I am much inclined to think, that the Government is now determined to take a very active part, in wresting South America, out of the hands of the Spaniards."[90] The receipt of this news in December, along with the advanced preparations for the impending invasion, led to sanguine expectations on the part of Miranda and his colleagues.

It is important to note that General Miranda did not ignore the propaganda commitment that was discussed aboard H.M.S. *Northumberland* in early November. Governor Hislop made the *Osprey* documents available; and he immediately sent copies to Colonel Rouvray in London. There was a triunvirate of documents agreed upon for the propaganda thrust to convince British ministers. The *Osprey* materials, of course, were basic. In addition, Colonel John Downie who remained with the Miranda forces serving as a rearguard on the Coast, near Coro, and later in Aruba, had written a lengthy report that underscored the model-like behavior of Miranda's forces during the second invasion—there was no plundering, Miranda had conscientiously guaranteed the sanctity of Venezuelan property during his stay there, etc.—all of which illustrated the point that English troops were unquestionably humane by contrast to Napoleon's plundering scoundrels. The Downie report arrived in Trinidad aboard H.M.S. *Lily*. A third letter, or group of documents, was given to Miranda by a Lieutenant Stout whom he met aboard the *Melville* when Miranda returned to Trinidad. Stout had also served on H.M.S. *Provost,* one of the vessels that had accompanied General Miranda on his second invasion. This British naval officer, it seems, was captured off Cumaná; and during his stay there, he was able to learn about public opinion among Venezuelan Creoles, especially how they felt about Englishmen as compared to Frenchmen. His comments reminded the British government of a point that General Miranda wanted emphasized: French forces had finally answered the call of their Spanish allies in Venezuela; the French were present and if Great Britain did not act soon she would lose all her opportunities in South America and the world's balance of power overseas would swing violently to Napoleon's followers. Creoles loved Englishmen, and they detested the imperious French with a passion.[91] This was very effective propaganda, to be sure. Whether the Downie or Stout documents were authentic, or merely the inventions of Miranda et al. in Trinidad, does not really matter. By early December, 1806, Miranda had forwarded all three sets of these documents to Count Rouvray in London.[92] He, in turn, submitted them to the British Ministers with great effect:

> I have submitted the three most interesting pieces for the scrutiny of Cabinet members, namely: Franco's letter—that by Downie, and Lt. Stout's report. They have been read and discussed with attention; and they have produced the effect that you had intended, that is to say, to convince the Ministers that there is not a moment to waste.[93]

The Miranda expedition of 1806 which twice attempted an invasion of Venezuela—one a disastrous failure but with world repercussions because of the North American prisoners and the other, a limited success but without an effective follow through—provided, nonetheless, a promising denouement that might bring about in Great Britain a commitment to intervention in northern South America—an objective that Miranda had tried desperately to achieve. The propaganda weapon held promise as the ultimate persuader.

Chapter Four

William Burke: Front and Center!

A pledge from Great Britain to assist these countries in asserting their independence and of protecting them in their enjoyment of it, would probably be followed by an immediate revolt. At any rate, the declaration that if they continue subject to Spain, they must have Great Britain for a determined and active enemy, till they are reduced under submission to us, would make them close with our terms without delay. We might then establish the most important commercial connections with them; and the commercial prosperity to which these noble territories, if independent, would probably soon rise, opens one of the richest prospects to this country, which can well be imagined.

Literary Journal, November 1, 1803.[1]

Miranda's program to revolutionize Spanish America and give life to his "Colombia" had a strong appeal among Englishmen like Thomas Pownall, who worked closely with his Venezuelan friend until his death in 1805. Another English collaborator, who shared many of Pownall's ideas, stepped in to fill the void. His name was William Burke, whose two treatises of 1807 and 1808 served to broadcast Miranda's message in meaningful and concise terms. Burke reminded his countrymen of the deep world crisis that they faced against a shrewd French enemy; and he offered them a choice between "Conquest" or "Liberation" in determining Spanish America's future. Later William Burke wrote a series of editorials that appeared in the *Gazeta de Caracas* (1810–1812) in which he advised Spanish Americans to follow the republican path of the United States of America, which embodied the best ideas and reforms of the Enlightenment. This particular English intellectual was thus a major influence in Miranda's propaganda movement for the liberation and modernization of Latin America and especially in Venezuela that became the first Spanish American Republic in 1811. Yet, it is rare that no one has been able to identify with certainty the *real* William Burke.

* * * * * * * * * * * *

Practitioners of history often encounter obstacles that are difficult to ignore.   As historians and human beings with all kinds of psychological baggage, they often proceed to write on controversial issues without explaining their qualifications for accepting certain conclusions, or interpretations. It seems desirable, therefore, to present a digression that might prove useful to the reader.

The origins of this Miranda study go back to 1975, on the eve of the "Bicentennial of the American Revolution," when I was asked to participate in a special program sponsored by the Library of Congress in Washington, D.C. The theme of the assignment was "The Impact of the American Revolution."   My bailiwick was the Spanish and Portuguese-Speaking World on a subject that had fascinated me for years.   My key inspiration had always been Professor Herbert Eugene Bolton of the University of California in Berkeley, who contended that the Americas had shared a common experience in breaking with the European mother countries from 1775 to 1825—the "Greater American Revolution," as he called it.   It was a convenient thesis, and term, for describing the first modern movement of anticolonialism in world history.   That was the hypothesis, or perspective, that I worked with on my Washington assignment.   Presented as a lecture at the national capital, it later was published in a compilation on the common theme.[2] During that period, I also finished another manuscript: *The Cádiz Experiment in Central America, 1808–1826* which analyzed Spanish liberalism and how much Central Americans had contributed to the movement.   It dealt in depth with the manifestations of anticolonialism in the Hispanic World, underscoring the importance of *laissez-faire* economics in that particular movement.[3]

During the academic year 1975–1976, moreover, I received a Fulbright Fellowship to continue my research on the theme of the American Revolution; and before long, it took the shape of a book published in Madrid entitled: *La revolución americana de 1776 y el mundo hispánico: Ensayos y documentos*. These essays expanded on the original lecture in Washington, D.C. and revealed new insights that I had gained on "The Greater American Revolution" up to the time of publication.[4] My objective then was a volume on Bolton's thesis about revolution in the Americas—a project that is now in limbo, although much research was completed on the Bourbon Reforms of the eighteenth century as they prepared the revolutionary climate in Spanish America.

When I returned to the United States, it was not long before I began to explore a facet of the revolutionary project that had intrigued me as I prepared the Washington manuscript: namely, the editorials written by a William Burke in Caracas from 1810 to 1812, which encouraged Spanish Americans to follow the model of the young United States in the establishment of nationhood. What I read in Burke's editorials was an amazing contemporary analysis of United States' history and institutions during the revolutionary and post-revolutionary eras, written by a man of vast intelligence. It would make, I thought to myself, an excellent chapter for the projected book on the American Revolution. Needless to say, I had to learn something about William Burke, who collaborated with General Miranda in those years. Later, when I reread the editorials in a more complete edition, published by the Venezuelan government, I recognized that Burke not only knew North America exceptionally well but also Spanish America since he compared developments and resources in both areas.[5] It was difficult for me, however, to accept the notion that one man could be that versatile and comprehensive, unless his Spanish translator was equally qualified on Hispanic America. Slowly, a new hypothesis began to suggest itself: Could it be that Miranda's propaganda team in Venezuela was using "William Burke" as a pseudonym in the program to persuade minds towards revolution? It was a daring notion since there seemed to be no question that a man calling himself William Burke lived in Caracas for those two years. The evidence, however, was suspicious and highly fragmentary. My doubts increased when one of Burke's editorials on "Religious Toleration" raised a storm of controversy in Caracas; and no one calling himself William Burke accepted the challenge—a suspicious absence given the nature of the debate. We shall say more on this point in a later chapter.

The search for William Burke's identity meant that I had to immerse myself in the voluminous literature on Miranda and his times. As much as possible, I placed my focus on Miranda's propaganda activities. The published *Archives of General Miranda* alone comprised twenty-four thick volumes of documents which cannot be absorbed satisfactorily in one reading.[6] Yet, it was here that I became acquainted with Francisco de Miranda, called by many of his contemporaries the "George Washington" of the Spanish world. I learned of his countless projects and read with excitement the ideas of a vast number of correspondents from all over the world. Fortunately, I had as guides the two-volume biographies of the Venezuelan diplomat and historian Caracciolo Parra Pérez and the North American historian William Spence Robertson.[7] I took extensive notes on those persons who were helping Miranda with his propaganda crusade: in Chapter One, we have already mentioned his North American friends; and the Europeans, especially Englishman and Spaniards, will receive more attention ahead. William Burke and Thomas Pownall have already been analyzed through 1808; and we still have to deal with such worthies as Jeremy Bentham, James Mill, and many others.

It was inevitable, of course, that this historian would have to return to Great Britain if he expected to make real headway. My first visit to England was during World War II, an excellent opportunity to meet Englishmen for the first time but hardly valuable as an experience in historical research, except as a participant in one of man's favorite activities. My next visit, in 1958, was another matter altogether which involved an impressive stint at the "old" Public Record Office in London that permitted me to prepare a volume on British activity in Central America in the first half of the nineteenth century.[8] Twenty-two years later, in 1980, and again in 1986, I went back to England to revive my keen interest in nineteenth century British history.

Prior to my visit of 1980, I had been able to read Burke's second treatise of 1808 in the University of California at Los Angeles Library; but the 1807 treatise was not in the area. My first priority in London, therefore, was to have it copied. That summer's work was indeed profitable from the standpoint of documentation, but I was not satisfied that I had found sufficient materials on William Burke to identify him as a London journalist, except for his publications. The William Burke that crops up occasionally in the Miranda documents was a merchant friend of John Turnbull. There were also some suspicious usages of the name "William Burke" that will be noted at the appropriate time. The 1986 visit involved further exploration in the research archives to

follow through on certain leads that would add to the weight of my
arguments or conclusions.

Venezuelans have displayed a keen interest in William Burke. They
have marveled at the mind that produced the famous editorials in the
Gaceta de Caracas—its masterful grasp of economics, history, political
science, and international affairs. The foreigner William Burke had a
mind that was equal, if not superior, to the better known Thomas Paine
whose ideas about the rights of man and the American Revolution were
widely read throughout the world, including Venezuela where his works
circulated in Spanish translation at an early date. Burke's writings were
also popular then.   Venezuelans admired his insights into
constitutionalism and government.   His controversial editorial on
"Religious Toleration" led some Venezuelans to conclude that Burke
was an ex-Irish Catholic. Perhaps he was the cousin of Edmund Burke,
that famous political philosopher of the late eighteenth century in
England. This popular view, unfortunately, committed a sin against
historical chronology.   Edmund died in 1797 and William, in the
following year.[9] They simply were not around to write treatises in
London and editorials in Caracas in the early nineteenth century!

Yet, the real Edmund and William Burke provided some tantalizing,
although marginal, connections with the Miranda story. There is no
evidence to indicate that the Burkes ever met Miranda, although they
were aware of each other. William Burke wrote a two-volume study
entitled: *An Account of the European Settlements in America* (London,
1757) that went through many editions. Edmund Burke helped to
revise one of the editions of this popular set which consisted of six
parts: the first and second dealt with the discovery of the New World
and "The Manners and Customs of the Original Inhabitants," a very
realistic as well as sympathetic description of the Indians; parts three
and four on the Spanish and Portuguese settlements; part five on the
French, Dutch, and Danish colonies; and the final section on the
English settlements. Well-written and soundly researched, Burke's
presentation stressed the economic potential of the Western
Hemisphere. It had a special appeal to Englishmen who might want to
expand their business to overseas markets. It represented the same
mentality as a Thomas Pownall and "our" William Burke. But it had
one striking characteristic: it was not the typical English interpretation
that was usually heavily-laden with "Black Legend" stereotypes about
the Spanish people.[10] Francisco de Miranda, it should be emphasized,

was deeply sensitive to this anti-Spanish prejudice in England, despite his role as a champion against Spain in America. If he had known the Burkes personally and had been able to peruse Burke's *Account*, he would have used it in his propaganda projects. Moreover, it is indeed strange that Pownall, well-acquainted with the Burkes because of their service together in Parliament, did not point out the Burkian synthesis of Spanish colonialism to his Venezuelan colleague.

The failure to meet the Burkes in the seventeen eighties and nineties was no doubt because of Miranda's presence on the Continent and his deep involvement in the French Revolution. The Venezuelan, however, came to the attention of the Burkes when they reacted vehemently to the Jacobin takeover in France. William Burke translated a lengthy document by Jacques Pierre Brissot de Warville to his constituents, in which he exposed the Jacobin activity in the National Convention. Edmund, who shared his cousin's conservative views, supplied the "Preface" to this much publicized pamphlet. The Burkes attacked Brissot as a brazen opportunist, worse than the so-called "anarchists," the Jacobins. It followed that Brissot's colleague from Venezuela was nothing but a first-class "adventurer."[11] General Miranda was always most sensitive to this uncomplimentary term that emerged from the "French Revolution;" and much of his propaganda campaign was aimed at proving his honorable intentions. When he returned to England, the Burkes were no longer alive. If he had known them, he would have tried to erase that concept from their minds. It should be emphasized that Miranda immediately published a volume about his role in France during the Revolution to erase the unfavorable image about him, to which the Burkes had contributed.[12]

There was another connection with the Burkes, a very human one, that was probably a mere coincidence. It was a mutual love and concern for an Irish painter. In 1809, Miranda had much to do with the publication of a two-volume study entitled: *The Works of James Barry, Esquire. Historical Painter . . . Correspondence from France and Italy with Mr. Burke*.[13] Born in Cork, Ireland, in 1741, this sensitive artist progressed on sheer native ability. In one of his earlier works, he followed an old, historical tradition when he depicted the first arrival of St. Patrick, the apostle of Ireland, on the sea coast. The painter subsequently had the opportunity to meet Edmund Burke; and in the late seventeen sixties Edmund and William Burke sponsored James Barry's education in Italy. During that period, William Burke wrote the letters included in the compilation of 1809. A meteoric climb to importance followed Barry's return to England. He became a professor in the Academy of Arts and later provided six major pictures that carried out the theme "The Progress of Human Culture." After the death of the Burkes, Barry's life slipped into a deep tragedy that expelled him from the Academy. He died virtually penniless in 1806. At the last moment, his friends rallied to provide him a most distinguished funeral.[14] Miranda was one of his dear friends before leaving for the United States in 1805. The news of Barry's death filled the General with overwhelming sadness. When he returned to London, he worked closely with the editor Edward Fryer in publishing Barry's volumes. Moreover, he asked his friend James Mill to see to it that the volumes were noted in the *Edinburgh Review*, where Mill was a regular reviewer.[15] It would be interesting to know what James Barry might have told Miranda in the years following the deaths of Edmund and William Burke.

Given your understanding of Burke's two treatises of 1807 and 1808, you are probably wondering why there is no extensive record of William Burke, the journalist, in London during those years. You can thus appreciate why a frustrated historian might begin to think in terms of a *nom de plume*, or a pseudonym. It follows that some detective work was in order. Since the historian had read the second treatise in Los Angeles, he immediately poured over the first treatise when he was able to examine it in 1980. It was clearly the same author who had written the sequel, both the products of an imaginative and philosophical mind. The cover page provided the first clue: the author had written another work in 1806. The complete title, which I found on the final page, read as follows: *The History of the Campaign of 1805, in Germany, Italy, the Tyrol.* It was published by J. Ridgway in London. Then, after this complete title, the publisher listed another work by William Burke: *The Armed Briton: or, the Invaders Vanquished. A Play in Four Acts.* William Burke was also a dramatist? Or was this just an advertising ploy? I suspected a ploy of the J. Ridgway Company. I then noted, at the bottom of the final page, and clearly separate:

Of J. Ridgway may also be had, just published, The Veterinary Tablet, or, a Concise View of all the Diseases of the Horse; with their Causes, Symptons, and most approved Modes of Cure. By a Veterinary Surgeon.[16]

Some cards in the Catalog of the British Library (formerly the British Museum) suggest that William Burke was a veterinary surgeon. We can readily see how that notion might have originated and how an investigator might have concluded that William Burke was a veterinarian.

Be that as it may, this historian opted to read the 1806 publication by Burke, the military historian, dramatist, or horse specialist. What a surprise! That writer, whatever he might have been, had nothing in common with "our" William Burke. At best, he was an amateur historian with a dull style and not a very imaginative mind.[17] Why then did "our" writer choose the name "William Burke?" In the absence of sufficient documentation, we can only speculate on his motive. I would guess that a writer in London of the early nineteenth century had to take on many writing assignments to maintain a decent livelihood. And if he already had a responsible writing position, along with the prestige that attended it, he might want to resort to a *nom de plume* or to write anonymously—alternatives that were common in those days. The editor of the *Literary Journal*, for example, commented cynically on the ruses employed by publishing houses to meet or surpass the competitive position of a rival.[18] If that were true, the Ridgeway Company might have been responsible for the deceit. And why stop there? Why not throw in a dramatist and perhaps a veterinarian! Besides, William Burke was a name that commanded attention; and, certainly, there would be no confusion with the earlier Burke. And if there were, so much the better—more sales on the streets! The pseudonym was likewise appropriate for the second treatise—the "Additional Reasons." In fact, given Burke's sympathy for the unpopular General Whitelocke, it was doubly necessary to continue the ruse. Francisco de Miranda had nothing to do with the deception; yet, in later years, he also opted to use "William Burke" in his native Caracas. To be sure, there is much speculation in the preceding lines, perhaps too much; but until further documentation throws light on that point, it at least offers a possible explanation.

There is another key document that bears close scrutiny if for no other reason than that it offers key insights into Miranda's unfolding propaganda campaign. It was a fascinating "Letter to the Editor" in the *Morning Post* (London) on August 13, 1806, under the heading "Peace or War." It was signed "W.B." This powerful editorial piece, especially considering the rumors and facts about the events that were transpiring in the Río de la Plata and in Venezuela, might have convinced "our" William Burke to undertake the writing of his first treatise. He had been thinking about it since the Truce of Amiens; and, now, it was time to revive the project. The conditions were right in view of the English excitement over Miranda's activities in the Caribbean. And there was no doubt at all in his mind, especially after September 13th, when Englishmen learned about the exploits of Popham and Beresford in the Río de la Plata. The author's pen went into action, determined to launch his crusade for England's emancipation of Spanish America.

"W.B." in the *Morning Post* was framing, in very belligerent terms, a call to arms against the "Foxite faction," the followers of Charles James Fox. From March, 1806, this controversial British minister had proposed negotiations for peace with France. It, therefore, revived pacifism in England and presumably led to the reports of Lord Lauderdale's overtures to Napoleon that provided the excuse for abandoning Miranda's invasion of Venezuela. According to "W.B.," it was a sheer travesty for British ministers to be seized "with the contagious panic," of the "great powers" of Europe that were degrading themselves "at the feet of the Corsican despot." British and Irish manufactures would thus be sacrificed not only in Europe but all over the world. Great Britain, "W.B." blustered, would gain nothing from "this perfidious treaty, this hostile truce, from which the enemy would reap innumerable advantages without surrendering to us any equivalent."[19] Many English service men shared W.B.'s vehement opposition to the peace program with France. Governor Hislop's letter to Miranda of September 22–24, 1806, announcing the "*Osprey*" documents, illustrates the point:

> Peace you will find is much talked of at home but it is impossible to believe that in the present circumstances of Europe it can take place and it is certainly not wished for by the People of England. Mr. Fox who is the great spring from whence these specific measures take their source is however in a deplorable State of health and is generally supposed to be near his end. . . . His death would undoubtedly occasion a change of the present measures. . . . By the continuance of War we have nothing to apprehend. By peace we have the Worst to dread.[20]

To be sure, Hislop and his fellow officers in the Caribbean wanted nothing to detract from Miranda's final victorious move in Venezuela.

Rather than a disgraceful program of appeasement, W.B. shamed the

English ministers for not opening up "New Markets" for British manufactures in "the three remaining quarters of the globe," especially in "*South America*, from the Mexico Gulf to Cape Horn," a rich continent that "they should have emancipated and rendered independent." W.B. warned them: "If this be not done before the signature of any treaty with France, the glorious opportunity will perhaps be forever lost to us."[21] He knew of William Pitt's interest in the emancipation of Spanish America and he evaluated accurately Miranda's role in stimulating the late minister. W.B. had participated in Pitt's invasion plans. The scheme's weakness, in his opinion, was that "Miranda was not sufficiently informed of the remote power we possessed to forward the emancipation of South America, by means of land forces transported from India across the Pacific Ocean." Claiming to be the author of an anonymous "military treatise" on this topic, W.B. elaborated upon the significance of South America's emancipation "to our East and West India trade." Peace was no solution; the only way to tame "this modern *Attila*" was "by force of arms, by well-timed and well-executed expeditions, and upon a great scale." England had to act immediately in support of General Miranda in the Caribbean; otherwise, just a truce of a month's duration would be sufficient to "exclude the British nation from any share of that lucrative commerce."[22] It is notable that in future publications on Miranda's plans in the Western Hemisphere, William Burke, or the man that I suspect was using that pen name, oftened displayed a great concern for the "India" connection and its potential impact on the Isthmus of Panama and on Europe as well.[23]

Despite the deliberate buildup of this frustrated detective story writer, it was not very difficult to establish the real identity of the writer posing as "William Burke." The surprise is that others had not pursued the search. As I perused the numerous volumes of Miranda's archives, I jotted down the names of his correspondents. From January, 1808, when Miranda returned to England, I noticed an extensive correspondence between the General and a young writer, just thirty-five, by the name of James Mill. In the summer of 1980, I expected to find additional documentation on what seemed to be a very intimate relationship in which young Mill veritably worshipped his sixty-year-old Venezuelan colleague. Miranda's library with its excellent coverage of the Greeks and Romans was a sheer delight to the young classicist, who was forever borrowing books from his friend, discussing and evaluating them in their long walks into the countryside near London or at their respective homes. Then it finally occurred to the unsuspecting historian that there was a precocious baby in the Mill family. The juices understandably began to flow! I turned to the studies of Alexander Bain on James Mill, the Bruce Maslish work on the father and son, and Joseph Hamburger on Mill and the art of revolution.[24] Later, I learned that Miranda and his young friend had written an article together in the *Edinburgh Review* of January, 1809. After reading that article, I guessed that "our" William Burke was James Mill. After investigating the publications of Mill cited by Donald Winch and other scholars, I became increasingly convinced that I was on the right track—a conclusion that we shall test for our readers to their satisfaction.[25] In the past decade, I have learned much about James Mill and his famous son John Stuart Mill, much more than I shall ever use. But it was imperative for me to learn in detail just what had attracted these two historical figures to each other, James Mill and Francisco de Miranda. Mill's reaction to Miranda's death in 1816, which appears in Francis Place's papers at the British Library, said it all for me—a feeling that I shall try to capture in subsequent chapters.[26]

A dramatic and convenient discovery for me was the fact that James Mill was editor of the *Literary Journal* in London from 1803 to 1806, a periodical that was on microfilm at the University of Southern California Library. It permitted me to penetrate the mind of this particular graduate of Edinburgh University and to learn of his exposure to key professors of the so-called "Scottish Enlightenment." The celebrated *Edinburgh Review* likewise commenced its long tenure at this time as a powerful intellectual force in nineteenth-century England and Europe. Young Mill, in London, was therefore competing with some of his former classmates. Not many years later, he joined them as a reviewer who mailed in his contributions from London.

* * * * * * * * * * * *

Sir John Stuart and James Mill, his protégé, rode into London in early 1802, one to occupy a position in Parliament that he had won in a recent election and the other, a "man of letters," to test his ability as a writer in the nation's capital. There was a strong bond between Sir John and young James. Trained as a lawyer, Sir John never practiced law; but when he recognized that young Mill had interests and talents similar to his, he was determined to promote and develop his ward's abilities to the utmost. Rather than see him educated at the University of Aberdeen, as James' father had planned, Sir John eagerly assumed the responsibility of sending him to the University of Edinburgh and paying all expenses beyond the Aberdeen level. Sir John more than complied with that agreement, taking young James into his home while he was in Edinburgh. This arrangement provided "many advantages," James Mill recalled in one of his letters to Francis Place: he "saw the best company and had an educated man to direct my education." Sir John also paid for "several expensive branches of education," which James could not have otherwise experienced. A grateful James Mill averred that he "had unlimited access in both town and country to well chosen libraries. So you see I owe much to Sir John Stuart."[27] It is not surprising, therefore, that the field of Jurisprudence and Government was well-known to the young scholar; and, as his biographer noted, James Mill in 1802 planned to get his law degree in London while, at the same time, offering courses in Law to meet his expenses.[28] It will be recalled, that "our" William Burke displayed an excellent grasp of "Natural Law" as he proceeded to undermine the Spanish title to empire. Mill's indebtedness to Sir John in the discipline of Law could also have extended to other relevant fields in History, International Law, Politics, Government, Psychology, and Economics. On the other hand, Mill's mother and Lady Jane Stuart likewise had a notable impact on young James' career from 1790 to 1798, in that his graduate work was in the Divinity School. His career as a presbyterian minister, however, was short-lived and unrewarding as a means of livelihood. So until his arrival in London, Mill managed to survive as a tutor in the household of some wealthy families, including that of Sir John Stuart, and at the same time he devoted himself to extensive readings in the fields that had captured his imagination. His specialty in "political economy" absorbed much of his time; and we know that on that subject he often dropped in to hear the eloquent lectures of Professor Dugald Stewart, one of his old teachers. Moreover, Stewart's influence upon James Mill in "Mental Philosophy," or Psychology, also helped to direct him in those fields of expertise. Indeed, the four years from 1798 to 1802 as a tutor and self-disciplined scholar—a period in which the documentation is nonexistent or fragmentary—was crucial in forming the mind of that young Scottish intellectual who arrived in London with Sir John Stuart in the beginning years of the nineteenth century. His experience as a tutor, especially in teaching Wilhemina, the Stuart's only daughter, provided him with a teacher/student model for his own daughters later, also Francis Place's Annie, the "Lady of Salsbury," and, lastly, for his own son, John Stuart Mill, an intellectual giant of the nineteenth century. James Mill's teaching ability, of course, permeated his writings.[29]

Armed with special letters of recommendations for intellectuals and administrators, supported by a well-organized nucleus of Scotsmen in London who opened up as many doors as possible, young James Mill made his presence felt in the national capital in short order at age twenty nine. Thanks to Sir John, he made acquaintances in the government and attended many sessions of Parliament; and by mid-1802, his writings began to appear in the Anti-Jacobin Review. As Professor Bain noted, he wrote a book review on the *Elements of Logic and Mental Philosophy* which already reflected professional calibre in a field that he excelled in many years later.[30] The publishing firm of Charles and Robert Baldwin, countrymen of young Mill, produced his first essay: "The Impolicy of a Bounty on the Importation of Corn," (London, 1804) and his first major treatise, or monograph: *Commerce Defended. An Answer to the Arguments by which Mr. Spence . . . and Others Have Attempted to Prove that Commerce is not a Source of National Wealth* (London, 1807), which focused attention on young Mill as a specialist of Political Economy. It also demonstrated that he was an advocate of Adam Smith who had original ideas of his own.[31]

But that was not all that this young, indefatigable Scotsman was able to accomplish in his first five years in London. C. and R. Baldwin Company accepted his prospectus to support a journal of "useful knowledge," an idea that had incubated in his mind for some years, perhaps since his "tutor" days. At age thirty, James Mill became the editor of the *Literary Journal: A Review of Literature, Science, Manners, and Politics*—a weekly that appeared from January 1, 1803, through 1805 and as a monthly through the final year of 1806. During those years, moreover, it seems that Mill also edited the Baldwins' *St. James Chronicle*, which Professor Bains described as a "clerical and conservative newspaper."[32] The Baldwins had no doubt about Mill's religiosity. Although there has been controversy since then about James Mill's religious beliefs, especially after his long association with Jeremy Bentham, that difference of opinion simply did not apply to the years before 1808. Like "our" William Burke, James Mill, the political economist, strongly believed that the laws of Providence were basic to a natural economy. As editor of the *Literary Journal,* and the defender par excellence of Adam Smith, James Mill made this point time and time again. A most convincing example of Mill's religious sincerity

was his translation into English of a book by C.F.D. De Villers, An
Essay on the Spirit and Influence of the Reformation of Luther in 1805,
totaling four hundred and ninety pages! Surprised by the Roman
Catholics' "liberality of view," young Mill decided to translate it,
adding copious notes that included quotations by such English authors
as "Dugald Stewart, George Campbell, Millar, Robertson, Hardie (his
Professor of Church History)."[33] According to Bains, Mill made some
disparaging observations about Voltaire on religious matters, an author
who on other issues Mill admired very much. Annoyed by Villers'
remarks about "the books of the Bible as mere scraps of the literature
of distant ages," James Mill sternly observed that "these books
comprise the extraordinary code of laws communicated by a benevolent
divinity to man."[34]   William Burke similarly believed in the
"benevolence" of "Providence" in setting down the laws for a natural
economy. What dedication and religious sincerity must have been
involved in Mill's translation of the work on Martin Luther, especially
in light of his demanding editorship of the *Literary Journal* and the two
economic studies that have been mentioned above!

Mill worked with special editors, most of them fellow Scotsmen
trained at Edinburgh. He put them in charge of sections on
"Literature," "Science," "Manners," while he took over the one labelled
"Politics." His assignment excluded current politics and instead
emphasized Political Science, Political Economy, Jurisprudence, and
Police. From January 1, 1803, Mill's leadership was dynamic and
imaginative. A "natural teacher," or publicist of rare talent, young
James suggested that all sections begin with background materials to
prepare the readers for the regular fare. In "Politics," Mill provided a
historical perspective for understanding the state of Europe in 1803, a
crucial year in which war and peace tugged at the Truce of Amiens,
threatening to bring it to an end. Just as Burke in the "Preface" of the
1807 treatise favored pacifism, Mill likewise began with a defense of
peace:

> It gives us the sincerest pleasure, that the result of our most serious, and
> as far as we were masters of our purposes, impartial enquiries into the
> state of the two nations, which at present divide the situation of Europe,
> is strongly for moderation; that these nations have every thing to hope
> from their government, and every thing to fear from their disagreement.
>
>   These opinions, if we can establish the grounds on which they rest,
> lead to the most agreeable consequences. They shall be laid before our

readers from time to time, with the facts from which they are deduced. Enough, in our opinion, and more than enough, has been said and done, on both sides of the water, for the purpose of exasperation. It is high time, that something should be attempted for conciliation. The wise men, in both countries should endeavor to meet on the neutral territory of candour and benevolence, and by mutual explanation, and mutual civilities, recover that good understanding, which is so advantageous to both parties.[35]

When the Truce of Amiens ended, the young editor felt a deep distress at man's resort to violence, once again. Determined to accept the reality, however, his objective now as an Englishman was to examine the French enemy carefully in order to bring about his defeat. Burke, four years later, made a similar decision despite his pacifism. In 1807, James Mill before the crisis of that year was again in favor of peace, as can be seen in his brilliant analysis of *Commerce Defended*. He concluded that waste in government and "the consumption of war" were the main causes of "wretchedness" in the world;

> The condition of the country therefore goes backward; and in general it is only after the country is so exhausted that the expense of the war can hardly by any means be found, that it is ever put an end to. When the blessing of peace is restored, the country slowly recovers itself. But hardly has it gained its former prosperity when it is generally restruck by the calamity of war, and compelled to measure back its steps. In this alternation between misery and the mere beginnings of prosperity, are nations for the most part, condemned to remain; the energies of human nature are exerted to no purpose; its beneficient laws are counteracted; and the happiness of society, which seems to be secured by such powerful provisions, like the water of Tantalus, is only allowed to approach the lip, that it may be immediately dashed away from it.[36]

Professor Winch graphically described the dilemma of stalemate that was tormenting James Mill:

> France controls the Continent, Britain the seas; neither side can gain by continuing a war which weakens both equally. In particular he is pessimistic about the possibility of raising an army or creating a stable coalition to defeat Napoleon. He believes that a truce could be drawn up which would accord with the self-interest of both France and Britain.[37]

Editor Mill's background sketches revealed an exceptional capacity for the study of history and an amazing command of historiography. A great admirer of his fellow Scotsman William Robertson and his studies of Spain under Charles V and his *History of America*, Mill relied heavily upon those interpretations of the Spanish empire. So did William Burke in his first treatise! Mill's preferences in History were: (1) the Classical History of Greece and Rome—and here Miranda's famous library pleased his tastes to the utmost, especially in preparing his thoughts on the theme of "confederation" in that area; (2) the ""Reformation," thanks to his theological training and a strong conviction that it had encouraged "progress" in Europe; and (3) the Eighteenth Century with its Enlightenment and modern vision, as well as the challenge of the French Revolution. On the Middle Ages, Mill's views were negative since he detested the nobility's exploitation of other classes and because it was a period that lacked progress in manufacturing and industry. Above all, Mill was a strong advocate of the "New History"—another point in common with William Burke—an innovative approach that dealt with the "silent progress of manners, of industry, of wealth, or poverty, and even of literature and civilization." Whereas his religious training reacted emotionally to Voltaire's impiety, Mill now could argue:

> It is to Voltaire that the introduction of these subjects into history has been generally ascribed. They are the most interesting and instructive particulars in the account of any people; and have received a large share of attention from almost every historian since the example was set by that celebrated author. Hume contrived to introduce deep political reasonings into his history; and his success has tempted many of his followers to imitate his example.[38]

The young editor of the *Literary Journal*, in short, had been trained as a serious historian at the University of Edinburgh or on his own. His performance as editor already gave evidence that some day James Mill would present the world with a serious historical production—his multi-volume *History of India*.

Editor Mill pointed with great pride to the progress in "happiness" that man and nation had achieved in the eighteenth century—the striking emergence and advance of the middle class; the forward thrust of scientific methodology with its contributions for a better life; the discovery of "political economy" by Adam Smith and the French physiocrats; the educational reforms and intellectuals of that great century of "Lights;" and the proliferation of newspapers and periodicals that stimulated concepts like "Public Opinion" and "Freedom of the Press;" and, finally, the controversy and tension created by the "French Revolution" and its impact upon Europe. On this last point, the indefatigable Mill poured over numerous French monographs and multi-volume documentary sets that supplied his readers with vital statistics about the government and economy of France. This master publicist, as his counterpart Burke, marshalled these facts to support his arguments for peace. Once war started again, Mill then used these materials to show why Great Britain had no reason to fear an invasion of its shores by the French enemy. In the event that he was wrong, the patriotic editor enlisted in a Scottish militia regiment serving in London.[39]

Indeed, James Mill and "our William Burke" were both dedicated reformers who were constantly writing about "ameliorations," "improvements," etc. for society. Burke's editorials in Caracas from 1810 to 1812 were in favor of "anticolonialism" first and then for the establishment of a modern, political order. He preached for political, constitutional, and economic reforms and offered or explained to his readers what projects and trends they should adopt in a modern republican system. With vital facts and statistics, for example, he underscored the significance of immigration to a young nation by providing a sufficient number of people to promote prosperity and to make stability a reality. Educational facilities for the nation had to be adequate and conceived with imagination—well-prepared teachers, sufficient funding for the system, etc. etc. All viable nations had to have a sound banking establishment to stimulate the economy and promote development, etc. etc. Religious toleration was essential for a young society; and divisive issues like the "Irish Catholic Question" should be avoided and discouraged, etc., etc. Economic progress was fundamental for the nation: the introduction of new technologies in agriculture, industry, commerce were imperative; the education of farmers, mechanics, artisans, and other workers should be promoted and modernized; new industries should be encouraged—fishing, woodcutting, shipbuilding, etc., etc. Moreover, governments should never forget their social and human responsibilities with regard to the poor. It was one reform after another; and whether writing in London or in Caracas, Burke was a conscientious advocate of reform.[40]

James Mill's reputation as a reformer is too well known to belabor here in any detail. It was already apparent in his role as editor of the *Literary Journal* where he had ample opportunity to make comments on necessary "ameliorations" in society. His writings on the British "Poor Laws" were persuasive, well-researched, and intellectually sincere —a harbinger of his subsequent works on that theme.[41] His remarks on education were well-conceived and modern; and his advocacy of Joseph Lancaster's system of education is well-known. It was through Mill, in particular, that Miranda chose to take plans with him in 1810 for the introduction of the Lancasterian system in Venezuela.[42] On the subject of banking systems and financial reforms, it would be difficult to find a more competent reviewer than young James Mill whose presentations, given the difficulties of the statistics and trends involved, were lucid and persuasive. The relevance for the Miranda story is that Alexander Hamilton was a very good friend of the General who shared with him his celebrated expertise and insights on financial systems. It would be a simple matter, therefore, for James Mill to use the Hamiltonian reports as the basis for editorials in the *Gazeta de Caracas*.[43] The assumption here, of course, is that William Burke was James Mill. The young Scot, moreover, wrote on the "Catholic Question" in the *Literary Journal*; and his views on religious toleration were on the same side of the ledger as Burke.[44] Mill's discussions on militias and the military, coupled with Miranda's documentation and talents along these lines, likewise point to another parallel that he shared with the essayist William Burke—both men were reformers par excellence![45]

To make our quest for the identification of William Burke much more meaningful, it is basic to recognize what that discovery might mean for the image of James Mill in history. It should support the contention of a well-known British authority—Donald Winch—on Mill as an economist. He maintains that Mill was the "midwife" of David Ricardo's *Principles of Political Economy* (1817) or the "link, albeit indirect, between the founder of classical economics and Ricardo, its next great exponent."[46] In his analysis of Mill's "Bounty" essay of 1804 and the *Commerce Defended* three years later, Professor Winch points to the strong influence of Adam Smith but he also acknowledges the original innovations of this young writer. Certainly, there is evidence in his editorship of the *Literary Journal* that he might have been Adam Smith's heir in classical economics; but the realities of his existence forced him into other channels of activity. When he met David Ricardo in 1808, he recognized his friend's native talents and encouraged him to realize his potential as the successor of Adam Smith. As the publicist for classical economics, however, there was no equal to James Mill, especially when we learn that he was also William Burke, the advocate of "Invisible Empire" in Spanish America.

Mill's commitment to the ideas of Adam Smith was superbly documented in a thirteen-page review of the work by Jean Baptiste Say: *A Treatise on Political Economy: or a simple Exposition of the Manner in which Wealth is Produced, Distributed, and Consumed* (1803).[47] "Political Economy," the editor began: "is a science altogether of modern growth, and the knowledge of its principles, and the power of making a just application of them to all the affairs of nations is yet very imperfectly distributed." The ancients, surprisingly, had no conception of this science. Mill continued:

> It was not early even in the history of modern science that any knowledge of political economy was obtained. So long as liberty was banished from the soil of Europe, the science of government, if the barbarian maxims upon which it was then conducted are not ridiculed by the term, was confined to the princes and ministers who exercised the powers of government; these stood ready to punish the first man who dared to think upon a subject which belonged exclusively to them; and no part of the science of the amelioration of human affairs received any improvement in their lands. Their major concern was to keep the people subservient to the passions and appetites of their superiors . . . and this was altogether incompatible with the means of rendering them wealthy and prosperous, and the nation, by consequence, at the same time. It is no wonder, therefore, that the science of rendering a nation wealthy and prosperous was then not understood.[48]

Professor Say's remarks about Adam Smith were not at all offensive to young Mill:

> In the year 1776, Adam Smith, reared in that Scottish school which has produced so many historians, philosophers, and men of letters of the first rank, published his book, entitled, *An Inquiry into the Nature and Causes of the Wealth of Nations.* When we read his work, we perceive that before Smith, political economy had no existence . . . Before Smith some very just principles had been several times advanced; he is the first who shewed the connection which they have with one another, and how they are necessary consequences of the nature of things; now it is acknowledged that a truth belongs not to him who first utters, but to him who first proves it. He had done more than establish truths; he has

given the true method of detecting errors. He had not permitted himself to make a single assertion, not even a single supposition which is not conformable to the most constant facts. His work is a series of demonstrations which have raised several propositions to the rank of incontestable principles.

On the other hand, James Mill regretted that Say's two volumes contained very little that was original: "Not only are the general principles copied from Smith, but almost the whole of the facts and illustrations." It would have been better if he had used a different set of examples, dealing with other countries and governments, thus buttressing further the Smithian argument. Say's clear presentation, however, was so indispensable because it clarified views that even readers of Smith had missed. "It will contribute in no inferior degree," Mill insisted, "to diffuse just notions on a most important subject throughout Europe." Referring to one of his professors at Edinburgh, Mill wrote:

> Although we in this country, have long been accustomed to read the same doctrines; though we have them taught to us not only with great clearness, but with great eloquence, so many of us are still prone to misunderstand them, that a view of them somewhat different from that to which we have been accustomed, may not be without its use. It may give at least to some persons, a more clear idea of their connection and consequences.[49]

Mill was referring to Professor Dugald Stewart's eloquence. He admitted to Macvey Napier, many years later, that "the taste for the studies which have formed my favourite pursuits, and which will be so to the end of my life I owe to Mr. Stewart."[50] Stewart, who had studied under Adam Smith, was the first to offer a course on "political economy" at Edinburgh.

James Mill was such an advocate and defender of Adam Smith that he often lost his temper and used strong words against writers who paraphrased Smith incorrectly or who were arrogant enough to criticize the Scottish giant. He attacked his classmate, five years his junior, and later a very close political associate, Henry Brougham, unmercifully for distorting Smith; and he also took on Professor William Playfair who dared to question his colleague Stewart's veracity on a issue involving Adam Smith. To spare the feelings of our reader, we shall cite only certain portions of this vicious attack: "this unhallowed conjunction

. . . a sacrilege . . . there was hardly a worse prostitution. Oh Fy! And this to have been perpetrated in a quarter where the immortal remains of that great man had such peculiar claims to respect."[51] Both James Mill and William Burke often assumed dogmatic stands out of a sense of righteousness, or just arrogance. Professor Bain astutely underscored a characteristic about Mill, namely, his use of ridicule against those who opposed him.[52] This was also one of Burke's traits, it should be noted! Both Burke and Mill were master debaters and publicists, as well as teachers. Jeremy Bentham observed, in a moment of pique, that Mill indeed had an arrogant and domineering attitude even in conversations.[53] Certainly, many readers of the *Literary Journal* shared Bentham's impressions of editor Mill, especially those who had presented books to him for review. They recognized, however, that the editor was an exceptional intellectual and a most effective writer.

On November 1, 1803, there was a notable editorial entitled, "Politics: Spain and Portugal," which demonstrated James Mill's interest in the emancipation of Spanish America, three years before William Burke undertook his quixotic crusade in that direction.[54] The opening quotation of this chapter appeared in that editorial. It is an excellent example of Mill's scholarship, the type of research that he practiced on a daily basis, and how meaningful his research of the moment was to the international scene. Moreover, it offers some hints on the identification of William Burke, which has so much consumed us in this chapter.

In the eighteenth century the dynastic tie of the Bourbons in France and Spain was vital in the constant balancing of power in Europe. The advent of the French Revolution, however, brought tension to the former amicable arrangement, forcing Spain to oppose her former ally. In time, however, the French republicans gained the upperhand. In the meanwhile, Portugal who feared a dependency upon her Spanish neighbor, continued her historical role as a "useful ally" of Great Britain. In time, of course, Napoleon's influence threatened to overtake Portugal. If Napoleon succeeded in this objective, war would be inevitable between Great Britain and Iberia—Spain and Portugal. The analyst Mill continued: "We are therefore highly interested in knowing what are the resources which France can draw from those countries to increase her power of injuring us." It was Mill's contention that Iberian resources would not be important. To begin with, the French did not need Iberian soldiers; and although the Spanish and Portuguese naval units might help to augment France's power, the facts and figures available to Mill indicated that the enemy's naval force still "would not equal one fourth of the navy of Great Britain." As for financial contributions to France, the prospects were bleak indeed. In fact, France would have to subsidize her Iberian allies; and here Mill's review of Spanish and Portuguese taxes, an "injurious" legacy of the "feudal system," worked against any substantial financial help for their French patron.

The Iberian weakness in Europe, however, might be overlooked in light of their holdings overseas. "Both countries enjoy," Mill continued, "the most valuable colonies in the world, but the poverty and degeneracy of the mother countries prevent them from deriving any considerable advantages from these colonies." These colonies, moreover, have "a most imperfect state of defence." So, editor Mill raised the vital question: "What could we gain by attacking those colonies?" Since the Iberians were powerless in Europe, Mill argued that "the advantage is altogether on our side with regard to the colonies. We can, in the first place, entirely cut off all communications between the mother countries and the colonies." Thus, the mother countries would lose whatever returns they used to get from overseas. Spain offered a good example of this point, cut off as she was for

> several years of the late war. The accumulated returns which she has obtained since the end of that war, are not equal to one half, probably not to one third of what she ought to have received, according to the rate of the yearly returns, before the war.

Mill, wise in the field of public psychology, explained that

> the misfortune which the mother countries suffer by the interruption of their communication with the colonies amounts to a calamity. During that interruption the colonies learn to do without the mother countries. After an interruption during some years of the communication between the mother country and a colony, it is not in the nature of things that the connection between them should ever again be so close and firm.

In short, Spain might soon find herself without any colonies and the same applied to Portugal. To illustrate this point, Mill, the teacher, took the case of the East Indies if a five-year break occurred with Great Britain. The results would be similar—a spirit of independence and self-government that could not be erased later without bloodshed. European colonials would not tolerate being stripped of the privileges that they had assumed during the interruption with the mother country. The "disjunction" of Iberia's colonies, Mill predicted, "is not very distant. This is a circumstance, which at present may excite the strongest alarm in Spain and Portugal."[55]

The Iberian mothers might deceive themselves into thinking that England could not take "their colonies by conquest," because of insufficient forces. "They do not reflect," Mill observed:

> that now France is cut off from the West Indies, and we have nothing to fear from her attempts, the force which we were obliged to maintain there as guard against her attacks, is nearly sufficient for the overthrow of all the Spanish and Portuguese force in America. They do not recollect too, that the military energy of this country is called forth to such a degree, that we have a greater disposable force than ever we had; and if Bonaparte would only give us an opportunity of chastising his presumption on our own shores, we have a force sufficient for much more arduous enterprises than the conquest of Mexico and Peru.

These were strange words, indeed, from a man who earlier in the year was a pacifist and who wanted the Truce of Amiens to continue. Once it did not, like William Burke later, he was ready to meet the French with violence.

Forcing his argument to a climax, editor Mill zeroed in on the decision that had to be made: "The Spaniards, and Portuguese, besides, are not aware that we can carry on a war against them in America, completely ruinous to their interests." Here were the alternatives: (1) the path of **CONQUEST**, or War: "*to reduce their dominions in that part of the world under subjection to us, to which the inhabitants could oppose considerable resistance*;" or (2) the path of **LIBERATION**: "*to free these countries from their subjection to their mother countries, in which we shall meet with the assistance of the inhabitants.*" The quotation that introduces this chapter was Mill's final statement: Spanish-Americans would welcome our pledge of independence and begin their revolt. If they were to resist us, we would have to put them down. Such a threat would bring them to terms immediately. Then, the great future of "commercial prosperity" would reign for Great Britain and "these noble territories." Four years later, William Burke used less threatening words but his goal of **LIBERATION** leading to "Invisible Empire" was identical to that of James Mill, that talented young editor of the *Literary Journal* in London.[56]

* * * * * * * * * * * *

Since there is no documentation linking James Mill directly to Francisco de Miranda prior to the 1806 expedition, it can be argued that young Mill wrote the first Burkian tract on his own initiative. To be sure, the editorial on Spain and Portugal in 1803 already indicated a strong commitment to the emancipation of Spanish America within the context of war with France. Three years later, in 1806, the dramatic events in the Plata and the Caribbean revived William Burke's earlier project that would have invited France to a free trade program in Spanish America hoping that this proposal would end the disastrous war between the two European contenders. That was his announced objective in the "Preface," as we have already indicated. The events of 1806 in the Río de la Plata, however, led to Burke's abandonment of the peace solution. He began the first third of his treatise with a theoretical presentation that questioned Spain's title to America and argued Great Britain's rights to challenge that title in defense of the long-suffering Americans whose natural rights had been violated. His training in jurisprudence and his familiarity with William Robertson's *History of America* (5th ed., 3 vols., 1788) were more than sufficient to carry the major theoretical thrust of both Burkian treatises. Through Robertson, Burke (Mill) was able to appreciate the Jesuit Order's role in defending and christianizing the Indians. In fact, Burke (Mill) had a more sympathetic view of the Indian's capacity and equality, although both Mill and Robertson had been trained for the presbyterian ministry. Moreover, coincidence would have it that James Mill reviewed the work of the Englishman John Constance Davie on Paraguay, an indispensable reference on the Indians trained by the Jesuits before the Order's expulsion from the Spanish Empire in 1767.[57] Mill also had the opportunity to consult the work of Anthony Z. Helm, a German mineralogist who served in Spanish America in the late eighteenth century. Mill quoted these key references on the isolation of the region and poor defense system of the Spaniards in South America.[58] They were especially valuable for Burke's long exposition on the oppression and tyranny which focused on the maltreatment of the Indians.[59]

A master propagandist, William Burke painted an emotional and powerful picture of Spain's abusive colonial system in South America. He had an intuitive sense for the words, the concepts, and the images that would sway his reader. This writer understood the human mind, how it would respond to certain stimuli, and what combinations of these might produce the desired response. Obsessed and inspired by the concept of "Progress," he believed with all his heart that "public opinion" could bring about constructive and necessary changes for a modern, rational order. Like the white man of Europe, the American "Indian" was rational and naturally good, as God had willed it. Even before meeting Miranda, William Burke (James Mill) was already sympathetic to the Jesuits' record in America. In addition to Robertson, John Davie encouraged the trend with the information he had garnered from the Dominican fathers who protected him in the Platine region. A father Hernández, a student of the Jesuit missions, informed Davie of the Jesuit practices that had won over the hearts and minds of their Indians. The Indians' hatred of the Spanish government intensified with the expulsion of their Jesuit *padres.* In this state of agitation, they understandably looked forward to cooperation with any prospective allies that promised liberation and justice, including foreigners. Davie's Dominican friends likewise pointed out that another key factor in the revolutionary climate of the times was the greater degree of enlightenment among Spanish officers and missionaries, some of whom incited the natives to rebellion against the injustice of the Spanish system. The ubiquitous poverty and mistreatment of the Indians who lived in Spanish urban zones were emotional eyesores that offended those Indians that did not. They continued to resent the offensive and abusive "work levies" that compelled these native Americans to work for a pittance on the white man's farms or in the unhealthy mines of South America. Helm and Davie both agreed that a disaster was in the wind. All was quiet in the late 1790s, Davie observed; but it was

> a deceitful calm that precedes a dreadful storm, which will, when least expected, break in fatal thunder upon the heads of the proud oppressors. Human patience in every state of life, may be stretched to its utmost limits, and yet forbear to turn; but let that limit once be passed, and woe to the tyrant who had tried how far he might injure with impunity.[60]

William Burke, or James Mill, put Davie's warning into these powerful sentences:

> The native American cannot forget the murder of his fathers. The massacres which depopulated his country, are handed down in melancholy tradition from father to son: he beholds the fields which once were the patrimony and scene of happiness of his ancestors, now torn from him: and stained with their innocent blood. He feels himself

a slave and outcast in his country; without property or security; and considered by the plunderers of the land of his fathers, merely as a beast of burden, formed only to labour for his oppressors—and to perish. The injured American carries his wrongs into the prospect of his posterity; he joins the future miseries of his children, with the afflictions of his forefathers; and sees himself the medial link of wretchedness between them. Gracious Heaven! Can it then be supposed that the native American, oppressed with such a lengthened chain of misery as he is forced to bear, can forget the cruel sufferings of three hundred years of massacre, plunder, slavery and blood; and become quietly reconciled to his tyrants? No—it is not agreeable to the nature of man—and they who suppose it to be so, know little of the workings of the human heart.[61]

William Burke's research in the first tract of 1807 was nowhere as extensive as that of James Mill in the *Edinburgh Review* article of 1809, which he wrote under the supervision of Miranda; but it was nonetheless of high quality. Although Burke did not provide many specific footnotes, nor full names of all of his authorities, it was no common writer who could quote Muratori on the slave raids upon the Jesuit missions of Paraguay or La Peyrouse's impressions on the fertility of Chile's soil and its food-producing potential.[62] Under Miranda, of course, he had a special library and a vast collection of materials that the Venezuelan had gathered during his extensive travels.

Although there is no direct evidence of Miranda's influence in Burke's first treatise, the same was not true in the second treatise of 1808, the "Additional Reasons" that is familiar to the reader. But there was also much documentation that came from the newspapers and periodical literature of the times: the materials on the Popham-Beresford fiasco; the "Recapture" of Buenos Aires only a few months after Popham's initial victory; the British reaction to Popham's success and the spirited build up of British expeditions that soon made their way to the Río de la Plata; the news and documents about the English victories at Maldonado and Montevideo; and, finally, Whitelocke's disastrous failure followed by the publications on his court martial, as well as those of Sir Home Popham earlier.

As in the first treatise, Burke continued and even intensified his treatment of the differences between "Conquest" and "Liberation"; moreover, he attacked unmercifully the faulted policy of Great Britain in the Río de la Plata. His expertise in international affairs, of course, provided this vital contribution with a special ring of authority. It was

James Mill at his best. From Miranda and his associates, William Burke was able to sketch for his reader the 1806 expedition of General Miranda in the Caribbean—both attempts to land in Venezuela; he had the opportunity to present to the public the *Osprey* documents and associated correspondence; and personal insights of Miranda's operations that he learned directly from the Count de Rouvray, the special envoy of General Miranda in England. By the end of 1806, moreover, Mill had in his possession the invaluable work on Venezuela by F. Depons. It was a key reference in the second essay "Additional Reasons" because of the facts and figures portraying Venezuela as the "Land of Promise." It also contained a biography of Miranda that was well-known in Europe—the one with some errors and distortions, that made Miranda four years younger, that depicted him as the son of a noble Venezuelan family, etc.[63]

The Count de Rouvray did not meet James Mill until he learned about the appearance of Burke's first treatise, sometime from April to July 1807, according to the listings of the *Edinburgh Review*.[64] On July 2, 1807, Rouvray sent a copy of the tract to Miranda, enclosed in a letter to Governor Hislop of Trinidad. Rouvray wrote jubilantly to Miranda that Burke's publication was creating "a sensation here, so much so that it may yet open the eyes of the most obstinate, if there is still in England anyone who can doubt the advantage that this country will reap from the independence of South America." The elated Rouvray remarked: "You should be extremely content with the style and ideas that this work contains, and if the author (whose name appears on the work) should write again on the same topic, I shall hasten to send you the new production."[65] Miranda was equally sanguine about Burke's tract when he received his first copy of it from General Bowyer in early July, 1807. On July 11, 1807, he wrote to Nicholas Vansittart: "It appears that even the Public Mind perceives now what was the sound Policy and Interest of Great Britain to have executed a long time ago."[66] To Admiral Cochrane, he noted that the Burkian analysis "appears well calculated to open the eyes of the public on this important subject." Miranda especially hoped that British Ministers would heed Burke's message: "May Providence open their eyes for the sake of themselves, as well as the interest of mankind!"[67] After thanking General Bowyer for the copy of Burke's work, Miranda recalled with some bitterness the fate of the project he had submitted to William Pitt:

And I leave to the consideration of any impartial Man, friend to Great Britain, friend to Humanity itself, to say, if this design was not more judicious, more practicable and beneficial to us all than the numerous Coalitions and bloody Wars that have been undertaken on the Continent, since the beginning of the French Revolution?

Perhaps, concluded the perennial optimist: "it will take place, for the mutual interest of Both Nations, and of Mankind in general." Miranda asked Bowyer to persuade a

Printer in Barbados to publish an Edition of the above mentioned Pamphlet. I do believe it would produce a good effect in the West India Islands, and I should gladly contribute to the expense of it—or to have some extract of the same Pamphlet, inserted in the Mercury of Barbados.[68]

When he acknowledged Rouvray's copy, Miranda noted with some sarcasm that Bowyer, who earlier had opposed the invasion of Coro, although now he was so eager to participate in Miranda's project, was the first to provide him with a copy of Burke's treatise: "What a pity that they did not open their eyes a year ago!"[69]

Despite the comforting discovery of a true ally in William Burke, General Miranda could not overcome the serious depression and despair that he had felt for months over events in London. Euphoric in the earlier weeks of the Rouvray mission in England, from the Count's arrival on December 17, 1806, to his agent's letter of February 7, 1807, in which he announced enthusiastically that British ministers were on the verge of action after reading the *Osprey* documents, Miranda's dreams began to dissolve as he experienced once again a familiar pattern of British procrastination and ineptitude. There were a series of delays, of unexpected obstacles, and of bureaucratic redtape. On this occasion, it seemed that the breakdown had been due to developments in the Río de la Plata. With the "Recapture of Buenos Aires," the Popham-Beresford dream lay shattered in a heap. The faithful Nicholas Vansittart, as Rouvray noted more than once, worked heroically to save Miranda's cause in London; but he was powerless to offset the stalling of British officials.[70] It would appear that English leaders were merely waiting to hear about the various expeditions that had been sent to the Río de la Plata since Popham's initial victory. Although Miranda did not express his real apprehension to the Count of Rouvray, it was implicit in his cynical remarks about Englishmen forever chasing rainbows—i.e. coalitions in Europe and selfish projects always had a priority over the emancipation of Spanish America.[71] Despite his constant lecturing and admonitions, he perhaps suspected that "Conquest" was what the English had in mind. This was reflected in the increasing anger and bitterness that Miranda felt toward Sir Home Popham, the prototype in his mind of the *Conquistador*.[72] He never could forgive him for his actions in the Plata. And all the while, the real enemy was threatening to make his presence felt in Spanish America. Some one hundred and eighty Frenchmen had been sent to Caracas in response to Miranda's maneuvers in the Caribbean. There were, moreover, constant rumors that Puerto Rico and Venezuela would be turned over to the French by Spain in exchange for Portugal, etc. Before long, it was apparent that the British were still very much in evidence in the Río de la Plata after their seizure of Maldonado at the mouth of the Plata estuary. Samuel Achmuty's expedition landed there and by April 12, 1807, had taken the stronghold of Montevideo.[73] British cavalry ranged the entire *Banda Oriental* (Eastern Shore, now Uruguay) as if preparing for a new attack upon Buenos Aires. There was a flurry of rumors that the Craufurd and Whitelocke expeditions were destined for the Caribbean to assist General Miranda. English officers working with the General assured him that these reports were true, although Miranda chose not to build up his hopes.[74]

By the time General Miranda received copies of Burke's first treatise, he was ready to return to England. In fact, John Turnbull advised him that he should return to help break the impasse in government over his project.[75] The Count of Rouvray likewise urged him to take over in London; but Nicholas Vansittart did not favor the move as yet. So Miranda waited and fretted.[76] When he learned that bookdealers in London were threatening to confiscate his valuable library, Miranda was beside himself, so disillusioned with Turnbull and others who had promsied to watch over his family and property in London during his absence.[77] He waited until early October; when he decided that he could no longer await Vansittart's letter of approval.

As it turned out, General Robert Craufurd's expedition left England for the Cape of Good Hope, presumably on its way to India. Then came the change in direction, as Craufurd's expedition sailed for the Río de la Plata.[78] Perhaps in order to camouflage the objectives of General Craufurd, the Count de Rouvray was told that at the right moment Craufurd had orders to announce Great Britain's firm commitment to the emancipation of all Spanish America and the impression was given that no conquest was intended. It was such an unbelievable fantasy that the English were embroidering, suspected the Count de Rouvray. He could not believe it. He was unable to resist adding, in his letter to Miranda, that if the British really had "Conquest" in mind, it would turn out to be a catastrophe.[79] In early September, 1807, Rouvray had a lengthy meeting with Lord Castlereagh in which it was obvious that the English would not support General Miranda at this time.[80] Once again, Miranda's project had been put aside by his English ally. Rouvray boarded a ship for his return to Barbados on September 10, 1807, a date that the reader should keep in mind because of its bearing on a subsequent discussion. General Miranda left Trinidad and arrived at Tortola by the end of October, 1807. He had a conference there with Admiral Alexander Cochrane for a few days. On November 4th, the Count de Rouvray joined his colleagues at Tortola, almost a year since initiating his mission to Europe.[81]

Thanks to a few facts from letters and other documents, in addition to Burke's second treatise "Additional Reasons," it is possible to reconstruct the Rouvray-Mill cooperation in London. Burke's strategy in the first work was to point out initially the evils of "Conquest," contrasting them to the positive model of "Liberation" in Miranda's expedition of 1806. Since Rouvray did not join Miranda until July 1, 1806, he could not provide more information to James Mill than what General Miranda had said or written before that date; thus, William Burke's second treatise lacks the information on the U.S. prisoners and the embarrassing trip after the defeat at Puerto Cabello.[82] Rouvray's information for the Coro invasion, on the other hand, provided almost excessive detail of an experience in which he had played a key role. It is reflected in Burke's portrayal of the Coro expedition. Rouvray, moreover, was given copies of Miranda's proclamations, publications, etc. and he could divulge the details of strategy in which he had been a participant. He also knew "Colonel" John Downie, who joined the Miranda group in Trinidad at the same time that the Count did—thus, impressions by Burke about Downie were from Rouvray. He also was the only one who could have provided Burke with the *Osprey* documents, Downie's correspondence, and the one letter by the captured English naval officer. Moreover, the second treatise contains copies and information of materials that Rouvray, along with Mill, were able to read in Miranda's home, thanks to the assistance of Sarah Andrews (Martin) the housekeeper and mother of Miranda's two boys. For example, shortly before Rouvray left London, there appeared a publication entitled "Letters addressed to the Right Hon. Lord Melville."[83] It evoked the malicious image of Miranda as a "Jacobin." William Burke, without knowing the General at all, denied the charge vehemently, by reproducing a document in which a Belgian bishop testified that Miranda was a great defender of the Catholic Church! These were documents that, at that time, were in Miranda's home.[84] Moreover, during Miranda's absence from London, Mrs. Martin received a copy of William Thomson's *Military Memoirs* in which he likened the Venezuelan to Scipio Africanus in Roman times. The reader will perhaps remember that particular quotation, which appeared in Chapter One of this book. Burke also used it in the "Additional Reasons," both the Latin and English versions.[85] Rouvray, in short, had been a major contributor to Burke's second publication.

There was one reference, or authority, in the second treatise that Rouvray had no opportunity to discuss with Mill, simply because he was not in London at that time. The reference in question was the Peruvian-born Manuel Padilla who had been in the Río de la Plata throughout the English invasions—from Popham-Beresford through the defeat of John Whitelocke in mid-1807. Padilla rushed to his native Peru after Whitelocke's defeat. He was the "Peruvian Gentleman" mentioned by Burke who had witnessed the wrath of Peruvians against the brazen British conquest in the Plata.[86] Certain "Peruvian manifestoes" and publications from the Plata were published in London after Padilla's arrival; we do not know if Mill had anything to do with these publications though it is likely that he did. John Turnbull, Miranda's merchant representative, complained that the Peruvian and Platine manifestoes were raising anglophobia to the point that commerce between England and South America was in serious jeopardy.[87] It was also Padilla who gave Burke specific information on how English atrocities at Montevideo and elsewhere had been responsible for the resistance of all classes in Buenos Aires that produced the death of so many Englishmen in the streets of the Argentine capital. Padilla's mission to London was to establish contact with General Miranda. By the time he arrived in London, much after September 10th, de Rouvray had left and Miranda's representative in London was James Mill.[88] Thus Mill, whose pen name was "William Burke," took Padilla's facts and introduced them into the second treatise. De Rouvray and Miranda were not privy to this information until months later.

Chapter Five

Miranda in London:
Response to Change, 1808

General Miranda . . . was the most proper person that could be thought of, for publishing and circulating proper sentiments of the British Government: that Conquest never entered into the minds of His Majesty's Ministers; that the Expedition against Buenos Ayres was perfectly unauthorized and that it had always uniformly been, and would always continue to be, the most zealous desire of His Majesty and his Ministers, to establish and promote the Independence and the Happiness of the inhabitants of South America.

John Turnbull, September 25, 1807[1]

As the dean of British merchants in London, always hopeful that Spanish American markets would open freely to his countrymen, John Turnbull, was one of Miranda's most trusted friends, whom he had known since the latter's service in Cádiz, Spain. Turnbull along with the Count of Rouvray, represented the General before His Majesty's Government.[2] At the time he wrote the lines above, however, he was emotionally distraught over the news that exploded in London on September 13th—that "terrible news" of Whitelocke's defeat in Buenos Aires. This emotional reaction, derived it seemed from a sense of guilt that he might not have been faithful to his charge on behalf of General Miranda. For several months prior to this letter to Nicholas Vansittart, his relationship with the General suffered an increasing strain that coincided with Miranda's disillusionment over British policy. "By your last three letters," snapped Miranda on June 10th:

I find a kind of incoherency in some things that ought to be very explicit and clear . . . I assure you I have been not a little unpuzzled in ascertaining the meaning or coincidence of them, particularly being in want of some of de Rouvray's letters, that might help me in clearing it up.[3]

Exasperated by the lapse in Rouvray's correspondence, Miranda suspected that perhaps the recent change in the British administration might lead to another abandonment of the Venezuelan project. "My agents in London tell me," he wrote to Admiral Cochrane on June 4, 1807, "that the change in ministry will not effect policy in the Caribbean." Yet, the news from the Plata reflected an incorrect stance by the British government:

A force more than sufficient to have opened all the Ports of South America to the commerce and Alliance of Great Britain, is now paralysed on the Town of Montevideo, and on the shores of the Río de la Plata, promoting warfare and resistance in the Country, instead of friendship, Trade and Commerce.[4]

A few days later, when Miranda learned that Lord Castlereagh would probably head the Colonial and War Departments in the new government, he advised him that "no conquest" was Britain's only effective approach in the Plata.[5]

Many contemporaries, including John Turnbull, recognized that the British swing toward confrontation in the Plata was a policy that Miranda did not like at all. Turnbull recalled the Venezuelan's strong reaction earlier to the Popham-Beresford intrusion. On May 6th, Turnbull expressed the opinion that Miranda should return to London to direct his own project—a recommendation that Rouvray also supported. It was assumed in London that Miranda would understand the recommendation. At first inclined to follow that suggestion, Miranda had second thoughts, knowing that Vansittart was not in favor of his return at this time. Vansittart, always loyal and consistent, had his reasons for thinking that he could turn things around in London on his own. Or so General Miranda chose to believe. Thus, he decided to remain in the Caribbean another month or so, hoping that the delay would not be ruinous to the New World.[6]

The following months were, indeed, ones of "ambiguity" or "incoherency" in British policy, to use Miranda's words. It was a phase described in the previous chapter—the speculation on the projected itinerary of the Crauford expedition, the ambiguous promises of English Ministers who favored independence of the Plata and other provinces of South America, etc., etc. Rouvray had doubts about the success of "conquest" in the Plata and on that occasion urged General Miranda to return to London at once.[7] Turnbull, during his "incoherency," repeated the same information in erratic sentences that reflected his own uneasiness. In the meantime, the merchant dean suffered a curious lapse, especially for a dependable and trustworthy businessman—the neglect of Miranda's family in London and the near confiscation of the General's valuable library by debtors. Bewildered and beside himself, Miranda could not believe that his trusted friend had allowed such a potential tragedy. Turnbull never again regained his colleague's confidence and trust.[8]

About three weeks before the Platine news reached London, Turnbull finally admitted to Miranda that "the Conquest of Buenos Ayres is highly probable." Although British ministers favored granting independence throughout South America, they could not, however, give up their possessions in the Río de la Plata. Those holdings might be useful as bargaining chips in subsequent peace negotiations! What an explosive fact for Spanish American patriots, arousing their emotions to a fever pitch. Imagine Europeans bargaining with a chip that happened to be their precious Independence movement for which they were willing to offer their lives! On the other hand, Europeans would find it difficult to forsake an established practice in the Old World's system of balancing power.[9]

On September 25, 1807, Turnbull wrote the letter to Vanstittart that introduces this chapter. In it, he referred to the conversation with Lord Castlereagh, on the previous day, concerning the psychological reaction of South Americans to Whitelocke's defeat at Buenos Aires and the English attempt to conquer the Plata by force. He told Vansittart emphatically that it was urgent "to counteract the injurious effects that the Peruvian Manifests and the publications from Buenos Ayres, must have produced in the minds of the South Americans, against the English."[10] Otherwise, British trade would inevitably suffer. Miranda's influence was therefore essential to prevent such an outcome. This belief bordered on the naive. How could Turnbull expect General Miranda to reverse this impossible situation? Miranda's credibility throughout the world would be put to a stern test. He might have argued that the Popham-Beresford intrusion was "unauthorized"; but to maintain that the Achmuty-Crauford-Whitelocke expeditions were intended to advance the "Independence and the Happiness" of all South Americans would have been ludicrous! Turnbull's wishful thinking merely documented the sense of guilt overpowering many prominent Englishmen, especially in government. Swayed by the "Platine Fever," they followed the line of least resistance—the urge to conquer. The ignominious defeat of Englishmen in the streets of Buenos Aires was a nightmare for them, leaving them enervated and disgusted with themselves for not following Miranda's more imaginative approach of "liberation." When they learned that the Venezuelan was on his way back to London, their spirits picked up noticeably as if an opportunity would soon arise to make amends for their grievous mistake.

As the conversation between Turnbull and Castlereagh focused on Francisco de Miranda, the merchant noticed that the Lord's sentiments "were very different from those which had been expressed to the Count de Rouvray" before his return to the Caribbean. The man responsible for Castlereagh's changed position was Edward Cooke in the Colonial Department. Lord Castlereagh thus argued that he felt no real obligation to General Miranda "as an Agent for the British Government." Castlereagh maintained that just the opposite was the case, especially when he learned that the General

> had left England contrary to the Opinion of the Administration: and has contrary to their wishes engaged in the ill-concerted Expedition to South America, which had been of Prejudice instead of Benefit to the Cause in question; and in regard to pecuniary assistance, if, as I had stated, the former Ministers had given General Miranda such Encouragement, as to induce him to incur Expense, it was incumbent on them to state in his behalf, that they had done so, and the Inducements that had operated with them as no papers whatever on the subject appeared in the War Department.

To offset the distortions Cooke had planted in Castlereagh's mind, Turnbull carefully presented the facts as he recalled them and as General Miranda had briefed him, mentioning the names of all officers in the government who had advanced money to Miranda and had encouraged his project. Lord Castlereagh, it appeared, was receptive; he "did not at all seem to have his mind made up against General Miranda." On the contrary, he wanted to see Vansittart to confirm this new interpretation. The merchant concluded that Castlereagh wanted to stop the French in Spanish America at all costs, convinced that

Miranda and the objective of independence was the sensible approach to take.[11]

John Turnbull, in other words, was setting the scene for the triumphant return of General Francisco de Miranda to London on New Year's day, 1808. The direction of Miranda's project, as far as Lord Castlereagh and the General were concerned, was now in the hands of Nicholas Vansittart, who in the previous months had very little impact on the government's direction.

* * * * * * * * * * * *

After a tempestuous crossing of forty-four days, from Tortola to Portsmouth, England, Miranda and a small cadre of followers: his secretary Thomas Molini and three of his veteran officers (Downie, Campbell, and Roorbach), entered the City on Friday evening, January 1, 1808. Although weary and tired from such a long trip, they anxiously looked forward to that moment in which they would meet their families and friends. Moreover, they were also excited about their mission in Great Britain and the leadership role that they would play in the impending crusade for the liberation of Spanish America. The group separated; and Miranda and his secretary headed for the General's home in London. It was a holiday weekend, and he thoroughly enjoyed himself with his two handsome sons and their mother Sarah. Friends poured into Miranda's house to welcome him back to the City; even Sir Home Popham, was there to give him "the most minute accounts and details about the transaction at his arrival in Buenos Aires."[12] "We found the Country in a great ferment with the events, that lately have taken place on the Continent," he wrote to Hislop in Trinidad: "I could not have arrived in a more critical and favourable moment, for the object that brought me here. His Majesty's Ministers have received me with friendship and attention; listening to my affairs with interest and concern."[13] On January 5, 1808, he spent the afternoon with Lord Castlereagh discussing his project in detail. On the 7th, he wrote to Hislop, Rouvray, and Cochrane about his success in London. He told Admiral Cochrane that the British government's commitment was positive; just keep it to yourself and make your preparations "as we did agree at the moment of our separation in Tortola."[14] Mr. Alexander Davison, a key supplier of the materiel for the projected expedition, was pleased to learn that Vansittart was "to have the entire direction of the business." He trusted him; he was not a bureaucrat who meddled with private enterprise.[15]   After the January 5th meeting with Castlereagh, Miranda and his assistants collected and put together the documents and position papers required by the English government. The political section was finished by the 10th, the military part by the 16th. Vansittart made some suggestions for the final draft; and the completed document was that of a professional writer, namely James Mill.[16]

At the November, 1807, meeting in Tortola, Rouvray had given Miranda William Burke's address in London along with the information that a second treatise was almost ready for the press.   Such a manuscript could be a valuable reference in the negotiations with the British. Miranda assigned John Downie to locate Burke. It was a task relished by "Colonel" Downie. According to his friend Rouvray, there were two letters of his in Burke's impending manuscript.   The Frenchman, it seems, took the liberty of promoting Downie to the higher rank! When he learned that piece of information, he was a great admirer of "William Burke," whom he assumed was a fellow Scotsman! There is a strange development in Downie's subsequent mission to Edinburgh that deserves to be underscored: "Colonel" Downie never learned that "William Burke" was really James Mill!   Everyone involved went along with this fiction: Mill, Miranda, and J. Lowe, a fellow Scotsman who worked with James Mill in Miranda's propaganda venture with the London press.   We shall provide examples of the Downie deception at the appropriate place. Moreover, there is another point to keep in mind: Burke's *Additional Reasons* was in manuscript form at this time; it did not appear in the bookstores until February 18, 1808, when Miranda began the distribution of copies to friends and institutions outside of England.   These friends, as it turned out, published editions of the treatise in the United States, for example, and in Barbados, where Burke's first treatise was already known.

In Miranda's previous experience presenting memorials to the English government, the Venezuelan called upon friends like Thomas Pownall to edit, and thus improve, the presentation of his message. In Pownall's case, the improvement in style was not especially notable; but at least it overcame some of the awkward words or constructions that a foreigner might add to the English language. The January 10th political manuscript was a qualitative improvement, one that a professional writer could bring to a manuscript. It is my contention that James Mill utilized here a remarkable synthesis of his second manuscript "Additional Reasons," which he highlighted with rather strong words or clauses to impress the English reader. As a specialist in psychology, who reveled in appealing to every English prejudice or sentiment, Mill wrote like a clone of "William Burke." A few examples of his style and approach should stir the reader's memory of Burke's talents in writing the second treatise of 1808:

> The failure of this attempt was owning not only to the bad faith of the agents of the American Government, who betrayed the secret to our enemies, but to the infamous and treacherous conduct of the American officers, entrusted with the direction of the ships composing the expedition. (See Note C)
>
> The subsequent attempt upon the coast of Caraccas in the districts of Coro, in August, 1806, supported by some ships belonging to a squadron of the Windward Islands, under Sir Alexander Cochrane, with whom a formal stipulation in favour of Great Britain was agreed and signed, would have succeeded, if the commanders of the navy had not peremptorily refused to continue any operations whatever on that coast, and forced us to retire (see Note D), under the apprehension that the preliminaries of peace with France must have been signed by Lord Lauderdale at Paris by that period. By the evidence of those that were on the spot at that time, and by the intercepted correspondence from the principal agents of the Spanish Government in the province, it appears that the point of the coast was judiciously chosen; their own evidence says: 'The situation is the most advantageous of any that he could possibly have chosen on all the coasts, on account of the Peninsula of Paraguaná, where they may form a second Gibraltar, as long as they are masters of the sea; so that this spark of fire, which appeared nothing, may ultimately devour the Continent, if the English give him any assistance'—and that the distress of the Captain-General and Intendant, for want of money, was so great, that it forced them to adopt the odious and violent measure of seizing some of the sacred property of the Church, with all the deposited money belonging to the poor, the dead, etc.
>
> So that if Great Britain had given us a decided support of any kind, not only those provinces, but the rest of the Continent of South America, would have been now totally emancipated from the dominion of Spain.[17]

Even before his arrival in London, General Miranda had a strong feeling that Lord Melville would be a vital influence in a government controlled by Castlereagh. So Miranda brought with him a letter from

Admiral Alexander Cochrane to his friend Melville; and Miranda, once he learned that Melville was in Edinburgh, sent off a letter requesting him to recommend his project to Lord Castlereagh. An expedition of four or five thousand Englishmen would be adequate for the task. Lord Melville replied immediately to Captain D. Campbell, who met him at a party in Edinburgh. In early April, 1808, Melville was back in London where he conversed at great length with General Miranda on how the project should proceed. By then, he had written a preliminary recommendation to Castlereagh, which he expanded upon on June 8, 1808. Lord Melville's recommendation was most helpful to Miranda's project. The Scotsman had learned the historical lesson of Whitelocke's defeat in Buenos Aires and the mistaken assumptions upon which British policy had been based.[18]

Lord Melville's empathy for the nationalistic and cultural concerns of the insurgents in South America was not just historical insight and the intuition of a sensitive British statesman. It was also a sentiment, or an appreciation, that Miranda strove to cultivate among his most intimate English acquaintances. The General sensed that Melville would incorporate this feeling in his assessment of Miranda's movement. He purposely raised these points in the discussions with Melville in early April, 1808, to great advantage. He did likewise in his frequent interviews with Arthur Wellesley, who was expected to head the projected expedition to South America. The advice of the Peruvian Manuel Padilla would be crucial to Wellesley. Padilla had been vital in the final phases of Burke's second treatise, providing evidence of the alleged atrocities committed by Englishmen prior to Whitelocke's attack upon Buenos Aires. Mill brought Padilla to Miranda's attention as the propagator of those "Peruvian Manifests and the Publications from Buenos Aires," that had so alarmed the merchant Turnbull. Padilla, for example, supplied Wellesley with copies of those documents describing the English sack of a Catholic church in Colonia del Sacramento, a village located across the estuary from Buenos Aires. Wellesley wanted more information on the general comportment of British forces in the Plata and met with Padilla, who subsequently described the major points of the meeting with Arthur Wellesley.[19] Melville, it seems, learned of these details, which accounted for his great concern that the English adopt a mature stand vis a vis the psychology of South American revolutionaries.

It was in Melville's native Scotland that General Miranda and his emancipation project received a most enthusiastic welcome, according to the reports of his agents. At home with his family, Captain D. Campbell seized upon the first opportunity to interview Lord Melville, delivering into his hands Miranda's request for a recommendation to Lord Castlereagh. It was at a social function in Edinburgh that the exchange took place; and Melville provided the "oral reply" to Campbell that the Scotsman would write to Castlereagh in Miranda's behalf.[20] On January 28, 1808, Campbell attended a large party in Edinburgh, in which there were repeated toasts to "General Miranda" by the leaders of that gathering. And Captain Campbell was proud to have been identified as a veteran of the Coro campaign in Venezuela. In closing his letter, Campbell stressed that there would be no problem in recruiting five thousand Englishmen for the next expedition to America; and he hoped that General Miranda would not leave him behind on that occasion.[21]

Captain John Downie, a "Colonel" in Burke's second treatise, was Miranda's most active agent in Scotland; but he was not able to leave London until the latter part of February, 1808, because of the assignments in getting Miranda's project together for the English government. Once the General obtained copies of Burke's second treatise—that is, by February 18th—Downie received a special assignment in his native Scotland in connection with the recent publication. He gladly went off to Paisley, Scotland, to visit his family, a convenient base for his trips to nearby Glasgow and to Edinburgh. In his first dispatch (March 5th) to Miranda, Downie reported on his visit with Lord Melville, who was about to return to London. The controversial *Letters to Lord Melville* came up in their conversation; and Downie displayed a document that explained "the purity of your views in your Expedition to Coro, both in principle and structure." This pleased the Lord, who had suspected the publication's veracity. In that same letter, Downie informed his chief that the military people in Scotland were solidly behind his project."[22]

Downie's second letter (March 22nd) expanded upon the topic of Miranda's support in Scotland:

In this part of the Kingdom, the wish for the Immediate Emancipation of S.A., or some part of it, is most general, and this Spirit is so universal, and so warmly embraced, that if the Government were only to give any assurance of aid and assistance in the undertaking, there is a readiness here in the minds of the people to come forward in support of the thing, by a general Contribution of both Men and Money.

In fact, Downie insisted that in a few weeks he could raise a regiment of two thousand "North Britons" for service in the New World. These were not just commoners; many "young Gentlemen of the first Families" had applied to him, men "who are full of ardour in the cause." Merchants in Glasgow and Edinburgh were protesting "that you have been so long in Britain, without a force having been furnished to follow up your Plan." The cause for their concern was obvious: if new markets did not open up within the next few months, one half of "our Merchants" will be bankrupt. Just before ending the letter, Downie raised a point that very much concerned his general—that is, England's propensity to spread herself too thin on European incidents that might distract her from a genuine national interest—namely, the emancipation of Spanish America. "I find we are sending a Force to Sweden," he wrote to Miranda, "just as if we could prevent Bonaparte from what he chooses with that Country: this will be a finishing stroke to our folly on the Continent."[23] Miranda, of course, suspected this possibility; but he refused to believe, in 1808, that England could make the same type of mistake again!

In his next letters (April 8 and 15), Downie played on the same themes. Although he was relieved to learn that English troops were not going to Sweden, he added a postscript of a rumor in the papers that Great Britain had offered Gustavus of Sweden the position of Sovereign of South America! (April 8th). By then, he still had not received a reply from Miranda; and Scots were desperate for a chance to enlist in his forces. There were also men in His Majesty's Service who wanted to request future assignment in the New World, etc. Downie was sending Miranda a letter from Glasgow merchants, anxious to trade with South America. The people of Scotland were all behind General Miranda whose "Noble and enterprising views would put the fear of God into Bonaparte!"[24]

John Downie's mission to Scotland had propaganda as its prime objective: to spread the word about Miranda's impending expedition to South America. As instructed by his chief in London, Downie had articles placed in the press hailing William Burke's recent treatise and its all important message on why England needed to support the emancipation of Spanish America. As part of his assignment, Downie was to seek an interview with Francis Jeffrey, editor of the *Edinburgh Review*, presenting him with a copy of Burke's latest treatise, ostensibly for its listing in the next quarterly bibliography, where the first treatise had been included. It was also intended to arouse Jeffrey's interest in the recent negotiations between the popular General Miranda and Lord Castlereagh. Although the evidence is lacking, we can assume that Miranda wrote a personal letter to the editor, along the lines suggested to him by James Mill, who knew Jeffrey since he was his editor. In that letter, Miranda perhaps suggested the inclusion of an article in the *Edinburgh Review* persuading the English public to support their nation's moves in behalf of Spanish American emancipation. James Mill was willing to cooperate in such an article based on Miranda's voluminous documentation and the two treatises written by William Burke. This article would focus on the famous work of Father Viscardo de Guzmán's *Letter to the Spanish Americans*, a book published in the late 1790s under the aegis of Francisco de Miranda. The title might be "Emancipation of Spanish America." This was the proposal made to Editor Jeffrey, who received it favorably. Considering the theme's notoriety at that time, as well as its significance for a periodical in its sixth year of modern tenure, Jeffrey welcomed the Miranda-Mill article that appeared in January, 1809. A second one followed six months later, when it became evident that the Burkian message was too long for one book review.

Students of either Miranda or Mill have known of the article's joint authorship. Miranda seemed an obvious contributor to them; and they wisely assumed that Mill, his close friend, was the authorized reviewer. What is surprising, however, was their ignorance of the sequel article in July, 1809, considering the frequent references in it to the earlier one. The new book-instrument to be reviewed was the work of another Jesuit Father: Ignacio Molina, *The Geographical, Natural, and Civil History of Chili.* This was the same work that Miranda had given to President Jefferson in his visit to the United States.

Downie's letters to Miranda provide interesting clues to the reconstruction that we have offered above. Here are some fragments from the letters of May 3rd and 15th: "I have attended to what you say [said?] about Mr. Burke, and his Pamphlet . . . and will still do more by inserting extra in some of our newspapers." "I am much pleased with what is in the London Courier of the 23 April"—an issue that we shall treat in detail later—"every one have [here?] sees with Mr. Burke's eyes. I beg you to Present my best comp.s to him and to Mr. Lowe." May 15th: "While I am in Edinburgh, I will again see Reviewers about Mr. Burke's Pamphlet. I beg to be kindly remember'd to him and Mr. Lowe." The identification of the person with J. Lowe as "William Burke" appears in two letters.[25] J. Lowe lived at

31 Charter House Square in London, where he and James Mill often conferred with General Miranda. On April 17th, Lowe wrote to Miranda that he had placed an article in the *Morning Post*, assuming that other newspapers would copy it. Miranda acknowledged the note a few days later and thanked him for the propaganda piece in question. Miranda then remarked: "as a new factor, not to forget the copying or substance, of in the Papers under His direction." This last remark suggested that Lowe and Mill had a responsibilty for certain newspapers in London—an interesting insight into Miranda's propaganda team in the City. Lowe also seemed to have a connection with the Murray group that published the *Annual Register.*[26]

General Miranda had good reason to be satisfied with Downie's mission in Scotland and he passed on the information of his good fortune in Europe to his friends in the Caribbean, especially to Admiral Cochrane and Governor Hislop. Thanks to these letters we have a fair barometer of the General's reactions to events in London. In January and February, 1808, his tone was still sanguine, perhaps because he wanted to believe all the good things that were coming his way. James Mill's intellect on his side was indeed comforting and even inspirational. It was the beginning of a long and fiercely loyal friendship between the two men. We suspect that Miranda was not able to add much to Burke's second treatise, just a few bibliographical items. Rouvray had done most of the work on the expedition of 1806. When *Additional Reasons* came off the press, Miranda immediately notified his two colleagues at Trinidad and Barbados. He told Cochrane, the publication was finally out: "shew it to de Rouvray and give him my compliments." It was his way of saying: "Thank you, Count, for your effort in carrying out this key assignment of your mission to England." To Hislop, he wrote: "The enclosed Pamphlet about South America is just come out; and the Public is reading it with interest."[27] Vansittart, in mid-April, 1808, asked Miranda for a copy of Burke's new treatise in order to counteract some "misrepresentations" he had heard to the effect that the Coro enterprise of 1806 was mere pillage. With both of Burke's works in his hands, he stopped the rumor in its tracks. Yet, he wondered how the "falsehood" originated and if Castlereagh had heard it.[28] Politics were in the air and there were men in government—Edward Cooke, for example, who wasted no love on Miranda. The problem, it seems, was the lack of executive leadership under the Duke of Portland's premiership. The government appeared to be in Lord Castlereagh's hands; and he hesitated, under the circumstances, to take decisive action.

General Miranda hoped that Lord Wellesley, brother of his friend Arthur Wellesley, would take over as prime minister and put Lord Melville in charge of the Admiralty, considering the apparent victory in Parliament on the evening of March 15th. Both men were well-informed on the "Colombian Continent" and would bring Miranda's project "to a head, especially as Whitelocke's trial was coming to an end." On this last point, Miranda reminded Admiral Cochrane of what he had said on the *Northumberland* in November, 1807. His prediction, Miranda noted proudly "was rather Prophetical."[29] In a letter to Rouvray, the General boasted that Whitelocke's case "has opened the eyes of the world" and, as a result, "has pushed our project forward again."[30]

In a restricted, or *secret* letter to Cochrane, Miranda told him that he had forwarded to Governor Hislop some secret documents about the Island of Trinidad and the Province of Caracas. These were documents that ex-Governor Picton, the first British executive on Trinidad in 1797, had allowed him to copy. These key documents, insofar as they reflected "the intentions and declarations of H.M. Ministers, so long ago as the year 1797 promising support, assistance and Independency to the said provinces. In fact, they go a great deal further than you and me ever thought." The General felt strongly that "Picton had no right to take such documents with him; it was unfair to Governor Hislop, depriving him and other commanding officers of His Majesty's Service of information they needed to have. It was improper, unjust, and injurious to the service."[31]

* * * * * * * * * * * *

Despite the overwhelming success of General Miranda upon his return to Great Britain in 1808, and his popularity in Scotland, he could not erase from his own mind Britain's vulnerability to Europe's system of power. He reluctantly, as we have noted in his correspondence with Downie, refused to believe that England would intervene in Sweden. Yet, it was in the southern most areas of Europe (Spain and Portugal) that a threat to his plans was about to materialize. In late 1807, Portugal, England's natural ally over the centuries, fell to Napoleon's forces. Fortunately, the British were able to convoy the Portuguese court to a new base in Brazil. Napoleon moved into Portugal to stop all leaks in his "Continental Boycott" of English manufactures. Would Bonaparte now turn against his ally Spain, removing the Bourbon monarchs and placing a relative of his on the Spanish throne? The recent events of March 19th at Aranjuez and Madrid seemed to announce the path of the future. By mid-April, Miranda knew conclusively that the "Spanish Revolution" against France was a stark reality! How would Great Britain face the new situation in Spain? Vansittart replied to Miranda's news on April 20; returning to London immediately to confer with him. They met on Friday, the 22nd, at 11:00 a.m.[32]

The decision arrived at by the two colleagues, and others that might have joined them, came out on April 23, 1808, in an editorial of the *Courier*. The controlling parties of that London newspaper were highly sympathetic to Miranda's project and its economic significance for England. Moreover, Miranda wasted no time in notifying Admiral Cochrane about the editorial "Our Future Conduct" on April 23rd in that paper. It revealed "what the future views and Plans of the present government actually are."[33] John Downie, it will be recalled, attributed the article to William Burke. Was Miranda the source for this insight, or was Downie just guessing? We do not know. The lines below contain telltale marks of a "William Burke" but not the pacifist—rather, the hard-nosed realist and imperialist. Here is how the April 23rd editorial opened its argument:

> Since it is at present in vain to attempt chocking the power of France on the Continent of Europe, this country should turn its whole thoughts and exertions to the creation of new connexions, new points of commerce, and new sources of wealth, with which to supply the place of those we are daily losing, and to counterpoise the increasing preponderance of the enemy. If France has acquired dominion over the Continent of Europe, England possesses the undisputed sovereignty of the seas in all parts of the world; and, if this country can establish herself in security against invasion, this state of things, so far from circumscribing her empire, may be the means of extending it, and exalting her in greatness under a wise and vigorous Government . . . The shores of the ocean have been at all times the birthplace of civilization and the arts, of wealth and of power. With these under our dominion, it may truly be said, 'the Trident of Neptune is the sceptre of the world' . . . Commanding the seas, nations must become our tributaries, or fall into sloth, poverty, and barbarism. The law of nations

must be made binding on France and her vessels, if England is to be bound by it; but while France tramples it under foot as convenience requires, we must do the same, or the law of nations will become our most dangerous enemy . . . If Bonaparte will become Emperor of Europe, the King of England should declare himself Emperor of the Ocean. We have as much right to the one as he has to the other, the right of conquest. It is only by a proud tone, and an assuming conduct that we can make the world feel our strength, and demonstrate our own confidence in its efficacy. It is not a question of right or wrong, but a question of power, that is to be decided. If we hesitate or compromise, we are gone.

The next statement revealed a common point that Miranda's writers would be making in the future, time and time again:

The great fault of which this Country has hitherto been guilty is, that instead of availing itself of its own means of attack against the most eligible points, it waits the attack of France, and then flies to render assistance against her. France generally has been left to choose the object of contest, the scene of struggle. We look on at her, watching what quarter she will next assail, and then we prepare to frustrate her designs, often when its too late. . . With so much disposable force, such an unexampled invincible navy as we possess, our main efforts should be directed toward, the dominions of Spain, in America, and India. To attempt the conquest of them is at once the most difficult, the most expensive, and the least secure course. Independence and alliance should be held out to them. Had this course been taken two years ago, the countries on the River Plate, Lima, the Caraccas, the whole of South America, would now have been in a state of friendship and close intercourse with us, consuming more of our manufactures, and employing more of our marine, than the present situation of the Continent of Europe, has affected.

The editorialist likewise attacked the misguided diplomatic tactics of governmental leaders in Europe. Referring to the mistakes made in the Plata area, he wrote:

They then sent out large armaments to conquer a place they had declared their readiness to relinquish on the first occasion, and the people of Buenos Ayres very naturally resolved to resist us rather than become an article of barter in another Negotiation. It is indeed a mischievous fault in all our Statesmen, that they take places in war with no other design than to surrender them as the price of peace. As a price of peace this may be well enough; but let us enquire into the ruin of character which it brings upon us. We rarely take a place in which there are not some considerable persons, perhaps considerable number, who do not favour our attack, or cordially receive and join with us when we have conquered. When the place is restored these persons are persecuted and ruined. By the repeated capture and surrender of Minorca, we have ruined our character in the Mediterranean, and by similar means have we lost all confidence in the enemy's colonies in the East and West Indies. Bonaparte, on the contrary, never gives up any people he has once taken under his protection, and hence the facility he finds in new modelling different States. The people of Buenos Aires, therefore, very naturally and very wisely, desired a permanent connection or none. In this respect, we should meet Bonaparte on his own way. In his negotiations he talks of the Kings of Holland, Spain, Wirtenberg, Bavaria, etc. as independent Sovereigns, his allies, of whom he cannot dispose, and to whom he cannot dictate. Were we to erect Buenos Ayres, Mexico, the Caraccas, Cuba, etc. into independent States, our allies, we might talk to Bonaparte in his own language. Instead of a long altercation about surrendering those places, we should have no negotiations respecting them. They could be our allies for whom to stipulate, not Colonies of whom to make a barter, and we should derive all the advantage of Colonies from the connection with them (except that of providing for the dependents of factions and rotten boroughmongers) without risk or expence. Our intercourse with the United States shews, that we may derive more benefit from trading with an Ally than with a Colony. The spirit of industry, the encouragement to enterprise is much stronger in one case than in the other. Colonists are confined in their industry; the sterility of slavery is in a degree spread over their country. Independence gives them a new impulse of action, which operates with great force, as the United States of America have shewn. Were we to declare countries independent and assist them in throwing off the yoke of our enemy, all the islands in the world would of necessity put themselves under our protection, and we should have in effect, though not in name, but one Colony from Hudson's Bay to Cape Horn. No great military or naval force would be necessary to effect all this; it would only be necessary to remain faithful to our engagements; and instead of feeling a loss of trade with the Continent of Europe, we should find trade, wealth, and maritime greatness beyond the dreams even of the most sanguine, far eclipsing France both in power and splendour. The time for the achievement of these great objects is fast passing away forever. France is possessing herself of Spain, and through Spain, will possess herself of the Spanish Colonies, to which she can spare an abundance of troops. Let us then no longer hear of dozens of Expeditions sailing from our coasts at once. . .let us see one great expedition going forth, four times as strong as is supposed to be necessary, thereby insuring success, and passing from place to place, emancipating countries from the yoke of our enemies, thus raising up a new world of friends to supply the place of the ones we have lost.[34]

Two years later, on June 23, 1810, the *Courier* again favored the liberation of Spanish America.[35]

The British Government responded aggressively to the clarion call in the *Courier's* April 23rd editorial: Napoleon had to be stopped and Spanish America should not be permitted to fall into his hands. This was exactly the response expected by Miranda and Vansittart. The editorial awakened British officials to the urgency of putting the final touches on Miranda's January project to emancipate South America. There could be no further delays. Full speed ahead in the month of May, 1808, as the French implemented their takeover of Spain in the usual manner. At Arthur Wellesley's request, Miranda met with him on May 4th. He brightened noticeably when General Wellesley informed him of the Government's decision to go ahead on his project. The decision was "according to our wishes," Miranda wrote jubilantly to Admiral Cochrane on May 5th. On that same day, he wrote to Rouvray promising to see him soon, as if a miracle was in the wind! In the meantime, he urged his friends to maintain secrecy.[36]

Thanks to the excellent, and detailed account of Professor William S. Robertson, we may dwell here on the general developments, emphasizing Miranda's thoughts about them. Although he was sanguine about his friend Wellesley's remarks on May 4th, the decision was not that clearcut. On the contrary, from the start there was a question whether the British should move first into Spain, or whether they should proceed with haste to the New World. In short, the ministers thought in terms of a "European" or an "American" thrust. General Wellesley, who it was assumed would be the supreme leader of the project, felt that the American invasion should have priority because of the preparations already taken since the return of General Miranda in early 1808. The ministers thus gave him the green light that preceded the interview of May 4th.[37] Preparations continued to send off eight thousand British troops to the Irish coast in the vicinity of Cork to await General Wellesley's arrival with the final orders to sail for the West Indies. In the meantime, however, another force of five thousand troops under a General Spencer was assigned to the Spanish coast, presumably to be used in Spain if it appeared that there was a significant determination on the part of the Spaniards to resist the French. This was, of course, a big "if," since it seemed more likely that Spaniards would follow the usual pattern in Europe of welcoming the French invaders. By June 6th, the favored, "American Thrust" was ready to proceed, along with potential plans for a West Indian option accompanying the major thrust into northern South America, all of which capitalized on Miranda's presence and influence in that area. In the meantime, there were heated deliberations between the two camps. Finally, it was agreed that the British troops bivouacked on the Irish coast should join General Spencer's force off the coast of Spain. If Spencer succeeded in his Spanish mission, then the entire effort would concentrate on the "European thrust" until a new decision were made concerning the effort in the New World. If Spencer's effort was fruitless, then all forces would proceed to the West Indies—Spencer's five thousand men with Wellesley's eight thousand from Cork.

For a man in his late fifties, with years of experiencing many highs and lows in his relations with the English Government, it is surprising that Francisco de Miranda could possibly think that this time it would be different. There was no question that he had the utmost faith in his friend Arthur Wellesley; and Miranda worked hard in stockpiling the materials needed for the South American project. In his moments away from work, his rational mind remembered his past failures in Britain. The April 23rd editorial had noted the British quirk of reacting instantaneously to Bonaparte's moves; could they be distracted now by the hopeless quagmire in Spain and thus abandon their true national interest in the emancipation of Spanish America? That would be a crime. The English could not be that irresponsible! The days passed. What was causing this delay? Perhaps he should write a letter to Lord Castlereagh, which he did on May 16, 1808, hoping that it would obviate the delay.[38] It was a pathetic letter; it was also a futile gesture, as it turned out.

The "late eventful occurrences in Spain," mentioned by Miranda in his letter to Castlereagh had reached the crisis stage by May 26th when he described them as the "late awful events" to Spencer Perceval and George Canning, the Chancellor of the Exchequer and the Secretary of Foreign affairs respectively. Miranda informed them that on May 2, 1808, the aroused people of Madrid attacked the hated French invaders with a ferocity and passion that shook the imagination of all Europe—a moment in history which Francisco de Goya, fortunately, captured on canvas for posterity, along with the fusillades of brave *Madrileños* on the following day. The famous *Dos de Mayo* (May 2nd) marked the beginning of Spain's "War of Independence" from France, also known as the "Peninsular War" in European annals. By May 8th, Napoleon had taken over the throne of Spain. It was his to give to his brother Joseph, a few months later. Thus ended the series of "awful events" depicted in the *Courier's* account of the "Spanish Revolution" on May 21, 1808. Enclosing a copy of the *Courier* selection in a letter of the 25th to Arthur Wellesley, Miranda promised to go to his office on the following day—an interview in which the two friends, it seems, agreed to insist upon the immediate action by the British Cabinet.[39] Miranda's letter to Castlereagh of May 16th would serve as the model for new ones to Perceval and Canning, demanding immediate action to save South America and England. These were appeals written by Miranda himself on May 26th. Canning chose not to answer his letter until June 18th, and then it was a curt reply that reflected some annoyance at the Venezuelan. Miranda received little satisfaction for his efforts in late May, 1808.

At five o'clock Saturday evening, May 28th, General Miranda attended a dinner with three English military officers. After a hectic and stressful week in trying desperately to convince the English government that any further delay would be suicidal, Miranda was exhausted, suspicious that perhaps another jolt from the English ally might be in the offing. It depressed him. When he got home that night he wrote in his diary that he had met the generals Loftus and Courtenay. There was a great deal of discussion about Buenos Aires and about "our America." The note in his diary ended with these words: "*Enemigos siempre de su independencia*" (Always enemies of her independence), followed by two exclamation points!![40]

The "late awful events" on the Peninsula stirred a violent nationalist reaction throughout the Spanish provinces. Regional *juntas* gathered to organize and arm their people for the bloody contest that faced them against Europe's best fighters. The notion of a united confederacy of these provinces was instantaneous; and its principal inspiration was the junta that gathered in Oviedo, Asturias, on May 24th. It seemed to have assurances from León and Galicia of cooperation in a common resistance movement against the French. It was agreed at Oviedo that two agents proceed to London to announce to King George III that Asturias had declared war on France and wanted the English nation to provide them with all the arms and munitions needed in Asturias, as

well as all the other interior juntas of Spain. A British warship on the
Cantabrian coast would also bolster the resistance movement. The two
Asturian agents moved swiftly northward to Gijón, boarding an English
privateer that carried them to Falmouth, where an English naval officer
guided them on the long journey to London. Early in the morning, on
June 8, 1808, the Asturians presented their case to George Canning,
head of the Foreign Office. The British, with little delay, accepted the
Asturian request. The leaders of the "European Thrust" were in
complete command of the situation. They could argue that British
intervention in Spain would only be temporary. If it failed—that is, if
the Spanish resistance faltered against Napoleon's forces—then England
could move to the "American Thrust," in order to save the Spanish
colonies. On June 9th, the Asturians presented their petition as
requested by Canning; and on the 10th, *The Times* reported that the
British forces at Cork, Ireland, were proceeding not to Venezuela but
to Spain![41]

Francisco de Miranda and his followers, as might be expected, were
at a loss to explain in rational terms this crucial decision to engage
once again the indomitable forces of Napoleon Bonaparte on the
Continent, especially within a week of a previous decision to lock horns
with the enemy in the West Indies, where the chances of success were
on the British side. It is doubtful that General Arthur Wellesley agreed
with the decision in favor of the "European Thrust," at this time.
Suspecting that they might prevail, he persuaded his old friend
Castlereagh to initiate the West Indian instructions on June 4th. But
that did not at all alter the final decision taken on Asturias; the orders
to Jamaica had to be rescinded.

Just when the Asturians were meeting with Canning, on June 9th,
Wellesley and Miranda had their own meeting to discuss the situation.
Miranda was disappointed, of course, but not shocked—it was an
English pattern that he knew only too well. The British decision to
join the Spanish guerrillas was not at all wise. As Sir Arthur knew
only too well, the resistance movements had not amounted to much in
Europe against Napoleon's forces. The French nemesis was a master
at tricking, or convincing the "people" to join his revolutionary crusade
in Europe. Spaniards would perhaps be much more successful than
other Europeans. After all, it was the "Asturi" and the "Cantabri" who
held up the Roman Conquest of the Peninsula for centuries and
tormented the Roman legionnaires with their fierce attacks. But that
was centuries ago! In the "modern" warfare of the nineteenth century,

the fighting was different, more scientific; and logistics were a serious difficulty in campaigns, etc. Miranda refused his friend's offer to join the English in the Spanish invasion. He simply could not do it; it was a point that he made clear to Pitt and others. He could only serve with the British in the liberation of Spanish America. He wished Sir Arthur the best of luck; and when the British recognized the futility of their decision, then perhaps they would return to the "American Thrust" without any further interruption. He honestly felt that the British intervention in Spain would not last more than a few months. There is no question that the future "Duke of Wellington" appreciated Miranda's logic and comments; for the next few years, whenever he returned from the Peninsular wars, he was forever asking him for advice about certain Spanish leaders and the obstacles that the English faced constantly in Spain, even those caused by their own ally.

And yet, even Sir Arthur, twenty seven years later, embroidered the historical cloth to satisfy a public that lionized him as the great military hero of the "Peninsular War," the Duke of Wellington. He described his meeting with Miranda on June 9, 1808, as follows:

> I think I never had a more difficult business than when the Government bade me tell Miranda that we would have nothing to do with his plan. I thought it best to walk out in the streets with him and tell him there, to prevent his bursting out. But even there he was so loud and angry, that I told him I would walk on first a little that we might not attract the notice of everybody passing. When I joined him again he was cooler. He said: 'You are going over into Spain. . .you will be lost—nothing can save you; that, however, is your affair; but what grieves me that there never was such an opportunity thrown away!'[42]

Whatever the merits of the British decision to ally themselves with the Spaniards, the die was cast by June 9, 1808. The implementation followed soon thereafter. Moreover, it was a momentuous decision in world history, for the Old and the New.

* * * * * * * * * * * *

General Miranda renewed old friendships when he returned to London early in 1808. He had much to say to Jeremy Bentham, whose relationship with the Venezuelan we shall discuss in our next chapter, and with the somewhat eccentric personality of Dr. William Thomson.

He was the British historian who applied the simile of Scipio Africanus to Francisco de Miranda, much to the latter's embarrassment. He was still grateful for Miranda's contribution to the second edition of his *Military Memoirs*. The relationship between the two men was even closer now and would yield some interesting strength to General Miranda's future propaganda activities in England. To begin with, Dr. Thomson provided a convenient vent for Miranda's bitterness and disappointment toward the British government. The intellectual exchange with this prolific writer was pleasant and stimulating, despite Miranda's occasional irritation at his friend's innate chauvinism. Dr. Thomson had writing projects galore—it was his life! He was forever asking Miranda questions about certain events, personages, and what-have-you concerning the Hispanic past: What books did he have on Philip II's reign? How would he assess the role of the Jesuits in Spain and her colonies? This curious Englishman, moreover, would start to write at a moment's notice! He had a trunk full of Miranda's books, always accompanied with exact lists of his borrowings from his friend's extensive holdings. James Mill followed this pattern of the trunk, but the difference was significant since he was writing projects *for* Miranda.

Dr. Thomson, moreover, was an expert flatterer; he was, forever, calling Miranda his "Mentor," etc., etc., etc.[43] He also strained to keep Miranda in a good mood, especially in the moment of crisis that he had experienced recently. "It was madness," he wrote on July 14, 1808, "to think of forming any lasting connection between South America and Britain otherwise than by the Emancipation of the Spanish Colonies." It was his way of saying: "I have just read Burke's second treatise that you loaned me recently." Thomson added: "All that could be done by the bravest, ablest, and wisest General was performed by General Beresford. Had General Whitelocke displayed the same talents and virtues Buenos Ayres might indeed have been retaken but not long preserved." Those last four words immediately covered his conclusion! Again, he was paraphrasing Burke. Then, he added some insights on an article he was preparing for the *Annual Register* and which Miranda had seen in draft form:

> Bye the bye, I have had for sometime past an opportunity of being most thoroughly convinced that General Beresford's merit had most injuriously been thrown into the shade by the vain Braggadocios of Sir Home Popham—though his own conduct was, in various respects, most reprehensible.

He knew, of course, that Miranda shared the same view! At this point, the old military historian turned to the Spanish situation, making these comments:

> You are my Master in the Art of war—Yet I will give my opinion of the present Great Conflict. As the Spaniards, including the Portuguese, possess a large and strong country and through the Alliance of Britain, the Command of a most extensive sea coast, by which means they can receive, from time to time, supplies of all kind; they will undoubtedly prevail.

"It is as much their interest to gain time, and to avoid a decisive action, as it is for Bonaparte to precipitate operations and to bring the contest to an immediate issue," he continued. "I do not know how the present aspect of affairs bears upon your grand design," he concluded, "But the fall of Bonaparte is at all events to be wished for by Europe." An imaginative strategy in Spain against the French might be successful after all—a conclusion that a demoralized Miranda did not wish to envision at this time.[44]

He felt compelled to lecture his friend as follows:

> I most heartily join you in wishing for the delivery of Europe, and for the re-establishment of its former independency; but it avails very little to the fate of mankind what your wishes or mine may be. It is the wisdom and conduct of those that are at the head and government of nations, that must produce those salutary effects. I am sorry to say that I do not see any change in their plans, views, or actions. The same selfish designs, illiberality, and duplicity, it appears to me, pervades most of them. For which reason, instead of any beneficial results, I am afraid we shall have mischief and calamities extended beyond the European Hemisphere and over the New World. The exertion in some of the Spanish provinces appear to me the work of fanaticism and disappointment, rather than patriotic views and designs of independency or freedom. Therefore, my hopes on this point are less sanguine than yours.

The General's lecture then turned to Platine matters. He noted:

> I have seen the greatest part of your manuscript upon General Beresford's conduct and justification at Buenos Aires. I have seen also numerous documents relative to the same subject communicated to me by a gentleman of the country [Manuel Padilla] that was chiefly

concerned in all those high transactions; from which I conclude much as you do, giving some credit to B. for his moderation while he commanded and much blame to the other [Sir Home Popham] for his sordid, selfish, and illiberal views which were the source of the incalculable mischief that followed afterwards, and that will be transcendant, yet I am afraid, against the real interest of England as well as South America. Whitelocke's instructions appear to me to be the result of the erroneous information transmitted to this country by the Chief of the Expedition and other mercantile adventurers, that consulted more their private interests (as they commonly do) than the benefit of this country or any other people upon earth! I sincerely believe that any officer or chief sent to that country with the same ridiculous and impolitical instructions, will come ultimately to the same result.[45]

Dr. Thomson received the General's comments with deep understanding. "It is still considerations of temporary expediency, the interest of Courts, that prevail—political, not moral principles."

Thomson's letter of July 19, 1808, informed Miranda of the savant's connection with the *Annual Register*, the most widely read periodical in London. According to the military expert, he had been a major force in reestablishing the periodical's reputation from 1791 to 1801. In that final year, however, he had to resign his editorial post when a new group of booksellers and tradesmen gained the ascendancy, preferring to accept the overtures of key politicians. "Politics" prevailed everywhere! Now, the power situation had changed again, and "the party, among the booksellers who protested against breaking faith with me has become a decided majority." Thus, Thomson opted to resume his duties on the *Annual Register* in early 1808, responsible for the next annual publication covering the year 1807. William Thomson's reappointment to the *Annual Register* in 1808 meant that the coverage of Hispanic events for 1807 would be favorable to the emancipation throughout Spanish America, thanks to Miranda's role as a consultant for his old friend Thomson.[46]

The opportunity was at hand—and Miranda wasted no time in capitalizing on it—to correct in the *Annual Register* the misinformation that was circulating in London concerning Miranda's expedition of 1806 to Venezuela. As the works of William Sherman and James Biggs came into the world market, and especially Bigg's English edition in early 1809, the reading public received a decidedly unfavorable image of General Miranda. Miranda was furious when he learned that the *Annual Register* of 1806 likewise shared in the distortion! It was an account in a "pseudo" journal, written by Dr. Thomson's predecessors in 1807, that only "an infernal imposter could ever devise!"[47] Needless to say, friend Thomson was asked to correct this travesty in the writing of history. He worked countless hours, in a state of anguish, to please his beloved "Mentor." Thus the publication of the 1807 "History" was delayed until December, 1808. With uncommon patience, Thomson persevered. He took advantage of, as he put it quaintly, "a natural opportunity of indulging though briefly, in some retrospective Glories."[48] With these corrective sections—all in a retrospective mood, of course—Thomson altered favorably the 1806 record of the Miranda expedition, as well as the Beresford-Popham invasion: now General B. was the "hero" and Sir Home, the "villain." General Miranda was ecstatic at his friend's accomplishments. He assured his correspondents that this version of his 1806 expedition was the "Language of History." By rights, Miranda should have given James Mill some credit, since the corrected version followed the Burkian second treatise almost to the letter. Nevertheless, it brought "high satisfaction" to James Mill that the 1807 "history" would effectively counter the distortions of Biggs and company. In a footnote on page 45, the readers of the *Annual Register* were urged to consult three references for "the principal facts authenticated"; first, the "Additional Reasons" of William Burke; second, the *Edinburgh Review* of January, 1809; and third, the *Monthly Review* of March, 1809—all three of which were primarily the creation of James Mill, in collaboration with Francisco de Miranda. Thomson's corrected account, as a separate pamphlet, or reprint, carried this title: *THE ANNUAL REGISTER OR A VIEW OF THE HISTORY OF POLITICS AND LITERATURE FOR THE YEAR 1807.*[49]

Miranda, the propagandist, circulated copies of this publication in English and Spanish to leading periodicals and institutions. He also sent them to friends in the United States and Spanish America where it was reproduced for local constituencies. Thus, the Venezuelan agent received the maximum coverage for his "Language of History."[50]

* * * * * * * * * * * *

After the emotional meeting of June 9th with Sir Arthur Wellesley, General Miranda found himself more and more isolated from the British Government. It gave Francisco de Miranda more time to think. In his sanguine moments, he convinced himself that the British effort in Spain would fail within a few months; then, all would be well again as the

English could turn to the "American Thrust" plan. The present set back was only temporary, as Sir Arthur had insinuated. Yet, how could he be so naive and gullible, in light of his twenty-odd years' experience with the governmental leaders of Great Britain? The naked reality was that Americans like himself were engaged in a bald deception. Egotistical Europeans, in their own minds, still wanted to be the masters of colonies in America; they had no sincere convictions in behalf of liberation movements to bring representative government to Americans. One of his greatest errors was the assumption that Spanish America, somehow or another, would follow the northern pattern by which European powers like France and Spain gave vital, indeed, indispensable support to English colonists. In the context of the Napoleonic Wars, it seemed that Great Britain, especially when she was cut off from Continental markets, had a strong enough motive to liberate Spanish America and to preempt for herself the new markets that would help her withstand Napoleon's threats in Europe. Yet, the notions of "Conquest" and "Monopoly" were too engrained in the European's psyche; and the loss of their European colonies was still a traumatic and unbearable legacy that tormented many British leaders. To support the liberation of other "colonists" from Spanish and Portuguese America was not a palatable task, devoid, as it was, of any real sincerity. Miranda's long experience with Englishmen made him appreciate that not all Englishmen fit that mould—Thomas Pownall, Alexander Cochrane, Jeremy Bentham, and James Mill, only to name a few. Nevertheless, in these months of retrospection and deep thought, General Miranda arrived at the conclusion that Spanish Americans, in the last analysis, had to direct the independence movement on their own, utilizing outside help whenever it was opportune. It was a serious mistake, however, *to count too heavily upon* the assistance—in fact, the leadership—of Great Britain. Such a dependency was unstable, as well as degrading; indeed, it might even harm the national objectives of Hispanic nations.

These sobering thoughts in the three months since the Wellesley meeting of June 9th were often recorded in moments of bitterness. Yet, they were fundamental in the formation of a new program, or policy, that slowly took shape in the Precursor's mind. On September 9, 1808, in a letter to Admiral Cochrane, Miranda outlined a position that has been called the "Mask of Ferdinand" in the historiography of the Hispanic-American Wars of Independence:

I do not believe that the Spanish Patriots, though defending a Right Cause with enthusiasm and zeal will be able to resist the prompt and most vigorous attacks that France may bring against them in support of her nefarious views and ambitious Plans of conquest. In this supposition I thought that the safest Plan for us to pursue was of simple Independence in the first instance, leaving the Question of sovereignty or form of Government for a future Period—in this mode **WE MIGHT IMMEDIATELY SEPARATE THE CONTINENT FROM ANY CONNECTION WITH FRANCE AND KEEP THE PROVINCES UNITED; FOR THE PURPOSE OF INTRODUCING AFTERWARDS WITH CALM AND UNANIMITY, THE FORM OF GOVERNMENT THAT MIGHT BE DEEMED MOST PRACTICABLE AND SAFE; WITHOUT RUNNING THE CHANCE OF HAVING DISUNION AND DISSENTION SPREAD IN SUCH AN EXTENSIVE COUNTRY, INHABITED BY SUCH AN HETEROGENEOUS MASS OF THE PEOPLE.** We must, however, act according to circumstances and without looking to past errors that are of no avail.[51]

To be sure, the "Mask of Ferdinand" was characterized by a "wait and see" approach by Spanish Americans before taking a final step toward independence in an given area; and Miranda explains why it would be expedient to follow such a policy. The loyalty expressed toward Ferdinand VII was popular and traditional: he was, after all, a prisoner of the hated tyrant Napoleon; and the masses were smitten with his image. He was a symbol of unity and harmony in a part of the globe that had so many discordant elements of race, culture, language, etc. Miranda wasted no love on Ferdinand; but that was beside the point. The Venezuelan preferred the Inca symbol; but his primary objective, after all, was to unite his people in this crucial moment of the Independence process, so that the future experiment in freedom and government might have time to form stable roots. Spanish American leaders appreciated the advantages of Miranda's logic.

Instead of the General's "Retirement" after Britain's decision to join Spain—the standard characterization about his career in those three months—he actually experienced a "Rebirth" that would fix his title as "Precursor" of Spanish-American Independence. In the following pages, we might conclude that "Primemover" might have been more accurate for that "Quijote" in that golden crusade of Spanish-American history!

Let us examine now the nature and the consequences of that audacious program that Francisco de Miranda created in a short period

after what seemed to be an apparent fiasco in his career. The telltale
marks of Miranda's initiative were soon evident throughout Spanish
America; in fact, it even touched Portuguese-speaking Brazil, where
Miranda had correspondents and agents familiar with his program and
ideas. Without Miranda's vast experience in the councils of the British
Government, the program outlined perhaps would not have gotten off
the ground. There was no question that James Mill and Thomas
Molini, Miranda's personal secretary, were vital factors in the
documentary collection that the program entailed—Molini as the
bibliographer and translator and Mill as the editor. Yet, the real genius
behind the program was Francisco de Miranda himself; he was the one
who took the risks and guided the program to its propaganda victories
in 1810.

From July 20th to October 6, 1808, General Francisco de Miranda
directed what might be called a "Paper Assault" upon the Empire of
Spain, ally of Great Britain. It produced a "library" of revolutionary
materials that became available to all parts of Spanish America,
determining tactics and the ideology of the "Wars of Independence."
The September 9th declaration of this campaign explains the motives
for this plan to his good friend Admiral Alexander Cochrane and the
latter cooperated in its implementation, at least until the British
Government, urged on by the Spaniards' cry of a "Conspiracy," took
steps to arrest its course. There are letters in July, September, and
October that record the "Precursor's" efforts in favor of Emancipation.
They were dispatched throughout Spanish America, along with their
enclosures. The British mail service, moreover, thanks to the Admiral,
delivered the letters to their destination.

On July 20, 1808, to begin with, he wrote a letter to the Municipal
Corporation (*Cabildo*) of Caracas, with a copy of it and its enclosures,
to a key Executive official—to assure the safe arrival of at least one
version of the original. To encourage the spread of these messages,
copies of the Venezuelan materials also went to the Cabildo of Buenos
Aires and to their key officials. On July 24th, Miranda wrote to the
Municipality of Buenos Aires a different letter with its own enclosures,
as well as duplicates to a key official in the Río de la Plata. The
Platine correspondence was also sent to Caracas.[52] Miranda, in addition
encouraged the duplication of materials sent to Caracas and Buenos
Aires among their neighboring kingdoms—Santa Fe de Bogotá and
Quito in the first case, and Peru, Chile, and Quito, in the latter. In
early September, Mexico City and Habana, Cuba, received letters from

the "Precursor," following the same procedure and receiving copies of the materials sent to Caracas and Buenos Aires earlier. In return, these South American cities received the Mexican-Cuban materials. The "Paper Assault," in short, reached all of Spanish America.[53] Admiral Cochrane and Governor Hislop were asked to aid the process by delivering the mail to its destination, receiving replies from Spanish America, and arranging for passage of American deputies to London. Clever and carefully worded letters to those British officials facilitated the exchange of correspondence in the initial phase of the "Assault." And, a cover letter to Lord Castlereagh cleverly protected Miranda's flanks.[54] It was an audacious venture but well worth the effort for a man facing the most serious crisis in his career.

The Caracas and Buenos Aires letters were intended to complement each other—they avoided repetition and thus added more material for each area. In the Venezuelan message, Miranda emphasized that Spain was "without a Sovereign" and Civil War on the Peninsula was between factions loyal to the French or to the English; these factions, advancing their selfish interests, aimed to involve the Americans "in a general dissension," thus minimizing their risks. "In the event of being subjected by France (which is the most probable result, although the least desired one)," Miranda added , they could "thus transfer to the Colombian Continent the same calamities, which because of their lack of prudence, or excess of bad conduct they had brought upon the unfortunate, oppressive, and corrupt Spain!" If this were the case, Miranda recommended the formation of "a municipal representative body," taking charge of the provincial government. Then, without delay, they should send to London their best people to discuss with the British the principal steps to take "for the security and future fate of the New World!" The following advice came from the authorized English translation of the letter:

> Your Lordships should on no account yield to the suggestions of interested Parties, and rashly adopt measures or offensive Alliances, that may bring upon our Country the same fatal consequences that the *Governors of Spain* have brought on their own, without having even consulted, or offered to us the least advantage in their vain and foolish Projects concerted with the other Powers of Europe! One thing however is evident; the views and interests of the present *Juntas of Oviedo, Sevilla, Madrid, etc.*, are altogether incompatible with the interests and rights of our Provinces in America.

In his final paragraph, Miranda urged the Venezuelans to send the same advice

> to the other neighboring Provinces (Santa Fé and Quito); for the purpose of bringing us all together, and enabling us to proceed with *unanimity* to the same end;—since by *disunion alone* in my opinion can our salvation and Independence be put in danger.[55]

This message, of course, applied equally to Caracas as to Buenos Aires, or other neighboring parts.

The Buenos Aires letter of July 24th, also part of the first batch of materials, discussed events in the Río de la Plata, with Miranda drawing his facts from their agent Manuel Padilla. The Venezuelan praised their stand against the British in 1807; yet, he informed them emphatically that the English had taken the action despite his "previous admonitions . . . as to the Impracticability of conquering or subduing our America." After repelling "such an odious attempt" with "heroical courage," Miranda continued: you offered your enemy "Peace and friendship, on the honourable condition of a solid and free Independence—this act was as glorious, as it will be memorable in the annals of the New World; and will serve as an inmortal Monument for the People and Magistrates of the City of Buenos-Ayres!"[56] Miranda's praise must have been welcomed in Buenos Aires; and other Americans reading that message could rightfully share in their pride and admiration. Miranda had accomplished a great deal in just two letters. Moreover, the documents in the enclosures were worth studying for all people of the Americas. These were the documents included in the "library" of Miranda's "Paper Assault":

1. His Britannic Majesty's declaration to the Province of Caracas, April 8, 1797, which Miranda reminded his readers, was the same as his agreement with William Pitt on February 14, 1790.
2. Lt. General Whitelocke's instructions of March 5, 1807.
3. General Craufurd's secret instructions, October 30, 1806.
4. H.B.M.'s speech to both Houses of Parliament, July 4, 1808.
5. H.B.M.'s Order in Council, [with] regard to the Spanish Nation, July 4, 1808.

On August 19th, General Miranda took the precaution of writing an informative and well-crafted letter to Lord Castlereagh. He perhaps suspected that some enemy of his in the British Government might prematurely expose his aggressive correspondence to Spanish America.

Since Arthur Wellesley's departure, Miranda explained, he had not been able to contact officials in the British Government because of their priority on Peninsular matters; nor did he want to bother Castlereagh who was busy on Spain as well, so he decided to handle the correspondence he had received from Trinidad and Caracas directly. On his own initiative, therefore, he commenced a correspondence with Spanish America. "The best advice I could give them [Spanish-Americans]," Miranda related:

> in the present most critical state of affairs, both with respect to the uncertainty of events in Spain and to the various sentiments and interests prevailing in South America would be to open a direct communication by authorized Persons with the British Government in order to concert with it such measures as circumstances might require without listening to the Juntas of Madrid, Oviedo, etc., whose interests were opposite.

At this point, the Cabildo of Caracas was

> to assume the Government of the Country themselves, having present among other Official Papers, H. Majesty's speech to both Houses of Parliament, and the late Order in Council relative to the Spanish Nation, which Documents regarded also our American interests, and gave an Idea of the views of the British Government, towards their mutual commercial interests, with our opulent Establishments in South America—recommending them above all, to act with *unanimity*, wisdom, etc.[57]

The distortion was more obvious here, since he did not mention that this was part of the letter to Buenos Aires (July 24th), nor did he mention the documents concerning English instructions in the Río de la Plata which certainly would have aroused Castlereagh's curiosity, no matter how hurriedly he was reading Miranda's letter. As stated, how could any good Englishman object to having foreigners learn from the King of England and an Order in Council about the Spanish nation. In short, the August 19th letter to Castlereagh saved Miranda considerable embarrassment; and Miranda could argue that he *had indeed* informed the English Government of this correspondence. What made the letter even more convincing was that half of it contained valuable information for England: the French in Caracas had returned to Guadalupe; there had been a disastrous fire on the Island of Trinidad, etc. Miranda, in other words, was able shrewdly to cover his tracks somewhat.

On September 9, 1808, Miranda wrote once again to Admiral Cochrane, this time defining his program, which we have identified earlier as the prototype for the "Mask of Ferdinand." As was customary, Miranda kept his friend up to date on Peninsula happenings—that dreadful situation that had deterred, and deferred, his expedition to the New World. An "unexpected change in Spain," he said somewhat ambiguously, "only make results more critical and eventful. We must be prepared to meet them and as sheet *Anchor* of Great Britain, there is and will always be, the friendship and Independence of South America."[58] To assure the "sheet anchor," Miranda asked Cochrane to forward the enclosed "*Duplicate letter for the Cabildo of Caracas: whose contents I have lately communicated to the Government here.*" Why did he emphasize those words? To persuade Cochrane that the Government was authorizing his correspondence? Miranda argued that this duplicate would have the effect of persuading "the South Americans to send some Deputies to this Country, who opening the views and feelings of those Provinces on the occasion may enable us to form a solid and well concerted Plan for the safety and happiness of both Countries."[59] Finally, on September 10th, Miranda added a letter to new recipients: Mexico City and Habana, Cuba, widening the net of his correspondents to include all of Spanish America!

In writing to the Mexicans and Cubans, Miranda also sent copies of that correspondence to the two South American capitals. General Miranda explained:

> The last accounts from Spain and Portugal sufficiently show what will be the result of my well-founded conjectures: and that the Colombian Continent can no longer be governed by Europe; whose *Political, Moral, and Civil System*, is totally different, and perhaps incompatible with the peace and welfare of America. Although Britain had changed her policy in light of events in Spain, her views nonetheless were the same toward Spanish America. Compared to France, moreover, the interests between us and Great Britain, are *solid, reciprocal, and most advantageous* for both parties; although the Government may have acted with a strange Policy at Buenos Aires, as well as in my Patriotic Expedition to the Province of Caracas! These hidden causes, and secret springs require that information and knowledge, that you can not acquire at such a distance, nor can I prudently communicate from hence, by writing:—In this supposition I earnestly entreat you to give credit and attention to a citizen and fellow Countryman whose doom is absolutely united to

yours, having devoted the whole of his life, and moreover, sacrificed considerable personal interests, for the welfare and happiness of his beloved Country.[60]

We know that the first installment of Miranda's correspondence (July 20–September 10) managed to reach its destination, either to the executive officer or the cabildo in question. The second installment (October 6–20) was less successful, since the British authorities stopped a substantial portion of it. Yet, this did not detract from the total effectiveness of Miranda's "Paper Assault." The reason for this is that *all* the letters and documents involved were included in Miranda's Documents of 1810, that we shall describe in our next chapter. By the end of 1810, therefore, all areas of Spanish America were in full possession of their "library." It formed a part of the general revolutionary resources of the Hispanic New World—a fantastic achievement for the Venezuelan Francisco de Miranda.

The second installment of correspondence dealt with the major news events of September, 1808—that is, the world's reaction to King Joseph I, Napoleon's brother as the new monarch of Spain; and secondly the spectacular clash of Anglo-French forces in Portugal. The disastrous news from Lisbon seemed incredible to an exhuberant British public that had first welcomed the military victories of August 17th and 21st—the Battle of Vimeiro, near Lisbon, with Wellesley the victor over his French rival General Andoche Junot. The pursuit of the enemy came to an end abruptly by orders of Sir Hew Dalyrmple, the British Commander who had not been present at Vimeiro. Dalyrmple negotiated the Treaty of Sintra on August 31st which, for all practical purposes, turned the British victory into a defeat. The French were allowed to evacuate the area—the net effect was that by December, 1808, those defeated French troops were available to Napoleon himself in upsetting the Spanish armies near the Ebro River.

An hysterical British public steamed with anger at the news of this diplomatic blunder! A broadside of September 24th, bordered in mourning black and priced at one penny, struck out angrily "On the late Infamous Convention in Portugal!!!" The author protested heatedly and exclaimed pathetically: "Where art thou, **WHITELOCKE?—HOLD UP THY HEAD!**—Behold a competitor, who disputes with thee precedence in the Temple of Infamy!" The Scot Dalyrmple was the main sinner: "Blush Scotland!—Blush England!—Blush human nature!" The author, incensed, spared no one, not even Wellesley:

What infatuation could make thee, Wellesley, tear the green laurels from thy brow, and yield them up to Junot? What could induce *thee* to give to the conquered all the honours and advantages of a conquest? What! Were you sent to Portugal to *recruit for Bonaparte*—to liberate his pent-up army from their dilemma and send them at the "**EXPENSE OF ENGLAND**," with all their plunder, the reward of sacrilege, rape, and murder, to act over again their hellish crimes among the Patriots of Spain; where some month or two hence, you will have again to fight them?

What the writer failed to mention was that Sir Arthur, disgusted with the decisions taken by his superior, submitted his resignation and returned to England by October, 1808.[61]

Miranda in his second letter to Caracas, October 6, 1808, allowed that same distortion of the Portuguese event to go forth in his message. Since he had predicted a British failure in Iberia from the outset, it was convenient to allow the distortion in support of his prediction! It was unnecessary, however, since the news of the following months supported his belief; in fact, Miranda's hopes were rekindled. Perhaps, the "American Thrust" might become popular again in London.

The October 6th letter to Caracas, moreover, came to the attention of the Spanish Government, who forever was spying on that "traitor" Miranda, that "*hombre revoltoso*" who was up to "his old ideas of upsetting the status quo in the Spanish possessions of America." Those were the remarks of the Spanish Minister in London, Juan Ruiz de Apodaca, who was determined to expose the Venezuelan's newest conspiracy. Juanito Sáenz, one of Apodaca's spies in London, reported that Miranda's October 6th letter was, in effect, a set of instructions to his agents in Spanish America.[62]

The notorious October 6th letter to Caracas went out to correspondents in Buenos Aires and Brazil; and, on October 20th, copies of it left for Mexico City and Habana, all of them including the valuable nine enclosures. Juanito Sáenz was right! This was a "revolutionizing" set of instructions! Therefore, let us examine the contents of that famous letter, remembering that it also went into the 1810 Documents sent out by Francisco de Miranda.

Miranda commented to the Caracas leaders on a report that Admiral Cochrane received from Captain Beaver of the *Acasta*, a British frigate that visited Caracas' port at La Guaira in mid-July 1808. She brought news of the Anglo-Hispano rapprochement to Venezuela, a visit that coincided with the appearance of the French corbette, *Serpente*, announcing the enthronement of Joseph I in Spain. Although Miranda as yet did not have the complete evaluation of the *A casta* report, the inferences in his letter provided a masterly political statement. Perhaps, Mill influenced the Venezuelan's viewpoint for he shared it entirely. At any rate, the gist of it was that the French mission was not well received at all; in fact, on July 28th, the Cabildo of Caracas beseeched the Captain General to establish a *junta*, following the precedent on the Peninsula, in favor of Ferdinand VII. Miranda commented in his ubiquitous diary: "If this story is true, it appears to me a favorable augury for the Independence of our America."[63]

Miranda continued the political analysis in detail:

> I greatly fear if his details are correct, that the diversity of Opinions between the European Governors, and the American People (creoles) may produce a contest fatal to the former and not very advantageous for the latter, if the People (and not the intelligent and virtuous Men) take upon themselves the Government.

In making that statement, General Miranda identified himself with a popular stand among the European elites and their views of the French Revolution:

> Consider, Gentlemen, the effects of the Revolutionary Government in France and what has lately occurred in many parts of afflicted Spain! It is certain, that the power of a state resides essentially in the People collectively, and without them no vigorous resistance can be made anywhere; but if they fail in obedience and subordination to the Supreme Government and to their Magistrates and Chiefs, instead of preserving and defending the state, they will infallibly destroy it by anarchy as we have evidently seen it in France, as well as in former times in Italy, Greece, etc.

Next, Miranda's attack upon Spain's leadership was equally masterful in the propaganda sense:

> The Directors of the present Revolution in Spain, for want of a Representative organization in the beginning, find themselves now obliged to form it appears an imperfect one (since the Provincial Juntas were not elected by the Nation) and so late that they will scarce have time to arrange a Plan of Defense, and general organization, before the

Enemy has invaded the greater part of the Kingdom; and the Person of
most weight and authority in the Country, disgusted with the excesses
and crimes of the anarchy has so far relented as not to wish to take part
in the common cause. These errors surprise me less, from having seen
in France, Persons of much more wisdom and experience, commit
similar blunders, merely from a want of practical knowledge in affairs
of this nature.[64]

This was an uncanny prediction into Spain's future within the next
several months. In early December, 1808, the Spanish armies suffered
telling defeats that soon gave the French, under Napoleon's personal
presence, the commanding initiative in the Peninsular war. Foreseeing
this consequence, Miranda urged his American compatriots to prepare
themselves to move with decision and information. It was his endeavor
to supply the materials and guidelines for making these crucial
decisions in their areas. Thus, he supplied no less than nine enclosures
in this second installment. Items One and Two, for example, dealt
with:

A Representative Organization and Government for our America, which
was framed here some years ago, and has met with the approbation of
learned and well-informed men in these matters, who have since
examined it, in England as well as in America; for which reason I
recommend it to your consideration at the present moment.

As for documents Three to Nine dealing with Miranda's career, the
Venezuelan remarked:

although on Personal affairs, [they] contain also facts and circumstances
relative to the Negotiations and efforts that I have made in this Country,
as well as in France and the United States of America, in order to obtain
the Liberty and Independence of these countries, our primary object at
present, and which claims the attention of almost the whole *Human
Race.*—Therefore, I beg you will examine them with care, as they are
the result of many years' studies and fatigues, accompanied by
experience acquired in the great Revolutions that have overturned nearly
all the old Governments, and institutions of Europe. I shall always
esteem myself happy if in any manner I can contribute towards the
prosperity of my Country, united with my beloved and virtuous
Countrymen.[65]

This section of the October 6th letter ended with praise for a special English colleague of his:

> The British Admiral who commands in those Seas and adjacent Islands Sir Alexander Cochrane a Person of great merit, and a strong advocate of our independence; you may with safety regard him as a friend and liberal Man—Any advice or Dispatch for me, will arrive with safety through his hands.[66]

It is not difficult to understand why the Spanish ally would insist on Cochrane's punishment, along with the "traitor" Miranda, for assisting in such a subversive set of "instructions."

Although there was much more in the October 6th letter to the Venezuelans, Miranda hoped keenly to make a favorable impression upon his own countrymen, identifying with the heroes of the 1797 abortive coup—Gual, España, and the "*Illustrious Americans*" who were treated and condemned as "Criminals." The Spaniards in Europe were now putting up a respectable fight against overwhelming odds, setting a good example for us:

> and since we have so long servilely copied them in their vices, let us now imitate them with satisfaction in their virtues; reforming our American Government, and claiming with dignity and judgement our own Liberty and Independence; points in my opinion indispensable and *sine qua non*.[67]

After sending off his "*lettre circulaire*" of October 6th to the "Colombian Continent," as he described it to Nicholas Vansittart, who was out of the City, an interesting exchange of letters took place between them. Aware of Miranda's correspondence campaign with the Americas, Vansittart wrote philosophically about Miranda's future role in the emancipation process. He had two alternatives, the Englishman noted: first, he could leave for Spanish America and take up his role as a military and political leader, for which he was indeed well qualified from experience. Or, secondly, he might consider remaining in Europe to represent the interests of Spanish Americans. Although Miranda had urged his correspondents in America to send their best people to Europe, the fact remained that only Francisco de Miranda, through years of experience and contacts, had the requisite ability and personality to represent Spanish America effectively in the capitals of

Europe. Whatever decision he made, Vansittart would do all in his power to assist him in carrying it out. If it were the second choice, he hoped that the General would come out to the country to spend a few days with him, so that they might discuss strategy, etc. When the Venezuelan replied on October 15th, he was noncommittal, although he appreciated his friend's advice. Since he could not visit him now, he promised to keep Vansittart posted on the October 6th letter.[68]

The Peninsular War had taken such a bad turn by the end of 1808 that Miranda, the perennial optimist, began to hope that the "American Thrust" might return as an alternative. He wrote to Cochrane on October 20, 1808, that because of the deteriorating situation in Spain: "Everybody begins to perceive now, that the only ultimate resource is South America; and to that point we ought to direct our particular attention."[69] It was the same chant on November 3rd. The situation in Spain and Portugal was even more alarming, he wrote to Admiral Cochrane. The people here are getting desperate: "Their ultimate hope, however, is placed in the Continent of South America, which is the only part of the Spanish Monarchy that can be rescued from the grasp of France, and protected by the British Navy." Referring to the April 23rd letter in the *Courier*, the one written by James Mill: "that you know better than anyone else . . . that the Idea was the solid good Plan that England had to pursue from the beginning. Lord Melville saw it always in its true light, and credit is due to his Lordship for being united with us in this grand and solid scheme."[70] By December 9, 1808, Miranda's letter to the Admiral was almost visceral:

> We have just received the news of the defeat and overthrow of the Armies of Spain acting by the direction and plans of their Juntas.—I never did expect other results from such an incoherent and indistinct set of principles as the leaders of those Juntas have been professing and practicing all along; their ignorance it appears, is as great as their presumption and superstitution, which circumstances diminish the regret.—What really gives us concern and interest is the position of the British armies that went to support their rights and Independence.—The British Generals as well as the Ministers here, have I am afraid placed too much confidence in the wisdom and abilities of the Spanish leaders at this momentous crisis, and God forbid they should be the victims of such rash and inconsiderate proceeding.[71]

In Miranda's letter to Cochrane of January 20, 1809, the news from the Peninsula was even worse: "The affairs in Spain I have no need to tell you are very near finishing and very nearly as unfortunate and disastrous as I scarcely foresaw." His prediction for the Peninsula made him sanguine that England would now revive the "American Thrust." In that same letter, the General acknowledged receipt of Cochrane's letter of October 30, 1808, thanking him for transmitting his letters to Caracas, Mexico, etc. "Indeed," he said,

> my conjectures have been found true in the result; and the measures that the South American Provincial Governments have begun to adopt are in fact perfectly agreeable to the advice I gave to them on this same subject—I hope they will continue to act upon this solid principle: that they will cut off all communication with the French or Spanish under the same influence; and to send Commissaries and Men of sense here, without delay. This is at least the hope and the wishes we entertain now.[72]

* * * * * * * * * * * *

In light of the disastrous turn of events on the Peninsula in the final months of 1808, as well as Miranda's sanguine expectations that the British were again ripe for the "American Thrust," the General felt that it was time to resume his contact with Sir Arthur Wellesley. After the latter's resignation in Portugal and his return to London, Miranda was able to learn what really happened at the famous Battle of Vimiero and its unfortunate aftermath. Thereafter, Wellesley followed his own domestic course; and the contact between them ended until December 12, 1808, when Miranda wrote to Sir Arthur asking for an interview to discuss some news of "highest importance" for Great Britain, "as well as for the future of mine."[73] Wellesley agreed to meet a few times; Sir Arthur was especially intrigued by what his Venezuelan friend had told him about his correspondence campaign in Spanish America. This led to a vital session between the two men on January 26, 1809. Fortunately Miranda recorded most of this meeting in his diary.[74]

The long conference on January 26, 1809, began with Miranda's recital of his activities since Wellesley left for Ireland in the previous June; then he asked Sir Arthur to examine the letters that he had written to South America, now translated into English. Curious and intrigued, the British general became so engrossed in his reading that he asked Miranda not to talk until he had finished the correspondence. After savoring the contents thoughtfully, Wellesley proceeded to express a verdict that caught Miranda somewhat offguard: "I can only tell you in all friendship and confidence that the Ministers, at present, do not have their views set on South America; it seems to me, therefore, better to leave that matter aside until the business in Spain has come to an end." Not entirely shocked, and after a brief pause, Miranda rallied: "Would you not agree, Sir, that England's attempt and plans to achieve the Independence of that peninsula are already frustrated." "Yes," replied Sir Arthur: "but we cannot deal with persons sent here from the Spanish colonies . . . without failing our Spanish Ally and dishonoring our Nation."   If England went out of its way to protect American Independence, Spaniards would reason that it might be best to dance to the French tune. Miranda's reply: "Then, dealing with me you would consider more incompatible than with someone else?"   Wellesley quipped: "Not at all, I have definite orders from the British ministers to receive any information from you that you consider convenient in these matters—but he could not communicate, nor receive any other persons, etc."   After an embarrassing moment, Sir Arthur asked how Spanish Americans would react to Spain's declaration in behalf of Joseph Bonaparte. Miranda did not hesitate in answering Sir Arthur: Americans "would favor *Independencia Absoluta.*" His English friend retorted: "*that is what we desire as well!*" Sir Arthur continued: "As for the type of government that they might want, that was their business, not England's." Miranda brought out some letters that he had received from agents in Trinidad, Curaçao, and Rio de Janeiro for his perusal. After a moment of examining them, Wellesley assured his Venezuelan friend that he would be happy to meet him in the future. When the "Spanish question is over," *which he did not believe would be too long,*" then, "we would return our exclusive attention to America!"[75] The session ended on this note.

What was the significance of the January 26, 1809, meeting as far as Miranda's project in South America was concerned?   According to his faithful diary:

> From this important Conference, we have culled the essence of this Government's thinking at this moment toward America, that is:
> 1st—that as soon as the Spaniards proposed an alliance against France; at that moment they abandoned us and sacrificed their own interest without the slightest regret. 2nd—when they perceived that we desired to be independent of the French, they then assumed an indifference, so as to sell their friendship or protection at the highest possible price. 3rd—and, as they noted that that continent does not

allow itself to be directed or influenced in matters of *Government and Commerce,* they prefer to display indifference as to form of Government that is chosen to adapt to the country—unless it is that of Ferdinand VII, their worthy Ally.[76]

Miranda's conclusions speak for themselves: he was back down at the bottom of the barrel again! There was not much difference in their conferences of June 9, 1808 and January 26, 1809, except that now there were no longer any illusions about reopening the "American Thrust," as the British Government had virtually promised him.

This alleged promise led General Miranda to direct an appeal to Lord Castlereagh in a letter of March 24, 1809. By then, the British decision not to abandon her ally Spain was known to everyone. In addition, the announcement was accompanied by the news that General Wellesley soon would take over in Portugal as Commander-in-Chief. To write to Lord Castlereagh with that news in mind was a gesture of futility. Miranda dared to hope, against all odds, that it was still possible to revive the "American Thrust." Lord Castlereagh, however, was in no mood to listen, especially now. He had never been too aggressive a leader in the past, at least not with regards to the South American issue. He followed his ministers' decisions closely, for the most part; and they favored a pro-Spanish stand. In fact, Lord Castlereagh had told Nicholas Vansittart that he did not want to be bothered personally on the South American project—a remark that the latter passed on to his Venezuelan cohort.[77]

Given these futile circumstances, Miranda's memorandum of March 24th merely permitted him to vent his spleen on the mistreatment by the British over the years. He also railed about the treachery of Spaniards, allies of the English etc., etc. There was, however, one item of information that did not appear in Miranda's diary concerning the Wellesley conference of January 26th: Miranda's offer to serve England in Mexico or Habana:

in Company of one or two English Commissioners that might explain to the constituted authorities of the country the favorable disposition of Great Britain in their favour; and after hearing and debating in presence of the English Representatives the interests on both sides, to come to a decision agreeable to their instructions; and upon which we could form a solid and general plan, to act upon, in the future operations and measures to be taken hereafter for the independency of that Continent.

Wellesley answered that "His Majesty's Ministers could not for the present enter into any further discussion upon the subject, while the Spanish attempt was pending." "These sad examples, and painful reflexions convince me more and more, My Lord," Miranda said near the end of the letter: "that the welfare and happiness of South America, never can come from Spain; but from her own uncorrupted children!" As for his major objective and plan over the years, Miranda concluded emotionally:

> It is surprising to me that a plan of this importance, and so essentially connected with the interests of this country should have been upon the point of execution by a series of administrations from the year 1790, beginning with Mr. Pitt; zealously adopted by Lord Sidmouth and St. Vincent; resumed by Mr. Pitt and Lord Melville, and ultimately embraced by Your Lordship and your colleagues, by some fatality unaccountable to me, have as frequently been defeated![78]

The Venezuelan diplomat for the Americas must have sensed that this was his last hurrah. Wellesley became the hero of the "Peninsular War"—the famous Duke of Wellington; and England ended the famous conflict victoriously. Yet, many English thinkers and statesmen were not at all convinced that the "European Thrust" was the only rational alternative. And champions of Latin American emancipation sorely regretted a British decision that deprived them of a tutelary influence that might have avoided the instability of the next half century.

Irony would have it that just as Wellesley and Miranda were meeting in London on January 26, 1809, another English officer, thousands of miles away, commenced a process that embarrassed the "Precursor"—the exposure of Miranda's "Paper Assault." Only the highlights of that investigation need detain us here.[79] Recently appointed the Governor of Curaçao, Sir James Cockburn informed Admiral B.S. Rowley of the Jamaica Station of certain developments that he considered to be against the best interests of Great Britain. Since Spain was now an ally, Sir James had done everything possible to establish "the most perfect confidence between the Government and the principal personages of Caracas and myself." Before long, he received a letter from the Captain General of Caracas concerning

> certain papers, which had been secretly left at the Marquis del Toro's House and immediately delivered up by him to his Government, purporting to be written by General Miranda under the sanction of the

British government, and urging the Provinces of Spanish America to throw off their allegiance to Ferdinand the 7th and to declare themselves independent.

It seems that Toro received his letter on October 24, 1808; and on the following day, he sent it to the Captain General, protesting his innocence and demanding that Miranda be punished for subversion and for implicating him, totally innocent and who had never met Miranda. Thus, the exposure of Miranda's alleged conspiracy proceeded on two fronts: the English with Cockburn's letter of January 26th, supplied with documents (copies of) from the Spanish ally; and the Spaniards own espionage organization.

The English soon learned how the letters, and their enclosures, proliferated throughout Spanish America. The investigation revealed that Admiral Cochrane had forwarded the packages under the authorization of the Secretary of State's office; and, in all, the British seemed to have detained the Habana-Mexico packages, as well as the second letter to Caracas. There was much verbiage in all the correspondence about what this represented for the Anglo-Hispano alliance in this crucial war, etc., etc. By December, 1808, Admiral Cochrane received specific instructions not to permit Miranda's mail to go forward without a legitimate authorization from Percival's office in London. Miranda learned of this prohibition in mid-February, 1809, and hastened to meet with Percival. He explained to him that the correspondence was authorized. General Wellesley and General Stewart, Lord Castlereagh's brother, had read the correspondence without complaint; in fact, they commended him on those letters.[80] Those were the major points in the early phase of the British investigation.

The Spanish Minister in London raised the roof when he learned of Miranda's new variation of treason. The Spaniards wanted his head, pure and simple; and they did not stop there. Admiral Cochrane had to be brought into line, so that he would learn to respect the Spanish-English alliance. Here is how the Minister in London (Apodaca) explained the situation to his superior in Spain. He analyzed George Canning's correspondence as follows: The English, under the present circumstance, could only censure Miranda, supervising him closely with the threat that he would be expelled from the British dominions if he persisted. On Cochrane's side, forget it—the English would not budge. Between the lines, Apodaca was saying, in effect—the English also

have their own *pundonor (point of honor* standard).[81] And that is how
matters ended between the allies.

The next evidence of importance appeared in a diary note of April
24, 1809, a month after Miranda's last letter to Castlereagh.   It
described the events on the evening of April 24th. After biding adieu
to some friends, Don Francisco decided to pass by Lord Castlereagh's
home near St. James Square. He had not seen or heard from him in
some time. Since generals Wellesley and Stewart were out of town, the
only other conduit to Castlereagh was that wretched character Cooke—"
(el infame C—" was the phrase in Miranda's diary).[82] This is the
General's entry on the unexpected meeting with His Lordship:

> I was just reaching his door, when I met *him* [as big as life], biding
> farewell to another person with whom he was talking, and I greeted him
> as I approached—he responded in a friendly tone, that he could not be
> detained at that moment, since he just happened to be on his way to
> meet with the Cabinet—I merely assured him that I did not want to be
> a bother but that *my papers,* promised me some time ago, I had not been
> able to collect as yet;—then coming toward me and in a reserved tone
> he told me: '*that they* (the ministers) *were not too happy with you
> maintaining so much Correspondence with the Provinces of South
> America—while at the same time receiving a considerable Salary from
> this Government!—and had not Mr. Cooke told you anything on that
> matter?*

Miranda answered defensively: "No Milord. I had seen Cooke only
once since returning to England; and I assured Castlereagh that I had
shown the correspondence to both Wellesley and Stewart, who had not
disapproved of it; on the contrary, they had commended it." That is
why His Lordship's words came as quite a surprise to him. He had
always been just a conscientious representative of his people in
London: "then, his facial expression becoming more relaxed, he said
goodbye: '*be on the safe side, not to write anymore on that topic, etc
. . .'*" The following conclusion informs us of Miranda's thoughts on
that occasion:

> This accidental discovery, and the conversation that took place with
> the minister as a consequence, have appeared to me as a favorable
> chance from Providence—to cut off in some way the wretched
> influence, with which C—procures to sow dissensions, and prevent
> (even when speaking evil of) the success of my Plans for the

Independence and Liberties of South America.—What then can we expect from a governmental organization in which its secondary members try to ruin, and destroy, what the principal Ministers have approved, and want to see implemented?—Such is, nevertheless, the monstruous system, of the executive branch of the corrupt British Constitution![83]

Miranda was not that surprised to learn from Lord Castlereagh that his aggressive correspondence campaign had finally been exposed, despite the precautions that he had taken to make it appear legal, or authorized. In this regard, we should note that General Miranda had spent most of that afternoon of April 24th with a group of political leaders in London who were not in agreement with the Castlereagh cabinet in abandoning the "American Thrust." Lord Grenville, the Duke of Gloucester, Lord Gray and possibly others met with General Miranda at *Camelsford House* (Oxford Road) for a lengthy orientation on South America—almost two hours, in fact. It seems to have been the idea of the Duke. He told Miranda, after the others had left, that this meeting would help in bringing about the

> execution of our plan for South America, if these men should enter, as it is possible, the ministry in the near future; and even if they do not enter the government, their influence would always cooperate advantageously with our views and ideas in Parliament. That is what I desire, and why I advised you meet with us here today; I expect that the results will be favorable to us in the future—and now let us go out for a walk.

They walked towards Bond Street and Picadilly, where Miranda said goodbye to the Duke; "leaving him with other friends of his that we met on the road; and that having heard my name mentioned by chance, they spoke with praise about the article on South America, in the latest number of the *Edinburgh Review*."[84] The reference was to the Mill-Miranda article of January, 1809, which will be discussed in the next chapter. Francisco de Miranda, in short, had not given up the ship yet, just because the Castlereagh ministers had reached a policy decision that worked against the interest of South American emancipation. He was willing to involve himself in "politics," if that was needed in the next phase of his stay in Great Britain. It was also necessary to continue in expanded form the propaganda movement to influence British opinion toward his project. The Mill-Miranda article noted above now joined the two by William Burke on the theme of Great Britain's need to help in the emancipation of Spanish America.

Chapter Six

The Propaganda of Liberation in Europe

It is now high time, for the people of Great Britain to view with courage and with wisdom those great interests of theirs which are involved in the fate of South America. The question is not about the destination of a sugar island, or the occupation of a barren rock in the Mediterranean;—it is about the fate of twenty millions of men, and of a country of such boundless extent and varied fertility, as to be capable, perhaps, of affording a luxurious subsistence to all the existing individuals of the human race.

Edinburgh Review, July, 1809.[1]

While General Francisco de Miranda was mounting the "Paper Assault" to gain support from South America's leaders, his associate James Mill focused upon persuading the British public to favor a New World strategy, much more meaningful to England than the misguided policy of fighting Napoleon Bonaparte on the Iberian Peninsula. Thanks to Mill and J. Lowe's contacts with publishers and editors in London, the Miranda writers were able to place key editorials in the *Bell's Weekly Messenger*, the *Courier*, the *Examiner*, *The Times*, the *Morning Chronicle*, and the French paper *L'Ambigú*—articles that kept major interpretations or facts before the reading public. In this manner, they hoped to persuade Englishmen to pressure the incumbent ministers or to support their political rivals at election time—for example, the vote scheduled in late 1809 gained much attention from Miranda's writers. It must be emphasized that, at that time, a veritable dogma prevailed concerning what public opinion could do that obsessed Miranda and Mill, in particular. Most reformers, as a matter of fact, shared this dream—the young graduates of the University of Edinburgh had this in mind when they reestablished their *Review* in the early years of the nineteenth century. And we have already seen that it was a major preoccupation for the young editor of the *Literary Journal* in London. Mill's spectacular publication on "Commerce," moreover, helped to win for him a reviewership on the *Edinburgh Review*, a connection that allowed Miranda and Mill to publish two major articles for their cause. During this crucial period, moreover, the *Edinburgh Review* published other articles of significance on the *Mercurio Peruano,* a key periodical for South America in the late eighteenth century; and at least two reviews on Alexander Von Humboldt's famous travels to Spanish America at the end of the same century. Thus, readers of the Scottish periodical had an excellent exposure to the area that provided a cultural setting for Mill's political analyses. Dr. John Allen, Mill's fellow reviewer, was the knowledgeable author of the complementary articles. His lifetime connection with Lord Holland allowed him to spend many years in Spain, where he became an accomplished linguist and was also adept at political and historical analysis. In fact, Allen and Mill's style of writing was deceptively similar; the saving grace was that one of these Scots was a conservative and the other, a liberal! In later years, these two friends of Lord Henry Brougham, the great political leader of Great Britain, advised him according to their political persuasion.[2]

Entitled the "Emancipation of Spanish America," the January, 1809, article in the *Edinburgh Review* started with the pretext of reviewing the famous *Letter to the Spanish Americans* by the Jesuit Juan Pablo Viscardo Guzmán, a native of Arequipa, Peru. Without wasting words, Mill explained:

> When the Jesuits were banished from all the territories of Spain, he, with the rest of his order, who, whatever may have been their demerits in other parts of the world, had been the chief benefactors of Spanish America, *[The footnote cited Montesquieu and Robertson in praise of the Jesuit Order] was deprived of his country, and took refuge in the dominions of the Pope in Italy. At the time when the dispute about Nootka Sound threatened to produce a war between Great Britain and Spain, and when Mr. Pitt, in the view of that event, had adopted the scheme of revolutionizing the Spanish colonies in America, he invited, at the suggestion of General Miranda, a certain number of the ex-Jesuits of South America from Italy, for the purpose of using their influence in

disposing the minds of their countrymen for the meditated changes. Of this number was the author of the present appeal, in which the inhabitants of South America are called upon, by every consideration interesting to human kind, to take the management of their own affairs into their own hands, and to establish a just and beneficent government, which may at once insure their own happiness, and open a liberal intercourse of benefits with the rest of mankind. This uncommon person, who evinces a share of knowledge, of thought, and of liberality, worthy of the most enlightened countries, died in London in the month of February 1798.[3]

It was General Miranda who immediately had the manuscript printed in various languages; Mill was using the French version; and Miranda, it will be recalled, distributed the Spanish version to Venezuelans in 1806. Just as William Burke, James Mill displayed a sincere admiration for the Jesuits; this proclivity was further accented in the July, 1809, article about another Jesuit Father in Chile. Under Miranda's direction, moreover, Mill did not employ the "Black Legend" to any great extent; on the contrary, he depicted this Peruvian Jesuit as a staunch believer in contitutionalism based upon the Spanish historical tradition of liberalism and "Natural Rights." James Mill—at this point in his life and development—was likewise a firm advocate of "Natural Law" in politics and economics.

Always well-organized, Mill continued his tight synthesis for another page of the text, highlighting Viscardo's principles of liberty in explaining Hispanic anticolonialism. Mill took note of Viscardo's historical models—the Dutch and Portuguese rebellions against the rule of Spain, which he likewise developed later in the essay. Moreover, he underscored a third model which the Miranda propaganda movement would emphasize more and more in the future:

the recent acquisition of independence by their neighbours in North America,—an event which had made upon them, as might be expected, the deepest impression; and concludes, in a strain of sublime piety, and genuine philanthrophy, which cannot be too much admired—including every nation upon earth, and even the Spaniards themselves, in his generous view of the blessings to be derived from the prosperity and freedom of that vast portion of the world.

Thus ended Mill's review of Father Viscardo's famous essay, only two and one-half pages in an essay of thirty four![4]Now, it was time to underscore the Miranda-Mill message to the British public:

The brilliant prospects which seem to be opened up for our species in the New World, and the cloud which still thickens over the fortunes of the Old, present, at the present hour, a subject of contemplation to the thinking part of the British people; than which, excepting the great question of slavery or freedom, we know not if one more interesting can be imagined. We seize, with avidity, the present opportunity of communicating to them such information on this grand topic as we have been able to collect; and doubt not that our readers will partake with us in the deep interest with which it has inspired us.

The master reviewer and propagandist, anonymous to his readers at the time of writing, was now ready to carry out his charge to his own conscience and to the model character who fortune had prepared for the task of emancipating Spanish America—General Francisco de Miranda. Like Thomas Pownall and William Burke before him, the young Mill was ready to present the Venezuelan's case once again, hopeful that this time it would receive attention and activize his audience.

Despite the wishful thinking of many Europeans about the alleged instability of the French regime, the despotic power of Napoleon Bonaparte was a fact of life in all of Europe that seemed endless and even limitless. Napoleon deprived his English neighbor from the markets of the Continent. Remembering the admonitions of William Burke, the author predicted that the contest overseas would be relentless and bitter. In that perspective, he concluded: "every eye, we believe, will ultimately rest on South America." Now, Mill sallied forth with some persuasion:

A country far surpassing the whole of Europe in extent, and still more, perhaps, in natural fertility, which has been hitherto unfortunately excluded from the beneficient intercourse of nations, is, after a few prudent steps on our part, ready to open to us the immense resources of her territory, of a population at present great, and likely to increase with most extraordinary celerity, and of a position unparallelled on the face of the globe for the astonishing combination of commercial advantages which it appears to unite. From the maturity for some beneficent change, which circumstances and events have for a series of years been working in those magnificent regions, and from the mighty effect they are capable of yielding for the consolation of afflicted humanity, it seems as if that Providence, which is continually bringing good out of evil, were about to open a career of happiness in the new world, at the very moment when, by the mysterious laws of its administration, it appears to have decreed a period of injustice and calamity in the old.[5]

Throughout this essay, James Mill wrote tightly digesting what Burke had spent pages on as in the first part of the quotation above: "after a few prudent steps on our part"—that is, the policy of "liberation" rather than "conquest" etc.; and note also the ubiquitous "Providence" of the writer trained in theology. He sensed very early that: "The subject is too extensive for an article in a Review. —And this the great difficulty," he told General Miranda: "It is hardly possible to place all the important points in the light which they would require. What we can do, will however, I think, produce a strong impression." Elsewhere, in another letter to the General, Mill revealed his tactics in writing the essay so that it would be effective:

> You will perceive that my great aim, in the part of the review, has been to present the subject, as strongly as I was able, in that particular aspect which would most fall in with the prejudices of this nation, and at the same time give instructions which might, as far as possible, prevent those who are to decide, from adopting any erroneous and pernicious plan of action. I know not whether making public the mode of procedure which you now propose will appear to you proper—if not, we can easily strike it out.[6]

In the quotations that follow, the reader should look for Mill's "strong impression," his instructions on what to do, and what prejudices he appealed to in a given case.

Since "William Burke" would write again in Venezuela, especially determined to highlight the North American model, it is interesting that Mill's next step was to add some proof to the above generalizations about South America. His appeal was, as he put it, "to experience and to fact." "We have," he wrote with pride,

> the grand experiment of North America before us, which the inhabitants of the South are so ambitious to imitate. The states of North America were our own colonies, and they had been always beneficently administered; yet has their independence been far more profitable to us than their subjection? What is the result with regard to commerce alone?—the very extraordinary fact, that for several past years we have exported more goods of British growth and manufacture to the United States of America, than to the whole of Europe taken together. If such are the benefits resulting from the prosperity of the United States, how many times greater will be those which must necessarily flow from the prosperity of South America? How many times more extensive is the

country which the Spanish Americans possess? That country, from enjoying a much greater diversity of climate compared with Europe, than North America, is much more richly provided with those commodities for which Europe presents the most eager demand. Of the soil of South America, a great part is much more favourable to cultivation, much more fruitful, and cleared by nations who had made some progress in civilization. Of all the countries in the world, South America possesses the most important advantages in respect to internal navigation, being intersected in all directions by mighty rivers, which will bear, at little cost, the produce of her extensive provinces to the ocean. If the population of the United States, amounting perhaps to 6,000,000 souls, afford so extraordinary a demand for British commodities, what may not the population of South America, extending already to no less than 16,000,000, be expected to afford? It is no doubt true, that the moral and intellectual habits of the people of South America are not so favorable to improvement as were those of North America. Their industry has been cramped,—their minds have been held in ignorance by a bad government; hence are they indolent and superstitious. But remove the cause, and the effects will cease to follow. So sweet are the fruits of labour, wherever the labourer enjoys them unimpaired, that the motives to it are irresistible,—and his activity may be counted upon with the certainty of a law of nature. The deduction, therefore, is so very small which, on this score, it will be requisite to make, that a very subordinate proportion of the superior advantages in soil and climate, which the South American enjoys, will suffice to compensate the better habits with which the inhabitants of the United States commenced their career.[7]

As might be expected, James Mill was especially effective in pushing the economic argument, so important to the Englishman's concern. Just as the United States, South America's orientation was agricultural; she would therefore depend upon imports of manufactures. And which country was best equipped to supply these manufactures? Great Britain, of course:

> So far before all other countries, in respect to manufacturing advantages, does she stand, that were the circumstances of Europe much more likely to encourage industry than unhappily they are, we could meet with no rival; and as we supply North America, so could we South, on terms which would infallibly draw to us the greater part of her custom. With this magnificient source of industry and wealth, the channels which Bonaparte can shut against us hardly deserve to be named,—since that even of the United States surpasses them all. With South America, then,

under a free and beneficent government,—though we might weep for the calamities heaped upon our brethren of Europe by an insatiable despot, who, with the words *liberty* and *good of mankind* on his lips, would rivet his chains on the whole human race, and expend their blood and sweat for his own momentary pleasure or caprice,—we might laugh the destroyer to scorn, and enjoy a prosperity which the utmost efforts of his power and his rage could never disturb.[8]

To get the reader's saliva flowing, so to speak, Mill the propagandist was ready now to reveal one of the great consequences that certainly would attend the emancipation of South America:

> the greatest, perhaps of all,—the mightiest event, probably, in favour of the peaceful intercourse of nations, which the physical circumstances of the globe present to the enterprise of man:—we mean, the formation of a navigable passage across the isthmus of Panama,—the junction of the Atlantic and Pacific Oceans.

This is not just "a romantic and chimerical project," it is "not only practicable, but easy." In scholarly footnotes, as well as commentary in the text, Mill's presentation was thorough and convincing.[9] His powerful mind and imagination had to savor such an historical accomplishment:

> We are tempted to dwell for a moment upon the prospects which the accomplishment of this splendid, but not difficult enterprise, opens to our nation. It is not merely the immense commerce of the western shores of America, extending almost from pole to pole, that is brought, as it were, to our door; it is not the intrinsically important, though comparatively moderate branch of our commerce, that of the South Sea whalers, that will alone undergo a complete revolution, by saving the tedious and dangerous voyage round Cape Horn:—the whole of those immense interests which we hold deposited in the regions of Asia, become augmented in value, to a degree which, at present, it is not easy to conceive, obtaining direct access to them across the Pacific Ocean. It is the same thing as if, by some great revolution of the globe, our Eastern possessions were brought nearer to us. The voyage across the Pacific, the winds both for the Eastern and Western passage being fair and constant, is so expeditious and steady, that the arrival of the ships may be calculated almost with the accuracy of a mail coach.*

In the footnote, Mill documented this generalization from the Appendix to the third volume of Sir John Dalyrmple's *Memoirs of Great Britain and Ireland*.[10] "Immense would be the traffic," he continued:

> which would immediately begin to cover that ocean, by denomination Pacific. All the riches of India and of China would move towards America. The riches of Europe and of America would move towards Asia. Vast depôts would be formed at the great commercial towns which would immediately arise at the two extremities of the central canal;—the goods would be received by the ships, as they arrived, which were prepared to convey them to their ultimate destination.

Then Mill went on to speculate about the cultural impact that Japan and China would receive from Europe. And South America for sure, Mill argued, would get a valuable supply of

> industrious inhabitants—myriads of laborious Chinese, who already swarm in all parts of the Eastern Archipelago in quest of employment and of food. This, to her, would be an acquisition of incredible importance: and the connection thus formed between the two countries, would still further tend to accelerate the acquisition of enlightened views and civilized manners in China herself.[11]

At this point in the essay, James Mill turned to a digest of the "Miranda Story" from 1785 to 1808 for the benefit of those who had not read William Burke's *Additional Reasons*, leaving his readers with a "strong impression"—in fact, many of them. There was no effort to correct biographical information about Miranda. Mill also chose the highlights in Miranda's career that Englishmen would consider impressive—for example, Miranda's stand in France against the Jacobins, etc. In the recent period, key documents in Miranda's possession were quoted in the text or in footnotes. Much information was drawn from the Popham and Whitelocke court materials; and the section ended with Great Britain's decision in mid-1808 to drop the South American project. Needless to say, Miranda's image was left clean and impressive for the English reading public.

Now, it was time to face directly Britain's present and future policy with regards to South America:

> We are now once more at peace with the Spanish nation; and, of course, all idea of using force to detach her colones is out of the question. We are not only at peace,—but we are in alliance with

her. . . . We are bound, therefore, by every consideration of national honour, to abstain, while this struggle lasts, from any step which might admit of being construed into an injury or offence to our allies.

In his usual "Burkian" manner, Mill teased his reader with some speculation as to what might happen, or what England might do, in light of the changed circumstances. The slight banter ended; and the mighty Scot came down hard:

> These, however, alas! are speculations in which it appears to us that no sober man can now allow himself to indulge. The fate of Spain, we think, is decided; and that fine and misguided country has probably yielded, by this time, to the fate which has fallen on the greater part of continental Europe. Her European dominions have yielded already to the unrelaxing grasp of the insatiable conqueror; and his ambition and cupidity have no doubt already scented their quarry in her American possessions. At this moment, we have no doubt, his restless intriguers are at work to poison the pure fountains of patriotism and concord in these distant regions; and forces are preparing to trample down those sparks of independence which the slightest stirring would now spread into an unquenchable blaze. A moment is yet left us, to resolve on what may soon be impracticable.

Another stimulating paragraph followed: should Great Britain look on passively while the despot advanced his cause in South America? Then, Mill introduced the quote that opens this chapter. He still was not ready to offer his answer on what England should do. So, he posed a ridiculous question, especially considering England's fate in the Río de la Plata: Should England undertake the conquest of South America? Heavens no! It would not be an "easy conquest. We mention this idea, therefore, only for the purpose of setting it aside."[12] So much for that, the clever Mill continued:

> There is another idea, however, which deserves the most profound and most respectful attention. If the King of Spain, or rather the late King of Spain, is stripped of his dominions in Europe, ought not his dominions in America to be preserved for him? With regard to this point, it is an unlucky circumstance to begin with,—that this ex-monarch is in the hands of Bonaparte. However, we are by no means convinced, that this is a difficulty which would be absolutely unsurmountable; and

our answer is, that, provided care is taken to secure liberty, by diminishing sufficiently the power left in the hands of the King, and placing a sufficient share in the hands of the people, we know of nothing so desirable as the establishment of a mixed monarchy for the government of South America.[13]

There were problems, however, to Mill's solution written in January, 1809. He had no way of knowing that Spaniards would survive the French presence in Spain and that "constitutional monarchy" would be the type of government desired by the provisional bodies of Spain during the French occupation. Yet, James Mill turned his discussion to a general issue in his suggested project:

The nation itself, however, there is reason to believe, would prefer a constitution resembling that of their neighbours in the United States; and if this preference should be very general and very decided, we hope there are no such bigoted partisans of royalty among us, as to think that we should take up arms to force them to resign it; and thus foment a civil war in South America, (the inevitable effect of which would be, to throw the country into the arms of France), merely to prevent a great and remote nation from choosing their own form of government. If, however, the people could be brought to submit to it, few things would afford us more satisfaction, than that a throne should be erected in South America, first for the aged ex-monarch of Spain and then for his son; for we can see no reason for respecting the feelings of the latter exclusively, and abetting all the revolutionary practices which have been used to dethrone the former.[14]

Mill warned his countrymen, however, that there was a formidable obstacle to the solution he had discussed above:

At all events, however, it is our decided opinion, that Great Britain is called upon, by the most imperious considerations of self preservation, utterly to reject and oppose any proposition *which may be made by Bonaparte*—and we are by no means sure that it will not be made—for the erection of such a kingdom, either for Charles, or for Ferdinand.

Well-versed in the tactics of the wily despot of Europe, Mill explained in simple terms how France would dominate South America by controlling cleverly the Spanish nobility that emigrated to the New World, by honoring their "properties and dignities" in Spain. Then, Mill concluded:

let him, by these means, teach the great men who would follow the monarchs, to fix their hopes and affections upon their ancient condition and property in Spain,—and in these silken and golden cords he would hold them bound as fast as by chains of adamant. Then would the affairs of South America be governed entirely at the nod of Bonaparte; and it would be easy for him, under ready pretexts, to introduce into that country his troops, till the time at last should arrive when he could declare it his own.[15]

For the remainder of the essay, James Mill, the "Burkian" teacher, felt that the English reader needed more information on the "disposition" of South Americans to appreciate how they would adapt to the momentous change of living in a free society. His approach was to discuss and evaluate authors and publications that readers might consult to deepen their insights about South America. On Venezuela, he recommended Depons recent work, despite a French bias and a desire to please his Spanish host. Even Depons noted that the 1797 conspiracy, if it had not aborted, would have ousted the Spaniards from Venezuela. From the *Trial of General Whitelocke*, Mill recommended the remarks of Sir Samuel Achmuty, as well as the "Instructions" of General Crawford, to determine the Platine people's deep sentiments for independence. Mill even cited, in a footnote, an anecdote by the French writer Segur L'Ainé concerning the hopelessness of surpressing a North-American type of revolution. "The disposition of the people," Mill averred,

we may conclude with safety, is adverse to every idea of dependence, but probably not yet attached to any particular plan of free government. It is pretty generally known, that they are enamoured of the happiness and prosperity which the Anglo-Americans appear to have procured for themselves; and the most precise conception they have formed of any line of conduct for themselves, is probably that of following the steps of those envied neighbours.

Mill's constant reference to the model of the United States, in the context of Miranda's correspondence attack and the possibility of its failure, suggests that the general and the writer were perhaps already discussing the possibility of a propaganda campaign geared to the Spanish-American public that would capitalize upon their sentimental attachment to the revolutionary experiment in the United States—a crusade in which "William Burke" would be the champion.[16]

As a student of "political science," Mill now turned "to the *manner* of the operation itself." Here we can see his remarkable mind at work:

> In all questions of political change, there are two dangers, of an opposite description, to be considered. The first is the danger of doing too little; the second that of doing too much. The first is by far the most common error; as timidity is a much more universal and powerful source of human misery than rashness; although the evils produced by the second, are much more simultaneous, and, for the moment, much more formidable.
>
> As there are few evils, in the mixed scene of human affairs, without some correspondent good, so the calamitous termination or change of the Spanish monarchy in Europe, has removed a considerable number of difficulties from the great measure of accomplishing the emancipation of South America. No contest is now to be maintained against the troops of Spain, or the ministers of the Spanish government, opposing the change. As those ministers can have no hopes whatever of transferring the government of the country to themselves individually, and as they will now look upon that country as their home, there is every reason to believe that they will cordially cooperate in effecting any beneficient arrangement in its general affairs.

Although Mill's last statement was far too sanguine for the actual history record, there were many examples of Spaniards identifying with the new governments. Mill's point, however, was to impress the English reader with the notion that South America, compared to the examples of revolution in Holland, the Independence movement in the United States, and even revolt of the British people against the despotism of the Stuarts, would have a much easier task of achieving their freedom from Spain. This permitted him to generalize as follows:

> Yet all of these experiments turned out well; and secured, at least for a long time, a greater share of human happiness within the sphere of their operation, than has ever been exhibited among any similar portions of the race. No difficulty appears to have been experienced, in any of those instances, in restraining the excesses of popular violence. How absurd is it, then, because *one* experiment—that of France —has failed, to entertain a prejudice against all changes of government, however urgent the circumstances which call for them; when so many more have succeeded, and above all, when the French attempt affords such instruction with regard to the causes of its failure, that the same event can hardly ever happen again.

While James Mill was composing the paragraph above, it occurred to him that the example of Holland, although in the seventeenth century, would be ideal for South America, since both were movements against Spanish rule:

> These successful experiments afford the most important instruction for the right conduct of the change which is meditated for South America. Let us select that of Holland for an example. The South Americans can hardly choose a wiser; and it possesses this remarkable point of resemblance, that it too was a revolt against the Spanish government. What happened when the Dutch declared their independence? All those offices and powers, which more immediately emanated from the Spanish monarchy, ceased to exist. These were the offices of viceroy or governor, the great military commands, the office of intendant or master of the revenue, and some others. But, besides these, there were other offices and powers, which might more properly be considered as emanating from the country. These were, the magistracies of towns and districts, the burgomasters, the officers of peace and of justice, the barons and landed gentry, with their natural influence. These remained, when the others were struck off; and the country still continued an organized whole. What then did the Hollanders do? They built upon this foundation. All the elementary organization of the country stood entire; and was only so far modified and altered as to accommodate it to the new institutions which were devised to supply the place of the powers rendered vacant by the expulsion of the Spanish authority.[17]

If you could find equivalent institutions in Spanish America, then it would be possible to have a stable transition from a colonial society to a new, representative government.

It was imperative for a political analyst of the Napoleonic period to insist on the avoidance of disruptive violence in adopting a republican system. Thus, James Mill, a leader of the Parliamentary Radicals of the 1830s in Great Britain, developed certain attitudes vis-a-vis the "people" that were brutally realistic and which we would now perhaps classify as "cynical." But it was a common position even among reformers of the so-called "Revolutionary Era" in world history, especially from 1775 to 1825. Mill's concern for a stable approach, following the Dutch model, was articulated as follows:

> The people,—whose ignorance and irritability may be worked upon by men of evil intentions, require, in the crisis of any political change,

the most sage precautions,—are never called upon for their interference. They remain at their homes. With regard to the institutions by which *they* are principally affected, the country appears to undergo no alteration; their passions have no opportunity of being inflamed; and in every instance where matters have been conducted prudently on this plan, the quiet acquiescence of the people has followed as a thing of course.

Political science has been principally obscured, and has become the prey of prejudices and of false alarms, by confounding things that are distinct. Thus, it is one thing to *form* a constitution;—it is another thing, and a very different thing, to *administer* a constitution, (or rather, the business of the nation agreeably to the constitution), after it is established. In regard to the first, we adopt, in its full extent, the proverbial maxim, 'That as much as possible should be done *for* the people,—but nothing *by* them.' In this case, the people are by no means qualified to determine what *is* for them. In the moment, too, of forming a constitution, it can hardly ever happen that sufficient checks exist upon popular violence. But in regard to the second particular—the conduct of the national business according to the rules of the constitution, the case is widely different. Here there is something which must be done by the people; or it is ridiculous to talk of doing any thing for them. Whenever the interests of two sets of people are combined together in one concern, if the entire management be left to one, it is perfectly clear that this managing set will draw, by degrees, all the advantages to their own side, and throw all the disadvantages to the other: and if the joint interest is so wide and unwieldy a concern as that of a nation, so far is this inequality sure to proceed, as to ruin the interest itself, and destroy all national prosperity;—witness Sicily, Poland, and all other countries where a feudal aristocracy has swallowed up the power of the people. So far, therefore, is it from being true, that, in carrying on the business of a constitution, you can do no good *with* the cooperation and influence of the people, that you can do no good *without* it. The constitution, too, can always be so contrived, as to afford, in its exercise, *after* it is introduced, abundant checks against any irregular impulse of the people: so that the operation of the power which, in this second stage, it is necessary to entrust to them, may be purely salutary.[18]

With these "general principles" in mind, James Mill was ready to apply the Dutch model to the South American case. After removing the Spanish hierarchy, Mill explained:

there remains, as there remained in the case of Holland, the local magistracies of the country, and these of a constitution originally peculiarly good; and there remains the natural influence of the people of property and character in the country;—all together, taken, as it must be, in conjunction with that extraordinary crisis which must unite, in a manner unparalleled, the views of all descriptions of the community in desiring a new and happy establishment of the national affairs, affording a more secure basis whereon to proceed in new modeling a government, than was probably ever presented to legislative beneficence before.

Drawing his specific examples from Depons' work on Venezuela, Mill highlighted the following institution in the historical tradition of Spain:

The *Cabildos*, for example, or what we would perhaps call the municipal corporations, afford an organization so complete, that the kings of Spain, themselves, have at times entrusted to them the entire government of whole provinces. The Cabildos of Spain were erected about the same time, and for the same purposes for which similar institutions, under the name of *corporations* in this country, *communautés* in France, *burgs* in Holland, etc. were erected throughout Europe. In no country, however, was the constitution of those municipalities more free than in Spain; and in no country do they seem to have acquired so great an influence in the general government.

Here Mill quoted Depons in French to the effect that the Spaniards' respect for municipal institutions explained the Conquerors' choice of Cabildos as the base for government in their new possessions overseas. Mill continued:

This, then, the acknowledged *basis* in America of the old government itself, remains when the Spanish authority is overthrown; and may become the basis of any new system which wisdom may choose to build upon it. The Cabildos, too, (and this may be contemplated as one instance of the manner in which the feudal institutions of Europe produce new consequences when transplanted into new situations), spread their influence beyond the limits of the town to which they nominally belonged. In Europe, the power and influence of the baron occupied all the country; and it was much if the town could preserve its own independence. In the new world, however, there were no barons; and the influence of the Cabildo extended to the whole district around. The whole territory, therefore, became divided among the Cabildos; and thus, the basis which they form for the erection of a new government is so much the more complete and satisfactory. The powers, too, which they engrossed, corresponded with their new situation . . . It is

abundantly evident from all this, that there exists in South America such
an elementary organization, emanating from the country, as affords a
security against confusion, and a foundation on which to build; in all
respects as good, to say the least, as existed in Holland, at the time
when she threw off her dependence upon Spain, and erected a
comparatively happy government for herself.[19]

At this point, the parallel with Holland ended, because she was
smaller in size and thus chose to form a confederation of her seven
principal municipalities. This was not possible in South America
because of its vast extent. Thus, Mill suggested:

> It is the representative system alone which, in circumstances like these,
> can ever afford a good government. The problem, then, with regard to
> South America, is, how the representative system can be ingraffed upon
> the Cabildos, and upon that stock of organization which is rooted in the
> country.

To make the problem more meaningful to the reader, James Mill
reminded him:

> The most important question which occurs here, is, whether the national
> representatives shall be elected by the *members* of the Cabildos, or by
> the *electors* of these members. Both plans are exemplified in Great
> Britain. In Scotland, it is the magistrates of the towns, corresponding
> to the *members* of the Cabildos, that vote for members of Parliament.
> In England, where the principles of freedom were always more
> powerfully asserted, it is the *electors* of the magistrates, the townsmen
> themselves, that generally chuse the representatives.

Here we have again the master teacher at work! Recognizing that he
was already somewhat overdrawn in the space allotted for his essay,
Mill had to come up with a

> grand principle which ought to guide in all deliberations of this sort.
> There is one danger in rendering the basis of a representation too wide.
> There is another danger in rendering it too narrow. In rendering it too
> wide, you incur the inconveniences of the ignorant and precipitate
> passions of the vulgar. In rendering it too narrow, you incur, what is
> still worse, the mischiefs of bribery and corruption.

His solution was, perhaps, to "establish provincial assemblies, for the

members of which almost all the inhabitants might have a vote, while
the great national legislator was elected by the members of the Cabildos
alone." In general terms, he followed Miranda's ideas on the type of
executive that was needed in Spanish America. In fact, Miranda, Mill
tells us in a footnote, preferred the name of "Inca, as a name dear to
South America."[20] And there was no space left for him to discuss the
judiciary branch of government: "which still, even in the best governed
countries, remains in so deplorable a state.—But we have already
exhausted our limits."

Fortunately, James Mill wrote on for almost three pages, giving us
even further insights into this remarkable mind, as well as his future
biography. If it seemed, he said, "to men wiser than ourselves, that any
good is likely to be derived from pursuing our speculations, we shall
gladly resume the subject on a future occasion." And this came to pass
in July, 1809:

> In the meantime, we are anxious to warn those persons, to whom the
> glorious talk of regenerating South America may fall, not be duped by
> the common division, on which so many changes have been rung, of the
> powers of government into the legislative, the executive, and the
> judicative. It is a division not inconvenient for the ordinary purposes of
> discourse; but at bottom so vague and inaccurate, that some of the most
> deep-rooted errors and greatest mistakes in politics have arisen from it.

He cited Jeremy Bentham in two of his works and recommended him
as an authority on the study of the "judicative branch, including both
tribunals and laws." Jeremy Bentham, young Mill continued: was "the
man, unquestionably, of all who have ever lived, by far the best
qualified to give advice on this subject."[21] Given Bentham's well-
known ego, the reader can probably imagine what might result from
this appraisal! Great Britain should do all that was possible to help
South America realize her independence. Needless to say, force, or
violence, was totally unnecessary. Rather, the English might heed
"some curious thoughts" written in 1780 by Governor Thomas
Pownall—those famous words that the reader has already seen in our
first chapter: "North America, building on the foundation of its
dominion as it lies in nature, has become a democratic or aristocratic
republic. The falling off of South America will be conducted, in its
natural progress, by the spirit of some injured enterprising genius
[General Miranda, of course]"[22]

As a follower of Adam Smith, the young Mill could not help pronouncing another word of caution to his countrymen:

"In looking to the advantages of friendship and of commerce, which will flow spontaneously in such abundance from the freedom and prosperity of South America, let them not be too eager to stipulate for monopolies." As William Burke before him, he pointed out that monopolies were deceptive:

> Monopoly, therefore, afforded us, in any quarter of the world, raises the price of all commodities at home; and that exactly in proportion to the extent, or, in the vulgar idea, to the value of that monopoly. The consequence of this necessarily is, to thrust us out of other markets. The creating, therefore, of a monopoly in our favour in one country,—is just creating a monopoly *against* us in all other countries,—the monopoly of nature; which executes itself; which needs no stipulation; no *guarda costas* [coast guard], nor revenue officers for its security.[23]

Compared to the uninhibited William Burke, Mill throughout this essay was much more diplomatic than he might have been otherwise; and there is an explanation for this toned-down, yet still brilliant, presentation. The Editor of the *Edinburgh Review* scrutinized Mill's pages closely, hoping to prevent any disagreeable reaction from an over-sensitive government. The high-strung author was furious, but Miranda had a calming influence upon him. Eventually, James Mill showed Francis Jeffrey's comments to Henry Brougham, who boldly supported his friend James. Well, the article appeared as we have seen it; clearly, young Mill thought twice about this key publication and what it meant for General Miranda.[24] Yet, he could not resist inserting these final lines:

> In submitting these views and these details to the consideration of our readers, we have been actuated chiefly by the desire of communicating to them those pleasing and comfortable impressions for which we would now look in vain in any other branch of political speculation. We have also been anxious, no doubt, to turn to the consideration of this most important subject the many powerful understandings to which it may not hitherto have presented itself; and thus to secure to the undertaking the benefit of a freer and more extended discussion than it has yet had the fortune to receive. Something, too, may perhaps be gained by interesting the nation at large in a project which has hitherto been almost exclusively the nurseling of

ministers; and thus binding the government to more prompt and effectual exertions in behalf of a cause which may have become popular as well as important. We have stated nothing that has not been long known to our enemies, both in Europe and in America; and nothing but good, it is evident, can result from its being generally known among ourselves.[25]

* * * * * * * * * * * *

The writing of the first article in the *Edinburgh Review* brought James Mill into a closer contact with Francisco de Miranda. He had used Thomson's simile in the second Burkian treatise; now, he was thoroughly convinced that Miranda, indeed, was a "Scipio Africanus," a "Renaissance Man," as well as a revolutionary giant who had fought in the American Revolution, the French Revolution, and now even a greater revolution to emancipate the Spanish New World, modernizing it along the lines of his countryman, Adam Smith, and hopefully for the benefit of Great Britain. His role in Miranda's crusade would inevitably take him to South America, thus securing his career and future for the rest of his life. This was a dream that he shared with another one of his heroes: Jeremy Bentham, whose linkage to Mill was imminent, thanks to Francisco de Miranda's friendship with that intellectual. In the final days of his editorship of the *Literary Journal*, James Mill recognized that this time-consuming position did not allow him to write and research a definitive study on a key area of the world. The project he chose dealt with the History of India; and his progress was substantial, until he opted to invent "William Burke," embarking on yet another extensive portion of the world. He did not lose interest in India. We have read about his insights on India in the two Burkian treatises and especially his fascination with the Isthmian Canal through Panama that would unite the markets of the East and West into a meaningful relationship. Now, it would seem, students of James Mill can appreciate why it took him a dozen years to complete his famous *History of India*. Circumstances forced him to put the project on a back burner, so to speak, while he tried his fortune on South America. If he had succeeded there, however, his Indian work might never have been written!

Throughout much of his life, James Mill suffered the embarrassment, or humiliation, of "dependence"—a difficult situation for such a proud and brilliant man. In 1814, the frailties of his body were taking their toll; he had learned of Miranda's defeat in 1812, thus bringing to an end one of his dreams; and he stayed on with Jeremy Bentham in order to complete his volumes on India. His good friends in London and elsewhere regretted to see him "struggling with poverty," as Francis Place put it. They, therefore, discussed the possibility of raising a 3,000 pound endowment for their colleague. Needless to say, they recognized that a proud James Mill would never accept such an arrangement.[26] These plans never materialized; but the mere fact that serious men in England recognized the pressing problem of Mill's existence underscores its seriousness. Within five years, thanks to his supporters, James Mill made the connection with the East India Company that solved his money problems. As an intellectual, he may not have been entirely satisfied with this new "dependence"; but he learned to live with it; and so did his famous son, John Stuart Mill.

When Mill's position with the *Literary Journal* ended in 1806, he seems to have made a connection with a fellow Scotsman, John Lowe. Mill's biographer maintained that J. Lowe was actually a drain on James' resources; but the documents in Miranda's *A.G.M.* seems to indicate that J. Lowe had the contacts in the publication business that helped Mill to survive in the London of that times. There is no question that Miranda considered John Lowe's services valuable, as we have already noted in the previous chapter; and in early 1809, he was especially useful in fighting the challenge of Biggs and Sherman's works against Miranda's expedition of 1806.[27] A March, 1809, publication was essentially Lowe's efforts, although James Mill also was of assistance at the time. By then, however, Mill was concentrating, more and more, on his second article for the *Edinburgh Review* in July, 1809. John Lowe, moreover, was in close contact with John Murray, a key publisher in London who was vital in the publication of the *Annual Register*. His offices were on Fleet Street. Murray, moreover, seriously considered publishing a volume on Miranda's expedition of 1806; and Lowe was the intermediary in this case, which also involved Dr. William Thomson. Be that as it may, it did not materialize; but it did leave open the prospects of Murray to support General Miranda in 1810.[28]

In late February, 1809, James Mill wrote to Miranda on the progress he was making for another Edinburgh publication, as well as the latest news on Biggs' challenge. "I send you an article I have cut out of the Morning Chronicle of this day," he began, "which serves still farther to shew us the point to which the public eye is beginning to be eagerly turned." Since the article in question was Mill's, it is indeed a revealing indication of the degree of independence in Miranda's team of writers. On their own, they planted articles; "I thought it would please you to see it," Mill proudly added. "You will see too by the advertisement I took out of the same paper at the same time that an enemy is at work [the reference was to Bigg's impending work]." But there was no need to worry, Mill told Miranda: "The Review will appear in good time to confound him. We might expect copies, I understand by Saturday." Mill was referring in this case to copies of the January, 1809, review. In the final third of this February letter, Mill discussed with Miranda a project on a book of documents, like the one published by Miranda *et al* in 1810. Miranda had asked him to review a French work, that might serve as a model. Mill's opinion was that it was a good book "but not exactly calculated for the purpose of distribution you appeared to have in view." Instead, James suggested another French work: the "Library of a Public Man" which, he explained, had "well chosen extracts from all the books we know, arranged in luminous order, and accompanied with judicious notes." That would be "the true thing," he told Miranda.[29]

The article that James Mill wrote on February 23, 1809, in the *Morning Chronicle*, a clipping that Miranda included in his folios of manuscripts now in Caracas, was typical of follow up articles, brief pieces for the most part, that kept certain arguments alive before the public. Moreover, it took liberties that Mill was unable to take in the January, 1809, article of the *Edinburgh Review*. He began with a pessimistic view of Spain's chances on the Peninsula—one of disastrous consequences with the prospect of a future breakdown and betrayal of the Spanish colonies. Mill, in other words, was focusing on the blunder of British ministers in choosing the Spanish option. His next point: Britain had often considered intervention in the Spanish colonies of the New World. Three years ago, a British officer attacked Buenos Aires on his own initiative; and a series of disasters ensued. The reason was simply selfish greed: "We went to South America in the character of plunderers, and we were punished for our rapacity. Had we gone as deliverers and benefactors, the two countries would long before this time have been connected by ties of the closest intercourse." The following point Mill had made in the *Courier* of April 23, 1808, but not in his recent article because of Francis Jeffrey's concern for the feelings of British ministers: "There has been throughout the course of the last sixteen years, a most mischievous error in our line of policy which is constantly deserting what ought to be our grand object, and turning off in pursuit of small ones."

Adam Smith would have been proud to read what a fellow Scot would write years after his death on the theme of colonialism and monopoly:

> In the present state of the world, it is hardly conceivable that it can be the opinion of any one, that the conquest of South America by this country is practicable, or, that if it were practicable, that it would be expedient. Our colonial territory is already far too extensive—to extend it, would be to increase an evil that has been long heavily felt—and it is now full time that we had renounced the extravagance of thinking, that the one half of mankind were made to be tributary to the other, any farther than a mutual supply of mutual wants may be called tribute. Not only is the prosperity of one State not incompatible with the prosperity of another, but it is in exact proportion to the flourishing condition of its neighbours. Were the most inconsiderable country in Europe to relapse into barbarism, this relapse would be felt as a common calamity. As in private society, the welfare of every individual corresponds with the general welfare, so in the community of States what contributes to the benefit of one will be found, when the matter is considered on a large scale, to redound to the advantage of all. Hence it is that by enlightened Statesman those treaties have been always judged to be best which are most impartial, i.e., from which both parties derive an equal portion of advantage; for when this advantage is all on one side, not only are the maxims of justice violated, but even the party which is an apparent gainer will eventually lose more from the permanent evil which he has done to others, than he will gain from the momentary result of an overstretched exercise of power. Were we asked what would contribute most to increase the prosperity of this country, we would answer, not monopolies of commerce, but all Europe being as flourishing as we are now, and the restoration of free intercourse between the nations; we would answer, not an enlargement of dominion, but an augmentation of the general stock of liberty and independence, which can alone render people powerful, great and happy.

The final paragraph was equally strong, and just as modern:

> What has prevented South America from hitherto becoming one great empire, like the Northern States? Is it not the circumstance of its having been kept in a state of vassalage to the Mother Country, and of its energies having been cramped and restrained by a code of most galling operations? When North America was a Colony of Great

Britain, its condition was not much better than that of Paraguay [here he means the Río de la Plata which included Paraguay] or Peru at this moment; and the same advantages which we have reaped from the independence of the Northern part of the Continent we may derive by propagating a spirit of independence in the South. Nay, we may reap these advantages in still a superior degree, if in the latter case we show ourselves the friends of freedom, instead of appearing, as we did in the former, in the odious character of its opposers.

This candid statement by James Mill about the American Revolution was not common in this period of English history.

Mill's conclusion was likewise provocative and went beyond what he had written in the January article of the *Edinburgh Review*. He argued, in short, that since Spain was irrevocably in Napoleon's possession Great Britain was free from any obligation under the Treaty with her: "we are released," he wrote,

from those scruples which are said to have been entertained about encouraging colonies to revolt from under the dominion of the mother country. In short, every thing is favourable to our views, provided these views are at once generous and wise; but if, on the contrary, they are selfish and narrow, BONAPARTE, who no doubt has many agents and partisans already at work in the colonies, will not fail to turn them to his own advantage. The great object with the American Spaniards will be the improvement of their condition, and whoever holds out to them, the fairest prospects of happiness and prosperity, will obtain their suffrage.[30]

It was during the first half of 1809 that James Mill arranged for the recognition of James Barry's work in the *Edinburgh Review*, a project that preoccupied General Miranda. This included preparing for Francis Jeffrey's visit to Miranda's home in London on May 9, 1809, where they also made the final arrangements for the second article of that year. Writing from his home at 12 Rodney St., Pentonville, Mill explained to Miranda what he had done:

My Dear General: I have now made appointments with all the parties concerned to visit the famous production of Barry in the manner you and I concerted. I shall accordingly be at your house on Thursday morning at half after ten. As I shall dislike the idea, however, of parting again for the day, I hope you have no objection to come on and dine with us. You need make no scruple of coming from any delicacy about putting us to trouble, for I ask nobody to dine at my frugal table

whose taste I know is not as simple as my own, and who will not be
content with the fare which I give to myself, and that of my son, whom
I destine to be an emulator of all the noblest benefactors to his race,
should hereafter be able to boast that he had seen General Miranda. My
wife too, has heard so much about General Miranda, that I can assure
you her female curiosity is at no moderate pitch.

Later, when James Mill began his famous connection with Jeremy
Bentham, we shall describe another touching document in Mill's
relationship with Francisco de Miranda.[31]

Before dealing with Mill's second publication in the *Edinburgh
Review*, let us consider a private letter that Miranda wrote to his old
friend William S. Smith in the United States. It provides a good
glimpse of Miranda's frame of mind during a most stressful moment in
his degenerating relationship with the British government. Since his
return to England in early 1808, he had twice, not once, been "on the
point of seeing wishes fulfilled at last and by some unexpected event,
suspended again!" The perennial optimist had not given up, however.
He wrote as follows:

Any *change* in the present administration, or *failure* in the attempt of
liberating Spain from the French (both very probable things) will
immediately give assistance, and execution to my Plans. Besides, I have
received within the last month, letters, and emissaries from South
America, inviting me (from different Provinces) come, and join them as
a leader, for the purpose of establishing our Independence, on free and
rational principles. They press me very much, at the present moment;
but I have resolved on waiting, until the grand result on the Continent
of Europe, is over; and then to proceed with solidity, in a general Plan
of Emancipation of our South America. At all events, *you* are the
person upon whom the eyes of my friends in South America are fixed,
and who possess their confidence in the United States;—your letter to
Yrujo, translated in Portuguese and Spanish, circulates now in Buenos
Aires, Peru, etc. with admiration—and has been read with general
applause over all Europe.[32]

The reference, of course, was to Smith's rejection of the Spaniard's offer
to free Smith's son from Spanish captivity.

* * * * * * * * * * * *

On July, 1809, the *Edinburgh Review* offered "*Molina's Account of Chile* with the following description : "ART.IV. *The Geographical, biographical, Natural, and Civil History of Chili, by Abbé Don J. Ignatius Molina; with Notes from the Spanish and French Versions; and an Appendix, containing Extracts from the Araucana of Don Alonzo de Ercilla. Translated from the Original Italian, by an American Gentleman.* 2 vol. 8 vo. Middletown (Conn.) 1808."[33]

James Mill opened the review with these words:

> We are particularly glad at the present moment to be able to direct our readers to the works of Molina, in their own language. Whatever is calculated to increase our knowledge of South America, is now of the greatest importance; and the region which is the subject of the work before us, is certainly among the most interesting of that neglected world. It occupies the space between the Andes and the Pacific Ocean; and, stretching from the 24th to the 45th degrees of south latitude, is universally described as a terrestial paradise, being blessed beyond any other country with a delicious climate, and a fertile soil; and exhibiting, in its varied scenes, at once the most grand and magnificent, as well as the most soft and engaging features of nature.

Despite Mill's frequent references to the Viscardo review of January, 1809, in the text and footnotes, the Molina article has been overlooked by the students of James Mill. The two presentations, moreover, are noticeably different: the first was the general background written with some restraints imposed upon him by Editor Jeffrey; the second was a veritable "attack" article with no holds barred! Just why Jeffrey permitted it, we are unable to say! Miranda and Mill must have thoroughly won him over. It leaves us with a priceless insight of a first-rate publicist whose emotional style at times reached artistic proportions—a great mind obsessed with a Smithian dream.

In two scholarly pages, Mill identified the two volumes: the first was Molina's *Natural History of Chile*, published in Bologna in 1782, an excellent "model of Chorography," and the second, his *Civil History of Chile* (Bologna, 1786), along with the Appendix cited. "It is not our intention," Mill indicated,

> to enlarge upon the contents of these works: the *Storia Naturale* is too well known to require it; and of the *Storia Civile* it may suffice to say, that it is a succinct and intelligent account of the state of the natives, when first discovered by the Spaniards; of the transactions, whether

warlike or peaceful, which have since taken place; and of the present state, diversities, and character of the population.[34]

Here, Mill again brought up the Jesuits:

He was one of those Jesuits, who were so cruelly driven from their country, when the court of Spain embraced the resolution of extinguishing the order within all its dominions; and was one of those, who, on that occasion, as we mentioned in a former article, took refuge in the dominions of the Pope in Italy. Clavigero [Francisco Javier], who has presented us with the celebrated history of his native country, Mexico; Molina, the histories of Chili; and Viscardo, a native of Peru, from whose pen we lately presented an interesting tract to the notice of our readers and who left behind him various manuscripts on the state of his country, which we have reason to believe were highly worthy of seeing the light, are three natives of Spanish America, and three of that handful of persecuted ecclesiastics, whom, in an equal number of any order of men, it will not be easy to parallel.[35]

Satisfied with his review of the text, James Mill got to the point of his piece:

The great political questions which regard Spanish America have not diminished—they have augmented in interest since the occasion which we lately embraced, of laying before our countrymen some of those statements and views which we conceived it important for them, at this juncture, to have presented to their minds.*" [The footnote referred to page 277 of the January 1809 article.] The appearance of the publication before us and, still more, our deep conviction of the value of the critical moment, in bringing good or evil out of such a state of affairs as just now presents itself in South America, have induced us once more to direct our pen to this interesting subject.[36]

Having thus re-introduced himself to the reader, James Mill's words began to flow with his uncanny ability for a synthesis of the past:

There is no former period of our history at which the emancipation of Spanish America, the removal of that dark, and jealous, and excluding government—which watched over its colonies as an Asiatic tyrant does over his seraglio—which feared the approach of a trader as an enemy, and shut out the world from all intercourse with so great and so fair a portion of the globe—would not have appeared an event to be numbered among the greatest which the course of human affairs could bring forth.[37]

It should be recalled that William Burke evoked a similar metaphor in his first treatise—the picture of a wall around that fertile garden that violated the rules of Providence! Then, Mill brought the British back into the picture:

> Witness the efforts which this nation has never ceased to make, to obtain even a diminutive share of the advantages which the intercourse with that country seemed calculated to ensure,—from the date of the romantic adventures of Sir Walter Raleigh, to the recent transactions of Sir Home Popham and General Whitelocke. Witness the importance which, throughout the history of British commerce, we shall find attached to the contraband trade with the Spanish Main;—the contract, on which so much stress was laid in the treaty of Utrecht;—the interest which has been so often excited by the question relative to the British right of cutting logwood in the Bay of Campeachy. Witness too the South-Sea Company, which absorbed to such a degree the attention of the nation. Witness even the importance which was so recently attached to the dispute about the wretched spot of Nootka Sound; the still greater importance which was, about half a century ago, attached to the possession of the Falkland Islands; and the weight which was ascribed to Trinidad, in arranging the treaty of Amiens.

There were not many Englishmen that could have written such a synthesis; but James Mill, directed or advised by Miranda, was able to do so with great effect!

Mill continued:

> But if ever the intercourse with South America was justly regarded as of importance to this country, that importance must be allowed to be augmented in a tenfold ratio, by the extraordinary circumstances in which the extraordinary events of the last twenty years have involved the nations of Europe.

Just as William Burke, that master teacher and propagandist, often turned to hypothetical cases to drive home a major conclusion, Mill did likewise:

> Let us suppose that, in our present state of embarrassment and alarm, South America had presented a prospect as barren of hope to us as

Europe itself; that, besotted with their bigotry to their exclusive religion, and their exclusive government, the inhabitants had rejected and abjured all intercourse with heretics and free men; and had driven us from their shores, as we have hitherto been driven by those who ruled over them; how deeply should we have deplored the misfortunes! How highly should we have estimated the resources so vast, and the demand so appropriate of the new world, had access to it been withheld from our beneficient enterprises, at the moment when the continent of Europe seemed closing upon our hopes! Formerly, when the emancipation of Spanish America, from an oppressive and degrading government was contemplated by the beneficent spirits of this country, as in the number of desirable events, the bigotry of the inhabitants, their hatred of heretics, their blind attachment, even to the government that oppressed them appeared to erect invincible obstacles, and were lamented as precluding the acceptance of aid, from the only government sufficiently liberal, and sufficiently powerful to hold it out. By the happy operation of knowledge and events, this bigotry has now given way; and a variety of causes have tended to weaken the chain which bound those colonies to the mother country; a chain which may now be regarded as broken, and impossible ever again to be joined. The inhabitants of the new world are holding out their arms to the inhabitants of the British isles, craving their assistance in the hour of need—and offering to them, in return, the most unbounded prospects of advantage which it ever was in the power of one nation to hold out to another.

How does one explain the inability to exploit such an opportunity in Spanish America? Mill's objective now was to lead his readers effectively towards that explanation. The master propagandist proceeded:

How, then, it may be asked, does it happen, that a state of things, which, while it was unattainable, was the object of so many eager efforts, should excite so little interest, and produce so few exertions to take advantage of it, now that it has spontaneously occurred? The truth is, that our hatred and our fear of France leaves us no room for any other feeling; and that the proximity and immediate interest of our daily manoeuvres against her, prevents us from descrying the superior importance, even as a measure of defence or hostility, or the great and easy exploit to which we are invited in another hemisphere.[38]

At this point, James Mill felt that he should present some documentary evidence to establish the fact that there were at least twenty million consumers of British goods in South America. The document that he examined in detail was a letter that Viscardo had received from Clavigero in Italy concerning population figures in Mexico and Central America. It was a very scholarly presentation of the materials, along with discussion of the sources and authorities—the type of treatment that Dr. John Allen had employed in his *Edinburgh Review* articles on Peru and Von Humboldt. It is not surprising, therefore, that the Review won international recognition for its thoughtful and well-researched essays. This section of the Molina article reflected Mill's conscientious study of the many volumes that he borrowed from General Miranda's celebrated library. Since the bulk of the population in Spanish America was Indian, Mill's next step was to prove that the harmful stereotype of the indolent and superstitious Indian was invalid. For Mexico, he drew from the writings of the Frenchman Mons. Thiery de Menonville; and for Chile, from Molina and the Frenchman La Peyrouse, whom we encountered in Burke's second treatise. The discussion of the Indians of Chile led to La Peyrouse's praise for Chile's fertility. After citing his references in French and Spanish, Mill, the experienced propagandist, offered his resumé, or digest:

> There are one or two of the statements here which cannot fail to attract, and that in no ordinary degree, the attention of the commercial and manufacturing world. A country, the production of which might be carried to that amount, as to feed the half of Europe, offers a field of extraordinary promise to the enterprise of the active nations of the globe. A country, of which the wools would supply the manufactures of both France and England, must be one of the most interesting regions on the face of the earth, to the country the most remarkable in the world for its woolen manufactures, at the moment when the great market of the raw commodity is in danger of being cut off from her.[39]

The next point of focus, naturally enough, was the Isthmus of Panama. If there were a convenient passageway in that vicinity, Mill noted with emphasis, it would bring

> Chili, as it were, to our door: and the wools of Chili may reach us at little more than the cost of Jamaica cotton. This circumstance renders the practicability of that navigation an object, if possible, of still higher importance. There are several circumstances in proof of its facility, which we are now enabled to add to the illustrations we presented in a former Number. The subject, indeed, is so interesting, and so little is

known about it, that we are anxious to give all the information relative
to it in our power.

Except for the spherical chart of Spaniards in 1805, Mill referred to
authorities of earlier centuries (Herrera, Gonzalo Fernández de Oviedo)
or of the last fifty years (Alcedo, Abbé de Pradt) to convince the
readers that the Panamanian or the Nicaraguan routes would open up
a passageway from the Pacific to the Atlantic[40] It was a convincing
presentation, reinforcing the earlier article in the *Edinburgh Review*
(January 1809).

With the historical and factual materials covered, Mill was ready to
open up a brilliant nine-page review and analysis of a policy for Great
Britain in South America. His organizational genius, his instincts as a
publicist, his historical perspective in international relations, his
political insights, his caustic commentaries, and his fiery commitment
to anticolonialism, laissez-faire economics, and Great Britain's economic
and political leadership in world affairs—are some of the conclusions
and observations that are discernible in this commendable display of
intellectual power. Mill's uncanny insight into the Cortes of Cádiz
experiment in liberalism and constitutionalism was a genuine surprise
to this author, having just spent over a decade studying that topic. Mill
was exceptionally accurate, for the most part, discerning the political
clash between Spanish Americans and the party of Europeans-Islanders
that brought down most of the Spanish Empire by 1825.[41]

Again, the teacher faced the problem of organization with
imagination and thoroughness, well-aware that repetition was the name
of the game. "The only satisfactory manner of discussing this
question," he began, "is to consider all the ways in which the present
crisis of South American affairs can possibly terminate; to fix the eye
upon that issue by which the interests of our own country are most
likely to be promoted; and to inquire what we can possibly do to bring
it about."

Mill proposed two possible outcomes:

I. Spain, the mother country, may remain independent and II. Spain
may become subject to Bonaparte. Furthermore, these sub-
classifications applied: I. If Spain remains independent, South America,
may, 1. remain united with her in the state of vassalage in which she
has hitherto been held. 2. It may remain united with her in her free
association or union, as that of Ireland with Great Britain. 3. It may

revolt from her by the assistance of Bonaparte. 4. It may revolt from her by the assistance of Great Britain. 5. It may revolt from her without any assistance. And the second classification: If Spain becomes subject to Bonaparte, South America may 1. remain united with her in the state of vassalage,—but not in a free association; because to a despotic crown there is no union of subjects otherwise than by vassalage. 2. South America may assert its independence with the assistance of Great Britain. 3. It may assert its independence without any assistance.[42]

Mill's development of this outline, or scheme, of exposition was uneven and discriminatory to prove his own thesis, as well as its component parts. The proposition that Spain would remain independent and Spanish America as her vassal was, of course, ridiculous since it would deprive Great Britain of her opportunity to utilize those overseas resources of Spain, thus strenghening Napoleon's strategy of boycott.[43] Having made this point, Mill now could attack the Treaty of Alliance between Spain and Great Britain—a major obstacle to British support of emancipation. As we shall see, Miranda's writers constantly attacked that diplomatic transaction as a betrayal of England. Here is how James Mill presented the problem:

In spite of all this, our Government, we find, has just entered into a treaty, guaranteeing the integrity of the whole Spanish dominions. If this means any thing else, than that, while that treaty subsists, we shall not ourselves do any thing to detach any part of these dominions, it means something which it would both be impolitic and impossible for us to perform. These colonies are in reality of no use to Spain. They would be of no use even to Great Britain, who is so much better able to turn them to advantage; and no wise man, we are confident, would advise this country to accept of such a sovereignty, even if it were tendered to her by the free will of the inhabitants. But the stipulation, in this sense of it, is fortunately as impracticable as it is impolitic. If, by engaging to guarantee the integrity of the Spanish monarchy, we meant to bind ourselves to prevent the South Americans from becoming independent. . .we shall only ask, whether, if we were to employ all the forces of Great Britain in such a conflict, they would be sufficient for the purpose? Could we, if we were mad enough to stake Great Britain upon the contest, prevent the independence of South America, if South America were resolved to be Independent?

This would be an impossible situation, argued the writer. Do we have the resources for such a commitment? Against the South Americans will? Then, the clever Mill turned on his make-believe strategy:

> But suppose the contrary; suppose we were actually in readiness to send a body of troops to resist the emancipation of South America; of all probable things the most probable—if we must not call it certain, is, that Bonaparte would offer his assistance to the South Americans, and that they would accept it. If so, we have abundant experience, that it is no impossible thing for him to send troops to South America; and it will be for us to consider in what manner, and to what degree a French army fighting in South America, on the side of the people, and against us, would be likely to promote the good, and prevent the evil of the British nation.[44]

The master debater was in good form!

In Part One, Section 2—Spain, independent; South America, free association, Mill's analysis was highly original, as well as accurate, since this was one of the viable alternatives open to Spanish Americans. "For this purpose," Mill commenced, "it is indispensably necessary that Spain should give to herself a free government. A despotical government in Spain can never do otherwise than govern the colonies despotically. There is no free association of subjects with an arbitrary crown:—it is a contradiction in terms." Only by adopting free institutions can Spain regain her independence, as well as maintain it:

> We hear of the national cortez [Parliament], and of the establishment of a representative government, in which the colonies are to be invited to partake; a liberal, it will be said, and beneficial proposal this, in which the suffrages of all reasonable men will unite.

Mill's political intuition concerning the Cortes of Cádiz—before it even convened—was indeed astonishing. He felt that he had to "unveil its real character." Mill continued:

> In forming a representative system for the different districts of a large country, the only safe and equitable rule perhaps is to follow the proportion of population, which always, on a large scale, gives you very exactly the proportion of property also. If you proceed on any other ground, you lay injustice at the foundation of your whole structure. On this principle, the representatives from South America in the cortez of Spain, must be nearly twice as numerous as those from Spain itself.

It was generally assumed at the Cortes of Cádiz in southern Spain that the overseas population was about sixteen million, whereas Spain and the nearby island groups had about ten and one-half million people. Mill was right; that was the problem at the Cortes of Cádiz when it held its first session in September, 1810. Mill's conclusion was also on the right path:

> The representatives from South America become then the governors of Spain, and South America is the metropolitan country; it ought therefore to be the seat of government, and would soon become so; for the preponderating representatives from South America would vote for the transfer. The consequence, however, would probably be, that the Spaniards would not submit,—and the union would be dissolved by a civil war nearly as soon as formed.

There was no question that Miranda's political insights on the fate of Hispanic constitutionalism must have influenced the writer's conclusion. Be that as it may, they were right! He said much more on this parliamentary scenario; and it was all very convincing. William Burke could not have done better.[45]

In Part One, Section 3—Spain, independent; South America, independent, French aid—James Mill, consulting Miranda closely, revealed a keen, as well as accurate, imagination. For all practical purposes, his explanation was close to what actually occurred in the next two years, but not necessarily because of Napoleon's assistance. "If we mistake not," he began,

> this is a contingency which, in this country, is not greatly apprehended. We trust to our fleets for keeping the transatlantic regions pure of the contamination of French armies . . . Suppose that Spain having fairly delivered herself from the arms of Bonaparte, and the colonies declaring their determination to be independent, Spain should, in pursuance of the treaty now existing, claim and receive the navy and army of Great Britain to aid in subduing what she could call the rebellion; in these circumstances, is it any thing less than certain that Bonaparte would both desire, and would be able to send an army to the support of the colonies? If the colonies, thus supported, would without any doubt baffle Spain and England attacking them, we should then have South America independent, united in friendship with France, and standing in enmity with England. If any thing more is wanting to complete the cup of English misfortune, it would be this. Another contingency, and one,

we are afraid, still more probable, is, that Great Britain hanging off, in consequence of the present treaty, in a state something between active discouragement and mere neutrality, the South Americans becoming divided among themselves, one party may call in Bonaparte, and by its efficacy give him the means of acquiring the ascendancy in the country.

James Mill, of course, had no trouble with Part One, Section 4—Spain, independent; South America free, English assistance—this was the main objective of the July, 1809, article. It was obviously the

most advantageous to our own country. The power of Bonaparte, not augmented, but baffled and impaired by the power of Spain, would cease to be formidable to us in Europe; while all the vast, and then rapidly improving, resources of South America, would become subservient to our aggrandisement and prosperity.[46]

William Burke's dream was still alive!

In James Mill's opinion, there was not much hope of Spain, independent, Colonies independent "without external help." He explained: "in almost all possible cases, if these colonies do not obtain the assistance of England, they will be sure to get that of France." There is no doubt, however, that they can oppose their mother country on their own. The interest of the "mother country is so low, that scarcely would there be found adherents of hers in the country, sufficient even to form a party, is more than probable." The problem here, he continued, was that "without some authority, to which all parties would look up, and Great Britain is admirably situated to perform the part of such a benefactor, there would be differences of views, which would be troublesome, and might prove mischievous." Despite this possibility, or weakness, the example of "North America" might guide them through such a crisis. Their course was plain, so that "two or three good heads, under the strong influence of good intention, would be sufficient to retain them in the salutary track."

A more likely scenario, Mill's argued, would be if Spain lost her independence:

This is the side of the alternative on which we lay by far the greatest stress, because it is to be considered as by far the most probable; but so much of what we have stated on the former side of the case is applicable to this, that we hope to be able to say what remains in few words. Nothing, if Bonaparte becomes a master of Old Spain, seems capable of preventing his becoming, at the same time, master of America, but the strong and irresistible determination of the American people to be no longer dependent. If that determination be, as we suppose it to be, already come to maturity, then will it triumph over all the obstacles which the power of Bonaparte can oppose to it.

"The determination of the South Americans to be independent," Mill observed, "is the only bulwark on which we have to rely, against one of the most calamitious events that can befall our country. The light which this throws upon the treaty under which we now act, is strong and instructive."[47] He would come back to this all important theme later.

James Mill preferred, at this juncture, to deal with his choice: Part Two, Section 2—Spain subdued; colonies for independence, aided by Britain. "By this assistance, "he beamed," the progress of that great revolution might be so guided, as to produce the greatest possible good at once to us, to the Spaniards, and to the people principally concerned." His optimism, however, soured as he remembered bitterly the mistake made by the British government in not recognizing that Spain, like other European countries, would fall to the Corsican. It was inevitable. How could English ministers have been so foolish! "To tie up our hands," the fiery Scot cut deeply: "by a treaty, from taking measures to prevent the extension of his [Napoleon's] influence to South America, was an instance of misconduct among the grossest to be found in the huge library of ministerial imbecilities." How did this sentence get past Editor Jeffrey's desk? Times were obviously changing. Mill followed this strong blast with these words:

> Never did a great event offer greater facilities in the execution, than the regeneration of South America by the helping hand of the British government. Little more, in fact, is necessary, than to go and offer to the people a rallying point, and to employ that wisdom and coolness which a third party might so easily possess, in preventing an inexperienced people, in the heat of a great change, from running into confusion. With what rapidity would the fruits of so noble a conduct begin to be felt! How sublime the distinction of having once again set an example of such beneficient interference in the affairs of nations! The revolt of the Dutch from the mis-government of Spain—a revolt so fruitful in benefits to the human race—was rendered triumphant, in a great measure, through British means. The wisdom of Queen Elizabeth and her ministers saw the magnitude of the occasion, and did not let it

slip. But what were the advantages immediately offered to Great Britain by the freedom of Holland, compared with those promised by the freedom of South America?

The historian, as well as ex-Presbyterian minister, made this point in sermon-like style:

> Great, too, as were at that time the dangers to this country from the enmity and power of a Philip the Second, the enmity and power of a Bonaparte are infinitely more formidable. In its wise and beneficient acts, it is happy for a country to emulate itself. For there are precedents which it is useful to follow; as well as others, the offspring of folly and minister interest—which it is no less useful to avoid.[48]

When he came to Part Two, Section 3—Spain under Bonaparte, South America's independence on her own, James Mill's anger against the guilty ministers had not yet subsided:

> If the alarming treaty so often alluded to, acting upon a correspondent state of mind in the rulers of Great Britain, shall so tie up the hands of this country, as to make her defer her interference till it be too late, it then remains for us to desire with inexpressible earnestness, that the South Americans may erect an independence for themselves; otherwise subjection under Bonaparte is the only remaining alternative.[*][49]

Note the asterisk. Here, Mill reported jubilantly what he had taken from the *Parliamentary Report* of June 1, 1809, footnoted at the bottom of the page:

> *We are happy at last to be able to say, that ours is not the only voice which has been lifted up to impress these salutary considerations on the public. On the 31st of May, Mr. Ponsonby said in the House of Commons, 'His opinion was, that the cause of Spain and Portugal would fail; and that, before long, the power of France would be as great in those countries as in the rest of the Continent. The conduct of our government, therefore, ought to be to secure their insular and foreign settlements.' He meant, that we should hold out to South America, etc. to become independent; that Joseph Bonaparte might not in reality, as he already was in name, be King of the Indies. 'To hold out the idea of Ferdinand the Seventh, as head of an American government, would be the height of folly. If the people of South America chose that he should be their king, that altered the case.' But he hoped there was nothing to

entangle this country with him, contrary to the inclination of those who had been his subjects. If this country, however, chose to put off the matter too long, he much apprehended, when the power of France was fully settled in Old Spain, it would be able to draw a great part of New Spain along with it. He stated this now, because 'next Session it might be too late.'

Supporting Ponsonby's argument, James Mill noted that England could be most helpful in the "work of regeneration" for South America.

As a student of public psychology, Mill had meaningful insights upon Great Britain as a moderating force in South America:

All those sudden and irregular impulses which were so apt to hurry into dangerous situations in a moment of change, the gentle influence of a moderating and friendly power, would be most salutary in allaying. All those dissensions which the passions of disagreeing parties are so apt, in similar situations, to inflame into open resistance and bloodshed, a protecting power, cultivating and deserving the esteem of all parties, might easily temper and guide. Who can contemplate the delightful results of such an interference as this, without lamenting the chances that it will yet be defeated? If so, if the people of South America must be left to themselves, it would be presumption in any one to pretend to foresee what may be the consequences. So firmly are we convinced that the minds of the South Americans are matured for a revolution, that we think the crisis still would end well. Yet, when the seeds of evil, which in such a situation can never be wanting, are allowed to spring and vegetate, without any exterminating hand; above all, with such a cultivating and fostering hand as that of Bonaparte to promote their growth; it is impossible not to dread what such a mixture of elements may bring forth. One thing is abundantly certain, that the people of South America, beholding themselves abandoned to all the hazards of a revolution, by a people who had the power, by little more than an act of volition, to save them from a peril so tremendous, must conceive an antipathy to that people, which ages may not suffice to eradicate.[50]

That was indeed a powerful ending for readers to ponder. The ex-Presbyterian minister had not yet forgotten his calling!

* * * * * * * * * * * *

Despite the harassment of Castlereagh's men, threatening to expel him at mid-year from British soil if he persisted with his treasonous correspondence against the Spanish ally, the beleagured Miranda at least had the deep satisfaction that his colleague James Mill was forcing Great Britain to reconsider its priorities. Shortly after the second essay appeared, Francisco de Miranda went on a vacation to Oxford University which provided him with a stimulating intellectual fare. He had interesting conversations with two students of government and international relations, Dr. F.S. Constancio and Gould Francis Leckie, who gladly joined his crusade to influence a change in British policy toward South America. Since Miranda was away, James Mill also decided to go into the country to get some relief from the weather in London, a practice that was possible for those Londoners with some means. Mill, of course, was not in that category, nor could he afford such an expense unless there was a good reason for it. The years in London, aggravated by his impossible schedule and unquenchable drive for intellectual goals, were beginning to show in the reoccurrences of what most thought was the gout. He considered it rheumatism. It was an infirmity, nonetheless, that would bring him down to his final rest in 1836. We shall come back to his vacation experience shortly.

A scholar, it seems, cannot go on a vacation without some notes or materials to peruse in the event an opportunity presents itself. Since Mill's stay in the country was much longer than he had expected, he composed an article for the *Bell's Weekly Messenger* that came out on October 15, 1809. Continuing the attack of the Molina essay, the result was a brilliant exposure of Spain's economic system and why Spanish colonials were desperate to escape the old shackles.

He noted that the Junta Central of Spain, in the past two weeks, had turned its attention to South America. It mortified him to learn that the Spanish Junta, in a sense, had returned to the old policies of monopoly. So annoyed by this event, Mill found himself overwhelmed by the Black Legend stereotype. The following paragraph could have easily appeared in the *Literary Journal*, edited by a young Scot:

> The French Revolution will certainly always be execrated, and justly execrated, for the mischief which it has caused; but amidst so many evils, it has likewise produced some good. It has moved and stirred up human reason; it set men upon thinking; and a civilized society never thinks in vain.

And the sermon went on. "Observe," he finally said, "for example, the fund of good sense and even of moral knowledge which pervades an audience at a theatre. How just are the sensations, and, where they are audible, the remarks on the performances even of the lowest amongst them." But Spain is impossible: "the only nation of Europe which has had nothing of this gradual progression." Her Government, Nobility, the Inquisition, Monopoly all stand in opposition to progress: "You hear much of the rights of the Crown, but nothing of the just expectation of the people."

With that introduction, Mill described Spain's old economic system in graphic terms and with a meaningful emphasis that is not readily available in discussing motives for the Wars of Independence in Latin America. Mill commenced:

> The System of the ancient Government of Spain with respect to South America was that of a double monopoly,—a monopoly of its produce, and a monopoly of its supply;—the Colonists were to sell only to Spain, and to buy only of Spain. Now Spain being unable to supply her colonies from her own industry, necessarily became a retailer;—she bought of England, and resold to the colonies. In this first step of the business, the Colonies were necessarily compelled to pay exorbitantly, because, instead of having to deal only with one trader, they had to deal with two;—instead of paying only the profit of the wholesale trader, they had to pay their own countrymen as retailers;—that is, had to pay a double profit on the capital employed to supply them. But this was not the whole. Being confined by the system of exclusion not to buy from any other, the Spanish merchant had the Colonial Market to himself;—he could raise the price as he chose; he had no other limits but those of his own cupidity, and those of their necessities. In this manner the Colonists have to purchase the most ordinary productions of Europe at the most extravagant prices. The necessary consequences was that all were compelled to buy less than they needed, and many could not purchase at all. Thus, with respect to the South American colonies, Europe almost existed in vain;—existed only to send them hungry Governors and starving tax-collectors, who receive all and give nothing.
>
> The monopoly of the purchase of Colonial produce had similar mischievous effects—it lowered the price of colonial commodities to an unnatural state of depression; the Spaniards only could buy and the Spaniards would buy at only the lowest possible prices. Colonial industry and cultivation were thus left without their natural encouragement, and accordingly the lands of South America are no further cultivated than is necessary for the immediate sustenance of the people. Unless by the bounty of nature, and the uncommon fertility of the soil, the South American Colonists would have been in a state of the

most extreme poverty,—compelled to purchase common comforts at the most exorbitant rate, and, by the discouragement of their own industry, restricted in procuring the means of purchase,—compelled to sell their own produce at half its worth, and unable to procure European articles except at double their value.

In the works of Burke and Mill, the metaphor of Spanish monopoly has been common: "the walled garden" and the "tyrant-seraglio" which Mill used in the July, 1809 article. Here he describes it once again:

> Such was the ancient system of Spain towards her Colonies, and such is the system which is now restored.—A system which has a necessary tendency to keep the Colonies,—that is to say, one-fifth of the earth in its present state of miserable depression and degradation.—A system, which perpetuates the poverty of the native country, because it renders it a pitiful retailer, instead of a wholesale dealer, and because it impoverishes their customs, and thereby necessarily diminishes their trade and profits,—And finally a system, which may be considered as a natural injustice by every other nation, because, contrary to the rights of nature, it cuts off the communication and mutual supply and exchange of Europe and America,—and, on a principle of selfishness and cupidity sacrifices a great common good to a trivial private advantage,—arresting the progress of civilization, and diminishing the stock of human comforts and enjoyments.—*Let it never be said of an English Administration, that it assisted in perpetuating a servitude like this.*

In the Caracas collection of Miranda's manuscripts, this last line was underlined in pencil. By Miranda?[52] We suppose so. The monopoly metaphor, though using different words, was also a major characteristic of the "William Burke" writings in the Caracas gazette.

* * * * * * * * * * * *

Even in the days of Napoleon, when a man turned sixty—born on February 15, 1748—he dreamed of faraway places like Mexico where a writer might extend his life by one-third without having to spend valuable time fixing fires during those bitter English winters. Jeremy Bentham, a celebrated English philosopher, political theorist, economist, and what have you, wrote to Lord Vassal Holland in Seville, Spain. It was six months after his sixtieth birthday. He wanted Lord Holland to seek permission for Bentham to establish a residence near Mexico City.

Gaspar de Jovellanos, a famous Spanish scholar and a member of the Junta Central, drew up a suitable petition for the license on personal grounds. For one reason or another, the Junta temporized; and, as the months passed, Bentham lost interest in proceeding to Mexico with Judge Herbert Koe, his assistant.[53] By November 1, 1810, Jeremy Bentham craved the terrestial paradise of Caracas, Venezuela:

> The temperature is delightful, summer temperatures all the year round. Within sight of the sea, though almost under the line, you have a mountain topped with ice, so that you may absolutely choose your temperature, and enjoy the vegetable luxuries of all countries. If I go thither, it will be to do a little business in the way of trade—to draw up a body of laws for the people there, they having, together with a number of other Spanish American colonies, taken advantage of the times, and shaken off the Spanish Yoke, which is a very oppressive one.[54]

On this occasion, it would be James Mill who was to accompany him to South America.

Bentham tells us that he first met James Mill in 1808; but his memory was not always too accurate. After returning to London in 1808, Miranda walked over to his old friend's house at Queen Square Place, Westminister. Bentham had sent him a note of welcome and a request to borrow some books from Miranda's library. Miranda, therefore, arrived at Bentham's home with some maps and books dealing with Mexico. The scholar was looking for more equitable climes. In return, Miranda borrowed Bentham's copy of a work by Gaspar de Jovellanos; and he also carried away some of Bentham's unpublished manuscripts. These were perhaps items that Mill had wanted to read. The exchange of materials continued throughout 1808; and Judge Koe was the intermediary for Bentham. In those final months of that year, Mill was very busy organizing the January, 1809, manuscript; and we do not know if he got to meet Judge Koe. A copy of Mill's first article on "Emancipation" was sent to Jeremy Bentham in late February, or early March, 1809. And we can just imagine Bentham's great satisfaction upon reading the praise that young Mill had expressed in that publication about his expertise. Bentham's over-sized ego, of course, went to work; and Miranda introduced his young colleague to his old friend. Within a month's time, on April 27, 1809, to be exact, we have the beginning of a correspondence between Mill and Bentham. Mill was helping him with certain legal cases, while commenting on the master's work on "Libel Law" and "Freedom of the Press." On this last theme, Mill mentioned the timid talk that he had heard at the House of Commons "on Monday night." "Oh, Gad," he exclaimed, "if they but knew what law is, and ought to be, as well as you can tell them on this most interesting of all points . . ." He signed this letter, and others that followed: "Your affectionate pupil."[55]

Jeremy Bentham and James Mill seriously began their long record of intellectual collaboration in August, 1809. Their contribution to "Philosophical Radicalism" was notable and well known to Englishmen. At the risk of appearing sacrilegious, we wonder how the historical record would have read if those two intellectuals, along with the child John Stuart Mill, had transferred themselves to South America with the "Precursor" of Spanish American Independence, Francisco de Miranda! That was a strong possibility at one time. Be that as it may, there are some interesting documents about their first serious attempt at intellectual cooperation in the summer of 1809, when the Mill family visited Bentham's Barrow Green House, in Oxted, Surrey, near Godstone where "the Brighton coaches all pass."[56]

James Mill wrote two long letters to General Miranda from Bentham's summer house in August, 1809. The first one, on August 11th, explained Mill's presence in Surrey as if it were actually a whim: "I must now inform you that I have been as great a truant from town, as any restless Englishman." Since Miranda had left London for the country, Mill and his wife decided that this would be a good opportunity to enjoy "the air and sight of the field. I have been running about the country in all directions. I have been at Tunbridge, and every place that was worth the going to in this part of Surrey and Kent." Then, in a very indirect manner, he admitted what was perhaps his real reason for coming out into the country. Mill was not one to waste time, unless it was to his advantage: "and among other things I have paid a visit to Mr. Bentham." And, of course,

> He has insisted that Mrs. Mill and I shall spend some time with him before we return to town; and as he has pointed out some thing in which I can be useful to him, and to the cause of good government through what he is doing for it, I have been the more readily prevailed upon not altogether to recede from his request. This will up a few weeks longer in the country than we had originally intended, which I the less regret, as I should have been deprived; at any rate, of the benefit of your conversation had I remained in town.

Mill asserted that Miranda especially needed to enjoy the countryside,

> and the more so, as your mind, more harassed with wretched
> interruption to your great designs, had more need of repose;—especially,
> too, as the play of events, in that curious and instructive scene which it
> is our lot to witness, had produced that temporary suspense, both on the
> continent of Europe, and in Great Britain, in which nothing remained for
> you but to sit still, and wait till the great results which had been just
> brought to pass should have time to work some of their natural and
> unavoidable effects.

He continued with details on events occurring on the Continent.
Napoleon already suspected that the Austrians were about to submit;
there were the usual lies about victories in Spain by the allies. Here
Mill found it difficult to contain himself:

> they tell lies because they have resolved to tell lies and to deceive the
> two abused nations, Spaniard and English, who are made to shed their
> blood, and waste their substance, in an unavailing struggle, for the
> gratification of a few villains in Seville and about St. James's . . . Did
> you ever see such a besotted cluster of fools entrusted with the affairs
> of a civilized nation? At any rate, I expect that our separation for a
> time in the country will render our conversation more interesting if
> possible.

The *Edinburgh Review* (July issue) would not be in London "for
general circulation, before the end of the month . . . It will give me
great pleasure to hear from you."[57]

Miranda's reply reached the Barrow Green House on August 24,
1809, bringing much excitement there. Mill tells us:

> Upon mentioning yesterday the pleasure I had received of a letter from
> you—and presenting Mr. B. and Mrs. M the compliments you did them
> the honour to send and upon Mr. Bentham's hearing that you *did* at
> times quit your headquarters in town, an expression came from him of
> a very strong desire that you would be prevailed upon to join, if it were
> but for a day or two, the rustic party.

Enclosed in Mill's letter of August 25th was one by Jeremy Bentham
himself: "Dear General: I have commissioned Mr. Mill, in quality of
my Chargé d' Affaires, *aupres de Votre Excellence* to say whatever he

wanted in order to bring you here for a visit." Overwhelmed by the suggestion: Mill wrote:

> I know few things that would give me greater pleasure than to meet with you here; where we could walk, and talk over so many things at leisure. A few days under the same roof, and at the same time, with you and Mr. B. the two men—(no offence to all the glory of Bonaparte)—whom I consider as more likely to fix the attention of a wise posterity, than any other men of their time, would be a trust to me indeed.[58]

Unfortunately, Miranda was unable to join Bentham's party at that time, due to the pressure of business that had come up during his vacation.[59]

Chapter Seven

The Year of Decisions: 1810

With a sincere hope that the year 1810 may produce something favourable to the liberty of the New World and that the Almighty may enable my General to sustain the conspicuous and glorious part of its first advocate.

S.C. Loudon (New York City), Jan. 24, 1810.[1]

My dear Sir: The object of the attached publication is to communicate to our Americans those documents and news items that seemed most relevant to their interests and security; and so by taking the most prompt and necessary measures in the present crisis, they might avoid with forethought and wisdom the imminent risks threatening them.

F. Miranda's Circular Letter (London), March 24, 1810.[2]

The collapse of Austria in mid-1809 and the French breakthrough to Sevilla, Spain, later in that year, compelled Americans and Europeans to make crucial decisions that were no longer postponable. Spanish Americans appeared ready to heed the earlier suggestions made in Miranda's "Paper Assault." Uprisings in La Paz and Quito by the end of 1809 were naked realities that challenged the Junta Central's power in the Empire. Unable to survive the enemy's advances, the Junta hurriedly transferred power to a Regency of five men who, in January, 1810, fled southward to Cádiz for a last-ditch stand against the French. If the Regency could not hold that port city on the Atlantic, it would have to move its capital to Mallorca, one of the Balearic Islands—an escape similar to that of Portugal from Lisbon in late November, 1807. Thanks to the aid of the British navy, the Portuguese Crown moved to Rio de Janeiro in Brazil. Or should the Spanish Regency also move its base to the New World, to Mexico or to Venezuela? Other questions arose as well: How would Spanish Americans react to the JC's transfer of power to the Regency? Would they accept a regency of five Spaniards, who only at the last moment agreed to include an American? Spaniards had issued a call for a national *Cortes* (Parliament) for September, 1810; but would Peninsulars and Islanders honor their promises of equal rights to overseas' delegates?

Thanks to the *Edinburgh Review's* articles, and their complements in England's newspapers, British politicians and intellectuals had good advice and information to make the changes necessary in England's policy. Frustrated by the financial drain and human losses of a "no-win" policy in Europe, the British opposition relentlessly attacked and challenged the "ministerial imbecilities," to use Mill's own words. The assault of Miranda's writers increased the sense of guilt among the government's ministers. Moreover, dissension within the cabinet of the Duke of Portland continued between the supporters of Lord Castlereagh and George Canning, leading to a duel between the two leaders. Subsequently, they both resigned; and Portland, in fragile health, gave up his office in September, 1809. The compromise leader that emerged was Spencer Perceval, the former Chancellor of the Exchequer, who held on as Prime Minister until 1812, when a fanatic shot him to death!

The turn of events in England might have played into Miranda's hands if Nicholas Vansittart, his good friend and constant adviser, had been present in London. Opposition leaders like the Duke of Gloucester, who since early 1809 was pushing many distinguished Englishmen to support Britain's advocacy of Spanish American emancipation, and William Wilberforce, the great champion in the abolition of the slave trade (1807), were both pressuring Perceval to bring Vansittart into his cabinet. This was a strong possibility since Perceval liked the suggested candidate personally. The problem was that from late 1809 through 1810 Vansittart suffered a deep tragedy—the illness of his wife that brought on her death. Her loving and supportive husband would just not leave her side, despite the impatience of Miranda and British opposition leaders. Vansittart tried to do his best at a distance, making suggestions to his allies; but this was not enough. The relentless crusader from Venezuela had not encountered such an obstacle before.

* * * * * * * * * * * *

Throughout his European career, Francisco de Miranda had always been regarded as a man of letters who looked forward to intellectual discussions. We have often commented on his use of that celebrated personal library of his in England—the exchange of books and articles with the prominent members of society and government. And, as we have seen in James Mill's case, he encouraged the careers of young intellectuals as personal friends who made his life more interesting and challenging. They were also his fellow workers in a crusade to influence public opinion in society and among officials in government to support the cause of *Colombeia*—all aspects of the Colombia theme. After his return to London in 1808, Miranda intensified his association with Jeremy Bentham; and the Mill-Bentham combination was vital to the emancipation of Spanish America. James Mill especially was indispensable to Francisco de Miranda in the period covered by this chapter. This was evident in the continued stream of newspaper articles and in the documentary collections that saw the light in 1809 and 1810. Mill would look over book catalogs periodically, suggesting to Miranda what should be ordered to strengthen his holdings. He even acted as his personal secretary on certain occasions to help Molini.

In this crucial period of history, Miranda was circulating copies of Depons *Travels* in South America that were being read by Lord and Lady Sheffield, William Wilberforce, Benjamin Waddington and family, etc. Another popular item, especially after the January, 1809 article in the *Edinburgh Review*, was Viscardo's *Letter to the Americans*. Miranda told Wilberforce that this little treatise had more between its covers: "than . . . all the speeches and assertions, about Spain and South America" that he had ever "seen or heard of from the noble Lord H___d [Lord Vassal Holland]."[3]

Francisco de Miranda, during his summer trip to Oxford, formed a very sound friendship with two English intellectuals: Gould Francis Leckie and Dr. F.S. Constancio. These men were well aware of "Colombeia; and they were most useful in Miranda's propaganda effort of 1809 and 1810. Unfortunately, we know very little about these two gentlemen, except for a few letters and publications. They were both highly knowledgeable in the study of government and international relations. Mr. Gould Francis Leckie was very close to the Duke of Gloucester, which helps to explain how he came to know Miranda. Mill had reviewed a book of his on British policy in Europe and was much impressed with his scholarship. The section on Sicily went into great detail on how the nobility had usurped the rights of the "people." Given Mill's hostility to the institution of aristocracy, he admired Leckie's conclusions.[4]   Leckie introduced Miranda to Dr. F.S. Constancio, a remarkable savant, as well as an enigma. James Mill agreed that Dr. C's talents would be indispensable to Miranda's crusade in South America.[5] Constancio's letters to Miranda were all in French, not in Spanish. He might have been Portuguese-born, thus explaining his connection with a Mr. Francis Egerton who in December, 1809, had paid for their tickets to Portugal. That trip, however, did not materialize, so Dr. C. spent the winter in London, working with Miranda. The mysterious Dr. C. had never been to Spanish America, so he claimed; but he could well have been the son of Spanish American parents who settled in Europe, where he was born. He had remarkable insights into the politics and history of Spain, as well as Portugal; he was at ease with an analysis of Napoleon and of French history; his real expertise, however, seemed to have been English politics. He might have been teaching at Cambridge temporarily; but in December, 1809, he was out of a job. That is why he contracted to accompany Mr. Egerton to Portugal. We have assumed, therefore, that he was free to serve Francisco de Miranda in whatever assignment might be given to him in Europe, or in America.[6]

Whatever their true biographies, Leckie and Dr. Constancio were key consultants to General Miranda in preparing his final strategy in Europe. They joined Mill in his attack on the British ministers from September to November, 1809, hammering away at their "imbecilities." The *Bell's Weekly Messenger* ran a series entitled "Illustration of the Politics of Europe," which Mill followed regularly and to which he contributed on occasion. He often loaned copies of it to Miranda. On September 10, 1809, there was an article that dealt with the British attack upon Santo Domingo, on the Island of Hispaniola [Haiti at this time]. After the capitulation, the British turned over the city to their Spanish ally. This infuriated the writer of the column, who could have been Leckie, or even Mill himself. "At present we have given the Spaniards a town which they cannot retain," he observed, "and which in true policy we ought not to have given them." The writer must have read William Burke's first treatise since he used the "walled garden" metaphor:

> If England can only be supported by her commerce, and that era is very fast approaching, surely nothing can be so absurd as conferring Colonies on a nation most proverbially anticommercial of any people in the world.—How long have the Spaniards possessed South America—yet is there more trade between Newcastle and London, and even between London and Madeira, than between all South America and all Europe?—The Spanish Colonists willingly submit to a kind of barbarism in preference to an intercourse with non-catholic countries—they consider the rich, the boundless Continent of South America, as a walled garden, and they keep it as such. Surely, therefore, it is not consistent with the principle of a commercial government to extend the possessions of such an anti-social power . . . Spain has truly been the Duenna of South America,—she has kept it in bars and bolts, till she has rendered it as feeble, as ugly, as emaciated, as herself.[7]

Miranda's writers were working the monopoly metaphor to its maximum.

In the remainder of the article, the writer ridiculed the theme of "Diversions in Favour of Austria." The sarcasm was typically Burkian (that is, James Mill's variety). He explained:

> The word 'diversion' has of late become a form of a wonderful use and most extensive application. It is the standing object of every expedition which appears to want every other. It is the prompt excuse for every foolish attempt,—the make-weight in every insignificant success, and the counterpoise in every serious disaster.
>
> If we fire a passing broadside at Boulogne, or draw up our ships to a line off Brest, what a glorious Diversion: We fight in Spain as a diversion for Germany, and in Germany as a diversion for Spain. It must indeed be most diverting to our enemies to see such repeated specimens of our folly. As well might we send a light-sailing frigate along the French coast,—and instructing it at every league to fire a broadside, all this keeping the enemy in alarm, and operating a diversion.

Despite the light sarcasm, the writer turned serious when he applied "diversion" to the Spanish situation:

The truth is, that the war has been all along a mere war of points and detachments,—a war of expeditions, in which the most complete success would have contributed but little to the main cause. If England be not equal to the sending of one army to the Continent, she is certainly not equal to sending two, three, or a dozen. If all our force, however, had been united in one object, and in one place, Spain, for example, we should have had a force which might have been efficient at least for an attempt. Two armies of twenty-five or thirty thousand men are good for nothing.—They are neither equal to a diversion, and most certainly not to the pursuit of any main absolute object. But one army of 75,000 men might have had some chance in Spain,—we might have borne the first brunt, and by our commanding strength and attitude, have formed the Spaniards into some shape. But what has Lord Wellington's expedition effected? He has penetrated into the depth of Spain, only that he may fight one battle and retire. He seems to have no object in view but fighting, without considering the value of victory, and the cost of the battle. A battle is necessarily a certain amount in the lives of men,—of money,—of human misery—it is therefore in itself a positive evil, and a very great evil. Unless there be something on the other side, it is so much dead loss—so many lives, and so much money thrown away . . . mutual extermination does not contribute to the main end of the war—at least not in the proportion of the actual cost. For what kind of victory would that be, in which all the vanquished, and nearly all the victors should be killed off; and nothing should remain to the conquerors but a small balance of blood in their favour. The true art of war, and the skill of a General, consists in buying victories at a cheaper price, and not in this kind of fighting it out.—The Congreve rockets and Shrapnell shells will never raise the military glory of our country.[8]

Dr. F.S. Constancio, for his part, published two outstanding articles in *The Statesman* (London) on September 13th and November 1, 1809. Here is how he opened the first piece: "Among the salutary plans proposed for the benefit of England, to serve as a counterpoise to the wide-spreading influence of Bonaparte, the most important is the emancipation of Spanish America, and to this point I wish to call the attention of the readers of *The Statesman*." He continued: Napoleon's "capricious violence" in Spain in early 1808, ursurping "the Crown of Old Spain," made many thinking Frenchmen recognize that he had thrown "the power and wealth" of Spanish America into the hands of the English. Their anxiety, however, was in vain. "Too little did they know," Dr. C. scored, "the men who had the management of the incalculable resources of the British nation!" These were the men, who in April, 1808, fully agreed on the importance of the independence of Spanish America, affirming "that the time for the achievement of this great object was fast passing away forever." Yet, these very men:

> suffered the best opportunity to slip, when the emancipation of that immense Continent was a measure as easy and politic as it was just, and all this to engage the nation in the baseless project of defending Spain against the power of Bonaparte, an undertaking which, in whatever light it is viewed, could never have produced more than trifling temporary advantage, in this country. . .advantage too dearly bought, at the expence of our blood and treasure.

Moreover, these ministers compounded their mistake by recognizing a Spanish Junta that was illegal. Here Dr. C. proved this point with a document written by the famous Jovellanos, which Miranda had in his archives, demonstrating the illegality of all of Spain's juntas. England had recognized a rebellion; and the learned doctor went into a detailed discussion of the steps in Charles IV's abdication, his son's disloyalty to his father, etc. etc. "It is rather strange," Dr. C. concluded with emphasis: "that an *anti-jacobin ministry* of England, the pupils of Pitt and Burke, the enemies of regicides, and defenders of the divine rights of kings, should be the first in Europe to acknowledge the right of the 'Spanish Malcontents' *to dethrone the lawful sovereign*!!!" They had other alternatives, which the learned doctor mentioned, but nothing, he emphasized

> ought to have retarded the execution of the grand plan of the emancipation of the inhabitants of South America, to whom, ever since 1790, Mr. Pitt and all his successors, *not excepting the actual Ministers*, have been promising their assistance to enable them to throw off the cruel and oppressive yoke of the mother-country, which has been so odious and intolerable to all the thinking natives of that rich continent.

Dr. C. always seemed to get around to how the "thinking" people felt about a certain point. Here was the manner in which "Las Casas,"—that is what he called himself in these two articles—described the ministers' "imbecilities":

> It is well known, that Ministers were on the point of sending an expedition to America, for the express purpose of proclaiming and protecting the independence of that country (the impracticable projects

of *conquest* having been happily relinquished after the *disgraceful transactions* at Buenos Ayres), when the arrival of some deputies of one of the *self-named* Spanish juntas disconcerted this most glorious project as effectively as could have wished any of Bonaparte's warmest friends. Ministers listened to their propositions, and not only adjourned, but afterwards gave up the intended emancipation, and absolutely sold the interests of this country, and those of eighteen millions of men, to the monopolizing views of the promoters of the insurrection in Spain. I shall not attack this measure on the ground of injustice and breach of faith, because I know that these are *mere trifles* for politicians of their school; but how can Ministers justify their conduct as to the real and dearest interests of their own country, thus so inexcusably destroyed?

Dr. C's relentless attack upon the incumbent ministers in London continued its punishing path, leaving them with no consolation at all:

Why, shall we ask, was there any stipulation made concerning America, with the Spanish patriots? Why did we pledge ourselves for the continuance of the slavery of our natural friends? Why not allow to *them* the same liberty of choosing a government which the Spaniards claimed? Had the self-elected Juntas acquired, or inherited, any rights over America? And had they not, on the contrary, acknowledged the very reverse, by having invited them to send deputies to the Cortes, for the avowed purpose of framing a constitution?

If we were determined to support the Spanish insurrection, we ought to have done it without binding ourselves to keep the colonies united with the mother-country. There was in such a treaty no sort of reciprocity; we gave the Spaniards ten times more than they could hope for, or ever be able to repay us, in the inadmissable hypothesis of their triumph of Bonaparte. Our policy was very plain, for any other men but the present ministers . . . to give whatever assistance we might judge proper to Old Spain, if we had any reason to expect that an effectual diversion could thus be operated in favour of Austria, if we thought a new coalition possible, or likely to have a better issue than the preceding ones; but never to stipulate against our interests and that of the Americans.

The errant ministers, Dr. C. conceded, might argue that Great Britain could always turn to the emancipation of the Americas, once they were satisfied that Spain's defense was no longer necessary. This "sophistical excuse," Dr. C. argued, failed to take into account the damage inflicted by not acting when the situation was ripe. What about the losses to

British commerce as a result of this procrastination? Besides, he said,

> let us see whether the main object itself has not been so much embarrassed by our misconduct as to render its execution problematic, while last year it was extremely easy and subject to no adverse chance. We shall find, on the contrary, that our enemy acquired a greater probability of accomplishing his designs on Spanish America, *whose subjugation I can venture boldly and confidently to predict*, if Ministers should persist in their narrow-minded schemes, and in their impolitic and unprofitable connections with Spain.
>
> After our attempt on Buenos Ayres and Montevideo, it is hardly to be expected that the Americans should look upon us as *their friends* . . . unless, indeed, we give them the most unequivocal proofs of our good intentions. What must the Americans think of a nation who, after having promised them liberty and independence, now offer them only slavery . . . Unless, then, we again address ourselves frankly to the Americans, laying aside our Spanish connections, it is impossible for our plans to succeed, while by our fruitless attempts we shall increase the influence of Bonaparte, when he is master of Spain, over the rich Continent of America.

Any attempts to put a foreign, or unwanted monarch on an American throne would only compound the mistakes made by the British ministers. Instead, Dr. Constancio recommended:

> *The sooner, then, England gives up all connection with Spain the better.* It is useless, as well as absurd and dangerous, to offer the Americans a King of Sicily . . . a Princess of Brazil [Carlota Joaquina, sister of Ferdinand VII and wife of the future King John VI of Portugal] . . . or an Infant Don Pedro, whom the inhabitants of Buenos Aires have refused to admit (in spite of the *insinuations* of Sir Sydney Smith) . . . as to take a shipload of Spanish nobles, friars, priests, and lawyers, to govern them. *Let the natives alone frame their own government* and all that we have to do, is to watch over the projects of the French, to intercept their agents and expeditions . . . *Honesty here, as in all other circumstances*, will be found to be our *best policy*, and the only atonement we can make for our past sins against Spanish America. LAS CASAS.[10]

On November 1, 1809, when LAS CASAS again took up the pen, the moment of great decisions was fast approaching in Europe. Although Spain was not yet aware of the collapse of Austria, the historical significance of this development was not wasted on Dr. C. Fighting mad, the scholarly writer opened with this grandiose view of European history:

> If the possession of the Netherlands, the limits of the Rhine, and the navigation of the Scheldt, were seven years back, considered by Mr. Pitt as threatening the very existence of this Country, what shall we say now that Bonaparte, as the sole Lord of the whole Continent, may whenever he pleases, realize his threat of the total exclusion of British vessels and goods from all the coasts and harbours from Constantinople round to the farthest limits of Russia! Nobody doubts his power of doing it, and few will deny his determined will to do every thing he can to accelerate the ruin of his only rival. The situation of this country is truly critical, and may become desperate, if an effectual remedy is not speedily adopted, which, however, from the present state of our Government, we can hardly expect.

LAS CASAS had little respect for those "superficial calculators" who maintained that "even the total loss of our European trade would have little effect on our prosperity and finances, it forming only a small fraction of the grand amount of our wealth." Nonsense! Dr. C. argued: "these gentlemen do not seem to be aware of the immediate and remote consequences of even a small diminution of our riches, while our expenditure is constantly and inevitably increasing." After offering an example of the West India trade, he continued:

> There is not a single branch of our industry that would not eventually suffer from such a state of things: the taxes would necessarily become less productive, the course of exchange still more unfavourable, the price of corn much higher, and, in short, this country must be brought into such a crisis as to force any Ministers to accept a peace almost on any terms that Bonaparte chose to offer; and this he will most certainly attempt because peace is as desirable to him, as it is likely to prove fatal to England.[11]

It is interesting to note that six months earlier, Dr. C. and Leckie had discussed the possibility of Napoleon offering peace to the incumbent ministers as part of his plan to offset any English-Miranda project of emancipation. By setting up Ferdinand VII in America, England might be duped into losing the entire area to Napoleon. It was somewhat far-fetched but it indicated how little faith Dr. C. had in England's ministers.[12]

There was still time to act:

> The Continent of America alone can save us from the gigantic power of Bonaparte: there we have a rich market for our goods, and which, both from its extent, and the nature of the return, is far more profitable than any from which the prohibitive policy of Bonaparte may exclude us—a market not only highly advantageous for the present, but whose importance must increase with incalculable rapidity, with the growing prosperity and population which cannot fail to follow the destruction of the monopolizing tirany of the most oppressive despotism.

He repeated the point that he had made in the September article:

> the existence of a new power in America will be to Britain's advantage—the only counterpoise to the unparalleled political influence of the new dynasty in Europe. The free intercourse with independent Spanish America will not only enable England to carry on the war for an indefinite length of time, but the establishment of a free government in the New World will greatly facilitate the final adjustment of a general peace. Bonaparte will be forced to recognize the independency of a country completely beyond his grasp; and if he wishes to procure to his subjects the advantages of trading with its inhabitants, he must grant the same privilege to the English in Europe. The erection of this new power will serve at once as a compensation for the immense acquisitions of Bonaparte, and as a pledge for the duration of peace, which I consider otherwise as ruinous, and almost impracticable.
>
> These truths are so evident, that they could only be overlooked by selfish and narrow Ministers, with whom the salvation of the country was but a secondary concern.[13]

In mid-October, it will be recalled, James Mill had attacked the Junta Central's revival of old economic policies in the Río la Plata and then explained how the monopoly worked, ending with the statement that he hoped Britain would not encourage such actions from an ally. To show how Mill and Dr. C. complemented each other, we shall return to the latter's presentation:

> We have therefore seen them lavish our immense resources, of which they have been more completely masters than any of our predecessors,

in the prosecution of objects of little or no value, and the attainment of which has even been frustrated by their incapacity. The Spanish war has not saved the House of Austria, but it has effectually prevented Great Britain from reaping immense commercial advantages, which must necessarily have been derived from a free intercourse with the Spanish colonies and I cannot contemplate without indignation, that while the precious blood of our countrymen is flowing in Spain, for the support of a Junta, now acknowledged to have been composed of every contemptible individual, the agents of these tyrannical monopolizers should be at the River La Plata, maintaining the old prohibitive laws of Spain, having actually expelled the English and their shipping, allowing them only a delay of 14 days!! With more insolence and intolerance than the former Government of Spain, we find these new upstarts enforcing the most odious and selfish colonial laws, intolerable to the natives, and most prejudicial to our trade; but we have no right to complain of these Spanish Pro-consuls; our Ministers alone are answerable to the nation for the culpable support which, in contempt of the dearest interests of their country, they have been giving to the monopolizing Colonial system of Old Spain.[14]

Dr. C., soon to be unemployed, did not seem to worry about his future! As James Mill subsequently remarked: Dr. C. was the type of man that would be valuable to Miranda in the future struggle for South America.[15]

"Our impolitic connection with Spain," the writer concluded:

has greatly complicated, and even rendered problematical, the execution of the long projected emancipation of Spanish America which at the beginning of the last year, might have been effected by a single act of our Cabinet, without any force being employed, or any expence incurred! What compensation have we derived from Spain, for the voluntary, and spontaneous renunciation of the immediate profits and future advantages which the independence of her colonies must have procured for us?

Not much and not very promising for the future, according to the author.[16] Constancio hoped that

a New Ministry may profit by his advice, before it is too late; and however they may find themselves embarrassed by the false policy, neglect, and mismanagement of their predecessors, much may still be effected by pursuing a system directly contrary to theirs, and by a steady perseverance in a line of conduct as profitable to us, as it is congenial with the feelings and interests of every native of Spanish America, a recommendation that can seldom apply to the schemes of the politicians of the Machiavelian School, which if they ever benefit one country, it is only at the expense of another.

LAS CASAS[17]

The publications of 1809, those analyzed in the last chapter and the new articles ending on November 1st, speak highly for General Miranda's propaganda campaign since his return from the Caribbean. In our day, an opposition movement of this nature perhaps would have brought about a dramatic change in British policy. But inertia, war-weariness, confusion, personalities, etc. seemed to be overwhelming deterrents; and the British government went on as usual even in the eventful year of 1810. Perhaps developments in the Americas would force a change; but then again, perhaps not.

* * * * * * * * * * * *

Francisco de Miranda, as we can see from his archives, exchanged letters with correspondents throughout the western world, especially in those areas vital to his program of emancipation. When he was in the Caribbean, one of his main sources of information in England was John Turnbull and Nicholas Vansittart. After his return to Europe in 1808, his major correspondents were in the Caribbean—Admiral Cochrane, Governor Hislop, and his special friend Francisco Febles in Trinidad. For reasons that we have already explained, Miranda seldom heard from John Turnbull again, except on matters dealing with financial obligations; but another Turnbull—young Peter—replaced his father from a seat of operations in Brazil. Miranda, thus, was able to receive some highly informative letters concerning Brazil's economy and the political developments at the royal court in Rio de Janeiro, where the Prince Regent João (future John VI of Portugal in 1816) attempted in vain to control the intrigues of his wife Carlota Joaquina, the sister of Ferdinand VII of Spain. Another correspondent in Rio de Janeiro was Dr. Saturnino Rodríguez Peña, who along with Manuel Padilla had left the Río de la Plata on foreign assignments for their cause. Padilla had been useful to Miranda when he returned to London in early 1808. Dr. Rodríguez Peña in Rio kept Miranda closely informed with letters, reports, and key documents on Carlota Joaquina. Back in August,

1808, this feisty lady reported to the Spanish world that she was the legitimate representative—the Regent, in other words—for her brother Ferdinand VII, as well as for the *Infante* Pedro, her younger brother who resided with her in Rio de Janeiro. Her ultimate objective was to take over the Spanish Empire before Napoleon got around to it. It was a much-publicized scheme because of the reams of paper—containing her speeches, documents, etc.—that circulated in all the major capitals of Spanish America. And as the future queen of Portugal, once her prince ascended the throne, she expected to unite the former colonies of Spain and Portugal under one head. Admiral William Sidney Smith encouraged this not-very-secret conspiracy; but Lord Strangford, the British Minister at Rio de Janeiro, stopped the project in its tracks. General Miranda resented Admiral Smith's meddling in Brazil; and he was especially annoyed at Carlota's brazen attempt to swing some of the Argentine revolutionaries to her cause. Miranda wrote to Vansittart: "I am afraid [he] has done very near as much mischief to the projected union and interest of this country, as the famous Popham did at Buenos Ayres, Maldonado, Isla de Lobos, etc."[18]

Felipe Contucci was another revolutionary correspondent from the Río de la Plata. He was the one who tried to get Miranda to lead the revolutionaries in the Platine area, a request which the Venezuelan turned down in early 1809. Several months later, the revolutionary climate throughout South America picked up momentum and Miranda tried to encourage his colleagues in Buenos Aires. In the meantime, he received a letter from Contucci which revealed that he had gone over to Carlota Joaquina's cause. Disappointed and upset, Miranda wrote back to him upon learning of the Caracas Revolution of April 19, 1810. That was the type of revolutionary procedure they should emulate: "I believe that it would be much better for you, than to embark on risky projects, for the introduction of foreigners and new sovereigns in those provinces."[19]

Captain Samuel C. Loudon, a former officer in the 1806 expedition, was General Miranda's most faithful and steady contact in the United States. Although his manner of expression was gruff and unpolished, the contents of his letters were most informative on United States' politics, as well as his analysis of Great Britain's actions and policy, or lack of same, with regards to South America. He had great faith in Miranda's cause and leadership of Spanish America's destiny; he was a strong and emotional champion of a republic as opposed to a European-style monarchy. In his most rhetorical moments, one cannot help but sense that he was too close to a bottle! Yet, Miranda thoroughly enjoyed the Captain's letters; and it pleased him when Captain Sam went out of his way to place informational pieces in New York newspapers, especially when he arranged for the publication of the Edinburgh article of January, 1809, in one of the leading periodicals of the East.[20]

There was a noticeable drop off in his correspondence from the Caribbean during the early months of 1809, after the investigation of the "Paper Assault" came into view. Admiral Cochrane was again in trouble for helping his Venezuelan friend; but Spaniards were unable to get the British Government to punish him, as we have already noted. Captain Beaver's account of Caracas' favoritism for the English, as opposed to the French, was good news for Miranda and to Englishmen as well. Miranda knew that Cochrane was a loyal ally; and he continued to be so after Miranda's return to Venezuela. During the correspondence blitz, however, Miranda began to suspect that General Thomas Hislop at Trinidad might hesitate to over expose himself for the Venezuelan's cause. When Governor Hislop hedged on a few occasions, Miranda's old companion Febles formed the same impression about him. So, the letters to Trinidad were not as frequent. However, any time that Miranda had literature to circulate on the mainland, he did not hesitate to ask Hislop to carry out the propaganda responsibility that they had discussed in their Caribbean meetings.[21]

Those were the correspondents that exchanged letters with Miranda in the second half of 1809, as the European developments reached their reckoning points. Also, there were three new faces that joined Miranda's team at this time, besides Leckie and Constancio. The three men in question—two Spaniards and one Ecuadorean—would carry over into the Venezuelan portion of this work that highlight the final chapters. First, in order of appearance in London, was Manuel Cortés Campomanes, born in Madrid; second, José María Antepara, a native of Guayaquil, Ecuador; and, third, José María Blanco y Crespo, who saw the light of day in Sevilla, Spain. The latter arrived in London in March, 1810.

The *Madrileño* Cortés Campomanes received a good education in the enlightened climate of the Spanish capital at the end of the eighteenth century—a sound exposure to the sciences and humanities. At the age of nineteen, this young liberal involved himself in the "Conspiracy of San Blas" (1796) against Manuel Godoy, the court favorite, for sacrificing the country's future. The men arrested were sentenced to death; but at the last moment, the authorities decided to send young Cortés to the prison at La Guaira, in Venezuela. In 1797, his name came up again in the "Gual-España Conspiracy" in behalf of Venezuela's independence from Spanish rule, another aborted revolution. Cortés managed to escape from the dungeon in Venezuela and reestablished himself in the French Antilles. He became a key official in the French forces, ending up as an aide-de-camp to the French leader at Martinique. When he heard of Napoleon's designs on Spain in early 1808, he immediately resigned his commission and returned to Europe to fight for Spain. The Junta Central's bumbling in the military arena, however, thoroughly disgusted him. The Junta, he felt, was not pursuing the proper path to a modern and liberal Spain. He then thought of his second *patria* (mother country) that he wanted liberated—Venezuela. So, he transferred himself to London in search of the famous Miranda. General Miranda, of course, knew of the young man's role in the Venezuelan conspiracy of 1797; and he could well appreciate the importance of his identification with the French in the Caribbean. He was a logical ally for the emancipation of "Colombia." Cortés Campomanes arrived in the English capital in mid-January, 1809; and, before long, he met with Miranda. The Venezuelan tried to get him on the payroll for the projected "American Thrust," especially since, by then, the British presence in Spain had not been successful. But Arthur Wellesley discouraged Miranda's project; and Cortés future looked bleak. Miranda introduced him to another Spaniard in London who could supply him with the bare essentials for survival; and that is how he existed until his return to Venezuela in late 1810, suffering from continued bouts of rheumatism. In his moments of health, however, Cortés proved to be a valuable "information gatherer" for Miranda. He got to know people in the Spanish diplomatic body that allowed him to copy important documents. He was also on the lookout for all new Spanish Americans arriving in London in this crucial period. He spent much of his free time working on memoirs of his military experiences in the Caribbean, which Miranda reviewed for him with valuable suggestions. This close relationship with Miranda was enough to guarantee the General that Cortés was not a counterspy planted in London to watch him. It also explained Cortés Campomanes' fierce loyalty and dedication to Miranda's cause in Venezuela. And his devotion to "Colombia" continued into the post-Miranda era in South America's emancipation effort.[22]

In August, 1809, Cortés Campomanes learned of the appearance in London of José María Antepara, a man who had been involved in Mexican mining and who had key contacts among Mexican creoles. From the start, it was obvious to Cortés that the Ecuadorean from Guayaquil was a highly-strung individual. Antepara, it seemed, had run into problems with his business—we assumed that it had something to do with the Mexican mines; and he was paranoid to the extreme, according to Cortés. To avoid any embarrassment to General Miranda, Cortés agreed to gather all the information that he could on Mexican plans for independence. Antepara had informed him that the Mexicans were anxious to push emancipation as soon as posssible; they could not be held up by European developments. Cortés' impressions of José María Antepara were indeed accurate, as Miranda soon learned to his own satisfaction. By the end of 1809, three Mexican notables appeared in London—the Marquis del Apartado, his brother, and a relative, Jacobo de Villaurrutia.[23]

The name of Villaurrutia registered loudly in this historian's memory; and rightfully so, since he was a recognized liberal leader of Central American history from 1794 to 1804, when he served on the Audiencia of Guatemala before returning to Mexico for a post in its head judicial body.[24] Here he was in London six year's later. This, indeed, had great historical implications. Dominican-born, Villaurrutia was related to the Mexican aristocracy. In pre-Independence Central America, this talented judge, who had also served in Spain, was a dedicated reformer, as well as a liberal, who advanced Hispanic America's cause everywhere that he went. If his two relatives in London had a similar ambition and training, then it was clear that these gentlemen, and their Ecuadorean front man, were the type of colleagues that General Francisco de Miranda needed desperately to advance the emancipation of Spanish America. And it was even more important since they had the financial support to offer to Miranda's team in London for the publication of their literature in behalf of the cause!

With Antepara and the Mexican creoles present, Miranda's projects reproducing important documents for the revolutionaries in Spanish America proceeded at a fast and steady pace in 1810. The major productions were three: two were overt and thus published officially, and one that was secretive, carried on by Antepara and the Mexicans. The first was the bi-monthly periodical *El Colombiano* (five issues starting on March 15, 1810, two in April, and two in May, ending with the issue of May 15th). The second project: *South American*

Emancipation. Documents, Historical and Explanatory Shewing the Designs which have been in Progress and the Exertions made by General Miranda for the South American Emancipation, during the last Twenty-five years (R. Juigné, London, 1810), edited by J.M. Antepara who finished the prologue in September, 1810. The third, the secretive project, constituted another edition of the Viscardo manuscript: *Letter to the Spanish Americans*, with a new "Amendment," urging the people of Spanish America to join the emancipation movement. It reflected the militant spirit of the Mexican financiers and their agent Antepara.[26] Miranda, for his part, agreed to send out copies of the "Paper Assault" documents that we discussed in the previous chapter. The Mexican secretive mailings of documents, as well as Viscardo's new edition, thus guaranteed the "library" that General Miranda wanted them to have in their hands as they launched their respective revolutionary movements throughout Spanish America. Miranda's circular letter of March 24, 1810, explains his purposes to Spanish Americans for sending those materials. That is the second quotation that introduces this chapter. What we did not include there was the rest of that letter, which explains that the so-called "Paper Assault" was the beginning of this process:

> so that forseeing in advance the lamentable consequences of the tricks and intrigues of the different governments of Spain, they might arrange for their own security and Emancipation.—These are essential points which cannot be doubted in the least at this time. My house . . . will always be the fixed point for the Independence and liberties of the Colombian Continent.[27]

In another letter, he mentioned that he was enclosing the first two issues of *El Colombiano*, which indicates that the second issue was already out at the time he sent this circular letter. The "Paper Assault" of 1808 was no figment of Miranda's imagination!

The *El Colombiano* project, which we shall evaluate later—and the secretive mailing of *legajos* (bundles) of documents to Hispanic revolutionaries were understandably the responsibility of the Mexican sponsors. But was this the case with the English volume of 1810 on "South American Emancipation?" Our hypothesis is that the financing of that volume was primarily British, for the reasons we shall present. Yet, unsure of this financing, Miranda tried to get a substantial contribution from the Mexicans, as a favor to him; in return, he would agree to put Antepara's name on the work, expecting him to write a Prologue for the compilation.

The 1810 work, in effect, was an autobiographical study of Francisco de Miranda as seen in the documents that he had collected during a twenty-five year period. The outline of the documents followed Miranda's notions of the highlights of his career; these documents, in turn, were filed in the legajos by Tomás Molini, Miranda's secretary, and were cared for in Miranda's house, where Molini also lived; and they were edited by its two editors since mid-1808: Miranda and James Mill. There are many references in Mill's letters to Miranda concerning such-and-such an appendix which substantiate Mill's editorship. He was also responsible for the "Explanation of the Plate"; only a classicist, familiar with Greek and Latin, could have done this. Within the frame surrounding Miranda's bust, was a cap of liberty; and below it, a picture of "The siege and bombardment of Antwerp," a glorious scene in the military annals of France, headed by Miranda. In Greek were the words "of Liberty" on the sword, denoting "the purpose to which, exclusively in the hand in question, the sword has been devoted." Mill continued: "witness the refusal to serve in the armies of France, from the moment liberty ceased to be her object, and the personal efforts against the arbitrary proceedings which ensued." This was a point of admiration in Mill's relationship with General Miranda. And Mill's touch was likewise evident in the final paragraph of the note:

> The Latin epigraph on the border of the socle, *Qui mores hominum multorum vidit et urbes*, is a quotation taken from the letter of the Bishop of Antwerp, who bore the testimony it contains, to the conduct and character, of which the writer had been a witness.

In his second treatise, William Burke had referred to the scene and to the document in question. Miranda, of course, helped his young colleague to put this in final form.[29]

From the standpoint of creativity, there was not much to do in this documentary collection. There were eleven sections to the volume: Section I, was the January, 1809, article of the *Edinburgh Review* on Viscardo's *Letter to the Spanish Americans*, pages 1–41. Since all the sections were in English, Spanish documents also appeared in English translation; thus, it can be assumed that the European market was the target of the 1810 volume. Section II, Appendix A, pp. 41–28, included documents of Miranda's travels in Europe. Section III, Appendix B, pp. 48–168, the largest bundle of documents in the compilation dealt with Miranda's experiences in France during the Revolution. Section IV, Appendix C, pp. 168–174, on Miranda's correspondence with Brissot concerning the projected expedition to the West Indies; Section V, Appendix D, pp. 174–177, more on Miranda in France, 1795; Section VI, Appendix E, p. 178, letter, Hamilton to Miranda on a projected expedition to South America. Section VII, Appendix F, pp. 179–217, key documents on Miranda's 1806 expedition, a touchy item with the general, it will be recalled. Section VIII, Appendix G, pp. 218–220, Governor Picton's proclamation of 1797. Section IX, Appendix H, pp. 220–265, miscellaneous documents revealing General Miranda's views and rebuttals to charges made against him. Section X, Appendix J, pp. 265–270, more documents on France; and Section XI, Appendix K, pp. 270–299, ending the volume, documents of F. Miranda since 1808. Very important here was the reproduction of documents, with English translations, of General Miranda's "Paper Assault" to influence Spanish American actions at the time of independence from Spain. Throughout the study, there were brief introductions to the materials, as well as defenses of charges made against General Miranda—his use of the title "Count" in his European travels, etc. This type of editorial remark James Mill could beat out as fast as he could write. Most of this work, moreover, was done before José María Antepara appeared in London.

In Miranda's circular letter of March 24, 1810, discussed earlier, there was a clue that suggested a possible source for the funds needed to pay for propaganda ventures, besides those offered by the Mexican group in London. Hoping that the recipients of those letters might subscribe to *El Colombiano*, as well as make some contribution to the expenses in publishing the documents, Miranda suggested that they either write to his home in London, or to the following banking firm on New Broad St: Messr. Boehm and Taylor. Nicholas Vansittart did his business there; and recently had helped to bail out General Miranda from a loan from Alexander Davison. To help José Antepara out of his financial problems, Miranda recommended him to the same firm, supporting his petition. The question that arises comes from the fact that Miranda asked Dr. Constancio to go along with Antepara; and, subsequently, these same two members of Miranda's team participated in meetings with leading politicians and figures in the English government, including even an admiral. We suspect that Antepara received assistance on his personal problem; and that the banking firm in question was also involved in the negotiations with members of the British opposition—William Wilberforce, for example, and other distinguished people. The presence of Dr. C. in these talks suggests strongly that the discussions dealt with the financing of Miranda's 1810 Documents, which, after all came out in English. We might also add here, although his name does not appear in these discussions, that the publisher John Murray was interested in publishing a more extensive volume on Francisco de Miranda, beyond just the expedition of 1806. He had expressed such an interest back in 1809 to William Thomson.[30]

The British opposition group that favored Miranda's emancipation of Spanish America recognized that the people of Great Britain needed to be educated to a more imaginative policy of their government on these themes. Wilberforce had expressed himself forcefully on this need.[31] The 1810 Documents, moreover, capitalized on Miranda's popularity and provided, in detail, a record of a hero that represented their epoch in European history—the long and fierce struggle against the disruptive French Revolution and its dreadful torchbearer, Napoleon Bonaparte. The *Edinburgh Review* article of January, 1809, demonstrated why England had to act now, or never. Moreover, what brought the sense of urgency into the picture was the celebrated "Exposé" of December, 1809, by one of Napoleon's spokesman. This so-called "French Exposé" received much attention in the world press.[32] The message was clear: Napoleon recognized Spanish America's dreams of achieving her independence from Spanish rule; he looked forward to trading with the new nations of America, bringing prosperity to both France and Spanish America, etc. etc. What was the catch? Spanish Americans, in return, were not to permit Great Britain any part in their trade relations! This was simply absurd! Now that Corsican fool wanted to exclude us from Spanish America! What would be next? In short, the British—and not just the opposition group that we have mentioned—understood that this was the last straw. They had to take a firm and decided stand; and funds—from one source or another—had to be found to subsidize Miranda's propaganda effort to convince the English public of the danger at hand. Thus, the support for the 1810 Documents that we have described earlier became a reality. As for Antepara writing the prologue in September, 1810, and being named the editor of the book, this was just a move to acquire some financial support from the Mexican group in London. That seems to be the plausible explanation, or hypothesis, on how Miranda arranged the financing of his three projects during 1810.[33]

The publication of *El Colombiano,* starting on March 15, 1810, was a risky venture for General Miranda, because it constituted a bitter attack upon Spain; and the English government had told him that any further aggravation of their ally's feelings would bring about his dismissal from the British dominions.   Nicholas Vansittart was definitely not pleased with Miranda's support of that periodical; he would have advised against it if he had been asked for an opinion. When the General answered his letter, he told him that the May 15th issue was the last one. Spain's representatives in England complained of the "traitor's" subversive publication; and *El Colombiano* shut down after its fifth issue.   It is not clear if the English government was responsible for the closure; or the appearance of *El Español* on April 30, 1810, made its continuation unnecessary.[34]

As most of Miranda's propaganda endeavors, *El Colombiano* was clearly a team effort. José María Antepara, representing the Mexican sponsors, was its co-editor along with Francisco de Miranda.   The reproduction of key documents was the primary format, along with occasional commentaries and essays. Miranda and Cortés Campomanes were competent reviewers of military matters; and the latter especially could provide insights into the Junta Central's administration of military policy. Dr. C. and Gould Francis Leckie, as well as James Mill, were knowledgeable on diplomatic documents and events; and Miranda also utilized materials from his own archives concerning Gaspar de Jovellanos' opinion on the illegality of Spain's various juntas. A very important contributor on the weaknesses of the Junta Central in Spain was Miranda's newest recruit, José María Blanco y Crespo, who left his native Sevilla in early 1810. He brought with him official documents from Spain, many of which he also highlighted in *El Español*. We shall say more about this gentleman later. What was lacking in *El Colombiano*—yet this was not responsible for its short tenure—was the unrelenting attack of Miranda's writers on the British ministers, in which case, perhaps, it might not have published its first issue!

On March 15, 1810, the editor provided a logical explanation for the periodical's need at this moment of crisis. The events on the Peninsula seemed pointed towards Spain's complete subjugation.   It was imperative, therefore, to provide in the pages of *El Colombiano* all the necessary information for the readers to act judiciously in their areas, given the situation in Europe.   The approach of the periodical was identical to that used by General Francisco de Miranda in his "Paper Assault" and the collection of documents for 1810. We suspect that the real editor must have been James Mill, who after all was an old hand at editing by this time. Like a typical historian, or editor, he pointed out to his Spanish readers that often these documents appeared first in French, English, Portuguese, and what have you; thus, there might be changes from the original text because of the translations that had taken place with the nuances supplied by different translators. Only a "perfectionist" editor like Mill was capable of bringing up such a point! The organization was again in Mill's style: introduction, caveats, and then point one: the Junta Central was illegal from the start. What better proof could there be than the statements of two members of the Junta Central: Gaspar de Jovellanos on such-and-such a date etc. etc. These documents, as mentioned earlier, came from Miranda's archives, for the most part. Some from contributors like Blanco-White.

The second and third issues of *El Colombiano* were routine documentary accounts of French military activity in Spain; the reproduction of the Regency's famous decree of February 14, 1810, promising Americans a new order and a life of "dignity," etc. Brief remarks followed on Spain by Sir John Moore and a speech by the Marquis of Wellesley, the new British Foreign Secretary, published on March 31, 1810, in the *Morning Chronicle* and *The Times* (London). Moore emphasized the imbecilic leadership of the Junta Central at war; and Wellesley's speech in Parliament placed the blame for English problems in Spain on the worthless Junta Central. His documentation was skimpy. So much for outside authorities on how bad the Junta Central was! Issue Number 3, April 1, 1810, reproduced Carlota Joaquina's "Manifiesto" (1808) along with documents.

Although the fourth and fifth issues followed the same documentary format, they were dominated by an exceptional article that was left truncated (*Se continuará*; it will be continued) in the final issue. Its title was "Thoughts of an Englishman on the State and Present Crisis of Affairs in South America." Who was the author? He was a man who had published much on the "future happiness" of the New World—ideas which he had recorded already "in one of the principal periodicals of England."[35] The reference was to James Mill's articles in the *Edinburgh Review* (January and July, 1809). Several months later, the first of those articles introduced the 1810 Documents, presumably edited by José María Antepara. This article: "Thoughts of an Englishman" was reproduced in its entirety (the two issues, that is, in truncated state) in the *Gazeta de Caracas* of January 25, 1811.[36]

Thoughts of an Englishman on . . . South America

After three centuries of the "vilest servitude" to a European power, America wants her freedom from the rule of foreigners. All of Europe has recognized America's longstanding desire for emancipation; and the voice of reason in civilized Europe "has pronounced loudly that the immense population of the New World cannot be well governed except by a government established in that area." Fortunately, the European oppressor country had been completely dissolved, thanks to an act of Providence. Thus, "the inhabitants of the New World have been called upon by the voice of God and of men to form a government for themselves and by themselves." Mill had not forgotten his training for the ministry! "Now," he continued, "all depends upon the wisdom and virtue of their conduct." The teacher commenced his civics lesson:

> What do we mean by a good government? A good government is the coordination of the people's affairs, by which all classes of the folk agree mutually to abandon, each on their own, for the love of peace and common happiness; all that might be prejudicial to the other [classes]: the rich man gives up all that might be against the well being of the poor: the poor man all that stands in opposition to the happiness of the rich: The people of one origin abandon all that might be injurious to the prosperity of the people of another different origin, so that in this way all of society might enjoy the greatest happiness possible. And this is the true sense of the word *Patriotism*.
>
> The establishment of a good government is founded therefore on the laws of God and of Nature, and depends upon the sacrifices made mutually in favor of the common happiness.

A bad government brings out the opposite—classes exploit each other; and people of one origin take advantage of another different group—for example, the Spartans tiranized the "Helotes." Anarchy takes over when contending groups fight for "unjust privileges," and are not guided "by a spirit of reconciliation." American sentiments should be

> *personal disinterest* and *docility*: the personal disinterest so that each class will not desire for itself more than what is compatible with the welfare of the remaining classes; docility to search for and follow the

necessary prudence and wisdom that must direct them in this important enterprise.[37]

There are very few societies, perhaps none, that have better circumstances and less difficulties to overcome in forming a good government. Now that the old oppressors were absent from the scene, all that Spanish Americans had to do was to seek unanimity on what is most convenient for themselves. It would be embarrassing for the inhabitants of the New World, as well as a setback for the rest of humanity, if they misused, or did not realize in full this favorable opportunity.

Just as Miranda had emphasized in his "Paper Assault," James Mill underscored this point:

The most frequent cause for the ruin of humanity's most beautiful hopes has been: that virtuous men, exaggerating the possible dangers to their interests, retire from the scene and take only minor roles in the great movements while corrupt and perverse characters offer their leadership and from want of opposition they direct affairs according to their evil motives: *the people*, that is all human kind, is then accused of perversity, because they follow the bad advice and scorn the good, when the truth is, that they have been deprived of the good advisors, or their good ideas were presented so weakly, that they lacked conviction and power to oppose energetically the bad advisors.

The second installment appeared on May 15, 1810, the last issue of *El Colombiano*. Despite the optimum conditions that existed in the New World, Mill opened, there still are some "difficulties" that may beset the Americans. The major danger would be the intrigues of the former government's agents to reestablish their control over society. Here are the steps that the "Thoughtful Englishman" suggested: "The first step that the inhabitants of the Colombian Continent must take in securing their independence would be to issue a decisive declaration that is much publicized on their resolution to create a government that emanates only from themselves." Here, Mill recommended the use of the *Cabildos* as the interim governments in all districts. To avoid any challenge from officials of the previous government, great care should be taken to select the principal inhabitants of each area to serve in the interim governments at the district level, elected by the people. Representatives from the cabildos sent to a provisional general government will thus form "an interim National Representation." The

net effect of this measure would be to discourage the actions of the
French and Spanish governments, as well as their former agents and
officials. This will also have the advantage of eliminating unjust and
illegal actions that are common in intervals of transferring power from
one government to another.   There Mill provided some practical
considerations that the Miranda team wanted to pass on to the future
leaders of Spanish American countries.

The next item of possible danger that James Mill brought up was to
have a crucial impact upon Venezuela. It was undoubtedly one of the
major problems, or characteristics, in the establishment of new Hispanic
nations for decades. In fact, it involved "William Burke" in a blistering
controversy—the most serious one among the editorials that he wrote
in Caracas from 1810 to 1812. The theme that he pretended to educate
Hispanic Americans on was that of "Religious Toleration." "The most
dangerous influence that the enemies of America's happiness could
possibly employ," the Englishman maintained, "would be the sacred
intervention of the Church [*la religión*]."

> The latter's object is to direct souls and lead them to heaven. Political
> institutions have as their objective the direction of acts of man for the
> good of society in this world. To mix religion with political questions
> is to deviate from its true objective, thus forming the chains of
> despotism, and man's slavery, with the pretext of religion. This amounts
> to profaning her [the Church] and producing traitors to the *patria*.

There was much food for thought in Mill's statement about the role
of the church in Spanish American society. It first appeared in the
Gazeta de Caracas on January 25, 1811, during a very agitated crisis in
the area. A few weeks later, William Burke published his controversial
article on "Religious Toleration."

Another "thought" that ended the second installment of Mill's article
was the absolute necessity of these young nations to provide for "*the
security of persons, and of their properties.*" With such a guarantee, the
process toward nationhood would be stable and smooth—one which
men of property could support heartily. Mill continued: "This sacred
principle should be engraved in all hearts and must be followed with
the greatest exactness."[38]

The essay by James Mill ended with a promise that it would be
continued (*Se continuará*) in the next issue of *El Colombiano.* Yet, in
the   Caracas   reproduction,   the   writer   merely   signed   off:

"El Colombiano," as if this were the author's penname. Be that as it may, the reader had reason to expect that other issues would be discussed that would be vital for the future leaders of Spanish American nations. We must not forget that in the Mill-Miranda article of January, 1809, in the *Edinburgh Review*, there was an acute awareness of the need to project the U.S. model, so much admired by Spanish Americans, in all its aspects. It was at this time, we suspect, that Miranda and Mill perhaps agreed to compose a series of essays dealing with the institutions and experiences of the first American republic from 1775 to 1783—the "American Revolution—and the post-War period from 1783 to 1809. Jeremy Bentham and James Mill began the preparation of materials for Miranda before his departure for Venezuela, which included an exposition of "freedom of the press" and connected issues, and congressional procedures. Eventually this also included essays on education with special emphasis on the Lancasterian system, which Mill was associated with in London. With the Mill-Bentham collaboration a fact from the summer of 1809 forward, James Mill—a veritable around-the-clock researcher and writer—commenced to organize the essays that came out under the rubric of "William Burke" in Caracas. Mill was the writer; but the ideas were not just his own; they also belonged to Jeremy Bentham, depending on the issue discussed. Whether or not Bentham was conscious of the Burkian series in Caracas, we cannot say; we suspect that he was not. He was perhaps satisfied with the assurances of his young colleague Mill that they were to be published in Venezuelan papers anonymously, or occasionally with the mention of Bentham's name. That certainly would have been enough for his ego. This, of course, is speculation at this point, that awaits future documentary discoveries.

Another key personage in this work, who also contributed to *El Colombiano* with his documents and comments on Spain's Junta Central, was José María Blanco y Crespo, better known to English readers as Reverend Joseph Blanco-White.[39] A mercurial personality, this native of Sevilla, Spain, was of Irish extraction on his grandfather's side and Spanish on his mother's side. He wrote extensively on his career in Spain prior to his arrival in London in March, 1810. His writings reveal the tormented thoughts of a man of the cloth, a Catholic priest who began to question his own religion and especially the dichotomy of the Church and State in the Hispanic world as a factor in despotism. Mill's remarks in "Thoughts of an Englishman" on a meddlesome Church may have been vital in the young Spaniard's decision to join the Anglican church. As a member of Miranda's team in publishing *El Colombiano*, he met James Mill, the ex-Presbyterian minister, exchanging notes on their respective careers. After Mill's death, Blanco-White wrote to John Stuart Mill that they were good friends in those earlier days after his arrival in England and that they might have proceeded in the same direction.[40] It would appear that he was referring to the career of publicists in the New World. But Blanco-White opted to become an Anglican clergyman, as well as operating his controversial periodical *El Español* until 1814. Then, he decided to finish his education at Oxford University; and subsequently changed his religious affiliation once again to that of Unitarian! Over the years, he wrote many publications exposing Catholicism, so he did not entirely abandon the role of "publicist." His role as an interpreter of Spanish-American Independence is our primary concern in this work.

At this point, however, we are still concerned with Mill's influence upon him on the theme of "Religious Toleration." If he had a weakness in that direction—or a strength along those lines—Mill's influence could have been crucial, especially since they both shared an innate hatred of that dreaded institution, the Inquisition. Blanco-White was no innocent: he knew only too well what resistance he would encounter from Spaniards and Spanish Americans, especially from the ultra-right Catholics but also the devoted group in the middle. Yet, this controversial ex-Catholic priest encouraged his readers in *El Español* to consider key reforms of that institution in the new Spanish system under the Constitution of 1812. When the liberals at Cádiz were too cautious in their changes of that institution, he accused them of being too traditional, insinuating that they had been hipocrites![41] As late as the 1820s, he embarked on a veritable crusade to convince the Spanish-American Republics that they had to dispose of the Inquisition and support "Religious Toleration" if they had any sincere hopes of modernizing their nations. It was a movement that was already implicit in the paragraph cited above by Mill in his "Thoughts of an Englishman." Needless to say, the ex-Catholic priest—and a Unitarian, no less—did not carry much weight among Spanish Americans, even or especially among the liberals who appreciated how sensitive this theme was in their countries.[42]

Except for Mill's personal remarks to Blanco-White on this theme, which are not at our disposal, they can be deduced from a review that James Mill wrote in the August, 1810, issue of the *Edinburgh Review*, just a few months after the demise of Miranda's paper.[43] Those interested in James Mill should welcome another brilliant example of this intellectual's dexterity, thanks to his training in history and religion. The book he was reviewing highlighted the lack of religious toleration in France since the revocation of the Edict of Nantes. The reviewer even mentioned his own translation of Viller's work on the "Reformation of Luther," which emphasized the major conclusion. The French bishops' intolerance, Mill insisted, extended not only to "*the liberty of the* press" but also to the "*liberty of conscience*"[44] We recall that Mill gave Miranda a copy of Viller's translated work for his personal library; and we suspect that Blanco-White perhaps received a copy of his own.

Mill's comparison of the "Liberty of the Press" and the "Liberty of Conscience" is a valuable intellectual exercise, which we have no time to explore here. His remarks on the so-called threat of the Catholics in Great Britain were clever and hilarious in places, as he ridiculed the alarmists.[45] And the reviewer used John Locke's writings effectively in defense of religious toleration. Mill's remarks on the Inquisition have a bearing on our concerns:

> Amid the calamities which this scourge of Europe has lately inflicted on the people of Spain, it is some consolation to contemplate the destruction of one of the most terrible instruments of hostility to the interests of human nature, which ever the enemies of human nature set up.

If Napoleon succeeded in accomplishing the destruction of the Inquisition, it would be a credit to his memory. The critic Mill then delivered his blow:

> A British ministry, distinguished for many things, but for nothing so much as an extraordinary horror for the abominations of the Catholic religion; a ministry, who had treaties to form with the Spaniards and Portuguese . . . that ministry did not think it worthwhile to make any attempt to abolish the human sacrifices of their allies, or to employ a word, when a word would have sufficed, for putting down the Inquisition.[46]

Mill's naiveté, however, revealed itself in this statement:

> If, however, while the Inquisition is destroyed in Europe by the power of despotism, we could entertain the hope—and it is not too much to

entertain such a hope—that the power of liberty is about to destroy it in America; we might even, amid the gloom which surrounds us, congratulate our fellow-creatures on one of the most remarkable epochs in the history of the progress of human society—the final erasure of the Inquisition from the face of the earth.

James Mill's final passage had special meaning for Spanish America:

> With this consolatory prospect, then, we close these observations; and shall only add, that, without freedom of conscience, there can be no free government. A system of intolerance affords such temptation and facilities to despotism, that the two are never found long asunder. If the awakening people of South America, therefore, desire at last to taste the blessings of a good government, they must fulfill the conditions which are essential to its attainment: They must not only proclaim their independence, but they must establish perfect toleration, and give their sanction to the exertions of a free press.[47]

This quotation indicates that James Mill was not only the reviewer of the book on "Religious Toleration" but also the writer of "Thoughts of an Englishman" in *El Colombiano*. Moreover, the objectives of "perfect toleration" and a "free press" were also those shared by the controversial Reverend Joseph Blanco-White.

* * * * * * * * * * * *

As resignations took place in the British cabinet, there were changes in the secretarial posts. Miranda especially enjoyed the departure of the obnoxious Edward Cooke, replaced by the amenable Mr. Herries. Vansittart's advice, from a distance, worked most effectively upon Herries, Miranda noted with satisfaction. The General finally was able to straighten out his financial business with the government; in fact, the Venezuelan even thought that the government was favoring him on occasion. In March, 1810, while busy with his publication projects, Mr. Herries informed him that Spencer Perceval was anxious to know if he had any available documents on the political situation in South America. In short order, the Venezuelan presented his wares to Perceval in a letter of March 31, 1810:

> In the annexed Memoir (which is the last official communication I had with Lord Castlereagh upon this important subject), you will find, Sir,

an accurate statement of the situation in which those Colonies were at that period:—and you will also perceive, that the conjectures about the state of Peru, Quito, etc. have not proved by the last accounts, to be unfounded.

He emphasized to Perceval, moreover, that recent information vitally concerned the interests of Great Britain in Spanish America. Miranda, therefore, suggested that Perceval appoint "some person, or persons of your confidence, with whom I might confer on this grave and most important subject . . . to rescue, if possible, those Colonies from the imminent danger of falling under the baneful influence of France." Such a disaster would surely lead to the "ruin of its innocent inhabitants, and an immense detriment to the commerce and interests of Great Britain." To encourage Perceval in the direction of a decision, he told him of the Mexican nobles who had recently arrived in London, anxious

> to know what England ultimately wishes, or intends to do, in favour of their Countrymen in S.A.—and their pressing applications are a new motive for me, to call to your attention at this present moment.—They sincerely wish to return soon to their native Country, and to impart some favourable news to its inhabitants; who have always placed great confidence and entertained high expectations, in the favourable disposition of the British Government, and in the friendship and intimate connexions that might be formed with the English Nation.

In his final effort to persuade Perceval, Miranda offered his services to the British Government, hoping thus to avert "the impending dangers that threaten S.A. both from France, and the internal popular tumults, that are so natural in a new country, situated as those colonies are at this peculiar moment." The cost of British assistance would be minimal by comparison to projects of the past favored by British ministers with regards to Spanish America.[48] The perseverance of the Venezuelan crusader was inexhaustible, it must be admitted!

In a letter to Perceval of April 26, 1810, there is evidence to suggest that Miranda, at last, was on a favorable tact with the British. He added a personal note to the effect that Mrs. Vansittart had another bleeding accident, just as Nicholas was on the point of returning to London. This, of course, meant another postponement of Vansittart's presence in the City; and Miranda still hoped that the Government would make a favorable decision on its own. Nicholas Vansittart wrote to Miranda on July 13, 1810, recognizing why no action had been forthcoming from Perceval's government: "I am sorry that my private misfortunes should again prevent me from meeting you and indeed from paying the affairs of South America that attention which their importance and urgency demand."[49]   By that time, a Venezuelan Commission had arrived in London to deal with Perceval's ministers.

There was a famous "Revolution" in Caracas, Venezuela, on April 19, 1810, from which would emerge the first Republic of Spanish America in 1811. Thus, that "Revolution" determined Francisco de Miranda's future, as well as the locale for our final chapters. This revolutionary movement followed, almost to the letter, the "classic" formula suggested by General Miranda to his countrymen in Venezuela, as well as the rest of Spanish America, in his daring "Paper Assault" of late 1808 and early 1809. Before a detailed account of the revolution appears, let us consider its impact upon the London press, especially on those periodicals used by the Miranda team in its intensive campaign to change British policy in South America. Of special importance was the first issue of *El Español* in London on April 30, 1810, a monthly periodical of immense importance to the Wars of Independence in Spanish America in their initial phase, as well as the constitutional experiment that took place in southern Spain, at Cádiz, and what it meant for the entire Spanish and Portuguese-speaking areas of the world. On July 31st, José Blanco-White made a commentary on the April 19th Revolution of earth-shaking proportions. The Napoleonic Wars had finally spread to the New World!

Bad weather conditions held up the news of the Venezuelan revolution for almost two months. The English government received its reports from Curaçao by early June; and it was perhaps Admiral Alexander Cochrane's command in the Lesser Antilles that supplied most of the details, including those that Miranda had in his possession by June 22nd. Miranda made these materials available to the *Morning Chronicle* in London, whose editor was a good friend of James Mill. On the 23d of June, the periodical published its first story; on the same day, the *Courier* editorialized on the historical significance of the Caracas uprising. Within a week's time *L'Ambigú* reported the event; and it was this version that first reached Venezuela, into the columns of the *Gazeta de Caracas*.[50]   Most London newspapers seemed to be drawing from the same body of materials. The presentation, in general, was positive: it was not a tumultuous uprising; the military force in Caracas soon shifted to the revolutionary cause, being rewarded by an increase in salary; there were from thirty to forty thousand people involved in the demonstrations; a *Junta Suprema* organized a provisional government headed by twenty-three of the city's leading citizens; the Junta promptly assured the other provinces of Venezuela that the movement's objectives represented the best interests of all the provinces in the former Captaincy of Venezuela; and the provinces were to elect deputies for a general government of the area. The Caracas Junta, moreover, soon issued reform measures to attract the support of the Indians, by relieving them of the onerous colonial tribute tax; the armed forces were promised higher pay; measures were taken to assure landowners of an adequate labor supply; and "free trade" was declared, thus lowering duties and opening up ports to outside powers. It was the type of information that pleased the English reader; yet, they also were able to read about how some Englishmen in the area feared racial disturbances. One Englishman reported that whites were a distinct minority—two hundred non-whites to one white; and the talk of equality and freedom for all seemed fraught with danger.

Some periodicals considered the historical significance of the April 19th Revolution in Caracas—what it might mean for Spanish America and for British policy, and what recommendations were in order. The *Courier* (June 23) opened with a sophisticated view:

> The intelligence received from South America, though important, is not unexpected. It will be more a matter of astonishment that that vast territory should have preserved its dependence upon the Mother Country so long, considering the total want of energy on the part of the Spanish Government, and its subserviency to the councils and commands of France, than that it should at last have disclosed a spirit of independence, and expressed a determination to exist as a separate State. Some of our contemporaries consider this event as having been solely produced by the military disasters of Spain. Those disasters may have accelerated it, but, the wish and the design had long been formed, particularly in that part in which the Revolution has broken out, the Caraccas. When the first disturbances took place in Spain, produced by the dissensions in the Royal Family, it was suggested in this Paper, that that was the proper time to strike a great blow in South America; not by attempting to effect conquests, or to extend the British arms, but by attempting to extend the British influence, by inviting the people to declare themselves independent, promising them the powerful protection of this country, the only country, on account of her naval sovereignty, that could effectually shield them from the power of France and

Spain—the only country, that could enable them to consolidate their freedom, and give strength and scope to their industry and their commerce.[51]

The reference here, the reader will recall, was the key *Courier* editorial of April 23, 1808, that inspired the British government to support the "American thrust" in the emancipation of South America. British ministers, however, were not consistent: Spain

> threw herself into our arms, and the Treaty was formed between the Spanish and our Government . . . That Treaty forbids our prosecuting any such designs as those we have mentioned, and prevents our acceding to the wishes of the Carraccas for our alliance and protection to enable them to establish their independence. Yet, that independence, which might have been established more promptly and more effectually had we encouraged it, will, we have no doubt, be established throughout the South American Provinces, whether we assist them or not.

These were prophetic words for the emancipation of Spanish America. Furthermore, the writer's message underscored the subsequent problems of the Venezuelan commissioners in their negotiations with the British government. Since James Mill, in our analysis, was the author of the celebrated April 23, 1808, editorial; it is likely that he also composed the editorial we have just examined; or at least, he was consulted. These were points that Miranda's writers had often stated in an earlier period.

All of the interpretive articles of the April 19th revolution were strongly influenced by Miranda's team of writers, although the authorship is difficult to identify. James Mill and Dr. C.'s writings, in particular, were well-known to other British journalists, so that it may have been one of their converts that produced the articles in question. Whatever may have been the case, the net result would be essentially to advance the cause of emancipation in the New World. *The Examiner* (London) of July 1, 1810, had an article of six columns entitled "Spanish South America." Miranda preserved a copy of it for his archives, making favorable comments in the margins. It was most likely written by a member, or members of his team—the evidence points to Gould Francis Leckie and Dr. F.S. Constancio—who, in the process, had digested thoroughly Mill's contributions to the same crusade. In short, it provides a good synthesis of the intellectual fabric

woven by Miranda's writers in behalf of the emancipation movement
for Spanish America:

> Positive accounts have at length been received of insurrections
> against the Spanish Government in the Caracas, the province in which
> such a spirit has manifested itself more than once. It has long been
> expected that some decisive revolt against their miserable Government
> would take place in the Spanish South American possessions. Europe,
> though filled with cares of its own that require a continued and anxious
> attention, has nevertheless, in every interval that allowed hope or
> speculation, turned an eager eye to the new world, as to a new channel
> for profitable exertion, a recompense for suspended industry, and even
> as to a new and more hopeful field for the structure of brilliant systems
> of policy. In these views, no European nation is so interested, with
> regard to influence, advantage, and social feeling, as Great Britain; and
> any new account or even rumour, respecting the above-mentioned event,
> ought to excite a powerful sympathy in every one of us,—in our
> merchants, for its prospects of great and laudable acquisition;—in our
> military and naval men, for it's prospects of that greatest of rarities in
> history—an unexceptionable field of exertion;—in our politicians, for
> the glory that would accrue to this nation, from a disinterested use of
> her assistance;—and in a word, in every thinking person, for the dawn
> of a new era in history, calculated to awaken all his speculation, to
> throw new lights upon systems, and to finish what has little more than
> commenced in human knowledge,—the education of *experience.*
>
> Disaffections and revolts in Europe are events so ordinary, that they
> can scarcely give a common relish to the news, and owing to a
> multiplicity of circumstances too well known to us, they excite almost
> as little sympathy as speculation. But it is far otherwise with
> intelligence from the Western world. Little of the past—and nothing of
> the present history of politics—apply to the prospects we see there; so
> that it presents at once all the charms of novelty; and what does apply,
> only gives fresh argument for hope both with regard to ourselves, and
> to those whom we may and ought to benefit. To revolt against tyranny
> in Europe is only to incur its sure and speedy vengeance; and why so?
> Because the very spirit which once rose against tyranny met not with the
> just or even the negative encouragement it deserved, and thus was
> converted into a more powerful tyranny itself. This is the first
> consideration that ought to strike an Englishman in contemplating the
> probable struggles of Spanish America.

Rather than burden the reader with details on Spain's oppressive
system and why her colonists anxiously looked forward to their

freedom, the writer recommended some readings from the *Edinburgh Review:* two reviews on Humboldt's *Travels* in No. 31, Depon's *Travels* in No. 15; "and particularly the remarks in No. 26, *on the Emancipation of Spanish America.*" If James Mill had been the author, he would not have forgotten the second article on Molina's book; and, certainly, he would have mentioned Burke's two essays! Then, the writer-scholar, much like Dr. C. did in his September 13, 1809, article, explained that:

> The object of the present article is merely to point out the obvious policy which this Country should observe towards Spanish America in case of a declared revolt, either of the whole or a part. Let any reflecting person, indeed, who estimates as he ought our conduct towards our North American possessions, present to his mind a set of Colonies retained against their will upon the same principle of monopoly, but infinitely worse administered, infinitely more oppressed and degraded, and without even a single habitual prepossession in favour of the mother country, and he will have no doubt of the policy to be pursued on such an event and in such an age.

Up to this point, the writer had appealed to "every thinking person" and "any reflecting person," thus exposing a mannerism that was noted first in one of Dr. C.'s earlier writings. Now, the writer in *The Examiner* presented an interpretation associated with Miranda's publicists and with a passion that revealed considerable embitterment:

> Of late years, however, it has been the misfortune of Great Britain, in spite of all that she has seen others suffer, and in spite of her own experience, to sacrifice great interests to small,—to render her high spirit subservient to petty minds and worse objects,—and to descend into the common work of corrupt governments, timid for themselves and ambitious against others. We have seen, that corruption, and corruption only, has been the sole efficient cause of the overthrow of other governments; and yet, whenever there has been even a sign of disturbance elsewhere, we began to tremble for ourselves; whenever another nation manifested an anxiety for decent freedom, we began to consider how far such a freedom would tell for or against our present relative situation in Europe;—we have discouraged all such attempts when they militated against a corrupt expediency, but at the same time have seized every opportunity of gratifying a paltry ambition, careless whom *that* might offend;—in fine, we have shewn a greater respect for positive corruption than the most probable blessings of society, and what

is worse, we have flattered or attempted to flatter our consciences that this was really the best and only *legitimate* policy. This distortion of our moral feeling led us into an approval of the American war; it led us into our schemes of unhealthy aggrandizement in the East; it led us into a war of repression and extermination with France; and *hitherto*, gathering obstinacy from consciousness, it has led us to treat the cause of South American emancipation first with coldness and afterwards with insult. Yet we have had glorious opportunities for its accomplishment. The Spanish colonies, connected with the mother country by a chain as brittle as it has been galling, seemed to want only some aspiring individual to give them the signal for bursting it. This individual was found in the person of Miranda, a native of the province now said to be in a state of insurrection, a gentleman well educated, thirsting for knowledge and its diffusion, and apparently of the most exalted intentions. Of his industry in the cause he gave long and unabated proof by traveling over Europe and engaging every friend for it he could find; and of his good motives and good policy united, there can hardly be better proof than in the tempered enthusiasm with which he went with the French as far only as liberty accompanied them, and with which he repressed their pretended ardour for his cause when he saw that they had degenerated from emancipators into conquerors.

At this point, the writer reviewed concisely the opportunism that guided British leaders in their negotiations with Miranda from 1790 to the present, not a very complimentary picture in the least. "Thus the English Court," the writer continued,

time after time, has sacrificed a great and glorious measure to wretched compromises with corruption; and the cause of emancipation has risen and fallen in this country, with as little good reason and infinitely less interest than the stocks in the city. A cause however, so just and so full of promise, wanted only to be cleared of the common *obstructions*; and the season is at length arrived, when its own energies, if not basely obstructed, are its best and sufficient helpers. We are told, that we ought not at the present moment to cooperate with the Spanish colonies in any attempt at a separation from Spain, because Spain is pursuing measures for her own independence, and we are her allies. But setting aside the likelihood of any such independence, Spain ought to have set a proper value on what she was demanding for herself, and regarded the decency of her claims on our assistance. Be that as it may, it cannot be doubted, I should think, for an instant, that if the Spanish colonies chuse to declare their independence, they have at least a full claim to our forbearance against them, and should be left to work out their

deliverance, on every ground of policy and natural right. To leave them
to themselves, at least with regard to armies and non-obstruction, seems
indeed to be the most politic as well as just assistance we could render
the cause. The mother-country can no longer even threaten them; they
are at a safe distance from the most formidable opposition in Europe;
and if they have a just sense of their situation and love of independence,
they cannot in the nature of things fail of success. A powerful ally,
going with arms to assist a rising nation, has a temptation before it,
which it finds very difficult to resist. The United States, who have
enough to do with their own possessions, and enough to acquire
whenever it suits them, may assist the South Americans by land; and
Great Britain, very much to their advantage and to her own profit and
reputation, may assist them by sea. But beyond this, help is
unnecessary, and interference would at best be suspicious and
perplexing.

As for the type of government to be established in Spanish America,
the writer insisted that it was the sole concern of Spain's former
colonists. Fascinated by "the prosperity of their Northern neighbours,"
they would like to follow that model with variations to take into
account differences in geography and population distribution. Miranda's
plan of an "Inca" sovereign, might be feasible. He added: "Miranda
himself deserves a crown, especially as he does not seek it under the
mask of wild theory and with French cant in his mouth." The
Edinburgh reviewers felt that a mixed, or constitutional monarchy,
might be advisable for the government of South America. Yet, the
author felt—and we should note the beginning words of this quotation:
"every thinking person will, I believe, agree with them;" but it is
doubtful whether their proposal of giving South American thrones to
"the aged ex-monarch of Spain and his son would give satisfaction to
any but themselves, or whether it is not in itself an impracticable and
somewhat ridiculous measure." He reasoned that "The passion for the
BOURBONS has pretty well gone by in every country, and it has not
been their fault, if they are respected by a single lover of freedom or
improvement. In another section, the author noted:

> Above all, our assistance, whether negative or positive, ought not to be
> founded on any ridiculous lingerings towards the old system, founded
> on the immediate use of **FERDINAND's** name. **FERDINAND** himself
> is now a mere name; and the freedom of millions is too substantial a
> cause to be made dependent on any such shadows.

Despite the writer's suggestions, he ended his editorial cynically with these words:

> Whatever we may do, will be done rather against **BONAPARTE** than for them,—rather against the overturner of old systems whom we have helped to make a powerful despot, than in favour of the overturners of old systems whom we may help to make friends and free men.

It would appear that Miranda, who read this editorial and the next one that we shall treat below carefully and marked them up with apparent enthusiasm, could thank his two intellectual friends of 1809 for this particular article, and the one that follows. Gould Leckie or Dr. Constancio, or even both of them, authored the blistering, but brilliant analysis, in *The Examiner* of July 1st, 1810, preparing the historical scene for our next chapter. Of the two, I suspect that Dr. C. was the main author, given his attention to the "thinking" or "reflecting" reader.[52]

On the same date, July 1st, 1810, another historical interpretation appeared in the *Bell's Weekly Messenger* (London). It was translated into Spanish and published in the *Gazeta de Caracas*.[53] Dr. C. was perhaps the major contributor, because of the analogies used in his 1809 writings. The report began:

> A revolution has broken out in the Caraccas, the professed objects of which are loyalty and allegiance to the expiring authority of Ferdinand: this we truly regret, because we are persuaded that the motive from which such revolution springs, is neither loyalty to Ferdinand, nor affection to a Monarchical Government.
>
> The truth is, the Governors of South America are very naturally desirous to retain and perpetuate their present power, which they can only lawfully derive from the grant and commission of the Spanish Monarchy; which Monarchy, if overturned, drags down with it the whole authority of the Colonial Governors. They would willingly, therefore, govern South America under the name and authority of Ferdinand; because they know that such government would be without responsibility or check—Their loyalty would be a cheap offering when made to a phantom and a prisoner, at the distance of three thousand leagues, and would cost them neither tribute nor submission—If a Revolution on these principles prevailed, South America would be governed by Ferdinand the Seventh much in the same manner in which Egypt is now governed by the Grand Seignor—A nominal sovereignty would be a mere cheat to delude the people, whilst all the efficient

power would be in the hands of those who, with a thorough contempt for the Monarch himself, would be most clamorous for loyalty and obedience in others.

We trust that these Mameluckes of South America will not effect their ambitious objects; and that Great Britain will not lend them a hand. Their attempt reminds us of the practice of some of the Eastern Governments, in which the Pashaw always takes care that the reigning Prince should be a minor or a madman; or, at all events, in prison during his life.

The final paragraph, as we shall see, justified the picture offered above; but the description was a distortion of the facts. Anyone reading the news items that came out on June 23rd, and the following days, could see that the "Colonial Governors"—in fact, all of the Spanish hierarchy—were captured by the revolutionaries in a bloodless coup on April 19th and sent off on a boat to distant shores. It was the revolutionaries, not the Spanish officials of the Old Order, that used the symbol of Ferdinand VII, although the publicist was correct in assuming that Spanish officials elsewhere might employ the tactics suggested. It should be obvious, however, that the revolutionaries themselves were using the same tactics, or the "Mask of Ferdinand," as it has been called.

The final paragraphs, nonetheless had deep meaning for the revolutionaries in Caracas, Venezuela. They read the Spanish translation carefully:

We should object indeed, without reserve, to the establishment of anything like a *Bourbon* Monarchy in South America. The Vineyard has already been too long neglected, and has been suffered to exhaust its natural luxuriance in weeds; to bring upon it a heavy blight of European ignorance and superstition would be a monstrous sin against humanity. It would be to inoculate with the old disease of Europe, and to bind to the carcase of a rotten monarchy, a country just emerging from barbarism into civilization.

We deprecate all attempts to transplant Bourbonism to South America—Let the principles of a generous Democracy, and a wise and grave Republicanism, (consistently with humanity) sweep that whole Continent . . . and we have no objection—Such principles are necessary *there* to rouse man to a due knowledge of himself; to stir up all that is active and generous within him; to strike out his latent qualities; to lash him till he *spins*, instead of wasting and consuming away like a piece of dead box.

The form of Government suited for South America is not Monarchy, but a Republic.[54]

The marks of a free press were evident in London when news of the Venezuelan Revolution reached there. Indeed, this was notable in the non-English press, especially in *El Español,* edited by a gifted interpreter—José María Blanco y Crespo, otherwise known in English history as the Reverend Joseph Blanco-White. *El Español* (1810–1814) was a major periodical in the Spanish world, vital for its insights and documents on Spain from May 2, 1808 forward, and the subsequent development of liberalism/constitutionalism in southern Spain, and for its thorough and emotional analysis of the Wars of Independence in Spanish America in its initial phases.

This young *Sevillano* at thirty-six, almost James Mill's age, became controversial from the time he appeared in London in March, 1810. As a matter of fact, he brought controversy with him from Spain, primarily because of his relations with the Junta Central that censored some of his writings as the political editor of the *Semanario Patriótico* of Sevilla. He left Spain to avoid capture by the French; but he also brought with him valuable documents that would prove embarrassing to the Junta Central while it controlled the provisional government of Spain politically and militarily. These documents, of course, facilitated his contact with Francisco de Miranda, just as *El Colombiano* came out with its first issues. In a sense, as we have already noted, *El Español* continued the work of Miranda's paper after it closed. From April 30, 1810, forward, *El Español* commenced the publication of documents on the Junta Central and the transfer of power to the Regency. Blanco-White expanded the harmful stereotype of the Junta which Miranda's team of writers had been spreading in order to further the cause of emancipation in Spanish America. Blanco-White, moreover, was a strong liberal who felt that Spain could no longer afford to follow erroneous policies with regards to the colonies. To keep them loyal to Spain, he advocated *real* and *sincere* reforms in the New World, not just theory, or words, when speaking of Americans' "equality." Blanco-White expected Spanish liberals to be sincere in establishing a modern, constitutional order in Spain. His criticism from London, exposing the liberals at Cádiz, kept them in a constant uproar against him. His reputation in Europe and America thus expanded accordingly. When Spanish-Americans later found out that he was actually a defender of "Enlightened Empire," and against any complete break with Spain, he became a controversial writer throughout Spanish America. The news that Great Britain had helped to subsidize *El Español*, as well as supplying a pension of sorts for Blanco-White, did not help his reputation among those opposed to him. His subsequent education at Oxford was also supported by the British government.

This brazen Spanish editor, of Irish extraction no less, poured out his ideas on the April 19th Revolution in Venezuela. These words would soon be read throughout the Spanish world, raising hackles in Blanco-White's *patria* (mother country) and nothing but praise from Miranda's patria and others throughout Spanish America: "Political Reflections—Venezuela."[55] "It would appear," Don José began,

> that the epoch of a great political happening has finally arrived, one that has been expected for a long time: the standard of independence has been raised in America; and judging from our calculations, of what we have seen about the revolution in Caracas, it is not a tumultuous or fleeting movement on the part of those *pueblos*; rather, it reflects a determination based on mature thought and knowledge, and put into execution under the best auspices: *moderation and beneficence*. That is what emanates from the proclamations and measures of the new government of Venezuela. If we had seen that revolution begin by proclaiming exaggerated principles of liberty, impracticable theories like those of the French Revolution, we would distrust the righteous intentions of the promoters, and would conclude that it was an action carried out by partisans, and not the practical decision of an entire people on the need for political change. But upon noting that they are only looking out for their security, and to do what all the *pueblos* of Spain have put into effect, that is, to form an interim government, during the absence of their monarch, or until the Kingdom is established on new and legitimate bases, it seems to us that we are witnessing in the Caracas movement the first steps towards the establishment of the empire that is to inherit the glory, the knowledge, and the happiness of the one that is about to perish on the continent of Europe at the hands of the most barbarous military despotism.

Having pronounced these grandiose lines to his brethren in Spain and America, Father Blanco-White had to summon his entire intellectual faculties to plead his case with both sides. And his imagination and intuition was uncanny, as if he could sense what the basic bones of contention would be in the next several years between Americans and Filipinos, on the one side, and the Peninsulars and Islanders on the other side. Thus, from 1810 to 1814, the Wars of

Independence became a reality in the Spanish world. Here was the argument presented by the Catholic *padre*:

> But what will become of Spain if the Americas separate from her? We can never believe that the Americas, even if they follow the example of Caracas, will forget those in Spain who are fighting gloriously against foreign oppression. Venezuela's proclamation breathes love for Spaniards; this is inextinguishable among Americans. The Americas—free of the yoke that some Spaniards have wanted to fasten around their necks, and others who still imprudently want to remain in power overseas—would be in an infinitely stronger condition to send aid to Spain.

Somewhat hesitant about his insinuation concerning some Spaniards, he blurted out:

> Well this is what it seems they want—those who became so upset on hearing about the independence of America. Americans will never believe in separating from the Spanish Crown, unless they are forced to do so by provocative governmental measures. Americans probably just want not to be awaiting government and direction from a country separated by an immense ocean, from a country almost occupied by the enemies, and where a government in perpetual danger, and that can barely look out for itself in the circumstances surrounding it, can do absolutely nothing about the extended countries of the New World, except to ask for aid and to send officials.

To be exact, this new, pugnacious champion of the Americas exposed the real culprit: "following a bad star"—*por una mala estrella*—the Spanish Government seems determined to support its predecessors' "numerous errors of administration concerning America."[56] Here, he exposed the Regency's rejection of a "Free Trade" measures for the Americans on May 10, 1810—an issue which thoroughly antagonized Americans everywhere, especially since the Junta Central had initiated the measure. The Regency denied that the document in question was real! To deny Americans free trade was an unwarranted travesty, that would certainly not encourage them to pursue a policy of "*moderación.*" Americans simply would not tolerate "the monopoly of the metropolis." Just as James Mill had described the monopolistic stages of Spain's economic system, Blanco-White blasted away at this unreasonable and selfish system. This was especially ludicrous in light of the fact that a royal order of January 22, 1809, had made the Americas integral parts of the Spanish Monarchy! If the Regency was the successor of the Junta Central, then how could it reactivate the antiquated and "prohibitive laws of the Indies."[57] His parting words of advice to the Spanish Regency were these:

> If you do not wish to agitate the Americans, in general, into a spirit of independence and even of hatred toward the metropolis [Spain], you must remove the shackles from your commerce, and dissuade the vested interests [in Spanish trade] from inciting the disobedience against the government. We note that in many parts of America new commercial measures are being taken; the need to seek export markets for their goods will bring on similar steps everywhere [in the Americas]. If the Regency opposes those [commercial] measures that will not stop them from continuing; they will be transformed by the opposition to the government to acts which they will call rebellion, and will thus obligate themselves, without realizing it, to join a complete revolution. Americans are the equals of Spaniards: if the latter enjoy the right to sell their goods to the best buyer, and selecting from the industrial products of all other nations what is convenient in exchange for their own products, any attempt to subject them [the Americans] to a monopoly that is contrary to their rights, is an injustice, that no law can authorize. The government of Spain, the general Spanish nation, cannot pretend to sustain it.
>
> These reflections are obvious enough; but because they are, we cannot help but repeat them. I have deemed it my obligation to pronounce them, despite the war that the special interest of many will declare against me for it. But I shall always appeal, above their interest, to the public, who in most cases is objective. If some how I am not permitted to reach it [the public], in Spain, I shall grieve over the fate that prevents that very noble kingdom from not advancing in the fields of liberty and political tolerance, the only cement that is left for her [Spain] future happiness.[58]

Father Blanco-White was a welcome addition to Francisco de Miranda's team in London. He was another fighter like James Mill.

Chapter Eight

The Caracas Revolution of April 19, 1810

> Who is this man called an American? What person of means . . . could
> view such contrast and injustice without being consumed with
> indignation? Who would not prefer to shed his last drop of blood to
> procure for his people those rights and benefits that God and nature
> have bestowed on them, rather than countenance, for even one more
> day, leaving his sword in the scabbard, tranquil and ignominious,
> witnessing such evil?
>
> But if every American is willing to shoulder his responsibility and
> strive to secure these rights for his country; he would not ignore his
> neighbor's experience to the North—their direct impact upon the
> increase of the population, upon the spread of their culture; upon the
> advance of manufactures, commerce, resources, arts, sciences, moral
> reforms—in short, of all those measures that constitute strength,
> civilization, happiness, and real glory for their nation.
> William Burke, Caracas, November 23, 1810.[1]

The Caracas Revolution of April 19, 1810, was a remarkable movement
for the times, so rational and just as José Blanco-White described it.
Conscious of its historical role in Spanish America, the Junta Suprema
of Venezuela weighed all its words and arguments carefully for local,
national, hemispheric, and world consumption. Inspired by Miranda's
earlier advice, the Venezuelan leaders appeared to be the logical
partisans of Francisco de Miranda's crusade for Colombia's liberation.
Juan Germán Roscio, who has been likened to Thomas Jefferson,
represented a powerful intellectual force in the decision-making of

Venezuela's provisional government. And as the Junta's Secretary of State, he wisely cautioned moderation. Since he was also the editor of the *Gazeta de Caracas*, he knew how to handle propaganda effectively, using "William Burke" to the greatest advantage.

This Thomas Jefferson of Venezuela needs to be explored in more depth, a prominent figure in Venezuela's birth, who had much to do with writing the Declaration of Independence on July 5, 1811. Born in 1769 to an Indian mother and an Italian father, young Roscio struggled valiantly against pressures imposed upon him by a rigid class and racist society. Thanks to the benevolence of certain parties, he managed to survive; and at the University of Caracas, he was soon recognized as an intellectual in the fields of theology and law. Finally, he opted for the doctorate in law, rather than theology. Race may have been a factor in his decision, as well as a strong concern—*obsession* might be a more appropriate word—for the abuses of the political-religious system in the Hispanic World epitomized by the Inquisition and the attendant consequences of fanaticism and superstition. The monopoly of Church and State was anathema to this otherwise calm intellectual; and some of his writings betray these beliefs that he had in common with another student of religion in faraway Spain—José María Blanco-White. This parallel is vital to our speculation on the authorship of the controversial editorial on "Religious Toleration," that appeared in the *Gazeta* on February 19, 1811 under Burke's name. Roscio authorized the publication of that piece.

As the key secretary of the Junta Suprema, it was Roscio's conviction that a moderate approach was essential to assure Caracas of a support system in the other provinces of the former Captaincy-General of Venezuela. Granted a superior status by the late Bourbons, Caracas experienced the envy and resentment of the *provincianos* that lived in outlying jurisdictions. Letters to provincial authorities were carefully worded to convince them that Caracas on April 19th had reacted to a danger that faced all of the Venezuelan provinces—namely, the French victories on the Peninsula that might result in the demise of the mother country. In the *Proclama* to the Provinces of April 20, 1810, the Junta Suprema in Caracas outlined a program for a Confederation Government of Venezuela in the near future. And it was indeed important to elect the best representatives to the Constituent Assembly that opened its doors on March 2, 1811. Roscio also put together an "Ordinance for the Deputies" that outlined election procedures for the provinces; it came out later in a series of instalments in the *Gazeta*. Despite the Junta's efficiency and concern for the provinces, it failed to win over three of them: Coro and Maracaibo in the "West" and Guayana in the "East". This recalcitrancy, as a result, brought moments of despair and chaos to the Junta Suprema and its successors in Venezuela.

As Secretary of State for Foreign Relations, Roscio sent out special commissions to notify the Venezuelan provinces and the English possessions in the nearby Caribbean islands about the April 19th events. A hostile audience greeted the two-man commission in the Province of Coro; then the commissioners left for Maracaibo and subsequently they were compeled to visit Puerto Rico, where the Captain-General imprisoned them for six months. Thanks to Admiral Cochrane's diplomatic pressure, the Venezuelan commissioners gained their freedom.[2] This was a good omen—Miranda's close relationship with Cochrane and other key officials in the English Caribbean that worked to the advantage of the Junta Suprema. Capitalizing on the British friendship for General Miranda, Roscio struck up a valuable correspondence with Lt. Governor John Thomas Layard of Curaçao and his chief secretary John Robertson. Since Roscio knew English, this contact with Curaçao was useful in dealing with other authorities in the Caribbean. Governor Layard, for example, put pressure on Coro's officials to collaborate and support the Venezuelan government in Caracas, which was also loyal to Ferdinand VII of Spain. In fact, that was the only government that Layard would recognize in Venezuela.[3] Admiral Cochrane, furthermore, had a few ships that guaranteed trade with the ports under the Junta Suprema of Venezuela. Not surprisingly, therefore, the Junta Suprema pushed free-trade reforms, in general; and specifically encouraged the English traders by giving them a one-quarter reduction on duties. The U.S. Commercial Agent to Venezuela, Robert K. Lowry, was somewhat annoyed with this favoritism to the English. But he did not push his complaint, at that time, because the British navy in the area was a strong guarantee for the survival of the Junta Suprema in Venezuela.[4] Roscio's letters with John Robertson revealed such key insights as: Spaniards were guilty of "hypocrisy" when they promised "free trade;" and the Caracas government would not continue its support of Ferdinand VII, if the latter became a mere puppet of Napoleon Bonaparte.[5]

An avid and critical follower of European developments since the French Revolution, when he was only twenty, Roscio read all the information available in the Spanish periodicals of that period, which were much more liberal than it is usually assumed. For example, these Spanish references covered the "American Revolution" in great detail. The grievances of English colonials were especially meaningful to thoughtful Spanish-Americans like Roscio who appreciated their implications for Venezuela.[6] During those years, Roscio gained a deep admiration for the institutions of the United States of America, the advantages of political and economic freedoms, and the faith in man's ability to progress to a more modern and rational existence. The Spanish Bourbons, for whatever the reason, allowed a reforming spirit to take hold. The colonials welcomed this progress in Europe. They were not impressed, however, when Spaniards were inconsistent, or selfish, in their reforms, while at the same time expressing attitudes of European superiority. Here were the bases for the grievances underscored by General Miranda in his propaganda movement for Spanish-American Independence. We are already familar with his techniques in getting his ideas and publications to colleagues in Spanish America. The writings of the Junta Suprema of Venezuela expressed Miranda's ideas and objectives, thanks to talented interpreters like Juan Germán Roscio. He was very sensitive to European motives and actions. Thus, Roscio suspected hypocrisy when Spaniards talked of "free trade;" as a serious advocate of Father Viscardo de Guzmán's ideas, he rejected the papal decrees of the 1490s that presumably established Spain's title to the Indies. His insights on the Treaty of Basle (1795), for example, led him to argue that Spain violated its legal codes (*Recopilación de Leyes*) in such-and-such an article when she allowed Napoleon to take over the Dominican side of the Caribbean Island of Española. He feared, moreover, that the provisional government of Spain, because of the military reverses in recent months, would lead to a similar violation that the Americans, who had not been consulted at all, would have to confront in the future. These arguments and parameters, at times legalistic and even paranoid, encouraged the proliferation of grievances against Spanish rule that attended that April 19th Revolution in Venezuela.[7]

In a letter of May 3, 1810, to the Spanish Regency, the Venezuelan Junta presented new complaints: a very important one in the days before April 19th centered on the electoral differences called for in the impending elections for a Spanish Parliament (*Cortes*): one deputy for every fifty thousand voters in Spain—the so-called "active voice"—whereas Americans and Asians were limited to the "passive voice"—that is, according to their representation in qualified municipalities, or corporations, in Spanish America or the Philippines. This major grievance, by the way, dominated the heated "American Question" at the Cortes of Cádiz and never was settled to a satisfactory degree.[8] Another complaint of significance, which underscored the Europeans' superiority at the office-holding level, was the Regency's determination to control appointments overseas. The Europeans at Cádiz assumed that their executive officers in America would implement reforms faithfully, thus choosing officers there on the basis of merit. The Venezuelan Junta pointed out caustically that the Regency's assumptions were erroneous, self-serving, and naive to the extreme.[9] And Roscio *et al* were right. Upon reading the Junta's sharp reply to the Regency, other Americans concurred with the Venezuelans, judging from their own experiences with arrogant Spanish officials. Other Americans, in short, understood the true significance of the April 19th Revolution in Caracas—a model that caught their attention and with which they identified. Before long, they also joined the cause of an "Independence," loyal to Ferdinand VII, following Miranda's suggestions. Moreover, on April 27, 1810, *La Suprema Junta Conservadora de los Derechos de Fernando VII en Venezuela* wrote enthusiastically to the *Cabildos de las Capitales de América* in these terms: "Caracas should find imitators among all the inhabitants of America. . .and her resolution should be applauded by all those *pueblos* who conserve any feelings for virtue and enlightened patriotism." In a Miranda-like manner, the Junta Suprema encouraged the Cabildos, as the best qualified instruments of power, to seize upon any opportunity that presented itself. "Our cause is one," the Junta implored with emotion, "our motto should be one: fidelity to our unfortunate monarch; war against his oppressive tyrant; fraternity and constancy."[10]

A major objective of the Junta Suprema of Venezuela was to send its best representatives to plead their nation's cause before the United States and Great Britain. The commission to Washington, D.C. consisted of Juan Vicente Bolívar (Simón's brother) and Telésforo de Orea; and, as Secretary, José Rafael Revenga. The reception of the trio in Baltimore was spirited and friendly, according to a report of June 4, 1810. North Americans shared Venezuela's hopes: "Our memorable resolution has filled with enthusiasm the Children of Washington and Franklin." The Baltimore *Evening Post* raved about the epigraph of the Caracas Gazette: *Salus populi suprema lex isto* (*The Welfare of the People is the Supreme Law*), a far better motto than "I the King: order and command." North Americans everywhere studied with admiration

Venezuela's statistics and industry; and "our manifestoes, proclamations, acts, regulations and other public papers" have appeared in U.S. newspapers "with the most honorable reflections."[11]

Despite the enthusiastic reception of the Venezuelan commissioners in the United States, this was a period of stress and strain for the young American nation that within two years would lead to war with Great Britain. In that context, the United States was not as free to support a new American country. And the old hard-nosed diplomats like Luis de Onís, the Spanish Minister in the United States, placed all manner of stumbling blocks in the path of the Venezuelan patriots, whom he regarded as traitors and rebels. Juan de Bolívar, therefore, failed to acquire the arms that Roscio had planned on when he wrote up the instructions. Onís and his consuls in the United States issued statements in the press making it clear that American ships entering "rebel" ports would be punished and confiscated. The wily Onís, in the meantime, persuaded American contractors to take arms to the "loyal" provinces of Venezuela: to Coro, Maracaibo, and Guayana. This was a key concern for Roscio when Robert K. Lowry appeared in Caracas in late August, 1810, as a U.S. Commercial Agent. Roscio insisted that President Madison had to stop Onís in his tracks. That vicious Spaniard, he pointed out, had earlier spoken disparagingly about the United States; and Roscio would show Lowry the pertinent documentation. Lowry sent copies of these papers to his superior in the State Department, who by April, 1811, was James Monroe. Without going into further details, the Venezuelan commission in the United States was not the success that Roscio had expected; and he tended to blame Juan de Bolívar; so, he recalled Bolívar and left Orea as the Venezuelan representative in Washington, D.C.[12]

Far more important in Roscio's thinking was the Venezuelan Commission to London. He wanted to be sure that the best men were chosen and that they knew exactly what to do and say to the English. His detailed instructions took the question and answer format; and considering the thoroughness of the document, it makes one wonder if Roscio's intuition had benefitted from Miranda's insights in dealing with the British government. Be that as it may, he sensed that Miranda's record and reputation on anticolonialism might be an obstacle and warned his commissioners not to use him—an inhibition which Roscio must have recognized his commissioners could not have observed. The top men chosen for the English mission were Simón Bolívar and Luis López Méndez, two members of the colonial aristocracy—the

Mantuanos. The third man, as Secretary, was Andrés Bello, one of Roscio's dearest friends and a fellow intellectual. Bello, at twenty-nine, just a few years older than his close friend Bolívar, was already acquiring prominence in Caracas as a leader, partially because of his editorship of the *Gazeta de Caracas*. In time, this young *Caraqueño* became one of the greatest minds in Spanish-American letters of the nineteenth century. Indeed, two of the three members of the Commission to England in 1810 were "greats"—one in the military-political field and the other, in the intellectual-artistic realm.[13]

In light of his importance in the "William Burke" story, Andrés Bello's background deserves further elaboration. Bello was the eldest son of one of Caracas most distinguished lawyers who died in 1805, leaving Andrés with the responsibility for a large family. Roscio knew the family well and offered his friend Andrés sound advice. At the University of Caracas, young Bello's interest focused on philosophy, science, and law; and he chose to follow his father's footsteps as a lawyer. Andrés Bello's advance in the colonial bureaucracy was dramatic and impressive for a Creole, who eventually worked up to a position that placed him in contact with the Captain General of Venezuela. When the *Gazeta de Caracas* opened its doors in 1808, Bello was its first editor. As a young man, he had the great opportunity to meet the famous Baron Von Humboldt in 1799, which helped to stimulate his keen interest in the geography of his native area. Later in his life, he expressed this interest in one of the great poetic works. When he began the *Gazeta*, he was planning to collaborate in the writing of a *Guide for Foreigners*, describing the beauties of his native land—the first of a series of distinguished works by the Venezuelan savant.

The assignment as editor of Venezuela's first periodical/newspaper was a fitting reward for his various talents. And from 1808 forward, there were less inhibitions on the freedom of expression, as the spirit of reform took over in Cádiz, Spain. Editing the Venezuelan gazette, Bello relished the permission that he was given to reproduce the editorials of a key Cádiz paper, *El Voto*, on the theme of freedom of the press. Its epigraph was "The Welfare of the People is the Supreme Law," which Bello took over as his motto for the *Gazeta de Caracas*.[14] The Spaniards' obsession with freedom of expression was more than welcomed in Caracas by the young editor. The first issue of the Gazette appeared on October 24, 1808, using the printing equipment brought from Trinidad by Matthew Gallagher and James Lamb. Before long these two Englishmen published Bello's *Guide for Foreigners* and William Burke's, *Derechos de la América del Sur y México* (2 vols., 1811), which we shall analyze later. Bello's first editorial highlighted the "Utility" of the press in keeping readers in touch with the advances in Agriculture, Commerce, Politics, and Arts, fields that were fundamental for economic development. Thanks to the Spanish Bourbons, this theme became popular throughout the Spanish-speaking world.[15] Not surprisingly, therefore, Juan Germán Roscio and his good friend Francisco Javier de Uztáriz decided on August 14, 1810, to call for the founding of a *Sociedad Patriótica de Agricultura y Economía*.[16] As Independence approached, many of these economic societies in Spanish America developed into political organizations. This happened in Caracas in January, 1811, thanks in large part to Miranda's support.

Secretary Roscio was strongly interested in the appointment of Andrés Bello as secretary of the Commission to Great Britain. Thus, he reassured himself that the two *mantuano* commissioners would follow the instructions to the letter. Roscio and Bello agreed to keep up a steady correspondence. We have most of Roscio's letters to Bello, thanks to the latter's Chilean biographer; unfortunately, Bello's letters seemed to have been lost, once they reached Venezuela.[17] We thus have only indirect evidence of what he told Roscio in them. What Roscio does not tell us, therefore, remains a mystery that forces a historian to speculate.

"Enlighten yourself as much as you can" in London, Roscio urged his friend, "so that you may enlighten your nation" upon your return, a cultural objective for young Bello in Europe. He wanted him to be receptive to all aspects of England's cultural, intellectual, and political life. Besides grammars, encyclopedias, and other instruments of study, Roscio expected him to purchase any works—books, monographs, articles—that would help to educate his nation. After all, London was where Viscardo's work and Rousseau's *Social Contract* had been published, he reminded Bello.[18] After meeting James Mill and Jeremy Bentham, Andrés Bello learned about their various publications. Mill must have shown him the two treatises of 1807–1808 by William Burke, and someone relayed that information to Juan Germán Roscio in Caracas. How else could Roscio have written what he did about the author William Burke on November 23, 1810? After Miranda returned to Venezuela, Bello remained in London to work with Mill and Bentham. Later, we shall explain the plans that Bentham and Mill entertained for transferring themselves to Venezuela, once it was certain that Miranda's career there was a success. Although this never happened, it none the less was projected and thus influenced our account. Here, Andrés Bello had to serve as a key figure in relaying materials and information back to Roscio in Caracas. We suspect that it was Bello who forwarded the initial Burkian articles to Roscio, since the latter took over as editor of the *Gazeta de Caracas* when Bello left. This fact would be certain if only Bello's letter of September, 1810, were extant. In its absence, a different hypothetical bridge must be employed to explain how the materials reached Caracas before November 23, 1810. It is conceivable also that the Venezuelan José de Tovar Ponte was the medium, since he returned to Caracas with letters from the Venezuelan Commission before that date.[19] A plausible explanation has been offered to our attention by the learned Professor Pedro Grases, that indefatigable Catalan scholar who has lived in Caracas for many decades studying Venezuelan history and letters. In one of his studies, he noted that on November 22, 1811, James Lamb, the publisher of the *Gazeta*, registered a legal complaint against the government. Certain facts emerged from this case that suggest the "bridge" that interests us. Clearly, a key objective of Bello's appointment was to purchase needed supplies and equipment for the *Gazeta* in Caracas that, in effect, would double its printing capacity—two composition sticks, a press, characters, paper, etc. These purchases were made in London; and they entered the port of La Guaira, Venezuela, in November, 1810, without the payment of duties. It seems likely that Burke's initial editorials, those that appeared before Miranda's team reached Venezuela, arrived in the *Gazeta's* shipment of supplies, along with a note from Andrés Bello with assurance that a more detailed book manuscript would follow. We suspect, also, that Burke's two treatises of 1807–1808, as well as other books purchased by Bello under his cultural assignment, accompanied that shipment of equipment and supplies for the Caracas gazette.[20]

* * * * * * * * * * * *

The Venezuelan commissioners were well-received in Curaçao on their way to England. Governor John Thomas Layard promised his continued support to Venezuela, and John Robertson, his secretary, and Andrés Bello became the best of friends. Admiral Alexander Cochrane, moreover, arranged to provide a ship that would carry them swiftly (31 days) to Great Britain. They arrived on July 10, 1810. The

Venezuelans were sanguine that the great British nation would not abandon them in this crucial moment. Some of their innocence evaporated as their hero Francisco de Miranda—and they stayed at his home—poured out the realities of his negotiations over the years with the English. The prospects were not promising at all. British ministers would be highly reluctant to admit to a faulty decision back in 1808, when they chose to fight Napoleon in Spain. The Venezuelan mission, thus, would be of short duration.

Yet, the climate of opinion in London was changing somewhat. The new Minister of Foreign Affairs, replacing George Canning, was the Marquis of Wellesley who had been in Spain, knew her problems, and had many friends in the southern part. Moreover, Lord Holland's influence in this change of British attitudes requires further investigation. Miranda, the reader will recall, wrote to Wilberforce that Viscardo's insights were superior to those of Lord Holland. That was in June, 1810, when discussions were taking place in Parliament on what England should do about the potential for revolution and independence in Spanish America. This was also when Wilberforce and other powerful leaders of the opposition were challenging the government's mistaken policy in Spain, as well as reviving the alternative policy of the emancipation of Spanish America. Lord Holland argued that Great Britain should be more understanding of the Spanish ally; England should try to influence Spain into adopting a program of constitutional reform that would save her Empire and the Allies' cause in Europe. Undoubtedly, Miranda recognized that Lord Holland and his followers were, after all, opposed to Spanish-American independence. The Venezuelan Commission, thus, came to realize that there were serious obstacles ahead.

The discussion that follows should provide some insights into the development of British policy vis-a-vis the independence of Spanish America. Here we must turn to a spokesman for the Holland group: Dr. John Allen, a Scot and a colleague of James Mill who was one of the original group of reviewers founding the modern version of the *Edinburgh Review* in 1802. At the advise of Sydney Smith, the first editor of the revised periodical, Lord Holland agreed to take Dr. John Allen with him to Spain as a health advisor and friend. From 1801 to 1805, Dr. John, a medical man with a deep interest in philosophy and the humanities, developed his linguistic and historical talents to the utmost in Spain. Proficient in Latin, Dr. John mastered Spanish to perfection; and emulated his patron, Lord Holland, as a student of

Spanish history and arts. He emersed himself in the study of Spanish constitutionalism from the eighth century forward: and he mastered the historiography of his subject with the attention and love of a real historian.[21] An 1808 review on Spanish constitutionalism demonstrated why this writer would eventually publish a significant monograph on English constitutionalism: *Inquiry into the Rise and Growth of the Royal Prerogative in England* (London, 1830).[22] After his return from Spain, Dr. John lived with Lord Holland and family until his death in 1843. In his final decades, he was the Master of Dulwich College. He was Lord Brougham's conservative consultant, whereas James Mill was the liberal counterpart. In their style and realistic common sense, these two Scots were very much alike. They were both adamant defenders of Adam Smith; and their arrogance was almost identical, one as a conservative and the other, a liberal.

Dr. John Allen shared the views of Lord Holland (Henry Richard Vassall Fox) in his speeches to Parliament in mid-1810. While the doctor was in Spain, he also cultivated an interest in Spanish America, especially as a prospective source of English economic activity. In 1807, he wrote a masterly review of the *Mercurio Peruano* (12 vols.,1791–1793), which prepared the readers of the *Edinburgh Review* for understanding the articles of his colleague James Mill in 1809. He did not, however, approve of Mill's recommendations in those two articles. Rather, Dr. John opted to question the attack upon the British cabinet by Miranda's publicists and the British opposition group, allied with the Venezuelan. Just why editor Francis Jeffreys of the *Edinburgh Review* would permit Allen to oppose Mill's stand in the 1809 articles, we do not know. Perhaps he felt that the importance of the controversy warranted the presentation of both sides. Be that as it may, it was a magnanimous decision on his part.

Dr. John Allen's opening assault on the Miranda-Mill program appeared in the April, 1810, issue of the *Edinburgh Review*, dealing with the works of Alexander Von Humboldt's travels to Spanish America. In the November, 1811, issue of the same periodical, Dr. John presented a strong attack on the First Republic of Venezuela and its leader Miranda.[23]

Dr. John Allen's ability as an historian, researcher, writer, and organizer was on a par with that of his fellow Scot, James Mill. In fact, it is difficult to tell them apart except for the criterion of language: Allen's command of Spanish was overwhelmingly superior. The ideological differences, however, were pronounced. On page 100 of the

April, 1810, essay, Dr. John identified himself as the scientist who ridiculed Humboldt for accepting Clavigero's estimates on Mexican population before 1492.[24]

The April, 1810, review began with a challenging statement that Robertson's *History of America* offered "scanty and imperfect information" about the Spanish colonies. This was not due to negligence but rather to Spain's "jealousy," unwilling to permit the diligent Scotsman to consult the voluminous documentation in that country. Here, Dr. John supplied another dramatic insight:

> Within the last thirty years, a great revolution has taken place in the maxims of the Spanish government with regard to its colonies; and in no particular has its change of policy been more remarkable, than in the dereliction of its ancient system of secrecy and concealment, in all that related to its American possessions.

Moreover, Dr. Allen continued: "the court of Madrid, with the violence natural to despotic power when, adopting a change of system, hurried into the opposite extreme, and seemed to glory in revealing to the world those secrets, which its former policy had been most sedulous to conceal." Squadrons and expeditions soon made the Spanish Empire an open book, so to speak. Baron Von Humboldt's travels from 1799 to 1804, with all the information that resulted from them, was a dramatic example of Spain's new policy.

"The first observation that strikes us on the perusal of this and other recent works on New Spain," Allen proceeded, "is the great and rapid improvement of that kingdom [Mexico: New Spain] within the last thirty years." This improvement in Mexico and elsewhere in Spanish America can be documented in the increase of population, the improvement of the highways and infrastructure in general, the greater productivity of the Mexican mines, and the increase in coinage and in commerce that mirrored the "spirit of improvement" in "all the Transatlantic dominions of the crown of Spain." Allen backed up these generalizations with impressive charts and figures.[26] This "fortunate Revolution" had resulted from three factors: (1) the "free trade" policies and experiments from 1765 forward, (2) the introduction of internal administrative reforms with the institution of the intendency, and (3) the reduction of the price of quicksilver, as well as other reforms that helped the miners.[27] The historiography of the reform era improved dramatically; and Dr. Allen displayed an impressive mastery of the sources and writers. This was an exemplary exhibition of historical analysis that twentieth-century scholars on Spanish America should peruse enthusiastically. Whether it was Mill or Allen, the readers of the *Edinburgh Review* received valuable information, as well as insights, with which to make up their minds on policy toward the area concerned. Dr. Allen assured his readers that England's present ally, despite former weaknesses, was now advancing to the model of a rational, modern country.

Yet, Dr. John insisted that "Old" Spain needed to be studied with care for the damage caused over centuries, in order to appreciate the obstacles that might still hold up improvement in Spanish America. Here again, we have another product of the University of Edinburgh with a remarkable organizational talent. The weaknesses of the Old Order were easily recognizable: avarice of the home government, "languor," and backwardness. There was also a "spirit of restriction and regulation" that was "useless," "capricious," arbitrary, and inconsistent. A key weakness was the government's "intermeddling" with the private concerns of the individual. As a champion of Adam Smith, Dr. John observed:

> The favourite maxim of its statesmen, that the government of a great empire ought to consult the general good of the whole, in preference to the private interests of individuals, is a doctrine of most dangerous and fatal application to commerce. For it continually happens, that, with the best possible intentions, the governments that act upon this principle, though expert enough in ruining the individuals, who stand in the way of their projects, yet seldom, by any chance, succeed in attaining the general good, which was the object of their schemes.

The net result was inefficient power overseas, because of the distances involved, the enormous expenses of that government with its extensive bureaucracies, and its vexatious system of taxation.[28]

In another well-documented section, Dr. Allen dealt with the problems of a "Class-Caste" system in colonial Spanish America—the jealousies of the "Whites," Creoles versus Europeans, the nervous fate of the "Mixed Bloods," or *Mestizos* (White and Red), as well as others below in the societal rankings. Moreover, there was discrimination in the judicial system, the sale of offices, etc., etc., etc. Dr. John spent much time on the "Indians," protected in theory by humane assumptions but abused in fact at every stage.[29] The result after centuries was that the Indian was "utterly unfit to be the governing caste." Here, Dr. John commenced his battle with the enemy:

"Speculatists, who have recommended the invasion of Spanish America, for the purpose of emancipating the Indians, have been utterly ignorant of their situation and character." To be sure, the Conquest was founded on injustice and cruelty; but, the writer maintained, "It would be a greater crime than all the enormities of Pizarro and Valdivia conjoined, to stir up the Indian population of the Spanish colonies to reclaim the dominion wrested from their ancestors." The Indians, he argued were

> improvident and brutal, cruel and tyrannical,—without a feeling of honour, or sentiment of shame,—the Indian may be reclaimed from his vices by a wise and enlightened policy; but to invest him with authority over the other casts, because his forefathers were the original proprietors of the Country, would, if practicable, be an act of wickedness and folly, exceeding the most pernicious schemes of religious or revolutionary fanaticism.[30]

Those were the highlights of Allen's well-conceived and informative review.

The political application of the materials presented was the concern of his last fourteen pages. The position of Lord Holland's group emerges from this analysis—ideas that henceforth found their way into the thinking of the British cabinet, just at the time that Venezuela's commissioners arrived in London.

As a hard-nosed realist and conservative, Dr. Allen discussed the future problems of Latin America with considerable insight. The observed weaknesses of the region might be "remedied by a government resident in the country." But, he argued,

> whether the prejudices arising from differences of cast, the most fatal obstacle to the union and permanent prosperity of the country, would not rather be strengthened and confirmed than dissipated or weakened, by the substitution of an independent in the place of a colonial government, may reasonably be doubted.

Buttressing this sensitive and controversial declaration, Dr. John offered an example from the United States: "the prejudices against the Blacks and Mulattoes have gained ground since the establishment of American independence," prejudices "so deeply rooted" that a former president in a recent, philosophical work "examines the question, whether it would not be advisable to expel the descendants of the Africans from this country, and assign them some place of residence, where they would neither offend the eyes, nor taint the blood of the Virginians."[31] Many Creoles in Spanish America, including Venezuelans, could identify with President Jefferson's remarks in his *Notes on Virginia*.

Nor did Allen have much confidence in the American Creole's ability to rule effectively in the region:

> The political independence of the Spanish colonies will be followed by great degradation and heavier oppression of the Indians; and experience suggests the apprehension, that the distinction between the Creoles and other casts will be more accurately fixed, and more sensibly marked, by a Creole government, than by one which was a stranger to the local prejudices and jealousies of the colonists.[32]

At this juncture, Dr. John became an apologist for Spanish colonialism, determined to prove that the Criollos were virtually alone in their grab for power. What proof did he offer? Dr. John listed the following:

> the progress of Spanish America within the last thirty years,—the gradual improvement of the colonial policy of the mother country,—the relaxation of her monopoly,—and the disposition which she manifested on every occasion to consult the good of her colonies, where it did not interfere with her own.

Moreover, Allen argued that Creole grievances did not represent, or excite, "general spirit of resistance in the colonists." Rather, there have been "speculative claims by a well informed, and comparatively free people, against a weak, indecisive unpopular government." Besides, the Criollos' revolutionary mentality was not comparable to that "of England in 1688,—of America in 1776,—of Ireland in 1782,—or of France in 1789."[33] Furthermore, the Creoles lacked the support of other groups in society. To have gotten their attention, the "higher casts" had to sacrifice "to the lower their privileges and distinctions." That would never have happened "in a country where the meanest White considers himself a noble, and looks down on his tawney countrymen as marked by nature to be their dependants." Criollos got excited about independence because they had been excluded from:

posts of honour and emoluments in the government of their country;—an exclusion, it is to be observed, not founded on law, but on custom;—irritating to them as individuals, but not degrading to them as a body,—capable of being removed at any time by a few concessions on the part of the government,—and, considering the growing wealth and information of the Creoles, sure, at no very distant period, to be gradually and silently abolished.[34]

Many of these Creoles "were ambitious minds, who looked forward to glory or power in the assertion of national independence;" others were "men of desperate fortunes, who saw nothing in civil wars and dissensions but a remedy for their own distress." But, Dr. John added:

the mass—the great body of the people—were firmly attached to the mother country, and would have resisted any attempt at separation, seems to us, from recent events, a proposition that can hardly be doubted. Even Humboldt admits, that the ideas entertained of the mother country in the provinces of New Spain, were extremely different from the sentiments expressed in the capital, by those who had made French and English literature their study, and imbibed from thence a more contemptuous opinion of Old Spain than it ever merited.[35]

Dr. John Allen now was satisfied that the British cabinet of 1808 had made the right decision:

What, then, would have been the consequence, if a formidable army had landed in Spanish America, offering independence to its inhabitants? Brilliant success would probably have attended its first operations; malcontents of all descriptions would have joined it; but the body of the people would have held back, till disease had thinned its ranks, and the sanguine expectations of its adherents had terminated in disappointment. A civil war would have ensued, in which the party supported by foreigners was sure to have become unpopular; and whatever might have been the ultimate result, the ruin and devastation of the colonies would have been one of the first and most certain effects of the enterprise.[36]

At this point, wishful thinking seems to have overpowered the learned doctor: "Fortunately, however, for Spanish America, she has been saved from this great, and, we are told at one time, impending calamity. The revolutionary sword, which an anti-Jacobin ministry had armed against her, was directed to another object." Dr. Constancio would have cringed upon reading those words; and even more so at the apologia that followed:

> The Spanish Junta has since proclaimed the independence of its colonies, by declaring, that its possessions in Asia and America are no longer to be regarded as colonies, but as integral parts of the Spanish Empire,—equal in rights, and coordinate in authority, with the European dominions of the crown of Spain.

Suspecting that he might be confusing theory with fact and that Peninsulars might nullify the "integral" thesis, Dr. John took pains to reassure the reader:

> This declaration, no future government of Spain can in honour or in policy retract. The Spanish settlements of the New World are, therefore, no longer dependent colonies, since they have been emancipated from that subjection by the sovereign authority of the state; nor can they be brought back to that situation without their own consent, or without a revolution imposed upon them by force.

The Venezuelan Junta Suprema certainly would have agreed with Dr. Allen on this point, as well as his conclusion: "Spanish America will be held as a constituent part of the empire, that owes allegiance to the Crown of Spain, but claims the same privileges with its European states."[37]

The British government sympathized with Dr. Allen on the following duties of Spanish Americans:

> While Spain maintains the unequal struggle in which she is contending for her independence, it is the duty of the Spanish Americans to continue the liberal assistance which they have hitherto afforded her: And, should the military superiority of her enemy, or the weakness of her own councils, bring the contest to an unfavourable termination for the present,—it will be the duty of America to offer an asylum to the vanquished, who prefer exile to slavery,—and provide for them, in their misfortunes, a place of refuge from the cruelty and vengeance of their oppressor.

If no counterrevolution to Napoleon emerged, America "will become the sole depository of the Spanish language, manners and institutions, the sole inheritor of whatever glory in arms or literature is attached to the Spanish name."[38] José Blanco-White evoked this same vision of Spanish America in his No. 4 editorial, defending the Venezuelan Revolution some months later. It also was characteristic of the Holland group.

As a champion of Adam Smith, Dr. John insisted that "free trade" should be the dogma of "integral" Spanish America: "Whatever trade is open to the Spaniards of the Old World, ought to be open to them, and on the same conditions." And, he added: "The internal administration of their affairs ought to be adapted to the circumstances of their present situation, as has been done in the different provinces of Spain." Venezuelans, and many other Spanish Americans, would have welcomed such a policy after April 19, 1810. Yet, Spain adamantly resisted British determination to encourage the "free-trade" proclivities of Spanish Americans.

Concerning the captive Ferdinand VII, Dr. John Allen made comments that impressed members of the British cabinet. "National enthusiasm," he wrote, "has attached every virtue to the name of Ferdinand VII:"

> His accession to the throne, the true epoch of the Spanish revolution, was the triumph of the nation over the satellites of the court. Too speedily bereft of power to have disappointed the expectations of his people, they have gratuitously conferred on him every good and great quality which a king ought to possess. No hero, sage or patriot ever enjoyed a name more adored and cherished in the popular mind. Under the auspices of that name, whatever is the government established, it will have all the illusions of loyalty in its favor, without any of the disadvantages which, it must be confessed, monarchy sometimes bring along with it. That the name of Ferdinand may long preside over the fortunes of his country, ought to be the prayer of every enlightened American.[39]

Yet, the good doctor had no illusions about Ferdinand, even though he was valuable to Great Britain. He noted:

> The mind of Ferdinand may be the seat of obstinacy and abode of prejudice; but these vices will be no obstacle to the execution of measures for the peace, union and security of his empire . . . his intrigues will never disturb or subvert the free constitution established by his people. Pity for his youth and unmerited misfortunes, suggests

fruitless wishes for his release; but if the good of his subjects only is considered, long may he reign at Valency.[40]

Dr. Allen might well have added: and also for the "good" of Great Britain! He was reminding British ministers that a fundamental point of English policy should be the insistence upon loyalty to Ferdinand VII, the great symbol of a European ally. And it did not matter if the king as a man was not worthy. So long as he stayed at the Palace of Valençay, Talleyrand's castle in France, Great Britain could advance her interests throughout the Spanish world as the champion of that symbol.

As for the type of government in Spanish America, Dr. Allen—and James Mill would have agreed with him on most points—affirmed:

> We trust, that the basis of their governments will not rest on any distinction of casts; that all free men will have the same civil rights; and that the qualifications for political power will be founded on property, and not on blood. A qualification of property will effectually exclude from political power the inferior casts, who are at present unfit to exercise it, without prejudice to themselves and to the state, while such a qualification will affix a stigma upon no one, as long as industry and fortune may open to him the road to power and preferment.

In keeping with the Holland position, Allen was urging the British ministers to insist on the sincere development of constitutionalism in Spain, so that Americans—the Creole elites, in particular—would not have to resort to independence.[41]

Dr. John Allen's article began to circulate in May, 1810, almost two months before the Marquis of Wellesley met with Simón Bolívar and Luis López-Méndez. This was ample time to influence British policy and to spark the debates in the British Parliament on the independence movement in Spanish America. The Venezuelan Commission arrived in England on July 10, 1810, and by the 16th and 19th it met with the Marquis of Wellesley. The Foreign Secretary based the British position on the January 1809 Treaty between Spain and Great Britain, whereby his country agreed to defend the "integrity of the Spanish Monarchy." Not long into the negotiations, he also made it clear that loyalty to Ferdinand VII was an essential requisite for the Venezuelans. Yet, because of the Treaty with Spain, England could not recognize the Junta Suprema of Venezuela. Wellesley then turned to the nature of the April 19th movement's grievances. Could they be satisfied, so that the Junta Suprema would then recognize the Regency? Bolívar replied categorically that Venezuelans had no confidence in the Regency, fearing a betrayal to Napoleon. As an "integral" part of the Spanish nation, Caracas had to secure herself against the French danger. His commission had been sent to England to seek British recognition, as well as materiel and ammunition for defense against the French. Despite his annoyance at the unwillingness to accept the Regency, Wellesley believed the Venezuelans were sincere on military and naval programs against the French. When the Venezuelans indicated an interest in opening up trade with the British—in fact, they soon would grant them a special reduction in duties—the British Foreign Minister was less demanding. Within three weeks of negotiations, a *modus vivendi* was in the making. In consultations with Miranda, who advised the economic concession that the English could not refuse, the Commission likewise volunteered to assist Spain in the war against France, assuring Wellesley that when a *bona fide* constitutional government prevailed on the Peninsula, Venezuela would cooperate in protecting their beloved monarch Ferdinand VII. Since Miranda and colleagues had studied Allen's interpretation, they understood what was necessary to assuage the climate of opinion in the London of mid-1810.[42]

In time, the Wellesley stand included the following items: 1. Great Britain would offer Venezuela naval protection against the French in behalf of Ferdinand VII's cause. 2. She also offered her services as mediator of differences between the Junta Suprema of Caracas and the Regency in Cádiz, as well as mediation with Americans supporting the Regency's lead. 3. Thanks to English support, Venezuela would assist Spain against France. Throughout, the basic component of British policy was loyalty to Ferdinand VII, the symbol of unity that would prevent the fragmentation of the Spanish Empire. Otherwise, the French might frustrate Britain's commerce in Spanish America.

The policy of mediation during the next four years floundered because of the conflicting interests of Spain and England. Spaniards adamantly resisted the "free trade" of her colonies with the English ally and raised impossible demands for the mediation process that thwarted it effectively, as we shall see in a future chapter. Taking Venezuela as an example, the Regency demanded that English officials in the Caribbean be reprimanded for encouraging the Caracas revolution. Spain especially called for action against J.T. Layard, Governor of Curaçao, who had recognized the Caracas government. Just as the

English earlier had spared Admiral Cochrane, they likewise hesitated to push Layard out of his post. In a letter of July 23, 1810, the English reprimanded Layard for action taken beyond his instructions; yet, an obvious concession to Spain would damage British relations with other provinces of South America. And Great Britain did not wish to help some provinces at the expense of others. England simply wanted these provinces to recognize the same monarch, to patch up their differences, and to work against Napoleon's France. She offered, and wanted, mediation "without intervening in questions of internal administration."[43]

* * * * * * * * * * * *

Despite its vaunted policy of "moderation," the Junta Suprema of Venezuela was unable to attract to its cause the three recalcitrant provinces of Maracaibo, Coro, and Guayana, all of which were accessible by water from Spanish bases in the Caribbean. Their defiance could last indefinitely if Spain, and her ally England, controlled the waters off the Venezuelan coast. Much depended upon how the English chose to perform. If they followed a "strict construction" of their nation's policy, the April 19th movement would find it difficult to survive without the help of another outside power. Yet, neither France nor the United States could commit their forces at this time. Therefore, it was to Caracas' interest to encourage an unofficial British stand—on the part of the Cochranes and Layards—by offering the one-quarter concession on customs duties. And this tactic was effective since officials in London likewise welcomed the commercial opening. The reality, therefore, was that both English positions had champions in the Caribbean area. Layard was not relieved of his command until almost a year after his reprimand; but when John Hodgson took over, a "strict constructionist" mode
went into effect—a critical change that helped to bring about the fall of the First Venezuelan Republic.

Geography was a dominant factor in the political development of Venezuela. Most of its population nuclei were on or near the Caribbean coast, or the Lake of Maracaibo. The historical experience during the colonial centuries, moreover, was one of loosely-controlled government, in fact, if not in theory. This historical-geographical proclivity encouraged the process of power fragmentation at the local (provincial) as well as the national (Venezuela) levels. For example, the intra-provincial rivalry between the capital Cumaná and its subordinate sister-city of Barcelona led the latter to establish a Junta Provincial of its own, prepared to recognize the Spanish Regency, whereas Cumaná was loyal to the Caracas government of April 19th. Despite Admiral Cochrane's efforts to keep the peace, this weakness in the April 19th movement persisted until October, 1810, when the Junta Provincial of Barcelona reversed its allegiances and joined the Caracas government as a separate unit. The Island of Margarita also parlayed its strategic location into a Junta Provincial! In short, there was considerable bargaining concerning loyalties, at this phase of the Independence movement. Even Angostura on the Orinoco (future Guayana) pretended loyalty to Caracas; but a faction of Spaniards there reacted and brought her into the Regency camp.

This is a complex syndrome but its potential can be illustrated well in the experience of the Maracaibo Province that remained loyal to Spain. Its military leader was the American Fernando Miyares, who had served as Governor of Cumaná in the colonial period, then went to Maracaibo as Captain General, presumably to take over all of Venezuela when the Caracas insurrection ended. Miyares almost succeeded in keeping Barcelona loyal to Spain; but, at the last moment, Caracas' persuasive powers reversed Miyares' strategy. Miyares' real problem, however, was maintaining Maracaibo's provincial integrity, confronted by the challenge and persuasion of the April 19th movement. A reporter from the Lake Maracaibo area presented the case graphically on October 17, 1810 when he wrote jubilantly: "the black vapors from the Lake of Maracaybo," could not contaminate the environs of Barinas, thanks to the winds of "liberality" that hailed from Caracas. Mérida near the Lake also "saw the light and detested the dark clouds" that were exposed by the beneficial movements in Caracas, Barinas, and Santa Fe de Bogota. *Mérida de Maracaybo* proudly changed her name to *Mérida de Venezuela*. Trujillo "has already opened its eyes"; or, more accurately, "has been able to use them, because of the enlightenment from Barinas and the force of Caracas." These two factors "have removed the cataracts" from Trujillo's eyes, formed by the "pestilential darkness of the Lake."[44]

Whether the problem was intraprovincial as in the Maracaibo case above or inter-provincial, the hostility of the outlying provinces vis-a-vis the capital city of Caracas and its province, the political situation in Venezuela exuded weakness at every turn. A small population of 700,000 to 800,000 inhabitants occupied a huge area in which the nuclei were located usually close to the water of the Caribbean or the Lake of Maracaibo. A rugged terrain in places also encouraged the process of fragmentation, a serious deterrent in uniting a future nation. Yet, the April 19th movement, guided by men like Juan Germán Roscio, did exceptionally well in holding the area together. Roscio's patience, however, was wearing thin with the stubborn resistance of the "*Maracayberos*" and the "*Corianos.*" In the final months of that first year, the Junta Suprema's spirit of moderation reached its breaking point.

A solution appeared in the pages of the *Gazeta de Caracas* on September 22, 1810, suggesting a confederation composed of Venezuela, Santa Fe de Bogotá, and Ecuador to form a united front against Coro and Maracaibo. As Secretary of State, Roscio took the initiative on this suggestion by encouraging the Bogotá and Cartagena governments, as well as other nearby areas of what is now Colombia, to maintain a boycott of the recalcitrant provinces of Coro and Maracaibo. This was the beginning of a key regional consciousness in the political development of northern South America, usually associated with the name of Simón Bolívar. As a matter of fact, Bolívar merely inherited this tendency, as we shall see.[45]

Roscio's determination to advance Venezuela's cause in late 1810 prompted him, as editor of the gazette, to utilize the publications of foreigners, such as William Burke whose first article appeared on November 23rd. Eleven weeks earlier, on August 31, 1810, Roscio eagerly presented the first number of *El Español* (London, April 30, 1810) edited by José Blanco-White. It was favorable to the April 19th movement and contained the first installment of "General Reflections on the Spanish Revolution." And on November 6th, Roscio praised this "impartial Spaniard" in the pages of the *Gazeta*, a writer "who was able to see the interests of America, not like the Merchants of Cádiz who were responsible for the Regency, but rather as reason and justice dictate to the lovers of humanity."[46] Pleased with the first issue of *El Español*, Roscio asked Bello to subscribe to the periodical. The Spanish priest, as one of the editors of the famous *Semanario Político* in Sevilla during the tenure of the Junta Central, spoke up courageously against that body and thus incurred its censorship. Roscio seemed to be aware of Blanco-White's reputation, or else Bello had told him about meeting this celebrity at Miranda's home soon after arriving in London. This latter possibility seems likely. As editors, Bello and Blanco-White had much in common, especially concerning the Venezuelan's cultural assignment in London. Thus, Blanco-White learned much about Roscio, his ideas and objectives as Secretary of State and Editor of the *Gazeta*. James Mill might also have gotten into their conversations since both Bello and Blanco could speak English; and one can imagine what must have been said on the subject of "Religious Toleration." Mill had his article in press on that subject, published shortly after this meeting (August, 1810, of the *Edinburgh Review*); and Blanco-White's obsession with that theme was well known to Mill by that time. The big surprise, however, was when Mill and his Spanish colleague learned from Andrés Bello that Roscio held a similar point of view, because of his experiences and training in theology at the University of Caracas. Allowing this speculation to continue, it might follow that the three men agreed to let Roscio know their common view on "Religious Toleration," if he should elect to write on that theme in the *Gazeta de Caracas*. Months earlier, Mill had authored "Thoughts of an Englishman" in *El Colombiano*, sounding the alert on this issue. Thus, it may not have been a coincidence that Mill's "Thoughts" appeared on January 25, 1811, in the *Gazeta*, several weeks before the publication of Burke's controversial editorial on religious toleration.

The Junta Suprema's policy of "moderation" convinced Blanco-White that it was genuinely sincere, so did his conversations with the Venezuelan commissioners and General Miranda. In Caracas, however, some major occurrences by mid-October, 1810, were forcing the Junta Suprema of Venezuela to abandon its "moderation" stand in favor of military action. The "flip-flop" of the Barcelona government perhaps resulted from the urgency felt in Caracas to make concessions in order to win its loyalty. More importantly, a riot took place in Caracas in which the *Canarios*, sympathetic to the Regency and the recalcitrant provinces, displayed their hostility to the Venezuelan Junta Suprema. On October 16, 1810, the Junta angrily informed the inhabitants of Venezuela that the Spanish Regency was unworthy of being obeyed; and the investigations of the defiant Canarians added fuel to the impending crisis in Venezuela. Then, the truth came out as to what had happened in Europe; and all the facts and documents appeared in the *Gazeta de Caracas*. According to a Spanish decree of July 30, 1810, effective on August 1, 1810, the Regency declared a blockade of the "Rebels" in Venezuela and issued instructions to officials in the Caribbean, especially the Captain General of Puerto Rico, to implement this policy at the first opportunity. In effect, the Regency had declared war on Venezuela, although previous steps taken against Caracas were virtually acts of war—i.e. Luis de Onís and his attempts to discourage and threaten ships from the United States that were thinking of sending aid and arms to the rebels in Caracas. We are already familiar with Roscio's reaction to that news.

The report of the blockade appeared in the *Gazeta* of October 30th with Roscio's comments on Puerto Rico's preparations. By November 6th, the blockade decree was reproduced; and on the 9th, there was a letter from Simón Bolívar in London, complaining that the ingrates in Cádiz had called the Venezuelans *rebeldes*. The nation's mission in London was over, for all practical purposes. By this time, *El Español's* articles in the *Gazeta* were popular. On November 6th, when the blockade documents appeared, Blanco-White's number four also was printed: the defense of the Venezuelan Revolution of April 19, 1810, that we covered in the previous chapter. It left a good taste in the mouths of Venezuelans—just what they needed in this critical moment of crisis. This Spaniard, as Roscio pointed out in the same issue, understood their Revolution and was thus attacking the ingratitude of the Regency. In that same issue of the *Gazeta*, one could read a "Letter of a Cádiz Spaniard to a friend of his in London," published in the *Morning Chronicle* (London) on September 5, 1810. It was an excellent commentary on the stupidity of the Regency's blockade policy—a piercing statement that bore all the earmarks of a discerning Spaniard, none other than José Blanco-White! He did not fool anyone by saying he was from Cádiz, rather than his native Sevilla!

To this southerner, the Regency's blockade was an "absurd measure" in light of Venezuela's "moderation" stance. Moreover, it was "ridiculous" since the Spanish government was broke; its policy reflected the hated monopolists of Cádiz. On their behalf, the Regency had undermined "free trade" for the Americas and prevented the English and Portuguese allies from trading with Spain's Empire. The Regency, moreover, assumed erroneously that Venezuelans wanted their independence. These Americans were not in favor of independence from "the Mother Country, nor of the Sovereign, but just of the Regency, whose legitimacy is in question in Spain herself." These were strong indictments which Blanco-White developed fully in later columns of *El Español*. The following statement gave Venezuelans much food for thought:

> Under the circumstances, the decree in question, should be regarded as an act of independence for America, since the weakness of the

government does not produce anything but displeasure and contempt of those affected by the measure, thereby assuring the necessary separation of the Provinces of Venezuela; and finally that of all South America. It is clear that once the natives of that region discover that neither their moderation, nor their adhesion to European connections, nor their financial sacrifices have acquired for them the respect and gratitude which they so deserved, they will raise the standard of independence, and they will declare themselves against Spain. And they will not fail to invite all the people of America to follow the same approach, and to pursue the same objective, and Americans everywhere will embrace eagerly the promising example of the inhabitants of Caracas.[47]

Simón Bolívar's letter of September 8, 1810, alluded to above, likewise foresaw the consequences of the Regency's blockade. He noted:

It is not easy to express to you what indignation and scandal the Regency's decree has caused in this country. The truth is that nothing so illegal and so monstruous has ever come out of the heads of its barbarous authors. They identify their usurped authority with the rights of the Crown, they confuse a security measure with an act of rebellion, and in the delirium of their impotent rage they themselves destroy the bounds that they propose to extend.[48]

After this fiery statement of September 8th in London, Bolívar began to prepare for his return to Venezuela, where he arrived on December 5, 1810. He immediately delivered his reports and documents to the Junta Suprema. Bolívar brought with him a letter from Blanco-White to Roscio, expressing the hope that the numbers of *El Español* had reached him. Blanco-White asked Roscio to send him whatever key information and documents that he might want to have reproduced in London: "The liberal ideas that the government of Caracas has expressed from the beginning," he wrote, "assure me that political tolerance would be one of its principal goals." Thus, he assumed that Roscio would welcome his writings, even those "where my opinions on the means to achieve reforms for America might not agree on occasion with those that might be adopted there." These were comforting words that Roscio cherished in the trying months ahead for his nation.

* * * * * * * * * * * *

When the Venezuelan Commission reached London on July 10, 1810, they wasted no time in contacting their famous legendary figure in England—General Francisco de Miranda. His home—27 Grafton Street, Fitzroy Square—was their base for the next three months; today, just several blocks from the University College of London Library. At dinners, the commissioners talked with other Spanish Americans visiting Miranda—the Argentine Irigoyen, for example, was present, as was José de Tovar Ponte, the Venezuelan who returned to his homeland shortly with the commissioner's first two letters of early August, 1810. The General, of course, had ample opportunity to discourse upon the problems he had encountered in his negotiations with the British over the years. He cautioned his countrymen about the attitudes they would face among British ministers. He also analyzed for them the significance of the debates held in Parliament on Spanish American independence, as well as Dr. Allen's opposing views in the recent issue of the *Edinburgh Review*. Miranda contacted his British allies and made arrangements to introduce them to the Venezuelan commissioners. These included the Duke of Gloucester, the thirty-four-year-old grandson of George III, and William Wilberforce, the great champion of "humanity." Jules Mancini, in his prize-winning volume described the experiences of the commissioners in London, as follows: "visits with key personalities, meals at the home of the Duke of Gloucester, walks [and rides] through Hyde Park and to Bond Street, nights at the opera and theatre. The gazettes were all commenting on the 'ambassadores of America' and Gill, a leading society painter, drew a picture of Bolívar."[49]

Jeremy Bentham's impressions of the reaction to the visitors and their cause were indeed meaningful. Writing to his cousin Mulford, he noted on November 1, 1810,: "A number of our considerable political characters, and even women too, are already looking to that country [Venezuela], and longing to go there." A case in point was "Lady Hester Stanhope, niece to Minister Pitt" who promised Miranda, that if he found things there settled to his wishes, she would go over to him, and superintend female schools for him." "Even Wilberforce," Bentham continued, "who gave them the entertainment t'other day, talked half jest half earnest, of paying them a visit." James Mill and Jeremy Bentham also wanted to go to Venezuela: "Our scheme, which we talked of for years, was to go to Caracas, which, if Miranda had prospered, we should have undoubtedly done." Bentham explained to his cousin that he had abandoned his earlier plans to visit Mexico in favor of Venezuela's idyllic setting and climate. Moreover, he argued,

> The good which I could do to mankind if I were in the House of Commons, or even if I were minister, is inconsiderable in comparison of that which I may hope to do if I go there; for having, by the ignorant and domineering Spaniards, been purposely kept in ignorance, they have the merit of being sensible about it, and disposed to receive instruction from England in general, and from your humble servant in particular. Whatever I give them for laws, they will be prepared to receive as oracles.

It pleased Bentham immeasurably that since 1802, when the French edition of his works on legislation appeared, the world was beginning to recognize his legal contributions to mankind.[50]

When Miranda left London in mid-October, 1810, he carried with him a manuscript on the "Liberty of the Press" which Jeremy Bentham had been re-working for almost two months. "He is to write me immediately on his arrival," Bentham noted, "and if things are in a peaceable state, I shall probably take a trip thither not long after I received his letter." In short, Bentham and Mill had reason to be sanguine about their future in South America. Moreover, they also provided valuable information on congressional procedures for Venezuela's legislators. It is difficult to say that James Mill and his colleague Bentham were collaborating on the Burkian editorials during Miranda's last few months in Europe, a process which we suspect Mill initiated back in mid-1809 when he finished his second article in the *Edinburgh Review*. Just before Miranda's departure, James Mill, thanks to Bentham, made the acquaintance of a key reformer in London: William Allen (F.R.S.—Friends of the Royal Society), who had just published the initial work of the *Philanthropist*. In a letter to Henry Brougham, he mentioned that Bentham and James Mill, whom he had just met, promised to help in his future publications. He gave this impression of Mill:

> indeed his heart seems warm in the cause of mankind and if I may form an opinion upon so short an acquaintance, he seems possessed of no ordinary powers. I consider a place in his regard as an acquisition for which I have reason to rejoice. He has been very kindly attentive to General Miranda who seems earnestly bent on introducing Lancaster's system of Education into the Caraccas. What a field of Philanthropic

exertion! I have assured the General that our Committee will yield every assistance in its power. He sets off in about ten days [letter of October 2, 1810] and intends to send two persons over to be instructed in the Plan.[51]

Mill became a member of the Lancasterian Committee, thus assuring Miranda's contact with that organization for the future. José Blanco-White likewise took advantage of Bentham-Mill's last-minute efforts to assist the Miranda expedition to Venezuela, which reflected his close connection with Miranda's group. He introduced the "Liberty of the Press" and a document on "Parliamentary Procedures" for his readers in *El Español*, hoping that it would assist the legislators at Cádiz. And Blanco-White also championed Joseph Lancaster's system of education that was popular throughout the Hispanic world.

As the Venezuelan commissioners informed Miranda on what had happened in their first two meetings with the Marquis of Wellesley, he realized that it was time, at last, to retire from the London scene. To relieve any suspicions that the Marquis might have that Miranda was pulling strings in the background, the General wrote to him on July 25, 1810, announcing his wish to return to Venezuela after decades of absence from his homeland. He thanked the British for their assistance during that long and crucial period in European history, vowing that he would do all he could in the future to advance British interests in South America. Miranda then suggested that passage on a British naval ship to any port in Venezuela would be an honorable manner of sanctioning his departure from London.[52] A similar letter went out on August 3rd to the Venezuelan government asking for permission to return home. At the same time, he congratulated the Junta Suprema on the calibre of men chosen to represent it in England.[53]

The startling news of the Spanish blockade in early September, 1810, put an end to the negotiations. The urgency now was to prepare an English ship for the commissioners' return to Venezuela. Miranda wrote to the British government in late August that the Venezuelans were anxious to return home at the earliest opportunity. Shortly thereafter, Simón Bolívar boarded the *Sapphire* for his trip home; she arrived in La Guaira on December 5, 1810. Of Miranda's followers, José María Antepara and Antoine Leleux joined Bolívar's party; interestingly, along with them were sixty-three folio volumes of documents and manuscripts belonging to General Miranda—his famous *Archives*. For reasons that are not clear—perhaps the British

Government was reluctant to permit his departure because of the blockade news—General Miranda did not sail on the *Sapphire*.[54] Nevertheless, he boarded another ship to the English Caribbean not long after Bolívar's departure, arriving in Curaçao in late November—according to a remark in Colonel Robertson's correspondence.[55]   Joining him on that voyage was his secretary Thomas Molini; and there may have been others. For example, Manuel Cortés Campomanes was desperately seeking passage to Venezuela and we know that he got there; he may have accompanied the General. It is conceivable that Dr. C. (F.S. Constancio) may have made the trip with Miranda at this time.   He did not go to Portugal, as he had planned; and later, it will be recalled he joined Antepara on a financial and propaganda assignment. He may have been on the *Sapphire* with Antepara; but there is no record of that. Considering his intelligence, his availability, and his devotion to General Miranda's cause—his letter of early December 1809, to Miranda bears out this point—he was a plausible choice to follow Miranda to Venezuela. His knowledge of British and European history and politics in general would have been useful to the General's propaganda system in South America. Moreover, Francisco de Miranda admired and liked him as a friend. If Doctor C. did reach Venezuela, as we suspect, then he would have been an excellent stand-in for "William Burke." His apparent weakness in the Spanish language, coupled with Burke's admission in the preface of Volume I that he knew very little Spanish when he started his publication, tends to support in a faint way the possibility that Dr. C. was the William Burke that was physically present in Venezuela. Other reports of William Burke's presence, as we shall see, were fictional, figments of Roscio's imagination. The curious might ask this pertinent question: if Burke did not know much Spanish when he arrived on the scene with his first editorial on November 23, 1810, how did he attain his mastery in such short order, or was there a Spanish translator in Caracas from the beginning? As we shall see in our next chapter, it was more likely that the translation occurred in Europe. It was perhaps no coincidence that Andrés Bello, the secretary of the Venezuelan Commission to England, remained behind in London to finish the translation assignment, working principally with James Mill.   Luis López Méndez also kept his post in London as Venezuela's main representative.

   If Robertson's claim is valid—Miranda arrived in Curaçao in late November—this would give the General a few weeks to reestablish his contacts in the English Caribbean and familiarize himself with developments in Venezuela since the news of the Spanish blockade. Thanks to Andrés Bello's friendship with John Robertson, Miranda stayed in the Canadian's home during his stop in Curaçao; and Robertson from this time forward, was one of General Miranda's key sources of information in the region.[56] So, from Colonel John he learned much about Roscio and other Venezuelans that he would have to deal with upon his return—what their objectives, ideals, and attitudes were all about, etc. Governor Layard was likewise most cooperative and informative about his colleagues: Hislop at Trinidad, Admiral Cochrane's actions vis-a-vis the Spanish projected blockade, etc., all of which assured General Miranda that his former program of collaboration in the English Caribbean was still intact, despite the addition of a Spanish blockade. It was obvious that without the cooperation of Britain's key officials in the Caribbean, the Spanish strategy of force was destined to fail. And that is the way it turned out in the late months of 1810 and early 1811, much to Venezuela's advantage and thanks to the "flexible" policy of British officials in the area, as opposed to the "strict constructionists" that we have mentioned earlier. The English, regardless of differences, all wanted free trade with Venezuelan ports, thus frustrating their ally's threats of violence. It should be noted that Governor Layard volunteered one of his ships to take General Miranda to La Guaira; and it is conceivable that the same ship carried him to other places where he personally contacted Hislop and Cochrane, for example, before pulling into La Guaira on December 11, 1810, to a hero's welcome.[57]

It appeared, moreover, that General Miranda arrived in Venezuela at the right time. The blockade news, for example, prompted the reinforcement and alert of the Army of the West under General Toro, whose forces made their way toward the City of Coro to fight the recalcitrants and bring them into the union with Caracas; hopefully, they would expect to go on into Maracaibo's territory. But there were delays and obstacles to these plans with the result that the campaign for Coro ended in a withdrawal of Venezuela's forces. This alleged defeat in mid-December, 1810, was utterly demoralizing for the unionist cause. Yet, with Simón Bolívar's arrival on December 5th and the news that General Francisco Miranda was on his way home, after so many years, was real music to their ears despite the reports of imminent failure in the western campaign at Coro. After greeting their hero at La Guaira—and Simón Bolívar represented the Junta on that occasion, along with Dr. José Cortés Madariaga—Miranda was made a Lt. General in the Venezuelan army at the suggestion of the Marquis del Toro, as well as "Inspector General" of the Army, presumably to shape it up for campaigns of the future against the hated Spanish foe. To reassure the people of Venezuela that a great hero had returned home to defend his country's rights, the Junta Suprema ordered all of the cabildos and major corporations in Venezuela to obliterate—there were no shredders in those days, at least as we know them—the Spanish documentation that had constantly referred to Miranda as a "traitor" for his exploits in 1806. It was a welcome that General Francisco de Miranda must have cherished.[58] Yet, an instant opposition arose to his presence making him out as a potential "Napoleon" of the Americas, determined to bring the bloody "French Revolution" and the Jacobin violence to his country. Unfortunately, much of that distortion still lingers on in the historiography of Venezuela—stereotypes that will be examined later in this work.

Chapter Nine

The Rights of South America and Mexico: William Burke et al?

> We have the grand experiment of North America before us, which the
> inhabitants of the South are so ambitious to imitate . . . If such are the
> benefits resulting from the prosperity of the United States, how many
> times greater will be those which must necessarily flow from the
> prosperity of South America? . . . If the population of the United States,
> amounting perhaps to 6,000,000 souls, affords so extraordinary a
> demand for British commodities, what may not the population of South
> America, extending already to no less than 16,000,000 be expected to
> afford?
>
> James Mill, *Edinburgh Review*, January 1809.[1]

The April 19th Revolution in Venezuela brought in its train intellectual
stimuli that prepared the "People" for the responsibility of freedom and
independence. As leaders of the prospective nation, *Caraqueños* and
the educated persons in all the provinces felt the urgency to upgrade
everyone's education and to develop the "public opinion" potential in
their areas to a competency level expected in a modern and progressive
order. This was a sensitive matter, considering the inherent proclivity
toward suspicion between rural and urban populations. To overcome
such weaknesses, or tendencies, it was imperative for the public to read
on a regular basis and to discuss their common problems and goals.
Books by thought-provoking authors should be encouraged to circulate
freely. Among the books selling in Caracas during these years, we

find, for example: Thomas Paine's *Common Sense*, Jean Jacques Rousseau's *Social Contract*, and William Burke's *The Rights of South America and Mexico*, just to name a few of them.

Juan Germán Roscio, moreover, was a positive model for his countrymen, a leader who encouraged them to improve their minds by reading every day. Within eight months of the April 19th Revolution, he had already set afoot a project to establish a *Biblioteca Nacional* (Public Library) for Venezuela; and, he contributed from his own personal library at least a thousand books.[2] He asked others to make their own contributions for their country's sake and the future. Roscio and Uztáriz, it will be recalled, promoted the establishment of an economic society (August, 1810) that led to the founding of the *Sociedad Patriótica de Venezuela* in January, 1811.   Under the editorship of Andrés Bello, the *Gazeta de Caracas* opened its doors in 1808 to promote useful knowledge and raise the public's consciousness to a higher level than ever before. After Bello's departure for London, Roscio took over as editor, a responsibility which he treated seriously. Thus, he welcomed the offerings of José Blanco-White and of "our" William Burke. Joining Roscio on the *Gazeta* was Francisco de Isnardi, born in Milan, Italy. From a post in Cádiz, Spain, he made his way to Venezuela, where he served as Associate Editor under Roscio. In early 1811, he also edited the monthly *Mercurio Venezolano* that reproduced key political and cultural documents for January, February, and March. After March 2, 1811, he assumed a major secretarial position in the Venezuelan Congress; and from July 4 through November 28, 1811, he also edited *El Publicista de Venezuela*, the official organ of Congress, reproducing its minutes and major Venezuelan documents.

Among the unofficially sponsored publications, there were two quality periodicals. The *Semanario de Caracas* was a weekly, issued in Caracas from November 4, 1810, to July 21, 1811, by two prominent men: the lawyer Miguel José Sanz, who directed the political section which tended to reinforce Burke's articles on political theory, governmental guidelines, and institutions. Sanz, who subsequently replaced Roscio as Secretary of State, was a dear friend of Francisco de Miranda. Sanz's co-editor was Dr. José Domingo Díaz, a scientist and statistician of note. He edited the second part of each issue on vital statistics concerning Venezuelan society, geography, and economy. Although brilliant in scientific matters, this verbose Caraqueño, a mulatto, became a controversial publicist for the Spanish royalist cause in a later period. And the second periodical, which showed great potential for the long run, was *El Patriota de Venezuela*, the organ of the Patriotic Society in Caracas. It published seven numbers from Independence to January, 1812—unfortunately, only four issues are extant. It was a newspaper that reflected the young patriots' view on Independence and government. The co-editors, both very good colleagues of Miranda, were Vicente Salias and Antonio Muñoz Tébar. Miranda encouraged this publication by contributing key essays on government and political developments in revolutionary France, which were of high calibre and very objective. Dr. Constancio may have had a great deal to do with the excellent quality of Miranda's contributions. The General also praised the institutions of the United States with special insights into Alexander Hamilton's financial program.[3]

All of the journalists mentioned were, indeed, articulate spokesmen for the Venezuelan people, fervently dedicated to the education of an enlightened electorate. They did their job well. Young Muñoz Tébar will be of special interest to us in our final chapter, since he served both Miranda and Simón Bolívar as Secretary of State. That young man reflected, perhaps better than anyone else, the strong influence of the Burkian editorials in northern South America.

* * * * * * * * * * * *

From his debut on November 23, 1810, to his editorial of January 8, 1811, William Burke regaled his readers with an exciting and attractive introduction to the projected two-volumes: *Derechos de América del Sur y México* (Caracas, 1811)—the Spanish title to our present chapter. Mill's genius revealed itself from the start. A critical and observant individual, he noted, was always aware of his environment at all levels. He asserted, for example, when some one tried to monopolize trade locally; this was unfair. At the regional, national, and international stages, it was still a notable injustice, which violated the rights of other individuals. Injustices, moreover, were the opposite of rights in society. If you were to read the ideas of Adam Smith, you would see, "with clarity that a free access and commerce between America and the rest of the world is one of your absolute and irrefutable rights."[4] This conclusion was the basic theme of William Burke's two treatises, published in London from 1807 to 1808.

We have already noted Burke and Mill's use of metaphors for the notion of economic monopoly. Burke, in the first London treatise, referred to the "walled garden," his metaphor in describing Spain's

monopoly of South America's resources—the wall around that fertile
South American garden which violated the natural laws of Providence.
Mill's review of July, 1809, on Father Molina's book, was just as
graphic: "the emancipation of Spanish America, the removal of that
dark, and jealous, and excluding government," watching over "its
colonies as an Asiatic tyrant does over his seraglio." On November 30,
1810, in the *Gazeta de Caracas*, William Burke offered his variation of
the metaphor: "*Fortaleza de America*" (Fortress America)—that unjust
policy of Spain for over three hundred years, a "cruel prohibition of
trade between South America and the rest of the world." Since this
Spanish colonial policy was the vilest of "injustices," South Americans
should stand up, therefore, and fight for their "absolute and irrefutable
rights." Mill used the term in both a negative and positive context: the
vicious monopoly over America and the great preserve of resources in
South America.[5]

As we can see in the opening quotation of this chapter, James Mill's
major tactic was to exploit Spanish America's strong sentiment in favor
of their brethren in the United States by convincing them that their faith
in the northerners was fully warranted. That was his goal in Caracas,
whereas in the European setting, his principal concern was to convince
Englishmen to favor a policy of emancipation that would open up the
promising market of South America to British goods. Regardless of the
audience addressed, the publicist used similar facts and arguments.
William Burke could have used just positive arguments in favor of the
U.S. model; but he also felt that perhaps initially he might employ a
negative slant in order to guarantee the South Americans' conviction
about the United States of America.

In presenting the negative side of the U.S. model, Burke emphasized
the hardships and disadvantages that North Americans had suffered for
so many years. Appearing in the New World back in the seventeenth
century, these latecomers had to settle in marginal areas where the
climate was harsh and the soils were decidely inferior to those of
Spanish America. By contrast, since 1492, Spanish colonists had
occupied an area three times that of the northerners, much more fertile
and with equitable climates. Moreover, Northerners suffered constant
warfare with the Indians and the French, making their existence even
more precarious and uncertain. Also, Great Britain's oppression drove
them to the breaking point. They decided, therefore, to free themselves
from the injustices committed upon them by the offending European
mother country. It took these English Americans almost nine costly

years to win their independence; and when they finally achieved their goal, they felt exhausted from the calamities and losses suffered in that long war. Deeply in debt, they struggled through an untenable financial situation of inflation and worthless "paper money." The American government after the "American Revolution," despite some tendencies, represented a less promising side of the U.S. model. By contrast, South America's existence appeared to have been tranquil and comfortable.

With this ominous and bleak picture in mind, the reader would better appreciate the "miraculous" transformation of the United States from 1783–1810. It took place in less than three decades. And the entire world was deeply impressed, especially the other "Americans" to the south. If Northerners could succeed so dramatically in a blighted area of harsh conditions, the future held even greater promise for Spanish Americans who lived in a larger portion of the Americas with much better weather, fertile lands, and greater resources. Burke—that is, James Mill—capitalized upon this Spanish American sentiment; and the strategy worked well. Whether it was Burke, or other publicists, the pro-Americas movement engendered much enthusiasm among the founding fathers of those countries; and it was a constant factor in support of progress in all fields. James Mill, in short, was a key contributor to this psychological phenomenon in the New World.

Burke's editorials recorded the U.S. "Miracle" in agriculture, industry, commerce, internal developments (infrastructure: roads, canals, bridges, development societies and devices, etc.), and morals, all of which fostered a sound basis for political freedom and self government. Some of Mill's quotations, illustrating these major themes, should be sufficient here. A key characteristic of the Burkian editorials was the quality and depth of documentation. Mill's great talent was the capacity to cover a fantastic amount of materials, producing a synthesis in a short period of time that was sound, insightful, and prophetic. He demonstrated this in his multi-volume work on the *History of India*. It was also evident in his analysis of the vast documentation that emanated from the New World during the last quarter of the eighteenth century and the first decade of the nineteenth. The United States government offered documentation on the economic, political, social, and cultural progress during the "Miracle" period (1783–1810); the Bourbons of Spain allowed the publication of much documentation, the gazettes of those years, the travel accounts of Humboldt, de Pons, etc. Mill also benefitted from the materials sent to the *Edinburgh Review*; the materials in the British Library; Miranda's extensive library and archival materials; and the presence of Andrés Bello in London. Bello lived in Miranda's home after the general's departure. He was a highly knowledgeable reference on the geography, and resources of Venezuela and South America. Some of the information in the Burkian articles derived from the *Gazeta's* staff—Roscio, Isnardi, Uztáriz, etc.

In his first editorial, William Burke announced—in his usual manner—what his publication strategy would be; and, as an expert publicist, he used catchy statements and figures to excite the reader's imagination. He noted, for example, that commerce in the United States of 1802: "without having gold or silver mines" added up to a "million American tons," carried by 5,000 ships of 200-ton capacity and manned by 40,000 sailors. Exports in that year totalled 80 million dollars (*pesos*); imports, 70 million; the Government received 15 million, leaving it with a profit, after expenses, of 1 and 1/2 million. After this barrage of figures, Burke teased South Americans playfully:

> While the United States was covering the Ocean with its ships and was enjoying the great and beneficient commerce with all parts of the Globe, South America, established twice as long before [the United States], her climates and soils more favorable to vegetation, and its products more numerous, varied and valuable, does not have at present even one merchant ship that belongs to her, nor a national flag to proclaim her name and existence.[6]

For shame! Another flurry of figures ensued on U.S. population: 1782—2 1/2 million; 1790—4 million; 1800—more than 5 million; 1810, about 7 1/2 million. Proud of their numerous, active, and enlightened countrymen, the Northerners boasted that their population was their nation's greatest wealth. Their numbers would double every 20 years, even every 15 years! In less than a century, their population would exceed 100 million from coast to coast. Immigrants—valuable skilled artisans—were reaching the U.S. at about 10,000 a year; and in his next installment, Burke promised to consider how Spanish Americans could achieve comparable figures.

It was in his second editorial (November 30, 1810), that Burke first employed the metaphor "Fortress-America," a land of 16 million persons. South America's territory, Burke stressed, exceeded that "of the greatest empire in the world, with a salubrious climate and richness of soil," twice the size of Europe and three times the United States.

Yet, if South America:

like North America, possessed her rights, and like the latter could expedite the increase of her people, she could look forward with certainty to a not very distant future in which her numbers would be twenty times larger. This is not surprising if we consider her potential in agriculture.

Burke's estimate of 320 million people was reached in the second half of the twentieth century and it is still going up! During the "Miracle" period, U.S. agriculture increased by seven fold at least: "What a beautiful field of contemplation and hope opened up before the agricultural estimates and efforts of South America and Mexico!" An elaborate description of South America's advantages and agricultural riches must have excited joy among Burke's Spanish American readers. South America's economic future would be freed from Spain's "cruel prohibition of trade." By stimulating agriculture, industry and commerce as the U.S. had done in the "Miracle" period, Spanish-Americans would likewise prosper while their population increased by leaps and bounds. Burke excited his readers in their aspirations for a free development of the "Fortress-America," one of the greatest reservoirs of resources in the world.

Using Alexander Hamilton's figures on industrialization in the United States, valued at about one hundred million dollars, Burke argued that South America might do better than that since Hamilton's total was only double the value of the gold and silver produced in South America and Mexico. Besides, they had all of the resources developed in the United States, as well as other useful materials. The potential for woods usable in a shipbuilding industry was indeed promising; and Burke—perhaps aided by what Bello had told him—described the famous Chacarandy wood in the forests near Lake Maracaibo. As for skins to elaborate, artisans in the South had some distinct advantages. And iron deposits, so important in the industrialization of the United States, were limited to Chile and Mexico. Yet, Burke maintained that a national government could utilize those resources to serve industries vital in supplying tools and farming equipment, as well as capital goods for those producing domestic utensils, firearms, etc. Burke also discussed all manner of resources in South America that had industrial application, hoping thus to aid them in organizing a sound and diversified economic base. Important to the Northerners' success, Burke added, was the industrious habits of the people, which South Americans should strive to emulate. Farmers' wives and their retinues were responsible for the spinning of cotton and the making of clothes, so that no matter where one travelled, the people were well-dressed, etc. etc. etc.

As a keen student of economics, James Mill ("our" William Burke) expressed some very modern anticolonialist arguments in this introductory section:

> If it circulates as it should throughout the region [referring to the gold and silver in South America and Mexico], this great origin of wealth, will serve like a vast and beneficent fountain, whose springs will activate the nation's agriculture, manufactures, commerce, and all the political economy, and which up to this moment has circulated without being of the slightest utility to the land that has produced it, and fostered it; inducing, on the contrary, the continuation of the monopoly that has oppressed it. But this unjust and denaturalized course already has begun to be altered; and America finally is drawing near to [the point of] utilizing her own products [for her own benefit.]

Bequeathed to South America by Providence, this national wealth would serve her own interests from now on, thus ridding herself of a dependency on other countries. The author concluded sagely:

> the genius of liberty, by activating industry, was unquestionably the key that worked such things [miracles] in the public revenues of the United States; South America's resources, assisted by similar advantages, should expect a proportionate increase and results equally beneficial.[7]

Commerce, the third theme, was a major contributor to the increased prosperity of the United States during the "Miracle" period. In this regard, Spanish America showed great promise thanks to the preparation allowed by the Spanish Bourbons in their program of "Free Trade." Burke described the famous reforms of that era that opened up Spanish America's economic system to a great extent. He also wrote of the neutral trade of the war years beginning with the American Revolution and proceeding into the Napoleonic Era. His description and evaluation of the contraband traffic contained valuable insights. His point was obvious: these examples of opening up Spain's colonial traffic reinforced the patent conclusion that Spanish America in a free-world economy had great potential for success. The discussion benefitted from the example of the commercial progress made by Venezuela since April 19, 1810. Perhaps, Andrés Bello in London brought these statistics with him, or Roscio added them to Burke's editorial in Caracas, thanks to his friend Uztáriz, who served the Junta Suprema on economic matters.

William Burke began his fourth theme on January 1, 1811, with the title *"Las Mejoras,"* the "Reforms" or "Improvements" that were essential for South America to become an active partner in the international economy. Here, Mill employed the term used by U.S. historians: "internal improvements," which dealt with the upgrading of an economy's infrastructure—roads, canals, harbors, new inventions and technologies, financial and development instruments, etc. For an author trained in the new economics of *laissez-faire* and a great admirer of Adam Smith, this indeed was an enjoyable editorial to write. Here we see James Mill, the great master of synthesis, revealing his identity with concepts and conclusions. He revived the historical dream that had always intrigued him, the Isthmian canal through Panama:

> The reforms that come to view, and which can be implemented in this great division of the earth, leads us into vast, profound, and pleasant meditations. To unite the Pacific Ocean to the Atlantic at a point near Darien, and to bind together the great rivers of South America by means of canals, are works that are worthy of the era of Colombian liberty and that would produce incalculable benefits to the area. The first [step] that can be taken on the Mexican side of the Isthmus would free the western shores of the American continent, so remote [as they stand], from the commerce of the eastern coasts [of the Western Hemisphere] and [from] Europe, whose ports would [now] find the trip to Lima and the coasts of the Northwest comparatively close and expeditious. The passageway, dividing America in her center, would also open up the eastern part of Russia, the East Indies, and New Holland; while it also unites the waters of the great rivers of South America, which are encouraged to do so particularly by their vast and numerous streams; communications would be established from the mouths of the Orinoco and the *Marañón* [the Amazon River] following their interior paths toward the Paraguay connections; and facilitating [new] settlements and the interior commerce of these vast regions—the generation that would carry it out [this grandiose project], would justly demand the admiration and gratitude of future ages.

At this point, the champion Burke picked up the sword for "internal improvements," so vital for the economic prosperity of "Fortress America." "Extensive and multiple roads, bridges, and barges," he added, "are another very essential "*mejora*" for the advances of such a vast country as this. Compelling the circulation of life and activity everywheres, they serve the Nation as do the blood vessels of the animal body." As he wrote this line, Burke (James Mill) remembered angrily the metaphors of the "walled garden," etc. He noted:

> Nothing could perhaps reflect more the shameful neglect of the former Government, and its cruel designs to subjugate the interests of this country than the absolute lack of roads in practically all places, and the unworthy condition of those that were constructed; that besides their usefulness for the carriage traffic, and the absence of lodging-houses, they are only passable for mules, and only miserable huts at stops [are found] for the convenience of travelers. On this point, South America exists like an immense and disorganized mass, without the advantages of connections and communications. It is well known that in many places the products spoil on the field where they were grown because they cannot be taken to market; and because of the excessively low price for them in the interior, the farmer never makes an effort to increase his production. Thus, a large part of this vast continent is without vigor and in the most sterile inaction; and what is even more lamentable yet, is the fact that many millions of our unfortunate European companions lack the bare essentials, unable to receive from America the surplus [of food] that it could provide for them. What a difference exists in North America![8]

There was nothing but praise for the amazing network of roads created in the United States. "The result," Burke explained,

> has been great waves of population and prosperity, in which a multitude of persons rush to occupy the new lands; and the astonishing rapidity with which new states, cities, and settlements have been formed, a thousand miles away from their old establishments near the coasts of the Atlantic sea; and it is likely that in less than fifty years, they will document their push by penetrating the West, settling and establishing themselves on the shores of the Pacific Ocean.

Burke explained the laws of the United States that guided the roadbuilding, how it was financed, etc., stressing the public-mindedless of everyone involved. Initially, toll roads met with considerable opposition; but it receded as people soon recognized that improved transportation paid off in every sense of the word. South Americans, Mill suggested, could use a portion of their gold and silver for these "internal improvements." Economic societies (chambers of commerce) were vital in sponsoring economic development; and Mill encouraged South Americans to follow suit. It would also be wise to establish hospitals, asylums of various sorts, etc. to assist in the "regeneration of South America."[9]

In the final theme of the introductory section, William Burke dealt with man's moral standards: "Morality is an essential requisite for the liberty and happiness of a nation." Without it, "there can be no true patriotism . . . and without love for the nation there is [a] lack of public spirit, which is necessary to protect their rights and defend their interests." As governments educate and provide the conveniences of life, a citizen learns to identify with his country and institutions. In the process, he appreciates and respects the rights of others. Therefore, Burke concluded: morality and liberty "work reciprocally: as each serves the other as cause and effect." This dichotomy, characteristic of each political entity of the North American model, coexisted harmoniously within a greater circle—the symbol that Burke would utilize to advantage in the next series of editorials. North Americans lived in a "vast and united family." There is trust everywhere; and one does not see "the frequent and severe punishments which degrade the European scene." Crime is virtually unknown, since everyone is working and has a stake in society. It would appear that Mill's presentation of U.S. society was too idyllic. It was nonetheless persuasive and thought-provoking on man's prospects of living in a rational society. The humane assumptions of the North American model were worthy of attention. Burke closed his introduction with these words:

> Every individual, wherever his place of birth may have been, who lives on this soil, and breathes the air of America, must consider himself now as one of her children, and as a member of the great American family: because of their overriding common interest, they must abandon from this time forward the vain distinctions of Spaniard and Creole; and [they must be] loyal to what they owe to the common father who protects and supports them, no one must abandon his tasks, until having perfected the great work in behalf of liberty and happiness; recognizing always that the highest title he can enjoy is that of being `one of the patriots who has contributed to the liberty of South America.`[10]

* * * * * * * * * * * *

A grave political crisis for Venezuela was evident in the first weeks of the new year: 1811. The withdrawal of Toro's forces from the attack on Coro in the previous month brought on a wave of disillusionment among Venezuelans. Moreover, on December 7, 1810, a letter written in Puerto Rico by Antonio Ignacio de Cortavarría, in behalf of the Spanish Government, demanded that the Junta Suprema capitulate to the Regency. Venezuelans dubbed this distinguished Spanish gentleman the "*Parlementario de Puerto Rico* (Spokesman)" . . . whose unbearable arrogance and conceit permeated the highly offensive letter, replete with platitudes, praises, and threats. "The good was bad" and vice versa, noted Roscio disdainfully. The combined news of impending defeat at Coro and the insulting missive by the "Spokesman" was the crowning blow to Venezuelan sentiments. To compound the insult, the hated Cortavarría himself appeared off the port of La Guaira, Venezuela, demanding a reply to his letter! He got just what he deserved: La Guaira's Commandant, confused and angered by the "Spokesman's" presence, ordered guns fired to frighten him off, causing the surprised Spaniards to sail away swollen with revenge. The Junta Suprema's answer to the "Spokesman" was just as direct. In effect, Roscio and partners told him to take his rhetoric some place else; Venezuelans were not about to kneel to the likes of the Regency and the Cortes at Cádiz, which had opened its doors on September 24, 1810. They did not approve of the Spaniards' terms for reconciliation; and, as usual, the Regency had no right to appoint Venezuelan representatives to Parliament on its own initiative. On January 21, 1811, as might be expected, Cortavarría reimposed the Spanish blockade on Venezuelan ports. And there were other issues in northern South America that aroused patriots everywhere: namely, a Spanish Bishop in the Ecuadorean area defying the patriot leaders of Bogotá. Roscio was beside himself with anger at this brazen defiance of the patriots' cause.

In this angry and bellicose context, Francisco de Miranda and the rest of his group reached La Guaira, several days after Bolívar's arrival, to a warm reception. This legendary hero, born in Caracas, had returned home just at the appropriate time to save his *patria*. The reception in Caracas was likewise spirited. Partly because of Simón Bolívar's enthusiasm for this famous warrior and traveler, the youth at the Capital hastened to greet him with open arms. Not surprisingly, the decision followed to found the *Sociedad Patriótica de Venezuela*, a move encouraged by Miranda. The Junta Suprema, for its part, moved rapidly to pave the way for Miranda's role in the government. As noted earlier, he was appointed Lt. General in the Venezuelan Army; and at the suggestion of the Marquis del Toro was also given the title of Inspector General, to organize and train the personnel along modern lines. The Coro type of military maneuvers would no longer be repeated. Roscio, as Secretary of State, pursued a valuable psychological objective by deliberately capitalizing on Miranda's presence in Venezuela during this period of crisis. It would bolster morale and courage among his countrymen, encouraging thus the movement toward independence. The Junta Suprema, it will be recalled, ordered all corporations to expunge from their records of the Spanish period anything that insulted the reputation of Francisco de Miranda. These meetings of the municipalities of Venezuela received broad coverage in the *Gazeta de Caracas*; and Roscio, on occasion, went out of his way to underscore the hero's valor and the admiration of many who walked miles to hear and see the General in person. Roscio's promotion of the hero's return, given the context of crisis, was a valuable step in preparing the nation for independence. Venezuela had in her midst a potential "George Washington."

Miranda, of course, cooperated with Roscio in every respect. He encouraged the self government and political virtues of the cabildos, so vital to Venezuela's future. Miranda, for example, thanked the Valencia government for praising him as a model for his compatriots: however, he reminded them that it was *their* exemplary conduct on April 19, 1810, that duly impressed the world, and the Americas in particular, for their decision, "to live like free men." Miranda, moreover, reminded the *Valencianos* of the sacrifices made by many of his own comrades in 1806 off the coast of South America:

> which the despotic and infamous Government, oppressing them at that time, wanted to obscure [their heroism], by condemning them [Miranda's comrades] with an unjust and slanderous punishment; that only such vile agents as *Jurado* and *Guevara* could have executed without scruples.

These bits of history were vital to Venezuelans in keeping up their spirits during the crisis of December–January.[11]

Documenting the close cooperation of Roscio and Miranda, the General wrote a letter to the Junta de Bogotá on January 22, 1811, on a theme that was dear to Roscio's heart: the union of Venezuela with the other nations of South America. Miranda congratulated the Junta for following Caracas' example in breaking with the Spanish government. He heartily approved, moreover, of the Junta's reply to the obstreperous Bishop of Cuenca. In so doing, the Junta of Bogotá had defended "the sacred rights and sovereignty of the Colombian *pueblo*" which included "the solid bases and reasons that justify our holy cause." Such incidents as these, Miranda stressed with strong feeling, would inevitably unite all of South America to repel "the contrivances of our enemies, who like Cortavarría, and the Prelate of Cuenca, never refrain [from using] indecent means in fooling or deluding the simple and honest inhabitants of these extended provinces." By way of contrast, Dr. José Cortés Madariaga, also a cleric, was not objectionable at all. On the contrary, he was a man of "high merit and distinguished patriotism." Miranda praised Dr. Cortés who was on his way to represent Venezuela in Bogotá. Cortés hoped to establish a political union between the "Kingdom of Santa Fe de Bogotá and the Province of Venezuela, so that forming together a single social body we shall enjoy now great security and respect." It will bring us glory in the future and "permanent happiness."[12]

As editor of the *Gazeta de Caracas*, Roscio's distress over the crisis in Venezuelan politics caused him to take whatever steps were necessary to influence public opinion along proper lines for Venezuela's survival and emergence as an independent power. We can only speculate as to who might have encouraged him to make these decisions. Certainly, his leading associates Uztáriz and Isnardi were consulted; and in light of what has already been mentioned, it is conceivable that Miranda might have also been a member of the decision-making body. Be that as it may, the *Gazeta's* three issues: January 11, 15, and 18, 1811 had a different "William Burke" at the helm, addressing himself to the December–January crisis that had caught Venezuela's attention. These were not editorials written by James Mill, although this new writer borrowed much that he had learned from the original author. This William Burke was clearly Hispanic and a student of Spanish law, politics, and history. The emotions and the national rhetoric was fervently and consistently pro-Venezuelan. Even though he may have drawn from a native Spaniard—Blanco-White, for example—the conclusions were his—a Venezuelan. The "new" William Burke was Juan Germán Roscio himself, aided wherever necessary by the men mentioned above. Our point here is to show the drift of these three key editorials with some pertinent quotations.

Gran Colombia

Projected: 1810 to 1819

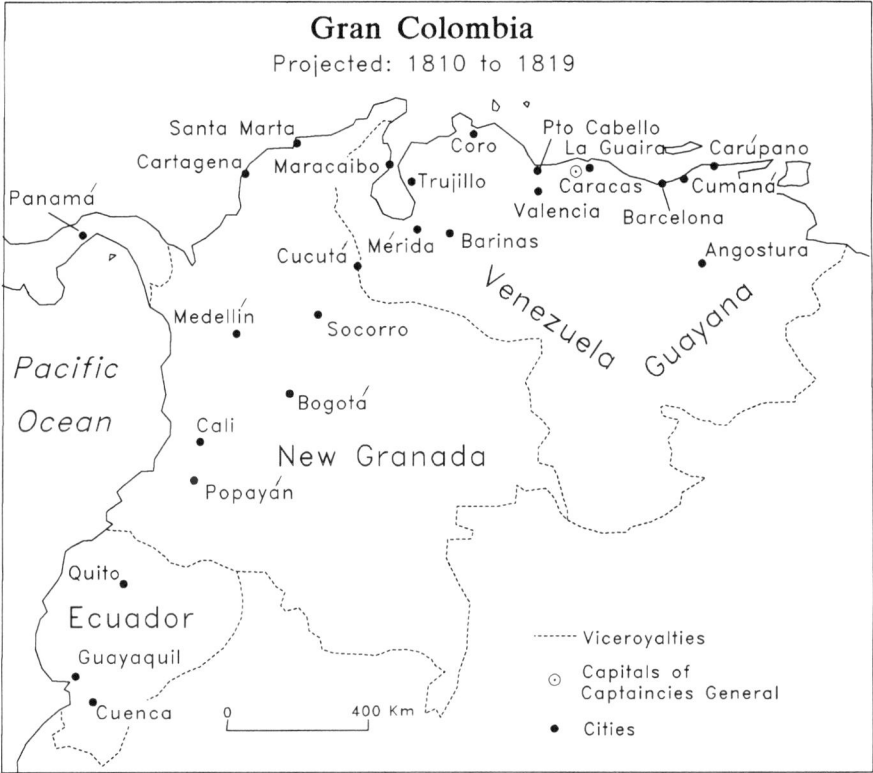

Santa Marta
Cartagena
Maracaibo
Coro
Pto Cabello
La Guaira
Carúpano
Panamá
Trujillo
Caracas
Cumaná
Valencia
Barcelona
Cucutá
Mérida
Barinas
Angostura
Venezuela
Guayana
Medellín
Socorro

Pacific
Ocean

Cali
Bogotá
New Granada
Popayán

Quito
Ecuador
Guayaquil
Cuenca

0   400 Km

┄┄┄┄┄ Viceroyalties

⊙ Capitals of
   Captaincies General

● Cities

Contrary to Mill's usual approach, the new Burke bypassed the expected high road—grandiose philosophical observations about opening up the "walled-garden," the "tyrant's seraglio," or the imprisoned "Fortress-America" for the world as a free and independent nation. This Burke was negative and threatening, one who was angry about the events of December–January (1810–11):

> If the people of South America do not understand that they have equal rights, as other nations, to liberty and happiness in their country; that their relations with God and nature are the same as the rest of humanity; and that their rights have the same origin as all of the others, it would be futile to arouse them here on individual rights in the present crisis, and this great continent would always remain exposed to the frightening evils of foreign ambition and slavery, and to being torn apart by domestic divisions and external wars.

Yet, the new Burke wanted desperately to believe that he was wrong:

> Believing, on the contrary, that they could not disavow their rights and that from the coasts of Caracas to those of Lima, and from the extreme limits of Mexico to those of Paraguay there are efforts towards union and the common independence of the country [Spanish America], we shall continue to examine them.

William Burke then launched a legal and constitutional theme that virtually obsessed Juan Germán Roscio since April 19, 1810: Ferdinand VII's rights to the Spanish throne. In the *Manifiesto* that followed Venezuela's Independence on July 5, 1811, attributed correctly to Roscio, he elaborated upon that theme at great lengths. At this point, the *Gazeta's* editor argued convincingly that Ferdinand VII's rights were based exclusively on "the will of the American people;" just as in Spain, it was the will of the Spanish people. Historically, the Revolution at Aranjuez, Spain, dethroned Charles IV and enthroned Ferdinand VII. In doing so, the "hereditary line" of the Spanish monarchy was broken; just as Louis XIV—the French Bourbons—had done to the Hapsburg line in the early eighteenth century when he established his grandson as King of Spain. Also, argued "Wm. Burke," this was the case when Napoleon imposed his brother Joseph on the Spanish throne. The argument, as Roscio developed it, was that the "People" had the right to depose their monarch for just cause and then to elect a new one—Ferdinand VII—or a new government if they willed it. It was immaterial that the man chosen for king at Aranjuez was the son of the ex-king. Spaniards could have chosen anyone else. It followed that the Spanish people did not have to stick to the Bourbon line if something happened to Ferdinand, still a prisoner of the French. They, the people, could elect, or choose, some other person. It was thus futile for any of the Bourbon pretenders to seek the American throne because of an hereditary link to Ferdinand. In this manner, Roscio conveniently disposed of Carlota's claims to the American throne, as well as those of her brother Don Pedro. Americans, Roscio argued, chose the same monarch as the Spaniards because of the exigencies of the times. Presumably, they could have chosen someone else, or they could have established another type of government, other than a monarchy. In short, the "new" William Burke provided a legal rationale for the independence of the Americas.[13]

There was much more in the editorials of this new "William Burke" that had nothing to do with James Mill, including the special terms and language constructions. The term "*amotinar*" (to encourage mutiny) was a common one used by Roscio and other leaders of the April 19th movement, referring to Spanish spies sent to Venezuela. "America," Burke maintained:

> does not need to direct her business a multitude of foreign courtesans, intriguers, corrupt, weak, tyrants, and accompained by a limitless retinue of dependents; all she requires is an honest an enlightened Government, composed of her own Citizens, interested in the liberty and prosperity of their country; and she, in my opinion, has resolved for her own convenience not to have [any] other but this [type of government].

This was unquestionably a fiercely nationalistic and pro-America stand. Roscio's attack continued in more and more detail, wreaking vengeance upon the Spanish enemy:

> May such slavery perish, [once and for all], as well as the usurped dependency, without any right or basis, and injurious and degrading to one and the other nation. For too long, America has bourne upon herself a shameful yoke; and Spain is now suffering the prize for her injustice.[14]

Vengeance was being served, and Roscio's wrath was likewise demonstrated in other articles of the *Gazeta*, not bearing Burke's name.

The "new" William Burke has thus provided us with a good account and feeling for the April 19th Revolution as it entered the new year of 1811. The realities of the December–January crisis had dispensed with the middle-of-the-road stance of the Junta Suprema de Venezuela. Up ahead, in March, the Constituent Congress of Venezuela would take over from the Junta, directing the movement for Independence.

The second editorial usurping "William Burke's" name will shock many students of Venezuelan history accustomed to a standard assumption in their historiography: that is, the alleged rivalry between Roscio and Miranda revealed explicitly in Roscio's famous letter to Andrés Bello on June 9, 1811. Although a rivalry of sorts—at least, in Roscio's mind—developed briefly in the relationship of these two Venezuelan heroes, it *was not* operational on January 15, 1811, when they collaborated under the aegis of the "new" William Burke! It may have been Miranda who strongly urged Roscio's aggressive propaganda move in order to speed up the pace of independence—an objective, after all, that had obsessed him for decades.

If we study the organization of the second editorial on January 15th, 1811, we note that the two men agreed to discuss the following themes: first, "It is an important fact that the present subjugation of Spain stems principally from her abuses with regard to America." And, it should be recalled that this notion was underscored by Roscio in the January 11th editorial, which we analyzed above. By rights, it would appear that Roscio, therefore, developed the discussion of that theme on January 15th in which he borrowed heavily from the ideas of James Mill. Roscio assimilated many of Mill's ideas; but he never could equal or master Mill's tight style of writing or his ability to synthesize, at least not to the same degree. For various reasons, some of which will come up later, it is my opinion that James Mill and Francisco de Miranda wrote the essay that was published in the *Gazeta de Caracas* on January 15, 1811, under Burke's name; moreover, I suspect that this contribution originally had been intended for publication in *El Colombiano* but was not published because of its short tenure in London. The essay, therefore, did not form part of the original Burke manuscript. It was introduced by Miranda, who brought it with him from London; and Roscio agreed to publish it as one of the three editorials in January, 1811. Now, we can turn to the editorial on January 15th; and leave Miranda's theme, or contribution, for the discussion that follows.

The theme of retribution for Spain's abuses was ready made for James Mill, if we recall his treatises:

If she [Spain] like England had treated her possessions under liberal principles, it is certain that America would have won her independence some time ago; but then the independence of the colonies, as happened with those of England, would have increased the royal forces and resources of Spain, she would have extended her commerce, increased her navy, and advanced her agriculture and manufactures, and would have been enabled to maintain an army capable of defending her in her peninsular location, and surrounded by her mountains, against any invader that would have dared to attack her.   But to America's misfortune, as well as that of Spain herself, the policy followed was completely the opposite.

This type of clever argument was something that Mill and his good friend Miranda might have discussed on one of their long walks in London.   Then, the economic discussion that followed was what we have seen and could expect from James Mill:

Since the first one [America] was only treated like a great silver mine, the other party [Spain] has directed its views and efforts in favor of the monopoly of this metal, for which she has sacrificed much more meaningful goals, and by which other products of a real and effective worth have been neglected; repressing the people's industry, while enslaving this same public.   Silver entered Spain in marvelous abundance; but the genuine elements of her power and prosperity immediately began to weaken. The Crown increased its prerogatives, and the freedom of the People diminished; riches could be acquired without work; and industry was exiled from the country; the forces and resources of Spain declined on a daily basis; and this Nation after having been reduced over a considerable period to the humble state of a Customhouse between her overseas possessions and the rest of Europe, has finally ended overwhelmed by the troops of an invader, attracted by her weakness, and taking over her crown, extinguished in one blow her dynasty and independence.[15]

"This melancholic catastrophe," Burke concluded: "has allowed us to recognize another important truth, that demands the attention of Americans."   This well-organized publicist thus introduced us to Miranda's theme: "that the despotism of the Spanish Government has been left virtually without *Pueblo* (Folk) in the true sense of this word."

In the January 15th issue of the gazette, Miranda commented on the scenario in Spain as Napoleon's troops poured into the Peninsula in 1808.   Much to the surprise of all Europe, Spaniards were initially victorious against the French. *If* Spain had been able to organize "a popular and energetic Government combining her true interests and utilizing the foreign aid that was available to her constructively, then the future might have been different." But Spain's record of despotism worked against that solution. Virtual slaves for such a long time, ten million Spaniards "were unable to take those vigorous measures that were necessary to save their nation." "They suffered," Miranda continued,

> a series of despicable and tyrannical cabals; each one of them feared most that the People would recover their liberty, rather than that the Nation might be taken prisoner by a foreign conqueror; they usurped the sovereign authority; and weakened their resources to such an extent that the invader was able in a new attack to see his desires fulfilled. Convinced of the ineffectual state of the Spanish People for an effective defense—that was the time when *the writer of these pages* [my italics] declaimed against the cause that promoted the resistence to this invasion, no matter how unjust it was; because that [the resistance movement], in the actual state of Europe [in 1808] would have no other effects but to bring desolation to the treasury and human blood, and the increase of evils that no real effort could avoid. The dramatic and fatal result has more than justified those thoughts, and the same firm conscience impels him now to lament the continuation of a desperate struggle, which cannot produce any more than a greater destruction of the unfortunate *Pueblo*, more confiscation of its resources, and greater facilities for the implementation of the ulterior designs of the invaders upon the country. Spain, in the meantime, is nothing more than a devouring whirlpool of its resources, without conceding the slightest benefit; and in the hands of Napoleon, she will be from now on a great sponge that will absorb all the aid that can be sent to her . . . In this manner, the despotic system of the Spanish Government is costly even after the loss of Spain. Such is the system that the enemies of America, and even some presumed friends of hers, have recommended that it should be transplanted overseas [to America.][16]

In the final paragraphs of that key January 15th editorial, "William Burke"—the "new one, that is—emphasized that Venezuelans must not doubt for a moment that Napoleon's conquest of Spain was imminent: "Let us, therefore, extinguish now every shadow of Spain's former protection over America." American rights are "absolutely free and unique," despite America's proclamation in favor of Ferdinand VII, following the Spanish lead:

Those rights, derive at present from nature and justice, eternal and abundant springs of all law; and Americans are already perfectly free, and can locate their edifice of liberty and happiness on the same unalterable bases as any other nation of equal independence, natural and civil.

Burke's editorial of the 15th was an explicit call for the Independence of Venezuela. There is no doubt on this point.

The interpretation that we have just presented was not original with General Miranda. Spaniards like José María Blanco-White and Manuel Cortés Campomanes, who was in Caracas at this time, held similar views on the subject; and Miranda, undoubtedly gained these insights from them. Besides, we are familiar already with his beliefs in 1808 that the resistance movement against Napoleon by the Spaniards was useless, as it had been in other European countries. He expressed this point to the future Duke of Wellington, it will be recalled. Moreover, he had a vested interest in the matter: if England stepped into the Spanish cauldron, it meant that she might, in the long run, abandon her complete plans for the emancipation of Spanish America. Mill and Miranda, also, had frequent discussions on Napoleon's tactics, military and in the propaganda area, all of which conditioned the Miranda interpretation at this point in his career. What is important, of course, is that this bold interpretation to influence Venezuelan minds appeared in the *Gazeta de Caracas* on January 15, 1811, using the penname of Miranda's dear friend James Mill. All the factors concerning the second editorial of the "new" William Burke suggest strongly the hypothesis that this particular article, which appeared in the gazette ten days before the publication of Mill's "Thoughts of an Englishman. . .," was first intended for publication in Miranda's London paper: *El Colombiano*; but, because of its sudden closure, was brought to Caracas by Miranda himself and offered to his collaborator Juan Germán Roscio, the editor of the gazette and Secretary of State under the Junta Suprema de Venezuela. This makes sense in light of the close cooperation between Roscio and Miranda at this time, including the proposed project to unite Venezuela with Bogotá's jurisdiction.

The third extra essay of January 18, 1811, revealed a classical and rhetorical style of a "William Burke," that was characteristic of the Junta's Secretary of State. "Oh Ye Americans," he began:

See here the glory of your present situation! Never has there been another equal one presented to the view of mankind. See yourselves finally placed in the fountain of your rights, receiving them directly from the beneficient hands of the Creator. . . See your country, one fifth of the inhabitable world, oppressed for such a long time and crowned with all the blessings that nature can provide, raise herself from her chains at this first opportunity, to implore for help, for the honor of creation, for your own good [and for] that of your brethen, and as a justice owed to the human race, whose rights have been cruelly violated, to consolidate forever your liberty and happiness. Ye Americans, observe your immense resources, and the limitless increase, which, as we have seen, you should receive from independence. . . Cast your views towards posterity, towards the interests of your country in the successive eras, in which your descendents by the millions, will bless or curse your memory, depending upon how you have acted in the present age.

At this point, Roscio resorted to a "What will they say about us?" session: if we opt for Independence, they'll hurrah us forever; if we don't, FOR SHAME! The author underlined both possibilities; the negative side, however, was longer and more emotional. Roscio, pleaded for "an absolute and complete independence."

Venezuelans, the "new" William Burke insisted, had to bring about "a *National Government*," facing head on the challenge of establishing nationhood. The world was watching them, hoping that they would be courageous.

There was nothing to fear; Europe was six thousand miles away, distracted and divided by war. The positive example of the United States was before them; and Venezuelans should not forget what happened to the counter-revolutionaries there, the tragic fate of the so-called 'Loyalists.' Moreover, Spain has left us no alternative, calling us 'rebels' and imposing an insulting blockade . . . You either '*sustain the rights of your country*,' or suffer the ridicule and oppression of unworthy Spanish leaders, who have constantly insulted your integrity and honor. Remember the horrible atrocities committed against your brethen in Quito?

They have promised you a general pardon "if you submit to them voluntarily," thus allowing you to return to a degrading slavery. What an insult! What an abominable offer by such "vile and infamous men." Throughout the heated harangue, it was obvious that Roscio despaired of those Americans who would help the tyrants against the interests of their own people. He reminded them of the positive accomplishments in Venezuela since April 19, 1810. He especially signaled out: *"personal liberty and the security of properties."* "Caracas," he added proudly: "will make herself worthy of imitation in forming her Provincial Government, just as she was the first to take on the emancipation [movement.]" Finally, Venezuelans should not overlook the glorious path set down for them by their North American brethren, "so worthy of the greatest attention in the present important crisis."[17]

Concurrently, in the *Semanario de Caracas*, editor Miguel Sanz pleaded the same cause with equal emotion and determination. The negative stance of *Coreanos* and *Maracayberos* was shockingly incomprehensible to him. In February 1811, he commenced a series of articles exposing their degradation and shame.[18] In short, patriotic Venezuelan editors performed an exceptional service in the early months of 1811, preparing their people for the Constituent Assembly that met in Caracas on March 2, 1811, bringing to an end the rule of the Junta Suprema of Venezuela. Roscio's role as Secretary of State for the Junta and as master propagandist in charge of the *Gazeta de Caracas* was especially exemplary and commendable. In late March, before stepping down from his two leading positions, he once again chose to impersonate "William Burke" with editorials of even greater historical significance.

* * * * * * * * * * * *

Political thought in Venezuela entered a brilliant phase from January 22 to March 29, 1811, in the *Gazeta de Caracas* with a series of about sixteen editorials. James Mill and his colleague Jeremy Bentham were responsible for the political wisdom that appeared in those columns of the gazette. What a fantastic discovery it would be for the world to find the original English manuscripts! For the present, however, we shall have to make do with the published Spanish version, which we suspect was by another famous world figure: Andrés Bello. In any case, we hardly would expect to find such a display of erudition and political common sense in northern South America at this particular time in history. It gives us some notion of what intellectual life might have been in Caracas if Mill and Bentham, along with the precocious John Stuart Mill, had realized the dream of moving to the New World to help Miranda modernize the vaunted Colombian Continent.

On January 22, 1811, the *Gazeta de Caracas* published the first "discourse" of William Burke's regular series on the political institutions of the United States of America. Its goal was to prepare Americans with a graphic overall view of the constitutional device agreed to by North American citizens. Here again, we observe the presentation of a master teacher and an expert in synthesis:

> The Republic of North America is composed of 17 independent States of which each one has a constitution, government and laws that are its own; but all are united by a Constitution and General Congress for the common defense, and other national objectives as we shall demonstrate in due time. In this way, each State retains its sovereignty and liberty with independence of the rest, and is only subject to the General Government in those matters that it has delegated to it without any other object—than the public welfare, and with the designation made in the constitution of the United States. From this form of Confederation results the great benefit of a General Government provided with sufficient powers to unite and defend the whole, and to regulate and promote the general interests [of all], while the individual sovereignties in their respective States present an insuperable barrier to the usurpation of other powers than those delegated specifically in the constitution, and serve as a shield for the interests of citizens in the different states against the attempts [that might be made on them] by the General Government; while at the same time each State possesses the advantages of having in its midst [center of power] its Government, laws, public pleasures: incalculable benefits in an extensive country, as that of those States. From this derives a system of Confederation adopted in that republic that can be extended to the ends of the North American Continent, without endangering the liberty of a single citizen.

Now, to keep this tight description in mind, Burke urged his readers to remember this "Grand Circle," or symbol:

> It is a multitude of political circles, of which each one has a political movement of rotation upon its own axis, and is disposed to unite itself to new circles, while a general influence presides over all [of them] preserving the harmony of their gyration, and restricting each one within the prescribed orbit by means of a constitution, without being able to obstruct or injure any of them. To understand more completely the advantages of this political structure, it is necessary to explain at least the plan of the constitution of the State, as well as the form of Government and the laws; and we shall make some observations upon

them by illustrating [those points] with principles of civil liberty, practiced in North America and in England.[19]

Just as he had promised, William Burke presented his readers with a general sketch of the "Grand Circle" that he specified above. All this in his first editorial of the regular political series, just enough to excite the readers about future discourses on the relationship between the Senate and the House of Representatives, their respective duties, etc.; the functions of the executive and judicial branches of government; the constitutions of the states and the general government, etc. "We the People" approve of the following constitution—was a concept that came up time and time again; the people were the source of power and sovereignty, etc. And he could not help going into more detail on the famous "Bill of Rights" of the various constitutions. He listed all of the pros and cons. As an historian and political scientist, James Mill wanted to know how the inherent rights of the individual and the sovereignty of the People had been abused, time and time again, throughout the ages. Editorial after editorial would clarify and expand upon those abuses and what steps had been taken to correct them, and how the United States model had pointedly tried to prevent any further abuses. And, of course, most of the examples were those familiar to Bentham and himself; and they perhaps agreed which ones would be utilized in the various themes. William Burke certainly set the scene well on January 22nd.[20]

In the *Gazeta*'s issue of January 25, 1811, Burke focused on the "Constitution" as a document that represented the People's sovereignty, which we shall come back to shortly. Roscio also decided, perhaps at the behest of Francisco de Miranda, to introduce his readers to another publication belonging to James Mill. So January 25th was Mill's day to sparkle in the *Gazeta de Caracas*. The only problem, however, was that the public did not know his identity—one was "William Burke" on the topic mentioned above, and the other was "Thoughts of an Englishman," which first appeared in Miranda's *El Colombiano* (London) in mid-1810. Mill's "*Pensamientos*," as we know, already previewed some of Burke's future editorials: those dealing with "Religious Toleration," "Freedom of the Press," advantages that Spanish America might have in establishing modern governments, etc. This suggests that editor Roscio, and his advisor Miranda, were preparing Venezuelans for controversial, or outstanding, topics of the future. Significantly, one of those key themes that Mill, the thoughtful

Englishman above, did not develop fully, only indirectly in a future Burkian editorial, was the potential of racial and cultural deterrents to impede success in Spanish America. This was a theme, it will be recalled, that Dr. John Allen, his colleague on the *Edinburgh Review*, highlighted in both of his articles: April, 1810, which we have discussed and the one on November, 1811, which we shall deal with in a later chapter.   Yet, it is conceivable that Mill did not participate in the selection of this controversial topic at all; Roscio and Miranda, as Venezuelans, realized that the discussion of racial and cultural deterrents was just too controversial, given the makeup and attitudes prevailing in their society.   Be that as it may, editor Roscio was preparing his people for those positive topics that might be tolerated in Caracas at least without damaging the impact of the Burkian editorials or manuscripts.   Andrés Bello, it can be assumed, would have also agreed with both Roscio and Miranda on the racial question.

Returning to the Burkian piece in the January 25th issue of the *Gazeta*, "our" William Burke felt the need for setting the proper historical background on constitutional precedents with regards to the People's sovereignty.   This authoritative synthesis followed:

> In all ages, whatever Nation has proclaimed its liberty, has viewed ╷ certain constitutional acts as the basis for its rights. Greece and Rome had their fundamental laws; Spain had its *Cortes*, and the constitution of Aragon; England maintains her *Magna Carta* and *Bill of Rights*; but we must confess that the constitution, which we have just reviewed, is the most perfect of its kind, and which has been best calculated, of all those that have been drawn up to this day, in order to assure the life, liberty, and property of the Citizens.

The U.S. Constitution is thorough in every respect, reflecting the norms of man's experiences in the past, incorporating the best in the knowledge and practices of the contemporary world; and a document that is not just theory; its ideas are being put into practice; and the mechanism is providing the world with demonstrable proofs. Compared to the U.S. document, the constitutional acts of many other nations are merely "unconnected fragments, produced by accident or violence during bloody wars and struggles" of very different and distant periods.   The evidence, moreover, has been distorted over the years. "Because of" these results, Burke concluded:

there has been the sad facility which we have seen of those governments usurping the rights of the People, enslaving them, pillaging them and submerging them in ruinous wars, due to the lack of a complete and defined constitution, that indicated limits and restrained the exercise of powers.

The pattern of abuse runs throughout this series of editorials: "We the People," he argued, was a phrase that demonstrated the "People's" assertion of their sovereignty. The Constitution originated with the "People," and the Government that emerged was the instrument of the "People." To prevent abuses, a series of checks-and-balances were necessary in the Constitution—the three-way division of power, an experiment that proved successful in England and the United States; two sections in the Legislature, both checking each other; elections and restrictions upon functionaries of government, and the omnipresence of the People's representation. The two "great principles *Representation and Elections*" are absolutely indispensable in a free state. Thus, you always have "a constant circulation throughout the political body, preserving its unity and integrity, and impeding the suppression of any of its parts." The election of government officials for short, specific periods, as well as other controls on them, are likewise good tactics.[21]

To convince his reader that history favored the "People," Burke assumed the mantle of philosopher/historian. "Man by his nature," he proclaimed,

and conforming to the designs of his Creator, expressed in the economy of his own organization and all that surrounds him, possesses certain essential and inalienable properties, whose enjoyment we call RIGHTS; and that are given by the Creator to fulfill innate obligations that he has imposed upon us on earth; no man can deprive another [of his rights], without committing an injustice, and without becoming a criminal for opposing frontally the beneficent intentions of the divine will. Thus, the eternal and imprescriptible rights of life, liberty, and the procurement of foods provided by nature, which belong to the being of man: they are the attributes of his existence, and as such, they belong to him in the savage as well as in the civilized state . . . Man, therefore, upon entering society, far from abdicating his useful and essential rights, increases the security of their enjoyment, in the reciprocal interest that all men should have in preserving their own rights and those of the rest; and there you have, [to sum up,] the true and only legitimate foundations of power and Government.[22]

After a lengthy philosophical discussion about man in society, Burke engaged his reader in an extensive historical analysis on the abuse, or usurpation, of the People's sovereignty. It is a discussion that raised all sorts of doubts about monarchy, as a form of government. The readers of the *Gazeta de Caracas* must have been deeply impressed with what Burke had to say on February 5, 1811:

> It is downright insolent language that is used by those governments who outlaw the sovereignty of the People that they have enslaved; and I am not sure who is more despicable: the despots that tread upon the rights of the nation, or the *pueblo* that puts up with it.

The language of all monarchies has been, Burke noted: "since the ancient and decrepit tyrannies of the feudal system, up to those that have appeared in the present: *'The pueblo* (public), *with respect to the Government, must do no more than to obey'.*"

As outlined by William Burke, the historical pattern of abuse began with the seizure of power by a political opportunist, or a military leader, to advance his own cause. Even if such a leader advanced the people's cause somewhat, in search of glory,

> what barrier would the People put up in opposition to the whim or tyranny of his successors, who forgetting the bastard origin of their founder, in their present state of aggrandizement, arrogated the government to themselves by right of descent, and abusing the name of Heaven, exercised all the horrors of slavery over the oppressed and unfortunate *pueblo*?

Their situation was hopeless. At this point, Burke hit hard with these conclusions:

> It is certain that all the strong or permanent executive powers, be they kings, dukes, consuls, or under any other title, will usurp, sooner or later, an unlimited power called falsely sovereignty; and [this usurped power] extinguishes by degrees even the memory that the true sovereignty belonged to the nation.

It follows, therefore, that:

> There is no monarchy in Europe that has not been imposed *upon the People* by force or by fraud. Intrigue or conquest provided the first

cement; and the absurd and insolent pretension of the right of inheritance, as if the inalienable rights of the nation were the private property of an individual, and the People transferable like a flock [of sheep], has secured the degrading tyranny, and has strengthened the chains upon the nation; no other way could we explain the insufferable oppression of the government, and the vile slavery and apathy of the people, that we have at present in many countries.

It is mindboggling to see people give up their rights into posterity to an arbitrary power. The "monstruous doctrine of the rights of kings" is a sham, Burke charged testily: "Some writers resort to a fantastic distinction affirming that the People delegate their sovereignty, or by an actual covenant, or by a tacit approval—all this is false, equally in theory as in practice." The so-called "compact theory" of government is a hoax:

> We have already said that all these pseudo-sovereignties have been established opportunely *upon the pueblo*, and against its approval; its posterity, born and educated in prisons, has had to bear chains that it has not been able to break, or has not challenged this injustice as much as it might have, because it did not have the opportuntiy of knowing the blessings of a free state. Besides the fact that no nation has more right to dispose of its sovereignty, than an individual has to dispose of his reason, which is part of himself. Both restraints have been given, as well as instilled, by a supreme artificer in the organization of man to serve as his guide and for his preservation and happiness. They, therefore, as the rest of the natural and essential rights, are inseparably united to his individual and general person; and the assumed right, or, more accurately, the crass error that a nation can alienate or transfer the exercise of them [the rights] to another, or many individuals, is tantamount to the treacherous authority acclaimed by a suicide victim to justify his death.[23]

At this point, William Burke reminded us of one of Mill's pet concerns: corruption in the British Government. Here, Burke remarked upon the "hypocrisy" that attended this corruption and its contribution to the abuse of the People's sovereignty:

> The supposition . . . that mixed governments are arranged by the equilibrium of their parts, in order to prevent the usurpation of the rights of the People by the executive, is more plausible in theory, than true in practice. I agree that these Governments, not having equal facilities,

and their situation demanding more caution in their procedures, do not become despots as fast as the absolute monarchies. But experience demonstrates that their objectives are similar; and even though there may be some difference in the mode, there is none in the objective desired. Even the most limited monarchies are converted ordinarily into arbitrary powers; that is their nature. The King, deriving his power from one of the two founts of such establishments, that is, force or fraud; or of both at the same time, far from permitting restrictions [on his power], he makes incessant efforts to advance it. He is aided in this by his nobles and by those sycophants that always surround the platform of the man who has power and positions to distribute; until the Crown's influence, obscuring the rights of the nation, gives the monarch the capacity to usurp the exercise of sovereignty and to proscribe as a crime of high treason even the memory of those [People's Rights]. From that point forward, the rights that remain to the nation do not exist except in name; and even personal liberty, reduced to the protection of the laws, reaching even to the representative bodies that form the popular arm of the government.

When the nobles agreed to unite and join "the same corruption," there was not much left to prevent "the usurper" from establishing complete tyranny, "equal to the most absolute and brazen monarchy" in existence. To sum up, Burke declared: "the establishment of a strong and permanent executive, whatever the denomination with which he cloaks himself, the first step is taken toward the usurpation of the exercise of the People's sovereignty;" and the regime that follows will finish up like all the present monarchies, either with a declaration of absolute despotism, or what is even more injurious and insulting, a tyranny produced by corruption, in the name of a constitutional right."[24]

The purpose of Burke's long and fascinating discussion on how the People's sovereignty had been abused historically was to demonstrate why North Americans had taken such trouble to avoid abuse ever again. The Constitution of 1787, in Burke's judgment, was a marvelous achievement of man's capacity to recognize and defend his "rights." "Finally," he noted,

we see the People dispose, also by delegation, of all the affairs of government; and we see each Citizen, by means of alternate elections, fill for short periods all kinds of positions from legislator to governor, and even to the post of constable. Thus, by means of the representative system the People assure themselves effectively of their right to sovereignty; and with this all the others: maintaining constantly its exercise [of sovereignty], so that it does not pass to other hands without the means of representation.

Fascinated by the concept of "Representation," Burke made this perceptive observation:

> It is a grand principle, understood indiscriminately by the ancients, unknown in practice by the despot Nations, omitted even by Montesquieu himself, and constituting the principal distinction between free Governments and the arbitrary ones; that the People enjoy liberty in proportion to the degree that they utilize representation. There is no representation in absolute Governments, because the People have no voice; and in the mixed ones, representation is partial and defective, because it is proportional to the small influence that the People have actually on the government. Of all of those in the world, only the United States has a perfect representation, because only there do the People have complete exercise [control] of their own sovereignty, without opposition, and without having to clash with the opposing interests of the Kings, and the nobles, or of any other power; and because only there do the People conserve in their hands, as all wise ones should, the administration of their affairs.

The proof of North America's achievement can be seen in the record of the last three decades—a period of peace and prosperity. In the meantime, Burke concluded,

> personal liberty [in the United States] has been constantly more complete; and since there are no parallels in the history of nations; they [the United States] have offered at one same time the most brilliant example and the most convincing proof of the superiority that its system of Government representation has over all the rest.[25]

A powerful and persuasive section followed in which the publicist was ready to make a practical application of all that he had been saying about the United States. Juan Germán Roscio, as we have noted, occasionally would embroider a clause or more onto William Burke's proposals to make them more believable to the Spanish American reader. The theme was still "representation" and Burke suggested an imaginative course of action:

> Venezuela, who has adopted this system, will undoubtedly apply it to all branches of Government, in order to facilitate her union with all the

remaining Provinces and States of South America and Mexico, and to
form a large, stable and general confederation instilled with these same
intentions, interests, and powers.

As might be expected, Roscio responded to Burke's notion of Spanish
American union with alacrity and conviction. After all, he had been
thinking along these lines since the Fall of 1810. The so-called "Quito
massacre" of August, 1810, convinced Roscio that, for defensive
reasons, Venezuela should join with the rest of Northern South
America. In Miranda's January 22nd letter to Bogotá, the political
motive was obvious, as the General supported the Cortés Madariaga
mission there in favor of union. Mill's suggestion, therefore, hit home
with Roscio and gave strong support, as well, to his friend Miranda's
dream of "Colombia." The unionist thrust in 1811, therefore, had three
enthusiastic champions: Mill, Miranda, and Roscio. And the readers
should keep in mind that the vaunted first Panama Congress was still
ten years away!

Here were Burke's principal arguments in favor of a Spanish
American General Government, later called "*The United States of South
America and Mexico*." First, without such a union, South America
would be so weak that it would disintegrate from internal strife,
following the example of Europe's weakness. A Napoleon would
emerge but that type of union would be nothing more than "degrading
slavery." The persuasive Burke added:

> What good is experience, if we do not take advantage of its lessons?
> The nature of man is about the same in all countries; and similar causes
> should always produce equal effects. Europe and North America offer
> two great and notable examples. The latter, is the result of a new and
> elaborative system of confederation, founded on equal rights, and
> reciprocal interests, and by which 17 large and independent States,
> among themselves, are intimately united by firm bonds of liberty and
> peace; and the former [Europe] is the result of a general humiliation and
> slavery, after a large and melancholic series of struggle, war, and
> misery, which has been the product of the fierce and unrestrained
> independence of the despots [and] legislators of their different States.

Anarchy and devastation has been the pattern. To a European who
grieves at that record: he wonders how long—"Oh if they were too
many [years]!"—before they could form a general confederation on the
North American pattern. Second, now is the time to erect your cement

pillars for "that great structure of Liberty and Peace in Southern America." It is important to remember that: "The separate and distinct Governments, established like those in Europe, according to the reigning passions," will all end up with "the same sufferings, and the same calamitous catastrophes that have overwhelmed Europe." Roscio joined the chorus at this point. It is time to act: "Colombians, the destiny of your country is in your hands." You can follow the European path to misfortune, or the American route to liberty and happiness.[26]

William Burke—more exactly, James Mill—not only elaborated upon and sold the "principle of representation" that sparked the first gleamings of a projected inter-American system for Spanish America; he was also the first to develop what has been called by Latin Americanists "The Western Hemisphere Idea." It was a sentiment shared by Americans of the New World that they were different from the Old World; their future was far more promising in every respect: political, economic, and social. It was an expanded version of the North American "Manifest Destiny," that U.S. historians have applied to the agricultural expansionism of their country. The late Professor Arthur Preston Whitaker of the University of Pennsylvania popularized the concept in a book entitled: *The Western Hemisphere Idea* (1954).[27] My work on the British influence in Central America demonstrated the practical application of the "Idea" in the British-American rivalry at mid-nineteenth century.[28] Therefore, it was a welcomed surprise to find out that James Mill, for all practical purposes, was the first to invent the "Idea"; and it was one that was very strong among Spanish Americans at the time of Independence.

It came up in the context of a publicist trying to sell the U.S. model to the "other Americans," that Mill felt it logical to develop—as we have already noted above—a scenario of two strong contenders: America versus Europe, or New World versus Old World. It was a clever argument, revealing a sharp mind at work. Here is how Burke presented it:

> Whoever does not perceive the total political and moral difference that exists between the circumstances of the new and old world, cannot help but have some very imperfect views of the situation relative to each other, or of the just and liberal policy which the grand interests of the former invite and demand.

To begin with, "the New World is 7 times larger than Europe; 14 million square miles versus 2 (with 150 million Europeans); and the Americas have only one tenth of that figure of '*población civilizada*' (civilized inhabitants)." Burke continued: "Besides, this population with regards to language, customs, government and laws, has only two great divisions which are the English of North America and the Spanish of the South." Europe, by contrast, consists of

> 100 distinct states, that have diverse languages, governments and interests and that almost always are engaged in disputes and internal wars. Finally, Americans, differing from the European People, possess a territory that demands at least a population 20 times larger than the present [one]: amounting to a ratio of *one person* for each square mile, whereas in the same space, there is in Europe *seventy persons*.

At this point, someone—not James Mill—added a question: "So where is the similarity between such a state of affairs and a part of Europe, that demands that we adopt the illiberal and restrictive policy of the latter, just because of injustice or the unfortunate circumstances that some of our states have followed her [Spain's] example?" The misguided states in question were those of Coro, Maracaibo, and Guayana in Venezuela—a statement that Roscio seems to have added. Or possibly it was the translator Andrés Bello.[29]

Burke's buildup of the "Western Hemisphere Idea" continued: European practices historically, or in the contemporary period, were not worthy of imitation: The Roman and Greek monopoly of citizenship, the pillaging of conquered territories and the enslavement of their people, "as if the Cities of Greece and Rome were the only ones on earth; and their Citizens the only portion of humankind worthy of being free." Is that the model that Americans should follow? Of course, not! Nor is the example of Europe's class structure—a violation of nature that separates the rich and powerful elite from the numerous poor: "the former of oppressors, the latter of the oppressed." We do not need to establish that same system here.

> Those who recommend the adoption of such elements do not have an exact idea of the real interests of that great Continent. No: The situation of the New World, entirely different from all parts of the old [Old World], dictates the need for a policy equally distinct. To be truthful, America is like no other nation: she only resembles herself;

and the man who cannot see her true point of view [essence] should have a very small influence in the determination of her destiny.[30]

The editorial continued in the February 26th issue of the *Gazeta* with a philosophical synthesis that reminds us of Whitaker's "Western Hemisphere Idea," as well as the "Manifest Destiny" view of U.S. historians, depicting the agricultural expansion of the United States in the first half of the nineteenth century. Burke expounded it in the following words:

> It seems that the New World was destined by providence, in the course of things, to be a beautiful area in which human happiness and reformed Governments would present themselves [to the World's eye]. The extension and fertility [of the area]; its small population and almost a uniformity of languages, governments, laws, customs, and even its location, sheltered from the disputes and the power [struggle] of Europe, all invite it to bring about the consolidation of a grand and beneficient system of union, liberty, peace, and industry founded on the rights and interests of all its Citizens. The northern part of the American Continent has begun this great work; it is now up to South America, following such a glorious example, to unite all the present States, and those formed subsequently, into a confederation, equally just and happy, of equal liberty and of equal rights to bring about the perfection of such a great enterprise. What other policy could guide us with more justice and utility than [the example] of that Nation that presents to us [a picture] of a happy experience of most fortunate successes? Americans need not retrograde to the free Peoples of antiquity, nor go over the ocean to find examples that might guide their political institutions among the oppressed nations and the remains of feudal Europe. In their own Continent, they have among themselves an incomparably superior model of those produced in the world; and despite the abuse of the enemies of liberty, it [the United States] cannot help but be, as they have been with good cause, to all sensible and honest men, the object of admiration and imitation of mankind . . . What other nation, until now, has established the system of its Government on equal rights, based upon the most perfect liberty, industry, peace, and prosperity for all its citizens? History does not register one. Only the United States of North America manifest the dignified and happy spectacle of a Government rooted in a genuine nature of man; who is formed by his admirable wisdom and to his advantage; that leads him constantly to his happiness via the sure path of labor and justice, and that rests on his concerns which are his firmest column, and should be the support of

such a Government. The latter evidently directs itself to put into action all the virtues of mankind, which are the object of its interests; while a sad experience [elsewhere] demonstrates that all other forms of Government sacrifice, to some extent, to their vested interest the People's welfare and [thus] produce in the society almost the same unfortunate effects as the sickness of the particular organs on the animal body, converting the marrow and the wholesome, healthy parts, destined for comfort and general well-being, into a corrupt mass of offensive and harmful disgusting matter. Thus, there emerges [in society] the extremes of luxury and misfortune, and the contrast of vice and virtue that we see in all ancient societies. Who can bear to see: in those countries where the multitude is destined to [a life of] indigence, and misery, and obligated by hunger and nakedness, and the terror of the gallows, the affliction and the infamy, to commit crimes that frighten their souls; where the hard-heartedness of the oppressors, never shows compassion for misery, refuses to hear the groans of the unfortunate, and raises a sumptuous splendor upon the remains and the tears, that its corrupt ambition and wanton greediness has afflicted upon the victims of oppression and poverty?[31]

Burke's concern for bad government and the abuse of popular interests still obsessed him in the editorials of March 1st and 5th, 1811. "Let us not insult Providence or Nature," he lectured, "attributing to each individual the evils of mankind, whose origin derive from the faults and vices of governments, and the ambition and selfishness of government officials." Good governments, however, like those in the United States, use constructive ideas and imagination in the operation of government. It is in this constructive vein, that the wise American nation

has sustained an uninterrupted peace for nearly thirty years, among the convulsions, the alternatives of incentives and threats, the plunder and insults of the rest of the civilized world; and she has served as a refuge for a large number of individuals, who, victims of the malicious guidance and the vices of their Governments, have become useful and important citizens, from the time they set foot in a free and happy land, attracted by its promise.

William Burke again sang the praises of the young American nation:

It is for this reason that the North American Republic is the first Nation, of which there is memory that has founded its polity upon just and equal rights, peace and the prosperity of the human race; and the only one whose example is worthy of being imitated by the People of South America upon establishing their glorious edifice to liberty and independence; and imitation which is the more necessary in view of the parallels of their circumstances; their interests, their own happiness, and that of their posterity.[32]

William Burke recognized that a vulnerable point in his argument in behalf of the U.S. model was the amount of territory that it could cover effectively and still achieve the same results. This is how he defended himself on that score:

This great Nation, as large as all Europe, demonstrates in practice [the reality], which is the best proof, that the extension [of a nation] is no obstacle to union, when a nation adopts a *free and representative plan*; and this system is capable, on the contrary, to embrace easily a much larger territory, without the slightest inconvenience or danger to the liberty of any Citizen, because in the North American Confederation, as we have pointed out* (footnote that cites a previous discourse), and will be further discussed later in a more extended form, each State retains its independence and individual sovereignty, and it has a constitution, government and laws of its own, is only subject to a General Government in matters dealing with union, defense, and prosperity of the WHOLE. Not important [here now] is the apparent difficulty in the communication of the diverse States: that [difficulty] will be less each day, in proportion to the increase in population and [internal] improvements; and this [the population] will increase marvelously under the system of a general confederation.

To prove the point that an American confederation could control an extensive area like Spanish America, the wily publicist reminded his readers that Spain, operating from a different continent, controlled the Americas for over three hundred years with a Council of the Indies. And she did this with an "anti-social and unnatural policy"—embodied in the "Fortress-America" metaphor that Burke had invented. If the tyrant mother country could do it, Burke asked:

could one say that a general free government, located in its own territory, founded upon the interests of equal rights of all its States, and administered by its own Citizens, for the strength and happiness of ALL, [and said government] could not be able to persuade all the settlements to subscribe to an adequate and unanimous cooperation?

Of course it could.   American patriotism would carry the day.
Assuming that he had convinced his readers, Burke urged them not to
waste any more time in preparing to enact their constitutions.   To
prevent any sabotage, they should move to limit executive power to its
expressed objectives, and no more; changing often the men who hold
that power. Above all, Burke urged South Americans to be cautious
and to consider events carefully.   All the while, "millions of
publications" should circulate preparing the people for their future
constitution.[33] By February 8, 1811, Burke and his editor Roscio had
done a good job of getting the Gazeta's readers primed for the opening
session of the Constituent Assembly on March 2, 1811.

Subsequent editorials in the series dealt with key documents and
constitutional highlights in the legal tradition of England and the United
States. "It is a maxim of British and American law," Mill asserted
proudly, "that everyone's house is his castle. It cannot be searched, or
anyone's papers or property be taken from it except as allowed in a
legal process . . . and in the space of time there is from dawn until the
sun set." He also explained the "Act of Habeas Corpus," how it
developed in English history, etc., etc.   Much time was spent on
discussing "Trial by Jury," and what procedures were in order. Mill
boasted that even at present it is one of the "great bastions of civil
liberty" in England and the United States, assuring the people of their
rights. "If my recommendation," Burke assured his readers, "could
influence the adoption here of this firm column of the Temple of
liberty, I would be pleased for the rest of my life, and perhaps even
proud with what I had contributed to the regeneration of this great
Continent." Mill's partner Bentham perhaps was the author of that
remark; it was more in keeping with his reaction to public acclaim. In
addition, "our" William Burke offered his readers: laudable principles
of "No Taxation without Representation," the prohibition of "ex post
facto laws," as well the celebrated amendment procedures to the
constitution. Since the Sociedad Patriótica de Venezuela was founded
in early 1811, Burke's remarks on the role of patriotic societies in the
United States were especially meaningful.   Their assistance was
invaluable in forming the bases for the new government. In Venezuela,
they could be helpful in furthering the cause of "UNION, LIBERTY,
AND INDEPENDENCE of the common Fatherland."   A patriotic
society could undermine the opposition to independence, preventing
them from reestablishing "their vile and abominable tyranny on the
ruins of our nascent LIBERTAD AMERICANA."[34]

It would be more appropriate for our next chapter to treat Burke's editorial of February 19, 1811, on "Religious Toleration," a key item in the Bill of Rights mentioned earlier in the *Gazeta*. It was also a key point in Mill's "Thoughts of an Englishman," published in Caracas on January 25th. In keeping with Mill's preoccupation for abuses of the people's sovereignty, religious toleration was an imperative in a modern democratic society. The past had shown how well the Church served the King in subverting the people's rights. Ironically, this controversial editorial on February 19th was accompanied by other articles in which Roscio commended, "The Mode of Procedure in the House of Commons of England," by Jeremy Bentham which Miranda had brought with him to Venezuela.[35] A second installment followed in the next issue of the *Gazeta*. The impending Constituent Assembly of Venezuela would welcome these guidelines in their sessions, thus preventing any repetition in Venezuela of the French "*sanculotismo*," the excesses reached by the disorderly revolutionary body in France.[36]

The right of suffrage and the topic of elections, as might be expected from James Mill and Jeremy Bentham, commanded a great deal of Burke's attention in the first regular series on U.S. institutions. The editorial on February 22nd was especially relevant, because it illustrated in masterly form man's advancement in representative government from the Classical Era forward with particular attention to the English contribution to the theme:

> The case study of England which is the cradle of the representative system, provides us with [a record of] its imperfect growth, [serving] more as an instructive lesson rather than a felicitous development of its most complete application.
>
> From its inception, there was evidently a great mistake in the application of the suffrage to certain properties and places rather than to persons. Thus, the state of the suffrage in England at present reveals all the defective variety and contradiction that might have been produced by such an imperfect institution in different times and circumstances. Only a small portion of the People is represented: only the man who belongs to a corporation has the vote, or who has an income from some small feud or rent; whereas the settlers that are unincorporated, or who have a personal property, a hundred times greater and acquired through industry and talents, are deprived of this right. The County of Middlesex, which includes the larger part of the population and riches of London, does not have more than 20,000 or 30,000 votes, and does not send to Parliament more than two deputies;

while the ancient Sahram, and other comparable *Villas* [Charter Towns] which do not have but a dozen inhabitants that belong to them, each sends two representative Deputies. The populous and opulent Cities of Manchester, Birmingham and Sheffield do not have any vote at all, because they were not in existence when representation was conceded to *Places*. Here is the origin for the imperfection and inequality in England's representation; here was the reason that a large portion of the population and riches of this country was not represented; and, finally, here was the principal origin of corruption in Government and the misfortunes of the People. It is a well known fact that a grand portion of the members in the House of Commons, or the popular branch of the English Parliament; have been restored [assigned] to the Towns belonging to the Lords, who appointed their political partisans to represent those places, filling the position the same as was done before by the original units. These representatives are required to follow the politics of their patrons, who with the influence of those [partisans] always acquire new powers and emoluments from the incumbent Ministers, and elevate their private fortunes upon the ruins of the People's freedom and the sufferings of the Country. Thus, the evildoers by corrupting the majority of the Houses of Parliament are able to emasculate the healthy brake of the People upon the Government. Their first step was to prolong parliament from three to seven years, by which they completed their corruption more easily. Having obtained a constant majority, the ministerial despotism has continued firmly [and] that has finally destroyed the name of English liberty, and has oppressed the country with harms and losses, unknown in the history of nations. If it had not been for the system of Ministerial despotism, the corruption that has resulted from a defective representation, the English ministry never would have succeeded in invading the just rights and liberty of the colonials in 1774, despite the interests and desires of the English public; nor would it have promoted fearlessly a war, which removed forever England's dominion over an important and large portion of the North American Continent . . . Such were some of the pernicious effects of the partial and imperfect exercise of the right of suffrage in England.[37]

Although James Mill and his colleague Dr. John Allen—one as a liberal and the other a conservative—had strong ideological differences, they shared similar views on laissez-faire economics, as students of Adam Smith; and they agreed that economic development in Spanish America should emphasize stability in which the non-whites would share in the prosperity, finally achieving political equality with the whites. The difference between the two Scots was who would control this protectorate system. Allen wanted the Europeans (Spaniards and those Creoles closely associated with them), working either under Spain or as an independent nation, to lead the country along benevolent and enlightened objectives, such as representative government and free trade. Mill, on the other hand, favored the American leadership to achieve the same objectives but without the outside influences; yet, he decidedly favored the point that compromise should guide the new Republic with no prejudice against Europeans willing to abide by national interests. Both Scots advocated property qualifications for voters; limited suffrage for non Whites as a reality until they satisfied the property requirement. Although they may have both started with more democratic objectives in the suffrage, the French Revolution, and its excesses, had tempered their beliefs along more moderate lines. This was typical for responsible people everywhere in the world; Allen and Mill were not exceptions at all. In Mill's discussions on the French Revolution and the Haitian Revolution of the 1790s, there was no question whatever as to his aversion to "mob" action of the masses, being mislead by irresponsible persons. Nevertheless, he had faith in the potential of the middle class to achieve the type of government that emerged in the United States of America. With much empathy, he described the various practices and restraints offered by the electoral system of the young Republic. On the suffrage issue, he felt that it was useless and inappropriate to divide citizens into "First Class" (*Activos*) or "Second Class" (*Pasivos*). Then, he provided a long explanation on his view of the vote.

> The right of suffrage, as I have said, belongs to the citizen by virtue of his natural right to govern himself. This is the only means by which the People generally or individually exercise their right of sovereignty; it is the origin of purity or corruption in Government; and the only restraint that the Nation can place on its governors. Let there not be more restrictions than those that the circumstances of the State make necessary for its security; and let us not mark the forehead of anyone with the degrading denomination of *pasivo* [second class]. Those who contribute honorably with their labor and industry to the support or defense of the State, are active [first class] citizens: but for the exercise of civil rights, they must be subjected to qualifications with regard to property; conforming with the just and equitable principle that, since the individual's independence is exposed to the influence of corrupt and ambitious persons, it is necessary that the person using the suffrage, votes in the affairs of the State, should possess property that would make him inaccessible to such a dangerous and injurious influence.

This requisite is of absolute necessity for the true liberty of the State; and should be approved by all well-intentioned and responsible men, even when he does not, at that time, have the necessary qualifications; because his rights of life, liberty and property, will be with such a precaution more firmly secured from the machinations of the intriguers.[38]

Dr. Allen, of course, would not disagree with this point of view.

By March 5, 1811, William Burke had almost finished his second series of editorials—the first, the introductory group; and, second, the one on political institutions. Having developed his main arguments, from now on, he summarized his findings and facts, bringing everything together for the reader. He reminded him of the importance of encouraging immigrants to South America, repeating what he had written before. This good teacher wanted his points to be thoroughly understood and incorporated into the knowledge of his students. "It is evident," Mill insisted,

that all countries where REPRESENTATION is the principal fount of government and of public and private rights, never will any precaution be superfluous in maintaining [the above] as pure as in their origin. To achieve this end, the laws of England and the United States supervise their elections with the greatest scrupulosity and delicacy. They are always public; troops can only be stationed at a certain distance from the place where they are celebrated; and no man can enter the election zone with offensive arms. If there is proof that bribery, intimidation, or undue influence took place, the corrupt parties are punished.

Such were the precautions for honest elections.[39]

"Freedom of the Press" was Burke's topic on March 5, 1811. "It is nothing else but," Mill lectured, "the freedom that the People have to express their opinions on the beginnings of government and the conduct of public ministers." Moreover, in all free countries, it has been regarded "as the most important in the conservation of the nation's liberty:" "announcing very early the approximation of despotism, declaring against corruption, and stripping away disguise or ambition, whatever its form might take." Proud of the English tradition, Mill continued:

no matter where we might begin the history of England since she has been known by the works of public writers, we can observe the benefits that the liberty of the press has conferred upon that country and the major part that it has played in the establishment and defense of popular liberty, a genuine origin of its actual power and greatness . . . The spirit of a free press was transferred from England to the savages of North America by her robust sons, which united to their formidable national sword, we have seen it [the spirit] perfect a revolution in time, favoring human rights and happiness, unknown in the history of the world. Although both nations [United States and England] love the liberty of the press, just as the People love their liberty, and appreciate [the free press] as principal distributor of the intellectual knowledge and pleasures, she is [still] restricted by distant and adequate laws so that it does not degenerate into license. Every man is free to publish what he wants; but he remains personally responsible for all that he has published.

Here, Mill went into details on how libel would be prosecuted and punished. "Thus," Mill concluded, "the fact is that although the press is free, each man must use it at his own risk."[40]

Those were Mill's concluding remarks on "civil rights"—an impressive and significant contribution to the ideology of Venezuela's independence movement.

Chapter Ten

Issues of a Precarious Independence

> We, therefore, the Representatives of the People of South America and
> Mexico, basing our pretensions on the eternal principles of justice and
> the imprescriptible rights of man, and of nations . . . in the name and by
> the authority of the mentioned People, we declare solemnly and
> proclaim:
>   That all the Kingdoms, Provinces and places of South America and
> Mexico; as much on the Continent and on their Islands, and formerly
> known by the name of Spanish America, are effectively, because of
> Spain's conquest, and what by right should be, *Free and Independent
> States* under the name and title of *United States of South America and
> Mexico*: that they, in future, are absolved from all alliance with the
> Crown of Spain; and of her political pretensions, or that of any other
> nation or individual.
>   Fundamentals for a declaration of INDEPENDENCE*
>   *Gazeta de Caracas*, March 29, 1811.[1]

Just as the crisis of "December-January" led to the intervention of Juan
Germán Roscio into the Burkian editorials of the *Gazeta de Caracas*, a
new critical situation confronted him on March 2, 1811. Congress
opened its sessions on that date, which meant that within a few weeks
the Junta Suprema de Venezuela would relinquish power to the
National Congress. Roscio gave up his post as Secretary of State to
Miguel José Sanz on March 16th; and before the end of that month, he
also turned over the editorship of the *Gazeta* to Sanz. Roscio's role in
Venezuela would now have to focus in the new congress, as the
recently-elected representative from his native district of Calabozo in

the Province of Caracas; and Francisco Javier Uztáriz, his intimate colleague on the Junta, won the post in the nearby district of San Sebastián. No matter where they served, they would be leaders because of their excellent qualifications. Yet, there was a drop in prestige, at least initially; and Roscio wanted to be sure that his projects would continue to flourish and be respected. It was therefore imperative for him to take over as "William Burke" for this final emergency; and, despite what he might have said later, it seems that he did not relinquish the Burkian manuscript to his successor Sanz; at least, not until he made final arrangements for the publication of the two volumes. That was after Independence on July 5, 1811; so that the Burkian manuscript remained in his hands and was silent as far as the continued publication of the last series of editorials by James Mill. This lapse in the Burkian schedule is explained later in the "asterisk caper," which arose from the editorial of March 29, 1811—Roscio's last intervention as "Wm. Burke" for several months. It is the footnote to the introductory quotation in this chapter: *"Fundamentos para una declaración de INDEPENDENCIA.*"

The first indication of Roscio's will to take over the pseudonym of "William Burke" was in connection with Mill's discussion on the "Freedom of the Press." Roscio felt that Venezuela would have to be an exception to that cherished concept. He explained: "But it is very opportune to observe that the perfect freedom of the press is more appropriate to a nation in [already enjoying] a state of liberty and security, than one in a transition from slavery to the enjoyment of its rights." Here, Roscio voiced the same concern we noted in Miranda's January letter to Bogotá: the innocence of a people corrupted by a vicious colonial system. This was a constant concern during the sessions of the National Congress in Venezuela before independence. Roscio articulated it well:

> The press in honorable and patriotic hands will produce an immense benefit, spreading just views of our rights and interests, especially in a country like this one, where the population is so dispersed. But we should all anticipate a corresponding danger in which she [the Press] might be a captive of intriguing and malicious people, taking advantage of her to carry out the criminal objectives of their perfidy and ambition. While a portion of the People is still ignorant of the true nature of its rights, it can be seduced by tricks and disguises.[2]

That was the gist of Roscio's qualifications to Mill's earlier remarks on freedom of the press in the English-speaking world.

From March 5 to March 29, 1811, the "new" William Burke did not abandon James Mill's influence from the earlier editorials; on the contrary, he merely hispanicized it; put it in an idiom that Venezuelans could recognize easily because of their customs and history. Roscio, moreover, clothed it with classical structures and flowery words that often characterized his own style of writing. His experience as a lawyer in the Spanish colonial system explains the terms and images evoked that a Scotsman would not have used without having lived in the area. Here is one of Roscio's typical speeches with my italics added:

> *Comparad*, Americanos [*Compare*, O ye Americans!] this free and rational structure of Government and of laws, derived with majestic simplicity from eternal justice and the rights of man, and whose shadow distributes to everyone equitably its protection and benefits; *Comparadla* [*Compare it*—the structure] with the horrible and odious tyranny, whose only basis is the most unjust and arbitrary power; its only objectives are oppression and pillage; and whose only restraint is the insatiableness and whim of the devourers under whom this country has groaned for more than three centuries. *Comparadla* with the apolitical system of the 'Council of the Indies' that kept you eternally in the weakness of infancy in order to monopolize the benefits of your labor and industry; compare her with the despotic rule of your Viceroys and Captains General, with the unlimited authority of your 'Courts of Appeal' and other tribunals, with their undivided power, their secret decisions, and arbitrary imprisonment; with the corrupt greed of all [of them], and the countless vexations and humiliations that you suffered from them; and finally with the nullity, or more exactly the imponderable abuse of having to appeal to the courts of your oppressors, and at a distance of 5,000 miles, against the excesses of the agents that they had sent here to keep you in [the state of] slavery. *Compárense* [Compare] such things and [then answer this:] Who is the honorable man, who is the man of means that will deny that the time of independence has arrived to dispense with the catastrofe of Spain, to remove the monsters causing such horrible evil, and to place the lives, liberty, and property of the American People under the safeguard of laws founded on the principles of equal justice and natural right? *Acordaos, Americanos* [Just remember, Ye Americans] that they were your rights [even] before Governments began. They are the patrimony of Heaven; and not any

corporation under any title or pretext whatsoever can legitimately
deprive you of them.[3]

Throughout the exhortations, Roscio blended his own experiences as a
lawyer under Spanish rule with what he had gleaned from Mill's wise
editorials on man and his government.

Mill's metaphor on "Fortress-America" was uppermost in Roscio's
mind as he prepared these final editorials of March, 1811:

> The fact is that even if Spain recovers her independence, for which there
> is no hope at all, you cannot return to your former dependency without
> sacrificing the dearest rights and interests of your country, your own
> honor, and your rights as men and as citizens, to a dependency marked
> with all the traits of the vilest external and internal slavery, that deprives
> you barbarously from all communication with the rest of mankind, that
> denies your country the common benefits of nature, closing your ports,
> suppressing your trade, impeding your manufactures, extinguishing
> industries, and paralyzing agriculture and the increase in population;
> thus attacking directly the origin of America's power and prosperity with
> no other object in mind but to assure the monopoly of your products.
> Add to this national system of external deprivation and slavery, the
> internal subordination, and the oppression in which the citizens born in
> this country have suffered, in which they have existed [virtually] without
> life, just to reinforce even more their chains and to maintain the line of
> their policy. What American could call himself free in his own country,
> [under those conditions]?

The patriot Roscio worked himself into a frenzy as he thought more
and more of Spain's "denaturalized system" of government in the
Americas. Spanish arbitrariness was unbearable, denying Americans
any say in the judicial, legislative, and executive branches of their
government. This was a "horrible oppression" that lasted three long
centuries! Is this what those persons "who counsel loyalty and
adherence to the Mother Country" want to restore? "You vile
hypocrites, simpletons!" "You must know," Roscio cried out angrily,
"that your first loyalty and attraction are towards your country; and that
it would be treason, a denaturalized treason, to permit her to be
devoured by a monster under the name of Mother."[4]

One of Roscio's greatest concerns—and which he lamented often
many years later—was the prospects of a grand betrayal on the part of
Americans themselves. He wanted so deeply to avenge the Spanish

massacre in Quito, Ecuador, in early August, 1810; but he felt that this might not occur because of the possibility of a cynical betrayal. The Bishop of Cuenca's defiance of Bogotá's government was a case in point, riling up Americans to support his treasonous actions. Suppose the new Archbishop of Venezuela, a Spaniard by the name of Narcisco Coll y Prat, should pose a similar threat to the Venezuelan nation in embryo. The Archbishop Narciso's speech to the Venezuelan Constituent Congress on March 2, 1811, emphasized the religion of Jesus Christ and its deep significance for man's history and future. This ex-student of theology had doubts about him; Roscio was becoming paranoid on this point. That is why he wanted independence as soon as possible, so that a potential betrayal would not force the stillbirth of his nation.

Connected with the concern of an American betrayal, Juan Germán Roscio likewise was obsessed with the prospects of a real challenge to Venezuelan independence coming from the so-called "Cádiz Experiment" in southern Spain—a reform program that, in effect, was outlining a liberal constitutional government for Spain. Moreover, it was humanistic as well as religious, at least in theory. That is what made it dangerous in Roscio's eyes, since it would be easy for Spaniards to persuade and fool the "people" of Venezuela to gather around the royalist side of the coin. Since the news reached Venezuela that on September 24, 1810, the Spanish Parliament opened its doors, Roscio, and his friend Uztáriz, had been attacking the much "ballyhooed" (*cacareadas*) *Cortes de España* as just another cheap distraction to fool the citizens of the New World. "There will be," Roscio's "Wm. Burke" pontificated: "the same sacrifice of America's great interests . . . under the mask of legal and constitutional forms." Alarmed at the possibility of transferring the Spanish monarchy to the New World once Spain fell to Napoleon, Roscio objected with vehemence and disdain:

> For this to happen, it would be necessary for America to continue being deceived with words alone; it would be essential for the American people to be *entirely incapacitated* and even *not to have the right* to administer their own affairs; and who, submitting their necks to the yoke of a foreign throne, which they solicited as convenient, would come here under the name of Ferdinand VII, or by right of their relationship in the event of death, captivity, or influence of France over the latter [Ferdinand VII], or to relieve the Americans of the annoying mandate

of governing themselves, and their extensive country. The Mines of Mexico and of Peru, Ah!, how many guileful glances are thrown your way from the other side of the Atlantic![5]

In paragraph after paragraph, the "new" William Burke pleaded pathetically for Americans to open their eyes and to take the initiative and declare independence, once and for all. If they failed to do so, he concluded dejectedly:

the progress of this great country would be miserably retarded; this would, indeed, give us nothing more than the [old] Spanish America; and in less than a half century; if the power of Europe does not forestall the event, the free and progressive population of North America, will extend itself toward the South and the West, attracted by the discontent of its oppressed neighbors; pour like a torrential wave over all of Mexico, and then all over South [America], uprooting the name and language of Spain, and taking over the countries that are unworthy of their exploitive Government. I am not prompted to say this, nor do I wish to suggest the slightest suspicion that the Government or the People of the United States, hold in their minds the idea of conquest. I am convinced of the contrary, that no other country has purer designs. But no one can respond to future events [only]; and the past experience of the world appears to teach us that a People that are incapable of enjoying and defending their country, should cede it, therefore, to those who can do this [for themselves]. Our entry itself on this earth, [the Conquest, that is], is a memorable case in point.[6]

At this juncture, Juan Germán Roscio felt that the time had come to advance the vaunted dream of union for all Spanish America that Mill had raised with his remarks on the "Western Hemisphere Idea" and which Roscio and Miranda pushed aggressively in late 1810 and in early 1811, during the December–January events. On March 19, 1811, the "new" William Burke proposed the following program of action:

The fact remains, Americans, that in order to conserve your country, and leave it to your descendants free and happy, as you should, it is absolutely necessary to repel from your midst the system of Spanish despotism, and proceed without loss of time to organize in all of the Continent a government founded upon the rights and interests of the American People, the only base upon which it can rest with justice and security. In this manner, you will put a stop forever to the injurious and degrading pretensions of all foreigners, and you will then witness the unfolding of the good things of which we have spoken, placing it in a high rank of prosperity and *as the great and permanent fortress* [these are my italics., M.R.] that her multiple proportions give her reason to expect by right and justice.[7]

James Mill should have been proud of Roscio's positive application of the metaphor "Fortress-America"—South America as a great source of prosperity!

On March 26th, Roscio introduced William Burke under the general title "Continental Congress," in which he proceeded to present much vital information on the project of "Union." To speed up the political process throughout Venezuela, he utilized Mill's "Summary" of the political editorials that ended on March 5th. This valuable digest assisted Venezuelans in the provinces in setting up their state governments and facilitating the election of their representatives for the National Congress. Many of the states, as it turned out, were unable to keep up with the pace set by the Province of Caracas; and by presenting Mill's summary, Roscio hoped to avoid any serious repercussions within the National Congress, dominated, as it was, by a huge majority of Caracas' representatives.[8]

Roscio's next move was to explain the project for a Continental Government, insisting upon certain shortcuts that would expedite its first meeting at Bogotá, the most favorable site for that purpose, in his opinion. The "new" William Burke suggested that representatives already elected for government in the cities of Caracas, Santa Fe de Bogotá, and Buenos Aires should proceed at once to the suggested capital city at Bogotá, permitting their elected alternates to take over the vacated offices in their respective governments. Thus, the Continental Congress could begin to operate immediately as a "rump" body until representatives from all over Spanish America arrived to take their seats in the new general government.

Bogotá's selection reflected well Roscio's political and organizational judgment: it was flattering to the people in New Granada's jurisdiction; Venezuelans and future Colombians could travel overland to that capital; Buenos Aires' agents were asked to proceed to Chile, embarking there with their Chilean colleagues to a northern port on the Pacific that would lead them to the desired location; Lima and contiguous regions could do likewise; and Mexicans had various options, via the Pacific to that northern port and via the Caribbean water route to the port of Cartagena, and other nearby ports that had routes up to Bogotá. At the temporary capital of Bogotá, the delegates to the General Continental Congress would elect a President and other officers of that body; they would commence the discussions on the State of the Union, what principles and objectives should be followed by their Continental structure; they would also declare the rights and interests of America, listing their grievances against the former mother country, and discuss the methods of implementing the Continental Government's laws, etc., etc. Roscio, the orator, could not resist this outburst: "Sublime Spectacle! How truly deprecating it would appear, by comparison, the vile and selfish ambition of any usurper whatever, even though he might try to disguise it with the ostentatious title of Emperor, Inca, or King."[9] There was no question about it: this "William Burke" was a "Republican" of the New World, as opposed to the "Monarchist" of the Old World.

In the final editorial of March 29, 1811, Roscio's "William Burke" presented one of the longest lists of grievances that this writer has ever seen—the faults that Americans had noted in their relationship with their European mother. The Secretary of State of the ex-Junta Suprema de Venezuela, in effect, had presented every grievance that he thought of before, during, and after April 19, 1810, with regards to Spain, as well as those that he had received from Americans all over the Western Hemisphere in his correspondence with them. Many of them were found in Venezuela's official documentation, many were published in the gazettes, especially under Roscio's charge, and many appeared in William Burke's editorials, mainly those of the "new" writer in the December–January epoch and now in March, 1811.

The final lines of this key historical document appear in the introductory quotation of this chapter. The project was most definitely inter-American and continental: "*United States of South America and Mexico.*"[10] Since Burke's editorials, and later his two-volume set, ran under the banner of "Rights of South America and Mexico," we can assert that James Mill, the "original" William Burke, who was determined to highlight the significance of the United States model, as well as the "Western Hemisphere Idea," had in mind the establishment of one super government of the former Spanish America that would join with the Northerners' equivalent in supervising the manifest destiny of the New World.

The last editorial of March 29th, it will be recalled, carried a subtitle: "Fundamentals of a declaration of INDEPENDENCE (*)" with its asterisk pointing to a footnote: "(*) *Entiéndese como teoría* *política.*" The English translation is: "Let this be understood as political theory." This "asterisk caper," which we shall develop in later sections of this chapter, demonstrated from the very beginning that the Burkian editorial of that date would be highly controversial. After all, it announced to the world that Spanish America was not only breaking her ties with European Spain, she was also about to establish a super government of Spanish America, following the example of the United States of America in the North. Who would be threatened by such an action? Certainly, Spain and her supporters in America would do their best to discredit and resist such a move! In the politics of Venezuela, of course, the "states' righters" would be unwilling to sacrifice their interests in their area for some super government in Bogotá, or elsewhere in South America and Mexico, etc. Opposition groups would challenge Burke's faith and interpretation of the principle of representation over such a large territory. They might tend to counter Burke's objective by insisting that two general confederations should be formed: one, at the capital in Mexico City and the other, the capital in Bogotá, etc. In short, however popular the movement might become with the Roscios and the Mirandas at the time of Independence, there would still be a constant and heavy resistance to the idea of union at any level. My point is that this resistance, whatever its intensity of feeling, was evident from the start. Miguel Sanz, the new Secretary of State in the Venezuelan government, placed that asterisk there, not out of meanness or because Roscio, his predecessor, had been responsible for the project, but merely because it might complicate Venezuela's relationship with Great Britain and other powers, etc. etc. Moreover, this resistance even reached the documents in question; new editions of editorials published, and especially in the varied sources used by contemporary editors, or revisors of the two volumes of Burke's essays, introduced new phrases or clauses that gave the impression that there were two confederations considered in the project. To complicate matters even more, there were concurrent articles in the various gazettes, including the *Gazeta de Caracas*, that further confused the issue. We do not wish to belabor the point here; suffice it to say, in another chapter where Burke dealt with the U.S. Constitution of 1787, he was aware of the fact that tampering had taken place in his original editorials; and he argued that the two-confederation approach had been used in the United States by the opposition to the Constitution of 1787; fortunately, he concluded, the opposition had failed to carry the day; and the United States Republic was born and soon became prosperous.

* * * * * * * * * * * *

"To mix religion with political matters," wrote an Englishman whose "thoughts" appeared in the *Gazeta de Caracas* (January 25, 1811): "is to distract it from its true goal." It only helped to "forge the chains of despotism, thus enslaving men under the pretext of religion, profaning the Church, and making men traitors of their country."[11] Those were prophetic words in the Venezuelan context; and they indicate that James Mill must have learned a great deal from his friend Francisco de Miranda on church-state relations in the Hispanic experience. And even more so from José Blanco-White in London, whose experiences in the Catholic Church had embittered him on the relationship between Church and King. The Venezuelan Roscio developed a similar phobia as a student of theology. We have already alluded to Roscio's reaction to the Bishop of Cuenca vis-a-vis the Quito Massacre of August, 1810; and his deep suspicions about the Archbishop Narciso Coll y Pratt who harangued the opening session of Venezuela's first congress on March 2, 1811. As a matter of fact, Narciso of Caracas made a diplomatic presentation on that date. Yet, Roscio chose to think that Narciso's sincerity was questionable, when he spoke of the need to follow the human values of Christianity in the all-important task of forming a government and drawing up laws for their brethren.[12]

Roscio perhaps feared that Narciso sounded too much like many of the legislators at the *Cortes* of Cádiz. Since most men-of-the-cloth born in Spain or the nearby Islands in Europe were forever encouraging their parishioners in Venezuela to follow the Regency's lead and then that of the Spanish Parliament in more recent times, Roscio just could not trust him. These clerics shared the same political views as their secular counter-parts—Catalan and Basque merchants or seamen, Canarians (*Islenos* was the term used by Venezuelans) in various economic activities. They also had close contact with Venezuela's non whites: Indians, Blacks, *Pardos*, etc. They, therefore, could persuade the masses to favor the "Cádiz Experiment" of modernization, or liberalism, instead of the action supported by Roscio and the April 19th movement. Despite Roscio's disparaging views, the Cádiz program favored a new order of reforms to uplift the lower classes, integrating them and providing them with a greater degree of justice. The religious reformers at Cádiz, moreover, advocated a constructive and educational role for the Church in society. From the political point of view, a key tendency of Parliament's reforms was to preserve, for the moment at least, the ecclesiastical *fuero*, or privileges, enjoyed by religious corporations in Hispanic society everywhere. At Cádiz, both Spanish and American liberals subscribed to the fuero concession in order to assure the Church's support of the entire liberal reform program. The loyalist enemy in Venezuela, therefore, was not as debased and reactionary as Dr. Roscio and his cohorts on the Junta Suprema would have their partisans believe.

It was precisely that credibility of Spain's liberal program that provided a real challenge to Roscio's independence movement. It might very well lead to the betrayal of some Americans, that Roscio feared so much. That also helps to explain Roscio's apprehensiveness with regard to the freedom of the press in Venezuela.

By the end of January, 1811, Rosico's patience with the loyalist opposition was wearing thin. On January 22nd, Burke mentioned "Religious Toleration" in his discussion of the "Bill of Rights." Three days later, the Englishman's "Thoughts" in the *Gazeta* spoke out against the dangers of religious intervention in society. On January 29th, it was perhaps no coincidence that Roscio, the editor, reproduced the key correspondence between the Junta of Santa Fe de Bogotá and the Bishop of Cuenca (now, in southern Ecuador).[13] The open defiance of Cuenca's prelate, coupled with the arrogance suffered by the Junta de Venezuela in its correspondence with the Church hierarchy in the rebel cities of Coro and Maracaibo, led the Junta to authorize the publication of a strong editorial in the *Gazeta de Caracas* on February 19, 1811. It took the form of one of William Burke's editorials, dealing with the theme of "Religious Toleration."

Who was the author of Burke's controversial essay? Accustomed to borrowing the penname "William Burke," the finger points at Juan Germán Roscio, an author who borrowed heavily from James Mill's editorials on the usurpation of the people's sovereignty by monarchs, "Divine Rights" of "kings," etc. So, James Mill has to be given credit for much of the text on background in the first half of the piece. On the other hand, Roscio must have received letters, or even a copy of Mill's article on religious toleration, from London that supplied the second half of the piece; and, here, José Blanco-White's influence was strong. Interestingly, his information on the effects of the Edict of Nantes seems to have been from James Mill's writings, or conversations with him. We must remember that Andrés Bello initiated the contact between Blanco-White and Roscio; and General Miranda, in this case as well, may have been the carrier of this special essay. If so, it was not a part of the original William Burke manuscript, the same situation as with Miranda's January 15, 1811, contribution to Roscio's *Gazeta de Caracas*. Miranda's reaction to the Bishop of Cuenca in his January 22 letter to Bogotá also should be recalled. All of this, of course, contains much speculation; but there seems to be no question that the authorship was multiple, brought together by Roscio and perhaps Miranda as well.

The text of the editorial also offers special insights to the question of authorship. To begin with, a special footnote accompanied the document, consisting of two parts. In the bottom part of the footnote, the editor explained that the Junta Suprema had authorized the publication of *"Don Guillermo Burke"* because of its importance and with the understanding that rebuttals would be included in subsequent numbers of the *Gazeta de Caracas*. The top part of the footnote was written by "the author," or, at least that was the impression given to the reader. Although the theme in question was a delicate one for Catholics, the author hoped that Americans, and their clergy, would give him credit for desiring "to reestablish the purest Christian charity, and to promote the happiness of the country"—these points were evident in the latter half of the essay. His ideas were not in error, he maintained, and he was willing to listen to opposite views. Then followed this ambiguous statement:

> He is not afraid of being branded as irreligious; despite having been born in a Catholic country, the whole world knows how much it costs Irishmen to be so and because of this they have suffered thousands of vexations and the harshest political deprivations.

The reader, of course, jumped to the conclusion that Burke was Irish, assuming that the "Catholic country" was Ireland. Yet, it could have been Spain, Venezuela, etc. Why did Roscio and the Junta Suprema publish the author's note? Were they trying to protect themselves against the expected reaction to the editorial? Perhaps this was the case; but it is also conceivable that they merely reproduced a section that was part of the original document. Be that as it may, William Burke henceforth was known as the "Irish Catholic."[14] It is noteworthy that such a note was not unusual for a certain Catholic priest from southern Spain who often mentioned his Irish ancestry—the famous José María Blanco y Crespo, or Blanco-White.

The first half of the essay reminds us of the hard-hitting prose and style of James Mill angrily relating the abuses committed upon the people's sovereignty, along with good sections of synthesis. It appears that Roscio was so strongly influenced by those passages and their style that he was unconsciously imitating it; and it was effective when applied to an Hispanic tradition and context. The opening charge was almost bellicose: how the "rights" of the people had been usurped by kings in Spanish history. Blanco-White knew that argument from reading Spanish historians of a liberal bent; and Roscio, of course, was familiar with the famous memorial of Father Viscardo de Guzmán, which we have noted in earlier chapters. "William Burke" wrote as follows:

> Since the conquest or the fatal event that reunited into one sole Empire the various monarchies that existed on the Spanish Peninsula, the people there lost all of their liberty and the wise constitutions of Aragon and Valencia were forced to give way to the will and the caprice of unbridled and arbitrary authorities. 'I, the King, and because it is my will': from that time forward, these [words] became the only sources upon which to found all laws and orders, whose exclusive object was to flatter the passions of the governors. But since the people could not be so indolent, that they would always view with an indifferent eye that iron yoke under which the tyrants had them oppressed, the first concern of the latter was to hide their injustices and arbitrariness under the shield of religion. They made everyone believe that the authority of kings was not delegated by society but derived from heaven; that their very persons, even when they were tyrannizing, were inviolable; that their will was that of God himself and that no one could be a Christian who proclaimed the rights of man and society. Those were the accursed maxims of the despots and of their Ministers.

Equally bombastic and to the point, the second paragraph opened:

> But the apostles of tyranny could have worked in vain if, inducing fanaticism, they had not also deprived [the people] of the freedom to think and [thus] sanctified ignorance. In that context, therefore, all books that might teach the people their rights found themselves prohibited on grounds of being heretical; all that was heard was the languishing voice of the humble vassal and there was no entry there for the citizen, nor the wise man; and [it was] just to exclude foreigners from the country and impede their communication and their introduction and the progress of all useful and liberal knowledge in Spain; and, in 1478, a tribunal emerged for the first time there that, under the pretext of defending religion against the Moors and Jews, also sustained the

tyrants and sanctified ignorance and despotism. It matters not that the
objectives of this tribunal were entirely distinct from the one established
in Rome by Innocent II in 1204; it was enough that it condoned the
usurpation of power, as well as the oppressors; it matters not that it [the
Inquisition] uprooted from Spain more than 70,000 artisans and farmers;
although the workshops remained deserted and the fields untilled and
unpopulated, it sufficed that the lands of their owners were later
recognized as the property and inheritance of the despots. It matters
not, finally, that a tribunal that even now is called holy, trampled under
foot the laws of the Gospel; the issue was to affirm repeatedly an
authority that oppressed and usurped; and [thus] that code of liberty and
charity was prostituted until it was converted into a shield for the
usurpers.

And there you have, Burke concluded: "the origin of the saddest
pages in history characterizing religious intolerance and the exclusion
of foreigners in Spain." Those were powerful words and statements
that questioned the "divine rights" of kings, the usurpation of the
people's rights and power by absolutists and their monarchs, the
religiosity of the Spanish Church and the famous "Inquisition" founded
by the "Catholic Kings" of Spain—Ferdinand and Isabela the Catholic!
Blanco-White was fully capable of writing this first half of the essay,
especially encouraged by his new English friend in London, James
Mill; but Roscio seemed to be the more likely author if we recall his
other writings as "William Burke." The parallels with Mill's editorials
on the abuses of the people's sovereignty were striking, satisfying
Roscio's temperament and emotions. On the other hand, Miranda and
Mill could have produced this part easily![15]

The remainder of the article on "Religious Toleration" was likewise
provocative but more intellectual and slightly less emotional. It
resembled the writings of Blanco-White supported by Mill's views on
the Edict of Nantes and its impact on the English-speaking world. This
"William Burke" sketched a documentary offering based upon the Bible
and other religious works. "No matter where we open that code of life
and health that our Savior of mankind left us," he declared solemnly
"we can only find advice, benevolence, [and] fraternal love; and it is
impossible that the Gospel, which is the science of charity, could ever
suggest violence or persecution to increase the number of disciples of
the truth." He quoted some of the apostles. These were "precepts of
tolerance" left to man by Jesus Christ and his disciples.

Let us agree, therefore, that God's law disapproves of intolerance; and since the principle objective of the Gospel is the establishment of a holy union among men, it inspires virtuous enthusiasm and those efforts capable of maintaining happiness among people, and condemns all enterprises that are aimed at upsetting that union.

It is certain that Jesus Christ did not favor cutting off the Christians' contact with foreigners. "Let us not be intolerant," the author pleaded: "Christianity will not progress on solid ground unless its directors follow the tracks of their Founder and his Apostles."

The Gospel's main objective was to promote morality and "the happiness of society"; and good examples of this could be found in England and the United States. Burke's praises of Englishmen and North Americans were persuasive, although perhaps too sanguine. England's progress in manufacturing was largely due to the "injudicious revocation of the *Edict* of Nantes, which forced religious refugees to seek asylum among the British." "It is an historical fact," Burke affirmed: "that the origin and increase of great industrial cities in England has been the result of the greater political tolerance enjoyed there." "An early tolerance" also flourished in North America's Pennsylvania. In his closing remarks, Burke pleaded for the acceptance of the historical premise that wherever "intolerance" was abandoned as national policy, "there has flowed immediately torrents of population, industry, enlightenment, riches and happiness to fertilize and beautify that country." Burke felt that he should be permitted "to direct my feeble words to the numerous and august clergy of South America." A policy of tolerance would pay off in the form of substantial immigration, bringing in elements that will strengthen and bring prosperity to their new land. On religious grounds, Burke urged them to welcome fellow human beings to South America's shores. Thus, they would be following "the spirit of the Gospel," setting up "a brilliant example of generosity, of fraternal love, and of *genuine Christianity*."[16] A Spanish priest, of Irish ancestry, found common ground in London with the ex-Presbyterian minister, a Scotsman, in their discussions. They were both excellent publicists, hoping that their presentation would go over well among South Americans.

Their hopes, however, were in vain! The reaction to Burke's exposition on "Religious Toleration" was an immediate, emotional, and voluminous rejection by Venezuelan spokesmen in Caracas and the nearby city of Valencia. During the next few months, in three voluminous treatises, religious leaders examined Burke's thesis line by line. They found it wanting, all agreeing that the "Irish Catholic" had distorted the meaning of biblical passages, had been misinformed on Spanish history since 1478, and had produced conclusions about the Church that amounted to "heresies." There was a great deal of emotion and dogma in their assertions; and, surprisingly, Burke did not reply to his attackers. Roscio made some educated comments; but no visible "William Burke" appeared to defend himself. Thanks to the publicity that attended the rebuttals to Burke's editorials in the *Gazeta*, the cause of Catholicism was strengthened throughout Venezuela.

What was remarkable about the opposition papers, two of which were by university professors, was the effective command they displayed of worldwide references on the theme of religious toleration and its history. They were thus able to challenge with documentation the intolerant tendencies of Englishmen and North Americans. Their research discredited Burke's favorable comments, making the rejection of his entire thesis possible. As propagandists, these Catholic professors were not amateurs. After all, they argued, William Burke merely reflected the thinking of the "*philosophers*," whose pernicious objectives were to encourage impiety and anarchy![17]

On April 22, 1811, the controversy produced a significant correspondence between the provincial government of Mérida and the national authorities. Formerly a part of Maracaibo's jurisdiction, Mérida was one of the seven political units that formed the Venezuelan Congress on March 2, 1811. Mérida's officials wrote on March 15, 1811, in complete disagreement with the Burkian contentions. Moreover, it was not a wise decision; in fact, it was politically naive to allow such a publication in the nation's present emergency.

> Although the corruption of customs has extended itself to all classes of the State, there has always been evident [among our people] an inalterable respect for religious beliefs, and almost natural horror for all sectarians [non-Catholics], and a general reluctance to deal and communicate with them.

Our enemies would seize this opportunity "to introduce among us, a religious schism more frightful in its results, than any civil war in all its furors . . . Coro and Maracaybo have said in their papers that all we aspire to is an absolute independence, and to the freedom of cults." With the discourse by "*Señor Burke*" in their hands, they would obstinately persist in their secession, and the heroic resolution of Caracas on April 19th, would be erroneously interpreted in light of the discourse in the Gazette of February 19th, in which Americans were exhorted to concede what is most sacred to them—religious freedom.[18]

Since the Mérida letter of March 15th was an attack on the ex-government—the Junta Suprema of Venezuela—the National Congress felt that one of the Junta's members should frame the government's reply to the Province of Mérida. Juan Roscio was the logical person, since he was editor of the *Gazeta* at that time; and he was the representative from Calabozo in Congress, as well as acting President of that body, when the letter of April 17th was sent off to Mérida. Needless to say, Roscio adamantly refused to admit that he or the Junta Suprema had made any mistake at all in permitting the publication of Burke's letter on "Religious Toleration."

The reply to Mérida of April 17th was well-organized and a clever exposition of materials intended to educate the readers of the *Gazeta*. These readers, by this time, had been exposed to Professor Antonio Gómez's description of the types of "toleration": political and religious. This, in turn, provided the clever student of the law with his way out. Given "the delicacy of the issue," the Government did not distinguish between the types that Dr. Gómez had mentioned. Its objective, instead, was to permit Burke's editorial to appear on the condition that there would be rebuttals also published in the gazette. That, as it turned out, was the essence of Roscio's long reply. Roscio, on the other hand, seized the opportunity to lecture his countrymen from Mérida as he proceeded to review and defend Burke's rational arguments.

The lecture began with an historical review of man's progress toward civilization up to the Conquest of the New World. Without trade and communication with each other, man came to realize that his progress would never occur. By communicating with each other, he learned that knowledge increased and the arts and sciences advanced accordingly. Man's world became larger and contacts spread from East to West and North to South, etc. The Greeks learned from the Egyptians, the Romans from the Greeks, etc. until the fall of Rome. Then man slipped back into an existence of ignorance and stupidity. Centuries passed; the dark cloud began to dissipate; the light again began to lead man to reforms and improvements; despotism was reduced from many to one tyrant; ideas spread with the expansion of commerce and communication; the Nations of Europe linked their interests together; and, "if they were not able to follow the same religion, this difference did not embarrass their trade, commerce and political communication."

The champion of Venezuelan independence, at this point, turned up the propaganda machine:

> Spain deprived America of these advantages that conceded a natural right to men and thus founded upon Americans' ignorance the lasting tyranny of her Empire, prohibiting through barbarous and inhuman laws the entry of all foreigners, which were not only punished to extremes but also branded with the stereotype of horrible wretches that impressed [Americans] from infancy, fostering an antipathy among the children, not in the least compatible with Christian charity, so as to obtain an end of making them loathsome and communication with them never desirable.

But the times have changed; and Americans having realized Spain's duplicity—continuing to trade with other nations of Europe and yet depriving Americans of this same right, etc. etc.

The great objective of the Junta Suprema de Venezuela in authorizing the publication of Burke's editorial on February 19, 1811, was to achieve American liberty and equality:

> This enfranchisement, this communication, this trade, this commerce with all men, free and encouraged by nature, prohibited and limited by tyranny and despotism with which America has been governed, by which it was administered and cultivated for the benefit of Spain—that was what your Junta had in mind.

It was not in favor of permitting religious cults to disturb our Catholicism. This "political" toleration, Roscio concluded,

> never has been contrary to the principles and dogma of our Catholic Religion; Rome herself and other [Catholic] Nations have provided a positive proof of this truth. That is why the Junta permitted the rebuttals to the Burke essay of February 19th.

In all, it was a brilliant and clever defense of the ex-Junta Suprema. Roscio ended it with this grand flourish:

Caracas since April 19, 1810, reclaimed her *Liberty*, and swore to conserve her true *Religion*, and this same oath she repeated with the greatest solemnity on the memorable day of the installation of the Congress of representatives of the People; the former [Liberty] demanded a free and secure exchange with all men; its communication and commerce, irregardless of their religious beliefs, for the State's happiness; and the latter [Religion] is not opposed to human Society's use of these means and of others that lead to its conservation, increase, and security, as Spain herself has practiced and continues to practice, and the remaining Catholic Nations of the world, without offense and repugnance of its dogmas and beliefs.[19]

That was the answer, in short, that Mérida had to accept: because of a commitment to "Liberty" and to "Religion," the Junta Suprema allowed Burke's article on February 19, 1811. It was not an answer that was entirely acceptable. Roscio was well aware of that; but, as a lawyer, there is no question that he had put up a respectable defense, for the time being.

* * * * * * * * * * * *

A disruptive factor in Venezuela's body politic, as much a sign of weakness as religious monopoly, was an exaggerated regionalistic tendency. History, geography, and population distribution contributed to a process of fragmentation that isolated Venezuelans from each other. This was not unique to colonial Spanish America; the United States' model also suffered along these lines before Independence. Decentralization and weakness characterized the "Articles of Confederation" before 1789. The urgent demand for reform, however, led to the adoption of the Constitution of 1787, ratified two years later. The Venezuelan case, however, was far more serious and chaotic. The rivalry of larger states that offset each other, guaranteeing more protection and equality for the smaller ones, was lacking in Venezuela's experiment of confederation.

The April 19, 1810, government, unfortunately, began its existence in a context of secession. The potential states, or provinces, of Maracaibo and Coro, plus Guayana later, refused to join the April 19th movement. This left just the provinces of Caracas, Barinas, and Cumaná, the only ones to join the Caracas government with provincial status from the old regime. Then, Barcelona, who years before had enjoyed provincial status for some time, broke off from Cumaná and demanded provincial rights under the Caracas government. Caracas honored the request, angering the authorities at Cumaná who often threatened to leave the April 19th movement. It was still an open sore on March 2, 1811, when Congress convened and again on July 5, 1811, at Independence. The two cities of Mérida and Trujillo, it will be recalled, seceded from Maracaibo and joined the Caracas movement as provinces, or future states, even though their numbers were small. If Maracaibo later had chosen to break with Spain, joining Caracas, there undoubtedly would have been much tension over the recognition of Mérida and Trujillo as equals, much like the hostility between Barcelona and Cumaná. The seventh province, the Island of Margarita, gained its status thanks to its strategic location near Cumaná's coast. These basic facts did not augur well for the future governments of Venezuela.

The most powerful political problem for the National Congress that assembled on March 2, 1811, was the overwhelming size of the Province of Caracas. According to the last census of the colonial era, it contained a population of 412,857, whereas the remaining six provinces totalled only 264,770 persons. When the National Congress convened, therefore, there were 24 deputies for the Province of Caracas and 23 for the remaining provinces, not all of whom had completed their elections in time for the convocation. Understandably, there was a strong demand in Congress for a more equitable "*división*" of the *Caraqueño* State if the Confederation of Venezuela were to continue to exist.[20]

The outspoken deputy from Mérida, Antonio Nicolás Briceño, did not show any compassion for the Caraqueños, insisting on the immediate division of their State:

> The province of Caracas includes within its boundaries today sixteen Head Districts among cities and *villas*; and more than five Districts that on their own have more population and wealth than the Provinces of Barcelona and Margarita. The cities of Barquisimeto, San Carlos and Tocuyo each exceeds 28,000, which is what Barcelona's [figures] reach; San Sebastián and Valencia have more than 50,000, and the District Capital at Caracas has 115,804 souls, without counting many who were omitted from the last census numbers . . . The wealth of each place and its public funds are all in proportion to its population; because the land is generally abundant and fertile; you can readily see how prejudicial it

would be, how many losses would be incurred by that portion of cities, *villas*, and places subjected to and dependent upon the city of Caracas.

All of them would have to go there with their judicial cases and disputes, with their political squabbles, and military ones; and they could not dispose of their own public revenues without the permission of Caracas, who because of distance, her population and the vast preoccupation with her Provincial Government, could not possibly be familiar with, let alone remedy the needs that each region faces, since there were not enough funds to open up new roads, repair existing ones, build new canals for trade and navigation, advance public education in the sciences and arts and foment agriculture, whose abandonment brings about the greatest evils.[21]

While Briceño represented Mérida, one of the so-called "Outside" provinces, he was speaking here primarily for the "Interior" districts of the Province of Caracas, where the "*división*" was most needed. It was from Valencia that Caracas received the sharpest criticism. Fernando Peñalver, a spirited intellectual from Valencia, argued effectively against the monopoly of Caracas in all spheres, shaming her for this predominance by comparing her rule to that of "odious" Spain. Other deputies from the "Interior" likewise clamored for "*división*." Peñalver's solution—a "pure" federalist at heart—was to reject the "status quo" arguments of the Caraqueños, who insisted upon the territorial limits of the former Spanish system. Instead, Peñalver argued, Congress should regard the Venezuelan area, as an "undefined" mass which should be divided into provinces of equal population and resources. His published report aroused considerable interest, but it had no lasting impact upon the Venezuelan polity. It was just another proposal that reflected suspicion and hostility towards the capital city of Caracas.[25]

Another deputy from the "Interior" [San Carlos: Francisco de Hernández], suggested the division of Caracas' province into four parts: the first would include Barquisimeto, Tocuyo, Carora, and San Felipe; the second, consisting of San Carlos, Araure, Ospino, and Guanare; thirdly: Valencia, Nirgua, Puerto Cabello, and Valles de Aragua; and fourth, the City of Caracas and her immediate environs. Basing himself on a government report that the Province of Caracas produced revenue worth one million *pesos* annually, the first three parts, with populations of about one hundred thousand, would each receive revenues totalling 200,000 pesos. The new Capital City province, which would include the districts of Calabozo; Villa de Cura, San Sebastián, and the Port of La Guaira, and with a population over 200,000, would receive about 500,000 pesos of revenue. It would still be, Hernández argued, "rich, opulent and flourishing" with this new "*división*." Although somewhat of a fantasy, it nonetheless reflected the "Interior's" concern for the overwhelming concentration of sources and population in their large state.[23]

Caraqueños and denizens of nearby districts, as well as the "nationalists" of the interior districts, mostly intellectuals, resented the clamor and emotion generated by the cause of "*división*." It hurt them deeply to hear the attacks upon their patriotism and the challenge to their motives in the emancipation of Venezuela. This was a horrible display of ingratitude in their eyes. As rational men, they understood that the preponderance of their Province might be regarded as a travesty; but in view of the security problem—the constant threat of a Spanish invasion—it appeared suicidal to distract and weaken Venezuela at this moment of crisis. Division could wait for more peaceful times in the future. But the opposition would not budge. It could not wait that long; besides it simply did not trust the vested interests of the Old Capital.

On the defensive, spokesmen for the larger province insisted that only citizens of the City and districts of the jurisdiction would make this decision of "division." And they would not accept—in fact, General Miranda made this point: that the limited documentation by "Interior" places favorable to division was not representative of all that hinterland. Miranda demanded a thorough survey of attitudes at the municipal level that included landowners, fathers of families, etc. As James Mill had indicated earlier, Miranda insisted that the *cabildos*, or *ayuntamientos*, should be the basic representative units. Fully aware of the urgent need to build up the defenses of Venezuela, General Miranda argued that "division" could wait until after Independence, when the nation was stable.[24]

As June turned into July, 1811, the controversy still raged on the political issue of division; no settlement was in view. A sensational news item, however, captured the attention of the people in Caracas and its environs—the desertion to the Spanish cause of Feliciano Montenegro Colón, a popular Venezuelan officer. Just a few months earlier, Montenegro had abandoned the Spanish service; now, with key documents in his possession, this traitor might trigger an all-out invasion by Spain and her loyalist allies. Fearful of the consequences of such treachery, Venezuelans put aside their differences and recognized that at last it was time "to unsheathe their swords," uniting under the standard of *absolute independence*! Although there were hopes that this action would be promulgated on July 4th, circumstances forced its cancellation for one day, until July 5, 1811.

* * * * * * * * * * * *

The following description of Caracas' Independence should have interest for our readers, as well as for the image that it left throughout the world. Just as Venezuelans learned about their model in the United States with great interest and attention, the same was true along the east coast of North America when the news of the April 19th, 1810, revolution reached there. The "other" Americans were following the North American example in breaking with Europe!

Capitalizing upon this curiosity, the ex-editor of the *Baltimore Examiner* did not hesitate to reproduce key documentation from Caracas in the second issue of his new periodical *The Weekly Register* (Baltimore), September 14, 1811. This periodical is best known to U.S. historians as the *Niles' Register* that recorded the genius of Hezikiah Niles. The documents translated from Spanish for the September 14th issue and others extending into October were the following: July 1, 1811, "A Declaration of Rights by the People of Venezuela," with sections on "Sovereignty of the People," "Rights of Man in Society," "Duties of Man in Society," and "Duties of the Social Body"; July 5, 1811: "Declaration of Independence"; and July 30, 1811: "A Manifesto . . . the Reasons which Influenced in the Formation of an ABSOLUTE INDEPENDENCE of Spain," a lengthy treatise written by Juan Germán Roscio.[25]

There was also a document from the Caracas State Government on the "Freedom of the Press," August 6, 1811, that immediately attracted the attention of Hezikiah Niles and James Giles, editor of the *National Intelligencer* (Washington, D.C.). Niles' comments bear on the theme of religion and politics. Editor Niles extolled the group of documents dealing with Venezuelan Independence and their significance for the New World at this time in history. But then he offered this gloomy note: "our joy was much damped by the appearance of a decree for `regulating the liberty of the press,' to which we are sorry to observe, the finger of the *priesthood*: at all times, and in all countries (where *established* religions exist) the inveterate enemies of reason, justice and truth." But there is hope, the editor went on condescendingly:

> We must, however, make great allowances for this new people, among whom the rights of self government, cannot be considered as more than a theory not yet practically understood as in the United States; whose inhabitants, always enjoying a representative system with a great portion of civil and religious freedom, and accustomed to think and reflect on all political matters, at the first glance would discern the natural and unalienable rights of man. The situation of our brethen of South America is materially different; and we have no doubt, they will cast off all the shreds of slavery, and put on the whole garment of freedom, pure and undefiled, in a short space of time.*

The asterisk above marked a footnote at the bottom of the first column explaining Niles' faith in the political future of Venezuela; the gentleman referred to was perhaps connected with the Venezuelan representative in the national capital. Niles explained:

> The editor has had the honor frequently to converse with a distinguished gentleman of that country, a man of high consideration at Caracas, possessed of a strong mind and very correct ideas of the great fundamental principles on which a free government should be constituted. On inquiry, some time ago, as to the part the clergy had taken in the revolution, he observed—they behaved better than had been expected; but, added he, we gave them some of their measures for the moment, to gain leading advantages to ourselves; well knowing that when the government was firmly fixed, they would not shake it, though at the outset they might complain on a great deal, if dissatisfied with our conduct, or words to this effect. The moment I read the decree for 'regulating the liberty of the press,' the remarks of this gentleman occurred to me.

Upon reflection, Niles concluded that the transaction in Caracas was "a *temporising* arrangement to effect some great and *permanent* good, or, in the language of the hardy fisherman of the eastern states, I compared it to `throwing out a mackarel to catch a cod.'"

Niles' criticism of the "Regulations of the Liberty of the Press" was accurate insofar as his assumptions about the Church. As in the case of the Cortes of Cádiz and subsequent liberal constitutions of Hispanic America, the dogmas of the Church as well as the moral standards of a Catholic society could not be violated under this projected ordinance of August 6, 1811, in Caracas. That is what Niles meant by using the word *priesthood*. The Church, in other words, had put certain traditional restraints upon this liberal law on freedom of the press; and there were laws to punish such violations. These were realities of life that liberal leaders in Iberia, or their American counterparts, could not overlook with impunity. Liberals, therefore, had to compromise with the Church to assure victory in other parts of their program of modernization and republicanism.

The North American Niles found these articles offensive:

Article 8: All writings are prohibited that are subversive of the system adopted and established in Venezuela, which consists principally of its liberty and independence from any other Power or Sovereignty situated beyond its territory.

Article 9: "Authors, editors, or printers of writings against the government established at Venezuela, as in article viii, *shall be punished with death*" [*serán castigados con el último suplicio*].

Since "Freedom of the Press" has been popular with Venezuelan intellectuals, as well as liberals throughout the Hispanic World, these two articles—for reasons that are not clear—have not received much attention in Venezuela's historiography.[26] *El Publicista de Venezuela* of July 25, 1811, was the first to publish the "Regulations" which included the two articles; yet, there was no indication that the Province of Caracas had drawn up the Ordinance on the Freedom of the Press. By that time, however, Congress encouraged the Caracas State Legislature to submit models for all potential states on major topics that would be incorporated into a national constitution. Thus, the Caracas state body drew up the "Freedom of the Press" ordinance that appeared in the *Publicista*; and the *Gazeta de Caracas* republished it on August 6, 1811, which mentioned its source as the state government of Caracas. That was the document used in Niles' paper. Moreover, on August 5th, the Venezuelan national government had authorized the "Regulations of the Liberty of the Press," for its entire jurisdiction.[27]

Perhaps through ignorance more than anything else, Niles failed to comprehend the Venezuelan historical context for those two articles. Independence day was July 5th; but on the 11th of July, 1811, a conspiracy was exposed in Caracas involving the Spanish enemy; and before long, it spread to the city of Valencia, where the rebellion led to a fierce resistance that was not quashed until early August by

General Francisco de Miranda. Venezuela, in short, was in a state of war; and on July 13th, Congress authorized the Executive to eradicate this dangerous threat to the nation's existence. There were also reports that a projected naval invasion of Spanish forces from Puerto Rico, Coro, and Maracaibo was about to take place. Martial law, therefore, extended throughout Venezuela until late November, 1811, when a pardon spared the lives of many conspirators. Unfortunately neither Niles or the other U.S. newspapers that used his documents bothered to explain the historical context for their earlier reaction to the "Freedom of the Press" issue raised by Niles. The European press repeated Niles' distortion, so that the world's image of the first Venezuelan Republic was not at all complimentary. It became part and parcel of a European publicist's program to discredit Miranda and the government that he represented; it will concern us again in a future chapter.

* * * * * * * * * * * *

The Independence of Venezuela could not escape the worldwide realities of the Napoleonic era and the stubborn resistance of a European mother country, determined emotionally to put down her upstart colonies overseas. Spain's weaknesses in Europe, draining her resources and manpower, compounded the costs and the humanity wasted in smothering the insurrection in Venezuela and throughout Spanish America. She refused to accept the inevitable failure of her program in colonialism. There followed, therefore, another decade, or more, of slaughter, instability, and destruction that prevented the revival of the Hispanic World's potential for a good part of the nineteenth century. The frailties of the Venezuelan political embryo have been noted as it approached the milestone of July 5, 1811, and the birth of the First Venezuelan Republic, which immediately faced the "Conspiracies" of July and August, 1811, weakening the national fabric even further.

In this precarious context, Francisco de Miranda returned to his homeland, offering a needed uplift to the Venezuelan government. He cooperated closely with Juan Germán Roscio in the propaganda campaign of "William Burke" and encouraged, with his correspondence, the movement to unite northern South America and someday, hopefully, all of Spanish America. He encouraged Venezuela's youth to seek the independence of their country through an activist mode within the *Sociedad Patriótica de Venezuela*; and his counsel in military and political matters—thanks to his popularity and acclaim throughout Venezuela, where he was considered a national hero fully capable of filling the shoes of a "George Washington" for his country. In the meantime, thanks to the gifted propaganda of William Burke—and his covert assistants—the road to independence exposed believers with grandiose dreams, extending beyond Venezuela's borders. Would their dreams survive? They thought so.

It is unfortunate, indeed, that Venezuelan historiography has not been able to capture the synthesis presented above. Despite their convictions, writers of Venezuelan history have tended to perpetuate a negative image, or sterotype, of General Miranda and the First Venezuelan Republic that he guided until its demise in mid-1812. This phenomenon, or distortion, requires an explanation. To begin with, contrary to the overwhelming materials available for the study of Miranda's career before landing at La Guaira on December 11, 1811, the documentary evidence of his activities in the first six months of his return is very sparse, except for the Burkian ideological story, which has not received any serious analysis until now. As for newspapers, there are vital gaps in the coverage that remain to be found, or unearthed. There is practically nothing of real importance on the activist drive of the *Sociedad Patriótica de Venezuela,* which could have revealed much on the political developments of this crucial period. The question remains: why has there been such a paucity of materials? The conditions of war from April 19, 1810, to July, 1812, destroyed much of the documentation, or were not conducive to writing much at that time. Some historians suspect that the victorious Spanish general Monteverde had much of this subversive documentation transferred to Spain, where presumably it awaits the conscientious researcher. That could be; but it will not be an easy assignment to carry out. More importantly, as our final chapter will demonstrate, the horrendous earthquake of March 26, 1812, levelled Caracas and other urban centers throughout Venezuela, no doubt destroying tons of precious documents that would have preserved a better approximation of historical realities in Venezuela. The change of capitals from Caracas to Valencia, Venezuela, as well as the chaos of the day and the earthquake aftershocks, destroyed whatever may have been left. The experience gained in the archives of Central America taught this writer to appreciate the historical significance of the lack of documentation in earthquake country—a problem that historians face even under normal conditions. Historians have little choice but to adapt themselves to the available documentation; thus, your author opted to emphasize the intellectual influences and manifestations exerted upon the Venezuelan story of independence and the establishment of nationhood.

This may come as a surprise to many readers: the Venezuelan who contributed substantially to the negative sterotype of Miranda was Juan Germán Roscio, a friend of his. The damaging evidence was in a letter that Roscio wrote to Andrés Bello in London on June 9, 1811. Published in 1882 by Bello's biographer, it strongly influenced and confused Venezuelan historiography *from that point forward*. This must be emphasized: much of the bad image of General Miranda emerged *after* 1882. Since we are not sure that contemporaries had copies of Roscio's letter, or were even aware of it, we have assumed that it was not politically important among contemporary Venezuelans. After the earthquake of 1812, on the other hand, Miranda's popularity plummeted with his defeat by General Monteverde, followed by the demise of the First Republic. In short, Miranda's bad image in the eyes of contemporaries, as well as many historians before and after 1882, was due to the unfavorable consequences of that key conflict of 1811–1812. The bad image, then, was reinforced, or magnified, after the appearance of the letter to Andrés Bello.

A few quotations from the June 9th letter, as well as an analysis, will be sufficient for now. In view of Roscio's close relationship with Andrés Bello and his young friend's great admiration for Miranda, it is almost impossible to explain such a vindictive and careless letter unless Roscio was mentally disturbed in May and early June, 1811, and in a veritable fit of anger at Francisco de Miranda.[28] What could have alienated him so much to make up such stories about a man from whom he expected so much a few months earlier? We shall attempt an explanation subsequently; now, let us study what was said in this famous letter of June 9, 1811. "Our *paisano* (countryman)," exploded Roscio, is a first-class ingrate and hypocrite—he said, in effect. Miranda felt that he deserved a higher military rank than what was given to him by the Junta Suprema; and, showing his poor taste, never expressed a hint of gratitude for the honors bestowed upon him by the Venezuelan government. We can imagine how stunned Bello must have been to charges that went contrary to what he had read in the *Gazeta de Caracas* in the early months of 1811! But since we do not have Bello's letters reacting to this one, we can only speculate! Elsewhere, Roscio noted that the Junta Suprema put Miranda in charge of a "Constitutional Committee" (Roscio, Uztáriz, Ponte, Paúl, and

Sanz) to prepare a charter, or the "bases for federation," to guide the National Congress on its installation (March 2, 1811). Roscio related how General Miranda presented a plan for establishing a monarchical system. From his description, although curt and sarcastic, it was clearly a reference to Miranda and Thomas Pownall's project with its two Incas as rulers. Uztáriz and Roscio rejected these plans outright. They were Republicans and wanted a federation form of government, like that of the United States. This meeting must have taken place in late February, 1811, before the installation of March 2nd. Type of government was the issue that commenced the break with Miranda, at least in Roscio's mind. The brilliant Uztáriz dogmatically rejected the "old man's" antiquarian notions; he was the major force behind the future Constitution of Venezuela (December 21, 1811). Except for Miranda, practically the same committee was selected on March 16, 1811, by the new congress—a point generally missed by most historians. When Uztáriz learned that Miranda had objected to his Constitution in December, he repeated his aversion to the "old man's" political aberrations. In the June 9th letter, Roscio remarked to Bello: "The political strategy of this *old man* is very unfortunate." (Italics by M.R.).[29] It appears safe to assume, therefore, that much of Roscio's anger at this point came from Uztáriz as a source.

Roscio's anger in the June 9th letter focussed also on the members of the Patriotic Society, the institution that Roscio and Uztáriz had made legally possible in the decree of August, 1810. Miranda's popularity with Venezuela's youth was understandable; and the burgeoning society before long had over two hundred members etc., etc., so we have here another factor upsetting to both Uztáriz and Roscio—envy of the popular military hero. Why else would Roscio write to Bello that these young hotheads had not produced a single reform of importance to the government; their role was negative and abusive to the Congress, etc., etc. etc. The recent news of Miranda's election to the presidency of the Patriotic Society undoubtedly triggered the abusive letter of June 9, 1811.

With these crosses to burn, Juan Germán Roscio punished his good friend in London with an unbelievable fantasy concerning Miranda and his minions in the Patriotic Society. It went something like this: this son of a "*Canario*" was certainly a "Napoleon" in disguise waiting to take over the Venezuelan government. His political orientation, moreover, was "Jacobin." He was a calloused opportunist, trying to win the hearts of the non-Whites—the *Pardos* of Venezuela, in particular. On the backs of the Black masses, he would seize power and level the "White Man's" society of Venezuela to his whim as *Caudillo* (strong man ruler). The picture becomes even more ludicrous when Miranda tells someone in the scenario that he did not like the United States, etc., etc., etc. And Roscio's version of the February 19th issue on "Religious Toleration" likewise strained the truth. The "Old Man"—an opportunist to the hilt—deliberately tried to play up to the Archbishop and others; but he did not fool them, Roscio tells us. They would not believe Miranda's claim that the real authors of the offending editorial were Roscio, Uztáriz, and Ponte! What an interesting revelation! And even more so when Roscio, and his sidekick Uztáriz, pointed out that in the Pownall instructions, there was a clause favoring religious toleration! The proverbial last straw in the fantastic story about Francisco de Miranda was when he compelled William Burke to resign from the Patriotic Society, as if this act would relieve Miranda of any responsibility for the misguided editorial in the *Gazeta de Caracas!*

This was an interesting use of "William Burke" by the former editor of the *Gazeta.* We already know how he used the Burkian penname to his advantage. And—surprise of all surprises—this was not the only way that Roscio used that name. For example, it was "William Burke" and not "Juan G. Roscio" who was a distinguished subscriber to *La Bagatela* of Santa Fe de Bogotá; that, of course, was a ploy to assure readers for the Caracas gazette. We also find an indirect clue to Roscio's anger toward Miranda in *La Bagatela*, edited by the famous Antonio Nariño. And here, we finally arrive at "The Asterisk Caper," if we can be permitted this levity of expression. The asterisk, it will be recalled, followed the Burkian title of March 29, 1811, "Fundamentals for a Declaration of Independence,*" with the footnote *"Let this be understood as political theory."* This article was read widely throughout South America, preparing them for the union-project that Roscio had elaborated upon in his March 29th editorial, which, as it turned out, was the last Burkian publication for over three months. At that time, the cessation of Burkian editorials annoyed Roscio—and this heightened further animosity towards the General—presumably because the new government was apprehensive that such editorials might alienate outside powers like Great Britain, thus frustrating independence altogether. Miguel Sanz, the new Secretary of State, apparently was hesitant about advancing Roscio's policy on independence at that time. And Sanz, a very good friend of Miranda, had the General's blessings for both of Roscio's positions in the government, including the editorship of the *Gazeta de Caracas*. With these facts in mind, the following incident presents a third factor for Roscio's anger and envy in writing the June 9, 1811, letter to Bello.

The *Argos Americano* of Cartagena likewise published Burke's essay of March 29th in its No. 40 issue, just as it had appeared in *La Bagatela* and the *Gazeta de Caracas*. The difference was that P.G., a subscriber, upbraided the editors of the *Argos* for using that objectionable asterisk on Burke's editorial. He assumed that it had been done by them and not by the Caracas gazette. P.G. argued that three hundred years of abuse by Spain put that theme out of the theoretical realm. Independence was a practical reality for all patriots of the Americas to achieve! And Cartagena followed Caracas' example on November 11, 1811. P.G. and other patriots in that famous port had taken William Burke's words seriously—that is, Roscio's words on immediate independence.

The incident received greater publicity when P.G.'s words and the *Argos'* correspondence appeared in the *Gazeta de Caracas* on October 1, 1811. Editor Sanz explained that the asterisk had been used to avoid any premature reaction by foreign powers on the theme of Independence. Juan Germán Roscio was furious upon reading Sanz's explanation; and immediately prepared a letter to Sanz signed by "William Burke," of all people. And the *Gazeta* in Caracas *refused* to publish it there! Now, Roscio was really upset and had his friend "William Burke" write another letter, this time to Antonio Nariño's *La Bagatela* in Santa Fe de Bogotá, complaining that the Caracas paper had refused to print his reaction. Here is what we learned from *La Bagatela* of December 22, 1811: first, Burke complained that Sanz had not made it clear in the *Gazeta* of October 1st that the asterisk had been placed "without my knowledge; [and] I feel it necessary to expose this fact." Initially, Burke had been annoyed by the asterisk; but did nothing about it. At least, that was the case until he learned "that the opinion, *not official*, of an individual, could possibly *endanger foreign relations!*" At this juncture, "William Burke"—or more exactly, his ghost writer—commented with sarcasm and bitterness essentially what P.G. had written in the *Argos* of Cartagena: no American patriot could agree with such an asterisk considering the "injustices" suffered over three centuries. Finally, Burke closed with a strong attack upon Editor Sanz for the censorship of the Burkian editorials that lasted "*three months*," by applying that "*nota* [footnote with the asterisk]" for allegedly "very powerful reasons." The public, therefore, was unable to read "discourses calculated to prepare the public mind for the reception of Independence."[30]   Months later, Juan Germán Roscio prepared an article for publication in the *Gazeta de Caracas* bearing the title: "Insurrection of Valencia." Valencia, he argued had no right to violate the "Declaration of Independence" of July 5, 1811, because of a well-publicized commitment to that historical movement. To prove his point, Roscio wrote the following:

> The model formula by which America should declare its independence was so well received in Cartagena that they [the people of Cartagena] were unable to tolerate the *nota* [the footnote] added by the Editor of the *Gazeta de Caracas*, to the effect that at that time it was merely a theoretical statement.

They objected to that asterisk and footnote as inconsequential and "scandalous" to consider "three centuries of effective evils" as just "theoretical."[31]   These facts came clearly from Roscio's hand—another use of the penname "William Burke."

Thus, we have a third factor that helps to explain the tragic aberration in Roscio's mind that led him to write that famous letter to Andrés Bello on June 9, 1811. Moreover, he was perhaps angry at himself for having rushed into publication those final numbers of the *Gazeta* in late March 1811. Yet, without the exposure of the "asterisk caper," Venezuelan historiography would have missed a key insight into Roscio's formidable contribution to the Independence of his nation and the significance of his "Inter-American" project in the Wars for Independence of Spanish America.

* * * * * * * * * * * *

Despite the torment that went on in Roscio's mind, he soon was able to observe that General Miranda was not his real enemy after all; Miranda's comportment was as it had always been with Juan Germán Roscio. After all, he knew nothing about the June 9th letter, or that Roscio and his friends were gossiping something to that effect. Miranda joined the Congress, as a representative from Pao, a district in the State of Barcelona. He consistently voted with Roscio and the *Caraqueños* on the "division" issue; and he continued to share Roscio's urgency to bring on the nation's independence. On June 25, 1811, for example, there was an extraordinarily knowledgeable discussion on the history of Bourbon Spain from May 2, 1808, forward. Roscio and Miranda demonstrated graphically at what point the Bourbons, including Ferdinand VII, had given up their claim to sovereignty in the Americas, thus justifying Venezuela's assertions to her sovereignty. They argued that political events in European Spain were no longer relevant to Venezuelans.[32]   Others welcomed the Roscio-Miranda arguments; and considered seriously how the United States and Great Britain might react to Venezuela's break with Spain. The British commitment to the name of Ferdinand VII would be a formidable stumbling block. The delegate from San Carlos (Francisco Hernández) noted:

> Besides this, it is highly probable that the *pueblos* might become alarmed, since many of them are still incapable of appreciating the good results that will come with independence: the masses (*el vulgo*) believe that Kings come from Gods, and this favorable view must disappear, as Mr. Roscio has explained so well: educate the *pueblos* to their rights; a well documented manifiesto has to precede the declaration of independence to prepare the peoples' minds [or spirits].[33]

The Hernández statement underscored the fact that independence was almost at hand and that the primemovers, which included Miranda and Roscio, favored the composition of a *"Manifiesto"* to justify in considerable detail why it was necessary for the people to repudiate their oath to Ferdinand VII. Roscio had been researching recent Bourbon history for months; and Miranda, through Blanco-White and others, had also garnered additional insights that complemented his colleague's research. Roscio was the logical person for the assignment, and there were hopes that the document would accompany the Declaration of Independence, if not precede it. Pressing concerns delayed its publication until July 30, 1811.[34]

Convinced that he had misjudged General Miranda unfairly, the bond of friendship between the two *paisanos* [countrymen] strengthened and so did the prospects for Venezuela's future. Roscio's next letter to Andrés Bello left the impression that all was well now between them.[35] Their most important objective was Independence for Venezuela and the real encouragement of the unionist movement throughout South America. Roscio and Miranda's group cooperated in the revival of Burke's editorials in order to influence, or commit, the Bogotá authorities to a republican form of government, as in Venezuela's model adopted on July 5, 1811.

The events in the former Viceroyalty of New Granada with its capital in Santa Fe de Bogotá were considered vital to Venezuela in achieving her independence and establishing the First Republic. On July 20, 1810, the Junta Suprema de Bogotá followed Caracas' pattern of April 19, 1810; and Venezuela's installation of Congress on March 2, 1811, produced the same results in Bogotá on April 4th. Named the State of Cundinamarca, the Bogotá government remained loyal to Ferdinand VII and encouraged elections in all the provinces of the extensive kingdom (now the modern countries of Colombia, Panama, and Ecuador). The syndrome of anarchy, fragmentation, secession, and civil war repeated itself in Cundinamarca to an even more exaggerated extent than in Venezuela. The significant difference between the two was that the State of Cundinamarca offered its people a liberal, monarchical constitution by May 10, 1811, as if its leaders felt compelled to anticipate the Cádiz project in Spain. Yet, the compromise tactic did not minimize differences with the Spanish-born officials of the Old Order, who still encouraged secession and violence in return for promises and *fueros* [privileges] to prospective loyalists. Instability was rampant, as well as expensive.

Upon learning the news that Dr. José Cortés Madariaga was in their jurisdiction and desired to seek an alliance, the authorities in Bogotá were beside themselves with excitement, as if Dr. Cortés from Venezuela was the "Ambassador" of a great power nearby. And, as the negotiations began, there were hints to the effect that Bogotá would be the capital of any prospective union resulting from the treaties between the two parties. These hints, of course, underscored Roscio's authorship of the Burkian editorials in late March, 1811. The publicity given to the negotiations, and especially to the popular Dr. Cortés, caused a sensation throughout both countries by late May, 1811. Further information, up to May 10th, with the news of Bogotá's new constitution, was in the hands of the Venezuelan government by July 5, 1811. And on the 6th of July, Venezuela's Executive congratulated President José Tadeo Lozano on the progress achieved by his State of Cundinamarca. At the same time, however, the Venezuelans reminded him that, just "yesterday," Venezuela had declared herself a Republic seeking absolute independence from Spain. Cundinamarca's recent monarchical constitution, still loyal to Ferdinand VII, was simply not compatible with any project of union with the Venezuelan Republic.

Understanding that the Lozano government would see the light in these matters, the Executive, nonetheless, waited with bated breath for a favorable answer. A negative reply would have been disastrous to Roscio's dream for a Confederation Republic in South America.

Once congressional leaders became privy to this information, they agreed upon a well-organized campaign to influence the Bogotá government and its electorate along Republican lines. There was agreement that Roscio, and other assistants, would get the "*Manifiesto*" out as soon as possible—a strong attack upon Ferdinand VII's rights to overseas territories, etc. Roscio, Miranda, and Miguel José Sanz felt that the William Burke editorials should be resumed; and there should be at least three editorials aimed generally at all Spanish Americans but especially at the subjects of Cundinamarca, attacking Ferdinand VII's credentials and preparing them to abandon their support of him, while at the same time explaining the world favorable conditions that made *absolute independence* a viable objective. In short, the same situation occurred as in early January, 1811, when the "December–January" crisis prevailed. There was a decision then to intervene with a new "William Burke" during the emergency. And the pattern of cooperation between Roscio and Miranda repeated itself successfully. Moreover, it would appear that the monarchical constitutional project was known as early as June 20th or so, which permitted Roscio and Miranda, at least, to think in terms of reviving the Burkian campaign and preparing it for potential unionist followers outside of Venezuela. There was a tight schedule here; but it was met by Roscio and his colleagues.[36]

According to Roscio, who controlled the manuscript, "William Burke" wrote the introduction to volume one on June 25, 1811. It was a strong prologue, in which James Mill explained how he had gotten interested in the anticolonialist movement of South America and his commitment to come to Venezuela once he learned of the heroic April 19, 1810, Revolution. Despite his weak command of Spanish, he convinced himself that he had to sacrifice his family and comforts in Europe in order to help eliminate despotism in Spanish America. He urged his readers—with Mill's typical optimism and pedagogy—to read and restudy his institutional proposals. It is not difficult to imagine James Mill writing those words back in the early summer of 1810 when the April 19th news reached London, as well as Bentham's agreement to go along with him. Leaving his family behind in Europe until the future was secure in America was also understandable. The June 25th date was Roscio's idea; it marked the beginning of his *third* intervention as "William Burke"; for Miranda, it was his *second*.[37]

Despite some premature announcements in the *Gazeta de Caracas*, the bulk of the five hundred copies per edition of Burke's two volumes appeared as follows: Volume I by July 12, 1811, and Volume II by October 3. It is important to keep in mind that words reached the Spanish readers in the two-volume format on the dates mentioned above. By October 3, 1811, a reader had in his hands all that Burke had written for the Caracas market with some minor revisions and a topical presentation. If that reader desired to learn what Burke had written on "Constitution," he would consult the index to volume two and turn to such-and-such a page. On the other hand, a regular subscriber to the *Gazeta de Caracas* would have to wait until early 1812 to read what Burke had to say on that issue —a delay of historical importance. The owner of volume two, in other words, was able to read in advance Burke's constitutional views whereas the periodical subscriber could not have this insight.

The Burkian editorials resumed publication in the *Gazeta de Caracas* on July 9th; but the uprisings in Caracas and Valencia in the following week postponed the second piece until the 19th; and the third one, on July 23rd. The contents of these three editorials, however, were in Volume I, published on July 12. Some copies, however, were available by July 6th; and they accompanied the Executive's letter to Lozano's government on that date. If our speculation is accurate, therefore, the Bogotanos soon reaped the ideas sowed by Roscio and Miranda to persuade them in favor of following Venezuela's declaration of absolute independence. By noting omissions in the *Gazeta*'s installment of July 19, 1811, we were able to establish that the book version was aimed at the Bogotanos and the *Gazeta*'s at the Venezuelan readers. Moreover, it was obvious to anyone that the three editorials in question seemed superfluous to Venezuelan readers who had already achieved independence on July 5th! The only other justification, apparently, was to reinforce the Venezuelans in their decision to favor independence, especially as "conspiracies" soon came to their attention.[38] Roscio's style, like in those of early January, reappeared in this new trio of editorials; and his expertise on the subject of Ferdinand VII was also well-established. The public soon read similar materials in the *Manifiesto* of July 30, 1811, mentioned earlier.

Miranda's contribution to the trio of editorials in question consisted primarily on the information he had received recently from

England—we suspect that they were letters from James Mill, dealing with politics in England during 1811. This was a crucial year in George III's reign because of his incapacitation; thus, the Regency, for a year's time, was put under the authority of the Prince of Wales. After that year, the heir assumed the Regency with full authority until his father's death in 1820, when he became George IV of Great Britain. Miranda knew the Prince; and through the Duke of Gloucester and other political leaders in London, it will be recalled, they hoped to change British policy in Spain and in Europe to the more imaginative tact of supporting Spanish America's emancipation and reform movements. Of special interest to South Americans was the potential assurance that Great Britain's new Regent and prospective King would be supportive of Spanish American rights and independence. In short, it removed all doubt about Britain's reaction to American independence. This information under the rubric of "William Burke" was reassuring to South Americans in general. Dr. Constancio, if he was present in Venezuela, also could have supplied this type of information to General Miranda.[39] By July 30, 1811, the original "William Burke" returned for his final series of essays that provided invaluable information and insights from two of Europe's great intellectuals—James Mill and Jeremy Bentham. We shall return to that series in the next chapter.

The impact of the Venezuelan project for republicanism in South America was vital to the governments of Bogotá and Cartagena. On August 21, 1811, just as General Miranda completed the finishing touches to his campaign in Valencia, bringing that "Conspiracy" to its end, the news of Venezuela's Independence (July 5, 1811), reached Bogotá, where the government and its citizens went wild with excitement, hoping that their own grand day of Independence would soon be a reality. President Tadeo Lozano assured his colleagues in Caracas that with patience the same consequence would take place in Bogotá. Yet, he cautioned that his government should not act prematurely; it had to await the verdict of "The General Congress of the Provinces" which soon would gather to take action on this measure, as well as that of union and others relevant to Cundinamarca.[40] Miguel de Pombo, one of the great liberal leaders of that area, wrote a letter to a Venezuelan friend—Roscio, we suspect, or perhaps Sanz—on August 22nd describing the pandemonium and enthusiasm in Bogotá's demonstrations upon learning of Venezuela's freedom. Pombo congratulated his friend and assured him that his name and those of other leaders in Caracas would be remembered into posterity on the

same level as those of "Washington, Adams, Jefferson, and Madison."
His descriptions of the celebrations were warm and emotional; and he
hoped that his country could reach the same heights, although he had
many serious doubts.[41]

On November 11, 1811, Cartagena's glorious declaration for
ABSOLUTE INDEPENDENCE from Spain was welcomed news
throughout South America. This dramatic stroke—undoubtedly
intended to force Bogotá's hand—brought the Independence movement
and the Union of all South America to its highest point. While Spanish
loyalists forces evacuated the provinces of Quito and Popoyán, thus
opening up communications with Lima, Peru, the Independence thrust
from Buenos Aires was in control of Upper Peru (Bolivia) and had also
influenced the Independence of Chile. In the meantime, Cartagena's
forces had infiltrated the jurisdiction of Santa Marta, the rival port
nearby that was a Spanish royalist enclave, much like Coro and
Maracaibo vis-a-vis the First Republic of Venezuela.

Heralding the second Spanish American Republic in Cartagena, the
Gazeta de Caracas issued an extraordinary edition on January 4, 1812.[42]
While the National Congress of Venezuela was in session, a spokesman
from the Executive Power asked permission to enter.   When
Congressmen heard the good news from Cartagena, there was a
thunderous ovation. This "*trueno espantoso* (frightful thunderbolt), as
one congressmen put it, should put the fear of God into all Spaniards
and their traitorous collaborators thought the Americas. Venezuela had
set the scene for the heroic action at Cartagena with her own stances on
April 19, 1810, and July 5, 1811. The spokesman from the Executive
Power—Miguel Sanz, we suspect—reminded his colleagues that it was:
"In the Castle of Boca Chica, where groaning and perishing under the
load of irons, were many of those illustrous sons of the immortal
Washington, who in 1806 approached our coasts to restore for us the
precious gift of liberty." Sanz's good friend Miranda had also praised
his former colleagues who lost their lives there.

A few days later, in an editorial entitled "Reflections," Sanz brought
out the real significance of Cartagena's independence on November 11,
1811:

> But it is not just the pleasure of imitation and the unity of sentiments
> that the Independence of Cartagena should inspire in us: it is, as some
> one put it, a "frightful thunderbolt" that will overwhelm with fear those
> conspiratorial assemblies [*conventículos*, he called them] in Puerto Rico,

Maracaibo and Guayana, and demonstrate to them that Venezuela's cause is that of all the Colombian Continent, and that our example shall have more influence in behalf of mankind than all the chimerical, criminal, and ephemeral projects which they abort continually in order to suffocate the natural and irresistible instinct that propels Americans toward their liberty.

Sanz was especially sanguine that Cartagena's action would secure the program of union in northern South America; and the dramatic news from Cartagena, moreover, improved the morale of republicans throughout the First Republic of Venezuela.[43]

There is no question that Venezuela's efforts to change the monarchical pattern in Santa Fe de Bogotá were instrumental in raising the political aspirations of all Colombia, as we know that area today; and the guiding presence of General Francisco de Miranda was most reassuring to everyone, especially after his convincing defeat of the two conspiracies in Caracas and Valencia. On July 14, 1811, in his first issue of *La Bagatela*, Antonio Nariño sounded the republican bell; Cartagena's conversion in November was a great advance; and by November 27, 1811, we have the framework, seventy-eight articles in all, for the first republican constitution for the "Confederation of the United Provinces of New Granada," just slightly two weeks after Cartagena's declaration. Editor Sanz, as early as January 17, 1812, announced the impending publication of this formidable document, which appeared in installments from January 21 through February 11, 1812, in the *Gazeta de Caracas*. The framers were rational and pragmatic men. They went out of their way to assuage the feelings of Spaniards living in their midst and to encourage commercial relations with Spain. They had ideas and suggestions that James Mill would have supported in light of the Hispanic past, except for the total commitment to the Catholic religion. But these men were realists; and they wanted this document to pass and to be accepted. Venezuelans seemed to be happy with the contents of this key document that reminded them of their own constitutional experiment, signed on December 21, 1811.[44] Moreover, the news from the Venezuelan agent in Bogotá was especially comforting: letters from Quito notified him that Chile had also adopted absolute independence, following Buenos Aires' pattern; moreover, the forces of Buenos Aires already were in charge of Upper Peru (Bolivia), and that General Castelli's victorious army was besieging Lima. Another important piece of news was that

Antonio Nariño had been elected to the Presidency of the Republic upon its establishment.[45] These were good signs, but the realities of the political environment were something else again.

Chapter Eleven

Divided Counsels:
A Venezuelan Polity Adrift

> We have expressed on many occasions, as a political axiom, that Independence is the only salutary move that remains to Americans; and nothing demonstrates it more than the system adopted by the Spanish Government to launch before the world a war of opinion emphasizing ambiguity, moderation, and apparent liberality, while it employs . . . and attempts in vain to gather troops with which to intimidate us, or attack us.
>
> Miguel Sanz, Caracas, January 14, 1812.[1]

> Ye sons of a new born world, heirs of liberty . . . we congratulate you on this auspicious epoch, which places you in an attitude of dignity; henceforth, let us be united by indissoluble bonds; then North and South America . . . shall show an example worthy of imitation, and admired by our fellow man of the old continent.
>
> *National Intelligencer* (D.C.), September 26, 1811.[2]

Upon returning to Congress after the Valencian campaign, General Francisco de Miranda welcomed the committee assignment to review the mission of Dr. José Cortés Madariaga to Bogotá, its expenditures, and the Treaty drawn up on that occasion. It was a project dear to his heart. Yet, the expenses of that mission were high, and revenues were never plentiful in his homeland since his return. According to an article in *El Patriota*, the April 19th Government went through two

million *pesos* that were left in the colonial coffers of Spain.[3] The
National Congress, starting on March 2, 1811, had no resources to
make ends meet, especially since commerce suffered from the piracy
that came in the wake of Spain's boycott of Venezuela. Just prior to
Independence, Miranda had complained to Congress that financial
reforms were imperative if Venezuela expected to defend herself
effectively and to establish a viable independent polity. The added
costs of the July–August "Conspiracies"—estimated at two hundred
thousand pesos—made financial reform even more urgent. The First
Republic had no future without it!

A flurry of paper bills went through Congress. On August 19th, a
Stamped Paper bill became law; on the 27th, the Law of Paper Money
passed, creating one million pesos. In October, 1811, other laws
created an additional million in coins of copper and gold. In November
1811, the Minister of Finances complained of "the extreme lack of
cash." There had been difficulties in implementing the "Paper Money"
legislation; it needed to be revised, etc., etc. By April 4, 1812—the
final session of Congress—the tragic story of the nation's financial
insolvency was still a reality!

The government of Venezuela simply could not get its citizens to
pay the increased tax bill for their new government. There were
additional political posts in the state and national governments that
required greater outlays of revenues, causing the less sophisticated to
wonder why these innovations had been made. Jobs simply were not
filled because of shortages. Possessors of capital, usually Spanish born
and their allies in colonialism, thus argued against Independence and
increased taxes. To be frank, their inclination was to get their money
out of Venezuela at the first possible opportunity; and their experience
under Spanish rule was an asset at this point. They were experts in the
secrets of the contraband trade. On July 4, 1811—the day before
Independence—Congress passed a reform of the Customs at the ports
of La Guaira and Puerto Cabello, intended to stop the vicious traffic in
the export of specie (gold and silver) that was threatening Venezuela's
financial stability. The drain of valuable capital was of no help to the
financial objectives of the First Republic.   The Minister of
Finances—the ubiquitous Roscio—proposed the prohibition of passports
to people leaving the country with their cash—a futile gesture, as it
turned out.[4]

In short, there was much talk about the need for revenues, but the
practical solution escaped the legislators. In one of his reports from the

battlefield, General Miranda continued to urge financial reform, so indispensable for the defense of the nation. He recommended the effective establishment of a credit system, very much along the lines that Burke was advocating in the *Gazeta* at that time. Yet, the pesky problem prevailed, and the First Republic limped helplessly toward its final demise. It resorted to forced loans, the sale of government properties, or other emergency measures, but without any long term results. During the Napoleonic Era, loans from Europe were not available to the first republic of Spanish America, as they were to others after 1815, another explanation for Venezuela's weakness.

Despite these financial shortages, the First Republic moved swiftly against the "Conspiracies" of July–August, 1811. It was indeed a trauma for many Venezuelans to experience a "rebellion" in less than a week after the Declaration of Independence. Yet, the threats of invasion had been constant prior to July 5th, which, in turn, influenced the decision for independence. In his first letter to Bello since the aberration of June 9th, Roscio provides keen insights into the conspiracies, as well as an implicit apology to his old friend for what he had said in his last letter: "In Caracas, it was contained [the Conspiracy] as it exploded because of the people's energy; and later, by the sentence of a judge that put seventeen to their deaths." Forty Venezuelans and three hundred rebels lost their lives in several weeks. Miranda was made responsible for Valencia, where he

> displayed the vigor of military discipline. As a result, there were some malcontents that condemned and accused him of excessive ambition. Others heaped praises upon him for his military expertise. Others attributed military inexperience and economic considerations for the spillage of blood in the vicious attack upon Valencia on the eve and on the day of its surrender . . . At last, we are free of the Valencian schism, originated in the malignity of European Spaniards; and we know well the good that this conspiracy has brought to us in order to embark upon the severe punishment of the delinquents and our enemies. Without this spilt blood, our system would have been too hesitant, and our Independence would not have been well established.[5]

Roscio's views on revolution were clear; and we wonder what Bello must have thought of Roscio's discussion on Miranda's evaluation as a controversial military figure!

Roscio's analysis will serve us well as a framework for the concurrence of factors that further weakened the First Republic—a syndrome that might be called: "Innocence" or "Irresponsibility" colored with some malice.

To begin with, there is the symbol of Francisco de Miranda, the Venezuelan "Napoleon," determined to force dictatorship upon his people. Since Roscio's June 9th letter was not published until 1882, it carried no weight in 1811; yet, there were constant rumors to that effect circulated by the Spanish loyalists and, perhaps, believed by many patriots. For example, on May 29, 1811, one hundred and seven *Valencianos* addressed a message to the Municipal Government of Caracas, hopeful that their words would reach the Congress of Venezuela. This forceful presentation brought out the entire "division" issue; and it was a rational, clear, and well-documented exposure. These Valencians believed that the offensive and exploitive concentration of power in Caracas during the Spanish regime was not a viable order for the future state of Venezuela. To persist with an identical concentration of power in a Republic would merely exasperate its people and produce interminable anarchy. From this frightening instability, there would arise:

> an ambitious and fortunate figure, who like Napoleon, might want to rule alone; to become a conqueror and devour all like a fire. What frightening ravages! What misfortunes! Just imagining it, horrifies us; but these are common cases in Republics, founded around large capitals.[6]

It is not difficult to imagine how these Valencians could have evoked the classical rise of a dictator in their midst, especially given the meteoric rise to power of a Corsican in the bloody European violence of the recent past. The elites of Europe and elsewhere lived in the constant dread of revolutionary change that might upset their societies. It came out in Roscio's letter to Bello on June 9th! This possibility could easily overwhelm less stable mentalities who desperately tried to attack, or insult, Francisco de Miranda in the halls of Congress and elsewhere. Not all of them were pro-Spanish and religious zealots; there were many persons who admired his military leadership. They dreaded, however, the possibility that this man might end up as Venezuela's Napoleon. After all, Miranda had been a French revolutionary general! They could see that he was a brilliant leader. This was evident in his speeches and positions taken in congressional discussions prior to Independence. He sounded like a sincere patriot;

but could he be swayed by the urge for absolute power, the ubiquitous "*suma del poder*" [total power] that obsessed so many Spanish-American *caudillos* of the nineteenth century? Burke's editorials constantly warned readers of the usurpation of power by the executive and the military; and Spanish-Americans went out of their way to avert this abuse of executive power in writing up their constitutions. It was like an obsession; and the Venezuelan Congress of 1811 was no exception.

As early as August 19, 1811, for example, deputy Briceño and others urged Congress to reconsider and reexamine the congressional grant of power to the Executive (July 13, 1811), now that the Conspiracy of Valencia was nearly over.[7] More rational minds recognized that such a premature display of no confidence would most certainly alienate the Venezuelan Executive Power—an unnecessary mark of ingratitude in view of its conscientious concern not to abuse *la suma del poder*. Of course, General Miranda was the real target to the Briceño group, since the Executive had passed on that absolute power to him. As Roscio indicated above, there were other cases of Miranda's enemies trying to discredit his facile victory over the Valencians. Dr. Miguel Peña, one of Briceño's good friends, complained that the General had arbitrarily forced his father, a native Spaniard, to contribute to a loan of money to help defray expenses in the Valencian zone. It created a sharp argument in Congress, which we cannot treat in detail. Suffice it to say that the defense of Miranda and the military tradition in war to collect money in this manner was well-established in world history. Miranda's defenders were, indeed, persuasive.[8] He soon learned of these charges and it bothered him deeply. He perhaps was beginning to wonder if such ingratitude would be his final reward for a career of lifetime devotion to "Colombia."

This irresponsibility toward a military hero was also present in the clemency movement that favored the *Valencianos*. Although understandable under the circumstances, the arguments of clemency partisans were not particularly impressive; seventeen lives were taken in the Caracas conspiracy; that should be enough to satisfy the "public vengeance." Besides, the Valencian conspiracy was a product of hated Spaniards and their despicable *pardos* who rallied the support of the non-white masses. This elitest view of the counterrevolution seemed to satisfy the Creoles of Venezuela. There were, of course, some misguided Americans who also went along with the uprising, etc., etc. General Miranda likewise felt that the victors should be magnanimous and that a general pardon should be forthcoming. It passed the Venezuelan Congress on November 21, 1811.[9] There were delays, however, in the implementation; and in late January, 1812, ten prisoners (*reos*), the real villains, were excluded from the pardon. The Franciscan Order had pleaded with Congress for mercy—not a very commendable action in light of the offensive role taken by their colleague Fray Pedro de Hernández. They asked for leniency on the grounds that it would encourage all of Venezuela to cooperate with the Republic. Finally, Congress yielded on the ten guilty prisoners.[10]

By sparing the lives of those prisoners, the Venezuelan Congress went against the historical precedent accepted in international law. Roscio, who headed the special six-man *Sala de Valencia* (Superior Tribunal on Valencia), adamantly disapproved of this deviation on the grounds that it weakened respect for the Republic and undermined the whole Independence process. Supporting him in the Sala were two other "founding fathers," as well as future historians: Manuel Palacio Fajardo and Francisco Javier Yáñez; the other members of the panel likewise agreed that clemency was ill advised; and their report of February 19 and 22, 1812, published in the *Gazeta de Caracas*, sustained their decision, despite the fact that Congress had already reached the decision of clemency for the ten reos. As a result, the Sala merely issued punishment to the prisoners that was entirely inadequate in view of the crimes committed.[11] The Sala's report, nevertheless, was an insightful analysis of the propaganda and illegal methods used by Venezuela's enemies in the "Conspiracies" of 1811 that would set the pattern for the future "War to the Death" in Bolívar's period.

The sentences of these six judges, along with their comments on the betrayal of their nation, must have had a sobering effect upon the *Gazeta*'s readers. Later, in 1812, the same tragedy came to the fore. The significant difference this time was that Venezuela lost the war! Would the Venezuelan precedent of clemency and understanding be followed by the Spanish victors? Not in the least. The Spaniards, according to Roscio, resorted to violence, cruelty, and vindictiveness towards Miranda's prisoners; and elements on both sides readily agreed on that judgment. The period of "Innocence" had come to an end. Henceforth, Simón Bolívar and his chastened Venezuelan supporters followed a policy based on experience: the "War to the Death" against the Spanish enemy!

During the emergency of the "Conspiracies," the National Congress was put on hold while its members assumed their duties in the military, judiciary, administration, or other assignments given to them by the Executive Power. In late August and early September, 1811, the congressmen returned to Caracas; and Congress began to function again. The key objective was to frame a Constitution for the Republic; and after three months of diligent labor and collaboration with Francisco Javier Uztáriz, the final document took form in December. On the 21st of the month, Congress signed the celebrated "Constitution of 1811."[12]

There were two major developments during those crucial months that had serious implications for the First Republic of Venezuela: first, the settlement, or compromise, on the troublesome "division" issue; and, second, the passage of a ban on corporate privileges (*fueros*). In the Hispanic world, this process of the *desafuero* (removal of the fuero) first occurred in Venezuela, then in the Spanish Cortes at Madrid in 1821, and thereafter in various republics of Spanish America during the early years of nationhood. For years and years, the desafuero became one of the most troublesome issues in the relationship between Church and State; it was the source of much political instability throughout the Spanish and Portuguese-speaking world.

Considering the acrimonious debate on "division" before Independence, it was a distinct surprise that Antonio Briceño, the leader of the anti-Caracas group, should propose a compromise solution that was acceptable to Congress as early as September 2, 1811. Perhaps this concensus occurred because of the victorious end of the insurrection at Valencia. Be that as it may, Briceño proposed the formation of a second state from the old Province of Caracas. There would be one state that included Valencia, San Sebastián, Puerto-Cabello, Calabozo, Villa de Cura, Nirgua, and San Felipe, totalling 150,245 people. This left a total of 262,612 persons living in the State of Caracas. Uztáriz agreed that two units, were adequate, as opposed to an excessive number of them without the financial potential to support them, thus causing political unrest and instability. After all, the United States of America only had seventeen states in an area that was larger than Venezuela, Quito, and Santa Fe de Bogotá combined. His suggestion that Cumaná, Barcelona, and the Island of Margarita should form a single state, however, received no attention. Instead, it was agreed to settle boundary disputes between Cumaná and Barcelona conscientiously. *Caraqueños* insisted that their State Legislature would assume responsibility for the surveys on local opinion, the elections for a capital of the second state, informing Congress of the results and recommendations. The division would take place in the future, at an appropriate time—one of stability and peace. The compromise of October 15, 1811, thus avoided a crisis that would have torn the Republic asunder in short order.[13] Yet, the factors of fragmentation, geography, and regional competition had not been erased, just subordinated for the time being.

Thanks to the compromise spirit in Congress, the constitutional work proceeded at a fast pace. Uztáriz was the major architect of the final document. He labored incessantly for three months before he put the major sections of the document together; then, Congress spent a month of morning sessions debating the projected constitution. The minutes of these debates went into a special volume: *Cuaderno de Debates* which, unfortunately, has been lost! The debates on the desafuero survived because they also appeared in the regular minutes (*actas*) of early December, 1811. Article 28 on the "Rights of Man," dealt with the equal rights of all citizens before the law, thus challenging the *fueros personales*: that is, the special privileges, rights, exemptions, etc. granted to men because of their military, ecclesiastical, and civil status, or corporate jurisdiction. Burke's editorial on this topic appeared in the *Gazeta de Caracas* on August 2, 1811. His treatment was brief and condemnatory—fueros resulted from monarchical tyranny. Although the military and ecclesiastical fueros had existed in the English and U.S. experience, the tendency was to make them subordinate to civil law and only applicable in very special cases. The English had brought their ecclesiastics under control in the past century and a half; and in the United States, where the Church hierarchy was minimal, the subordination to civil justice went unquestioned.[14] In Caracas, the opposition to the religious fuero likewise maintained that monarchy had been responsible for the practice; and the monopoly of political power had been the motive for the concession to the Church.

The Venezuelan Congress approached Article 28 (Rights of Man) in a logical fashion, seemingly unaware of the pioneering effort toward the desafuero. The first vote proposed by President Toro (from Valencia—his V.P. for the month of December was General Miranda): should all fueros personales be abolished, or should all citizens be equal before the law? There was a plurality for the affirmative, although many present had a host of reservations that they would have liked as amendments. The discussion then focused on the numerous reservations which made it clear what consequences might result from the first affirmative vote. So, President Toro offered a second proposal: should Article 28 pass in its literal sense of absolute extinction of all fueros. Again, the vote was in the affirmative. In short, the two votes had voted clearly for the desafuero. At this point, a large number of clerics in Congress registered their discontent with the two votes. They argued once again that the ecclesiastical fuero was of divine origin, documented in the Council of Trent, etc., etc., etc. Their major point was obvious: it was inopportune to take such action at this time, as if threatening that the alienation of the Church would undermine the Republic's future. The third vote: "It is inopportune to abolish all fueros at the present time?" The vote was seventeen in the affirmative, thirteen in the negative. There was, indeed, confusion at this point. The first and the third votes contradicted each other, as one congressman observed. Some one suggested a compromise: to add a footnote to Article 28 that the abolition of the ecclesiatical fuero was inopportune to implement at this time, saving it for a subsequent vote of the people in a time of peace. By this time, tempers flared in Congress; and the vote taken under those conditions supported the desafuero in the Constitution by itself, no footnotes! The die had been cast.[15] There was a last effort at compromise on December 16th, but it likewise failed.[16] On December 21st, most members were present to sign the Constitution, even many clerics who nevertheless maintained that the two contradictory votes relieved them of their responsibility. Henceforth, absenteeism was common in Congress and it was difficult to get a quorum to hold sessions. Later, when the Archbishop of Caracas relayed to Congress a complaint signed by clerics against the unconstitutional decision on the desafuero, the situation was acute, even before the famous earthquake of March 26, 1812.[17] The entire incident, once broadcasted to the world, must have provided food for thought to the liberals at the Cortes of Cádiz who in their Constitution of 1812 chose not to offend the Church at this time.

Because of his military responsibilities, General Francisco de Miranda was not able to return full time to his congressional seat until early November; and by the end of that month, he was elected Vice President of Congress for December. He was not present, therefore, in late October to vote on the bill making Valencia the new federal capital of Venezuela. In early January, 1812, he voiced his strong opinion against such a move, because of his concern for national security. Despite his recommendation for the Pardon Law of November 21,

1811, it is doubtful that he favored the clemency granted to the ten *reos*, again for national security reasons. Yet, Miranda did not enter his protest into the minutes of the congressional record.[18]

Before considering Miranda's objections to the Constitution that he signed on December 21, 1811, it should be pointed out that by this time the General was deeply concerned with the prospects of civil war again in Venezuela. By late 1811, there was a revival of rumors about the oft-threatened invasion from Puerto Rico. Miranda knew that his ally in Curaçao (Layard) was no longer Governor; the new Governor John Hodgson, on the other hand, was fully capable of siding with the Spanish ally. And that constituted a real difference in the equation. Venezuela was in danger. As early as October 15, 1811, Miranda notified Congress that the threat of invasion by the Spanish enemy this time was real; and he urged his colleagues to speed up the process of developing financial resources for the defense of the nation.[19] When Miranda returned to Congress by November 5, 1811, he was a valuable resource for his colleagues on issues of defense, security, and finances. From December 18, 1811, forward he had much to do with the investigation of the defense effort in Trujillo, weakened, it would appear, by unnecessary expenditures from the tobacco revenue. During these troubled financial times, the Venezuelan Congress was providing amounts of money from 25,000 to 1,000 pesos to the provinces of Cumaná, Barcelona, Trujillo, and Mérida for defense purposes.[20] Since Caracas ended up paying the bulk of the 200,000 pesos for the pacification of the "Conspiracies," it was evident to Caraqueños that they were the only taxpayers of importance who footed the bills of government.

On January 21, 1812, General Miranda urged his colleagues to prepare for war. The latest news, Miranda noted: "that coincided with a thousand other symptoms observable in Valencia and the suspicious conduct of the present Government of Curaçao"—all added up to the need for a general plan of defense, well-thought out by Congress. His colleagues agreed; and a Committee of three, including Miranda, was authorized to consult with the Executive Power. The urgent needs of the Government were: (1) to augment the nation's forces, (2) to construct new batteries and repair old ones, (3) to pay off the debts that are in arrears, and (4) to increase the emission of paper money. One congressman observed shrewdly: what is needed is "more money and troops."[21] In an extraordinary evening session of January 27, 1812, Miranda reported on his Committee's work with the Supreme Executive

Power. The Government had learned that foreign troops were in the Western sector near Agua Negra; moreover, the Commandant at La Guaira had reported the sighting of ships near Choroní. Orders went out to meet both threats; and Miranda suggested that it would be wise to replace the commandants at major ports with American officers. His colleagues thought that such action would be "impolitic," so they ignored Miranda's suggestion. A subsequent report on the ships near Choroní indicated that they were merchant ships.[22]

Finally, in his own irresponsible and reckless manner, Antonio Briceño blurted out that the Executive Power had exploited the services of the congressional committee. Congress, however, disagreed with him, approving of the Executive's actions. Embarrassed by Briceño's charge, the Committee of three submitted their resignations, which Congress refused to accept.[23] Miranda's patience with Briceño was wearing thin. By January 30th, the Committee and the Executive Power agreed on the following measures: to increase the line forces and budget for the construction of new batteries and repairing old ones; to increase the number of garrisons and the payment of outstanding debts; and to establish a new veteran batallion consisting of nine companies, along with a commitment of financial resources by the Treasury Department.[24] The financial predicament of the First Republic was serious, to say the least. If we add to these new defense outlays, the expenses of moving the federal capital from Caracas to Valencia by March 1, 1812; plus the added strain of a natural disaster in Venezuela in late March, 1812, and the costs of fighting the dreaded enemies for many months—the situation for Venezuela was hopeless! General Miranda no longer returned to Congress after the last episode with Briceño. He had to get ready for his next military assignment, perhaps the most important challenge of his long career.

Francisco de Miranda's ideas on government are well-known to the reader. Aware of the racial and cultural differences in Spanish-American society, the lack of education of the masses, and other traditions and customs that would resist change and modernization, Francisco de Miranda favored a strong executive power to direct the new nation, to enlighten and spur its people to a better life, and to insist upon a just and representative government that would guide its people to higher levels of achievements and happiness. A constitutional monarchy, along the lines suggested by Governor Thomas Pownall, was acceptable to Miranda because of its symbolism, so important to a people steeped in tradition. Yet, Miranda felt that the U.S. Constitution of 1787–89 was likewise acceptable because it was more centralist than the Articles of Confederation that preceded it. William Burke comprehended the real differences between the two. If Venezuelan deputies had purchased Burke's two volumes, which were available before the signing of the new Constitution on December 21, 1811, they would have realized that Uztáriz's brand of federalism was closer to the Articles of Confederation in the United States experiment. The real problem, however, was that Venezuelans merely wanted to follow their own historical instincts for local autonomy that would free them from a centralized capital, or authority. Spiritually, they wanted the old classical confederation; and Francisco de Miranda was intelligent enough to know that such a governmental trajectory would end in dismal failure. Miranda's political ideas in late 1811, like those of Bolívar in his period, were vitally influenced by a concern for military security and victory for his nation. They were brutal realists on this score, like many other political leaders in South America during the long Wars of Independence.

It is not surprising, therefore, that Miranda's colleagues were upset by what he had to say about the Constitution of Venezuela on December 21, 1811:

> Considering that in the present Constitution the powers are not in precise equilibrium, nor is the structure or general organization sufficiently simple and clear to be permanent, which besides is not adjusted to the population, usages and customs of these regions, from which may result that instead of uniting us in a general mass or social body, it may divide and separate us to the disadvantage of our common security and independence. I submit these corrections in fulfillment of my duty. Francisco de Miranda.[25]

The reaction of his colleagues was strong and varied. We are already familiar with the Uztáriz declaration on the "Old Man's" awkward notions on government; others complained that it was not fair of him to wait so long before making such a critical statement about a covenant upon which everyone had worked so hard. When Miranda retorted that Congress had given the ecclesiastics that much leeway in expressing their ideas about the *fueros personales*; he therefore had the freedom to do likewise. And there were other complaints of this nature. Yet, many of Miranda's critics could see that a triumvirate Executive to protect against the abuses of Executive Power was not the ideal situation in the long run, unless it was also expected to resort to a classical dictatorship in periods of emergency, as was the case in July and August, 1811. Yet, Miranda's popularity with Venezuelans did not suffer too much. Venezuelans realized that he was deeply concerned with the security of his country and that in the year of his return to Venezuela, his hands had been tied on almost all occasions by a powerless *Supremo Poder Ejecutivo* [SPE] (Supreme Executive Power). It is interesting to observe that in voting for a new SPE that would serve under the Constitution of 1811, the seven provinces voted initially as follows on the top three: Francisco Javier Uztáriz, 65 votes; Juan Germán Roscio, 21; and Francisco de Miranda, 17.[26]

* * * * * * * * * * *

The final third of Burke's editorials in the *Gazeta de Caracas* dealt with major themes and institutions that legislators and citizens needed to know in order to form a stable and prosperous society. The model, of course, was the United States during the "Miracle" decades. In summary, the topics included: "National Militias" (*Gazeta*: Sept. 6–27, 1811), "Public Revenues" (*Gazeta*: Oct. 1–22), "South American Commerce" (*Gazeta*: Oct. 29–Nov. 19), "Public Credit and Banks" (*Gazeta*: Nov. 26, 1811–Feb. 4, 1812), and "Constitutional Issues" (*Gazeta*: Feb. 11–March 20, 1812). The format was similar; outsiders posing as "William Burke" were not frequent; Bentham's influence was less conspicuous; and Mill's training and expertise in economics and finances predominated, as a disciple of Adam Smith. There were many reminders of that young Scottish editor who took over the *Literary Journal* of London in 1803.

Since Juan Germán Roscio controlled the manuscript before its publication in book form: Vol. I (July 12th) and II (October 3rd, 1811), his influence remained strong throughout, although Miguel Sanz, as Roscio's successor, likewise intervened with a few essays. One of Roscio's interventions involved his close colleague Francisco Xavier Uztáriz, whose talents included economics and constitutional developments. As a member of the famous Uztáriz family, so closely identified with the Bourbon reforms of Spain and Spanish America, we suspect that he had many documents on that subject in his family's library; and Uztáriz's post within the Junta Suprema government likewise involved economic matters. Thus, on November 19, 1811, "William Burke" was Uztáriz providing his readers with a detailed evaluation of Spanish taxes and a careful analysis of the Bourbon program of Debt Consolidation (*Consolidación*) for Spain in the 1790s and for America in the early nineteenth century. That is an exotic topic for serious Latin Americanists even today! The Uztáriz piece and other modifications of editorials in Volume II were interventions that Roscio allowed earlier in 1811 when he first received the manuscript from London.[27] Once Roscio made the changes intended to persuade readers in New Granada in favor of republicanism, editor Sanz intervened with two essays as "William Burke" providing a brilliant philosophical presentation on the significance of the 1811 "Conspiracies."[28] Readers of the *Gazeta* must have wondered about Burke's rare intelligence on so many different topics!

Mill's brilliance in historical synthesis was again evident in the priceless evaluations of national militias and confederation governments from the classical era to modern times. Employing an involved construction, this Scottish intellectual explained the rationale for the establishment of "National Militias:"

> Under the principle that the free citizen has rights to lose, and that it is safer and more natural for a man to be his own defender, rather than to trust the defense of his rights, jointly with his weapons, to some one, who can turn them against him, it is obviously to his interest, as well as the obligation of each citizen, who wants to conserve [the] liberty of his country and his own rights, not to separate his security from his person, trusting it to the care of mercenaries; rather he himself should be at all times, in common with his fellow citizens, the trusting, quick, and efficient protector of his rights and liberty. This principle, understood with more or less perfection seems to have been originally the general practice, as much in the ancient as in the modern nations.[29]

The old tradition of national militias eventually gave way to standing armies, the nemesis of Burke's synthesis. The artful writer explained:

> The ambition, nevertheless, of the sovereigns and their thirsts for conquests, one after the other, gradually changed the more natural and constitutional mode of defense among the nations, introducing permanent armies and, with them, almost always, constant wars, foreign subjugations and, in some cases, even the extinction of entire states. The permanent army of Philip of Macedonia finally subjugated the republics of Greece, and after them, the great empire of Persia. The

destruction of Carthage and the conquest of all the civilized nations of the Ancient World took place with a similar instrument in the hands of Rome. After the fall of this empire, the feudal governments that emerged from the ruins introduced by stages permanent armies, towards the end of the VIII century; from which period up to the French Revolution, a time span of almost 1,000 years, Europe has manifested almost an uninterrupted, horrible scene of wars, devastation, slavery and blood; and at this moment, the entire civilized world finds itself threatened by the armies of the renovated France, with a second subjugation to this modern Rome.[30]

In *Commerce Defended* (London, 1807), James Mill, whom we have quoted in an earlier chapter, emphasized that waste in government and "the consumption of war" were the major causes of human "wretchedness" in the world. As "William Burke," he expanded upon these "evils":

> The operations of war are costly: large armies must be supported either by the spoils of the enemy, or with what they can rob from their own people; they never produce for themselves, and subsist entirely from the work of others. Their maintenance is, for that, an onerous weight and their expenses an absurd loss, except in cases of necessity, for the countries that maintain such establishments. The immense charges that burden the monarchies of Europe, the weight of the debts under which they are saddled, the oppressive taxes that grind and impoverish their people, which at one stroke rob the fruit of their industry and exhaust their means [of livelihood], repressing in this way the public and individual prosperity, and the progress of civilization—all of which has originated principally from the large and costly armies that the ambition, or the needs of Princes, has forced them to pay and maintain.

What future was there for mankind in view of Burke's penetrating analysis of constant wars with their institutional consequences? James Mill thought deeply about the question and then came up with a surprising evaluation, one that a serious economist and a former student of religion might write—in short, a pacifist:

> Our reflection on these matters leaves us, nevertheless, with one consolation: namely, that the rapid accumulation of the expenses of such establishments, doubling themselves, as it happens in some states, with each new war; that [accumulation] resulting from the increased

value of human labor with proportion to the progress of general and [technological] improvements, will contribute in large part to limiting, if not destroying entirely, the inhuman practice of war and, with it, the then useless and exhausting system of permanent armies. We have already seen the insolvent monarchy of France, despite the vast resources of that great nation, submerged under the accumulated expenses of her wars: a similar destiny, accelerated by the new order of things, probably awaits all the other military despotisms of Europe. England supports her immense annual expenditures, that ascend at present to more than 300 million *pesos*, from the profits of a commerce without precedent; and an extraordinary crisis, as well as the spoils of the continent are necessary to maintain the present and gigantic military power of France. These things, however they may be, since they are beyond the ordinary course of nature and since they are incompatible with the fixed and permanent condition of nations, should, sooner or later, come to an end; when the devastating and ruinous system of permanent armies, which they maintain, gives way to the return of reason, justice and peace between nations.[31]

As expected, "William Burke" had much to say about the armies' role in the state's denial of individual "rights" and the paring down of the "people's" sovereignty. In remarkably modern idiom, he spared no one:

We note, besides, that permanent armies, shortly after their establishment, place themselves on the side of arbitrary power; and have been, almost universally, the instrument by means of which tyrants and usurpers have diminished or destroyed entirely the liberty of their own country. Caesar's permanent army destroyed the Roman Republic. Cromwell's army expelled the English Parliament from its Hall of Sessions. Gustave III, likewise employing the same means, reached the point of trampling upon the constitutional laws of Sweden, and, finally, Napoleon, with his soldiers, has overthrown the Republic of France. These are the necessary consequences of the nature and makeup of permanent armies. All such bodies are like a distant power [prop] of the State's power, whose authority is, by its essence, disposed towards usurpation, from the moment it has the force for it. Since this body is separated from the connections and solicitudes of the rest of the citizens, without wives or children, or fixed dwellings, it forms a distinct body of its own, with different interests and views. They are also different in their principles and customs. Fear and prompt and instantaneous obedience are the soldiers' principles; and accustomed, as they are, of being attended by their chief in all that concerns their [daily] life, with regards to eating, drinking, sleeping and dressing according to orders, and visibly depending upon him for all that he enjoys and desires, it is evident that a body of men worked into that mold, without the bonds that unite the rest of the citizens to the liberty of their country, and possessing in their hands the security of their force, all that is needed is sufficient numbers and to be directed by an ambitious and enterprising *caudillo*, to take advantage of the first favorable occasion to bring down the sovereignty of the State, able to dominate it with its power. The ancient military monarchies of Europe try to avoid this army usurpation by having its own sovereign as *generalisimo*, and having him appoint the principal part of his officials, under his authority, from the aristocratic estate.

After briefly describing the French system, Burke went into specific detail on the English example:

In England, besides the prerogative of the King, as head of the executive, has the direct authority over the army, and makes all the appointments, and besides his close links with the nobility and persons of property, and since the commissions are saleable, the people through their representatives in the House of Commons, who keep their hands on the purse of the nation, has still another brake over the army, by conceding subsidies to its maintenance only from year to year, as well as by decrees of the other two branches of Parliament, what is called the "*bill de motin*" [Mutiny Bill], which is, in effect, the legal authority by which the executive can maintain the army together, only for the period in question. To be sure, it is true in the present imperfect state of England's representation and other defects in the House of Commons, this wise and constitutional safeguard, which would prevent the dangers of a permanent army, is, like the greater part of other healthy restraints, reduced almost to a shadow, and the English monarchy, in this respect, comes close to the military structure of other European monarchies. Despite, therefore, all the precautions and restrictions that one might employ, the nature of a permanent army is always the same; and it will always reveal its genuine character, from the moment that circumstances permit it to shake off the brake that restricts it. This is the experience of history, as we have shown, and can be proved even more by the practice of Turkey, where the army, lacking that restraint that controls the military bodies of other monarchies, imposes and disposes of emperors when it desires. And there cannot be any doubt that a free and representative republic, in which the head of the Executive is not necessarily any soldier, and is elected for a short period of time, and in which there is no aristocracy to blend in with its officers, the danger should be even more, because of the greater opportunity for usurpation; and such a republic could not hope to survive, except for a short period, before the establishment of some permanent and numerous army.[32]

With these caveats in mind, Burke recommended the U.S. model which revived the historical tradition of national militias composed of citizens defending their nation. According to the Constitution:

> There is to be no appropriation of money to maintain an army for more time than two years," and "no State can maintain troops in time of peace without the consent of Congress, or engage in war, unless it has been actually invaded, or in such imminent danger that would not admit delay.

There were to be no peacetime armies in a State, except militias authorized to take up arms in cases of emergency. In the United States, all able white free men from 18 to 45 years of age were required to serve in state militias—estimated at one and one-quarter of a million men "the most constitutionally efficient" body of citizens brought together for "the ends of defense and security."[33] Burke surmised that South America and Mexico could get by with a militia force of one-half to one million men. He urged a general militia force, not one left to the states; and he favored cavalry units, dressed up in green uniforms to blend with the countryside, etc. etc.[34]

Cost was a key concern for William Burke; he ended the section on "National Militias" with that preoccupation in mind; and began "Public Revenues" with the same theme.[35] This provocative hypothesis immediately caught the reader's attention:

> One of the greatest principles of *representative and confederative* Government is that, [by] uniting different nations and people in harmony and peace upon one same continent, it can impede those wars and fear of them that otherwise would be the natural result of separate and entirely independent sovereignties; and prevents by these means the costly military establishments, as well as others, that are essential in a state of separation; and which are, as we have already demonstrated, the cause of the principal charges, oppression and poverty of the great body of Europe's people.

At his point, the propagandist revived the "Western Hemisphere Idea" to persuade his readers:

What wars, what expenses and sufferings has the confederative system of the United States of North America spared its people! A principal part of the people's work in Europe is dedicated to clothing, feeding, and maintaining armies to promote the destructive traffic of wars. And to what end? On the one hand, to place ambitious rulers in the state of establishing their power and monopoly over other nations; on the other [hand], to resist those usurpations. For this [reason], the industrious man is robbed of a major part of what he acquires by his sweat, and he remains with his family, subject to deprivations and sufferings, while under the free confederative system, in which everything is peace and confidence because the different individual governments are restrained by a civilized union through a constitution of general government, industry enjoys fully the benefits of their efforts, and the State thus offers prosperity to its citizens.[36]

To convince his readers that cost differences were impressive, Burke pointed out that Republican government was kept simple and more frugal in operation: "the people manage almost all the affairs of the nation gratuitously." The exceptions were the salaries provided for the top posts in government, diplomacy, and the armed forces. The civil lists of the U.S. Government involved a total expenditure of no more than one half a million annually, "which is less than one fifteenth of what is paid for the same service in monarchical countries." And the latter do not cover more than one twentieth the area of the United States! The tax structures were likewise more favorable in the Republican system. Whereas English taxpayers averaged out at from "10 to 12 pesos per head, the people in the United States who, in the general sense, are equal to paying as much in taxes as any other people on the globe, does not pay more than one and three-quarters pesos per individual." That is why they love their Republican institutions![37] These were persuasive comparisons between the two forms of government; and it may be no coincidence that Spanish Americans often boasted of the Spartan manner of their lifestyle by comparison to effete Europeans!

"The legitimate object of all public revenues," Burke maintained,

should be to pay the expenses of the State that are necessary and useful for the security and well-being of the whole. All citizens are interested in public defense, in the distribution of justice and the advancement of their country. It is therefore to his own benefit that each one contributes according to his capacity, to support those institutions that confer upon him the protection and means of increasing those advantages that he enjoys in society. But it is equally obvious that the objectives of the budget, as well as the total administration of its expenses, should be fixed and defined at all times by the legislature, and not to be left arbitrarily to the will of the Government. To do otherwise, would be to fall into the mold of European despotic governments, where corruption was endemic. Such procedures would invade the right of property, one of the fundamentals of civilized society, and of each free state; it would amount to subjecting the property of the nation to just the will of the few that control the Government, and to precipitate [the country] into the most unlimited despotism and extravagance.

The main emphasis in organizing an efficient system of control should be "*not to provide temptation to vice.*"[38]

According to William Burke, the revenue system of the United States involved some fourteen to fifteen million dollars annually. In his account, Burke dealt with the northern Republic's commercial potential by comparison to that of South America and Mexico. He also treated the extent and utilization of public lands as a source of revenue in the United States, as well as the public credit and financial institutions of that country—all of this in amazing detail. That story, unfortunately, we cannot accommodate here, since our primary objective is to emphasize the presence of this valuable interpretation during the Independence of South America, guiding its leaders and intellectuals. Some of Miranda's speeches and letters reflected closely Burke's suggestions on economic and financial reforms. Since "Paper" money in the United States was a key issue for years, Burke's discussion of this problem was vital to Republicans in Venezuela in their time of crisis. The problem was not just peculiar to them. The U.S. model, in this case, was a true catastrophe; and Mill indicated ways in which South Americans might avert such a drastic result. Economic historians of the United States of that period will appreciate Mill's exceptional grasp and analysis of Alexander Hamilton's financial reforms.[39] Those reforms, of course, prepared the United States for its remarkable economic recovery and prosperity—the miraculous period in U.S. history that formed the basis for Mill's manuscript in behalf of Miranda and Venezuela's Independence.

Gifted in the study of economic institutions, James Mill was also well-endowed in the disciplines of the historian and the political scientist. What "William Burke" had to say about "confederation" and "constitutions" in history was of great importance to the young nations of Spanish America, especially because of his preference for a Republic.

As an excellent teacher, Mill wanted his public to review all the fundamentals: what was a confederation, the two types of confederations in the Greek World and how they succumbed to outside elements: the Macedonian invaders under Philip, in one case, and the Romans in the second place. In the modern era, the confederations of Germany, Poland, Switzerland, and Holland also ended in failure. And the United States, in the New World, almost reached its fatal point in the 1780s, despite its heroic union and defense that made the independence of the United States possible. Burke's analysis was concise:

> The great error and cause of weakness was the imperfect principle of legislating for States instead of individuals. We have already demonstrated that such a principle was the father of anarchy and the cause of the destruction of all the ancient and modern confederations that have existed; and it could very well have produced the same catastrophe for the American republic. Congress passed laws in vain, when it had no power to put them into effect. Each State adopted the right to dispute the propriety or convenience of the General Congress' rights, and frequently the interest of a sole State was opposed to the interest of all of them. The Confederation also needed a sanction for its laws. Congress had no power to compel obedience to its resolutions, by means of fines, or other methods.

Burke pointed out all of the weaknesses of the General Government. The results, of course, were, as might be expected:

> The resolutions of Congress were not well attended by the States; only a few of the legislatures obeyed the requisitions to supply the union's treasury; there was barely enough money to meet the expenses of the civil list; British troops still retained their posts within the Confederation; the credit of the United States declined rapidly in other countries, while Congress was losing its rightful respect in its own sphere; and thus it appeared that the seeds of a general anarchy were planted, and that the union was approaching a rapid and violent dissolution.[40]

> Other circumstances added to the danger of the crisis. Large amounts of foreign goods flooded the markets after the war, the paper money, that previously had been the means of circulation [payment], now loses its value, and cash was being sent to Europe to pay for the

imported goods. The consequence was a total scarcity of money in the
country. To remedy the bad situation, some States asked for letters of
credit. This tactic, notwithstanding, after producing a temporary relief,
was followed by bad results. At first, it raised, or increased, the price
of gold and silver, which had the effect of stunting all types of
commerce and industry, etc. etc.

Anarchy was in the offing and business came to a halt; distrust and
discontent was everywhere, "and even some of the States were
threatened, or actually experienced some dangerous insurrections."

"What aggravated even more the calamities of those times," Burke
continued, "was that the principal European powers passed prohibitive
measures that were highly injurious to American commerce." Despite
the actions of some States to counter with their own taxes against
foreign goods, they were helpless without a General Government to
direct them: "The interest of one State was opposed to that of another;
their restrictions were useless; irritation and contrariness followed; and
the end would probably lead to the most fatal consequences."[41]

The rest of the story is well-known— the celebrated Convention that
met in Philadelphia in May, 1787, producing the world's greatest
political documents. The required nine states ratified the Constitution
of the United States in 1789. Yet, William Burke's observations
concerning that historical process are well worth noting:

> In the meantime, there were numerous individuals, however, some
> because of their vested interests, others from ignorance, and some also
> because of hatred for liberty, who opposed the adoption of the new
> Constitution, based on grounds that it embraced principles and views
> that were new in politics, that although they appeared plausible in
> theory, they could not be implemented in practice, that the extension of
> territory and commutable distance of the States was too great to be
> included under one Government; and, finally, that it might be seen how
> two or three Confederations would be better. The friends of union and
> of America happily parried those arguments: they made people realize
> that force, security and prosperity of all the States depended upon being
> closely united; that this, far from admitting difficulties, was practicable
> and easy and that the plan of Constitution recommended was the best
> that could have been invented to bring about effective union.[42]

Finally, the time had come for the great master to sum up the moral
and the significance of this celebrated event in world history:

We have presented this historical sketch to the reader, with the double objective of demonstrating the impropriety of a confederation based upon imperfect principles of union and legislation, and of placing before his eyes the example of one of the most important and interesting revolutions that has ever taken place—revolution in which a people of an extensive nation, or perhaps we should say of thirteen nations, serene and judiciously, without any bloodshed whatsoever, put aside their old structure of general Government and erect in its place a better one—the result of a profound consideration and of experience. History does not offer another example to equal it; while it is certain that this glorious and, for the human race, happy revolution, only was able to happen through means of the great principle of representation.[43]

Never have the effects of any other political revolution been so sudden, great, and beneficent. The confederation, which only recently was in a state of rapid disunion, approximating anarchy, war, and slavery, is now situated on new and secure fundamentals. With confidence and security, peace and harmony are recovered in just a little time. Industry and commerce revive; credit is established within and outside of the country; public securities go up 40 percent in price in their market; the value of lands, which had dropped 50 percent after the revolution as a result of insufficient capital and the bad state of business in general, receives [now] a rapid increase; and all this is born by simply perfecting the general government, remodeling the confederation, and placing it on the true principles of union. The creation of resources for the public debt and the establishment of Banks, complete the work of national betterment. These things, as we have said, because they increased the capital and means of the nation, adding to the force and efforts in all lines. America now assumes an attitude of importance and respect in the eyes of foreign nations; she cleans her territory of foreign posts and fortifications; she concludes advantageous commercial treaties abroad; unfolds the powers of her industry and opens to her citizens a career of enterprise and prosperity without rival in the history of nations.[44]

In an earlier chapter, we emphasized that Burke's proposal of March 29, 1811—the asterisk document associated with the "caper"—called for the establishment of *one* state, or confederation, for all of former "Spanish America": the "United States of South America and Mexico." Yet, for various reasons, as subsequent documents were modified by certain clauses, etc., Spanish Americans began to think in terms of two confederations. We suspect that Roscio's influence tended in that direction; and the non-Burkian portions of the *Gazeta de Caracas* reflected this view, as Roscio's opinion or that of some other publicist with whom he agreed. We suspect that Andrés Bello and James Mill discussed this matter and decided to write to Miranda about it in mid-1811, sending him new or modified articles for publication in Volume 2. In short, Mill felt that he had to counteract that notion of two or three confederations, knowing that the opposition to the U.S. Constitution of 1787 had used that tactic before. Spanish Americans, therefore, should be made aware of that destructive device by the enemies of union. Given Mill's temperament, he also was annoyed that his ideas had been distorted and tampered with, giving the appearance that he was inconsistent. Perhaps the only one he revised was the editorial that appeared on February 11, 1812, in the *Gazeta de Caracas*—the first of the series on constitutional issues.

As a skillful debater, always looking for the best technique to impress his readers, he wrote as follows:

> With these ends in view, we have proposed that South America and Mexico form themselves into two great and distinct confederations, basing themselves on similar principles and with concurrent views; and united the one to the other, as well as to the United States of the North, in friendship and equal alliance. The Colombian Continent thus, would comprehend three great representative republics, whose distribution of power would favor the conservation of peace and happiness, and in case of disagreements between two confederations, the third would be able to intervene as a friendly mediator to settle the difference and restore harmony as before.[45]

Mill's Burke, of course had *not* said that at all! Yet, Mill chose this tactic to protect Roscio's use of his penname. The rest of this article, double the size of most of them, proceeded to demonstrate conclusively how erroneous the two, or three, confederations of states had proven to be in history! The argument was scholarly and clever; and the number of times he blew history's trumpets were indeed revealing, reminding us of the original Williams Burke published in London. And what is truly interesting is that among his various historical examples there were two dealing with India!

In the study of confederations, there are certain errors that must be avoided. To begin with, you should not confuse a representative republic with a mere democracy, which leads to "the erroneous supposition that a republican government cannot embrace a vast space of territory." "Nevertheless," Burke continued: "nothing could be less accurate, as much in principle as in practice." A democracy, because of its nature, is limited to a smaller zone. On the other hand, if you adopt

> the modern principle of representation, reuniting the people and administering government by means of deputies and agents, you can use the republican system to almost all extension as we have demonstrated in the practical example of the United States of North America.

And, not understanding "sufficiently the distinction between the two forms of government, gives birth as well to the harmful opinion: 'that leagues and alliances among numerous and distinct confederations, will take the place of a general confederation, founded on true principles for the union of the whole.'" This is humbug!

> The nature of these things and the world's experience proves, that nothing could be farther from the truth. An alliance is nothing more than a contract between two or more independent states, in which each one enters because of its own particular views, and which can be observed or broken, whenever it desires, conforming with his sentiments of interest or whim.

Burke was now ready to get back to his major objective:

> Let us suppose that South America is divided into different confederations, united by means of treaties. Should we not fear those same evils with which similar divisions in the other parts of the globe have been overwhelmed? Where is that district on the face of the earth . . . that has not been at one time or another soaked with blood and tears, and finally brought down to the condition of conquest or slavery, conforming to the temperament of the invader, because of a bad distribution of its powers, through the destructive system of numerous and distinct sovereignties or federations held together solely on the sandy bases of treaties, or united with such weak bonds? Ancient history is a fountain of proofs that treaties did not last more than while contracting parties believed that it was to their interest to observe them; that they generally ended in war and, one or the other, invited to their own country a foreign force to assist them against the adversary; and thus they paved the road for the conquest and enslavement of all. In modern history we see the same consequences born from similar causes.

The examples flowed; British kings, five kings of Ireland, etc. etc. And, Oh, yes: the "Princes of India opened up the road to the subjugation of their Continent," etc. To think otherwise "is to contradict the experience of the world and to misjudge the nature of man." The persistent Burke returned again to the Spanish Americans:

> Even if we supposed that three or four confederations might grow up in South America based upon equal principles and fundamentals, and with all the circumstances of mutuality; everything considered, the natural progress of things would create a distinction among them, and it would lead to differences. One confederation would be more industrious, populated, and powerful than the other; she would like to be the leader; the others, jealous of her achievements, would agree naturally to measures against the threat posed by the superior state.

The situation would not be any better in a "League" of nations in South America; or even a "confederated republic based on erroneous principles. History has shown, time and time again, that these types of organization" ended in disaster. The explanation, or remedy, that Burke was hinting at was what he had concluded about the Articles of Confederation in the United States. The great error was the "imperfect principle of legislating for States in place of individuals."[46] Instead of "States' Rights," Burke seemed to be saying, you had to have the "unionist" orientation of the Constitution of 1787. Throughout Spanish America, the words were different: the unionists were called *unitarios* (unitarists) or *centralistas*, etc. At any rate, that was the message that James Mill was preaching to his readers. It is interesting, however, that he had to resort to this special technique in order to convince his readers that he was back on the "consistent" track. During the time of the First Republic of Venezuela, Venezuelan readers had an opportunity to judge for themselves the historical pattern and examples supplied by James Mill, who sensed that Spanish Americans might fall into the same historical trap, which they did! He pleaded with them not to forget how the enemies of union in the United States used the same technique: two or three confederations to throw the unionist solution out of the window.

As William Burke in his final editorials of 1812 pleaded his case emotionally in behalf of a single General Confederation for the former Spanish America, he could not ignore the issue of distance. On February 25, 1812, he admitted that "The most plausible objection to a general confederation of South America is that of distance."[47] And he likewise admitted that "the force and resources that emerge in a general union, would be the most efficient means to destroy the enterprise." However, alliances were no solution at all, returning to his chant that history could prove it. "What American, therefore, would want to trust confidently his liberty and happiness of his country to such an uncertain guarantee?" Time and time again, he would return to the example of the United States who, "equal to all of Europe now, makes her governmental system work expeditiously with deputies from the representatives from states that traveled 400 to 600 miles, and those in the Western states, 800 to 1,000 miles," etc. etc. Judging from the U.S. system, he concluded "that the confederative, representative system is capable of including any extension of territory that can be traveled conveniently by the members of the General Congress." With a good Constitution, and "with the distant situation in which America finds herself vis-a-vis Europe," the urgency is lessened. In South America, therefore, it would suffice for the states near the capital to form a "quorum" in an emergency while other members made their way to the seat of government. Thus, the national business would go forward, etc. etc. Distance, thus, is not the great problem, he argued, citing the example of Greeks traveling two thousand miles in their defense; and, in India, a British army penetrated Hindostan for about two thousand miles to the borders of the Persian empire.[48]

William Burke's last editorial appeared on March 20, 1812, and presumably it was to be continued [*Se continuará*]. But on the 26th, an horrendous earthquake hit the city of Caracas; thus, Burke was discontinued—no more of his essays for the *Gazeta de Caracas*. In the final paragraphs, William Burke waxed philosophically by returning to the "Western Hemisphere Idea": "The New World is entirely a new scene; it is, compared to the Old [World], a state of nature."[49] These were reflections that we learned earlier from the old master.

* * * * * * * * * * *

Once England committed herself to face the French enemy in the Peninsular War, her options with regards to South America changed dramatically. The Treaty of Alliance with Spain was a serious deterrent in advancing British commercial interests in Spanish America. Despite the Anglo-Hispano Alliance, the historical antagonism of Spain and

England continued to fester over the British desire to trade with Spain's overseas possessions. This hostility, moreover, manifested itself over the direction and leadership of the war against France. Nationalistic tendencies flared up against the English in the Spanish port of Cádiz especially.

The "American Question" at the Cortes of Cádiz further aggravated the feelings between the two allies, as Spanish Americans sided with England in seeking "free trade" for Spain's allies in Europe—Great Britain and Portugal. And, it will be recalled, that there was an interesting dichotomy in British policy, especially with regard to Venezuela. Alexander Cochrane and Governor Layard of Curaçao encouraged trade relations with Venezuela, leaving the impression that they favored Venezuelan Independence; whereas Governor John Hodgson, Layard's replacement, favored the ally Spain as opposed to the freedom fighters of Venezuela.

On March 2, 1811, the establishment of a National Congress in Venezuela was critical in forcing Great Britain's hand. Although still loyal to Ferdinand VII, Venezuela reached a new governmental level that, in due time, would lead to Independence, thus setting the pattern for all of Spanish America. Buenos Aires, for example, followed suit in May, 1811, and others soon did likewise. England now had no alternative but to order a consistent policy of "mediation," which meant, in effect, following the precedent set with the Venezuelan Commission of mid-1810. The British Ambassador to Spain, the Marquis of Wellesley, offered a proposal for mediation to his ally. Although Spain hesitated, she then agreed to England's conditions, adding some of her own, and forwarded Wellesley's proposal to the Spanish Cortes. By late June, 1811, the Spanish Parliament announced its nine articles on mediation.

With this background in mind, let us turn now to the related topic of propaganda that each side would use to win the approval of world opinion for their respective causes. We are familiar with Miranda's propaganda over the years, so that we have a good idea what mediation would mean for the American cause. We need, however, to have some understanding of Spain's side of the ledger to be able to reach a more valid judgment.

Nevertheless, let us review briefly Miranda's career in convincing the world that Spanish America's emancipation was in the air. Governor Thomas Pownall, his good friend, fostered the vision of a cultural and economic union of the Old and New World—the English in Europe and the ex-colonials of Spain and England in America during the final decades of the eighteenth century. James Mill took up the English mantle after Pownall's death; and in the Burkian treatises of 1807–1808 encouraged the British Government to involve itself in Spanish America's Emancipation, thus outsmarting Napoleon and creating an "Invisible Empire" of free trade for England's future prosperity and world leadership in politics and commerce. And the publications of Miranda's writers from 1808 through 1810 influenced emancipation pressures in Europe and especially in the New World. The editorials of William Burke from 1810 to 1812 were vital, we know, for northern South America; but we know less as to their real impact elsewhere in Spanish America. Thanks to Francisco de Miranda and his Mexican associates, propaganda bundles circulated throughout Spanish America, emphasizing continental solidarity and revolutionary procedures. Miranda's group in Venezuela, and especially Roscio's contributions as Secretary of State and Editor of the *Gazeta de Caracas*, sent copies of Burke's essays throughout the New World. Miranda's message likewise received support in London from Blanco-White's *El Español*, as well as the Portuguese counterpart in that city, *O Correio Braziliense*. The editor of the "Brazilian Post" was a close friend of Miranda; and they both dedicated themselves to keeping the Americas informed of the emancipation story in the New World. After April 19, 1810, Roscio also seized every opportunity to send documents of the Venezuelan story throughout the Americas and Europe. As a result, the Independence movement in Spanish America received a good press in most of the world.

There was no question about receptive audiences in the North American Republic, whose citizens were thrilled that their example was being followed in the lands to the South. A case in point was the letter printed in the *National Intelligencer* (Washington, D.C.) from "The American Patriot" to the "Friends of Good Government, Liberty, and Independence." He reminded his colleagues that since 1776 there had been three "extraordinary revolutions:" the American, French, and now South American. The Patriot asked emotionally: "Who amongst us does not exult at the intelligence received from that abused and long oppressed people? What bosom does not bounce with rapture almost ecstatic, on reading the declaration of independence by the inhabitants of Venezuela?" The Patriot turned up his rhetoric: "Ye sons of a new born world, heirs of liberty . . ."[50] That was the second quotation that introduced this chapter.

This pro-Independence image making has concerned us throughout this work; but, now, what about the Spaniards' version of the same events? On January 14, 1812, Miguel Sanz wrote a fascinating and historically valuable essay in the *Gazeta de Caracas*. After studying the newspapers in Spain and Puerto Rico from September through October, 1811, he evaluated their propaganda vis-a-vis the events transpiring in South America and especially in Venezuela and neighboring jurisdictions. Despite the observer's partiality, Sanz, nevertheless, provides us with some interesting insights on what the enemy was saying during the so-called "Conspiracies" of July–August, 1811, in Caracas and Valencia. A good friend of Francisco de Miranda, Miguel José Sanz objected vehemently at the picture of Miranda as the arch-villain of the Venezuelan rebel movement. These offensive reports were fabricated in the *conventículos* ("special offices, laboratories, etc.) in Puerto Rico. It was there that Cortabarría and his minions prepared their vicious projects, as well as their propaganda, to keep the Spanish Mainland of South America loyal to the Cádiz government. These men cared nothing about means; their objectives, or ends, were a complete victory over the rebel Americans.

Deeply disturbed by the vicious stereotypes that he saw in those papers, Miguel Sanz feared that propaganda of that type might have a crucial impact upon the final results of the conflict between Spain and her ex-colonies. Sanz again repeated his political axiom that, as a result of Spain's policy of insincerity, ambiguity, and hypocrisy, Americans had no alternative but to fight for their Independence. Spanish strategy was simple: create a false illusion of military victory in Buenos Aires and Mexico so that everyone would assume that an expeditionary force from Puerto Rico as its base could easily take Venezuela or the neighboring jurisdiction of Santa Fe de Bogotá. Understandably, Sanz resented the personal attack upon Miranda, which at the same time discredited the Venezuelan Revolution as nothing more than a French experiment of blood and lust. In this light, the "Conspiracies" of July–August, 1811, appeared in the enemy papers as liberating crusades against the bloody "Dictator Miranda," supported by the villainous members of the *Sociedad Patriótica de Venezuela*. Half-truths and bald-faced lies were common:

> that Miranda at the head of the Sociedad Patriótica, has dissolved the Congress of Venezuela having shot down some of its members . . . It would appear that Miranda has set himself up as an independent tyrant

and that he is marching with some troops against Valencia and the
Valles de Aragua where the congressionalists are defending themselves.

By the time this distortion reached London, via Cádiz, the reader
learned that the Sociedad Patriótica had stormy rump sessions at night
in which its members arbitrarily determined who was to die on the
following day!

Sanz's interpretation of the Spaniards' propaganda barrage reveals
insights into the Spanish-American position with regards to the British
mediation proposal that commenced seriously in 1811. Sanz was
highly suspicious, as the following remarks indicate:

> Under the veracious and honorable auspices they [the enemy writers in
> those *conventículos* of Puerto Rico] try to form public opinion in Spain,
> as well as to surprise that of England by persuading [the English] that
> the Regency in Cádiz is sacrificing a great deal in accepting mediation
> with America.

This was a sham; a real mediation move should be proposed, and
directed, by the British along the lines followed in September, 1810,
with the Venezuelan Commission to London. All the while, Spain has
been frustrating Americans with all manner of fakery—those abusive
Royal Commissions, like the one sent to Venezuela, and the other
exasperating tactics. All of this has compelled Americans to violent
and desperate measures. Spain "has done all that was possible to attract
us and deceive us." Unable to defeat us by force, Spain has pretended
to help her ally England on a program of "mediation;" later, she will
undoubtedly reward the English by excluding them from the "free trade
that she [England] already enjoys with the American countries." By
declaring their independence, "Americans have made themselves
superior . . . to the mediations, and other devices, which have been
used alternatively to maintain Europe's hegemony of America under
Spain's monopoly."[51]

As Editor of the *Gazeta de Caracas*, Sanz challenged his readers to
look at the papers in question and to examine what Spanish policy was
towards America. Was it truly liberal? Did it reflect good faith in the
concepts of "reconciliation" or "mediation?" Or was it the usual
insistence of Spaniards on the "submission, obedience, vassalage, and
degradation of America, gilded with the specious titles of fraternity,

loyalty, gratitude, compassion forming the deck of words that they deal us in their overseas planning rooms?" Blanco-White used similar expressions in describing his countrymen's hypocrisy and arrogance in dealing with American rivals. Sanz was furious: Americans were fed up with the continual denials of their natural rights. "Time and time again," Sanz concluded: "we discover the impotence of our enemies, the fraudulence of their promises, the wild fancy of their expeditions, and the falsity of their papers."[52] These were powerful remarks by a responsible Venezuelan patriot. They did not offer much hope for England's program of mediation.

Wise counsels emanating from the Lord Holland group in London might have saved England's mediation plans for America. At that stage in the anti-colonial movement of the New World, however, the eurocentric emphasis of its writers would have been too much for Americans to accept. The advice offered by José Blanco-White and his good friend Dr. John Allen was in agreement on most points. Both gentlemen were "cultural imperialists," one representing a "glorious Spain" and the other a "glorious England." They expected their mother countries to assume a respectable, reasonable, and modern stance on government for the New World. Both Blanco-White and Allen offered programs that in a less agitated world might have helped Latin America to form a stable base for the modernization of her societies.

Reverend Joseph Blanco-White became a celebrity throughout Spanish America when he defended the April 19, 1810, Revolution in Caracas; and by the Fall of that year, he also attacked Spain's blockade of Venezuela, bitterly assailing the wrong-headed policy of the Spanish leaders at Cádiz. Juan Germán Roscio, on two occasions, showered the Spaniard in London with praises for his exposure of ill-advised colonial practices of Spain. On July 11, 1811, *Don José* composed a lengthy letter to the Venezuelan Government, answering their January, 1811, message of praise. It should be noted, that the letter in question did not reach its destination until the late summer—in fact, it was written almost a week after Venezuela's birth as a Republic. It appeared in No. 16, *El Español* (London), July 30, 1811; but the Venezuelans chose not to publicize it in their *Gazeta*, for reasons that should be apparent in the discussion that follows.

Why did Blanco-White wait so long to reply to Roscio's favorable letter? By studying the letter of July 11th, we can see that *Don José* had been pondering the implications of the blockade news upon the Spanish Americans; it would probably lead to a wide-scale

Independence movement; and the thought of this infuriated him with the stupidity and hardheadedness of his countrymen. Thus, when he learned that the Venezuelans brought together their first National Congress of March 2, 1811, he knew in his heart that Independence would be the result; and if Venezuela took the first step, the rest of Spanish America would follow suit; and the Spanish Empire overseas would crumble. The news that Great Britain was going to sponsor a "mediation" program, had the effect of reviving his hopes; and Blanco-White's relationship with the Lord Holland group intensified. For example, Dr. John Allen's essay that we shall discuss later was also published in *El Español*, so that Spanish readers would listen to Allen's cogent message. Blanco-White, moreover, provided the background information for Allen's article.

Blanco-White's letter of July 11, 1811, marked the beginning of a shift in the relationship with his American admirers, who now recognized, for the first time, that his motives were less altruistic than they had appeared initially. After thanking the Venezuelans for their good feeling towards him, he reviewed what they all knew about him and how he had arrived at the conclusion that "*Conciliación*" between Spain and Spanish America was the desirable goal, so that if Spain vanished under Napoleon's heel in Europe, she would live on in a free Spanish America. In effect, he was suggesting a course of action similar to what Portugal had experienced in Brazil from 1807 forward.

Yet, it was so difficult to sustain his faith for a program of "Conciliation." It was so much to expect Americans to be patient in view of the constant finagling of Spanish governments that went from bad to worse. But then, he argued with himself, as if to seek pity: the Americas could survive and certainly they would not turn their back on Spain "on these people worthy of the admiration and compassion of the entire world, (and above all, of their brethren)." Although, he admitted:

> I could not come up suddenly with the details of a plan that would combine the interests of one and the other, I saw clearly and decidedly that they could be conciliated—and from that point on I dedicated my weak efforts to this truly grandiose object.

Then, the Spanish Regency started its "blood and fire" strategy to blockade Caracas. What hope was left? The only hope left for conciliation was the convening of Parliament, followed by the reversal of the Regency's policy. That turned out to be a dismal mistake:

beautiful and democratic verbiage but the reality was that the Regency's despotic acts were left in place! Blanco-White thus concluded—and he underlined it: Parliament left it all up *"to despotism to limit the logic of Americans!"*[53] In short, he had arrived at Sanz's political axiom: Americans had no other alternative but to seek Independence in view of Spain's strategy in dealing with them.

Blanco-White's letter of July 11, 1811, was a revealing confession of a Spanish intellectual whose dream of a "glorious Spain" was evaporating before his eyes. And he was pathetically desperate in his appeal to Americans to have a heart, be humane, understanding, and forgiving. Towards the end of his letter, he finally admitted that there was little hope that either side would accept "this rude sketch, and even if it were a plan infinitely better arranged."[54] And as he dared, almost shamelessly, to propose what Americans should do in their contriteness—turn their cheeks again—he recognized that this was all unreal and farfetched: "Perhaps what I propose to you will appear like the virtue of a novel." He raved on: "The example of the United States was not applicable to Spanish America"—that was his dogma; Spanish Americans should not contribute "to the dismemberment of the Spanish Monarchy." They should remain within the Spanish Commonwealth, whose capital would be in Spain! The government would be a constitutional monarchy: the program outlined by his friend John Allen for self-government was also his wish. He believed in a gradual approach, not a revolutionary one. It would bring prosperity and happiness to Spanish America in the long run, etc., etc., etc.

On occasion, this desperate publicist turned to threats to bring Spanish Americans into line. If you persist with Independence, Great Britain, because of its treaty with Spain, might force your acquiesence. Then, Blanco-White stopped that approach and shifted to a more positive line: what was needed was a "powerful mediator." "The only power that can mediate under the present circumstances in Europe" was Great Britain. The time was ripe for Americans to unite in their respective congresses, to draw up "a solemn, although moderate manifesto, explaining the reasons for your conduct, and your dispositions not to abandon Spain, despite the fact that they are aggrieved by the war she is waging upon them." "That war of Spaniards with Spaniards is horrible," exclaimed Blanco-White: "All that is directed to extinguishing it is very noble and glorious."[55]

After this lengthy, and pathetic, plea for "Conciliation," *Don José* unexpectedly confessed to his Venezuelan admirers:

the American affair is for me not only the most important of those that interest the Spanish Nation, but also because it is my own affair, a matter that I have identified with my person, since, because of it, I have found myself persecuted, insulted, and perhaps already proscribed from Spain.

"The Americans," he continued:

honor me by saying I am impartial; many Spaniards insult me by calling me a rebel; but the testimony of my conscience tells me that I am not one or the other. I vehemently desire the happiness of Spain, and on this issue, I am *a passionate believer.*[55]

This was an amazing testimonial by one of Spain's intellectuals, the leading publicist of his day who witnessed the birth of Spanish liberalism, Spain's "War of Independence" against France, and the "Wars of Independence" in Spanish America.

Dr. John Allen, whose July, 1810, article we have already studied, published a sequel in the *Edinburgh Review* (November, 1811), the one that Blanco-White translated into Spanish for his periodical. "Since the appearance of our former article," Dr. John began: "a lamentable revolution had taken place in Spanish America." "Colonies, which were at that time the abode of peace and industry, have now become the seat of violence and desolation," he added. Civil war and bloodshed were rampant everywhere. Dr. John Allen doubted seriously that Independence was worth the price being paid by the Americans; and he objected to Spain's exaggerated obsession in fighting the insurrection. Mediation and reconciliation should be the major objectives of both parties. He hoped to persuade his countrymen that mediation should be Great Britain's policy in this draining conflict, that was holding up England's stand in the Peninsular War, as well as playing havoc with British trade.

With the assistance of Blanco-White, Dr. Allen sketched in the historical background: Spanish history from the time of the Junta Central forward, the Regency's problems with the Americans, and the issues at stake in the April 19, 1810 revolution in Venezuela during its first year of existence. This was a good historical analysis. But objectivity was completely lacking from July 5, 1811, forward, as the Doctor drew primarily from the accounts of Spaniards, even though he had some doubts about their accuracy. On events in the Río de la Plata, New Granada, and Mexico, he utilized the reports written by

Blanco-White for the British Foreign Office. Although years earlier, Miranda had received praise in the pages of the *Edinburgh Review*, in Allen's second article his name was not mentioned at all! Just as March 2, 1811, the opening of Congress in Venezuela had impressed Blanco-White as the beginning of the end, Dr. John Allen noted that a "different spirit" henceforth prevailed in that area because of the "unhappy ascendancy in the colony" of agitators. "A refugee from America," Dr. John elaborated:

> whose lifetime has been spent in stirring up enemies to Spain, had been permitted, by the English government, to return to Caracas, and had there contrived to get himself elected member of Congress by one of the most inconsiderable towns of the province. A patriotic club was got together, and a newspaper set on foot, with the imposing title of the 'Patriot of Venezuela'; having for its professed object to discredit and destroy the system of moderation on which the leaders of the insurrection had hitherto proceeded. These arts were as usual successful. On the 5th of July, 1811, the deputies who had so lately renewed their oaths to Ferdinand, abjured his authority, declared themselves absolved from all allegiance to the Crown of Spain, and constituted the provinces which they represented into free and independent states, with the title of United Provinces of Venezuela.[57]

Dr. John's description of the conspiracy period was not objective at all:

> Many persons have been arrested on suspicion, and thrown into prison; some banished, and not a few put to death; and to strike greater terror into the disaffected, the heads of the sufferers have been fixed on poles at the gates of the city, as a warning to the unwary, not to question the legitimate authority exercised by the free and independent states of Venezuela. Such are the happy auspices under which South American regeneration has commenced, and such the benefits of a leader experienced in revolution![58]

What a strange way of presenting a villain without even mentioning his name. Did it have something to do with Francisco de Miranda's popularity in Scotland back in 1809?

Here, it should be noticed that Blanco-White's description of Venezuela in the "Conspiracy" period was just as superficial: the French Revolution was being repeated in the streets of Caracas and throughout Venezuela. Proof of this contention: the document on "The

Rights of Man" and the brazen denial of freedom of the press—the documents that the *Niles' Register* had published earlier which also reached Europe shortly thereafter! It would appear that the ex-Spanish liberal in London was beginning to develop a phobia for *"francesismo"* (Frenchified political doctrines?), as he later described it. That revolutionist Miranda, and his blood-thirsty minions in the *Sociedad Patriótica de Venezuela*, had gone beserk rejecting their King and their old mother *patria*. *Don José's* bitterness and anger was apparent to all readers of *El Español* who received the numbers 17 through 19 in late 1811. Spanish-Americans, as might be expected, became thoroughly disenchanted with their former champion who pleaded for British "mediation" while at the same time insulting Miranda.[59]

Blanco-White's aberration in the propaganda struggle of late 1811 did not go unanswered. Two Spanish American patriots—the Colombian Manuel de Pombo and the Mexican Fray Mier Noriega y Guerra (José Servando Teresa de)—fiercely attacked Don José editorials in Nos. 16–19 of *El Español*. Fray (Friar) Mier's critique appeared in *Carta de un Americano Español sobre su número XIX* (Letter of an American Spaniard on [*El Español*] No. XIX). Father Mier, a distinguished Mexican deputy at the Cortes of Cádiz, knew Spanish liberals as well as Father Don José Blanco. He took the distortion on the Sociedad Patriótica de Venezuela—cases in which the members decided who would die on the following day—and made Blanco-White look ridiculous. He lectured *Don José*: if you had read the *Gazeta de Caracas* on such-and-such a date, you would have realized that the death penalty was being applied for violating the Freedom of the Press in the war crisis of that emergency. To insinuate otherwise was a deliberate falsehood! What was Blanco-White's answer? It was unbelievable: my hypothesis was as good as yours. I, at least, started from the premise that independence was bad for America, etc. etc. The year 1811 was a stressful one: first, Juan Germán Roscio, and then Joseph Blanco-White, both intellectuals and colleagues of Miranda. Roscio salvaged his relationship with the General; and, interestingly, as the Spaniard recovered somewhat from his aberration, *Don José* wrote, in 1812, that the Spanish military leaders in Venezuela were no match for General Francisco de Miranda![60]

Dr. John Allen's article of November, 1811, continued:

> After this historical review, which we have endeavoured to make as concise as possible, consistent with our object of pointing out the nature,

extent and causes of the present troubles in America, we shall, in a few words, state our reasons for thinking, that it is not for the interest of the Spanish colonies to declare themselves independent, or to separate entirely from the mother country, unless compelled to it by the unreasonable obstinacy of the government at Cádiz, or by the complete conquest of Spain by the arms of France.

Dr. Allen's analysis was elitist in spirit but it was also a realistic program of action for the Hispanic America of the early nineteenth century. To begin with, Dr. John stressed that Independence now was too costly since it involved civil war—lives lost, fantastic expenditures, and instability for decades to come.   The facts were compelling, reflecting keen insights into the society of Spanish America. Europeans in their area constitute a key factor in the equation, Dr. John argued: because of

> the power they possess; the union that subsists among them; the influence they derive from property, from intermarriages and other connections with Creole families; their activity and habits of business; the respect in which they are held by the inferior casts, and by the Creoles themselves; and even the ideas of their own superiority, in which they have been accustomed to indulge, render them, though the smaller party, a formidable body, which ought not in prudence to be exasperated.

Venezuelans could certainly relate to Dr. John's insights. His second point was also realistic: a sudden change in government could be dangerous without some experience in government.   "Freedom to be well-enjoyed, must not be seized immaturely . . . attempt no more than the necessities of the time require, and the state of public opinion warrants."

Dr. John Allen's third point met the basic issue of race and culture in Spanish America head on, just as he did in his earlier article. These were the facts:

> The character and composition of society in America greatly increase the difficulty and augment the danger of a thorough revolution of its government. The property of the country is chiefly in hands of Creoles and Europeans; while the majority of the population consists of Indians, Mulattos, and Mestizos. These casts are not more distinguished from one another by differences of physical constitution and appearance than alienated by sentiments of mutual prejudices and aversion.

Once he presented the essence of Spanish America's most fundamental problem, Doctor John raised a series of explosive questions leading to the obvious conclusion: to achieve political stability in Spanish America it was essential to have respect for authority. It would take time, Dr. Allen maintained,

> to consolidate such mixed and discordant materials as compose the present population of America. In the meanwhile, will the pride of the Creole admit the Indian and Mulatto to a real equality with himself? Will the hatred and jealousies of the inferior casts suffer the political power of the state to become the exclusive patrimony of the Whites? On what foundations shall we raise the new political structures that are to adorn America? If property is made the sole basis of political power, how will the subordinate casts be reconciled to a system which will leave them, naked and unprotected at the mercy of their old taskmasters and oppressors? If population is preferred, and mere numbers regulate the government, what security would there be against the gross ignorance and blind fury of an uneducated multitude, invested with the whole political power of the state?[61]

Dr. Allen made it clear that the "revolutionists" in Spanish America were not to be trusted with promises of stability and a better day for the non-Whites. On the one hand, Dr. John argued cleverly, they used the concept of "natural law" to resist the mother country Spain. What will they do when the same doctrine is used by the "inferior casts" to justify their freedom from the whites?

> If Creoles should have recourse to artifice or chicane for the purpose of excluding their sable or copper-coloured brethren from an equal participation of political power, do they suppose that, fresh from these lessons of natural right, the degraded casts will submit quietly to the disfranchisement?

"The eager friends of American independence," Dr. John suspected, "will accuse us of partiality to the mother country in these remarks." He was right, of course.

At this point, Dr. John Allen outlined the obligations of Spain in the "mediation" program if she expected her colonies to come back to the fold. Dr. John, moreover, was correct when he said that "the politicians of Cádiz will be still more offended" with him "for the observations that are to follow." If the mother country failed to give the Americans what they wanted, in justice, to have, then the colonists should persevere in their "insurrection, and obtain by force that redress for the past, and security for the future, which pride and avarice withheld from them." America should be in the hands of Americans; so that no matter what the fate of Spain was in Europe, the "independence of America will be secure." Americans should hold all types of offices, along with those "Europeans long settled in the country, who have an interest in its safety and welfare equal to that of its native inhabitants." As a good Englishman believing in *laissez-faire*, Dr. Allen insisted upon the Americans' right to trade freely with the allies of Spain. Local legislatures were responsible for levying whatever duties were appropriate, etc., etc., etc. Abuses of the past would end. "To carry this system of conciliation into effect"—note the use of Blanco-White's term "conciliation,"—

> there must be provincial legislatures in America, invested with the sole power of imposing taxes; and with the consent of the Crown, of making laws . . . A representation, founded on property, will not exclude the inferior casts from political power and consideration, and yet leave, in fact, to the whites, where it can best be lodged, a preponderance in the Legislature; while the authority and influence of the Crown will secure to the Indians and Mulattoes a protection and defense against oppression.

Dr. Allen expressed his desire that the model of Great Britain and Ireland be applied to the relationship of Spain and Spanish America, etc., etc. etc. Apply the experiment first in Mexico, Peru, and Guatemala which the Spaniards control; then extend it to the "insurgent provinces"; "if they refuse" these reasonable terms, "let war be made upon them." Dr. John's final sally was priceless: "in the meantime, let Spain reserve her troops in Gallicia for a different enemy." The British needed Spain's best troops on the Peninsula, not in America where the Spanish government insisted stubbornly upon using them![62]

* * * * * * * * * * * *

Once war commenced in South America, "Mediation" never had any real chance of succeeding. So long as Spaniards were recklessly committed to the violence of a "Reconquest" of Spanish America at any price, accompanied by a no-holds-barred propaganda assault upon world opinion, Americans like Miguel Sanz had no alternative but to declare their Independence from such a vicious "Mother Country," or as the militants called her: *"Madre Chocha"* (Crazy Mother). Blanco-White knew this in his heart; but he still had to go through his "aberration" of blaming "Revolutionists" in the Americas like his good friend Miranda, until mid-1812. At that time, the Spanish Cortes rejected "Mediation" entirely, thus shamelessly telling the world that they never believed in it from the start. Now, Blanco-White joined his colleague John Allen in telling the Americans that they had no alternative but to go for Independence. We suspect that the Scotsman Allen knew it all the time; so did most of England's leaders who were in a constant anger over the puerile decisions being made on the Peninsula and in America by their ally Spain.[63]

Although José Blanco-White lost his credibility among Americans for his numbers 16–19 (*El Español*: July 31, August 31, September 30, and October 31, 1811), he still reinforced the Americans' determination to fight the long War of Independence against Spain by his general and relentless attack and exposé of Spain's hypocrisy, arrogance, stupidity, and viciousness. As Miranda's government fell in Venezuela, Spanish Americans developed their own crusade of "War to the Death;" and Simón Bolívar and his followers resorted to the same tactics of war. Thus, the topic under discussion here had real implications for contemporaries.

On June 19, 1811, the Cortes of Spain, in secret session, agreed to a nine-article program for mediation. A month later, the *Morning Chronicle* in London hinted at the Spanish program; whereupon Blanco-White's agents got ahold of a copy of the nine points and published them in Number 17 (August 31, 1811). Although No. 16 never was published by the Venezuelan gazette, No. 17 did appear in late 1811.[64] Like a scavenger at his best, Blanco-White picked away at the nine articles: their language, assumptions, and stupidity. Americans had to recognize the Spanish Cortes, no ifs, ands, or buts! Americans might present their grievances and that "in due time" justice would be served! Great Britain would be allowed to trade with the Americans during the fifteen months allowed by the mediation process. Article eight: if the process ended in failure, the British would cease any further dealings with the Americans; then they would assist their Spanish ally in reducing them to loyalty by force! This notion infuriated Blanco-White! The spirit of Parliament's propositions was "to gain through Great Britain's mediation all that she [Spain] had lost without it; and in the extreme case to take advantage of a [world] power to overcome the Americans, which her own forces had been unable to accomplish." This was the last straw! "Why should she go there, with her hands tied by Parliament, to mediate in America, without taking anything to offer the Americans, so that within 15 months, she would have to bear arms against them . . . What for?" The demands of the Spanish Cortes were not "mediation" at all. Rather, the Cortes merely wanted to commit England to Spain's *"tenacity* and *false policy."*[65]   The British government was likewise annoyed by the Spanish demand; and, for a time, it appeared that there would be no mediation program. According to Venezuela's agents in London—Andrés Bello and Luis López-Méndez—however, public opinion in Great Britain strongly favored the American cause; thus, the Government yielded to it, by naming British commissioners. Spaniards did likewise. But that is as far as the process got; there were no further meetings of importance.

The Andrés Bello and López-Méndez letter, written in early October, appeared in the *Gazeta de Caracas* on November 29, 1811, a document of great significance. Along with the remarks on English public opinion, the two men provided other examples of the real tension existing between England and Spain. The situation on the Peninsula looked almost hopeless from the military point of view; and the bickering among the allies did not improve the prospects for victory. It was generally believed that Spaniards had no faith in mediation; they only agreed to it: "under two conditions among others: that Parliament's sovereignty be recognized; and that in the event of resistance by the Americans, that England contribute to the effort of reducing them."   Bello and López-Méndez also recommended that Venezuela try to form a "general league" of American States, in which they agreed not to sign any other diplomatic documents with other powers dealing with the common interests of the league. This would permit a more salutary presentation of American rights in international affairs. Editor Sanz, who discussed their letter, thanked the deputies in London for their observations, proving that Spain could not be trusted on "mediation." Spain wanted to rule America as if it were still the sixteenth century. The suggestion on the "League" prompted Sanz to make this meaningful statement:

> The identity of principles that reign in all of free America, make it very necessary for the large States that have followed the example of Caracas to cooperate simultaneously. She [Caracas, or Venezuela] has taken

steps in this direction, despite the distance, and already has relations with Quito, Buenos Aires, and Santa Fe [Bogotá]; with the latter, she has just signed a solemn treaty of alliance, that will be the basis for binding and important relations; and in our answer to Parliament's request [to join the proceedings at Cádiz], we have declared that we were unable to resolve this matter for ourselves until we learned what was the general will of the Southern Continent, of which we are a part, on this [request].[66]

This statement placed Roscio's "Union" project in a clearer perspective.

On December 30, 1811, the *Argos Americano* (Cartagena) reviewed and published the documents that Blanco-White had treated in his No. 17 (*El Español*).[67] The footnotes to the documents are priceless in raising the same points Sanz had been making all along in the *Gazeta de Caracas*. The nine points from Cádiz were just "inadmissible," so much so that it compelled the editor of the Argos to supply five articles for the American side. They read as follow:

I.   Spain must swear solemnly to recognize the Absolute Independence of the American Provinces, and must treat them as such.

II. Once the previous article is fulfilled, hostilities will cease,followed by the exchange of prisoners from both parties, presenting two Americans for each Spaniard.

III. The claims that are made on the properties of Spaniards that exist here, will be heard and will be taken care of *as justice will permit* [the same terminology used by the Cortes in their 9 articles].

IV. To give Spain proof of our gratitude, in the event she agrees to these propositions, we offer to admit her ships in our commerce, and an asylum to Spaniards that wish to live with us, providing that they come here within 20 years of this date, if by some miracle Spain recovers [her freedom].

V.   In the event that the reconciliation does not follow these terms, England shall separate herself from the alliance with Spain, and will assist America, who offers her henceforth a free trade in her ports.

With tongue in cheek, that is how Cartagena reacted to the vaunted "Mediation" program of Great Britain and Spain.[68] It was too absurd, as well as too late for Spanish Americans that had moved beyond the "myth" of Ferdinand VII to their "Declaration of Independence." Free at last!

Chapter Twelve

The "Earthquake Republic:"
The End of the Road

The earthquake that took place last year in the territory of Caracas . . .
This extraordinary commotion was still being felt in the month of
December, 1812. The details of that memorable catastrophe . . . are
replete with interest and we think that we perform an agreeable task for
our subscribers by making available to them all the circumstances and
all these details.[1]

Editor, Le Journal de Paris, May, 1813.[1]

This is a death blow to Miranda and his followers if the adherents
of Ferdinand the Seventh, do not lose time in taking advantage of the
effect this calamitous visitation has had on the minds of the populace.

Captain Thomas Forrest, Caracas, March 30, 1812.[2]

Holy Thursday, March 26, 1812, promised to be an exciting religious
celebration for Venezuelans, especially since two years earlier on that
holiday—April 19, 1810—the doors opened wide for the glorious
Independence of Venezuela. Denizens of Caracas, the city of "Eternal
Spring," thanked God for their healthful existence in a priceless valley
at three thousand feet above sea level, surrounded by majestic
mountains, beautiful trees, and luxuriant vegetation—all within fifteen
miles of the port of La Guaira on the Caribbean. Jeremy Bentham and
James Mill often interrupted their labors to talk about their future life

in that terrestial paradise. After Miranda's departure from London, they waited patiently for that call to reunite with him in the New World.

The call from their erstwhile Venezuelan colleague, unfortunately, never reached them! On March 26, 1812, a devastating earthquake leveled the beautiful city of Caracas and its environs within a matter of minutes. The shaking earth destroyed most of La Guaira and much of Venezuela's territory within the radius of three hundred miles. It hastened the fall of the First Republic of Venezuela, leaving her with the uncomplimentary rubric of "Earthquake Republic." It also tarnished General Miranda's record as an historical figure.

There were two famous earthquakes, during Miranda's lifetime, that affected coastal areas of the Atlantic Ocean inhabited by the heirs of Roman Hispania. In 1755, Lisbon's earthquake terrified Europe; and European intellectuals, among them the celebrated Voltaire, studied that heralded phenomenon for its meaning to man. It marked a milestone in European thought that characterized the second half of the eighteenth century. Indeed, these two Hispanic quakes raised identical questions: Was this the wrath of God punishing his children for their sins? Or was there a rational, scientific explanation for the catastrophe? In Portugal, the vaunted Jesuit Fathers insisted upon the first point; they scolded their followers that man's only choice in this crisis was to do penance and thus accept his fate for having sinned. The Marquis de Pombal—the dictator emerging from Lisbon's ruins and dominating Portugal as a prototype of the "Enlightened Despots" of that era—insisted that the cause of the earthquake was scientific and that man was fully capable of determining his destiny by introducing reforms. Pombal soon commenced, moreover, the process of expelling the upstart Jesuit Order from Portugal's domains in Europe and overseas. Before long Spain and France followed suit as European monarchs strove to control their religious establishments and to centralize power in their hands.

Venezuela's earthquake of 1812 likewise had major political and psychological consequences. The Parisian editor, we have quoted in the introduction, appreciated the historical significance of that "commotion." The text of that document belonged to the Frenchman Louis Delpech, who married into a prominent Venezuelan family. He was, moreover, a key supporter of General Miranda who at one time recruited soldiers from the "Colonies," meaning the islands of the Caribbean. A liberal in his political orientation, somewhat suspect on the role of the Church in Hispanic society, Monsieur Delpech had an imaginative curiosity, which makes his description of the Venezuelan earthquake somewhat suspicious on religious points. But there is no question that Delpech's presentation succeeded in impressing thoroughly his countrymen and other European readers. Delpech provided a copy of his manuscript to the British Foreign Office. Our readers, we expect, should enjoy saboring this striking piece of literature:

> On March 26, 1812, at five in the afternoon, the first commotion became apparent. The air was still, the heat excessive; nothing preceded or announced the terrible occurrence. The first shake that we were able to perceive was sufficiently strong to start the bells ringing. This lasted barely six seconds. During the interval of ten to twelve seconds that followed, the earth commenced shaking in an undulatory movement similar to that of the sea in a period of calm. We were hoping, at this moment, that the crisis was over, but soon we heard subterranean noises and electrical detonations much more violent than thunder claps. The earth, shaking at a velocity that I just could not possibly describe, seemed to be boiling like water exposed to the heat of a violent fire. During three or four seconds, a deafening roar overwhelmed the scene; a few minutes later the earth suffered further agitations in the opposite direction. From North to South. From East to West. This short period of time was enough to destroy the city of Caracas from top to bottom. More than thirty other cities, farmhouses, and numerous dwellings that populate the surface of this delightful province in an instant all were destroyed over an extension of some three hundred miles. Ninety thousand persons ceased to exist and thousands fled [from the city] horribly wounded.
>
> Situated at the foot of the highest mountain, called "*La Silla*" ["The Chair"] and at the entrance of a vast plain watered by various rivers, the city of Caracas rose considerably above the sea level and enjoyed constantly a fresh and pleasant temperature. That day (it was Holy Thursday) the inhabitants had flocked in mass to the city Churches; which—[as it turned out]—served them as a tomb. The churches *La Trinidad* and *Altagracia*, the closest to the mountain, also suffered the most terrible effects from the extraordinary commotion; even though some had been lifted to more than one hundred and fifty six feet off the street level, the ruins did not exceed more than five or six feet in height; which permits us to form an idea of the violence of the shock that rattled those enormous buildings, if we consider that they were supported by columns and pilastars thirty to forty feet in circumference, of which there remained practically no evidence. An eminent row of two-story buildings with a capacity for four thousand men and which served as an artillery depository experienced the same fate. A line

regiment on its way to join a religious procession, was almost entirely devoured.

It was difficult to describe the terror and desolation that later engulfed the inhabitants: the confusion, the disorder, the desperation, the misfortune and [the] religious exhaltation were at their peak. In the beginning, everyone saved himself as best he could, falling to his knees to implore divine clemency. Those who were near death's door, and the wounded as well, covered with dust, their clothes in tatters, carrying in their arms children, the sick, and the wounded, provided a heart-rending spectacle. From the first moment of terror, during which the desire to conserve oneself muted all other considerations, the wretched living dead scurried distressfully in search of the most sorrowful mementos; everyone, in a painful anxiety, was looking for a relative or a friend, informing himself with glances of fright. Among those bloody and deserted ruins one could see some of those unfortunate whose lives had been spared, straining to unbury—without any other instrument but their weak and trembling hands—the live persons and the dead ones that were interred there. All ran, hither and yonder, over this vast cemetery, throwing themselves into the middle of the rubbish, with their ears cocked to hear the groans of those still alive; some of them entombed forever in those same dwellings where minutes before they had enjoyed a tranquil happiness.

The rest of that day and the entire night they were dedicated to that merciful occupation. The following day it was necessary to render the final rites to the dead, but it was impossible to carry out the customary funeral ceremonies; it would have been impossible to find the sufficient number of persons or the necessary instruments; with the objective, therefore, of avoiding an epidemic that the infectious air would have caused, they piled up the cadavers in different places and set them afire, using the wood pulled out of the ruins. That is how the survivors of that catastrophe employed those sad moments that followed. Other equally deplorable tasks remained to be carried out.

Supplies, furniture, clothing, all that was necessary for life, had been destroyed or plundered by the mob . . . Everything was needed. Such a violent shock had destroyed the aqueducts; the small rivers had dried up or changed their course. There was no water in the city; there was a lack of containers to fetch it and it was necessary to travel far in search of a sufficient amount to calm the thirst and to employ the hands to bring it to the public's mouth.

Devoured by hunger and thirst, without asylum, those who owned farmhouses took refuge there, but—unfortunately!—nothing had been spared. The nation was just a vast extension of ruins. They returned to the city, where their companions in misfortune, seemed less wretched.

The silence and solitude of the countryside, without question, added to nature's sinister appearance.

The markets lacked food supplies; the farmers did not bring anything to the city. After searching in vain everywhere for sustenance, various persons died of hunger; those who survived were not able to get their sustenance except with great difficulties; if they had not saved certain amounts of cacao, sugar and corn (which was sold in small containers [*detal*] at exorbitant prices), hunger would have killed a greater number of persons than the actual effects of the earthquake.

Three thousand wounded from all classes were gathered together at the edge of a river under the shade of some trees, but everything was lacking, even the most indispensable items. Words of consolation were the only remedy that could be given to their ills. They were told that they needed to resign themselves to the decrees of Providence and that all happened for the best . . .

Holy Thursday is, without a doubt, the most imposing of Catholic holidays; it is the celebration that should inspire the most pious reflections, but in Caracas, as in many cities, on that day, ladies preoccupied themselves with their coiffures, and they appeared to be more concerned with pleasing the eyes of men rather than honoring the Almighty; they thought only of pleasure. But the moment that they felt the earthquake, they believed it to be a punishment from an irritated Heaven, determined to bring sorrow to all mortals for their sins; instantly, they stripped off their elegant fineries, and as a sign of penitence, they put on coarse dresses. Voluntarily they submitted themselves to a monastic discipline and beat their chests unmercifully, only recently adorned with the most precious jewels. As for the men, most of whom dropped any further notions of gallant intrigue, they were converted into fanatics and, with expectations of calming the anger from Heaven, they marched in procession without any other dress than a wide belt, their feet unshod and with long beards, wearing around their neck a cord that secured a large rock and on their shoulders a wooden cross, whose weight was from one hundred to one hundred and fifty pounds. In the city and throughout the nation all one could see were processions night and day. Every mountain was transformed into a calvary; where the people, dying of hunger, implored the heavens for divine clemency and kissed the relics of their tutelar saints.

Everyone blamed himself for attracting the wrath of God and inflicting this universal misfortune [upon others]. Those who were unable to find a priest shouted their confessions publicly on the major roads and admitted to robberies and deaths that they had committed secretly.

Within two days, almost two thousand individuals (who ordinarily would never have had the intention of doing so) were married. Relatives which before had been scorned or rejected on grounds of poverty, were then welcomed back to the fold.   Many children, unfortunate products of the illegitimate traffic, who had never known their parents, were now discovered and made legitimate. There were many restitutions and various cases [in court] ended. But at the same time, a singular and contrary scene was discernible to the philosopher's view: while a portion of the inhabitants hastened to atone for their past sins, the rest, composed of persons who perhaps never had committed major crimes, but whose conscience was not too scrupulous, took advantage of the confusion to blame themselves for all the excesses.

Nevertheless, the shocks continued; every day and every hour ruins tumbled down that had been shaken by the first convulsions. On April 5th, at four in the afternoon, there was such a violent clash that various mountains were cracked and split apart, some had their center of gravity shift and enormous rocks broke loose and rolled down towards the valleys.

From that moment until nine o'clock the following morning, the shocks were so violent and so frequent that there was only an interval of about five minutes between one and another and, during those short lapses subterranean noises were heard and the earth was in constant agitation.

These extraordinary disturbances did not end until the month of December, 1812, the period in which I left that unfortunate nation; and people considered the most tranquil days those that had only experienced nineteen or twenty shakes. All was destroyed, the walls of La Guaira that were about twenty feet in depth were completely knocked down to the ground. It was noticed that many rivers had grown considerably, a natural consequence of the mountains splitting open, formerly containing great water deposits. Many high mountains had been split in half, and the celebrated "*La Silla*" had descended six fathoms [thirty-six feet]. It is difficult to predict the end of this terrible event, but we can risk the conjecture that it will finish with the opening of various volcanoes. While waiting, the unfortunate inhabitants of these territories, chained to their native soil and unwilling to abandon the ashes of their parents, have constructed, in moments of deep grief, rude dwellings in which they await with stoic resignation the end of their troubles.[3]

Delpech's figures of ninety thousand deaths are a gross exaggeration. The reference cited by U.S. agents in Venezuela placed the count at one third that number; and modern authorities estimate the death toll at twelve thousand. An English observer came close to that mark—some fifteen to twenty thousand dead.

Captain Thomas Forrest of His Majesty's Ship *Cyane* made this estimate in a letter dated March 30, 1812, only a few days after the catastrophe. Describing his experiences at La Guaira on that trembling occasion, Captain Forrest was one of the first Europeans to sense a psychological change in the people of Venezuela as a result of the March 26th catastrophe. The Venezuelan Commandant at La Guaira, distressed by the prospects of an epidemic, asked Forrest to use his sailors in burying the dead. At this point, the Englishman wondered why the officer had not compelled the "numerous parties of idle negroes and soldiers who were sunning themselves" to do the task that he had asked English sailors to perform. The Venezuelan replied that he could not get them to work. This incident provoked the following conclusions from Captain Forrest, supplying a key insight into the final days of Venezuela's First Republic. "This is a death blow to Miranda" [see the second quotation introducing this chapter], which Forrest explained as follows:

> it having happened upon Holy Thursday, a solemn Festival, and while they were in Church, gave a degree of solemnity to the calamity, which was truly awful, and inspired very generally an Idea that it was a judgment of the Almighty upon them, manifesting his displeasure at this defection from Loyalty to their Sovereign.

"This want of authority," the Captain continued,

> which I remarked in the Commandant and the hasty information I gathered from the few English here, convinced me it has this operation on the minds of the mass of the people and as it is probable that this sentiment together with their present defenceless state, from the destruction of their Fortifications, may materially change the political state of this part of the World.[4]

Another European, a Scotsman, offered the following insight. Writing jubilantly to his brother in the United States, he exploded: "I count myself among the living." He had survived the Caracas ordeal! Moreover, Providence had saved "all my English and American friends," despite the fact that they had witnessed the crisis in La Guaira "which has suffered proportionately much more than the capital." "Let me hasten to mention the Americans," he added, "just in case you might recognize one of your friends: Alderson, Depeyster, Shotwell and Burke." What a coincidence—a Burke survived the earthquake of 1812! We wonder if he was a North American? And what might his first name have been?[5]

The National Congress of Venezuela, now located in Valencia, met in extraordinary session on March 30, 1812, to relieve the "misery" in Caracas and other hard-hit areas of Venezuela, supplying the food and other necessities needed by their afflicted countrymen. What aggravated the earthquake emergency in Venezuela was the concurrent news that Spaniards, from Coro as a base, had finally begun their threatened invasion of Venezuela by seizing the town of Carora and thus exposing the nation's western provinces to a takeover by the royalists. The dual challenge of Mother Nature and the inveterate Spanish enemy was a serious imposition on the financial resources of Venezuela—an impossible situation that cast a threatening shadow on the First Republic's existence during the next three to four months of heavy warfare. Legislators in Valencia immediately sensed the nation's danger to the dual threat before them: it was imperative to control public opinion in Caracas and other troubled zones in the country. The trauma of the earthquake had caused confusion and great anxiety. The government had to reassure and comfort the people. Fortunately, Manuel Palacio Fajardo, recognizing the seriousness of the crisis urged his fellow legislators in Valencia to act on two measures: first, to tranquilize the public mind with reassuring messages; and, second, to centralize government in the hands of the Executive Power during the emergency. The future historian of the First Republic, in other words, recommended the establishment of a "dictatorship," following the precedent of the previous year, during the "Conspiracies" of Caracas and Valencia. By April 6, 1812, the proper document for an emergency grant of absolute power went into effect. It was the legal basis for the *Supremo Poder Ejecutivo*'s subsequent action granting its military leader—General Francisco de Miranda—full power as "dictator" of Venezuela, as well as the title of *Generalisimo*.[6]

Just as Captain Forrest had recognized the political implications of the change in the public's mind because of the earthquake, Venezuelan patriots like Palacio Fajardo and Miguel José Sanz, among others, developed a special interpretation of what happened in Venezuela from the time of the Earthquake, coupled with the Spaniards' invasion, to Miranda's defeat in July, 1812. It has been called the "*nueva teoría del terremoto*" (New Theory of the Earthquake), or sometimes the new

Doctrine (*doctrina del terremoto*). According to the "Earthquake Theory/Doctrine," the enemies of the Republic, and especially Spanish clerics, deliberately exploited the trauma of the masses, brought on by the Earthquake, for the benefit of Ferdinand VII's cause. This was precisely what was indicated in Captain Forrest's letter; and, more importantly, the precedent had been set during the abortive "Conspiracies" of 1811 at Caracas and Valencia, where dissident clerics like Fray Pedro Hernández and others had spread dissension among the masses through the confessionals and/or from the pulpits. Thus, the "people" turned against the "patriots" and their darling "republican" experiment. Indeed, there was much to justify the patriots' explanation for the failure of the Republic. It served as a convenient rationalization for their defeat—the exaggerated clericalism of the old Spanish Order led to so much ignorance and superstition among the people that republicanism never really had a chance to flourish. The later writings of Miguel José Sanz and Juan Germán Roscio provide classic expressions of the "Earthquake Theory/Doctrine."[7]

Although the interpretation above reflected the "patriots" disillusionment with the "people," it does not do justice to the faith, optimism, and "common sense" that these patriots brought into the experiment initially. They fully appreciated that "public opinion" had to be swayed to the conviction that the earthquake catastrophe had a rational explanation, as well as a religious justification; and man should be wary of the political and selfish motivation of those agents of evil and superstition that raised contrary and superficial explanations for natural phenomenon. Venezuelan patriots and republicans, in short, sided with Voltaire and Pombal on the celebrated contoversy over earthquakes.

The State Legislature of Caracas distributed and published, on April 9, 1812, its "earthquake" message to its countrymen. It was a statement by rational men to their frightened brethren explaining why the Creator had allowed Nature to test man's courage and virtue. Thus, man could more easily understand and appreciate "the infinite wisdom of God." "That is why," the explanation followed:

> the drought sterilized the fields; the superabundance of rains floods them; the hail destroys the grain; the thundering and lightening frightens [all life]; the heat suffocates; the cold is inconvenient; the volcanoes erupt; the earth is disturbed; cities are destroyed; the plagues attack; kingdoms are transformed, nations disappear; new ones come to life

. . . And it is because of this that the same water that refreshed him [man], drowns him; the fire that comforts him, burns him; the food that sustains him, can kill him; the land that supports him, frightens him; the roof that defends him, destroys him.

What was that horrible occurrence that surprised Caracas and other parts of Venezuela on that tragic March 26th? How does man explain it? In the negative explanation, for example,

The superstitious and fanatical man will tell you with exaggerated gestures, that it is a special punishment from God, who, furious and angry, especially against his flock, displays, in this way, his vengeance . . . The man of bad intentions will suggest to you that you need not expect anything from a city despised by God for having proclaimed its independence and taken a stand against the tyranny of the ambitious . . . The enemy of liberty and equality of men will try to persuade you that the glorious resolution with which Caracas detests the tyrants, and makes war upon despots, is the cause of this catastrophe; and that if you were to change your opinion, and return to the chains that you broke, you would placate God's anger.

On the other hand, there is the other explanation by a "truly Christian" man, who is an

observer of the doctrine of Jesus Christ, disinterested and barren of puerile preoccupations. He would tell you that his earthquake of March 26th, just like all the beauties and horrors that daily affect the human species in all parts of the world, are necessary effects of nature, disposed by God so that man will admire his omnipotency and will adore him in all his works . . . He will tell you also that in this way God wants to test your constancy, and make you worthy of the liberty that you have conquered from your tyrants; that this is such an important good, that cannot be deserved, enjoyed, and conserved without a virtuous heroism: patience in your works, courage in moments of adversity; firmness in your resolutions; valor against the tyrants; and if you were to faint in the holy work that you have undertaken against the ambitious [and designing enemy], you shall return to the condition of slaves for your unworthiness to be free men.

Your government is taking constructive steps to return to normalcy and to resume its progress into the future. Be patient:

Citizens: your representatives are speaking to you, be Christian men to adore God in all his works; be constant men to deserve your freedom; be men to unite yourselves truly to your compatriots; be men to recognize the equality of rights of all men and be men to show the world that you are men, and that you deserve to be respected as men.[8]

It took the facile mind of Miguel José Sanz—philosopher, political theorist, sociologist, historian, lawyer, statesman, etc.—to capture on paper the psychological phenomenon of March 26, 1812, and what it meant for the First Republic of Venezuela:

The frightful earthquake of March 26, 1812, and the circumstances that attended it, decided the battle [of idealogies in Venezuela], declaring the victory against Liberty. We should expose the moral effects of this unexpected event, so as not to transmit to posterity the shameful mortifications of a People led towards extravagance by superstition; but it is worthwhile for men to learn for themselves so that they are on the alert against the deceits of ambition when it appears to speak by authority of God. They were led to believe that the phenomenon was a special punishment for Caracas, for having separated herself from Spain and denied obedience to the King. The deceit gained in strength, the proclamations of the authorities were ineffectual, the insinuations of learned men were diabolical, delivered to persuade [the people] that the earthquake was a natural development. No one listened; the indifferent joined the faction of the ignorant to save their souls; the enlightened muzzled [their ideas]; the system of independence vanished; the Republic was overturned and with her disappeared the brilliancy, magesty, and decency that Venezuela was beginning to achieve. All was exaggerated acts of penance, all was shrieking noises, slovenliness, and abandonment. The streets and homes were in a horrid solitude after being pillaged; the neighboring hillsides resounded with the mournful voices of superstition; wandering men, frightened women; wavering judges; shortages, poverty and misery; that was the true picture of the city of Caracas in those sad and unfortunate days! Only those who were taking advantage and mocking the excessive credulity of the People were satisfied.[9]

* * * * * * * * * * *

General Miranda sounded the alarm in the National Congress, during the final months of 1811, that a Spanish invasion was imminent. The base of operations, as expected, was still in Puerto Rico where troops from Europe disembarked and recruitment for the invasion took place all over the Spanish Caribbean. Miranda emphasized that the perennial threat of invasion was serious this time because the British were also behind it, thanks to the new governor of Curaçao, General John Hodgson. Heeding Miranda's arguments, Venezuelan legislators took emergency measures to augment and improve military units and fortifications. The stumbling block, however, was Venezuela's chronic and pitiful financial condition. Deputies again resorted to "paper money," a device that, for all practical purposes, was not implemented until the earthquake emergency. There were also new outlays of coins planned and loans negotiated from various sources. The results were meager and insufficient to mount a respectable defense effort. The expenses of the earthquake emergency further aggravated the finances of the Republic and seriously limited Miranda's plans and strategy in the coming months of "Civil War" and combat with the royalist invaders. The trauma of the populace increased the General's anxieties; his people desperately needed food and housing; the cost of living skyrocketed, discrediting the "paper money" issued by the Venezuelan government; young men hated service in the army, and when forced to join, they deserted at the first opportunity. As time passed, the "Earthquake Theory/Doctrine," seduced the "People," who flocked to the royalist invaders with open arms and hungry stomachs: "Long Live Ferdinand VII," they shouted with anticipation. That was the easy way out for most people, even in the eastern sectors of the country during the final days of the Republic. These depressing trends increased the number of royalist forces and, at the same time, lessened Miranda's prospects for a military victory. His only alternative, it would seem, was to follow a defensive strategy that would buy time for him, as he put together a long range program.

On March 25, 1812, General Domingo Monteverde and some four thousand followers easily took over the town of Carora, a strategic point in the western sector of Venezuela. When government soldiers in Barquisimeto learned of the royalist attack, they prepared to meet the enemy. As they were about to leave their barracks on March 26th, the horrible earthquake stopped them in their tracks, burying them under the ruins of their quarters. It was a tragic stroke of nature, one that left Monteverde unchallenged. The popularity of the Spanish royalist cause gathered momentum by leaps and bounds. An unnerving situation henceforth in General Miranda's conduct of the war was the sudden and unexpected desertion of military units from key positions on the battle lines. Angrily, Miranda's top officers recorded these acts of cowardice and treason for their general.[10] What was worse, these traitors joined the enemy in making war against their own country!

General Francisco de Miranda's mettle as a soldier and political figure suffered a severe test in the next four months of war, so decisively favorable to the Spanish royalist cause. Many emotional contemporaries, frustrated by the prospects of imminent failure for the First Republic, harshly judged their Venezuelan military leader as unfit and cowardly. This bias, so damaging to the historiography of this great figure, was so emotional that it has ignored many factors and constructive plans of that period that might have reversed the fortunes of war in 1812. Moreover, Miranda's complete devotion and lifetime commitment to the cause of "Colombia" certainly justifies a fuller and fairer reading of the 1812 crisis that brought down the Republic and its leader. An objective approach is far more rewarding than the emotional stereotypes and distortions that have resulted from the bitter accusations and controversies of that fatal year in Venezuela. Also, by viewing the crisis in its hemispheric setting—the subsequent Wars of Independence for Spanish America—it makes this particular episode in Venezuelan history much more meaningful and historically significant.

In any war, the receipt of good intelligence reports are vital to military leaders; and General Miranda was notably proficient in his use of intelligence. From the Caribbean area, and especially from Curaçao, directly across from the mainland base of Puerto Cabello, Captain John Robertson was a major informant. This Canadian-born military officer, who served as Governor Layard's Secretary until mid-1811, was well known by Roscio, Bello, Isnardi, Miranda, and other patriots. Bello and his partners on the Venezuelan Commission to England (1810) further developed the Robertson connection; and because of Bello's warm friendship with the Canadian, Miranda stayed at Robertson's home for several days before returning to Venezuela in late 1810. The Canadian also headed the British mission to Caracas that negotiated the favorable trade concession in the nation's trade. Robertson greatly admired Venezuelans, favorably impressed with their enthusiasm and optimism for Independence—an objective which he, as an "American," could fully appreciate. While Layard was governor, the friendly relations between Curaçao and Caracas were a constant that Roscio and others counted on to catapult Venezuela into the independent column. The substitution of Governor John Hodgson, however, brought about a distinct change in British policy at Curaçao. And this reversal embittered Captain Robertson and prepared him for the decision to join Miranda's army in June, 1812, the beginning of his long career and dedication to South America's Wars of Independence. Given his military training and experience, he was Miranda's logical choice to implement needed military reforms and disciplinary patterns for the Venezuelan armed forces. "Colonel" Robertson joined Miranda's General Staff in the final days of the military campaign; and he became an invaluable asset to Simón Bolívar in the future.[11]

Before joining the Venezuelans, however, Robertson had forwarded vital information to Miranda via letters to Francisco Isnardi. These messages confirmed the obvious fact that Governor Hodgson was decidedly hostile to the Venezuelan Republic and that Robertson's relations with the new executive were becoming increasingly unbearable to the Canadian. Under Hodgson's stewardship, Curaçao became a mere logistics' base for the Spanish ally. Spanish merchants were favored in Curaçao; the flow of troops and supplies from Puerto Rico easily passed on their way through Curaçao to the royalists' strongholds on the Venezuelan mainland at Coro and Maracaibo, as well as to the port of Santa Marta, the Spanish base near Cartagena. The republican allies of Venezuela and Cartagena, therefore, shared a common grievance against Hodgson's pro-Spanish actions. Spain's blockade of Cartagena and Puerto Cabello likewise gained from the English assistance. General Miranda's accurate reports from Robertson and other informants in the Caribbean zone helped to convince him in early 1812 that the perennial invasionary threat by Spain was now a reality. Thus, preparations took place accordingly in Venezuela. If financial resources had been adequate, it follows that Spain's invasionary force under Monterverde might have faltered in its initial stages, even before the boost provided by the earthquake of March 26, 1812. These are the types of "ifs" that sometimes are overlooked in judging campaigns and battles.

The political weakness of the Venezuelan Confederation was obvious to many of its leaders prior to the disaster of March 26th. That is why the Federal Government in Valencia was given emergency powers to meet the crisis, which the Executive Power subsequently delegated to the "Dictator" Francisco de Miranda. Operating from the city of Valencia—scene of the "Conspiracy" against the Republic months earlier—was not to Miranda's liking. He had objected strongly to moving the nation's capital there; and any serious military leader could appreciate the security risk involved in having his general headquarters in that dangerous locale. Not surprisingly, therefore, he abandoned Valencia soon after the victorious presence of Monteverde's forces at Carora. This was a wise decision in his defense strategy to force the Spaniards beyond their logistic capabilities. At the appropriate time in the future, Miranda planned to retake Valencia and force Monteverde's men to flee in the direction of Nirgua, where Colonel Simón Bolívar and his men, from their base in Puerto Cabello, would destroy the enemy in retreat. Bolívar received specific instructions to furnish intelligence on all routes that the enemy might take in retreating from Valencia—a project which the famous Venezuelan general and tactician hoped to implement against Domingo Monteverde.[13]

Again, General Miranda went out of his way to learn what he could about the calibre of Spanish officers facing him. Domingo Monteverde's record in Spain against the French was not especially commendable. He, therefore, was assigned to Cuba and from there reassigned to Maracaibo and later to Coro. As a native born *Canario*, Monteverde might be able to attract the substantial and influential group of Islanders (*Isleños*) in the Venezuelan area. With some imagination, as well as deception, Miranda hoped to trick Monteverde into overreaching his logistics' base. On four occasions, we are told, he succeeded in this tactic. It is interesting to note that contemporaries were well aware of the "cat" and "mouse" game between Miranda and his Canarian foe; and there was no dirth of second guessing by "armchair generals."[14] The conditions that helped to increase the size of enemy forces after the earthquake, however, apparently minimized the possibility of Monteverde's entrapment. Yet, Miranda's activity in behalf of this strategy should not be faulted. It might have worked! As late as the final days of June, Miranda had hoped that he might still cut off Monteverde's supplies. The reversal at Puerto Cabello, however, doomed those expectations forever.

A vital factor in Miranda's strategy for those crucial four months in 1812 was the receipt of supplies and troops from the Venezuelan states outside of the Caracas-Valencia zone. There, the "Dictator" Miranda's tactics were at the mercy of local conditions and factors which he could influence only from a distance. Although he supplied the theoretical system of control for the nation—the dictatorship that the Executive Power had authorized—the implementation of this centralism depended, in the last analysis, upon the state authorities. And their unwillingness to cooperate with the core area of Caracas-Valencia reveals the major weakness of the Republic in mid-1812. In short, the fact is that there was no real dictatorship in the final days of the Republic, which raises serious doubts concerning the responsibility for the military failure of Venezuela's first government after Independence.

The *Llanos* (plains) of Venezuela were all-important in providing the food supplies for a nation that had just suffered a serious dislocation caused by a severe earthquake—the damage to its communication system, and the need to repair it, and the dispersal that occurred to its population. The Province of Caracas, at the time of Independence, constituted about one half of Venezuela's population and resources with a heavy concentration in the highland mass south of the port of La Guaira up to the city of Caracas and its extensive hinterland in the highlands to the West. In the other direction, the population current proceeded into the eastern valleys and elevations towards the coast and the Caribbean Leewards in the direction of Barcelona and Cumaná. Here, the traveler encountered the "upper llanos" that led into the interior to the Orinoco river basin where he had the option to proceed eastward to Guayana or westward around the Caracas highlands complex to the "*Llanos del sur*" (southern plains). From Caracas, the major line of descent to the west was towards La Victoria, Maracay (at the eastern end of Lake Valencia), and then to Valencia, which was slightly southeast of Puerto Cabello on the coast. This population cluster was still part of the colonial jurisdiction of Caracas; and, by using the llanos nearby the traveler could visit the highland complex to the west in the direction of Barquisimeto, Barinas, and Mérida, or proceed into the interior towards the Orinoco river basin. Key settlements on the backside of the Caracas highlands complex were San Carlos and Calabozo, both of which were attacked and taken over by Monteverde's royalist forces.

The llanos area provided a convenient route to agricultural lands that supplied cereals, etc. and pastoral regions for the meat supply that Miranda needed for his army and the Venezuelan markets as well. It also was a key zone to recruit cavalry contingents—the cowboys, horses, etc. To exploit the valuable resource area, the Venezuelan government issued permits to three major entrepreneurs who were to assemble about two thousand *llaneros* (plainsmen, or cowboys): (1) José Ignacio Briceño, who was to recruit in the Barinas area; (2) the Marquis del Toro recruited closer to Coro in the western zone; and (3) Nicolás Ascanio, who worked more into the interior around Calabozo. For various reasons, the first two men encountered obstacles and were unable to complete their contracts with the government; they both moved to the llanos on the eastern side of Caracas, expecting to realize their objective there. The third entrepreneur, annoyed at having to share his business with the others, managed to deliver parts of his contract; but the main obstacle was Monteverde's penetration all the way to San Carlos and Calabozo.[15] This prevented the much-needed meat supply for the Caracas market from getting through. Another factor, only hinted at in the documentation, was the infestation of certain valleys by highway robbers. Many of these criminals, as it turned out, were fugitive slaves; and this report raised the ever fearful possibility that a race war, as the one in Haiti during the 1790s, might become a reality in Venezuela. During the Valencian "Conspiracy," for example, there were accounts of Spanish plantation owners using their slaves against Miranda's forces, only to find out that the slaves eventually turned on their own masters. These stories, by the way, came up again the final month of the 1812 conflict, when General Miranda, as "Dictator" decreed that ex-slaves might win their freedom if they fought valiantly for the Republic. Both sides, it seemed, were willing to use ex-slaves in this "civil war" between whites. It set a pattern for the era of the "Wars of Independence" in South America.

Nevertheless, Miranda's failure to secure an adequate meat and food supply for the Venezuelan masses, at reasonable prices, helped to alienate his confused countrymen. The ex-colonial Spanish system seemed a more reliable alternative in their eyes, especially since the royalists' propaganda trumpeted the new system of constitutional monarchy.

Of the seven "States" in the Venezuelan Union, the western ones of Barinas, Mérida, and Trujillo did not offer much resistance to the Spanish enemy. The earthquake damage in Mérida was crucial in weakening its assistance to the union; and the other two units failed to get the support they wanted from Cartagena and neighboring states of New Granada. Miranda counted heavily on the realization of the South American union with Bogotá *et al*; but the internal dissensions and instability of those neighbors nullified that political dream at this time. Yet, the expectations of such an alliance had a high priority in Miranda's thinking. This was evident in his appointment and use of Dr. José María Salazar, a good friend of Bogotá's Antonio Nariño, as Venezuela's representative to Cartagena and Bogotá. Dr. Salazar left for his assignment in late June and early July, 1812, providing General Miranda with priceless intelligence of what he had heard and seen in

Curaçao with reference to developments in Puerto Cabello while proceeding to his destination.[16]   Although we lack any further documentation on Salazar's mission to Jamaica and then Cartagena, it nonetheless indicates that General Miranda was vitally interested in stimulating the cooperation of the two areas against the common enemy. It also tends to support the contention of Dr. Pedro Gual many years later that General Miranda, in 1812, entertained plans of moving to New Granada in the event the military situation in Venezuela worsened.[17]   Be that as it may, there is no question that it was one more plan that General Miranda considered as he surveyed the military situation in those four crucial months of war in defense of his country. Was it a mere coincidence that within a year's time of Miranda's defeat, Simón Bolívar followed Dr. Salazar's trek to Cartagena and before long was back in Venezuela to challenge and defeat Monteverde's forces with elements of the projected alliance of Venezuela, Cartagena, and Bogotá?

In General Miranda's immediate context, however, it was the potential of the "Eastern" states of the Venezuelan Union that might allow Miranda to build up a well-trained body of men that could recapture Valencia and overwhelm Monteverde's forces. He counted heavily upon receiving a few thousand men from the "Eastern" states of Margarita, Cumaná, and Barcelona in addition to the foodstuffs for his army and for Venezuelan survivors of the dreadful earthquake.

The eastern project seemed to have the potential of realization. Trade in that area had not suffered the same losses as the zone from La Guaira to Puerto Cabello; the East, in short, was in good shape to bring about the reconstruction of the afflicted West, which also was fighting for its life against the Spanish enemy. Although the Briceño and del Toro interests had failed to realize their llanos objectives in the West, they both concentrated in the eastern llanos where there were greater opportunities for success. Moreover, in June, 1812, John Robertson arrived in La Guaira with his mind made up to join Miranda's army; with him was George Robertson, one of Curaçao's prominent merchants who had accepted a contract with Miranda's government to transport the "Eastern" troops to La Guaira, as well as the traffic in foodstuffs for the war effort in the Caracas-Valencia zone. The merchant George was no relative of Colonel John; but they were both on the side of the Republic. George Robertson, it seems, communicated with Briceño and del Toro who reportedly were willing to cooperate; these reports, of course, sustained General Miranda in his expectations that before long troops and food supplies would be pouring through La Guaira on the way to the battle lines.[18] Miranda, moreover, had great confidence in the military leaders from the East—Vicente and Antonio José Sucre and Manuel Villapol, among others. So that by the end of June, 1812, there was still hope that the Republic of Venezuela might reverse the military odds and defeat the royalist enemy.

* * * * * * * * * * *

To save the Republic, each of the Venezuelan states would have to be willing to support a government that would achieve national objectives for everyone; and victory was only possible if there were sweeping economic, financial, and political reforms. The SPE (*Supremo Poder Executivo*) could not meet the emergency confronting the nation under the Constitution of 1811; therefore, Congress granted it emergency powers to confront the crisis, just as it had done on July 13, 1811. The SPE, in turn, chose General Francisco de Miranda as the instrument of dictatorial power during the emergency. In early May, General Miranda asked to meet with the representatives from the Federal Government and from the State of Caracas, the largest and wealthiest of Venezuela's seven political units. These men negotiated the so-called "Martial Law" of May 19, 1812.[19]

In realistic terms, the "Martial Law" project was a device intended to make palatable to the State of Caracas the Miranda dictatorship, as authorized by the SPE. After all, the former Province of Caracas was still the richest and most powerful in the Confederation—the real issue of the "*división*" controversy. The obstacle was that the Caracas interests were still miffed at the general sentiment against them by the other states of the union. In the early months of 1812, moreover, the State Legislature of Caracas had made it clear that it would not accept blindly the actions outlined by the Federal Government in Valencia, or by its chosen "Dictator." In other words, we have here the makings of a "States' Rights" defiance that was very similar to that of the "Southerners" in the United States of America a half century later. And Miranda was unable to control this problem before the Republic's fall in July, 1812. The "Eastern" States, moreover, compounded the tragedy by joining the defiance against the alleged dictatorship of Francisco de Miranda. They refused to accept the constitutionality of a "Martial Law" agreed to by federal representatives and those of Caracas.[20] In short, considering James Mill's views of "imperfect" confederations, the fall of Venezuela's First Republic was due to its deficient power organization. And this illustrates the point that many have suspected: that is, that Miranda's dictatorship was a *myth*. This "Dictator" counted heavily upon the "Eastern" troops and supplies to save the Republic; but that assistance, as we shall see, was not forthcoming. Thus, the "States' Rights" defiance was primarily responsible for the failure of the war effort and the demise of the Republic.

Under the Martial law of May 19, 1812, the *Generalísimo* had the power to appoint anew the military and civilian chieftains of the nation's administrative units. To secure final victory against Spain, priority always favored the military over the civil branch. General Miranda's choices as military *jefes* were young, eager, and devoted nationalists, men like Simón Bolívar, assigned to the key Puerto Cabello, and Manuel María de Las Casas, the military chief at the port of La Guaira, and Dr. Miguel Peña, as the civilian chief of La Guaira. A major objective of the May 19th project was to reorganize the nation's financial structure in order to guarantee a sound banking system and an efficient collection of tax revenues, so sorely needed for the war effort. The unanimous choice for Director of Revenues was the Spaniard Antonio Fernández de León, the Marquis de León. The Martial Law also called for the appointment of super administrators like Miguel José Sanz, Pedro Gual, and Francisco Paúl, well known to the Dictator. General Miranda, the politician, expected this martial project to implement his dictatorial authority in a conciliatory fashion so that the nation, and her patriots, could get on with the business of winning the war against Spain, while establishing a much needed and sounder basis for the nation's finances.

Despite the good intentions of General Miranda, as well as those of the Marquis de León and other appointees, the *Ley Marcial* was unable to succeed in the long run because of the bitter opposition on all sides. Patriots, for example, wondered politely why their hero had chosen a Spaniard for the treasury post, especially since it was alleged that León was the "agent" of the rich, peninsular magnates that were still in Venezuela. Miranda's reply was forthright and realistic: the nation needed capital desperately and these men had that commodity that could reconstruct the economy, recently devastated by a killer earthquake. Thus, Spaniards should be given the chance to show their loyalty to Venezuela. Needless to say, this involved great risks; but what other alternative was there under the circumstances? The nation's "capital" should not be allowed to take flight in this moment of great crisis. And Spanish capitalists, it should be recalled, had resorted to that possibility from the first whisper of independence in Venezuela.[21]

In the aftermath of that horrible earthquake, the hostility between "Americans" and "Spaniards" had intensified to the point of polarization. This was especially true as time passed and the war's ferocity was evident. In a letter to General Miranda, one patriot noted that Spaniards, so unbearably arrogant, had assumed that León's appointment as Director of Finances would allow their clique to continue to occupy key positions in the government of Caracas, etc. etc. Presumably, they had a monopoly of the food supply and other services; and they distributed those scarce items amongst their friends, leaving the poor of Venezuela to starve to death, etc. etc. etc. The masses apparently resented Spanish abuses and demanded that these "internal enemies" be imprisoned, before their departure into the next world![22]

Tensions in late May and all of June, 1812, went from bad to worse, as the State government officials resisted the implementation of the "Martial Law" with delaying tactics that bordered on treason; they likewise opposed the appointments of the super-administrators like Sanz and Gual; and revealed an undisguised hostility to the new appointees for the military and civilian posts. Miranda sent commissioners to insist upon compliance with the law, but with not much success. By the end of June, and in the early days of July, 1812, Miranda's agents began to round up the key Spaniards and Islanders, who were supposedly fomenting the State Government's resistance, or preparing to deliver Caracas to Monteverde's army. In early July, 1812, a wave of anti-Spanish phobia, or hysteria, came to a head with the first reports that Monteverde's forces were beginning to enter Puerto Cabello, the last bastion of defense. At this point, two striking developments occurred; first, a paralysis, or almost complete breakdown of the nation's economy; and, secondly, many connected with the Spanish interest began to take flight from the ex-capital via the eastern descent to Guatire, Capaya, Curiepe toward the Leeward coast. The spread of royalist revolution into this new area was financed presumably by "Catalan" money and led by the Spaniard Gaspar González and the *hacendados*—the Llamozas and Vaamonde families—who were intimately connected with Father Quintana, a cleric leading the royalist supporters in Venezuela.[23] General Miranda realized that the war in Venezuela was nearing its end, as the dreadful news from Puerto Cabello reached him. He tried to send some troops to the new front in the Guatire-Capaya area; and Las Casas at La Guaira managed to send a fifty-man force to Chuspa on the coast, to block any Spanish support or supplies into the interior. In the meantime, Miranda waited hopefully for the reinforcements from the "Eastern" states. These were last minute gestures; and they were too late. The war was over!

General Francisco de Miranda was not alone during those last months of the war crisis. He corresponded with many persons who influenced his policy, bolstered his morale, and offered him keen insights into this enigmatic period of Venezuela's history, so bereft of documentation. His old friend Miguel Sanz kept him well informed on the opposition in Caracas, as well as providing a great deal of information on the last royalist front in the Guatire zone. He had property there, and knew many of the families in Capaya, where his own wife and daughters were living.

When Don Miguel first learned that Miranda had been given unlimited authority to save the nation, he veritably exploded with joy: "*Victory, Victory, Victory!*" Sanz can now sleep in peace: "Miranda is in charge; external and internal enemies are trembling. Justice has finally succeeded; all we need now is for fortune to triumph."[24] With the tenacity of a hawk, he watched the anti-*Mirandistas* in the Caracas government, exposing their hypocrisy and obstructionism. Pedro Gual likewise defended Miranda's views in the Caracas legislature. Both men, and other allies, fought tenaciously any resistance or delay in the implementation of the "Martial Law," as well as their own appointments under that Law.

In his special philosophical manner, Don Miguel always had advice for his dear friend;

> General Miranda knows very well that a nation beginning [its existence] is in more need than the established [ones] of virtue in its individuals: [who are aware] of the national character within her, and the knowledge of her interests. General Miranda has much to do by insisting upon forming a nation: population, arms, justice, good faith and customs.

Sanz elaborated upon these themes in this letter and future ones. He assured Miranda that he desperately wanted him to succeed.

> Command is a very slippery and dangerous [situation] and the friends who see their friend in danger, should place themselves at his side to support him and give him their hand so that he will not fall.[25]

Sanz offered Miranda the following advice on June 14, 1812, which the latter heeded in his final month in government:

> The case is accurate: we cannot sustain ourselves without agriculture, population, commerce, arms, and money. The major part of our territory is occupied by our enemies and the internal ones are waging the crudest and most dangerous war against us . . . If you wish to achieve the glory of making your country independent, so that she might enjoy her liberty, it is indispensable that you do not trust exclusively the means that are available to you here; look for them in the outside [world].

With the nation on the verge of bankruptcy, Sanz assured Miranda that León, the Director of Finances, was a conscientious worker who was fully capable of reversing the trend toward a financial impasse.[26]

Sanz's recommendation that Miranda look outside of Venezuela's borders for effective assistance had been made in earlier letters; and, as a matter of fact, had formed point two in the *Ley Marcial* of May 19th. As secretary of state in the pre-Independence government, Sanz had urged the executive power to issue corsair licenses to help offset the Spanish blockade, while at the same time stimulating traffic with foreigners for ammunition, guns, and food products in general—advice which at that time went unheeded. Miranda, on the other hand, acted immediately by assigning Louis Delpech—the author of the earthquake description—to prepare for the issuing of corsair licenses, along with a program of recruitment in the "Colonies" of the Caribbean. The recruitment of foreign officers, especially Frenchmen, had started earlier; now Colonel J. Du Caylá went along with Delpech to attract more officer talent into the Venezuelan army. Englishmen like John Robertson and Sir Gregor Macgregor and others likewise signed up for duty with Miranda's army. The General needed professional officers with experience in the Napoleonic wars to match the talents of the Spanish officer corps that was leading the invasionary forces. Some Venezuelans have objected—unrealistically, it would seem—that General Miranda should have counted more on native sons for leadership. Yet, Miranda had not overlooked that resource at all; he had worked with them in the conflict of 1811; and these young men were his choices for the military posts under the *Ley Marcial*. The fact was that they were not numerous enough, or that experienced, at the time; and the reality was that foreign officers were available to Miranda on a barter basis: their services for concessions, land grants, etc., rather than money.

As the British connection with Curaçao and the English Caribbean cooled in the post-Independence era, Sanz encouraged Miranda to seek out other foreign nations to assist Venezuela in return for commercial exchanges, strategic concessions, etc. Napoleon's France and Russia might be interested, Sanz suggested to the General. Although the suggestion concerning a mission to Napoleon's France caught Miranda's attention, the follow through was too late to have a bearing upon the First Republic; and at the time the negotiations would have been possible, Napoleon's political downfall in Europe was a virtual reality. Manuel Palacio Fajardo, the historian and former legislator in the Venezuelan Congress, whose name has come up before in these pages, was Miranda's representative in Europe assisted by the ubiquitous Louis Delpech.[27]

As for relations with Great Britain and English subjects during Hodgson's presence, the Venezuelan government had to consider indirect ways of obtaining support. Miranda decided to withdraw López Mendez and Andrés Bello from the London post. He replaced them with Thomas Molini, the General's private secretary, who was more familiar with Miranda's old contacts in London, including the financial agents there that had represented Venezuelan interests. But since Miranda was defeated in mid-1812, the substitution of Molini had no direct impact on our story; as a matter of fact, Molini was unable to do much for Francisco de Miranda in his final years of incarceration in Cádiz, Spain. Thanks to the documentation of Francisco de Iznardi, we know that the Federal Government in Valencia tried to carry out a financial scheme involving English interests in the Caribbean. It was a plan favoring the support of Francisco de Miranda's efforts against the Spanish invaders. It involved the attainment of letters of credit in exchange for Venezuelan commodities; the amounts were not very large, totalling, it seems, about twenty thousand pesos. The major English operator was a Scotsman by the name of William White, some of whose letters appear in Miranda's general correspondence. White operated, among other places, from Martinique, Jamaica, and Trinidad. For reasons that are not clear, Isnardi was removed from the operation, replaced by Martín Tovar whose wealth, it would seem, might advance this mysterious project. That is all we know about it; it does not seem to have materialized in time to supply the financial assistance needed by Miranda.[28] Yet, the episode underscores the fact that Miranda and his associates were exploring every possible avenue of financial assistance from outside of Venezuela. Perhaps, further investigation might document a connection between William White and George Robertson's contract to transport the troops from the "Eastern States" to La Guaira. Be that as it may, considering Miranda's longstanding friendship with British interests B.H. (Before Hodgson), it would appear logical that the connection should have survived.

In his more pensive moments, General Francisco de Miranda could remember an even longer connection with English-speaking people who also called themselves "Americans." They had helped him to form his revolutionary model and objectives; William Burke had underscored North American principles of freedom and representation in the *Gazeta de Caracas*; and their program of economic development and prosperity embodied the same objectives and way of life aspired to by "Americans" in the Hispanic sections of the Western Hemisphere. The United States of America rejoiced at the news that on July 5, 1811, the Republic of Venezuela was taking root in South America, setting the scene for the emancipation of the entire New World. The United States prudently watched international affairs and articulated its policy cautiously, so as not to offend the British, French, or Spaniards. The world situation, however, changed dramatically in the winter of 1811–1812. War seemed to be on the horizon for the United States; and Hodgson at Curaçao was destroying the bond between Great Britain and the Republic of Venezuela. General Miranda's realization that the Spanish invasion of Venezuela was imminent also prompted the reality that the United States of America was the logical outside ally, or foreign power, to join with the Venezuelans in saving republicanism in the Americas. This helps to explain General Miranda's great emphasis on fortifying the U.S.-Venezuelan connection.

In late January, 1812, while General Miranda served on the Legislative Commission to prepare Venezuela's defenses against invasion, he went out of his way to talk with Robert K. Lowry, the "Marine" agent for the U.S. This was an informal title that later was changed to "Consul" for the port of La Guaira. Miranda described his nation's political situation and expressed the hope that the United States might consider offering substantial military and financial support to her sister republic in South America. Lowry indicated that perhaps some aid might be forthcoming, if the Venezuelan government were to draw up a candid statement on its military condition. Lowry learned in his conversation with Miranda that there were only about six thousand

weapons in the nation that were functional, plus another two thousand
that were virtually useless.[29]   When Miranda urged Lowry to sail
immediately to the United States to arrange for the arms assistance, the
latter declined to do so. He did not offer any more information on his
negotiations with Miranda! Undoubtedly, official messages were sent
to Telésforo Orea, Venezuelan representative in Washington, D.C.; but
the documentation is lacking. General Miranda, however, did not
abandon hope with regards to the United States; and he readied agents
to proceed to Washington, D.C. for further negotiations with the United
States government. Miranda first turned to Guillermo Burke to carry
out the assignment; and Burke proceeded to La Guaira in June, 1812,
to set sail for the United States. We know this because the military
chief at the port, wrote to Miranda saying that he would not permit
Burke to get on any ship until he supplied a license from the General.[30]
Was this Burke the survivor of the earthquake? We cannot say; but he
obviously was a man known in the United States and England because
Miranda informed that letters concerning him had reached his hands;
and the General wanted time to study them before authorizing his
license to sail to the United States.[31] Miranda subsequently decided to
appoint Dr. José Cortés de Madariaga, the Chilean who had negotiated
with Bogotá on the alliance with Venezuela, as the new agent for the
Washington D.C. assignment.[32] In early July, however, Miranda opted
to send Dr. Pedro Gual to the United States, accompanied by William
Burke. Gual expressed his approval of having a man of Burke's
intellectual ability assisting him in the United States.[33] We shall leave
our final speculation on the identity of this "William Burke" for our
conclusion.

An unexpected surprise for the Venezuelan Republic was the
donation of food supplies by the United States Government for the
survivors of the March 26th earthquake. On June 9, 1810, the first of
five ships from the Baltimore, Philadelphia, and New York area arrived
in the devastated port of La Guaira. As the Frenchman Delpech noted,
it could not have been sent at a more appropriate time, just as hunger
was claiming victims throughout Venezuela.[34] Ten days later, the
Marquis de León reported to Miranda that all ships had reached the
Venezuelan port of La Guaira, bringing a total of 1,782 barrels of flour
and 400 sacks of corn, About one-quarter of the food went to the
needy poor throughout Venezuela and the remainder was made into
special food rations for the army, hospitals, and charitable agencies.[35]
In a letter to Miranda, Louis Delpech estimated that, for the army's

share, there would be food to last another four months if distributed efficiently. This estimate entered into Miranda's reckoning in mid-June, 1812.[36] The donation of food, was the idea of Alexander Scott, the man first assigned as a political agent to the Venezuelan Government by James Monroe, the Secretary of State of the United States, shortly after the earthquake news was known in the United States. Congress immediately accepted the program and made the donation of the five American ships an exception to the embargo that was then in effect. As expected, Venezuelans thanked their northern neighbors for the generous act of charity. And the Venezuelan representative to the U.S. government officially expressed his nation's gratitude.[37]

Although the political appointment of Alexander Scott augured well for the future recognition of Venezuela, this depended upon her survival and victory over the invaders. Despite Scott's sensitivity in suggesting American aid to Venezuela, his personality and quirks undermined his mission from the start, as he and his wife became victims of the earthquake, so to speak. In one of his reports to the State Department before leaving for his post, Scott made the dogmatic statement that after shocks were *not* characteristic of earthquakes! When his wife experienced one of those shocks in La Guaira, she insisted upon being placed back on the ship that had brought the family to Venezuela! Las Casas related to Miranda that Scott was even more fearful than his wife and simply refused to go forward to Miranda's general headquarters. In fact, Scott allegedly insisted that he was returning to the States, a threat which he later abandoned.[38] Scott's comportment at La Guaira, unfortunately, precluded any real success for his mission; and Miguel José Sanz, in particular, regretted that Miranda's enemies had been able to distort Scott's views about Venezuela and her future.[39] General Miranda did his best to encourage the northerner's visit, although somewhat annoyed by his fears of the shaking earth. These were critical days; and Scott dallied in his trip up to Caracas and then the descent to the general headquarters at Maracay; and he did not reach there before July 16th. The war was over by then; and the General advised him to return to the States, which Scott refused to do because he was concerned for the interests of U.S. citizens. While passing through Caracas, Scott had an opportunity to converse with Dr. Pedro Gual, a talk that seemed to hold some promise for U.S.-Venezuelan relations and raised Miranda's expectations. But that was all. There is no evidence of what was said at Scott's meeting with the General except what has been noted above; but Scott's portrayal of Miranda was that of the tyrant-scoundrel, which permeated his various letters to the State Department. He had been exposed to all of the stereotypes on the Dictator's worse features. Despite this hostility, Scott did not register any complaints concerning an action taken by General Miranda before their meeting.[40]

On June 26, 1812, Miranda issued an order, which has been called an embargo of the port of La Guaira against foreign ships, preventing them from leaving the harbor. This embargo applied to the "donation" vessels and the one that brought the Scott family to Venezuela. Since this affected the rights of American citizens, it is noteworthy that Scott did not complain until months later when Spanish authorities, allied to Great Britain, insisted upon taking over the American ships.[41] The War of 1812 was then a reality.

Miranda's embargo of June 26th seemed to apply only to North Americans and to certain Spaniards, seeking to leave Venezuela with their capital. It did not apply to "national" ships that were involved in the coastal trade for foodstuffs or the transfer of loyal troops to La Guaira. Nor did it discourage the normal traffic of foreigners that the Marquis de León was welcoming to stimulate the economy of the nation. In short, military objectives apparently determined its implementation. With regards to subversive foreigners—Spaniards, for the most part—it made sense; but why would it apply to the personnel on the ships that brought the heralded "donation" of food to Venezuela? As a brutal realist, General Francisco de Miranda recognized that Venezuela's cause could be precarious if certain actions or objectives were not forthcoming: first, if the "Eastern" States hesitated or delayed too long in sending troops and supplies—here we must remember that as late as July 16th Miranda still did not know if those troops were in La Guaira; second, if Puerto Cabello should fall to Monteverde's troops because of desertion or what have you; and third, if the new royalist front in the Leeward coast and the highlands leading to Caracas were not contained and the "slave" revolts were allowed to spread into Miranda's battle grounds, etc. etc.

Controlling the U.S. ships at La Guaira, therefore, was a wise maneuver to protect the remnants of Venezuela's forces from being wiped out completely; even a small maritime force of this type could help evacuate the best men and officers left in Miranda's army to carry on the battle against the "New" insurrection in the Leewards area, or from bases in nearby Barcelona, Cumaná, or Margarita Island. That was one possibility; but there was also the possibility of evacuating those troops under Miranda to Cartagena, where they could regroup and increase their forces for the reconquest of Venezuela from Monteverde *et al.* At the same time, such a move would realize Miranda's old dream of a military alliance with other Americans for the final eradication of Spanish power in northern South America. This was a dream that fell to Miranda's heir, the young colonel that for several days after June 30, 1812, had to shoulder the responsibility for the fall of Puerto Cabello to the Spaniards. That catastrophe, which everyone sensed upon learning about it, meant the demise of the First Republic of Venezuela; it also served, in the long run, to inspire Simón Bolívar—the colonel in question—to pick up his general's mantle and carry on the emancipation of South America to a successful conclusion. In light of the Puerto Cabello disaster, Miranda's earlier decision to keep the American ships at La Guaira in reserve for an emergency proved to be an imaginative display of foresight and intuition. By July 16, 1812, the American ships were in the final stages of readiness for their prospective assignment.[42] The military chief at La Guaira, M.M. de las Casas, had received by then full authorization to finance the "Maritime" force with the money in the Republic's coffers, totalling over thirty five thousand dollars.[43] Following Miranda's orders, moreover, the Director of Revenues had arranged for other sums of national money in those final days before the ships sailed to whatever their destination might be. Ironically, or tragically, it was these amounts of money that some disgruntled and misguided Venezuelans later chose to believe was the booty the "traitor" was taking into exile!

To provide a more expanded context for the historical development described above, we should note the following preparations that were taken by General Miranda shortly after he negotiated the "Martial Law" of May 19th. He urged his good friend Dr. José Cortés Madariaga to meet him at general headquarters for a discussion of foreign policy, bringing with him as well Dr. José María Salazar and the General's secretary Thomas Molini. If Dr. Cortés was unable to attend, he should not fail to insist that Salazar be present; his intelligence was vital for the decisions that had to be made. Such an invitation could not be refused; and all three men mentioned attended the meetings at La Victoria on June 3rd forward. Three major diplomatic missions emerged from the discussions: one to Great Britain to be headed by Molini, replacing the López-Méndez and Bello representation, as we have indicated before; second, the U.S. assignment under Dr. Cortés Madariaga; and third, the Bogotá-Cartagena posts for Dr. José María

Salazar. All three missions, it would appear, were closely related in Miranda's mind.[44] The receipt of arms and other assistance expected from the United States would be of immeasurable significance in turning the emancipation struggle around in favor of the Venezuelan-New Granadian allies, once and for all. Just how Molini's trip to London would assist the project, it was not clear; but it probably had something to do with gaining specific financial support from the Taylor banking interests and the contributions of Miranda's former allies in England. Why even Blanco-White was asked to help in the enlistment of recruits, as one authority has noted! We can be sure, therefore, that even more dependable friends of his could be counted upon for some real assistance.

The three men returned to Caracas to make preparations for their departure, securing the necessary documents that were available in the city, and arranging for financial assistance with the Director of Finances, as well as their passages on ships. Cortés and Salazar, it seems, would depart together; but this was not possible at the last moment because of Dr. Cortés Madariaga's additional duties in Caracas, as one of the three commissioners representing Miranda on the martial law project which encountered exasperating resistance. Thus, Dr. Cortés became involved in those acrimonious negotiations along with his colleagues Roscio and Juan Paz del Castillo. So valuable was Dr. Cortés to this political struggle, especially considering his role as a clergyman in favor of the Republic, that Miranda kept him in this capacity and decided to use Dr. Pedro Gual and Guillermo Burke for the U.S. assignment.[45]

So, Dr. José María Salazar departed for La Guaira on his own. On the 16th of June, he encountered Colonel John Robertson who was on his way to join Miranda's forces; and the Canadian gave him an additional letter to his colleague Best in Curaçao. Robertson unquestionably informed Miranda of the latest news on Curaçao, preparing him for the two letters that Salazar wrote to Miranda on June 22 and July 8th. With the information that Robertson gave Miranda orally, and Salazar's letter of the 22nd, Miranda had a good feeling for the role that Spanish interests in Curaçao, and their agents in Caracas, were playing in the game of smearing the Republic and its leader. Thus, the June 26th embargo would put a stop to the subversion from Caracas to Curaçao, as well as the exporting of capital that might be attempted. Salazar's July 8th letter wrote of the provisions that were leaving shortly to support the royalists at Puerto Cabello. Salazar was hopeful that the Republic's ship *Zeloso* would cut off these supplies, thus ending the royalists' bid for power. On July 9th, Dr. Salazar headed for Jamaica for a few days before proceeding to Cartagena. The Salazar mission was clearly intended to revive the "Union" that we have traced in earlier pages; the attraction to seek Inter-American assistance was even more alive as the Republic of Venezuela was being threatened by disaster. Therefore, Dr. Salazar's mission supports Pedro Gual's assertion, many years later, that General Miranda in those final days was considering the transfer of his best troops to allied positions in Cartagena or New Granada.[46] He tried desperately in the Armistice of July 12, 1812, to extend the document's jurisdiction to the sea, meaning the port of La Guaira and its coastal area. Monteverde doggedly resisted because he would thereby have to abandon any royalist attempt to supply aid to the "new" front of the Leeward coast leading to Caracas. The Spaniard's resistance on this point, as it turned out, seemed to militate against Miranda's evacuation scheme. Instead, it bolstered the will of those Venezuelans at the port of La Guaira who were considering the possibility of saving their necks at the expense of their nation's interests.[47] In the cauldron of controversy over Venezuelan events in that fateful month of July, 1812, this speculative point of mine should add to the emotional irritation.

In the "Martial Law" of May 19, 1812, a major ingredient was the assignment of the Marquis de León to reform the nation's economic and financial structures, an objective, which we recall, had received much attention since the outbreak of Independence but little achievement by comparison to the expectations of those who dreamed of "modernization." Antonio Fernández de León held the post of Director of Revenues. Although the documentation is poor to fragmentary, there is still some evidence that León's experiment was not all hopeless. On the contrary, this Spaniard brought a sense of excitement to the program, judging from his initial letters to Miranda concerning the *mejoras* (improvements) that he had in mind. Aspiring to build an efficient model for the nation's customhouses, León hoped to equalize the tariffs for all imports. He, therefore, recommended the abandonment of the special British concession of 1811, a concession that the American agent Lowry had resented since his arrival in Venezuela and which General Miranda agreed with him should be changed. The General perhaps had authorized León to proceed on this reform, especially meaningful considering the hostility of Hodgson at Curaçao. With the emphasis on "free trade," León hoped to promote the sale of Venezuela's products. He reduced the tax on gunpowder to stimulate the sale and import of that item, so necessary in time of war; and León insisted upon the improved collection techniques that would maximize commercial fees. To increase revenues, he reestablished the franchise on playing cards and stimulated tobacco sales—these were hardly popular measures! But Miranda and others recognized that tobacco had been one of Spain's best revenue sources in the colonial era; and the war crisis demanded the continuation of the tobacco tax. By July 3rd, León had issued additional measures to free the salt trade and reduce all duties on major food items: flour, salted meat, corn, and rice—concessions extended five months to foreigners and ten months to national merchants. By that period, moreover, a trio of capitalists (Gerardo Patrullo, Joaquín Joves, and another merchant from La Guaira) accepted a government contract for key supplies, which by July 5th also obligated Patrullo to produce twenty barrels daily of military rations. The hard-working León, it would appear, was beginning to turn Venezuela's economy around.[48]   Some of Miranda's friends discerned this progress. For example, Vicente Salias, editor of *El Patriota* (Patriotic Society), was a case in point; and he wrote to the General that once the military situation improved, Venezuela would emerge in prosperity and complete her freedom as a nation. Miguel Jóse Sanz was likewise sanguine about León's work. The opinion of these two patriots sustained Miranda's own expectations for León's program under the martial law project.[49]

It is manifestly difficult to arrive at a serious evaluation of Venezuela's economic condition in the months following a drastic earthquake, not to mention the additional drain of a war crisis, that destroyed not only buildings and lives but also the documents that might have given us more than a fragmentary view of the conditions prevailing in the tragic days of defeat. Yet, there are some statements by contemporaries that are suggestive, if not conclusive. To begin with, there is no question that Miranda's young appointees to the military and civilian posts of leadership proceeded to alienate many groups of people who resented the discipline and ironclad dictatorship of Miranda's young, enthusiastic, nationalist followers who annoyed their seniors with their excessive zeal in executing the laws. Perhaps that Commandant at La Guaira was right all along when he told Captain Forrest that he could not get those workers to do anything. The trauma of the earthquake must have had something to do with this. The people resented Miranda's youngsters, the new "bossy" military and civilian *jefes* (chieftains). Vicente Salias and Francisco Paúl wrote to General Miranda on this problem. The intellectual Salias perhaps displayed an exceptional intuition; he had known many of these young men in the early days of the Sociedad Patriótica when their imaginative minds wanted to construct an ideal blueprint for their new nation. Salias noted that men like Las Casas and Peña, the military and civilian jefes at La Guaira, were overzealous in their goal to send all the men possible to the warfront. They should realize that the prosecution of a war also consisted of men working in agriculture, commerce, etc. So, there had to be balance, more perspective, etc.[50] Less constructive in his criticism, Francisco Paúl praised General Miranda for the inspiration of the Martial Law program—the theory was commendable while the implementation was harmful to the nation's interests. The General should use more dependable leaders, the cynical observer concluded without any explanation of importance.[51] There was no attempt, however, to explain the other side of the story—the resistance and alienation of certain groups in society that frankly were no longer interested in the survival of republicanism.

The letters of La Guaira's civil leader, Dr. Miguel Peña, illustrated the hostility of local groups to Miranda's dictatorship, or the implementation of the martial law program. On June 14, he told the General how the "old" civilian leadership had opposed him at every turn. "My charge" [under the May 19th project], Peña added: "does not recognize any dependence on anyone except you." Peña, however, promised to follow Miranda's suggestions, doing his best at all times to get along with the former leaders.[52] On June 26th, Peña's letter provided a sobering message for Miranda's conciliatory dictatorship. La Guaira's civil chief described a mission that he had sent to the "Eastern" states in order to purchase supplies for distribution along the coast from La Guaira to Puerto Cabello. José de Jesús Goenaga was in charge; and he was given "paper" money to cover the purchases. As mentioned earlier, the government's "paper" money was not well received by Venezuelans. The reception to Goenaga's mission more than illustrated that point! The governments of Cumaná and Barcelona publicly resisted the payment. Moreover, Peña noted: "the authorities condone those contracts in which the product sold has a much higher price in paper money than in cash; and that in Margarita [Island] the government is so weak that paper money does not circulate, or if it does circulate, it is at a ridiculous discount." At Pírutu, south of Barcelona on the coast, Goenaga bought some cattle "and when he tried to pay with paper, they threw out the contract with impunity."[53] The complaint about officials permitting the discrimination against "paper" money, despite the penalties in the law against such action, was common in Caracas and elsewhere in Venezuela; and León, the Director of Finance, complained to Miranda in late June and early July that contractors were rejecting governmental orders based on paper money.[54]

The implications of Goenaga's failed mission to the "Eastern" states were not wasted on Dr. Peña:

> My General, if paper money does not circulate, our liberty is lost; what
> it lacks in credit because of defective national funds, it is necessary to
> put energy into the authorities. If they are weak or authorize this evil,
> the time has come in which our enemies will triumph irremissibly.

This was a good point that Peña was making: defeat was inevitable if the martial project could not be implemented. And that is one explanation for the unpopularity of Miranda's young *jefes*, military and civil. Goenaga had further reported these infuriating facts: there is "great abundance of supplies and in the island of Margarita there is much corn and casaba that can be exported without harming its inhabitants." Moreover, the states of Cumaná and Barcelona "are carrying on an active contraband [exchange] in money with the colonies [foreign possessions in the Caribbean]."[55] The Goenaga mission, in other words, documented a lack of empathy in the "Eastern" states for the economic plight of the Caracas-Valencia heartland of Venezuela, the area that was fighting desperately for its life and the existence of the nation. What might be expected from those states on the political and military request for help? General Miranda learned that answer in the correspondence with his friend Colonel Vicente de Sucre, whom he had recommended for the post of military governor of Cumaná under the Martial Law of May 19, 1812. The Cumaná government rejected the appointment on "constitutional" grounds, according to its judicial officers.[56] Other documents from the "Eastern" states told Miranda essentially the same thing—excuses for not coming to the nation's rescue, all couched in the usual verbiage of loyalty. Colonel Sucre, at least, kept his word, reaching Pírutu on July 10, 1812; but it was too late by then. Most of the "Eastern" states were now favoring, or caving into, the Spanish royalist cause.

There was a nervous hiatus throughout Venezuela on July 5, 1812, the first anniversary of the Republic's Independence. Miranda insisted upon a respectful commemoration to honor the nation's commitment and future existence. Bitter enemies of the Republic observed the ceremonies in Caracas mechanically, barely able to contain themselves in an unfriendly environment. The latest news was that the tide was turning at Puerto Cabello; Monteverde's forces would soon take over the key port, the nation's last bastion. The patriots suffered the news with gravity, sorrow, and anger. Miranda's commission to Caracas fulfilled its assignment in a dignified manner, overseeing the holiday schedule with patience and benevolence. By this time, it had harnessed the dissidents in the Municipality and the State Legislature of Caracas. It had announced, moreover, Miranda's decree to free the slaves willing to fight for the nation's liberty, a proclamation that angered and surprised many Spanish and Creole landowners; and the commissioners also imprisoned many Spaniards and *Canarios* (Islanders) whom they suspected of aiding and abetting the enemy.[57]

This historical pause on July 5th was just the prelude to disaster. The polarization of society in Caracas was almost approaching its final climax, while militants at both extremes pushed their hardest to win over the "People." Miranda, it seems, did not realize the situation was that bad, because he sent an agent to interview the Marquis de León, hoping to learn what had upset him in the political arena. As late as July 3rd, Miranda had no inkling of the fact that León, fearing for his life, would ask him for a passport to leave the country. Instead, on that date, Miranda wrote optimistically to León:

> I hope that you will reunite all the Europeans and encourage them with their persons, with their talents, and with their wealth, to confer on the nation the greatest possible good. Bring them together, my friend, and lets see if we can win over this worthy group of citizens who will help to extricate us from our troubles.[58]

León's reply of July 5th opened Miranda's eyes to the grim realities in Caracas. To bring together these Spanish capitalists would not help much; then, mustering up his courage, he stated categorically:

> It is impossible for any nation to exist under the present circumstances: without agriculture, without commerce, without income, without merchants, without laborers, and without security in the government and without the nation's confidence in its people, nor they in it.

Miranda's presence here for a few days to rectify matters, was the only solution possible.[59] On July 6th, León wrote again, asking for his passport. He mentioned that a calumny against him was threatening his family's existence in Venezuela. When Miranda learned this news, he urged Don Antonio to ignore such malicious tales; after all, "you and I are one."[60] Reassured, the Marquis de León continued in office until the end, carrying out Miranda's orders faithfully. It could be that Miranda's defense of this Spaniard, along with the fact that his own father had been a *Canario*, were mixed emotionally in the inflamed minds of many patriots during the Republic's last moments. Whatever the situation may have been, there was an inclination among Venezuelans to blame Miranda for the impending disaster.

Suspecting that perhaps his commission to Caracas had been overzealous, he sent an agent (Juan Echezuría) to interview León on what the real situation was in the former capital. León's evaluation of July 10, 1812, is a valuable document capturing the mindset of both sides. He claimed that his opinion was shared by many "sons of the country, sensitive and judicious, and who have the greatest interest in the government, deserving, at the same time, your full confidence." He explained the crisis in these words:

> When the first manifestations appeared, I thought that they were the result of one of those weaknesses to which man is prone. I expected that once a lawsuit began that society would recognize the justice of this measure; but the arrested parties ended up in shackles and chains, and it is known positively that there is no law case, a truth that is also obvious from the release and liberty [from prison] for one or another, according to the influence of those who have interceded and imposed their attention.

In short, this polite and timid Spaniard claimed that there were arbitrary arrests committed in Caracas by government officials, that led to imprisonment under ball and chain and without trial, and that release was possible if influential parties could speak in their behalf or supply the wherewithal to make it possible!

Perplexed, the Marquis de León could not understand why such tactics were chosen, even though it might have resulted from a "general lack of confidence" for Spaniards or Islanders. If these arrested parties cannot be useful to Venezuela, then remove them from the area, especially the doubtful ones. But to apply such measures to *all* foreign-born Hispanics, just does not make any sense whatsoever. Nothing good has come from this, and it puts you and your government in an untenable situation. Your feelings on this matter "are quite distinct [and] are well known to me." Those measures have gone against what my objectives were from the start: "to augment the treasury revenues and meet the key expenses of the day." León emphasized that he counted heavily upon many of those who were arrested, hoping to win their confidence so that they could be useful to the government of Venezuela. What especially annoyed León was that not even the most patriotic Europeans were excluded,

> nor those whose connections in this country, having their sons employed in the government and closely associated with the cause of [independence], it seemed that they had a veil of protection and appreciation and not the stamp of persecution! That, therefore, is what has happened and I do not know what consequences might result from it . . . It is up to your talent and knowledge to resolve what you may think to be most useful and convenient.[61]

We do not have Miranda's reaction to this important letter; but he understood only too well its implications with regards to the polarization of opinion in Caracas. The Repubicans of Caracas in July, 1812, had pioneered in a tactic of arbitrary arrests that became standard under Miranda's successor.

* * * * * * * * * * * *

Five of Venezuela's prominent figures made their way on July 12, 1812, to a secret meeting called by General Francisco de Miranda at his headquarters in La Victoria. Antonio Fernández de León and Francisco Paúl, the Director of Finances and the Representative for the State of Caracas respectively, had ridden in from Caracas; Francisco Espejo and Juan Germán Roscio were there in behalf of the Executive Federal Power; and José de Sata y Bussy, a former deputy of the National Congress, was on Miranda's General Staff. Grim-faced, Miranda solemnly described the nation's critical military and political situation which resulted from

> the loss of the *Plaza* and *Puerto de Cabello* and the coast of Ocumare and Choroní, occupied by the enemy, less by force of arms, than by the influence of treachery, fanaticism, and fraud, which instead of diminishing, is increasing and offering new advantages to the enemy,

without having received any assistance whatsoever from the Confederated Provinces, nor do we expect fundamentally to receive it, since some of them are under the enemy's rule, and the others, poorly instructed in the obligations of the federal pact, or [even] prepared with regards to the true situation of things, or without sufficient arms to help the army of the Confederation, which almost in its entirety consists of troops and officials of these provinces, of which two thirds of them, more than less, are in the hands of our rivals, including all of the *llanos* and cattle ranches, to such an extent that all that is free from the invasion and occupation of the enemy is the head district of the capital of Caracas [State] and La Guaira, without counting those on the leeward coasts and valleys of Capaya, where the evil of subversion also has favored the enemy.

Such were the realities of Venezuela, according to General Miranda. He, therefore, proposed an armistice to the Spanish General to bring about a cease-fire and halt the bloodshed. Thus, the peace negotiations could begin "according to the mediation offered and published by the generous English nation, or its government."[62]

Miranda's advisors agreed to this armistice proposal unanimously, leaving its "execution and fulfillment to his prudence and military and political expertise." Except for the psychological clash of Americans versus Europeans in Caracas, the General's assessment of the crucial facts and developments involved was thorough and relevant to the armistice decision. From the diplomatic point of view, Miranda's willingness to accept Britain's mediation was a stroke of genius! Later, as the negotiations on the armistice were advancing, Venezuelan representatives added the theme of constitutionalism, since the Spanish Constitution of 1812 had already been published. This was another imaginative addition that critics of the final Treaty of San Mateo have tended to overlook. Later, when General Monteverde ignored the Treaty and thus violated Venezuelan rights, it was General Francisco de Miranda, a prisoner in the dungeon at Puerto Cabello, who complained in great detail—using the Constitution of 1812 as his basis—about the *Canario*'s violation of the compact. Miranda directed his appeal to the Audiencia de Venezuela, the supreme judicial body for the area.[63] Despite all the writings about Miranda's Treaty of San Mateo, blaming the General, it should be noted that his patriotic opposition constantly took up the same defense of Venezuelan rights, as well as the terms of that treaty. It became a legitimate grievance in their long war with Spain.

The notions of British mediation and Spain's constitutional experiment did not wear well upon Spanish minds; in fact, it seems to have provoked an extremism on their part that further aggravated the polarization between Americans and Europeans. By July 12, 1812, General Miranda knew that British mediation in Venezuela was going nowhere: the Americans were not sanguine about it, for reasons that Sanz had noted; and Spaniards detested the entire process, thus leading to its rejection at about the time that General Miranda decided in its favor! Miranda also recognized that Great Britain wanted to avoid further conflict in Spanish America in order to preserve its commercial expectations there. It might even have occurred to Miranda back on June 3, 1812, when he met with Cortés, Salazar, and Thomas Molini on their diplomatic assignments. Moreover, there was already talk about Napoleon's days being numbered in Europe; and that also excited the English Government on mediation and ending the conflict in the New World. This would assure Great Britain's future prosperity in pursuit of James Mill's objectives, so familiar to us. Miranda saw the picture from his own perspective: Great Britain's commitment might save the day for the reconquest of Venezuela, as well as the future union of Venezuela with Cartagena and Nueva Granada. If these thoughts passed through Miranda's mind, he was surely a man of vision and foresight. Spaniards hated him with a vengeance: this "old man" had been in their hair too long; and perhaps the mediation tactic was just another one of his tricks to capitalize upon an obvious bone of contention between Spain and England. Spaniards, like General Monteverde, resented Miranda's constitutional argument in defense of the Treaty of San Mateo and his Venezuelan heirs' constant bickering about their rights under the Cádiz Constitution. It smacked of hypocrisy to them and thus pushed Spaniards onto the defensive. In their rage against the hated Americans, they resorted stubbornly to dictatorial and vindictive measures that further inflamed the polarization of opinion. The patriots' arbitrary arrests of Spaniards and *Canarios* shortly before Miranda's capitulation did not help matters at all; in fact, it provided an excuse for Monteverde's reciprocal program of vengeance, notwithstanding the terms of the Treaty. Not surprisingly, his fellow *Canarios* in Venezuela encouraged this streak of vindictiveness. It kindled the vicious warfare that followed, the "War to the Death," of Bolívar's period.

The First Republic of Venezuela perished in the final days of July, 1812, the ill-fated "Earthquake Republic." It also ended the career of one of Venezuela's greatest patriots, Francisco de Miranda. It was a thoroughly frustrating and disillusioning experience for him, especially its ignominious ending. After all, he was leader of the side that lost that unequal conflict; understandably he had no real bargaining power in the negotiations on an armistice and treaty; and there was no time to discuss the bones of contention with Monteverde, who was in no mood to compromise at all! The uprising of Miranda's own men in the general headquarters' zone, even though it was suppressed, was ennervating, to say the least. The General made his final arrangements for packing and transporting his valuable papers and documents—the subsequent Archives of Miranda that were sent to Curaçao—and he instructed the Marquis de León on how to dispose of the governmental funds in Caracas. By July 17th, Mariano María de Las Casas, as military chief, had full authorization to proceed with the naval force at La Guaira.[64] One of Miranda's favorites, young Las Casas opted to betray his General. He managed to convince other young officers—most of them Miranda's candidates for military and civil posts under the Martial Law of May 19th—to join the "Conspiracy." Simón Bolívar and Miguel de Peña were among the conspirators. The story of betrayal, not one of Venezuela's best historical episodes, is too well known to bear repetition here. It was not an unexpected result in such a highly polarized and emotional war for young men to seek a scapegoat for their failure by turning on their great leader. Two years later at Carúpano it happened to Bolívar himself but with a different ending, compared to Miranda's future.[65]

Francisco de Miranda, thus, had to step down from his historical platform to spend the rest of his life in jail. Sent to Puerto Cabello's famous dungeon by General Monteverde, the prisoner Miranda had time to reflect upon past events. In the early months of 1813, he wrote that lengthy document to the Audiencia de Caracas that we mentioned above. It was his last historical contribution. Thereafter, the Spanish Government moved the prisoner to Puerto Rico and finally to Cádiz, Spain, for his last incarceration. On July 14, 1816, at 1:05 A.M., General Francisco de Miranda expired.[66] *Requiescat in pace* (MAY HE REST IN PEACE).

Epilogue

Bolívar's Reconquest and the Miranda Legacy

> The hatred [Spain's] that animates her against us, is not like other sentiments, a passion that is more or less inflamed; it runs in her blood, a poisonous envy corrodes her entrails upon witnessing our glories . . . You [Bolívar] should confuse the pretensions of that savage Nation, our enemy. You have trampled under foot her flags after immortal victories. You have forced her to yield in battle, trembling and covered with shame, her violent usurpations in America. Lets hope that with her armies shattered in the dust, the Councils of Cádiz will tremble, and receive in America the law imposed on them by victory!
>
> A. Muñoz Tébar, Caracas, December 31, 1813.[1]

The reins of Venezuela's emancipation passed from Francisco de Miranda's hands to those of Simón Bolívar, the Liberator who reconquered his native land in 1813, just a year after the First Republic's demise. From Cartagena as a base, Bolívar commenced a dazzling series of victories against his Spanish enemies that caught them completely off guard. He emerged, almost overnight, as a man of destiny in the crucible of a "War to the Death" against Americans' hated oppressors. Although the principles of the Venezuelan Revolution remained intact, the new leadership was far more realistic, or cynical, about man's destiny: ends, rather than means, seemed to have priority. This was not a surprising development in the context of perennial war. Bolívar's patriots seldom mentioned the Precursor's name; and they often ridiculed the weaknesses of the First Republic. Having being trained and nurtured under the Martial Law of 1812, however, they adamantly maintained the "Old Man's" fervor for a modern and efficient Venezuela. By continuing to implement much of Miranda's program, they were effectively recognizing the importance of the former model in their own experience. The historical significance of the continuity with the Miranda period was striking and pervasive; and the realization of this historical fact should help to deemphasize the futile and emotional squabbles over the demise of the First Republic.

To begin with, Miranda's dream of "Union" with Cartagena and Nueva Granada permeated the documentation of Bolívar's reconquest of Venezuela and its new government until it own tragic end in mid-1814. Under the banner of the ally Cartagena, Bolívar went into battle again in the Magdalena river area; then, he headed the force that was assigned to attack and capture the royalist base at Santa Marta, Cartagena's traditional enemy. His remarkable success thoroughly surprised and upset Spain's defenders; and Bolívar compounded the defeat by capitalizing upon the enemies' disorganization.[2] The victors poured through their lines and were irresistible. Inspired by the slogan "War to the Death"—and Monteverde's record of abuse in Venezuela incited the Patriots to give the hated Spaniards an example of their tactics—added an element of ferocity that fully justified the slogan. The practice that the Patriots had learned in Caracas on the eve of Miranda's defeat now became institutionalized: Spaniards and *Canarios* were incarcerated as a matter of course to supply the patriots' expenses, or meet an untimely end! Needless to say, this further polarized the relationship between Spaniards and Americans. The "War to the Death" begat a "War of Plunder"—in short, a vicious and ferocious war of "brothers," as Blanco-White described this nightmare that tormented his thoughts. It came to pass; and it lasted so long! It alienated many of the Liberator's followers and held back, if not destroyed for decades, the economic development of all Spanish America.

Antonio Muñoz Tébar was a dominant and remarkable figure of the "Reconquest." This young intellectual joined the *Sociedad Patriótica de Venezuela*. He was the co-editor of *El Patriota de Venezuela*, along with Vicente Salias; and he became a good friend of Francisco de Miranda; in fact, he served as his Secretary of State in the last days of the First Republic. Simón Bolívar likewise respected and admired Antonio's brilliance in economics and international relations; and those were the first two portfolios assigned to Antonio Muñoz Tébar by the

Liberator. By mid-1814, he also assumed the secretaryship of War. He was, in short, the Liberator's right-hand man in every sense: his voice, ideas, and his actions as Liberator. It was a remarkable relationship, leaving us with the feeling that Bolívar learned a great deal from him, which he never forgot after 1814. Young Muñoz Tébar was a devoted intellectual; he learned much from his friends in the Patriotic Society, from Miranda and Salias, as well as Juan Germán Roscio. He borrowed books, articles, etc. from them. In view of our study, it is important that he read all of Burke's materials in London and Caracas; and Miranda must have loaned him a copy of Thomas Pownall's major work. This young man applied the ideas that he had learned; writing them up in position papers and articles in the *Gazeta* to educate and persuade Simón Bolívar on what measures he should take. Muñoz Tébar realized that his friend Bolívar had "greatness" in his future; and it was his responsibility to develop these indications to the maximum.

As the Reconquest movement settled down in Venezuela, the theme of "dictatorship" vitally concerned Simón Bolívar and his advisors. There was general agreement that Miranda's dictatorial rule had been justified in the last days of the First Republic; and Bolívar wanted to justify his rule on the same basis. Bolívar, however, felt that the dictator Miranda had no right to sign a treaty with the enemy that gave up the Republic's existence—that, in his eyes, was Miranda's greatest sin—and his fellow liberators shared this sentiment, or dogma.[3] It is interesting to note that a few months after Bolívar commenced his series of victories from Cartagena as his base, the government of that Republic also expressed the view that the grant of dictatorship should not allow its recipient to sign away a Republic's existence. The rationale was contagious, it seemed, since it appeared plausible to emotionally distraught minds, unable to face the real fact of failure.

In the instructions prepared by Muñoz Tébar for Venezuela's agents to Great Britain, the Liberator admitted his preference for "centralism" in government. "The central authority is sovereign," the instructions concluded,

> and the Peoples' influence consists of the selection of their Representatives that form the Legislative Council, and [it also consists of] the private property protected by a Supreme Court. These conditions do not apply exactly at this moment because the form of government depends upon the extraordinary circumstances of the war that had compelled us to form a dictatorship.[4]

In time of war, therefore, both Miranda and Bolívar agreed that Confederation government was not acceptable.

An interesting feature of the Reconquest was the campaign by Muñoz Tébar and Bolívar to convince their countrymen that Miranda's "dictatorship" should automatically go to the Liberator. They, therefore, called upon Francisco Javier Uztáriz to draw up a project for a provisional government of Venezuela establishing a strong executive—that is, a dictatorship. By this time, the major author of the Venezuelan Constitution of 1811 had learned from experience that the excessive idealism of the former document was impracticable in these new conditions. The "Old Man"—it was Uztáriz who gave him that nickname because of his ideas on government—would have smiled with satisfaction upon knowing that he was not as outmoded in his political thinking as Uztáriz used to believe.[5]

Two men, familiar to our readers, published their opinions on the Uztáriz project in the *Gazeta de Caracas*, which is understandable considering the campaign of Bolívar-Muñoz Tébar. Dr. Miguel de Peña was one of the informants and Miguel José Sanz, the other. The latter, Miranda's dear friend, favored the dictatorship on the same ground that he had argued for it in Miranda's case. Dr. Peña specifically noted that Bolívar, as Miranda's successor in power, deserved this same authority. With these arguments, fortified with many other rationalizations, the dictatorship was acclaimed by the public in early January, 1814.[6] It is doubtful that the opposition could have resisted this campaign, because dictatorship, whether anyone disapproved or not, was a fact of life in Venezuela from the time that the liberators got there.

The trend toward *la suma del poder* was not peculiar to Venezuela alone. The entire "Union" area of northern South America engaged in the same debate over the "states' rights" and the unitarist (centralists) type of government. Antonio Nariño in New Granada believed, as Miranda and Bolívar did, that a unitarist government was far more efficient; and the Cartagena document mentioned earlier likewise subscribed to this point of view. This did not just apply to emergencies, requiring a dictatorship; they sincerely believed that even in normal times, a strong executive government of a republican nature should embody unitarist theory of government. In short, any unionist government in Northern South America, consisting of Cartagena, Nueva Granada, and Venezuela would, by choice of their leaders, have been unitarist.

Muñoz Tébar's ideas on "Union" and Foreign Affairs provided an excellent illustration of the continuity between the Miranda-Bolívar years. In addition, it also reflected "William Burke's" influences upon the ideology of those two governments. On December 31, 1813, Bolívar's Secretary of State for Foreign Affairs surveyed the Liberator's first four months in power in the most complimentary terms. Although Muñoz Tébar's remarks were highly negative on the First Republic, the young secretary underscored Bolívar's determination and great concern for achieving a strong alliance with New Granada which, in turn, would provide a united nucleus for a potential American system. Following Burke's thought in March, 1811, Muñoz Tébar asserted:

> The enemies of the American cause will tremble before such a formidable Body, that in all places will resist them united. The Power and internal prosperity [of the Americas] will reach its peak, when directed by a common impulse; our elements of Power and prosperity, will gather together to form a great whole. While we promote our National greatness, we shall extinguish among ourselves all germs of division, and thus avoid, what already has happened in New Granada on one occasion, when her regions opted to engage in battle which destroyed them mutually, and caused the barbarous Spaniard to laugh, seeing his enemy weaken himself without any risks [to the Spaniard].[7]

History favored the cause of "Union" in South America:

> If in those ignominious centuries, in which a Continent with greater population and riches than Spain, was the victim of the perfidious glances of Madrid's Cabinet; if the latter at two thousand leagues' distance, without enormous forces, could control America, from New Mexico to the Magellans, [by placing her] under a hard despotism: why could not New-Granada and Venezuela join into a solid unity? Even more, why could not all of South America unite under its own central Government?

At this point, Muñoz Tébar paraphrased the ideas supplied by James Mill as Burke in the *Gazeta*:

> The lessons of experience should not be lost to us: the spectacle that Europe offers us, flooded in blood for trying to establish a balance [of power] that is always disturbed, should serve to correct our policy, in order to save it from the bloody rocks [of disaster]; if our Continent would divide itself in Nations, as in Europe; if the American Government followed the principles of that area [Europe], we would

also have the oscillations of a Continental balance [of power], and we would shed our blood as she [Europe] sacrifices at the feet of that idol that her policy worships.

Now, the young secretary brought his master into this great scenario:

We are now in the best circumstances, without an obstacle, to give our policy the most convenient orientation. Your Excellency [Bolívar], victorious in the eyes of America, who is the admiration and hope of its Citizens, is the most appropriate [leader] to unite the votes of all the Southern Regions; and to occupy himself from this time forward to form the great American Nation in one fell swoop, thus preserving her from the evils inflicted upon Europe by her system of Nations.

Besides, explained the Secretary:

In addition to the Continental balance [of power] that Europe seeks where she is least likely to find it, in the midst of war and agitations [of all types], there is another equilibrium, Your Excellency: which concerns us deeply: the equilibrium [balance of power] of the Universe. The ambition of European nations has fastened the yoke of slavery on the remaining parts of the World; and all of these regions of the world should try to establish a balance among themselves and Europe, in order to destroy the preponderance of the latter. I call this [new balance] the equilibrium of the Universe, which should enter into the calculations of American policy.[8]

Earlier in his presentation, Secretary Muñoz Tébar had stressed that the U.S. Congress on December 5, 1811, had already envisioned the historical significance of Venezuela's emancipation. The President told Congress that he would continue to report on similar moves in other parts of the Western Hemisphere. Muñoz Tébar interpreted this to mean that the United States intended to recognize Venezuela's independence as soon as New Granada and other regions made an identical commitment:[9]

These are the votes [desires], Your Excellency, of that Nation of the North, that the great Washington led to victory, and whose policy should unite with ours, to combine our mutual resources, like an insurmountable barrier to Europe's ambition.

Thus, it would appear, that Miranda's long-standing notions of hemispheric unity, expressed also by William Burke in the *Gazeta de Caracas*, now developed into a policy statement by a Venezuelan Secretary of State, anticipating the famous James Monroe message of 1823 by nine years! And Muñoz-Tébar wanted Simón Bolívar, the man of the moment, to be the standard-bearer of the Western Hemisphere Idea's defensive strategy against the Old World.[10]

The inspirational message of Antonio Muñoz Tébar in his position paper of December 31, 1813, guided the Liberator Bolívar for the rest of his public career. After the *Informe* appeared in print, the news reached Curaçao that Napoleon's forces had met defeat at Leipzig in the fighting of October 17–20, 1813, a decisive turning point in world history. As editor of the *Gazeta de Caracas*, Muñoz Tébar welcomed this great news in the February 7, 1814, issue:

> America should rejoice for the triumph of the allied arms, which have so gloriously defended the cause of Independence [in Europe]. [America] should not fear any attempts from Spain which she can no longer execute. The war has exhausted her Treasury, and the concessions gained against the French, even though they will increase her territorial possession, they still cannot provide her with a Navy, which she lacks, and without which her threats against us are ridiculous; because of the major Allied successes and Lord Wellington's presence, Great Britain has gained a predominance over Spanish affairs that it can even destroy her system [Spain's] against the Independence of the New World. No one should doubt that the powerful Nation that has constantly defended the Independence of Europe should hesitate to defend equally that [the Independence] of America, if she were attacked. On the contrary, let us rejoice for the irresistible ascendancy that she will assume in both Hemispheres to assure the liberty of the Universe.[11]

The mutual economic interests of Great Britain and Spanish America, Muñoz Tébar argued, as if he had James Mill at his elbow:

> Our products until now have been without value, our agriculture has been dispirited, [but now] they will emerge from their condition of nullity because of the compensatory factors offered to the Laborer with the rise in prices of products he grows; in the context of the opening of Continental Ports of Europe to British ships, they will carry our exports of coffee, cacao, indigo, cotton, etc. etc., that are in much demand [in Europe]. Stagnant for such a long time, our maritime commerce suffered wherever the Napoleonic influence reached, Europe was deprived of many goods of prime necessity [for] them, and we also

suffered as exporters of those goods that stimulated our commerce and the advantages of our Agriculture.

The commercial interest and policy of Great Britain and Spain are diametrically opposed with respect to America. Now that Spain can no longer enslave us peacefully, she is still determined stubbornly to exterminate us; [whereas] England is an advocate of our Independence and interested in our prosperity. Since the North and South of the New World has decided to uphold their liberty at all costs, even though Spain should send the most numerous Armies, they would merely come here to be destroyed by us, without being able to conquer us. England will not abide a hateful war, a futile effort at best, which without offering any hopes to Spain, will only end up ruining this beautiful half of the earth.[12]

For the next few weeks, articles in the *Gazeta* elaborated upon the nature of the Spanish enemy and his obsessive hatred for the Americans, underscoring the introductory quotation of our epilogue. In Curaçao, the nucleus of a Spanish colony, along with their American faithful, held open rallies in which they vented their vitriolic anger against Bolívar and his ilk. General John Hodgson, much to the surprise of some observers, protected this vocal group of foreigners in his midst, despite some of their harmful antics vis-a-vis the natives of Curaçao, who favored the Republican cause of Venezuela. But there was a serious incident, involving some deaths, that forced Hodgson to conduct an investigation. Henceforth, he was less supportive of his fiery allies.[13] Showing no remorse whatsoever, the latter wrote angry letters to the authorities at Cádiz, demanding the immediate formation of a large scale expedition of Spanish troops to reinvade the Venezuelan mainland. Some forces were sent but not enough to turn the tide against Simón Bolívar's republic. From Curaçao, the poisoned pen of Dr. José Domingo Díaz, that "miserable Venezuelan" and "vile man," irritated his mainland readers with his apologies for the Spanish royalist cause. An observer in Curaçao, who regarded Bolívar's regime favorably, captured the venomous spirit of the Spanish exiles on the Island, and their spokesman Dr. Díaz:

> Those insurgents . . . those rebels, that gang of traitors defend themselves like lions, they fight like desperate men. That mad Bolívar . . . frustrates all of our best projects, the best organized designs; but [this will change] once that the great Nation sends ten thousand men to bring Caracas down [to her knees], [who will then] pass over to

Santa Fe, [then] a tour [south] to Buenos Aires, and as they march [around the circuit] they will not leave one insurgent alive.[14]

In early October, 1813, these Spanish exiles in Curaçao finally were given a serious hearing in Cádiz, Spain, where their merchant allies applied unbearable pressure on the government.[15] They received the green light to proceed in the preparation of a royal expedition consisting of over ten thousand Spanish troops; its destination was initially: the Río de la Plata. But in its final stages, the expedition's objective was Caracas, Venezuela, the first step in the circuit of conquest outlined in the quotation above. And that was achieved by the famous expedition of General Pablo Morillo in 1814–1815. Governor Hodgson received orders from London to force all Spaniards to remove all their goods from Curaçao; and, on April 3, 1814, five ships left the Island for Coro with substantial supplies, accompanied by about one hundred Spaniards. The Curaçao exiles, in the meantime, made plans to send eight to ten agents to the Venezuelan mainland to "revolutionize" the area, getting slaves to join the war against the Republicans.[16] In view of the disastrous defeat of Bolívar's forces in mid-June, 1814, it would appear that Muñoz Tébar in his editorials had misjudged the power of the Spanish enemy. It proved to be a costly mistake for him since he lost his life in one of the battles that month!

The Caracas gazette of May 23, 1814, published an insightful letter by an Englishman, residing in America, to a friend in Jamaica. It dealt with "England's commerce and the war in America." "My respectable friend," he began,

> we would have to close our eyes to reason, if we could not see the enormous harm inflicted upon the cause of Great Britain's commerce by the civil war of the Americas. Just keep in mind that the arms of farmers are being employed in the armies without discernment, that, as a result, the harvests of all types will be delayed noticeably, that is, if they are not extinguished altogether in many branches of agriculture. At least, in the region where I live, I can testify to you that in the past year there had not been a new planting of cacao, coffee, indigo, or cotton, and that the latter had disappeared entirely, having lost the major establishments and the other three branches have also diminished. Even when the war ends, many years will go by without being able to resume cultivation; and Great Britain will be deprived for a long time of the profits that it made from the transport of tropical products.[17]

The ruthless atrocities and the great devastation of the lands and resources can only mean: "Soon these people will not have goods to exchange, or metals with which to buy commercial goods from England." And what will be the result "of such a horrible destruction?" The Englishman answered:

> That European Nations will be deprived of the precious goods from America, and they will not have a place to dispose of theirs; in short, that agriculture and American populations will decline everywhere, and that because of a frightening retrogression, things will return to the state in which they existed three centuries ago. All of these regions are being converted into deserts, and or transformed into impenetrable forests.

Even Spaniards have admitted that 200,000 men have died in Mexico without any benefit from "such a horrible butchery." The patriots are determined more than ever to become independent. "This war," he repeated,

> does not produce any other effect than the annihilation of trade, which already begins to decline noticeably because of a lack of exchangeable specie. Those two hundred thousand victims sacrificed by the Spaniards' barbarism have brought about an irreparable reversal in the work of the mines. The same has happened in Peru and in New Granada. What will they use henceforth to pay the merchandise of the English trade? Purchases diminish rapidly and the prices of clothing should fall because of the lack of moneyed species; and from the paper that the new governments have been forced to put into circulation, and the Spaniards as well have done so in the areas that they retain.

The amazing fact was that Spaniards, he noted,

> have not wanted to admit England's mediation, despite the fact that their authority over the Americas is ending every moment; and it even can be said that it no longer exists since, even in the places that they retain, they merely rule half way, from fear that the towns will give up their allegiance to them, and because the justice and smoothness of the liberal Governments established by the patriots, oblige Spaniards to temper their natural ferocity. But this will only last while the people are learning to become civilized. Before long, they will not have a single soldier, when all Americans recognize that their interest consists in struggling for liberty. Then, Spaniards will learn that America is no longer in a state that permits her to be conquered.

Preparing for his conclusion, this English sage had some good advice for his countrymen:

> It is my contention, therefore, that Europe's interests consists in allowing America to prosper in liberty. Agriculture and the mines will produce infinitely more, under the new Governments, than they produced under the monopoly of Spaniards: in this manner those regions will open up into immense markets for the manufactures of Europe, which will concede an advantage to the truly industrious nations of the world, and not to the Parasitic monopolists, that have not permitted the extension of cultivation in the Americas. Great Britain would benefit most from these favorable circumstances because of the preference that their merchandise deserves, and because of the disposition that the natives of those countries display in trading with the subjects of that nation.

The advice that he gave the British Government was especially worthy:

> It is time for the English to take stock of themselves and recognize how ruinous it would be to our industry and to the final settlement of the present war struggle, for the extinction, or at the minimum, the great decadence of our trade in the Americas because of the unjust depradations of the Spaniards. I assure you, Sir, that if the American war is prolonged for one more year, the exportation of colonial products will be suspended almost entirely, and just as bad, there will be a deficiency of cash, because the warfare occurs principally in the mining countries. Capitalists are avoiding all types of negotiations because of the prevailing circumstances; as a result, all is lapsing into lethargy. I believe that the merchants of that island [England] had better start recognizing that peace has to be restored in these regions in order to revive agriculture, without which there is no commerce. What good is it for Great Britain to have free access to those coasts if before too long there will not be any colonial products?[18]

Following Miranda's pattern, Bolívar and Muñoz Tébar recognized the importance of British assistance in achieving peace and stability. On May 4, 1814, Muñoz drew up fourteen articles as instructions for their agents assigned to London: Colonels Lino de Clemente and John Robertson. On May 9th, five additional notes were added to these instructions.[19] The Venezuelan mission, of course, never reached London because of the disastrous defeats of mid-1814; yet, these instructions provide valuable insights on the objectives of Bolívar's reconquest and its continuity with Miranda's legacy. These orders

highlighted the efficiency and centralism of a powerful American ally
that would have included Venezuela, Nueva Granada, and Cartagena—a
rich and vast area that offered great advantages for England's economic
future.

The Venezuelan Government began its proposal with a righteous
statement on the region's "neutrality" with the rest of the world and "its
inadmission of privileges in favor of any government." And yet,
Clemente and Robertson had authorization to reciprocate with the
British if they conceded special advantages that promised an equal
exchange. If the British offered to advance "sums of money," the
Commissioners could grant them favorable commercial concessions,
which is what the Venezuelan leaders did in 1811, when Robertson was
the negotiator from Curaçao. With the money allowed them, they
would request "armed ships for the protection of our coasts, for a short
time," until the General Government of Northern South America were
operable. They would also purchase guns, ammunition, and other types
of materiel, according to the terms of the agreement. England's major
obligation was to get Spain's recognition of their regional independence,
or at least, to force the cessation of hostilities by whatever means
possible—war against Spain if necessary. After all, the instructions
read: "since nothing could be more dismal for British commerce than
the prevailing war of destruction, by which the plantations, our cattle,
and all that we have is being decimated by the Spainards." Clearly,
Bolívar and Muñoz Tébar were in complete agreement with the English
gentleman-farmer we have quoted extensively above.

Instruction number ten offered a clever justification for the "War to
the Death":

> As for the motives of the war to the death that we declared against
> Spaniards, the first one; since they from the outset, not only brought
> death to our prisoners of war, but also to men of peace, children, and
> women, burning and destroying entire defenseless populations; second,
> the violation of the capitulation of San Mateo [Miranda's treaty with
> Monteverde]; third, the violation of all the rights of people and nature,
> committing such unheard of horrors of which there are hardly any
> former examples; fourth, the promotion of liberty for slaves has riled up
> a large number of those in Venezuela; fifth, the arousing, in general, of
> all people of color against the whites.

This last charge is significant, providing some insight on the racial
implications of the emancipation movement in South America. Because

of the destruction of documentation for the Miranda years, the evidence is silent or fragmentary; but there is documentation available in Bolívar's reconquest period, as well as later years, for a better understanding of the problem. The mere fact that the point was raised in these instructions is significant in itself, as well as a promising vein to study in greater detail.

The instructions also suggested some modern concepts in world and inter-American relations. Articles 11 through 13, indicated that if a world congress should convene in Europe after the war with Napoleon ended, Bolívar's agents were to ask England to help sponsor inter-American representation at that world conference. She could encourage a Venezuelan to represent his region there or support him in behalf of "all the new republics of America." If other American representatives were sent to Europe, Venezuelans promised to cooperate with them in some form of joint representation. Moreover, Venezuelans agreed only to act in conjunction with the wishes of all. The final article urged the British to help bring about "improvements" (*mejoras*) in agriculture and mechanical arts, sending to Venezuela skilled artisans in industry, as well as the machines and instruments that are sorely needed here.[20]

Simón Bolívar's influence predominated in the additional notes of May 9th, because of his experience in London with Miranda and the 1810 Commission. He advised his agents that if Great Britain were not ready to act promptly in Venezuela's behalf, they were authorized to proceed to northern Europe to find a nation best suited "to recognize and protect our independence." He must have remembered that Miranda had taken that position at one time. By coincidence, Russia was the most likely candidate in view of its "actual connections with Great Britain and her relations with the United States." Note five emphasized a policy of inviting non-Catholics to South America, employing the same standards as those offered by Brazil.[21]

In the month followed the writing of the instructions, Muñoz Tébar devoted much of his time to preparing his readers in the *Gazeta* on the major themes that he had emphasized in Spanish America's future relations with the world. The first topic, which came out in two parts, dealt with "*Neutralidad*" (Spanish America's Neutrality). This had been mentioned in the Instructions as one of America's major principles. Actually, what the writer meant by this term was the "non-entangling alliances" referred to by President Washington in his Farewell Address of the 1790s. Paraphrasing the U.S. President, the editor wrote:

> Nothing is more essential than to exclude the lasting and inveterate
> antipathies against certain nations, and the passionate connection with
> others, cultivating respect for all the sentiments of friendship and justice.
> The great rule of conduct for us with respect to foreign nations, is to
> extend our commercial relations, while politically having with them the
> least connection possible.[22]

The second theme, appearing on June 9, 1814, carried the title:
"Refections upon the Present State of Europe with Relationship to
America." Here, Muñoz Tébar brought together ideas he had learned
from reading the Burkian articles published in 1807–1808 in London.
Miranda, or Roscio, must have allowed him to read their copies of
those treatises; or perhaps Dr. Constancio had them as well. Be that as
it may, Bolívar's Secretary of State concerned himself with the
prospects of a new "Balance of Power" system in Europe and how it
would impact upon the Independence of Spanish America. It was the
eighteenth century power system that produced the first major steps
toward American Independence:

> France helped the North with troops, as well as war vessels, not because
> of any sense of philantrophy, or because of love for the American
> people, but because having lost her establishments in Canada, it was
> necessary to despoil her rival of the other Northern Provinces, and thus
> diminish her influence in the balance of power.

Spain had a similar objective in thwarting England's power. "The
present political situation in Europe, however, was totally different":
Great Britain is "the only maritime nation of the Universe" and it is not
likely "to lend itself to a situation in which Spain again tries to
guarantee her domination here." No league of her former allies in
Europe could force her to accept Spain's continued dominance in the
New World. Spanish America's emancipation has always been of
interest to the British Cabinet: "Great Britain, located between the
ancient and old Continent, via the new equilibrium of the Universe, will
finally achieve the apex of political greatness to which no people of the
world have dared to dream." Although he did not seek to challenge the
more profound thinkers "on the question of *imperio* of the seas"
[dominion of the seas], a humble Muñoz Tébar remarked: "We can just
see at a distance, a Great Britain, confused and overwhelmed by the
enormous weight of her riches, and an America forming the most
powerful empire of the earth." Such an overwhelming optimism makes

one wonder if, by chance, Miranda also loaned his friend Muñoz Tébar a copy of Governor Thomas Pownall's book on the prospects of an Anglo-Hispanic American union!

Having stated his major thesis, the "Equilibrium of the Universe" controlled by England and America, Muñoz Tébar added some interesting rationalizations:

> Our revolution, on the other hand, has contributed an aspect, so important that it cannot be suffocated by force. Mexico, Peru, Chile, Buenos Aires, New Granada, and Venezuela today form through their identity of principles and feelings a formidable league, incapable of being destroyed no matter how hard their enemies may try . . . It should be a great consolation to us to know that any outrage whatsoever that is committed against a small portion of the Colombian soil, will be avenged by an infinity of brethren States scattered throughout this new hemisphere.

Venezuela's Secretary of State for Foreign Affairs was sanguine about his thesis concerning England but he likewise felt that he had to explore all possibilities to satisfy his readers. They might be fearful that Spain would find allies in Europe to help in the reconquest of Spanish America. But that would just mean the continuation of the Emancipation movement for many more years with more destruction of Spanish America's economic life; all that the Europeans had realized in three centuries would be lost forever. Besides, he argued, anyone supporting that solution could not simply understand how valuable Spanish-American products have been to Europeans; if they did, they certainly would not want to have them cut off. Besides, England would not permit it. So, Muñoz Tébar shifted his approach:

> Fortunately, America also finds herself in circumstances of not inspiring misgivings among those who live from trade and from industry. For a long time, we cannot be anything but an agricultural people, and an agricultural nation capable of handling the most precious materials in the markets of Europe, the best [nation] calculated to foment *friendly* connections with the merchant, and the manufacturer. Once our independence is recognized, and these countries have been opened to all foreigners on the same basis, we cannot imagine how much public demand will increase every year. Export articles will multiply to infinity, and the imports will be trying always to strike a balance with our products.

By this time, Muñoz's description was approaching the clouds. The emancipation of America would bring unknown prosperity to the world: "in a word, in the customs of mankind, it [would bring us] a revolution much more frightening than the one produced by the Discovery." Muñoz Tébar also included Mill's conclusion that an independent United States was much more profitable to England than the former dependency; and he likewise emphasized Mill's notion that Spanish America's potential wealth was superior at that time to that of the United States. It was also clear that Mill's ideas on Britain's role in the Universe especially fascinated Simón Bolívar's Secretary of State. He promised to expand his discussion in future editorials of the *Gazeta de Caracas*—a promise that he was unable to keep.[23] This was his last publication. On June 15, 1814, at the Battle of La Puerta, Antonio Muñoz Tébar lost his life! What a shame for Venezuela and the emancipation of Spanish America—an exceptional mind that appreciated James Mill's ideas and tried to apply them to the New World. Muñoz Tébar also supplied us with an excellent illustration of the continuity of the Miranda-Bolívar years. The Bolivarian reconquest ended, for all practical purposes, with Muñoz Tébar's death.

Conclusion

During the brief visit to Philadelphia in late 1805, Francisco de Miranda greatly impressed young Richard Rush. On one occasion, the General emphasized to him that "it was wonderful how much one man could do" in shaping the great events of history. Other sage observations by the famous visitor made Richard assume that he was in the presence of a key historical figure. Our assumption is the same as that of young Richard: Miranda deserves to be recognized as a great influence in the Spanish-speaking world during the Revolutionary and Napoleonic eras. Still, he would have been the first to point out, from his own personal experiences, that there were stubborn obstacles, personages, and entrenched power groups in government that constantly scattered impedimenta along his career's path. He struggled in vain for years, even decades, to get a definitive British commitment for the emancipation of Spanish America. Yet, this "prince of visionary schemers," as Lt. Biggs once called him, refused to give up. When he learned from General Arthur Wellesley on June 9, 1808, that Great Britain had decided to intervene militarily in the Iberian Peninsula against Napoleon's forces rather than support Miranda's plans to liberate Spanish America, the Venezuelan strategist mastered his deep disappointment with the British and conceived the ingenious "Paper Assault" upon the Spanish Empire. This was within six weeks of that celebrated interview with Wellesley, the future Duke of Wellington. Miranda's new strategy included the well-known concept, or device, of the "Mask of Ferdinand" to justify, as well as initiate, a movement that would unite the Spanish Americas for their eventual Independence. Thus, he has been called the "Precursor" of Spanish American

Independence. Taking into account the revolutionary propaganda and materials involved in the "Paper Assault," we might even be justified in calling him the first "liberator" of Spanish America: not in the military context, but certainly in the ideological sense. This is especially true when we consider his contribution to William Burke's invention of the "Western Hemisphere Idea" and the beginnings of "Inter-Americanism," as proposed in the editorials of late March, 1811.

Although Francisco de Miranda won immediate worldwide fame for his military exploits and talents in the American and French Revolutions, and later in the Emancipation of South America, it should not be overlooked that much of his universal reputation stemmed from an exceptional personality and image as a man of letters who felt at ease with philosophers of the "Revolutionary Age." Dr. William Thomson did not err when he likened Miranda to the Scipio Africanus of the Roman period—hero in war and an intellectual leader in peace that fomented the spread of knowledge and wisdom in his midst. As early as 1785, in the *Political Herald and Review* (London), the impression that Miranda had made upon leaders of the American Revolution followed him to the British capital:

> He is a man of sublime views and penetrating understanding, skilled in the ancient and modern languages, conversant in books, and acquainted with the world. He has devoted many years to the study of general politics; the origin, the progress, and the termination of the different species of government: the circumstances that combine and retain multitudes of mankind in political societies; and the causes by which these societies are dissolved and swallowed up by others. (Ch. 1,11)

His library in London, as well as his collections of art, coins, and other valuable souvenirs of the past, brought great joy to his friends there; and the ubiquitous diaries of his world travels made him a brilliant conversationalist at all gatherings. We have mentioned the publication of his U.S. diary; others are now being published in the monumental *Colombeia* set of *all* of Miranda's manuscripts (63 folio volumes). He was a great memorialist of his period—a tireless and brilliant recorder of what he saw in different lands—a man whose linguistic talents were especially valuable in writing tracts of descriptive contemporary history.

As an intellectual himself, who had a deep faith in the need to formulate public opinion, Miranda enjoyed the friendships and cooperation of profound thinkers of his day who shared his crusade to liberate the Spanish American people so that they could experience a new order of political freedom and representation, a modern and just society, and full participation in an international economy of "free trade." Miranda learned much from his European collaborators; he understood their motives and national objectives; and they, in turn, came to appreciate and understand the spirit and goals of the Americans in the New World. Miranda's long relationship with Thomas Pownall (1790–1805) was especially meaningful in supplying the Venezuelan patriot with the grand setting for the *Colombeia* project—all aspects of the Colombia dream that obsessed Miranda. Pownall had sketched it in his famous *Memorial* to the monarchs of Europe in 1780 (later editions in 1783 and 1803). The *Memorial* called for a union of the Anglo-Americans in the New World and the British in Europe to sponsor international free trade and constitutional monarchy throughout the world. After 1790, Governor Pownall and Miranda endorsed the addition of Spanish Americans to that union, or alliance, with Great Britain. As the European power with great potential in manufacturing, shipbuilding, and other advantages that could help develop the economies of the New World, Miranda was able to appreciate these economic realities that in the long run could bring modernization to Spanish America. The Pownall-Miranda vision, in effect, was the first real expression of many aspects of the "Western Hemisphere Idea"—a concept that "William Burke" expressed so effectively in his editorials of early 1811 in the *Gazeta de Caracas*; and, as we have seen in the Epilogue, Bolívar's Secretary of State (Antonio Muñoz Tébar) wanted his famous master to implement that "Idea" for the Americas while aligning his people with Great Britain and her powerful navy. In this light, Francisco de Miranda's historical stature deserves to be enhanced. Following a clue from his old friend Pownall, Miranda told young Richard Rush in 1805: "The inhabitants of North and South America should, in their government and interests, copy the union of the vast continent upon which they both live."

The "Age of Revolution" in the Western World commenced in the English colonies of North America, setting off what Professor Herbert Eugene Bolton has aptly called the "Greater American Revolution" (1763–1825) that liberated most of Europe's possessions in the Western Hemisphere. That wave of anticolonialism, moreover, inspired republican precedents that influenced the Old World itself in the French Revolution and the Napoleonic Era, which vitally concerned the writers and thinkers that we have treated in this volume.

As Napoleon Bonaparte consolidated his control over the French Government via the Consulate and then the Empire in 1804, his strategy was to nullify Britain's opposition by resorting to economic warfare. This led to the "Continental System" (Berlin decrees of November 21, 1806, and those of Milan on December 17, 1807), whose objective was to wreak havoc with the British economy, blockading its goods from the continental markets of Europe, as well as applying other restrictive devices. These economic pressures brought near panic to British merchants and interests, thus encouraging England to entertain Francisco de Miranda's projects for the emancipation of Spanish America, in search of new commercial markets for her goods. Yet, at the last minute, the English would back out of these projects for considerations that involved the balancing of power in Europe—a frustrating pattern that disillusioned the Venezuelan advocate. Admiral Horatio Nelson's defeat of a combined French-Spanish naval force off the Cape of Trafalgar, near Cádiz, Spain (October 21, 1805), turned the tide for England. This great victory assured her control of the seas and also prevented Napoleon's invasion of England from taking place. It was a key consideration also in Sir Home Popham's plans, who presumably on his own initiative embarked upon the "Conquest" of Buenos Aires in June 1806. It reflected a British challenge to the Corsican's economic program, so the French leader responded stubbornly with his decrees in Berlin and Milan (November, 1806, and December, 1807). In the meantime, the British Government armed three separate expeditions to consolidate the English presence in the Río de la Plata area. This involvement led to two defeats: the "recapture" of Buenos Aires within a few months and the tragedy of John Whitelocke's loss, in mid-1807, of some two thousand five hundred Englishmen, who died on the streets of Buenos Aires!

Concurrently, Miranda's expedition to Venezuela, in 1806, was no more effective than the Platine adventure. It suffered a bad defeat, as well as a second invasion that withered away from want of adequate British support. On the plus side, however, Miranda's expedition sailed under the banner of "Liberation," rather than that of "Conquest." Moreover, Miranda, along with a coterie of British allies in the Caribbean, accidentally ran across some convincing evidence of Spain's defensive weaknesses on the Spanish Main. There was reason to believe that a third invasion of Venezuela, strongly supported by the English, would easily topple the Spanish foe. This would bring independence to Miranda's people and, at the same time, provide the

British ally with new markets for their goods, as well as additional strategic positions to guarantee a continued presence in the Caribbean. Thus, as 1808 opened, Miranda appeared to be on the verge of success after so many years of failure.

The South American invasions of the North (Venezuela) and of the South (Río de la Plata) provided the springboard that brought a young journalist to the attention of readers in London. Using the penname of "William Burke," his meteor flashed across the literary horizon for a six-year period, from 1807 to 1812. His first two treatises came out in London during 1807 and 1808, dealing with the Platine tragedy and stressing England's need to help forward the cause of Spanish American Emancipation. Rather than pursue a policy of "Conquest" that led to Whitelocke's disaster, the young writer urged upon his countrymen the more imaginative approach of Miranda's "Liberation" model in Venezuela. The use of a pseudonym in these works permitted the young intellectual to express his views candidly, without incurring a reaction against him for exposing the wrong-headed policy of the English Government that resulted in a disastrous defeat. By way of contrast, Miranda's exploits on the Spanish Main garnered considerable sympathy from the people there and would have been successful if the British Government had not withheld some support from him at the last moment.

Despite considerable speculation, no one seems to know much about this writer who challenged Spain's title to the New World, presenting anticolonialist views that we have heard recently during the quincentennial celebrations of America's discovery in 1492. Champion of the Americans' "natural rights" to seek their freedom from Spain's long rule of colonial tyranny and injustice, young Burke encouraged England to help the Americans achieve their liberty on humanitarian grounds. Besides, it would pay off in the form of new markets for British goods, offsetting the Corsican's strategy against England; and, for the future, at a minimum expense, it would assure a long-range prosperity for the English and Spanish Americans under a relationship of "free trade." In effect, Burke was arguing for an "Invisible Empire," thus applying Adam Smith's "Invisible Hand" to America's alliance with Great Britain. The analysis was brilliant, following the best ideas of the "New History" and the emerging "social sciences."

Who was this young writer? In Chapter Four: "William Burke: Front and Center," I explained how I arrived at my answer: it was James Mill, one of Miranda's closest friends, and the father of a precocious child, John Stuart Mill. He invented "William Burke" in London and the one that reappeared in Caracas, Venezuela, from November 23, 1810 to March 20, 1812, writing editorials in the *Gazeta de Caracas*. These essays also appeared in a two-volume work that came out in 1811. Here, James Mill advised his readers to study carefully his analysis of the "American Revolution" and especially its miraculous development in the years from 1787 to 1810. It provided an exceptional political, economic, and social model for the young nations of Spanish America to follow. Most of the editorials belonged to James Mill, reflecting his style, methodology, and concepts in various disciplines; yet, many of the ideas also belonged to Jeremy Bentham. In short, the editorials represented two powerful English thinkers of the early nineteenth century. If I am correct, it suggests the hypothesis: that Bentham and Mill's cooperation in writing these editorials for their friend Miranda, beginning in 1809, may have been the reason initially for the close collaboration of these two English thinkers that continued after 1812, leading to their contributions to "Philosophic Radicalism" in British political history, and reforms, of the first half of the nineteenth century. What I found fascinating was that these two scholars, writing in 1809 and 1810, were strong advocates of republican government as opposed to monarchy; yet, as realistic monarchists and good, patriotic Englishmen, they were visibly proud of key British traditions and precedents. They did not hesitate, however, to expose the injustices suffered by the English "people" at the hands of their kings, nobles, and assorted sycophants. It provides us a remarkable view of English practices, good and bad, often comparing them to French equivalents or differences.

Upon General Miranda's return to London on January 1, 1808, he was greeted enthusiastically by Lord Castlereagh and his colleagues. It seemed to him that the fortuitous circumstances in the Caribbean during the late months of 1806 were still operative. Castlereagh had assured him that England was vitally interested in supporting his plans for a third invasion of Venezuela. Preparations commenced and progressed noticeably in the following months, organizing an expedition that would be headed by General Arthur Wellesley and assisted by his Venezuelan cohort. It seemed unbelievable that this time around the British Government would follow through with its commitment to his project. By May, 1808, however, the annoying historical pattern repeated itself: delays, hesitation, and abandonment! Miranda was not happy to see this happen again; but he was not entirely surprised by the turn of events in mid-1808, as it is usually believed.

As he recalled the events of late 1806 and most of 1807 in the Río de la Plata, Miranda pondered their implications for his objectives in the Caribbean. He was in Barbados with Admiral Alexander Cochrane and others when the news of Popham's victory in Buenos Aires reached them. Popham's invasion, he predicted to his English friends, would end in failure since it clearly had "Conquest" in mind; and, as it turned out, that happened at the time that he was making the prediction! The British follow-through expeditions to the Plata in 1807 would have the same fate, he warned the British Government, reminding his allies that only expeditions of "No Conquest" or "Liberation" would have any future in Spanish America. The surge to welcome his third invasion of Venezuela, however, raised the following questions in Miranda's mind: Was this conversion to "Liberation" a sincere one? Or did it result from a "guilty conscience" in not following his advice on what approach was necessary in Spanish America? And other questions occurred to him, as he noted the first manifestations of delay in March and April of 1808. Were Europeans—and the English especially—really sincere about freeing Americans from Spain's tyranny? Or were they all *conquistadores* at heart? Angry that their ex-colonials in North America had broken with England, could they really believe in a process that reached the same results against another European mother country? After all, those were Americans who killed their countrymen on the streets of Buenos Aires! Questions of this nature tormented General Miranda *before* and *after* his famous interview with Wellesley on June 9, 1808.

Disappointed to the core, Miranda and his writers did not remain idle in any way; on the contrary, they set upon a propaganda project that would engage their attention for the next few years. Since Miranda's return to Europe, James Mill and the General immediately organized an education program to win over Englishmen everywhere to the cause of Spanish America's emancipation. For this objective, they exploited the appearance of Burke's second treatise—*Additional Reasons for our Immediately Emancipating Spanish America* in the spring of 1808. At the same time, they gained the approval of two essays to be published in the *Edinburgh Review* in January and July of 1809, dealing with the theme of emancipation. In short, the bad news of June, 1808, merely intensified the propaganda effort, drawing into the group of Miranda's writers Gould Francis Leckie and Dr. F.S. Constancio. Within six weeks of the Wellesley interview, Miranda also launched his "Paper Assault" with two letters dated July 20 and 24, 1808, to the municipalities of Caracas and Buenos Aires respectively.

The questions raised in Miranda's mind as he witnessed the reappearance of England's pattern of delay had the effect of changing Miranda's policy for the rest of his career. Now, he recognized that his major weakness in dealing with the British Government had been an exaggerated dependency upon Great Britain in plans to achieve his cherished objectives in South America. It was one thing to take advantage of outside help, as the English colonists had done with France and Spain in their Revolution, controlling their own national destiny; but it was another matter altogether to become too subservient upon that outside power. This could easily undermine the nationalistic objectives of the Spanish American Revolution. In the last analysis, Spanish Americans had to lead and control their own revolutionary cause. These were facts of life that Miranda had recognized earlier in his career; but now, the difference was that he was mentally prepared to adopt more aggressive tactics—for example, the bold "Paper Assault" against the Spanish Empire.

It should be recognized initially that only Miranda, among Spanish Americans, had the experience—his many years of dealing with British governmental officials, his personal contacts throughout the English imperial system, etc.—to execute the tightly-organized "Paper Assault" of 1808. The well-balanced content of the various letters involved also indicates that James Mill's organizational talents helped this propaganda campaign immeasurably. An important part of the process was Mill's psychological analysis of his countrymen's proclivities, as well as those of man in general. Moreover, the follow through upon this "Paper Assault"—that is, after the exposure of Miranda's conspiracy by Spanish and English officials—made this movement one of the most imaginative propaganda coups in history. It established a unified pattern of revolutionary procedure and content for the Spanish American Wars of Independence. General Miranda assumed the major risk; thus, he deserves the main credit. James Mill's contribution, however, also merits the plaudits of History.

To assure the receipt of the two letters, plus enclosures, to the *cabildos* of Caracas and Buenos Aires (July 20, 24, 1808), Miranda sent duplicate packages to executive figures in both cities. He urged the two focal centers to send out copies of the materials to neighboring political units: Caracas to Bogotá and Quito; Buenos Aires to Lima, Santiago de Chile, etc. The two centers, moreover, received copies of Miranda's letter to the other. The two letters, also, did not compete in contents; instead, they complemented each other intentionally. By September 10, 1808, the same procedure applied to new focal centers: Habana and Mexico City, who were given different materials, which were copied and sent to the South American focal centers; and copies from the South American centers also reached the Middle American points. On August 19, 1808, Miranda, and his colleague Mill, wrote a clever cover-up message to Lord Castlereagh, as innocent and distorted as one might expect in order to avoid a sudden exposure of the correspondence campaign. Interestingly, this aggressive correspondence seemed to be under the nominal supervision of Minister Spencer Perceval; and Admiral Alexander Cochrane's forces in the Caribbean distributed the letters. Most of the first batch of letters (July through September) reached their destination; but much of the second batch (October 6 through 20, 1808) was intercepted by suspicious English officers. Spanish agents likewise discovered Miranda's new "Conspiracy." Spain screeched to the high heavens: Miranda had to be stopped in his tracks; he should be eliminated! Admiral Cochrane likewise deserved severe punishment. England's "point of honour," however, would not allow this last demand. Thus, Miranda's friend got off easily; and Miranda was told to desist, or be expelled from British territory! Although not all of Miranda's message in the "Paper Assault" got through to Spanish America in late 1808, new copies were made by Miranda's team; and, thanks to Mexican financial assistance, *legajos* (or bundles) of those documents, as well as others, circulated throughout Spanish America by the end of 1810.

The total output of correspondence, plus the accompanying enclosures, added up to a full manual of information for all good Americans in the New World that wanted to start their own regional revolutions. It provided the best advice that Miranda and Mill could offer them: how cabildos throughout Spanish America should take over their provincial areas; they were told that Spaniards had betrayed Americans and had failed to consult them on government and strategy; thus, their governmental orders should be ignored; they were given the details of the victorious *Porteños* of Buenos Aires, their valiant defense of the Río de la Plata, and all the pertinent English documentation that they should have at their disposal to enact wise legislation and policy for their respective areas; they were sent copies of Miranda's key documents in the various revolutions of the late eighteenth century, etc. etc. They also received in the enclosures political documents on how to set up their national government, following the advice of political philosophers in Europe, etc. etc. Just as the Spanish spies had noted: the "traitor" was sending out complete "revolutionary instructions" to the municipalities of Spanish America! Yes, indeed! By following the "Mask of Ferdinand," Spanish Americans could buy time to establish governments in their own lands, thus avoiding any immediate clash of the different races and cultures in Spanish America and unifying the Americas for their glorious historical role in the future. General Miranda supplied this explanation for the "Paper Assault" on September 9, 1808, in a letter to Admiral Alexander Cochrane. We have reproduced it in Chapter Five.

By the early months of 1809, as the British Government became aware of Miranda's subversive correspondence with Spanish colonists, his publicists—James Mill, in particular—had commenced a "Public Assault," encouraging English public opinion to reconsider the policy that the Government's ministers had taken to fight Napoleon in the Iberian Peninsula and to insist upon launching Miranda's abandoned project of emancipating Spanish America. Mill and Miranda have both been publicized as authors of the January, 1809, essay in the *Edinburgh Review*. James Mill composed the essay in his usual, effective way, while Miranda advised him on what facts and documentation from his archives could be brought to bear on the argument. They worked well together; and Miranda, of course, would not permit any of the "Black Legend" slips that had gotten into "William Burke's" accounts. Presumably just a review of the Peruvian Jesuit Vizcardo de Guzmán's *Letter to the Americans*, the bulk of the essay provided a synthesis of Burke's earlier treatises, citing new facts and figures that would persuade English readers to regard favorably their country's assistance to the Independence of Spanish America. Such a policy would obviate Napoleon's economic restraints upon Great Britain and insure continued prosperity into the postwar world with strong allies in Spanish America. In retrospect, we can already see in this January, 1809, piece, the points of view that would be developed fully in the Burkian articles of 1810–1812 in Venezuela: the overwhelming attraction of South America's resources, human and otherwise, that would be advantageous to the allies in question; the opening of an Isthmian passageway through Panama that would revolutionize the flow of world traffic from East to West, etc. etc. And of vital interest was Mill's recognition that

Spanish Americans admired their Northern brethren and were eager to follow the model provided by the United States of America from 1787 to 1810, which was precisely the period emphasized in Burke's Venezuelan editorials. As most anticolonialists of this period, moreover, James Mill, as well as William Burke, often underscored the fact that U.S.-British trade *after* Independence was far more significant than before 1763. The first *E.R.* essay of 1809, in short, was a sophisticated and diplomatic presentation in favor of British intervention in the emancipation of Spanish America. It was intended initially to draw the attention of the British public in favor of Miranda's project *before* it was abandoned by British ministers; now, it was equally significant to impress those readers with the mistake that had been made in mid-1808 by English officials.

The July, 1809 issue of the *Edinburgh Review*, dealt with the publication of another Jesuit Father from Chile. Although overlooked by earlier students of Mill and Miranda, the review of Father Molina's work was no longer diplomatic in its approach; it was a veritable "attack" document against the ministers who committed the betrayal of England in mid-1808. Considering the record of futility against Napoleon's superior forces on the Continent, it was presumptuous, as well as stupid, to expose British manpower and finances in an unrealistic cause. Here we have again, Mill reminded his readers, another grim example of "ministerial imbecilities"!! Perhaps, irritated by the exposure of Miranda's correspondence with Spanish Americans, Mill's emotions had gotten out of control; and it was indeed a mystery that this language passed the editor's glance without action. Apparently, the exposure of the "Paper Assault" did not mean that Miranda *et al* would remain silent. On the contrary, the "Public Assault" against "ministerial imbecilities," as James Mill put it, had just begun. Dr. F.S. Constancio opened up his cannons against the ministers in the columns of *The Statesman* (September 13 and November 1, 1809), signing off as "LAS CASAS." In two exceptionally well-organized and scholarly essays, Dr. C. asked in awe: Who could ever imagine such stupidity on the part of British Ministers? And to pay such a high price in life and money, as well as sacrificing the immense commercial profits that would have accrued to British investors. Instead, these Machiavellian agents entered into a Treaty with Spain that unnecessarily made concessions to the Spanish ally, while at the same time sacrificing the rights of Spanish Americans. Dr. C.'s friend, Gould Francis Leckie, likewise joined in the minister-bashing, which encouraged a significant political opposition in Parliament that insisted upon a change of British policy, considering the unfortunate results of the Peninsular War. Thus, the "Public Assault" program by Miranda and his publicists brought about a new atmosphere in 1809 and 1810, which helps to account for the appearance and the success of Miranda and Mill's publication projects in Spanish America and Europe.

The most important projects of the Miranda team in 1810 were as follows: (1) Thanks to the presence of some rich Mexican Creoles and their Ecuadorean agent (José María Antepara), arriving in London in late 1809, General Miranda won their financial support in March, 1810, for sending bundles of documents throughout Spanish America—that is, the "Paper Assault" documentation of the earlier period—and other revolutionary materials: a new printing of Father Vizcardo de Guzmán's Letter with a fiery amendment added, and copies of *El Colombiano*. (2) Antepara and the Mexicans also supported the periodical *El Colombiano* for five issues: the first on March 15, 1810, two in April, and two in May, 1810. Like the documents of the old "Paper Assault," the issues covered international relations and topics that the Hispanic revolutionary leaders should know while establishing their respective governments. James Mill, who did most of the editing of Miranda's various collections, or books, also wrote an article entitled "Thoughts of an Englishmen" on matters in Spanish America, which may have been the first of a series of articles that he had been planning. It promised a sequel on May 15th, but the periodical never got around to another issue. We also see here the outline of some of Mill's topics for the Burkian editorials in Venezuela. The "Thoughts" article appeared again in the *Gazeta de Caracas*, but not within the original book manuscript conceived by William Burke. (3) Later in 1810, there appeared in English a book of documents entitled *South American Emancipation. Documents . . . by General Miranda for the South American Emancipation, during the last Twenty-five years* (London, 1810) edited by J.M. Antepara, who finished the prologue in September, 1810. The real editor was James Mill, assisted by Miranda and Thomas Molini. According to my case, the British opposition in Parliament helped to subsidize this publication in an effort to persuade the British public to line up behind Miranda, a great military hero before the emergence of Napoleon, and the man who the English should support in the liberation of South America—a major objective that held so much potential for England's prosperity in the long run.

On April 19, 1810, the Caracas Revolution in Venezuela, following the guidelines set by their hero in London, announced to the world that Spanish America was beginning her "Wars of Independence" that, as it turned out, would liberate Venezuela and lead her to establish the first Spanish American Republic in the New World. It was a momentuous event in world history, especially if Great Britain were to recognize, as Miranda's writers insisted, her own genuine interests in helping Spanish Americans to achieve their freedom. When the news of that Revolution spread to London, it was no coincidence that Miranda's publicists, or their converts, told the world, in no uncertain terms, what the historical significance of that Revolution in the New World would mean for mankind. Was this a case, as Miranda told young Richard Rush, of "one man" shaping key events in history? Perhaps!

A notable Spanish intellectual, José María Blanco y Crespo, arrived in London in March 1810, and before long joined Miranda's group of publicists who contributed to *El Colombiano*, especially with documents concerning recent Spanish politics and history. A strong liberal, this man was a priest, of Irish lineage on his father's side; and his immediate goal in London was to start a monthly periodical (*El Español*) which first appeared on April 30, 1810. He is known in English history as Reverend Joseph Blanco White. His impressions of the April 19, 1810, Revolution in Caracas won him instant popularity among Americans, while his countrymen in Spain began to think of him in terms of a "traitor." The Venezuelan Revolution was "moderate" and reasonable in its declarations. It was time that Spain awakened to reality; she could not continue her abuses against the colonies; she should try to bring justice to her system overseas. Otherwise, Spain would lose her Empire. Blanco-White's editorials on the constitutional experiment in Cádiz, Spain, were indeed perceptive but also critical—another source of irritation with his countrymen, especially among his colleagues, the liberals. The Venezuelan leaders, on the other hand, welcomed him and congratulated Blanco-White for his demands to reform Spanish governance overseas.

Following the "Mask of Ferdinand" technique, the Caracas Junta declared its loyalty to Ferdinand VII of Spain, who was a prisoner of the French; but the Junta would not recognize the Regency government in Cádiz. The Caracas government conducted a fiery correspondence with the Regency, copies of which circulated throughout Spanish America to win sympathy for the April 19th Revolution. Also following a recommendation made in the "Paper Assault," the

Venezuelans sent commissioners to London. As the Secretary of State for the Junta Suprema in Caracas, Juan Germán Roscio favored the following delegates: Simón Bolívar, Luis López Méndez, both members of the Creole aristocracy, and Andrés Bello, as the Secretary of the Delegation. There were two future "greats" in the history of Spanish America on that Commission: one, the famous "Liberator" who inherited Miranda's mantle of leadership in Venezuela; and Bello, one of the great literary figures of the nineteenth century. According to my hypothesis, Bello worked with Mill and Bentham in translating the Burkian editorials. The three commissioners stayed in Miranda's house; and he prepared them well for their deliberations with the British Government in mid–1810.

Despite the "Mask of Ferdinand" and the "Moderation" of the April 19th Revolution in Caracas, the Spanish Regency regarded Venezuela's actions as rebellion; thus, it declared a blockade of Venezuela. This declaration of war reached London in early September, 1810, and Caracas two months later. It put an end to the commissioners' work in London, and it alerted Venezuela's forces for war—"Moderation" was a thing of the past! In London, Blanco-White denounced his countrymen's stupidity and the irresponsibility of the Regency, etc. Roscio, as Venezuela's Secretary of State and Editor of the *Gaceta de Caracas* congratulated this special Spaniard for his approval of their Revolution and for condemning Spain's ridiculous blockade. Spain could not implement such a blockade without the aid of her English ally!

One of the grim realities of the Peninsular War in Europe was that Spain and England, inveterate historical enemies, wasted no love on each other, despite their Treaty of Alliance. Thus, weaknesses were observable everywhere on the battlefield and overseas. In London, the British welcomed the "Mask of Ferdinand" tactic of the Venezuelan commissioners. They worked out an arrangement, short of Venezuela's recognition of the Regency, that allowed them to receive arms and supplies to defend themselves against the French enemy in return for "free trade" status for the English in South America. England's ally, of course, adamantly rejected any British contacts with her former colonies—a policy, of course, which Spain could not enforce. The net effect was an unofficial traffic which English officials overseas were wont to condone! Thus, the blockade of Venezuela was a joke. The Venezuelan Junta and its successor, the Constituent Assembly that opened its doors on March 2, 1811, welcomed the "unofficial" support and commerce from British Trinidad and Curaçao in the Caribbean.

These friendly relations, however, ended with the arrival of a new governor at Curaçao (J. Hodgson) in mid–1811. He took a "Strict Constructionist" approach in favor of the Spanish ally. This turnabout worked against the interests of Venezuela's First Republic, thus contributing to its final demise within a year's time.

Derechos de la América del Sur y México (The Rights of South America and Mexico) appeared in Caracas in two volumes: the first, on July 12, 1811, and the second, on October 3, 1811. This major publication was also available in editorial form in the *Gazeta de Caracas* from November 23, 1810, to March 20, 1812. Its author presumably was *Guillermo Burke* (William Burke)—the penname used by the same writer who published two treatises in London from 1807 to 1808. He urged Great Britain to assist South America in achieving her emancipation from Spanish tyranny.

James Mill, as we have already indicated, was the inventor of "William Burke," in order to allow him to speak out candidly against Britain's policy in South America. From my research in Europe, I have explained when and why Mill and Bentham put together the contents of the Venezuelan Burke's editorials and publications. The individual editorials in the *Gazeta de Caracas*, enhanced by other comments and reports in each issue, helped to identify the editors and what ideas they shared on various topics. Thus, when an editor stepped in to use the name "William Burke" with additional materials or to influence public opinion on certain issues, it revealed how the Burkian editorials of European authors were being used in Caracas or in other regions of northern South America. Somewhat nebulous and speculative, this procedure was nonetheless rewarding. From the very beginning, I was much impressed with the penetrating sagacity of William Burke's remarks, insights, and conclusions, especially in describing English institutions or precedents. It revealed to me instantly that a great mind, or minds, was at work here.

Although I was concerned initially, perhaps too much, with the identity of the Venezuelan "William Burke," much as I had been with the one in London, it soon became obvious to me that it was really the *ideas* being expressed in South America under the name of "William Burke" that were the historically significant findings of my investigations. In the process, we have noted that editors, and other writers associated with them, used the name of "William Burke." Roscio, in particular, employed the term in a fictional sense, as we demonstrated in the "Asterisk Caper." I still suspect that Dr. C. (F.S. Constancio), dedicated as that European savant was to Miranda's cause, was present in Caracas and may have been extremely useful in Miranda's writings and speeches to the Venezuelan Congress. He could well have been the William Burke that was to accompany Pedro Gual on the assigned mission to the United States; but then that Burke may have also been the North American who had the luck to survive the catastrophic Earthquake of March 26, 1812. Yet, it is difficult to forget Gual's comments on Burke, a man of great intelligence. Gual, however, may have been confusing the North American Burke with the Burke in the editorials! Considering the great amounts of materials destroyed in those hectic years from 1810 through 1812, we perhaps will never know!

In the *Edinburgh Review* of January, 1809, James Mill noted that Father Viscardo's *Letter* had praised the example of the United States to all his Spanish American readers. Mill also concluded, thanks to Miranda's perspective, that Spanish Americans felt a deep affinity to the experiment taking place in North America. Here, in my opinion, was the moment of conception for William Burke's publications on Spanish America, employing the U.S. model. Mill and Miranda apparently agreed to work up units of materials along these lines. Given the format of the book manuscript, and considering Mill's expertise as a teacher and organizer, it is reasonable to assume that his first objective was to catch the attention of his public in Spanish America with a brilliant introductory section. Since the project was conceived in late 1808 or early 1809, while Miranda's "Paper Assault" was reaching its public, it may have been Mill's intention, approved by his ally Miranda, to send the introductory section along with the other enclosures in Miranda's final letters. Certainly, it was excellent material to include in the *legajos* (or bundles) that accompanied Miranda's circular letter of March 24, 1810. That was the secret project that José María Antepara and his Mexican sponsors financed for shipments throughout Spanish America, along with a special printing of Father Vizcardo's *Letter*. Since this might have been the case, I should like to urge my readers in Spanish America to check in their archives for a collection of documents associated with Vizcardo's letter. That would be an interesting "discovery" in support of my speculation; and it would save me much time, especially since there is not much of it left!

A final reading of the Preface (June 25, 1811) to the two-volume publication of Burke's editorials provides some interesting clues on the Miranda-Mill project in Europe. To begin with, the date assigned to it by Juan Germán Roscio was not the original one. Rather, it was changed to conform to Roscio and Miranda's decision to resume the publication of Burke's editorials in the *Gazeta de Caracas* in July, 1811, and to publish the two volumes in time to persuade the New Granada allies to reconsider the governmental form of a republic rather than that of a monarchy. From the contents of the Preface, the actual document might have been signed "William Burke" by James Mill as early as June 23, 1810, a year earlier. The day before that—June 22nd, 1810, was when Miranda received news of the April 19th Revolution in Caracas; and on the 23rd Mill wrote his sophisticated editorial on the significance of that Revolution. Be that as it may, the *real* author offered us a few clues. First, he dedicated the Preface to those people who took part in the April 19th action. He felt especially satisfied on this point since he was able "to know and to have dealt with many of you personally, and to be cognizant of the integrity of your views." He continued:

> Let us hope to the high Heavens that the same zeal and integrity be universal among all the people of America. At that point, in truth, this great Continent will not have to depend upon the strange circumstances of the other hemisphere to secure its just and necessary rights!

This passage could have come out of Burke's "Western Hemisphere Idea" in the March, 1811, editorials, that came *after* the introductory section, ending in early January. Another interesting clue in the Preface was the following:

> I hastened to visit your shores, from the moment that I heard about your revolution, abandoning my domestic tranquility, parents, and friends, I decided to risk my repose and security in the revolutionary scenes of a distant country, whose language was still unknown to me, with the end of contributing with those efforts I was capable of for the good success of your cause. (Wm. Burke [2 vols., Caracas, 1811], Vol.1, 41–42)

The major clue in the Preface, however, was the reference to "the first publication of this work," which was offered "to the public incompletely and separately." There was an asterisk here, explaining that this referred to the editorials in the *Gazeta de Caracas* beginning on November 23, 1810. This is the clue that supported my conclusion that the introductory section of editorials (November 23rd, 1810 to January 8, 1811) might have accompanied the bundles of documents associated with Antepara and his Mexican associates. In addition, Burke commented favorably on "the impression that it has caused in different parts of the Continent." This, again, supports the interpretation above of the "bundles" circulated by Antepara *et al.* It also suggests that the full Burkian publication may have been intended for all of Spanish America, not just Venezuela and northern South America.

What other conclusions can we draw from the Preface published by Roscio and Miranda in mid–1811? To begin with, this Preface did not reach Venezuela until December 5, 1810, with the arrival of Simón Bolívar and Miranda's archives, or on December 11th, when Miranda arrived at La Guaira. The introductory section of editorials, as I pointed out in Chapter Eight, perhaps arrived with Andrés Bello's shipment for the *Gazeta de Caracas* in November, 1810, or via the Venezuelan (José Tovar Ponte) who was in London when the commissioners arrived on July 10, 1810. Burke's admission of having met people who participated in the April 19 Revolution refers to the Venezuelan gentleman mentioned above or the three commissioners: Simón Bolívar, Luis López Méndez, and Andrés Bello. Of the three, I suspect that Bello made the deepest impression upon James Mill ("William Burke"). Although Thomas Molini, Miranda's secretary, was perhaps the first to translate Mill's editorials; Bello would continue after his arrival in London. Finally, Burke's decision to come to America was one made by James Mill at this time; and we know that Jeremy Bentham also shared that dream of visiting Miranda's cherished homeland in America. It demonstrated James Mill's firm commitment to Miranda's cause of emancipation.

The Junta Suprema of Venezuela welcomed General Francisco de Miranda to his homeland, after such a long absence. Their "Washington" had come back just at the right time—the December–January stalemate with Spain—and the Junta expected him to reorganize Venezuela's armed forces along modern standards. As Secretary of State for Venezuela, Juan Germán Roscio capitalized on Miranda's presence in time of peril, broadcasting his reputation throughout Venezuela in order to rally the people in the impending conflict with the Spanish enemy. Since the previous Fall, Roscio had recognized the need for union in defense of northern South America with other jurisdictions in the region; he, therefore, assigned a mission to Bogotá and asked General Miranda to write a supporting letter in behalf of what later would be called "*Gran Colombia*." This was in late January, 1811; and Miranda, of course, was a fervent advocate of unionism in the Spanish Americas. This cooperation, as it turned out, led to the first elaboration of an Inter-American system in the pages of the *Gazeta de Caracas* by March 29, 1811. "William Burke" and his sponsors—Miranda and Roscio, in particular—all favored this worthy cause.

In mid–January, 1811, after Burke's introductory section ended, there were three editorials in a row that were not part of James Mill's manuscript for Venezuela, yet they all bore the penname "William Burke." In times of crisis—like the December–January one—the editor of the *Gazeta* would intervene in the original manuscript by introducing special Burkian editorials concentrating on the problems besetting the nation. Roscio's oratorical style was evident, divulging insights that only a lawyer of the old regime could relate and working himself into emotional states that had not been evident in the earlier "William Burke." The internal evidence in the January 15th editorial exposed the handiwork of James Mill and Miranda in a serious interpretation of Spanish history that must have been written for *El Colombiano* but never got published. This might also have been the case for the Burkian article of February 19, 1811, on "Religious Toleration," although there were additional contributors to that particular essay. In March, 1811, there was a second major intervention by Roscio that followed up on Burke's theme of "The Western Hemisphere Idea"—a topic that has been popular in the past three decades because of Professor Arthur P. Whitaker's book of that name. By emphasizing the New World as opposed to the Old World, Mill encouraged a hemispheric nationalism and pride on the part of Americans everywhere. It was an ingenious invention; and it followed that a single governmental body for all of Spanish America—the "United States of South America and Mexico," would join hands with the United States of America in the North to shape what we might call the "Manifest Destiny" of the New World and its favorite children. Roscio took this notion and spelled it out in detail in the last editorials of March, 1811. James Mill, his colleague Jeremy Bentham, and the other writers in Caracas, posing as "William Burke" for their special projects and concerns, were responsible for a persuasive educational program in the *Gazeta de Caracas*, leading Venezuelans toward the declaration of their Independence on July 5, 1811.

After the three special editorials of mid-January, 1811, James Mill's language and ideas took over again. It was his first installment of editorials dealing specifically with the political details of the U.S. experiment. The master teacher was again at his best. Judging that Spanish Americans would soon embark on the implementation of the program, he wanted to impress them with a symbol—the "Grand Circle" of the celebrated North American Republic:

> It is a multitude of political circles, of which each one has a political movement of rotation upon its own axis, and is disposed to unite itself to new circles, which a general influence presides over all [of them] preserving the harmony of their gyration, and restricting each one within the prescribed orbit by means of a constitution, without being able to obstruct or injure any of them.

The constant repetition of this symbol would fascinate South Americans with the clocklike precision and beauty of the confederation system created by the Constitution of 1787 in the United States of America. Masterful presentations followed on "Habeas Corpus," "Trial by Jury," "Public Tribunals, *a viva voce*," the "Bill of Rights," and ending with "Freedom of the Press." He also added a summary chart that prospective citizens should study at all times to remind them about the North American system. This section ended in time for the Constituent Assembly in Caracas on March 2, 1811.

Although the People's "Rights" were his primary concern, the master organizer wanted his readers to appreciate fully what challenges had existed throughout history against those "Rights." As he had pointed out in his first editorial (November 23, 1810), "Injustices" were the opposite of "Rights." James Mill and Jeremy Bentham were at their best exposing those abuses, so that readers would comprehend fully why North Americans insisted upon a Constitution protecting them against such abuses and injustices, making the principle of "Representation" inviolate. In this regard, the record of monarchies in human history had been deficient. In fact, they had been aggressively abusive of the People's "Rights time and time again, in violation of the Creator's intentions." Even in England the principle of representation was flawed from the beginning by putting an emphasis upon *place* and not *people*. The writers of William Burke's words even questioned such concepts as "Divine Kingship," the "Compact Theory," and the "Church-State Conspiracy" of King Ferdinand and Queen Isabella, the "Catholic Kings" of Spain. All this being written in Venezuela in the early nineteenth century, in behalf of modern constitutionalism and "Religious Toleration." Venezuelans did not react to these heresies when the example was English or European, except for that of Iberian Spain. That man in Caracas: *Guillermo White* was obviously an "Irish Catholic," whose brain had been tampered with by the French *Philosophes*!

Carried away with the example of chronic "injustices" in the Old World, it seemed logical to "William Burke" to contrast this picture with a "New World," a comparatively virgin and uncorrupted land where these new men—"Americans"—could carry out their "Manifest Destiny." British colonists, following the best English precedents, and not the abuses recounted earlier in Burke's essays, flourished in the New World. They took a "Republican" system, which failed miserably in Europe, and breathed a new spirit into it to prevent the abuses of the past. The new men of Spanish America were just as likely to succeed: their bountiful resources and fertile soils would become an asylum for the poor of the Old World, giving them a new lease on life. Roscio became so fascinated with Burke's words that he spelled out a project in the final editorials of the *Gazeta* in March, 1811, calling for the establishment of the "United States of South America and Mexico." This one single State of Spanish America would join hands with its northern counterpart to control the fate of the Western Hemisphere! Roscio was not solely responsible for this grand project: Miranda's continental vision a la Pownall was a major precedent, and the English writers as "William Burke" likewise were key contributors—Mill and Bentham. That was some cast!

When Roscio later added the date of June 25, 1811, to Burke's Preface to his two volumes, we came to realize how important the concept of a "Greater Colombia" was in bringing about the Independence of Venezuela on July 5, 1811. Moreover, Roscio and Miranda intervened once again with the original Burkian manuscript, in hopes of assuring the victory of REPUBLICANISM over MONARCHISM in the ex-Kingdom of New Granada at Bogotá. The emergence of the Republic of Cartagena in November, 1811, seemed to assure that republican unionism was Gran Colombia's choice of governance. In Roscio's project for a United States of South America and Mexico, he suggested Bogotá, thanks to its centrist geographical position, as the initial capital of a new super government for the former Spanish America. The precedent for a general government, thus, was set historically and it was Simón Bolívar who would carry out this dream, as we have shown in the Epilogue of this work.

In William Burke's last installment of editorials, James Mill's talents as an economist, financial expert, and student of classical confederation were most evident, reminding us of his earlier writings in the *Literary Journal* of London. Mill expertly digested Alexander Hamilton's famous reforms to reconstruct the national economy and build a strong national government. A pacifist as well as an economist who wrote about the wastefulness of war in *Commerce Defended* (London, 1807), Mill's modern elaboration of that theme as "William Burke" was easy to identify. When Mill learned that South Americans were considering the formation of two or three confederations for the former Spanish America, he hastened to point out in Burke's final editorials that such a mistake was almost made in the United States of America. Fortunately, Mill concluded, the unionists were able to stop that subversive tactic. Confederations, Burke argued, had always ended up as ridiculous absurdities in European history, whether in the classical or more recent periods. The key prerequisite was a unified government that could act directly upon the people and not on political organizations called states. Those were wise words that circulated throughout northern South America in the first third of the nineteenth century.

Wherever possible, I have been concerned throughout this work in throwing light upon some of the exaggerations and sterotypes that still persist in Venezuela's historiography. For many years after the events described in this book, it was common to refer to the First Venezuelan Republic as "*La Patria Boba*" (The Foolish Mother Country). This term, by the way, also appears in the history of other countries in northern South America. It refers, in Venezuela's case, to the period from July 5, 1811, to Miranda's defeat in late July, 1812—a most tragic year in the nation's experience. Overwhelmed by the grim reality of initial failure, Venezuelans tried to explain the horrible experience as follows: Our country was young and naive, so much so that she foolishly believed that the only course of action was to follow the brilliant example of the North Americans in the United States, especially in light of the fantastic progress made by them in a quarter of a century since Independence. That northern example, however, simply did not apply to Venezuela because of the wretched colonial experience under the Spaniards. It never occurred to them that English colonials might have had an even more wretched experience than the Spanish-Americans, as our "William Burke" noted accurately in his introductory section of editorials for the *Gazeta de Caracas*. Moreover, considering their natural resources and fertile soil, Spanish American leaders had no reason to feel inferior to their northern brethren; they just had special deficiences or problems in their society that had to be overcome in order to modernize their regions. These leaders were constructively optimistic; and their approach, contrary to what many have believed, was decidedly pragmatic and not doctrinaire, except in the eyes of those opposing change in a traditional society. Those at least have been my findings on the Cádiz experiment in Spain, Central America, and now in Venezuela.

The stereotype of "*La Patria Boba*" is an emotional and simplistic explanation of a very complex period of historical change from a colonial to a national existence. The serious historian must try to record *all* those factors in a particular environment that might have influenced the process of reform on the positive or negative sides. Our background study of Venezuela demonstrates that geography and cultural factors have been strong influences in the story of failure. Seven hundred thousand people in such an enormous and varied country with its settlers isolated from other population clusters by topographical obstacles, so that contact most always was by water; a society of different cultures and races controlled by a minority oligarchy of White families, etc. etc.—all these characteristics offered obstacles to the establishment of a modern nation. We recall the exaggerated "*división*" issue in Venezuela's congress in which the "states' righters" threatened to secede if the powerful state of Caracas was not stripped of its potential power; the role of the Church in this type of divided society helping the elites to control the Non-Whites, etc. etc. The unreal expectations of ex-colonials, their misunderstanding, or unwillingness to comprehend the demands of a new system with more officials than the old one. Their unwillingness, or inability, to pay the new taxes needed by their young nation was, indeed, a critical problem. Without money how could the First Venezuelan Republic survive as a government, especially when confronted by the ravages of Nature—the terrible Earthquake of March 26, 1812, that devastated the nation for months; the invasion of Spanish forces that attracted the people so distraught with the natural disaster;

and the demands imposed upon the government by the final military
maneuvers of General Francisco de Miranda? Those were the *real*
problems besetting the First Venezuelan Republic that could not obtain
loans from outside powers, as was the case elsewhere in Spanish
America *after* the Napoleonic Wars. The ban on clerical
privileges—the famous *desafuero* that plagued the Spanish American
nations everywhere during the establishment of nationhood was first
implemented in Venezuela with disastrous consequences in the crisis of
war and earthquakes! Clergymen rallied their parishioners to the
Royalist cause in those final, tragic days, as the first Spanish-American
republic of the Western Hemisphere withered away its existence.

Within a week's time of the Republic's birth, the "Conspiracies of
July and August, 1811," tried viciously to overthrow it; but the
Independistas rallied in defense of the nation, led by a courageous
military leader: Francisco de Miranda, who was given dictatorial
powers to quash the rebellion, which he achieved in early August,
1811. This victory, as Roscio noted, could have been Venezuela's
baptismal of fire that might have saved her. It was here, however, that
the *bobos* appeared, irresponsible voices in Congress that furthered the
path toward disintegration. They had the temerity to charge their
military hero of abuses in the war against Valencia, etc. etc., charging
him with being a "Dictator," a potential Napoleon in their midst etc.
etc. They also led the nation into a policy of "Clemency" toward the
rebel city of Valencia and climaxed this madness by declaring her the
new National Capital to replace Caracas! In this period of insanity at
the end of 1811, Congress passed the *desafuero* with its unfortunate
consequences in the future months; and on December 21st, they signed
the nation's constitution. Did they follow the U.S. Constitution of 1787
that would have strengthened the national government? No, they chose
the equivalent of the Articles of Confederation in the U.S.
experience—the "States' Rights" type of government that came closer
to following the "Home Rule" proclivities of the Spanish colonial
system. No wonder that Miranda did not give his full approval to the
Constitution of 1811. It was too weak an instrument for the type of
crisis facing Venezuela in 1811–1812. "William Burke" was unable to
convince Venezuelans that such a "Confederation" government could
not work—a conclusion established in the history of that type of
government in Europe. Therefore, in 1812, when the earthquake and
the Spanish Invasion hit almost simultaneously, the only recourse that
was left to the nation was to give Miranda the emergency power that

he had used back in 1811 against the "Conspiracies." Thus, the charges of "Dictatorship" were again raised against Venezuela's hero—a stereotype, by the way, that entered into the world's propaganda organs wishing to discredit General Miranda and the April 19th Revolution that led to the First Venezuelan Republic. Unfortunately, Blanco-White in London by this time was a serious enemy of his former friend Francisco de Miranda. The program of denigration of Miranda's world image, along with the theme of "Mediation" in the early Wars of Independence in Spanish America, have also been examined in this book.

In light of the world's attention upon the fate of the First Venezuelan Republic and its famous leader, well known to Europeans, it is not surprising that distortions would also plague the military accounts of Miranda's defeat on the battlefield and his alleged treasonous conduct in the Armistice proceedings, etc. etc. It was easy to blame a dictator, who was piling up his fortune to spend it abroad, and who capitulated to the Spanish General Monteverde at every turn, etc. etc. It was a ludicrous and yet a pathetic story illustrating how much people who believe in a cause could not fully accept the realities of a defeat—they felt an excruciating need for a scapegoat! In one of Antonio Muñoz Tébar's *informes* to Bolívar, this intelligent human being maintained that Miranda's forces gave up to the Spaniards without any real fight—a betrayal considering the larger forces that were at Miranda's call elsewhere in the nation! What was the basis for that rationalization, which runs contrary to all that we know about the military activity of that period? Was this a sanguine belief based on the expected aid from the Easterners that never materialized? If so, Miranda certainly waited as long as any prudent military leader could have under the circumstances that prevailed. Or was it just a rationale to justify their actions of frustration and angry revenge against their great leader? In combat, such a mental state is not unusual.

"The Foolish Mother Country" thesis, moreover, does no justice to the general theme of this book. The First Venezuelan Republic, perhaps more than any other Spanish American country, had within its reach unquestionably more information on the U.S. model than others in South America, thanks to the presence of a "William Burke." Many of Burke's ideas were reflected in the Constitution of December, 1811; but my reader would agree that the U.S. Constitution of 1787, which Burke discussed so fervently, had no impact on the Venezuelan charter at all. The only vestiges of American influence derived from the

Articles of Confederation "states' rights"; and even there it was the "homerule" tradition of the Spanish colonial past that was asserting itself. We must realize, moreover, that for all practical purposes, the Venezuelan Constitution of 1811 was in a state of abeyance, once emergency powers of a "dictatorship" were conceded to the Executive Branch of the government. That practice of resorting to a dictatorship goes back to Roman times; and Miranda and Thomas Pownall included it in their governmental projects for Spanish America.

Our final word on the "*Patria Boba*" interpretation is that there were other factors, much more complex and significant, that explain the weaknesses of the First Republic, as we have described them in the final chapters of this book. It therefore makes it all the more important for young historians of the Americas to immerse themselves into whatever documentation is available to them in order to ferret out those factors that caused or resisted change in a given historical situation. It is hard work but it is most rewarding!

Notes

Chapter 1.   A SCIPIO AFRICANUS FROM CARACAS

1. William Burke, *Additional Reasons for our Immediately Emancipating Spanish America* (London, 1808), p. 65 which contains both the Latin and English texts (Hereafter: *Burke*, II, 1808).

2. Francisco de Miranda to Dr. William Thomson, London, February 24, 1808, *Archivo del General Miranda* (24 vols., Habana, 1929–1950), XXI, 53 (Hereafter: *A.G.M.*, Vol.).

3. "Papeles de Familia," España, 1771–1773, Francisco de Miranda, *Colombeia* (5 vols. to date, Caracas, 1978–1982) I, 157–167 (Hereafter: *F.M. Colombeia*). This series, entirely in Spanish, amounts to the beginning of a second edition of the *Archivo del General Miranda*, containing new documents and enclosures of the original 63 folio volumes of the Miranda Manuscripts that were not included in the *A.G.M. (1929–1950)*. Dr. Josefina Rodríguez de Alonso, the Director of the new series, provides us with digests of the materials in each volume and historical articles as well. For example, in Volume I she wrote "Bosquejo biográfico de Francisco de Miranda," 27–121. Volumes in the future will follow the same format.

4. Patente de Capitán, Madrid, January 7, 1773, *F.M. Colombeia*, I, 306–307; also see 27, 140, 297–305.

5. "Notes of Conversation with General Miranda," Philadelphia, December 4, 1805, Richard Rush Papers, Manuscript Division of the Library of Congress, Washington, D.C., MMC–1712 and OVSZD3 DI, folio 3 dorso (Hereafter, R. Rush: "Interview").

6. *F.M. Colombeia*, I, 327–412 on Melilla in 1774 and 1775.

7. William S. Robertson, *The Life of Miranda* (2 vols., Chapel Hill, N. Carolina, 1929), I, 56. (Hereafter: W.S. Robertson, *Life*).

8. Martens to F.M., Cartagena, March 19, 1776, *F.M. Colombeia*, I, 440. We do not know this correspondent's first name; he always wrote in French to

Miranda. When he said "*Mi querido indio*," he really meant "American" from the Spanish Indies, not a racial Indian.

9. Ibid., pages 487–489 and 492–493 (sloth); art and architecture, 476–490.

10. "Lista de libros comprados por Miranda en Madrid," Cádiz, April, 1780, ibid., 312–318.

11. Typical of the literature on this theme are: John Tate Lanning, *The Eighteenth-Century Enlightenment in the University of San Carlos de Guatemala* (Ithaca, 1956); Arthur P. Whitaker, ed., *Latin America and the Enlightenment* (2nd. Ed. Ithaca, 1961); Richard Herr, *The Eighteenth-Century Revolution in Spain* (Princeton, 1958); and my own *Cádiz Experiment in Central America* (Berkeley, 1978).

12. J. Kibblewhite to Alexander Davision, London, August 17, 1807, *A.G.M.*, XX, 367–368, who estimated the figure cited; also see, W.S. Robertson, *Life*, II, 241.

13. Many works deal with Spanish intervention in the American Revolution: see, for example, John Caughey, *Bernardo de Gálvez in Louisiana, 1776–1783* (Berkeley, 1934); Buchanan Parker Thomson, *La ayuda española en la guerra de la independencia*, (Madrid, 1967); and my own: *La revolución americana de 1776 y el mundo hispánico: Ensayos y documentos* (Madrid, 1976), citing the key works and articles on the period. An indispensible study for French, as well as Spanish, naval power is: Jonathan Dull, *The French Navy and the American Revolution* (Princeton, 1976).

14. Miranda compiled a fantastic number of documents on the conflict in Pensacola, West Florida; and the military events in the Bahamas, 59–227, *F.M. Colombeia*, Vol. II; and in the charges against him, 230–493, plus the appendix of documents that follow.

15. Francisco de Miranda left Cuba on June 1, 1783. His "Diario del Viaje por los Estados Unidos," the original Spanish version begins on that date: *F.M. Colombeia*, Vol. III, 35–358; which was followed by a diary from Boston to London, December 15, 1784 to February 1, 1785, 361–373.

16. *The Diary of Francisco de Miranda: Tour of the United States, 1783–1784*, the Spanish text edited by William Spence Robertson (New York, 1928). Thanks to the University of Oklahoma Press, we have an attractive edition: Francisco de Miranda, *The New Democracy in America, Travels of Francisco de Miranda in the United States, 1783–1784* (Norman, Oklahoma, 1963), translated by Judson P. Wood; see his excellent introduction: "The Man, the Country, and the Diary," xv–xxxii.

17. *F.M. Colombeia*, III, "Diario," 68, 77–79 (letters in last three pages).

18. Ibid., 68 and David Ramsay to Rev. Smith, Charleston, S.C., October 29, 1783, 87–88.

19. Ibid., 85–86 (the two letters of Cagigal to Rendón and Washington, dated Habana, May 18 and 26, 1783, respectively); also see, "Diario," 103–104.

20. "Diario," December 12, 1805, *A.G.M.*, XVII, 290.

21. William Duer to F.M., New York, May 28, 1784; Duer to Sayre, June 3, 1784; and Sayre to F.M., no date, 199–200, *F.M. Colombeia*, III; and see Duer's letters to key people in the British government, 381–383 in ibid.

22. Susan Livingston to F.M., New York, February 28, 1785, ibid., 387–389.

23. F.M. to Henry Knox, Paris, November 4, 1792, *A.G.M.*, XV, 146–147.

24. Henry Knox to F.M., Boston, November 23, 1784, ibid., 75–77.

25. Considering the documentation, there is no question that Francisco de Miranda's birth date was March 28, 1750; but, for a long time, some writers used the date June 9, 1756, applicable to a younger brother. Yet, after Miranda's return to England from the Continent, where he had been received as "Count" Miranda, he wanted the public to regard him as of noble origin; and he used the birth date of 1754, slicing four years off his real age. The new year of birth and his pretention to nobility appear in many publications of the period. Take, for example, the testimony of one of his recruits in the 1806 expedition: James Biggs, *The History of Don Francisco de Miranda's Attempt to Effect a Revolution in South America, in a series of letters* (London, 1809 edition based on the first one in Boston, 1808), Letter 2, February 9, 1806, 8–9: "According to his own account he is in the fifty-second year of his age. His appearance is that of sixty" (Hereafter Biggs, *Revolution*). The 1754 date is also in William Burke, *South American Independence: or, the Emancipation of South America, the Glory and Interest of England* (London, 1807), 66–67 (Hereafter *Burke*, I, (1807). It was used subsequently in the *Edinburgh Review* of January, 1809.

26. "Tarjetas de visita y direcciones de Londres," *F.M. Colombeia*, III, 410–417.

27. "Salida de Miranda y el coronel W.S. Smith para Prusia," London, August 9, 1785, ibid., 443.

28. John Turnbull to F.M., London, August 9, 1785, ibid., 442.

29. Correspondence from April 10, 1785, F.M. to Conde de Floridablanca and "Representation" to Charles III, London, April 10, 1785, ibid., 421–431; also, other replies, and the exchange between Miranda and Bernardo del Campo in London, May 25, 1785, 420–434.

30. Note, Smith to Miranda, London, July 4, 1785, ibid., 401.

31. "Salida de Miranda . . . Prusia," ibid., 443–444.

32. "Diario de Holanda, Electorado de Hannover, y Ducado de Brunswick, August 10, 1785, London, ibid., 447; and entry of August 13th, 454.

33. James Penman to F.M., London, August 26, 1785, 72 and enclosure: article from *Morning Chronicle* (London), translated here into Spanish, 73–74, *F.M. Colombeia*, IV.

34. *Political Herald and Review* (London), Vol. 1, 29–30. Miranda and an ally used it effectively in the *Edinburgh Review*, Vol. XIII, January, 1809, 286–287, citing the first portion of the editorial. William S. Robertson, *Life*, I, 62–63 provided the last part of it.

35. John A. Schutz, *Thomas Pownall, British Defender of American Liberty*:

A Study of Anglo-American Relations in the Eighteenth Century (Glendale, California, 1951), 267–271. (Hereafter Schutz, *Pownall*).

36.Colonel Smith's concluding remarks in the "Diary," *F.M. Colombeia*, IV, 157, followed by W.S. Smith to F.M., Vienna, October 26, 1785, "Crédito," totaling 230.15 pounds sterling.

37. W.S. Smith to F.M. Paris, November 10, 1785, ibid., 335, (English version).

38. W.S. Smith to F.M., London, April 8 and 11, 1786, ibid., 321 (for the 8th) and 322 (the 11th, with the quotation cited).

39. William S. Smith to F.M., London, March 26, 1788, ibid., 329–334 (English version); see, two copies of Spanish version: 323–329 and 336–342; and French version, 343–348.

40. See footnote 34.

41. Dr. Matthew Guthrie, the British doctor at the Russian Court wrote a series of letters to his father and to distinguished leaders in his native Edinburgh from September 3–5, 1787, which captures Miranda's image throughout Europe: *F.M. Colombeia*, Vol. 5, 443–452.

42. William S. Robertson, *Life*, II, 238, quotes Professor Pictet from Geneva.

43. "Diary: Vienna, 1785," October 26–28, 1785, *F.M. Colombeia*, IV; 162–163.

44. Passport for Francisco de Miranda, issued by Emperor Joseph II, Vienna, October 24, 1785; ibid., 159–160; also see, Passport issued by Joseph II's Minister Plenipotentiary (Herbert Rathkeal) to the Ottoman Empire, Constantinople, September 22, 1786, 468, which will serve as the basis for the rank of "Count" in the remainder of Miranda's trip through Europe.

45. Ibid., 183–359 (Diary, Italy); 363–390 (Diary, Greece).

46. Ibid., 393–470 (Diary, Turkey).

47. Ibid., (See footnote 44 above).

48. F.M. to Catherine II, St. Petersburg, August 5, 1787, *F.M. Colombeia*, V, 391–392, and F.M. to Prince Potemkin, St. Petersburg, August 22, 1787, 422–424. Also see the financial documents: 380–382, 405–409. In all, as a final payment, Miranda received well over two thousand pounds sterling.

49.The Crimean Diary started in *F.M. Colombeia*, IV, 483–541 (October 7, 1786 to January 5, 1787), and in ibid., V, 43–74; the Diary for Poland, ibid., 132–145 (March 14–19, 1787); and the rest on "Russia," with emphasis on Kiev, Moscow, and St. Petersburg. The meetings in Kiev and St. Petersburg with Catherine II of Russia are impressive, as far as royal society life was concerned.

50. Ibid., 332–334, 369–370, 393–395, 422–424.

51. F.M. to Prince Potemkin, St. Petersburg, August 22, 1787, ibid., 423.

52. Circular Letter . . ., Kiev, April 22, 1787, ibid., 373–374; and the Imperial Passport, St. Petersburg, August, 1787, 374–375.

53. The Swedish diary, ibid., 457–548 will be finished in volume VI when it comes out; the other diaries for the rest of Miranda's trip to the continent will also be included at that time. Also see, William S. Robertson, *Life*, I, 81–89, for a spirited coverage of Miranda's travels in those countries.

54. Ibid., 90–91.

55. Stephen Sayre to Samuel Ogden, London, June 29, 1789, cited in ibid., 90.

56. Schutz, *Pownall*, 166, 176, 179–180; 184–194; 240–244.

57. Ibid., 279.

58. Ibid., 227–228.

59. John Turnbull to F.M., Bath, January 28, 1790, *A.G,M.* (1929–1950), VI, 19.

60. See footnote 41—Dr. Guthrie's remarks on Miranda.

61. *Memorial . . . Sovereigns of Europe* (London, 1780), 26–27.

62. "Conference with Pitt—1790," Pownall's report, January, 1790, *A.G.M.*, XV, 106–109. Also see the excellent articles by John A. Schutz, "Thomas Pownall's Proposed Atlantic Federation," *Hispanic American Historical Review*, XXVI (May, 1946), 263–268; and "Thomas Pownall and his Negro Commonwealth," *The Journal of Negro History*, XXX (October 1945), No. 4, 400–404.

63. Miranda drew up a specific proposal on March 5, 1790, embodying the points discussed on February 14th: see the Spanish and English versions in *A.G.M.*, XV, 111–114 (Spanish) and 114–118 (English). See also the statistical section on 121–126.

64. F.M. to William Pitt, London, August 2, 1791 and March 17, 1792, ibid., 132–137 and 142–144 for Miranda's grievances and disappointments.

65. Miranda's arrival and activities in France are presented in a "Note" by Francisco de Miranda, ibid., footnote 4, 144–145.

66. Loc. Cit.

67. William S. Robertson, *Life*, I, 120–141, offers the details of Miranda's military career in France.

68. Jean Brissot de Warville to General Dumouriez, Paris, November 28, 1792, *A.G.M.*, XV, 148–150 (English version), the French version, 150–152.

69. F.M. to Jean Brissot de Warville, Liége, December 19, 1792, ibid., 153–154; and other correspondence on this topic: 155–164.

70. Ibid., 145–148, including letters F.M. to Alexander Hamilton, November 4, 1792; ditto to Henry Knox, same date; and W.S. Smith to F.M., London, November 24, 1792.

71. The details of Miranda's experiences in France from 1793 to 1798 are treated in William S. Robertson, *Life*, I, 142–160.

72. F.M. to W. Pitt, London, January 16, 1798 and March 17, 1799, *A.G.M.*, XV, 209–211 and 344–352; Also, 277–278 (Preamble).

73. F.M. to John Turnbull, Paris, September 26, 1797 and November 7, 1797, ibid., 177–178 and 196–197; Instructions of Junta, Paris, December 22, 1797, ibid., 198–205.

74. "Plan Militar," London, August 1798, ibid., 287–295.

75. F.M. to W. Pitt, London, January 16, 1798 and March 17, 1799, ibid., 209–211 and 344–352.

76. Thomas Pownall to F.M., Bristol, February 11, 1798, ibid., 215.

77. William S. Robertson, *Life*, I, 170–171; 176–181; 184–186, dealing with the United States and the projected expedition of 1798.

78. "Notas de Diario 1799–1800," *A.G.M.*, XV, 355–359; Note of F.M., London, September 1, 1799, ibid., 374–376.

79. See "Miranda's Last Visit to France," 212–220, W.S. Robertson, *Life*, I.

80. "Proclamations," F.M., London, 1801, *A.G.M.*, XVI, 104–159, in Spanish and French.

81. "Memoir of Sir Home Popham," London, October 14, 1804, ibid., XVII, 88, 93.

82. F.M. to Sir Evan Nepean, London, February 5, 1805, ibid., 144–145.

83. F.M.'s Note, Diary, London, August 5, 1805, ibid., 248.

84. F.M. to William Pitt, London, June 13, 1805, ibid., 215–218.

85. On July 13, 1801, Miranda met with key officials of the Addington government in which this nationalistic and emotional debate took place. For an excellent analysis, see William S. Robertson, *Life*, I, 240–243.

86. F.M. to William Pitt, London, June 13, 1805, 215–218 and F.M.'s note, Diary, London, July 5, 1805, ibid., 218–219.

87. F.M.'s note, Diary, London, May 24, 1805, ibid., 208–209; Biggs, *Revolution*, 264.

88. F.M.'s note, Diary, London, July 16, 1805, *A.G.M.*, XVII, 246.

89. F.M.'s note, Diary, London, August 5, 1805, ibid., 248; also, see note on 247; and F.M. to Joseph Lambot, London, August 30, 1805, 329–330.

90. W.S. Smith to F.M., New York, January 14, 1806, ibid., 298–299.

91. F.M. to W.S. Smith, New York, January 20, 1806, ibid., 300–301; Also see 348, 351–352.

92. F.M. to Nicholas Vansittart, New York, January 4, 1806, Private, ibid., 331–332.

93. William Armstrong to F.M., New York, December 30, 1805, ibid., 307–309; also see F.M. to Christopher Gore, New York, November 27, 1805, 278–279; and F.M. to H. Knox, New York, November 27, 1805, 277.

94. John Turnbull to Nicholas Vansittart, Barnes, September 25, 1807, *A.G.M.*, XX, 375–378, relating an interview with Lord Viscount Castlereagh that noted his mistaken notions, thanks to Cooke's misinterpretations. Castlereagh was favorable to changing his stand if warranted and wanted to talk to Vansittart about Great Britain's support to General Miranda.

95. F.M.'s Diary, November 29 to December 3, 1805, *A.G.M.*, XVII, 279–282.

96. Ibid., 283–292.

97. Ibid., 286.

98. Ibid., 287.

99. Ibid., 288–289.

100. F.M. to Rufus King, New York, December 30, 1805, 300–301 and F.M. to Nicholas Vansittart, New York, January 4, 1806, 331–332, ibid. There is a note or postscript, dated January 22, 1806, on 332, confirming the commitment.

101. *The Trials of William S. Smith and Samuel G. Ogden for Misdemeanors* (New York, 1807) 1–287, Microfilm Roll 21 of Miranda's manuscripts: Colombeia, Academia Nacional de la Historia, Caracas, Venezuela (April 1, 1806 to July 1806 for both trials).

102. F.M.'s Diary, Washington, D.C., December 13, 1805, *A.G.M.*, XVII, 290.

103. F.M. to Thomas Jefferson, New York, January 22, 1806, ibid., 346–347.

104. F.M. to Nicholas Vansittart, New York, January 4, 1806, to John Turnbull, same date, to William Brown and Joseph Lambot, January 27, 1806, ibid., 305, 331–333, and 351.

105. See footnote 5 for full entry of R. Rush: "Interview." Notes refer to the folio page of the manuscript, dorso or verso.

Chapter 2.   A BRITISH STAR IN EMANCIPATION

1. William Burke, *South American Independence; or, the Emancipation of South America, the Glory and Interest of England* (J. Ridgway, London, 1807), 22. (Hereafter: *Burke*, I, 1807).

2. Home Popham, *Minutes of a Court Martial, Holden on Board His Majesty's Ship Gladiator in Portsmouth Harbour, on Friday, the 6th day of March, 1807, including a complete copy of his defence* (London, 2nd ed., 1807), hereafter *Minutes of a Court Martial (Popham)*.

3. *The Morning Post* (London), March 14, 1807, commenting on the public's dilemma; *The Times* (London), January 5 and March 16, 1807, especially the editorial in the latter which reviews the press coverage of the trial.

4. *Minutes of a Court Martial (Popham)*, p. 188.

5. Home Popham, *A Full and Correct Report of the Trial of Sir Home Popham . . . Together with a Preface containing a further Vindication of Sir Home Popham, particularly against certain attacks made upon him since the Trial* (London, 1807). The edition used is in the British Library (North Library), G 19449. It is especially valuable because of the handwritten comments of Popham's naval critics in the margins. They are lengthy and revealing, not only about Sir Home but of his adversaries as well [hereafter, *A Full and Correct Report (Popham)*]. Also see *The Morning Post* (London),

March 14, 1807, which focuses on the vindictiveness of the "present administration" with respects to Sir Home Popham.

6. Ibid., March 19, 1807, article "Sir Home Popham."

7. Loc. Cit.

8. *The Times* (London), January 26, 1809, article "Comparative Services of the Remonstrating Captains, and Sir Home Popham's."

9. William Spence Robertson, *The Life of Miranda* (2 Vols., Chapel Hill, N.C., 1929), I, 260.

10. *A Full and Correct Report* (*Popham*), XX.

11. Reviewed in the *Literary Journal* (London), Vol. 1 (1803), p. 430.

12. Home Popham to Lord Melville, London, August 17, 1804, f. 33, Melville Paper, Series II, Vol. II (Sir H. Popham), Additional Manuscripts 41,080, British Library, Manuscript Division, London. Also see, *Minutes of a Court Martial* (*Popham*), 78, alluding to the discretionary authority allowed Popham by his political superiors.

13. *A Full and Correct Report* (*Popham*), XII–XIV, critic's note in the margin.

14. *The Times* (London), May 23, 1808; *Minutes of a Court Martial* (*Popham*), 78.

15. *A Full and Correct Report* (*Popham*), VII in the margin.

16. *Minutes of a Court Martial* (*Popham*), 134. Melville was Secretary of War (War Department) then.

17. Ibid., 135–141, especially his testimony on p. 137.

18. Ibid., 78–90.

19. Ibid., 87.

20. Ibid., 80–81.

21. Ibid., 81–82.

22. Home Popham to Lord Melville, Downs, December 10, 1804, Melville Papers (see footnote 13), in which Sir Home wrote "I am anxious for a Spanish war." Also see other letters from December 4, 1801 forward in the same documentary reference.

23. *Minutes of a Court Martial* (*Popham*), 111.

24. Home Popham to William Marsden, Buenos Aires, July 6, 1806, in *The Times* (London), September 15, 1806 (hereafter "Popham's").

25. Ibid., which includes: W.C. Beresford to William Windham, Buenos Aires, July 2, 1806 (hereinafter: "Beresford's").

26. "Popham's."

27. "Beresford's."

28. *The Times* (London), January 27, 1807.

29. Ibid., September 15, 1806, article: "Terms granted to the inhabitants of Buenos Ayres and its Dependencies by the Commander-in-Chief of his Britannic Majesty's Forces by Land and Sea," Buenos Aires, July 2, 1806, signed by W.C. Beresford, Home Popham, and José Ignacio de la Quintana.

30. Ibid., "Proclamation by the Commander-in-Chief of his Britannic

Majesty's Forces by Land and Sea," W.C. Beresford, Buenos Aires, June 30, 1836; also see letter to Editor, *The Morning Herald* (London), September 16, 1807, by "Recollector" referring to the "Illusion of Trinidad."

31. "Resolution of the Town of Manchester Congratulating him on capture of Buenos Ayres," September 25, 1806, Auckland Papers 776, Vol. XLVI (Correspondence 1806–1809), Additional MS 34, 457, British Library, Manuscript Division, London; also see, *A Full and Correct Report (Popham)*, XVI.

32. *The Times* (London), September 20, 1806; *The Morning Herald* (London) September 20, 1806; *The Morning Advertiser* (London), September 20, 1806.

33. *The Times* (London), September 13, 1806.

34. *The Morning Advertiser* (London), September 15, 1806.

35. *The Times* (London), September 15, 1806, editorial.

36. Loc. Cit.

37. *The Times* (London), September 25, 1806 under title "Buenos Ayres" and "Account of the present state of that province;" ibid. September 20, 1806; and *The Morning Advertiser* (London), September 25, 1806.

38. *The Times* (London), September 19, 1806.

39. *The Morning Herald* (London), September 22, 1806, reporting the figure: 27 tons, 18 cwt, and 4 pounds of silver.

40. *The Times* (London), September 19, 1806.

41. *The Morning Herald* (London), September 22, 1806; also in *The Morning Advertiser* (London), September 22, 1806.

42. *Minutes of a Court Martial (Popham)*, 69–70 reproducing William Marsden to Home Popham, London, September 25, 1806.

43. *The Times* (London), September 16, 1806.

44. *The Morning Advertiser* (London), September 22, 1806, describing the Order in Council of September 17, 1806.

45. *The Times* (London), September 26, 1806, on Wellesley; and ibid. October 1, 1806, on Beresford.

46. Ibid., September 29 and October 9, 1806.

47. Robert Craufurd, *An Authentic Narrative . . . Montevideo . . . Buenos Ayres . . . by an Officer of the Expedition* (London, 1808), a pleasurable account with remarkable insights upon the entire Platine action in mid-1807; also see *The Times* (London), March 11 and August 8, 1807.

48. For a more complete discussion of this topic, see my studies: *The Cádiz Experiment in Central America, 1808 to 1826* (Berkeley, Los Angeles, and London, 1978), and "The Impact of the American Revolution on the Spanish and Portuguese-Speaking World" in *The Impact of the American Revolution Abroad* (Library of Congress, Washington, D.C., 1976).

49. *The Morning Herald* (London), September 16, 1807.

50. *The Morning Post* (London), September 28, 1807, reproducing materials from the Madrid Gazette, August 25, 1807, especially "The *Publicista* of

Buenos Aires to Señor General Beresford." Also see the volume of documents in the British Library Manuscript Division, London, Additional Manuscripts 32,607, "Papers of the Government of Buenos Ayres: English Invasions," folios 17 verso to 39 dorso.

51. *Minutes of a Court Martial (Popham)*, 107, reproducing the letter, Home Popham to Admiral Charles Stirling, Maldonado, December 3, 1806.

52. Ibid., 69, 105–106, 108.

53. *The Times* (London), April 15, 1807.

54. *The Morning Post* (London), September 14, 1807, containing the letter, John Whitelocke to William Windham, Buenos Aires, July 10, 1807, with the General's version of the battle.

55. The description draws from Whitelocke's account, ibid., from the testimony in *Trial of General Whitelocke . . . by Court Martial at Chelsea College . . . 28 January 1808 . . . March 24, 1808* (London, 1808), and the Spanish version in *The Times* (London), November 13, 1807, by a merchant: "True Account of the Proceedings of the Forces of His Catholic Majesty, under *Jago Liniers* and *Bremont*, Viceroy, Governor and Captain General of the Provinces of the Río de la Plata and those of the Forces of Lieutenant General John Whitelocke, from the period of their disembarkation to the attack on said Capital until the surrender on the 7th of July, 1807," Buenos Aires, July 16, 1807. It should be noted that the expression *"Santiago y vitoria"* in the latter account harks back to the Crusades in Medieval Spain when Spanish Christians went into battle shouting: *"Santiago y Cierra, España"* which in translation is: "Saint James and Close in, Spain."

56. Ibid., Spanish version of the battle.

57. *The Morning Post* (London), September 14, 1807 (Whitelocke's version).

58. *The Times* (London), September 14, 1807 (editorial).

59. Ibid., August 19, 1806, and August 27, 1807—the latter reveals the newspaper's inconsistency on this issue.

60. Ibid., January 26 and May 23, 1808; also see the bitter remarks on the Popham promotion in the Wellesley Papers (Series II), Vol. XI, Additional Manuscripts 37, 284, folios 152–159, verso and dorso, British Library, Manuscript Division, London.

61. *The Times* (London), March 15 and 25, 1808; and *The Morning Post* (London), September 14, 1807.

62. John Whitelocke, *Buenos Aires. Truth and Reason versus Calumny and Folly* (London), 1807), a well-organized and rational defense of the General by a writer who felt it was unfair and tragic for the public to expect nothing but success in a military situation; also see, *The Times* (London), March 26, 1808, commenting upon Whitelocke's sentence:

> Poor consolation this is for the two thousand five hundred men, who were slain, maimed, or captured, in the streets of Buenos Ayres, by an

undisciplined rabble of townsmen! . . . But still the country is and must be dissatisfied. Two thousand five hundred of its bravest troops have been lost—a whole army disgraced and defeated by a herd of mechanics; and what is the ample vengeance which has been afforded us for such misfortunes? *One General has been cashiered*!

63. *The Times* (London), September 14, 1807.
64. Hereafter as *Burke*, I (1807) and *Burke*, II (1808).
65. *Burke*, I (1807), Preface, iii–iv.

66. Ibid., iv–vi.	88. Ibid., 30–31.
67. Ibid., 1–2.	89. Ibid., 36.
68. Ibid., 2–3.	90. *Burke*, II (1808), 1–2.
69. Ibid., 3–4.	91. Ibid., 3.
70. Ibid., 5.	92. Ibid., 3–5.
71. Ibid., 6–7	93. Ibid., 9–10.
72. Ibid., 8–9.	94. Loc. cit.
73. Ibid., 10.	95. Ibid., 11–12.
74. Ibid., 11–13.	96. Ibid., 12–14.
75. Ibid., 13–15.	97. Ibid., 15–16.
76. Ibid., 15–16.	98. Ibid., 16–18.
77. Ibid., 17.	99. Ibid., 18–20.
78. Ibid., 17–18.	100. Ibid., 21.
79. Ibid., 18–19.	101. Ibid., 22–23.
80. Ibid., 19–20.	102. Ibid., 23–24
81. Ibid., 20–21.	103. Ibid., 24–25.
82. Ibid., 21–22.	104. Ibid., 25–26.
83. Ibid., 22–24	105. Ibid., 27–30.
84. Ibid., 25.	106. Ibid., 30, 32.
85. Ibid., 25–26.	107. Ibid., 32.
86. Ibid., 28–29.	108. Ibid., 33–34..
87. Ibid., 29–30.	109. Ibid., 41.

Chapter 3.   THE EXPEDITION TO VENEZUELA

1.   Rolla, "General Miranda," *The Barbados Mercury*, September 6, 1806, Archivo de la Academia Nacional de Historia, Caracas, "Papeles de Caracciolo Parra Pérez, 1790–1806," Tomo 15, fol. 296 (Hereafter: Rolla, "Miranda"). "Rolla" was the pseudonym of William D. Robinson, a British merchant who had spent almost seven years in Caracas.
2.   *Burke*, II (1808).   See Chapter Two, footnote 64, for original entry.
3.   James Biggs, *The History of Don Francisco de Miranda's Attempt to Effect a Revolution in South America* (London, 2nd. ed. 1809), based on the Boston edition of 1808. Hereafter. Biggs, *Don Francisco*; John H. Sherman,

A General Account of Miranda's Expedition (New York, 1808), hereafter: Sherman, *General Account*.

4. Clippings, Sarah Martin, Archivo del General Miranda, *A.G.M.*, XXIII, 141–249 (Hereafter: S.M.'s Clippings, *A.G.M.*, XXIII).

5. Rolla, "Miranda," fols. 298–299.

6. Biggs, *Don Francisco*, 1–10; Sherman, *General Account*, 15–25.

7. Biggs, *Don Francisco*, 11.

8. Sherman, *General Account*, 26–27.

9. Loc. Cit.

10. Biggs, *Don Francisco*, 11–13.

11. Ibid., 30–31.

12. S.M.'s Clippings, *A.G.M.*, XXIII, 166–170.

13. Biggs, *Don Francisco*, 16.

14. Ibid., 32.

15. Sherman, *General Account*, 29.

16. Biggs, *Don Francisco*, 33.

17. S.M.'s Clippings, *A.G.M.*, XXIII, 148 (Sayre's letter); also 141–144.

18. Ibid., 141.

19. Ibid., 142.

20. Ibid., 165–166.

21. Ibid., 148–149.

22. Ibid., 150–151.

23. Biggs, *Don Francisco*, 32–35; Sherman, *General Account*, 29–42.

24. Rolla, "Miranda," fols. 298–299.

25. Sherman, *General Account*, 42–43.

26. *Burke*, II (1808), 43–44.

27. Sherman, *General Account*, 43–44; Biggs, *Don Francisco*, 66–67.

28. Ibid., 68–70.

29. Ibid., 69; Sherman, *General Account*, 45.

30. *Burke*, II (1808), 44.

31. Sherman, *General Account*, 46–65; Biggs, *Don Francisco*, 74–85.

32. *Burke*, II (1808), 44.

33. Biggs, *Don Francisco*, 87, opening Letter XII, May 9, 1806.

34. Ibid., 88–89.

35. Ibid., 89–90.

36. Ibid., 91–92.

37. Ibid., 93–94.

38. Ibid., 97.

39. Governor of Grenada to William Marsden, Grenada, May 29, 1806, AANH, Caracas, "Papeles de C. Parra Pérez," fols. 240–241.

40. *General Advertiser—Aurora* (Philadelphia), October 15, 1807, under the title: "The Miranda Expedition," copy seen in the AANH (Caracas).

41. Lt. Sherman was sentenced to ten years of labor at Omoa, Honduras; see the chart of prisoners: Sherman, *General Account*, 119–120.

42. *Aurora* (Philadelphia), October 15, 1807, third column.

43. Loc. Cit., fourth column.

44. *The Times* (London), August 28, 1806, reproducing letters: Marquis de Casa Irujo to William S. Smith, Washington, D.C., and the latter's reply from New York, June 30, 1806; also in *A.G.M.*, XXIII, 196–199. Miranda wrote to Smith, London, July 3, 1809, *A.G.M.*, XXII, 368–369, praising his stand.

45. See footnote 39: Governor of Grenada to Marsden, Grenada, May 29, 1806, fols. 240–241. (Original documents in the Public Record Office in Great Britain, Admiralty 1/327, copied for the Parra Pérez Collection).

46. Miranda to Rouvray, Trinidad, September 7, 1807, *A.G.M.*, Vol. XIX, 141; Miranda to Nicholas Vansittart, Bridgetown (Barbados), June 17, 1806, ibid., Vol. XVII, 405–406.

47. William Marsden to Alexander Cochrane, London, June 6, 1806, AANH, Parra-Pérez Collection, Tomo 15, fol. 242 (PRO., Admty 1/327).

48. Alexander Cochrane to Earl Spenser, *Northumberland* off Martinique, June 12, 1806, ibid., fol. 288 (PRO., Admty 1/327).

49. Treaty of June 9, 1806, Cochrane-Miranda, Barbados., ibid., fols. 242–245 (PRO., Admty 1/327).

50. Cochrane to Spenser, *op. cit.*, fols. 289–290 (PRO., Admty 1/327).

51. William Armstrong to Francisco de Miranda, Port-au-Spain, June 20, 1806, *A.G.M.*, Vol. XVIII, 6–9.

52. William Armstrong to Donald Armstrong, Trinidad, June 7–15, 1806, *The Times* (London), August 27, 1806; also in *A.G.M.*, Vol. XXIII, 194–196.

53. Rolla, "Miranda," *The Barbados Mercury*, September 2 and 6, 1806, AANH, "Papeles de Caracciolo Parra Pérez, Tomo 15, fols. 294–295 and 296–305.

54. Ibid., September 2nd, fol. 295.

55. William D. Robinson (Rolla) to Alexander Cochrane, Barbados, September 10, 1806, AANH, "Papeles . . . Parra Pérez," Tomo 15, fol. 262.

56. Rolla, "Miranda," September 6th, fols. 300–301 (also: PRO., Admty 1/327).

57. Ibid., fols. 301–302.

58. Ibid., fol. 304.

59. Ibid., fols. 304–305.

60. Robinson to A. Cochrane, September 10th., *op. cit.*, fols. 262–263.

61. Ibid., 264–265.

62. *Burke*, II (1808), 49–51.

63. George Dundas to William Marsden, *Elephant*, off Aruba, September 22, 1806, AANH, "Papeles . . . Parra Pérez), Tomo 15, fols. 271–272. (Also: PRO., Admty 1/327).

64. Loc. cit.

65. Miranda to a British financer (unnamed), Trinidad, pvt., February 17, 1807, *A.G.M.*, Vol. XVIII, 336–337.

66. Biggs, *Don Francisco*, 114.

67. Ibid., 115–116.

68. Dundas report, September 22, 1806, op. cit., 272.

69. *Burke*, II (1808), 50–51.

70. Biggs, *Don Francisco*, 236–237.

71. *Burke*, II (1808), 51–52.

72. Ibid., 51.

73. William Marsden to Admiral Alexander Cochrane, London, July 17, 1807, AANH, "Papeles . . . Parra Pérez, Tomo 15, fols. 309–310 (also: PRO., Admty 1/327).

74. Biggs, *Don Francisco*, 236.

75. John Turnbull to Francisco de Miranda, London, November 20, 1806, *A.G.M.*, XVIII, 325, and following document, 326–327.

76. *Burke*, II (1808), 52–53.

77. T. Hislop to Francisco de Miranda, Trinidad, September 22, 1806, *A.G.M..*, Vol. XX, 161; the entire document: 161–165 also entitled "Intercepted Correspondence on the Coast of Caracas by H.M.S. "Osprey" in July or August 1806."

78. Ibid., 162.

79. Ibid., 164.

80. Ibid., 164–165 (Franco's letter).

81. *London Evening Post*, November 9, 1806, "West-Indies—Miranda," ibid., Vol. XVIII, 317–320; *Spanish Main* (Barbados), September 23, 1806), ibid., 321–324; *The Statesman* (London), October 25, 1806, Vol. XXIII, 229, followed by *Bells' Weekly Messenger* (London), November 9, 1806, 230–233.

82. Ibid., XXII, 226–227, reproducing sections of Lord Castelreagh's speech to Parliament (December 22, 1806).

83. Miranda to Nicholas Vansittart, *Northumberland* in Carlisle Bay, Barbados, November 3, 1806, ibid., Vol. XVIII, 201–203, and documents that follow: 204–211.

84. Rouvray to Miranda, Samede Barbade, November 8, 1806, ibid., 239–240.

85. Rouvray to Miranda, London, December 18, 1806, ibid., 333–334.

86. Miranda to Cochrane, Trinidad, March 5, 1807, ibid., 361–362.

87. Miranda to Vansittart, Trinidad, April 7, 1807, ibid., Vol. XIX, 8–9; also Vol. XVIII, 314 (February 12, 1807) and 378 (March 9, 1807).

88. Miranda to Sir Home Popham, Trinidad, April 7, 1807, ibid., Vol. XIX, 9–10.

89. Miranda to Rouvray, Trinidad, March 7, 1807, ibid., Vol. XVIII, 376–378.

90. John Turnbull to Miranda, London, November 20, 1806, ibid., 284.

91. *Burke*, II (1808), 54–64 reproducing the major portions of these three key documents.
92. Miranda to Rouvray, Trinidad, December 4, 1806, *A.G.M.*, Vol. XVIII, 258–259.
93. Rouvray to Miranda, London, February 7, 1807, ibid., 389–391.

Chapter 4.   WILLIAM BURKE: FRONT AND CENTER

1. *Literary Journal* (London), No. 8, November 1, 1803, 499.
2. Richard B. Morris, ed., *The Impact of the American Revolution Abroad* (Washington, D.C., 1976), 100–125: "The Impact of the American Revolution on the Spanish-and-Portuguese-Speaking World," by Mario Rodríguez.
3. Mario Rodríguez, *The Cádiz Experiment in Central America, 1808 to 1826* (Berkeley, Los Angeles, London, 1978).
4. Mario Rodríguez, *La revolución americana de 1776 y el mundo hispánico: Ensayos y documentos* (Editorial Tecnos, Madrid, 1976).
5. *Gaceta de Caracas* (6 vols., Paris, 1839), a facsimile edition published by the Academia Nacional de la Historia, Caracas, Venezuela. Later, I consulted a more complete edition, also by the same Venezuelan Academia, in its *Biblioteca de la Academia Nacional de la Historia* (30 vols., Caracas, 1959–1960), vols. 21 and 22; and now, an exhaustive collection of the *Gaceta de Caracas* and other Venezuelan newspapers from 1808 to 1822 (Caracas, Vols. I–XI, 1983–1986) with valuable introductory essays and notes edited by Dr. Manuel Pérez Vila.
6. Francisco de Miranda, *Archivo del General Miranda* (24 vols., Habana, 1929–1950). (Hereafter *A.G.M.*, Vol.).
7. Caracciolo Parra Pérez, *Historia de la primera República de Venezuela* (2 vols., Caracas, 1939); for the revised and expanded second edition, see *Biblioteca de la Academia Nacional de la Historia* (Vols., 19 and 20, Caracas, 1959). Also see: William S. Robertson, *The Life of Miranda* (2 vols., Chapel Hill, North Carolina, 1929).
8. Mario Rodríguez, *A Palmerstonian Diplomat in Central America: Frederick Chatfield, Esq.* (Tucson, Arizona, 1964).
9. Dixon Wecter, *Edmund Burke and his Kinsmen, a Study of the Statesman's Financial Integrity and Private Relationships* (Boulder, Colorado, 1939).
10. William Burke, *An Account of the European Settlements in America* (1st ed., 2 vols., 1757) which appeared anonymously; later ones carried William's name; Edmund helped to revise the 1760 version.
11. Jacques Pierre Brissot de Warville, *Letter to his Constituents*, translated by William Burke and the preface by Edmund Burke (London, 1794).
12. Francisco de Miranda, *Correspondance du général Miranda avec le general Dumouriez, les ministres de la guerre, Pache et Beurnonville* (Paris,

1793) and Miranda's translation of this correspondence into English (London, 1794).

13. There is a copy of the set in the North Library, British Library in London. The editor was Edward Fryer.

14. "Memoir of James Barry, Esq." in *The European Magazine and London Review* (April 1806), 247–250 followed by a portrait of Barry's house, which I consulted in Miranda's manuscript collection (63 folio units). It is an enclosure that was not published in *Archivo del General Miranda*. The original folios are in the Academia Nacional de la Historia in Caracas, Venezuela. Also see William L. Pressly, *The Life and Art of James Barry* (New Haven, Conn., 1981).

15. See the correspondence in *A.G.M.*, Vol. XXII, 341–353, between Miranda and James Mill, Edward Fryer, and Francis Jeffry, editor of the *Edinburgh Review*, during early May, 1809.

16. William Burke, *South American Independence: or, the Emancipation of South America, the Glory and Interest of England* (London, 1807). Opposite page 82, the final page would be 83 if numbered. In the British Library, it is number one of the ten pamphlets (*Political Tracts, 1807–1856*).

17. William Burke, *The History of the Campaign of 1805, in Germany, Italy, the Tyrol, etc.* (London, 1806). The card in the British Library catalog (reading room) indicates that Burke was a "Late Army Surgeon."

18. *Literary Journal* (London), number 11, June 16, 1804, 675.

19. *Morning Post* (London), August 13, 1806, *A.G.M.*, XXIII, 189–194.

20. Governor T. Hislop to Francisco Miranda, Trinidad, September 20–24, 1806, ibid., XX, 161–162.

21. *Morning Post* (London), August 13, 1806, op. cit., 190.

22. Ibid., 193.

23. Art. II. *Lettre aux Espagnols Americains. Par un de leurs Compatriotes* (Juan Pablo Viscardo y Gusmán), *Edinburgh Review*, January, 1809, 277–311.

24. Alexander Bain, *James Mill, A Biography* (London, 1882); Bruce Mazlish, *James and John Stuart Mill* (New York, 1975); Joseph Hamburger, *James Mill and the Art of Revolution* (New Haven, Conn., 1963).

25. Donald Winch, ed., *James Mill: Selected Economic Writings* (Chicago, 1966); also see footnote 23 above, a review written by James Mill and Francisco de Miranda.

26. Francis Place to James Mill, London, September 15, 1816, Mss. Div. British Library, Add. 37, 949, fols. 212–214, replying to a recent letter from his friend at Fort Abbey, where he was working with Jeremy Bentham.

27. James Mill to Francis Place, Fort Abbey, October 26, 1817, Mss. Div. British Library, Add. 35.153, fol. 26.

28. Bain, *James Mill*, 38.

29. Ibid., 13–21, 28–30; James Mill to Francis Place, Fort Abbey, October

26, 1817, Mss. Div. Brit. Lib., Add. 35.153, fol. 26; Place to Mill, London, September 15, 1816, Mss. Div. Brit. Lib., Add. 37,949, fol. 214.

30. Bain, *James Mill*, 41.

31. Winch, *Selected Economic Writings*, 23–29 in which Professor Winch analyzes Mill's "Early Economic Writings: 1804–1808." In the documentary section, page 91, there is a reproduction of the title page of *Commerce Defended* (2nd. ed., London, 1808), published by C. and R. Baldwin.

32. Bain, *James Mill*, 53.

33. *Ibid.*, 51–52.

34. As quoted in Bain, ibid., 52.

35. *Literary Journal* (London), No. 5, February 3, 1803, 155.

36. *Commerce Defended* in Winch, *Selected Economic Writings*, 157–158.

37. Ibid., 159.

38. *Literary Journal* (London), No. 5, September 16, 1803, 257; also see Nos. 6 and 7 in October, 1803.

39. See, for example, the issues of the *Literary Journal* on: March 31, April 14, August 16, and September 16, 1803; also February, 1805.

40. My first discussion of the Burkian reforms appeared in: "The First Venezuelan Republic and the North American Model," *Inter-American Review of Bibliography*, 37, No. 1 (January, 1987), 3–17.

41. *Literary Journal* (London), No. 6, June 1805, reviewing George Rose's *Observations on the Poor Laws, and the Management of the Poor, in Great Britain* (London, 1805); ibid., No. 11, November 1805: Michael Nolan, *A Treatise of the Laws for the Relief and Settlement of the Poor* (2 vols., London, 1805). In Francis Place to J. Mill, London, September 14, 1815, Mss. Div. Brit. Lib., Add. 35,152, fol. 168, Place comments on Mill's article "Mendicity" which appeared in William Allen's *Philanthropist*; subsequently Mill also wrote an article "Mendicity" for Macvey Napier's *Encyclopedia Brittannica*.

42. James Mill to Francis Place, Fort Abbey, December 4, 1814, Mss. Div., Brit. Lib., Add. 35,152, which includes a discussion concerning the latest developments in their organization, the West London Lancasterian Society.

43. *Literary Journal* (London), No. 4, April 1805, dealing with the history of public revenues in Great Britain by John Sinclair.

44. *Edinburgh Review*, Vol. 16, Art VIII. *Relexiones Philosophiques et Politiques sur la Tolerance Religieuse*, par J.D. de Nxxx (Paris, 1809), 413–430. Although it is difficult to identify reviewers, the internal evidence indicates that it was James Mill—his reference to Villers' work on the Reformation, the arguments favoring the Catholics in England, and the reference to South American hopes of introducing "Religious Toleration" in the future coincide very closely to Mill's previous statements and his commitment at the time in the Miranda propaganda movement. Also see Mill's work: *The Principles of Toleration* (London, 1837).

45. See "The Military Spirit" in *Literary Journal* (London), No. 10, August 1, 1803; also, ibid., No. 5, September 16, 1803.

46. Winch, *Selected Economic Writings*, 23.

47. *Literary Journal* (London), No. 4, April, 1805, 412–425.

48. Ibid., 412–413.

49. Ibid., 414, 418, 425.

50. James Mill, East India House, to Macvey Napier, July 10, 1821, Mss. Div., Brit. Lib., Add. 34,611, fol. 428.

51. This was the review of Henry Broughman, *An Inquiry into the Colonial Policy of the European Powers* (2 vols., London, 1803) in *Literary Journal*, No. 9, November 16, 1803; and No. 11, November 1805, 1130, for the Playfair quotation.

52. Bain, *James Mill*, 426–427.

53. John Bowring, *The Works of Jeremy Bentham* (11 vols., Edinburgh, 1843), Vol. X, 450–451.

54. *Literary Journal* (London), No. 8, November 1, 1803, 492–499.

55. Ibid., 497–498.

56. Ibid., 498–499.

57. *Literary Journal*, No. 1, February 1806, 200–207: John Constance Davie, *Letters from Paraguay; Describing the Settlements of Montevideo and Buenos Aires* (London, 1805).

58. *Burke*, I (1807), 45–46; Anthony Z. Helms, *Travels from Buenos Ayres, by Potosí to Lima* (London, 1806), also reviewed in the *Edinburgh Review*, Vol. 9, Art. XI, 168–176. Helm's work first appeared in German, and was published in English to meet "the public curiosity about South America," after the capture of Buenos Aires by Popham.

59. *Burke*, I (1807), 52–63.

60. *Literary Journal*, No. 1, February 1806, 206.

61. *Burke*, I (1807), 53–54.

62. Muratori cited on 55 and La Pérouse on 69, ibid. Lodovico Antonio Muratori, *Il cristianesimo felice nelle missioni de'Padri della Campagnia de Gesú nel Paraguai* (Venice, 1952) was a famous Italian scholar (1672–1750) whose work on the Paraguayan Indians is known only to specialists; and the navigational exploits of that famous Frenchman Jean François de La Pérouse (1741–1788) whose posthumous volumes appeared in 1797: *Voyage de la Pérouse, autour de Monde*.

63. F. Depons, *Voyage à la Parte Orientale de la Terre-Firme, dans l'Amèrique Meridionale, fait pendant les Annèes 1801, 1802, 1803, et 1804* (3 tomes, Paris, 1806), which *Burke*, II (1808) referred to as *Travels in South America*, 66; see pages 66–72 for Miranda's biography and 88 on Venezuela, land of promise. Also see the *Edinburgh Review* of July, 1806, Art. IX, for an analysis of the work.

64. Ibid., Vol. X (July, 1807) and its "Quarterly List of New Publications," 241.

65. Count de Rouvray to F. Miranda, London, July 17, 1801, *A.G.M.*, Vol. XIX, 122–123.

66. F. Miranda to Nicholas Vansittart, Trinidad, July 11, 1807, ibid., 104.

67. F. Miranda to Alexander Cochrane, Trinidad, July 22, 1807, ibid., 104–105.

68. F. Miranda to General Bowyer, Trinidad, July 30, 1807, ibid., 107–108.

69. F. Miranda to Count de Rouvray, Trinidad, September 7, 1807, ibid., 141.

70. Rouvray to Miranda, London, December 18, 1806, *A.G.M.*, Vol. XVIII, 333–334; Rouvray to Miranda, London, July 1, 1807, ibid., Vol. XIX, 124–126.

71. Miranda to Rouvray, Trinidad, March 7, 1807, ibid., Vol. XVIII, 376, in which General Miranda said: "Believe me, my dear Count, that so long as the British Government sees any hope whatsoever (even the most illusory) of a European coalition, it will not come to our assistance willingly."

72. Miranda to Rouvray, Trinidad, March 7, 1807, ibid., 377; Miranda to Cochrane, Trinidad, June 4, 1807, ibid., Vol. XIX, 46–48.

73. Ibid., 46–48; Miranda to Rouvray, Trinidad, September 7, 1807, ibid., 142.

74. John Turnbull to Miranda, London, March 9, 1807, ibid., 24–26; Miranda to Cochrane, Trinidad, January 17, 1807, ibid., Vol. XVIII, 298; John Downie to Miranda, London, January 1807, ibid., 299–300.

75. Turnbull to Miranda, London, May 6, 1807, ibid., Vol. XIX, 87–89.

76. Miranda to Nicholas Vansittart, pvt., September 4, 1807, ibid., 143–145.

77. Miranda to Turnbull, Trinidad, September 4, 1807, ibid., 139–140; Sarah Martin to Miranda, London, June 23 to July 4, 1807, ibid., 129–138.

78. Robert Craufurd, *An Authentic Narrative of the Proceedings under the Command of Brigadier-General Craufurd until it Arrived at Montevideo; with an Account of the Operations against Buenos Ayres under the Command of Lieut. Gen. Whitelocke by an Officer of the Expedition* (London, 1808).

79. Rouvray to Miranda, London, August 8, 1807, *A.G.M.*, Vol. XX, 332–333.

80. Rouvray to Miranda, Barbados, October 17, 1807, ibid., 334–337.

81. Miranda to Turnbull, Tortola, November 6, 1807, ibid., 343.

82. Gaston Comte De Rouvray was in charge of "De Rouvray's Hulans," and he is listed as a Colonel, beginning July 1st, in the Chart of officers with General Miranda, *A.G,M..*, Vol. XVIII, 84. See the previous chapter for the reported omissions.

83. This is listed in ibid., Vol. XIX, in the section for early 1807 when the Count de Rouvray left for the Caribbean.

84. *Burke*, II (1808), 73–76.

85. Ibid., 65.

86. Ibid., 41.

87. John Turnbull to Nicholas Vansittart, Barnes, September 25, 1807, *A.G.M.*, Vol. XX, 375–378.

88. Miranda to Rouvray, Trinidad, February 12, 1807, ibid., Vol. XVIII, 345, a reminder of a specific instruction he had received in November, 1806, concerning the appointment of his replacement.

Chapter 5.   MIRANDA REACTS TO CHANGE (1808)

1. John Turnbull to Nicholas Vansittart, London, September 25, 1807, *A.G.M.*,, Vol. XX, 375–376.

2. F.co de Miranda to Lord Castlereagh, Trinidad, June 10, 1807, ibid., Vol. XIX, 55–58; idem to Nicholas Vansittart, Trinidad, July 11, 1807, ibid., 102–103.

3. F. Miranda to John Turnbull, Trinidad, June 10, 1807, ibid., 50–51.

4. Idem. to Alexander Cochrane, Trinidad, June 4, 1807, ibid., 46–48.

5. Idem. to Castlereagh, Trinidad, June 10, 1807, ibid., 55–58.

6. Idem. to Vansittart, Trinidad, July 11, 1807, ibid., 102–103; J. Turnbull to Miranda, London, May 6, 1807, ibid., Vol. XVIII, 87–89.

7. Rouvray to Miranda, London, August 22, 1807, ibid., Vol. XX, 332–333.

8. F.co de Miranda to Turnbull, Trinidad, ibid., Vol. XVIII, 139–140.

9. Turnbull to Miranda, London, August 22, 1807, ibid., Vol. XX, 324–325.

10. Idem. to Vansittart, London, September 25, 1807, ibid., 376.

11. Ibid., 377.

12. F.co de Miranda to Rouvray, London, January 7, 1808, ibid., 387–388.

13. Miranda to General Thomas Hislop, London, January 7, 1808, ibid., 390–391.

14. Idem. to Alexander Cochrane, London, January 7, 1808, ibid., 388–389.

15. Alexander Davison to Miranda, London, January 8, 1808, ibid., 392–393.

16. Memorandum, Miranda to Castlereagh, London, January 10–16, 1808, ibid., Vol. XXI, 18–35, consisting of initial drafts with some amendments; military memoir of January 16th starts on 27; the final memo sent to Castlereagh; Castlereagh, Viscount, *Memoirs and Correspondence of Viscount Castlereagh*, edited by C. Vane, Vol. VII, 405–412; and also see Archivo de la Academia Nacional de Historia, Caracas, "Papeles de Caracciolo Parra Pérez, 1790–1806," Tomo 15, VII–15, fols. 27–35.

17. Ibid., fols. 29–30 (C. Parra Pérez).

18. Miranda to Melville, London, January 4, 1808, *A.G.M.*, Vol. XX, 382; idem. to idem., London, February 20, 1808, ibid., Vol. XXI, 68–69; Melville to Lord Castlereagh, Dunira, June 8, 1808, ibid., 116–117.

19. Miranda to Arthur Wellesley, London, March 13, 1808, ibid., 100; Manuel Padilla to Wellesley, London, April 8, 1808, ibid., 128–132, and his documents: 88 and 172–175; on Melville, 116–117.

20. Miranda to Melville, London, February 20, 1808, ibid., 68.
21. D. Campbell to Miranda, Edinburgh, January 30, 1808, ibid., 54–55.
22. J. Downie to Miranda, Edinburgh, March 6, 1808, ibid., 84–85.
23. Idem. to idem., Paisley, March 22, 1808, ibid., 112–113.
24. Ibid., 121–123 (April 8th) and 144–145 (April 24th).
25. Ibid., 156–157 (May 3rd) and 168–169 (May 15th).
26. Ibid., 140–142.
27. Ibid., 66 (Cochrane) and 67 (Hislop).
28. Ibid., 135 (Vansittart).
29. Miranda to Cochrane, March 18, 1808, ibid., 103–105.
30. Ibid., 109 (Rouvray).
31. Ibid., 104 (Cochrane).
32. Nicholas Vansittart to Miranda, Shottesbrook, April 20, 1808, ibid., 144 and Miranda's note to the letter.
33. Miranda to Cochrane, London, May 5, 1808, ibid., 154–155.
34. *The Courier* (London) April 23, 1808.
35. Ibid., June 23, 1810.
36. Miranda to Alexander Cochrane, London, May 5, 1808, *A.G.M.*, ibid., 154–155 and 150 (Rouvray).
37. Arthur Wellesley to Miranda, May 4, 1808, ibid., 148.
38. Miranda to Lord Cochrane, London, May 16, 1808, ibid., 167–168.
39. Ibid., Miranda to Wellesley, May 25, 1808, 176; also 177 (Perceval) and 178 (Canning), both dated May 26th; also 191, for Canning's answer of June 18, 1808.
40. Diary note: ibid., 175–176.
41. *The Times* (London), June 10, 1808.
42. W.S. Robertson, *Life*, II, 23, for the Wellington quote; in that same chapter XV, see "Climax in English Policy," 1–27, for a lively discussion of the Spanish issue in English politics.
43. Miranda to Dr. William Thomson, London, February 2, 1808, *A.G.M.*, Vol. XXI, 53, with regards to the simile; also 51–53—Thomson: "mentor" etc.
44. Dr. William Thomson to Miranda, Gravel-Pits, Kensington, July 14, 1808, ibid., 311–312.
45. Miranda to Thomson, London, July 16, 1808, ibid., 313–315.
46. Thomson to Miranda, July 19th, ibid., 316–317.
47. Miranda to Thomson, London, November 23, 1808, ibid., Vol. XXII, 105–106, in which the Venezuelan concluded: "I beg you to excuse so much trouble, but the cure of disease *Calumny*, can be obtained only from its contrary, *Truth.*"
48. Thomson to Miranda, November 23, 1808, ibid., 104–105.
49. Title as in the text: *A.G.M.*, Vol. XXI, 145, 2d item.
50. Among the recipients were Samuel Loudon in the United States (Miranda to Loudon, December 6, 1808), ibid., XXIII, 258–259, Felipe Contucci in

Buenos Aires (Miranda to Contucci, January 17, 1810) ibid., 271–273, Thomas Hislop in Trinidad, ibid., 341–342, and John Downie in Portugal (Miranda to Downie, January 6, 1810), 264–265, now an Assistant Commissary in the British Army, in which the General told his friend: "This will be probably the Language of History where truth at last commonly prevails: *Magna est vis veritates.*"

51. Miranda to Cochrane, London, September 9, 1808, ibid., XXI, 352–353.

52. Ibid., 321–28 for letters of the 20th (Caracas) and 24th (Buenos Aires) plus English translations, etc.

53. Ibid., 368–377 for letter of October 6, 1808, plus documents and translations for the second batch of materials, as well as the Habana-Cuba additions.

54. Miranda to Castlereagh, London, August 19, 1808, ibid., 339–342.

55. Ibid., 321–326.

56. Ibid., 327.

57. Ibid., 340 (Castlereagh's letter of August 19th).

58. Ibid., 353 (Cochrane's of September 9th).

59. Ibid., 352.

60. Ibid., 353–354 (Habana, Cuba letters of September 10th).

61. Broadside, September 24, 1808, located in the Miranda manuscript collection in Caracas, Venezuela, fol. 136.

62. Spanish Government to Viceroy of Buenos Aires, Sevilla, November 9, 1809, and Captain General of Caracas, November 8, 1809, Archivo General de Indias (Sevilla, Spain) Estado, 71, 181–182.

63. Miranda's diary, *A.G.M.*, Vol. XXI, 374.

64. Ibid., 374–375.

65. Ibid., 376–377.

66. Ibid., 377.

67. Ibid., 376.

68. Vansittart to Miranda, Worthing, October 6, 1808, ibid., 378–379.

69. F.co de Miranda to Alexander Cochrane, London, October 20, 1808, ibid., XXII, 96.

70. Ibid., 97 (November 3, 1808).

71. Ibid., 125 (December 9, 1808).

72. Miranda to Cochrane, London, January 20, 1809, ibid., 196–197.

73. Miranda to Wellesley, London, December 12, 1808, ibid., 126–127.

74. Diary note, F.co de Miranda, January 26, 1809, ibid., 208–210.

75. Ibid., 209.

76. Ibid., 210.

77. Vansittart to Castlereagh, Great Malvern, August 21, 1809, ibid., Vol. XXIII, 50–51.

78. F.co de Miranda to Lord Vincent Castlereagh, London, March 24, 1808, ibid., Vol. XXII, 246–250.

79. Governor of Curaçao (James Cockburn) to Vice Admiral B.S. Rawley, Curaçao, January 26, 1809, and pertinent documents from the English and Spanish authorities, are in the AANH, Caracas, "Papeles de Caracciolo Parra-Pérez, 1790–1806, Tomo 15 (VII–15), fols. 81–112.

80. Cochrane to Miranda, December 12, 1808, and Miranda to Cochrane, February 17, 1809, *A.G.M.*, ibid., 228–231.

81. See footnote 79, fols. 100–101: Spanish Minister (Juan Ruiz de Apodaca) to Martin Garay in Madrid, London, June 9, 1809.

82. Diary note of Miranda, April 24, 1809, *A.G.M.*, Vol. XXI, 301.

83. Ibid., 302–303.

84. Ibid., 301.

Chapter 6.   PROPAGANDA OF LIBERATION

1. *Edinburgh Review*, July, 1809, 345.

2. This point can be tested in the Henry Brougham Collection, University College of London Library: on John Allen, see Ms. 10,027 (1827), attacking the "Benthamites, Political Economists and Utilitarians;" and on Mill, see Ms. 10,759 (1821) discussing political strategy with Brougham.

3. *Edinburgh Review*, January, 1809, 277 (hereafter, *E.R.* Jan. 1809).

4. Ibid., 277–279.

5. Ibid., 280.

6. James Mill to F. Miranda, London, January 4, 1809, *A.G.M.* Vol. XXII, 183, as well as the following letter, also in January, 184.

7. *E.R.*, Jan. 1809, 280–281.

8. Ibid., 281–282.

9. Ibid., 282–285.

10. Ibid., 284 and also footnote.

11. Ibid., 284–285.

12. Ibid., 299.

13. Ibid.

14. Ibid., 299–300.

15. Ibid., 300.

16. Ibid., 302–303.

17. Ibid., 304.

18. Ibid., 304–305.

19. Ibid., 306–307.

20. Ibid., 308.

21. Ibid., 308–309.

22. Ibid., 309.

23. Ibid., 311.

24. Mill to Miranda, early January, 1809, *A.G.M.*, ibid., 189–190; and the letter of mid-January, 193–194.

25. *E.R.*, Jan. 1809, 311.

26. Edward Wakefield to Francis Place, Fort Abbey, October 1, 1814; Francis Place to Edward Wakefield, London, October 7, 1814, Mss. Div. British Library, Add. 35152, fols. 85-87.

27. John Downie to F. Miranda, Coruña (Spain), March 19, 1809, *A.G.M.* Vol. XXII, 251-252.

28. Wm. Thomson to F. Miranda, Gravel Pits, March 21, 1809, ibid., 240-242, plus enclosure from John Murray; also in *A.G.M.*, Vol. XXIII, 407-408, another letter by Thomson to Miranda (May 1, 1810), plus Murray's enclosure.

29. James Mill to Miranda, London, February 13, 1809, *A.G.M.*, Vol. XXII, 224.

30. *Morning Chronicle* (London), February 23, 1809, Miranda manuscripts (Caracas), Roll 20, Tomo 15, folios 95-96.

31. James Mill to Miranda, London, May 7, 1809, *A.G.M.*, Vol. XXII, 344-345.

32. Francisco de Miranda to William S. Smith, London, July 3, 1809, ibid., 368-369.

33. *Edinburgh Review*, July, 1809, 333-353.

34. Ibid., 333-334.

35. Ibid., 334.

36. Ibid., 334-335; thus far, Mill's connection with the January and July articles has been mentioned three times.

37. Ibid., 335.

38. Ibid., 336.

39. Ibid., 336-342.

40. Ibid., 342-345.

41. Mario Rodríguez, *The Cádiz Experiment in Central America, 1808 to 1826* (Berkeley, 1978). Hereafter: *Cádiz.*

42. *Edinburgh Review*, July, 1809, 345.

43. Ibid., 345-346.

44. Ibid., 346-347.

45. Ibid., 347-348.

46. Ibid., 349.

47. Ibid., 350-351.

48. Ibid., 351.

49. Ibid., 352.

50. Ibid., 352-353.

51. *Bell's Weekly Messenger* (London), October 15, 1809.

52. Miranda's Manuscripts (Caracas), Roll 20, Tomo 17, fols. 71-72, with the last sentences of the article underlined in pencil *Bell's Weekly Messenger* (London), October 15, 1809.

53. John Bowring, ed., *Works of Jeremy Bentham* (11 vols., Edinburgh,

1843), X, 438–448, containing the letters from October 31, 1808 (J.B. to Holland) and Lord Holland to J.B., February 18, 1809, on the Mexican request. Hereafter: Bowring, *Works*, Vol.

54. Jeremy Bentham to Mr. Mulford, London, November 1, 1810, ibid., 457.

55. James Mill to Jeremy Bentham, London, April 27, 1809, British Library (London), Manuscript Division, Add. 33,544, fols. 432d–434v; also see fol. 449.

56. James Mill to F. Miranda, Oxted, Surrey, August 25, 1809, *A.G.M.*, Vol. XXIII, 54.

57. Mill to Miranda, Oxted, Surrey, August 11, 1809, ibid., 13–16.

58. Mill to Miranda, Oxted, Surrey, August 25, 1809, ibid., 52–54, plus enclosure by Bentham on the same date.

59. Miranda to Bentham, London, August 31, 1809, ibid., 57–58.

Chapter 7.   THE YEAR OF DECISIONS: 1810

1. Samuel C. Loudon to Francisco de Miranda, New York City, January 24, 1810. *A.G.M.*, Vol. XXIII, 427–428.

2. Circular letter, Francisco de Miranda to Whom It May Concern, London, March 24, 1810, ibid., 367–368.

3. Miranda to William Wilberforce, London, June 4, 1810, ibid., 426.

4. *Edinburgh Review*, October, 1808, Article XII. *An Historical Review of the Foreign Affairs of Great Britain* . . . By Gould Francis Leckie (London, 1808), 186–200, noting Mill's remarks on "Aristocracy," 196–199.

5. James Mill to F. de Miranda, May ?, 1810, *A.G.M.*, ibid., 410.

6. F.S. Constancio to F. de Miranda, Harwich, December 7, 1809, ibid., 123–124.

7. *Bell's Weekly Messenger*(London), September 10, 1809, in Miranda Mss, Roll 20, Tomo 17, fols. 54–55.

8. Loc. cit.

9. *The Statesman* (London), September 13, 1809, Miranda Mss, Roll 20, Tomo 17, fols. 57–58.

10. Loc. cit., Someone wrote "Dr. Constancio" in the left margin, identifying "Las Casas."

11. *The Statesman* (London), November 1, 1809, *A.G.M.*, ibid., 103–108; also fol. 84 (see footnote 9).

12. *A.G.M.*, Vol. XXIII, 7–9, for Leckie's letter to Miranda, August 2, 1809.

13. *The Statesman*, November 1, 1809, *A.G.M.*, ibid., 104–105.

14. Ibid., 105.

15. See footnote 5, 410, in which Mill stated: "The Doctor is not only a man of talents and information but appears to have that discretion and practical common sense, which joined with the others, fit him to be highly useful in the present crisis of South America."

16. *The Statesman*, November 1, 1809, *A.G.M.*, ibid., 106–107.

17. Ibid., 108.
18. F. Miranda to N. Vansittart, London, January 1, 1810, ibid., 252–253.
19. Ibid., 489 (Miranda to Felipe Contucci, London, August 2, 1810).
20. Loudon to Miranda, New York City, January 24, 1810, ibid., 427–428.
Captain Sam noted: "Herewith I send a file of "Spectator" in one of January
6th [1810], under the Extract of a Letter from London October 28th you will
perceive a piece which he readily inserted and was much gratified to give
currency to what it contains." Miranda had sent an envoy to Loudon with
copies of the first Edinburgh article, as well as an anti-Biggs article of March,
1809. His reference above was to the January 1809 article by Mill and
Miranda.
21. Ibid., 500–512 (letters between Febles and Miranda and Hislop and
Miranda).
22. Pedro Grases, "*Estudio histórico-crítico sobre los DERECHOS DEL
HOMBRE Y DEL CIUDADANO* (Caracas, 1959), 105–121, dealing with the
two conspiracies mentioned in which Manuel Cortés Campomanes was a
participant. This is vol. 5 (*Derechos del Hombre y del Ciudadano*) published
by the *Biblioteca de la Academia Nacional de la Historia* (30 vol., Caracas,
1959–1960,hereafter *BANA*. Professor Grases, in his various works on this
period, has done more than anyone else on Cortés Campomanes role in history.
23. Manuel Cortés Campomanes to Miranda, London, August 23, 1809,
A.G.M., ibid., 49–50; also a December 30th note, 137–138, announcing the
arrival of the three Mexican nobles.
24. Dewitt S. Chandler, "Jacobo de Villaurrutia and the Audiencia of
Guatemala, 1794–1804," *The Americas*, Vol. XXXII, No.3 (January, 1976),
402–417; also see my *Cádiz* book, 19–23.
25. Francisco de Miranda, *El Colombiano* (London, 1810; facsimilar
reproduction, Caracas, 1966). Professor Grases has edited the manuscript, along
with an editorial note and background section. There is much material here on
the main contributors, including Manuel Cortés Campomanes and his letters to
Miranda. Grases also reproduced a key document "Alerta" (xxviii–xxix) which
documents the Mexicans' interest in *El Colombiano*. Grases was kind in
allowing me to copy the original manuscript of "Alerta" for my files.
26. Miranda to Thomas Hislop, London, February 8, 1810, and Miranda to
Francisco Febles, London, February 8, 1810, *A.G.M.*, ibid., 341–343, are crucial
in documenting these facts; interestingly, in the reproduction of Viscardo's
Letter, Antepara wrote the militant "*adición*" or amendment, signing it "*un
colombiano de Guaiaquil*"—the same manner in which he signed off on the
1810 Documents, thus reinforcing the point that the Mexicans also helped to
subsidize the 1810 Documents. It suggests, moreover, that perhaps the Mexican
sponsors chose to use Antepara's name to throw off suspicion from their
participation in the publication of documentation by Miranda!

27. Circular Letter (see footnote 2), 367–368.

28. Miranda to Hislop, London, March 23, 1810, ibid., 366–367.

29. *Burke*, II (1808), 73–76, the "Additional Reasons . . ." treatise. The "Explanation of the Plate" came right after the frontispiece and before the "Preface" of *South American Emancipation, Documents* . . . (London, 1810).

30. William Thomson to Francisco de Miranda, Gravel Pits, March 21, 1809, and its enclosure from John Murray (written on Sunday), *A.G.M.*, Vol. XXII, 240–243, in which the latter was not in favor of publishing an account on Miranda's expedition of 1806; rather, he said:

> I am extremely desirous of giving to the public a complete narrative of the role of the General's transactions not only in regard to his grand object of emancipation but during the time that he served in France and respecting all of which, he has probably retained official documents and notes in this way it could prove very interesting to the public . . . a genuine, interesting and valuable work. I beg the favor of your further consideration of this matter (p. 241).

31. William Wilberforce to Miranda, New Palace Yard, June 6, 1810. *A.G.M.*, Vol. XXIII, 426–427.

32. Francisco de Miranda to Nicholas Vansittart, London, January 19, 1810, *ibid.*, 275, discussing the dangers presented by "*l'Exposé* de Bonaparte." Geared for action, members of the British opposition included Wilberforce, Sidmouth, and Grenville. Also see documents that precede this letter: ibid., 267–274, 276–279, revealing elements of the financial negotiations for propaganda and action against the enemy, including Dr. C. and Antepara.

33. R. Juigné to Thomas Molini, January 24, 1810, ibid., 280, reveals Antepara's use as a front for the Mexicans, as well as Miranda's interests. Here the publisher Juigné tells Miranda's secretary about the publication of 700 copies which he had just turned over to Antepara, pointing out that it was cheaper if he had taken 1,000 copies. This tract, of course, was the Viscardo pamphlet that we have cited. This was Antepara's role vis a vis the 1810 Documents, also published by Juigné.

34. Nicholas Vansittart to Miranda, Torquay, April 20, 1810, ibid., 405–406, and Miranda's answer in June, 1810, ibid., 424–425.

35. *El Colombiano* (London), 31.

36. *Gazeta de Caracas*, January 25, 1811, in the four columns that followed William Burke's editorial for that date.

37. *El Colombiano* (London), p. 32.

38. Ibid., 40.

39. Martin Murphy, *Blanco White, Self-Banished Spaniard* (Yale Press, New Haven, Conn., 1989), provides an excellent European background for his American role.

40. *The Life of the Rev. Joseph Blanco White*, written by himself, edited by John Hamilton Thom (3 vols., London, 1845), which contains letters to John Stuart Mill (1835–37 period); Vol. II, 242–245).
41. Mario Rodríguez, *Cádiz*, 90–99, provide examples of his attacks upon the Spanish liberals.
42. His writings on this theme are in another periodical that he edited: *Variedades, o Mensagero de Londres* (2 vols., London, 1823–1825), published by R. Ackerman.
43. *Edinburgh Review*, Art. VIII. *Reflexions Philosophiques sur la Tolerance Religieuse* . . . (Paris, 1809), Par J.P. De N***, 413–430.
44. Ibid., 416–417.
45. Ibid., 426.
46. Ibid., 428–429.
47. Ibid., 429–430.
48. Francisco de Miranda to Spencer Perceval, London, March 31, 1810, *A.G.M.*, XXIII, 369–370.
49. Miranda to Perceval, April 26, 1810, ibid., 406; and 455, Vansittart to Miranda, Rochampton, July 13, 1810.
50. *L'Ambigú* (London), June 30, 1810, in the *Gazeta de Caracas*, September 14, 1810.
51. *The Courier* (London), June 23, 1810.
52. *The Examiner* (London), July 1, 1810; also in Miranda Mss (Caracas), Roll 21bis, Tomo 19.
53. *Bell's Weekly Messenger* (London), July 1, 1810; also in Miranda Mss. (Caracas), Roll 21bis, Tomo 19.
54. *Gazeta de Caracas*, October 23, 1810, last two pages under title "*Noticias Extrangeras*."
55. *El Español* (London), July 30, 1810, 314–320.
56. Ibid., 317.
57. Ibid., 318–319.
58. Ibid., 320.

Chapter 8.   THE CARACAS REVOLUTION

1. *Gazeta de Caracas*, November 23, 1810. This was William Burke's first editorial published in Caracas, Venezuela; the Editor (Juan Germán Roscio) introduced him as an "author of some works dealing with the happiness of America,"—a reference, it seems, to the treatises of 1807 and 1808.
2. Most documents of this critical period were reproduced in the *Gazeta de Caracas*: the "*Proclama*" to other areas of Spanish America, April 20, 1810, appeared in the *Gazeta* of April 27, 1810; on January 1, 1811, we have the December, 1810, documentation on Admiral Cochrane's negotiations with the

Puerto Rican authorities; and the key facts in the text are taken from the gazette, unless otherwise indicated.

3.   *Gazeta de Caracas*, June 8, 1810, reproducing the May correspondence between Layard and the Coro authorities.

4.   Robert Lowry to Robert Smith (U.S. Secretary of State), La Guaira, August 30, 1810, and idem to idem, September 6, 1810, plus enclosures, National Archives (Washington, D.C.), U.S. State Department, La Guaira, Volume 1 (F.M. 84 File Microcopy).

5.   Juan Germán Roscio to Colonel John Robertson, Caracas, September 7, 1810, in Juan Germán Roscio, *Obras* (3 vols., Caracas, 1953), III, 186–196, and especially 189; other letters follow for Robertson and Layard in the months of September–October, 1810—documents that come from the War Office (London): W.O. 1/105, folios 361 forward.

6.   Mario Rodríguez, "The Presence of the American Revolution in the Contemporaneous Spanish World," *Revolution in the Americas* (Proceedings of the Pacific Coast Conference on Latin American Studies), Vol. 6, 1979, 15–24.

7.   Most of them appear in the *Gazetas* after April 19, 1810; and, after awhile, compilations were made of them: see *Gaz.* December 4, 1810 noting the presence of one. It will also be evident in the discussion of Burke's articles.

8.   See my *Cádiz* volume, 53–74; also, my article: "The `American Question' at the *Cortes* of Madrid," *The Americas*, Vol. XXXVIII, No. 3 (January 1982), 293–314.

9.   *Gazeta de Caracas*, June 2, 1810, which includes copies of the Regency's order of February 15, 1810, and the blistering reply of the Junta Suprema in Caracas on May 20, 1810—the first three pages of that issue.

10.   Ibid., April 27, 1810, letter of "The Supreme Conservative Junta [to conserve] the Rights of Ferdinand VII in Venezuela" to the "Cabildos [Town Councils] of the Capitals of America."

11.   "Estados Unidos de America. Baltimore 4 de Junio," *Gazeta de Caracas*, July 20, 1810. Based upon the Baltimore *Evening Post*, Editor Roscio commented enthusiastically on its contents, as well as the remarks of those sending and bringing this material to Caracas.

12.   Robert Lowry to Robert Smith (Secretary of State), La Guaira, September 6, 1810, National Archives (U.S. State Dept.), La Guaira, Vol. 1 (see F.M. 84, File Microcopy) with information on the exchange between Roscio and Lowry.

13.   Miguel Luis Amunátegui, *Vida de Don Andrés Bello* (Santiago de Chile, 1882) is the classic biography of the Venezuelan savant, also containing the extant correspondence with Roscio and others, including James Mill. A key letter, which we shall cite later: Juan Robertson to Andrés Bello, Curaçao, December 10, 1810, 95–98, concerning Miranda's stay in his home before proceeding to Venezuela.

14.   From April 19, 1810, forward the *Gazeta de Caracas* adopted the motto

used by *El Voto* (Cádiz), which discussed the term in its No. 5 (January 10, 1810), 61–72; *El Voto's* issues are available in the British Library (London).

15. *Gazeta de Caracas*, October 24, 1808, its first issue; by February 17, 1809, when Bello praised the "Freedom of the Press" in the Cádiz papers.

16. *Gazeta de Caracas*, August 24, 1810, with a copy of Roscio's measure of August 14th, along with the support of Francisco de Ustáriz, serving as *Intendente* at that time.

17. Amunátegui, op. cit., for Roscio's letters to Bello of June 29, September 10, and September 24, 1810, see pages 82–87; the last one reveals that the letters from London arrived in Caracas on September 23, 1810, referring to those written by Bolívar et. al. on August 3–4, 1810.

18. Roscio to Bello, Caracas, June 29, 1810, ibid., 82–83 in which he wrote: "*Ilústrese más para que ilustre a su patria*," the quotation cited above in English.

19. In fact, it was José de Tovar Ponte who delivered the correspondence of August 3–4, 1810, London, mentioned in footnote 17.

20. Pedro Grases, "Estudio Bibliográfico," 27–30, preceding Vols. 21 and 22 (*Gazeta de Caracas*) of the *B.A.N.H* (30 vols., Caracas, 1959–1960).

21. Gaspar M. Jovellanos, *Cartas de Jovellanos y Lord Vassall Holland sobre la guerra de la Independencia* . . . (2 vols., Madrid, 1911), I, 35–41, 108–109, especially *Nota* 20 on John Allen. The prologue and notes are by Julio Somoza García-Sala.

22. *The Holland House Diaries, 1831–1840* (London, 1977), which also contains extracts from the diary of Dr. John Allen; edited with introductory essay and notes by Abraham D. Kriegel. Also see the new edition of Allen's *Inquiry* . . . (London, 1849) with biographical notices.

23. *Edinburgh Review*, April, 1810: Art. IV. *Essai Politique sur le Royaume de la Nouvelle Espagne*. Alexandre de Humboldt. Paris, 1808–1809, 62–102; also see ibid., January, 1807, 433–458, on the *Mercurio Peruano*.

24. Ibid., 100 (April, 1810).

25. Ibid., 63–64. A good example of the literature on expeditions: Iris H.W. Engstrand, *Spanish Scientists in the New World. The Eighteenth–Century Expeditions* (Seattle and London, 1981).

26. *E.R.* (April, 1810), 65–76.

27. Ibid., 77.

28. Ibid., 80–81.

29. Ibid., 83–85.

30. Ibid., 86.

31. Ibid., 88.

32. Ibid.

33. Ibid., 88–89.

34. Ibid., 89.

35. Ibid., 89–90.

36. Ibid., 90–91.

37. Ibid., 91–92.
38. Ibid., 92.
39. Ibid., 92–93.
40. Ibid., 93.
41. Ibid., 93–94.
42. See the studies: Cristóbal L. Mendoza, *Las primeras misiones diplomáticas de Venezuela* (2 vols., Madrid, 1962); and Carlos A. Villanueva, *Historia diplomática de la primera república de Venezuela* (Caracas, 1969).
43. Lord Liverpool to Layard, Secret and Confidential, July 23, 1810, Public Record Office (London), F.O. 72/103.
44. *Gazeta de Caracas*, October 19, 1810.
45. Ibid., September 22, 1810.
46. Ibid., November 6, 1810.
47. Ibid., October 30, 1810, and November 6, 1810.
48. Ibid., November 9, 1810.
49. Jules Mancini, *Bolívar y la Emancipación de las Colonias Españolas desde los orígenes hasta 1815* (Paris, Mexico, 1923), 315 for the Spanish version and translation by Carlos Docteur. It was page 321 in the original French edition of 1911.
50. Jeremy Bentham to Mr. Mulford, November 1, 1810, Bowring, *Works*, X, 457–478, and 483 for the Mill-Bentham quote.
51. William Allen to Henry Brougham October 2, 1810, Henry Brougham Collection, University College of London Library, Box 17, No. 10,950.
52. Francisco de Miranda to Marquis of Wellesley, London, July 25, 1810, *A.G.M.*, Vol. XXIII, 476–478.
53. Miranda to Junta Suprema of Venezuela, London, August 3, 1810, *Gazeta de Caracas*, November 20, 1810; Miranda to Fernando Rodríguez del Toro (Governor of the City of Caracas), London, *A.G.M.*, ibid., 523–524.
54. Ibid., 528 (Miranda's note to Wellesley of August 29, 1810), and 531–532 (Vansittart to Miranda, August 30, 1810), indicating that it might be wise to take a different ship, thus minimizing any reaction from the Spanish government.
55. Amunátegui, op. cit., 95–98, John Robertson's letter to Bello, December 10, 1810, on Miranda's stay in Curaçao.   *
56. Ibid.
57. See endnote 43 for Lord Liverpool's annoyance on allowing Miranda the use of that ship.
58. The *Gazeta de Caracas* supplied the facts presented here: December 21, 1810, announcing Miranda's arrival on the English ship, the *Avon*; January 11, 1811, Miranda's appointment on the previous day to the rank of Lt. General and Inspector General; and the January 18 and January 22, 1811, issues commenting on the celebrations and promises of various municipalities and corporations to remove the spiteful documentation concerning Francisco de Miranda.

Chapter 9.   BURKE'S ANALYSIS OF RIGHTS

1. *Edinburgh Review*, January, 1809.
2. Juan Germán Roscio, *Obras* (3 vols., Caracas, 1953), compiled by Pedro Grases and Prologue by Augusto Mijares, Vol. II, 13–14; the original broadside is in the *Biblioteca Nacional* in Caracas, date is unknown but the evidence points to late 1810, early 1811.
3. The *Biblioteca de la Academia Nacional de la Historia*, cited in earlier chapters as *BANH* (30 vols., Caracas, 1959–1960) has published the newspapers cited: Vol. 8: *El Publicista de Venezuela*, facs. ed; Vol. 9: *Semanario de Caracas*, facs. ed; Vol. 25: *Mercurio Venezolano*, facs. ed.; Vol. 37: *El Patriota de Venezuela*.
4. *Gazeta de Caracas*, November 23, 1810.
5. Ibid., November 30, 1810.
6. Ibid., November 23, 1810.
7. Ibid., December 21, 1810.
8. Ibid., January 1, 1812.
9. Ibid.
10. Ibid., January 8, 1812.
11. The *Gazetas* of December, 1810–January, 1811, provide copies of the documents cited, as well as the facts indicated. For some unknown reason, perhaps security purposes, some of the documents did not appear in the gazette until mid 1811, as for example, Miranda's letter to the Valencia municipality on February 18th, not published until the *Gazeta* of June 28, 1811.
12. *Gazeta de Caracas*, June 25, 1811, including Miranda's letter to Bogotá, January 22, 1811—another case of delayed publication, clearly for security reasons.
13. Ibid., January 11, 1811.
14. Ibid.
15. Ibid., January 15, 1811.
16. Ibid.
17. Ibid., January 18, 1811.
18. See the February issues of the *Semanario de Caracas*.
19. *Gazeta de Caracas*, January 22, 1811.
20. Ibid.
21. Ibid., January 25, 1811.
22. Ibid.
23. Ibid., February 5, 1811.
24. Ibid.
25. Ibid., February 8, 1811.
26. Ibid.
27. Arthur Preston Whitaker, *The Western Hemisphere Idea: Its Rise and Decline* (Ithaca, N.Y., 1954), lectures that he delivered at Cornell University.

28. Mario Rodríguez, *A Palmerstonian Diplomat in Central America: Frederick Chatfield Esq.* (Tucson, Arizona, 1964), Chapter Eleven, "Brother Jonathan and the Tiger," 295–326, which provides the ideological battle between Chatfield and the U.S. agent Ephraim George Squier. Chatfield referred to the W.H. "Idea," as the "American System" and had his allies in Costa Rica fight it tenaciously; his allies in Guatemala likewise cooperated, while the "center states" of Honduras, El Salvador, and Nicaragua followed Squier's appeal for "Americanism."

29. *Gazeta de Caracas*, February 22, 1811.

30. Ibid.

31. Ibid., February 26, 1811.

32. Ibid., March 1, 1811.

33. Ibid., February 8, 1811.

34. Ibid., February 12th and 15th.

35. Ibid., February 19th and 22nd.

36. Ibid., February 19, 1811.

37. Ibid., February 22, 1811.

38. Ibid., March 1, 1811.

39. Ibid., March 5, 1811.

40. Ibid.

Chapter 10.   PRECARIOUS INDEPENDENCE

1. *Gazeta de Caracas*, March 29, 1811.

2. Ibid., March 5, 1811.

3. Ibid.

4. Ibid.

5. Ibid., March 12, 1811.

6. Ibid. It would appear that Roscio had read William Burke's first treatise in London: *Burke*, I (1807), 76, in which James Mill brought up the threat of a U.S. takeover in Spanish America. The difference, however, was that Mill used it in his essay in order to frighten the English to take action in 1807, thus beating the North Americans to the area; whereas Roscio here was merely trying to shame his countrymen into action before it was too late.

7. Ibid., March 19, 1811.

8. Ibid.

9. Ibid., March 26, 1811.

10. Ibid., March 29, 1811.

11. Ibid., January 25, 1811.

12. Ibid., March 8, 1811: "Harenga," March 2, 1811.

13. Ibid., January 29, 1811.

14. Ibid., February 19, 1811; the footnote is at the bottom of the left column.

15. Ibid.

16. Ibid.

17. Ibid., see especially the issues in April: 9th, 12th, 16th, and 19th; the report of the University Corporation came out on June 6, 1811.

18. *Gazeta de Caracas*, April 22, 1811.

19. Ibid., which contained both the Mérida letter of March 15, 1811, and the Government's answer of April 17th, signed by the President of the Executive Power; yet the letter was written by Roscio, in his capacity as acting President of Congress.

20. Antonio Nicolás Briceño, "Exposición en Pro de la División de la Provincia de Caracas . . . ", Caracas, August 14, 1811, *BANH*, Vol. 37, 29–57, especially the introductory pages (29–31).

21. Ibid., 40–41.

22. Fernando de Peñalver, *Memoria* to the National Congress, Caracas, June 26, 1811, *BANH*, Vol. 37, 11–26.

23. *El Publicista de Venezuela* (Caracas), August 22, 1811, producing the congressional session of June 27, 1811, 67–68.

24. Ibid., August 29, 1811, also reproduced part of the congressional session of June 27, 1811, 65–67.

25. *The Weekly Register* (Baltimore), September 14, 1811, Library of the Archives of the United States (Washington, D.C.), Vol. I, 105–110, 121–125.

26. Dr. Manuel Pérez Vila, Editor of the recent volumes on the *Gazeta de Caracas* does mention the incident without explaining it in any detail, perhaps because he understood its context; there seemed, however, to be an unawareness of the impact that this incident had throughout the world.

27. *El Publicista de Venezuela* (Caracas), July 25, 1811, 29–30; *Gazeta de Caracas*, August 6, 1811.

28. Miguel Luis Amunátegui, *Vida de Don Andrés Bello* (Santiago de Chile, 1882) has been cited in earlier Chapters: Here we prefer to use Roscio's *Obras*, III, letter number 9: Caracas, June 9, 1811. Roscio to Bello, 23–36.

29. Ibid., 28.

30. *La Bagatela* (Bogotá), December 22, 1811, containing most of the documents in this incident plus Burke's final remarks.

31. *Gazeta de Caracas*, February 15, 1812.

32. *El Publicista de Venezuela* (Caracas), August 8, 1811, reproducing minutes of the session on June 25, 1811, 41–46.

33. Ibid., September 12, 1811, reproducing session of July 3, 1811, 83.

34. The "*Manifiesto*," Caracas, July 30, 1811, attributed to Roscio, appears in many references: the *Gazeta de Caracas* published it in several installments; the *Niles' Register*, as we have already noted; and in a volume that was published in London, 1812, in English and in Spanish: *Interesting Official Documents Relating to the United Provinces of Venezuela*, 105–148, and which also reproduced the Venezuelan Constitution of December, 1811.

35. Juan Germán Roscio de Andrés Bello, Caracas, July 31, 1811, Roscio, *Obras*, III, 37–38.
36. *Gazeta de Caracas*, July 9, 1811, which reproduces the letter of July 6th to the President of Cundinamarca.
37. William Burke, *Derechos de la América del Sur* (2 vols., Caracas, 1811), *BANH*, Nos. 10–11, Vol. 1, 41–44; William Burke "To the Patriots of Caracas," Caracas, June 25, 1811.
38. *Gazeta de Caracas*, July 9, 19, and 23, 1811, with special attention to the remarks of the editing commission on the issue of the 19th.
39. Ibid., July 23rd for the information supplied by Miranda.
40. Ibid., October 11, 1811, President Tadeo Lozano to President of Executive Power (Venezuela), Bogotá, August 21, 1811.
41. Ibid., Miguel de Pombo to "my dear friend," Bogotá, August 2, 1811.
42. Ibid., Extraordinary Edition, January 4, 1812.
43. Ibid., January 7, 1811.
44. Ibid., January 22–February 11, 1812.
45. Ibid., February 15, 1812, plus enclosures published.

Chapter 11.   DIVIDED COUNSELS

1. *Gazeta de Caracas*, January 14, 1812, editorial by Miguel Sanz.
2. Letter, "The American Patriot to the Friends of Good Government and Independence," *National Intelligencer* (Washington, D.C.), September 26, 1811. See the Spanish version in the *Gazeta*, November 29, 1811.
3. *El Patriota de Venezuela* (Caracas), November, 1811), No. 3, 372, *BANH*, Vol. 37.
4. *Libro de Actas del Supremo Congreso* (Venezuela), *BANH*, Volumes 3–4: Vol. 3, 315, 328–330; Vol. 4, 89 (Miranda), 111–114 (Treaty), and 121, 141, 181. Also see: *Gazeta de Caracas*, July 5, 1811.
5. Juan Germán Roscio to Andrés Bello, Caracas, July 31, 1811, Roscio, *Obras*, Vol. 3, 37–38.
6. Representation of 107 *Valencianos* to Municipality of Caracas, Valencia, May 29, 1811, in *Gazeta de Caracas*, June 25, 1811.
7. *El Publicista de Venezuela* (Caracas), Sessions of August 19, 20, 1811, in the issues of October 17 and October 24, 1811, 122–125, and 129–30, *BANH*, Vol. 8.
8. *Libro de Actas del Supremo Congreso* (Venezuela), Vol. 4, 61–62 (October 1, 1811), 160 (November 16, 1811), and 161–162 (November 18, 1811).
9. *Gazeta de Caracas*, December 10, 1811, with the *Indulto* (Pardon) of November 21, 1811.

10. Ibid., February 4, 1811; also *Libro de Actas*, Vol. 4, 290–295, for the full discussion in Congress, and its decision on January 27, 1812.

11. *Gazeta de Caracas*, February 19 and 22, 1812.

12. Ibid., December 27, 1811.

13. *El Publicista de Venezuela*, Session, September 2, 1811, 130–131, issue of October 24, 1811; *Libro de Actas*, Vol. 4, 99–100 (Extraordinary session of October 15, 1811).

14. *Gazeta de Caracas*, August 2, 1811.

15. *Libro de Actas*, Vol. 4, 190–193 (Session, December 5, 1811).

16. Ibid., 208–209 (Session, December 16, 1811).

17. Ibid., 218–232 (Session, December 21, 1811); see 363–365 for Archbishop's petition (Session, February 20, 1812).

18. Ibid., 259 (December 9, 1811).

19. Ibid., 96–98 (Session, October 15, 1811).

20. Ibid., 211–214 (Session, December 18, 1811) and other pages: 233–234, 265–266, and 276–277.

21. Ibid., 280–281 (January 21, 1812).

22. Ibid., 296–297 (Extraordinary Session, January 27, 1812).

23. Ibid., 297.

24. Ibid., 304–305 (January 30, 1812).

25. Ibid., 232 (December 21, 1811, Miranda's evaluation).

26. Ibid., 369–370 (Extraordinary Session, March 21, 1812).

27. *Gazeta de Caracas*, November 19, 1811.

28. Ibid., August 13, 23, 1811, were written by Sanz, and possibly the issue of August 20, 1811, as well.

29. Ibid., September 6, 1811.

30. Ibid., also see William Burke's book: Vol. II, 28.

31. Ibid., September 6, 1811; *Burke's II*, 29–30.

32. Ibid., Vol. II, 31–32.

33. Ibid., September 10, 1811: Vol. II, 33.

34. Ibid., September 21, 1811.

35. Ibid., September 27, 1811; and then on October 1, 1811, he began with the quotation that follows in the text.

36. Ibid., October 1, 1811, and Vol. II, 57–58.

37. Ibid., Vol. II, 58–59.

38. Ibid., Vol. II, 59, 61.

39. Ibid., October 18, 22, 29, 1811 (Finances and Commerce) and December 24, 1811, January 3, 10, 1812 (Banks, Paper Money, etc.).

40. Ibid., February 22, 1812; also Burke, Vol. II, 168–169.

41. Ibid., Vol. II, 169–170.

42. Ibid., Vol. II, 171–172.

43. Ibid., February 25, 1812; Vol. II, 173.

44. Ibid., Vol. II, 174.

45. Ibid., February 11, 1812. The statement, in the first column, was followed by five and one-fifth columns, ending with "*se continuará.*"

46. Ibid., Vol. II, 174–177.

47. Ibid., February 25, 1812.

48. Ibid., March 6, 1812.

49. Ibid., March 20, 1812; Vol. II, 197–202, bearing the title "Liberty as a Universal Principle."

50. See footnote 2 in this chapter.

51. *Gazeta de Caracas*, January 14, 1812.

52. Ibid.

53. *El Español* (London), No. 16, July 30, 1811, including Roscio's letter to Blanco-White, Caracas, January 28, 1811, and Blanco-White's reply of July 11, 1811, 294–296 and 296–309 respectively.

54. Ibid., B-W's reply, 307.

55. Ibid., 307–308.

56. Ibid., 308.

57. *Edinburgh Review* (November, 1811), review by John Allen of Art. VII. *Essai Politique sur le Royaume de la Nouvelle Espagne.* Par Alexandre de Humboldt. Paris, 1809, 10, 11, 164–198.

58. Ibid., 171.

59. *El Español*, a monthly, published Nos. 16 (July), 17 (August), 18 (September), and 19 (October) 1811, by the end of each month; the Venezuelan and New Granadian newspapers reflected the Spanish American reaction, as well as the two writers mentioned in footnote 60.

60. Manuel de Pombo, *Carta a Blanco-White sobre la independencia de América y Filipinas,* 212–242, a pamphlet that exists in the Biblioteca del Archivo Nacional de Historia (Caracas), written probably in 1812 (Bogotá); Fray Mier's pamphlet is number 16, in the British Library (London): *Carta de un Americano al Español sobre su número XIX* (London, 1811), 59 pages; on page 6 he begins the attack on the distortion concerning the members of the Sociedad Patriótica de Venezuela. Blanco-White's rebuttal appeared in El *Español* (London), No. 24 (April 30, 1812), 409 forward and especially on 411–412. Blanco-White's political ideology was suffering a cynical streak at this time in his life, which, fortunately, he disposed of in later years. See footnote 63 for a quotation by Blanco-White concerning his old friend Miranda.

61. John Allen's review, 177–179 (See footnote 57).

62. Ibid., 182.

63. Blanco-White published the Spanish translation of Dr. Allen's second article of November, 1811, in *El Español* (London), No. 22, January 30, 1812, 241–269. In Number 28 of *El Español* (London, August 29, 1812, Blanco-White published the secret minutes of the Spanish *Cortes* (July 10–14, 1812), rejecting the continuation of "Mediation" by a vote of 101 to 46. Furthermore, he was ready to predict that General Miranda would be the victor in Venezuela:

"General Miranda, whom we cannot deny, has talents and superior knowledge by comparison to the Spanish leaders there, and it is very probable that before long he will not only cut short the progress of his rivals but will most likely end the war in his favor, by taking over the dissident cities" (page 324; and the minutes, 324–327).

64. *Gazeta de Caracas*, December 10, 1811, which reproduced Blanco-White's No. 17, *El Español*, August 30, 1811.

65. Ibid.; B-W's analysis of the "mediation" process to that point was, indeed, perceptive.

66. Ibid., November 29, 1811, including the letter by Bello and López-Méndez, as well as Sanz's commentary.

67. *Argos Americano* (Cartagena), December 30, 1811, with Blanco-White's No. 17 and the 9 articles of the Cortes.

68. The above documentation and commentary was published in the *Gazeta de Caracas*, March 10, 1812, with the congratulations of editor Sanz.

Chapter 12.   THE "EARTHQUAKE REPUBLIC"

1. *Le Journal de Paris*, May, 1813; Louis Delpech wrote the original manuscript in French; the Spanish translation appears in Jesús Rosas Marcano, *La Independencia de Venezuela y los periódicos de París, 1808–1825* (Caracas, 1964), 135–140; the English translation is mine (M.R.).

2. Thomas Forrest to Charles Stirling, Caracas, March 30, 1812, P.R.O., London, F.O. 72/157.

3. Jesús Rosas Marcano, op. cit., 135–140.

4. See footnote 2.

5. John Semple to Mathew Semple, Caracas, April 3, 1812, in *Tres Testigos Europeos de la Primera República* (Caracas, 1934), 86–87; the other Europeans were Louis Delpech, H. Poudenx, and F. Mayer.

6. *Gazeta de Caracas*, June 2, 1812, which reproduces Miranda's letter to José Sata y Bussy, Maracay, May 21, 1812; it records that the power was given to Miranda on April 26, 1812, clarified on May 4th, and incorporated in the Martial Law on May 19, 1812; also see Palacio's contribution in *Libro de Actas del Supremo Congreso*, Vol. 4, 384–402, including the sessions of March 30th through April 6, 1812.

7. Roscio expressed it well in the *Gazeta de Caracas*, May 6, 1812, which included his letter: the SPE to the Confederated States of Venezuela, La Victoria, May 6, 1812.

8. State Legislature to the People of the Sovereign States of Caracas, Caracas, April 9, 1812, *A.G.M.*, Vol. XXIV, 388–391.

9. Miguel Sanz, "Bases para un gobierno provisional en Venezuela," 1813, *BANH*, 37, 217–218.

10. Typical of their complaints were those mentioned in Juan Paz del

Castillo's correspondence with Francisco de Miranda, *A.G.M.*, Vol. XXIV, 283–293; also see 51–53, Sanz's letter to Miranda on desertions.

11. For an excellent and thorough study of John Robertson, see Carlos Pi Sunyer, *El General Juan Robertson; Un prócer de la Independencia* (Caracas, 1971).

12. Robertson's letters to Isnardi, May 8–31, 1812, *A.G.M.*, Vol. XXIV, 247–254.

13. Ibid., Francisco de Miranda to Simón Bolívar, Maracay, May 21, 1812, 437–438; Carlos Soublette (Miranda's secretary) to Simón Bolívar, June 5, 1812, 447–448.

14. For a good discussion of Miranda's tactics by contemporaries, see Miguel Sanz to Miranda, Caracas, June 21, 1812, 49–50, ibid.

15. Ibid., 315–325, for Nicolas Ascanio's correspondence with Miranda, which also provides insights into his competition, especially the Marquis del Toro.

16. Ibid., "Cartas de J.M. Salazar," 294–296.

17. José Félix Blanco and Ramón Azpurúa, eds., *Documentos para la historia de la vida pública del Libertador* (14 vols., Caracas, 1875–1877), III, 758–759, reproducing a Bogotá publication of 1843. Manuel Palacio Fajardo, the author of *Outline of the Revolution in Spanish America* (London, 1817), claimed that Miranda, when he arrived in La Guaira in late July, 1812, was planning to sail to Cartagena: see the Spanish translation by Carlos Pi Sunyer; *Revolución en la América Española* (Barinas, Venezuela, 1973), 72.

18. George Robertson to M.M. de Las Casas, Barcelona, July 5, 1812, *A.G.M.*, XXIV, 101–102, and idem to idem, Cumaná, July 8, 1812, ibid., 115–116, which ended with the remark: see you in "3 or 4 days" and in the postscript: "P.S—I beseech you to inform the *generalísimo* of the content of this letter." In short, Robertson, his troops, and supplies expected to be in La Guaira by July 12, 1812; since they were not there by then, Las Casas knew that perhaps they had been held up. This may have encouraged his betrayal of Miranda!

19. *Ley Marcial* (Martial Law), La Victoria, May 19, 1812, ibid., 405–410. To assure its implementation within a month's time in all the states, however, they dated the law for June 19, 1812, in this document. See 400–402 for the original document dated May 19, 1812.

20. Ibid., 497–500: Vicente de Sucre to Francisco de Miranda, Cumaná, July 11, 1812, *Año II de la República*, especially 497–498.

21. Ibid., 306–307: Patricio Padrón to Francisco de Miranda, Caracas, May 22, 1812; his letters (301–310) kept Miranda informed of the patriots' views and normal people in general.

22. Padrón, in particular, brought out such points in ibid., 301–310.

23. Miguel José Sanz to Miranda, Caracas, June 15, 1812, ibid., 40–41; Sanz's letters to Miranda (ibid., 9–71) were the best sources of information for

what was going on in the eastern zone, as well as in Caracas. And he received more replies from the *generalísimo* than other correspondents in Vol. XXIV *(A.G.M.)*.

24. Sanz to Miranda, Caracas, April 8, 1812, ibid., 9.

25. Sanz to Miranda, Caracas, May 26, 1812, ibid., 16–20, especially 17–18.

26. Idem to idem, Caracas, June 14, 1812, ibid., 36–37.

27. Ibid., 35–37.

28. Ibid., "Cartas de Francisco Isnardi," Caracas, May 15, 23, 1812, 241–243.

29. Robert K. Lowry to James Monroe, La Guaira, February 2, 1812, National Archives (D.C.), F.M. 37, Roll No. 4, (Despatches from Special Agents, 1794–1837).

30. Manuel María de Las Casas to Miranda, La Guaira, June 2, 1812, *A.G.M.*, XXIV, 77–78.

31. Ibid., 83–84 (Carlos Soublette to Las Casas, Maracay, June 16, 1812).

32. Miranda to Dr. Cortés Madariaga, Maracay, July 5, 1812, ibid., 456–457.

33. Pedro Gual to Miranda, Caracas, July 15, 1812, ibid., 216.

34. Louis Delpech to Miguel Sanz, La Guaira, June 30, 1812, ibid., 57.

35. Marquis de León to Miranda, Caracas, June 29, 1812, ibid., 138–139.

36. Delpech to Miranda, Caracas, June 4, 1812, ibid., 352–353.

37. Telésforo de Orea to James Monroe, Washington, May 15, 1812, thanking Congress for the donation, and assuring Monroe that Alexander Scott would be well-received in Venezuela; this follows Lowry's letter to Monroe of June 5, 1812 (see footnote 29).

38. The military chief of La Guaira, M.M. de Las Casas, wrote a series of letters to Carlos Soublette, Miranda's secretary, from July 3 to 8, 1812, recording the various activities of the frightened Scott family: *A.G.M.*, XXIV, 88–100.

39. Miguel Sanz to Miranda, Caracas, July 4, 1812, ibid., 55.

40. Alexander Scott to James Monroe, Caracas, November 16, 1812, F.M. 37/4 (National Archives, D.C.); by December 1, 1812, in his next letter to Monroe, General Monteverde ordered all citizens of the United States to leave the country immediately; on January 1, 1813, he was given forty eight hours to get out, convinced that "British counselers" had influenced the decision; and the British authorities at Curaçao did not allow him to stay there very long—the War of 1812 was a great determinant at this point.

41. Francisco de Miranda to Marquis de León, Victoria, June 26, 1812, *A.G.M.*, XXIV, 131.

42. Ibid., 156–157 (José Alustiza to Marquis de León, La Guaira, July 16, 1812).

43. Ibid.; and León's reply of July 17, 1812, 158.

44. Miranda to Dr. Cortés Madariaga, private, Maracay, May 20, 1812, ibid.,

432–433; 445–446 (pvt. to León) and 27 (pvt. to Sanz); and Madariaga to Miranda, Caracas, June 8, 1812, ibid., 193–194.

45. José Cortés Madariaga to Miranda, Caracas, July 5, 1812, ibid., 203–204.

46. Ibid., 294–296, Salazar's letters of June 22, July 8, 1812.

47. See footnote 18; this speculation also results from Las Casas' ailments and quarrels with Miguel Peña that alarmed Miranda in those final days; it may have hurt his feelings; and when it was clear that the "Eastern" troops were not coming as scheduled, he decided on betrayal, which capitalized upon the younger men's disillusionment.

48. These facts come out in Antonio Fernández de León's correspondence with Francisco de Miranda: ibid., 118 (May 29, 1812 forward), 158.

49. Ibid., 172–173 (Vicente Salias to Miranda, June 22, 1812); Miguel Sanz to Miranda, June 14, 1812, ibid., 34–38.

50. Ibid., 173–175 (Vicente Salias to Miranda, June 25, 1812).

51. Francisco Paúl to Miranda, Somos, July 7, 1812, ibid., 210–213.

52. Ibid., 229–230 (Miguel Peña to Miranda, Guaira, June 14, 1812).

53. Ibid., 230–231 (idem to idem, La Guaira, June 26, 1812).

54. See, for example, 149–150 (July 8, 1812) and 158 (July 17th), in which León insists that contracts have to be paid in paper money.

55. See Miguel Peña's letter above in footnote 53.

56. Ibid., 497–500 (Vicente de Sucre to Miranda, Cumaná, July 11, 1812).

57. See, for example, ibid., 54–56 (Sanz, July 4th), 198–200 (Cortés Madariaga, July 5th), 286–288 (Paz y Castillo, July 5th), and 308–310 (Padrón, June 20, 1812).

58. Miranda to Antonio Fernández de León, Victoria, July 3, 1812, ibid., 146.

59. León to Miranda, Caracas, July 5, 1812, ibid., 146–147.

60. Idem to idem, Caracas, July 6, 1812, ibid., 148; Miranda's reply, 149.

61. León to Miranda, Caracas, July 10, 1812, ibid., 153–155.

62. "Capitulación de 1812," Victoria, July 12, 1812, ibid., 509–510.

63. Francisco de Miranda to the Audiencia (Venezuela), Puerto Cabello, March 8, 1813, ibid., 536–545.

64. José Alustiza to Marquis de León, La Guaira, July 16, 1812, and León to Alustiza, Caracas, July 17, 1812, ibid., 156–158).

65. John Lynch, *The Spanish American Revolution, 1808–1826* (Norton: New York, 1973), 206; Bolívar and Mariño were allowed to sail for Cartagena.

66. Pedro José Morán to Duncan Shaw Co., Hoy, July 14, 1816, ibid., 553.

Epilogue   THE BOLÍVAR AND MIRANDA LEGACY

1. *Gazeta de Caracas*, January 3 and 6, 1814, two installments of the "Informe," Antonio Muñoz Tébar to Simón Bolívar, Caracas, December 31, 1813. On that same date, the position papers of Muñoz Tébar and two other

secretaries were presented; they appeared in the *Gazeta* during the month of January, 1814.

2. Ibid., January 24, 1814, "*Informe*," of the Secretary of War, Tomás Montilla, reporting on Bolívar's campaign from the time he arrived in Cartagena until he entered Venezuela victoriously.

3. Ibid., January 3, 1814, Antonio Muñoz Tébar's first installment of his report to Bolívar, December 31, 1813, in which he underscored that dreadful Treaty that Miranda conceded to the enemy. It continued with a supporting statement, which seems to have been part of the dogma created by Miranda's former supporters to justify their actions: "Miranda's forces *doblemente superiores* [double the size of the enemy forces], surrendered to Monteverde, who by virtue of the Treaty agreed upon, occupied without resistance cities and Provinces, that could have been disputed successfully to a victory."

4. Instructions to Venezuelan Agents: Great Britain, Caracas, May 4 and 9, 1814, Carlos Pi Sunyer, *El General Juan Robertson: Un prócer de la Independencia* (Caracas, 1971), 295–299.

5. *Gazeta de Caracas*, March 17 and 20, 1812, for an article discussing the protests; also see the constitutional discussion in *Libro de Actas del Supremo Congreso* (Venezuela), *BANH*, Vol. 37, IV: Session (December 21, 1811), 218–232, and Session (December 24, 1811), 236–238; also see: Francisco Javier de Uztáriz to Francisco de Montero, Caracas, March 1, 1812, *A.G.M.*, Vol. XXIV, 384–391.

6. *Gazeta de Caracas*, October 21, 28, and December 2, 1813, with Peña's dated October 18, in the first two *Gazetas*; Sanz's dated September 26, 1813, in the October 28th issue; and a third consultant Ramón García Cádiz, dated October 13th, in the December gazette. Also see, *Gazeta* of January 3, 1814, that reports on the public session in which Muñoz Tébar and other secretaries presented their reports; it also reproduces Bolívar's speech and those of other dignitaries that attended that reunion, confirming the fact that Bolívar had been given total power until the war was over.

7. Ibid., January 6, 1814, 118 (Muñoz Tébar's Informe).

8. Ibid.

9. Ibid., 117.

10. Ibid., 119.

11. Ibid., February 7, 1814, 154–155.

12. Ibid., 155.

13. Ibid., February 7, 1814, which reproduced a letter from Curaçao to a friend in Caracas, which in addition to announcing the recent news from Leipzig, described the violent acts and language of Spanish exiles, and the incident involving several murders. Hodgson, at that point, began to take steps against any repetition of such incidents.

14. Ibid., May 12, 1814, 261–262, in which the author of the quotation used the penname of "Chaleen."

15. Ibid., May 2, 1814, 250–252, which includes a letter of October 6, 1813, to the Regency, reviewing their requests for a sizeable expedition of Spanish troops for Venezuela; this letter insisted that the situation was now desperate—Bolívar's regime had to be eradicated in short order.

16. Ibid., May 19, 1814 270 under title "Miscellaneous."

17. Ibid., May 23, 1814, 274–275.

18. Ibid., 276.

19. See footnote 4.

20. Ibid., Instructions, 297–298.

21. Ibid., 298.

22. *Gazeta de Caracas,* May 30, 1814, first installment of article on Neutrality, 282–283; on June 2, 1814, ibid., the second installment followed.

23. Ibid., June 9, 1814, "*Reflexiones,*" 293–294.

Index